Mummies, Cannibals and Vampires

Mummies, Cannibals and Vampires charts in vivid detail the largely neglected and often disturbing history of European corpse medicine: when kings, ladies, gentlemen, priests and scientists used and consumed human body parts to treat a broad variety of common ailments of the time.

Conventional accounts of the Stuart kings of England omit the fact that James I refused corpse medicine, Charles II made his own corpse medicine and Charles I was himself made into corpse medicine. Ranging from the execution scaffolds of Germany and Scandinavia, through the courts and laboratories of Italy, France and Britain, to the battlefields of Holland and Ireland and on to the tribal man-eating of the Americas, *Mummies, Cannibals and Vampires* argues that the real cannibals were in fact the Europeans.

Often presented as a medieval therapy, medicinal cannibalism was in fact at its height during the social and scientific revolutions of early modern Britain. It drew strength from the formidable weight of European science, publishing, trade networks and educated theory, and for many it was also an emphatically Christian phenomenon. It survived well into the eighteenth century, and among the poor it lingered stubbornly on into the time of Queen Victoria.

Richard Sugg is lecturer in Renaissance Literature at the University of Durham. His previous books are *John Donne* (Palgrave, 2007), and *Murder after Death: Literature and Anatomy in Early Modern England* (Cornell University Press, 2007). He is currently working on three new books: two examine the physiology of the soul in classical, Christian and early modern literature and history, whilst the third looks at the vampires of folklore and fiction.

Mummies, Cannibals and Vampires

The History of Corpse Medicine from the Renaissance to the Victorians

Richard Sugg

Routledge
Taylor & Francis Group

LONDON AND NEW YORK

First published 2011
by Routledge
2 Park Square, Milton Park, Abingdon, Oxon OX14 4RN

Simultaneously published in the USA and Canada
by Routledge
711 Third Avenue, New York, NY 10017

Routledge is an imprint of the Taylor & Francis Group, an informa business

British Library Cataloguing in Publication Data
A catalogue record for this book is available from the British Library

Library of Congress Cataloging in Publication Data
Sugg, Richard, 1969–
  Mummies, cannibals, and vampires : the history of corpse medicine from the
Renaissance to the Victorians / Richard Sugg.
     p. cm.
  1. Medicine–Europe–History. 2. Medicine–Religious aspects–Christianity. 3.
Cannibalism. I. Title.
  R484.S84 2012
  610.4–dc22
                    2011001662

ISBN: 978-0-415-67416-4 (hbk)
ISBN: 978-0-415-67417-1 (pbk)
ISBN: 978-0-203-15418-2 (ebk)

Typeset in Bembo
by Taylor & Francis Books

Printed and bound in Great Britain
by CPI Antony Rowe, Chippenham, Wiltshire

For my mother,
for Les and Doug,
and for Chris and Danni,
and their great adventure.

Contents

Acknowledgements

Many people have assisted generously in the development of this book by reading, responding to queries, or voluntarily supplying data and advice. Warm thanks are due to Christine Alvin, Rachel Bailin, Martyn Bennett, Oliver Cooper, Alice Eardley, John Henry, Frances Hornyold-Strickland, Arnold Hunt, Paul Jump, Louise Leigh, Elaine Leong, Willey Maley, Irene Miguel, Kaja Murawska, Richard Newell, David Porter, Joel Rasbash, Barbara Ravelhofer, Krista Shaw, Alison Shell, Jerry Singer, Leona Skelton, Mauro Spicci, Chris Sugg, David Thorley, Jonathan Trigg, Keir Waddington, and Danielle Yardy.

For attempts to raise the public profile of this topic I am very grateful to Andrew Abbott, Marc Abrahams, Philip Bethge, Dionne Hamil, Bill Hamilton, Leighton Kitson, Dave Musgrove, Andreas Weiser and Claire Whitelaw and all those involved at Wildfire television, particularly Rebecca Burrell and Ben Steele. Thanks to Vicky Peters at Routledge for her initial interest and her ongoing help with various queries, to Laura Mothersole for prompt help during the latter stages of writing and editing, to Jayne Varney for her excellent work on the cover design and to James Thomas for his meticulous copy-editing. Thanks are due, also, to the four anonymous academic readers for their thorough and often generous comments. Staff and students at Durham's Department of English Studies have again helped to make the period of research and writing more a pleasure than a job. I am particularly grateful to the departmental research committee for the financial assistance which has made it possible to publish a work of this length. Special thanks once more to Daniel Hartley, whose enthusiasm and insight helped nudge an idea towards a book.

Abbreviations

Unless otherwise stated, all references to Shakespeare's works are to: *The Riverside Shakespeare*, ed. G. Blakemore Evans *et al.* (Boston and New York: Houghton Mifflin Company, 1997).

Complete Works of Ben Jonson
The Complete Works of Ben Jonson, ed. C.H. Herford and Percy and Evelyn Simpson, 11 vols (Oxford: Clarendon Press, 1925–52).

Diary
The Diary of Samuel Pepys: a New and Complete Transcription, ed. R. Latham and W. Matthews, 11 vols (London: Bell, 1970–83).

Letters
Edmund Gosse, *The Life and Letters of John Donne*, 2 vols (London: William Heinemann, 1899).

Poems
John Donne: The Complete English Poems, ed. A.J. Smith (Harmondsworth: Penguin, 1971; repr. 1996).

RCP
Annals of the College of Physicians of London, trans. J. Emberry, S. Heathcote, and M. Hellings, 5 vols (Wellcome Library, RCP, London).

Sermons
The Sermons of John Donne, ed. George R. Potter and Evelyn M. Simpson, 10 vols (Berkeley and Los Angeles: University of California Press, 1953–62).

Thorndike, *History*
Lynn Thorndike, *A History of Magic and Experimental Science*, 8 vols (New York: Columbia University Press, 1938–54).

Works of Thomas Nashe
The Works of Thomas Nashe, ed. Ronald B. McKerrow, 5 vols (A.H. Bullen, 1904; repr. London: Sidgwick & Jackson, 1910).

INTRODUCTION

One thing we are rarely taught at school is this: James I refused corpse medicine; Charles II made his own corpse medicine; and Charles I was made into corpse medicine.[1] This alone is a quite unusual view of England's first three Stuart monarchs. To clarify it, we must also add that James I was very much in the minority, and that Sir Theodore Turquet de Mayerne, the doctor who prescribed powdered human skull for him, was one of the most eminent practitioners in all of Europe. We must add, too, that royal cannibals such as Charles II, Francis I, Christian IV of Denmark and William III were just the tip of the social iceberg.

For well over 200 years in early modern Europe, the rich and the poor, the educated and the illiterate all participated in cannibalism on a more or less routine basis. Drugs were made from Egyptian mummies and from the dried bodies of those drowned in North African desert sandstorms. Later in the era the corpses of hanged criminals offered a new and less exotic source of human flesh. Human blood was also swallowed: sometimes fresh and hot, direct from a donor's body; sometimes dried, powdered, or distilled with alchemical precision. Human fat was one of the most enduring substances of all: it was usually applied externally in the form of ointments or plasters. Certain parts of the bone of the skull were swallowed as powder or in liquid distillations. In London chemists' shops one could see entire human skulls for sale. Some had a growth of botanical moss, which could be powdered and used to treat nosebleeds and other forms of haemorrhaging. Both skull bone and the moss of the skull should – most authorities agreed – be derived from a man who had met a violent death, preferably by hanging or drowning. These were the most common drugs derived from the human body. But, as we will see, for certain practitioners and patients, there was almost nothing between the head and the feet which could not be used in some way: hair, brain, heart, skin, liver, urine, menstrual blood, placenta, earwax, saliva and faeces. Medicinal cannibalism was practised to some extent in the Middle Ages. But, with nice irony, it became most popular and pervasive in the era when reports of

New World cannibals were circulating amidst the outraged Christians of Rome, Madrid, London and Wittenberg.

Just who were the real cannibals? Was it those without books, without guns, given to wearing fewer clothes, and worshipping lesser-known gods? Or was it those who, in their determination to swallow flesh and blood and bone, threw cannibal trade networks across hundreds of miles of land and ocean, established cannibal laboratories, sponsored cannibal bodysnatchers, and levied import duties on human bodies and human skulls? The reader must, of course, make their own decision at the close of this book. But one basic point should be established before we begin. Such medicines were not merely a matter of abstract theory. They were used. The employment of different substances certainly varied across nations and social classes. The educated, for example, were probably less likely to swallow fresh human blood; and the poor could rarely afford exotic corpse medicines such as Egyptian mummy. Allowing for these variations, we can again state emphatically that cannibal medicines were swallowed, rather than just written about. In the late sixteenth century Ambroise Paré asserted unequivocally that mummy was 'the very first and last medicine of almost all our practitioners' against bruising.[2] In the seventeenth and eighteenth centuries, corpse medicines and body fluids feature in family medical recipes, which at times cite precise cures or names of patients. In Germany and Denmark, poorer citizens paid whatever they could afford to drink human blood at execution scaffolds. Perhaps most basically of all: Egyptian mummy was sufficiently popular to generate persistent counterfeiting. Fraudulent substitutes were on sale in London apothecaries well into the eighteenth century.

We will have much more to say about all these substances, and about consumers eminent and obscure, in following chapters. Returning to the Stuarts, let us just briefly touch in some more detail on the cannibal habits of Charles II. As Antonia Fraser notes, Charles became an enthusiastic and reasonably skilful chemist during his youthful exile in France.[3] He later appointed the renowned and relatively avant-garde French scientist Nicasius Lefevre as royal chemist. Charles had his own private laboratory, and is supposed to have paid £6,000 to Jonathan Goddard (Professor of Physic at London's Gresham College) for one particular chemical recipe.[4] This, sometimes called 'spirit of skull', became so closely associated with Charles that it was also known as the King's Drops. On 2 February 1685, Charles awoke, 'feeling ghastly'. He was indeed seriously ill, and just four days later he would be dead. The first remedy he reached for (perhaps as automatically as you or I might take paracetamol or echinacea) was this distillation of the powder of human skull.[5] High doses of this medicine were also given to Charles by his physicians as he lay on his deathbed. Some months before this (Fraser tells us) the king's increasing frailty had meant that his 'long walks were reluctantly cut down'. Accordingly, 'his keenness was now channelled into his laboratory, where he would devote himself to his experiments for hours at a time' in an 'obsessional manner'.[6]

A newspaper reporter to whom I spoke in 2009 seemed especially intrigued that this famous monarch (often presented as an epitome of elegance and wit) should be distilling the powder of human skull in his own laboratory. Part of this surprise may stem from the oddly sanitised view of the Restoration which has somehow come down to us. Much of this book is what might be called Dirty History. And Charles too was in many ways part of that dirty world. For all his supposed ease and gentleness, he was quite ready to have a prisoner deliberately placed 'in a dungeon in the Tower where mud and water came up to his waste', and moved only when it was reported that he was dying as a result.[7] As we will see in chapter two, it was in or shortly before the time of Charles II that uses of the human body became most ruthlessly thorough and (in our eyes) often disgusting.

'Why don't I know about this?' These are the words of Dr David Musgrove, editor of *BBC History* magazine, during a conversation in 2006 about a future article on the subject of medicinal cannibalism. Three years later, after Internet versions of a *Der Spiegel* story on this topic quickly circulated on the web, I began to suspect that many of the general public were obliquely echoing his puzzled query. For some, the most potent core of the present book lies not in another neglected chapter of medical history, but in a very basic revision of the history of one of our deepest taboos. You do not eat people, and those who do are always savages (or, later on, savage psychopaths).

Why do so few people know about this? This question will be tackled in detail in chapter eight. We can say here that, at least for early generations of medical historians, cannibalism did not seem to be an acceptable element in the stories they wished to tell. Amongst those who have covered this topic in the past thirty years, perhaps the most prominent figures are Karl H. Dannenfeldt, Piero Camporesi, Louise Noble, and Philip Schwyzer. None of these figures are medical historians. Like myself, Noble and Schwyzer were originally trained in literary studies; whilst Camporesi's unconventional attitude to traditional historical narratives arguably makes Dannenfeldt the only historian in the group.

One other point on the history of neglect is also worth adding. I myself was initially guilty of treating the subject in rather too narrow a fashion. Academics can sometimes lose sight of certain basic general questions as they pick through the complexities of detail attendant on modern specialisms. One of the benefits of teaching is to have students occasionally insist on those questions which one has come to treat in a 'purely academic' way. It was a Cardiff University student, Daniel Hartley, who did this after reading my article on medicinal cannibalism. Many of my sometime colleagues at Cardiff will probably still recall Daniel. I myself can still recall the raw fascination and enthusiasm of the message he wrote me. These (along with some ingenious points of detail) have returned to me time and again during a long process of research and writing, and have helped me keep sight of some of the more urgent and basic questions embedded in this topic.

Mummies, Cannibals and Vampires is organised in four broad sections. First: what was medicinal cannibalism and who was involved in it? Second: what was New World cannibalism? What did it mean to its participants and to European commentators? Third: how did therapeutic cannibalism thrive and endure in the face of such a powerful taboo? Finally: what negative or ambivalent responses to this phenomenon existed in the early modern period? When and why did it end? And why did certain historians all but try to pretend that it had never really happened?

Chapters one and two show how widely and deeply corpse medicine pervaded European society, from the time of Columbus to that of Robert Boyle. Interspersed throughout these opening chapters are a number of case histories, drawing on the theory or practice of some of the era's more eminent and influential doctors, scientists, thinkers and leaders. These pages detail a systematic cannibalism, underpinned by educated medical theories, and by global trade and commerce. They show that corpse materials or body fluids were used not just by doctors and apothecaries, but as treatment for hawks, as fish baits, rabbit food, and cosmetics. Perhaps most importantly, they emphasise that corpse medicine (still occasionally referred to as a 'medieval' phenomenon in recent discussions) gained its fullest reach and popularity in the time of the so-called Scientific Revolution, from the Interregnum through the late Restoration period.

Chapter three turns to the various sources of human body parts and fluids. Many of these sources were conveniently distanced in some way from those trading, mixing or drinking them. Egyptian mummies were (or were thought to be) ancient; and they, like the desiccated victims of North African sandstorms, were also thoroughly dry, and usually anonymous. The same went for the bones and skulls which were plundered from graveyards or lonely battlefields (with Ireland being an especially popular choice for English traders).

Matters get a little less distant when we come to the recently dead bodies of those felons who were sold by executioners, used by anatomists, or mutilated as they hung from gibbets. In the case of blood therapies, the beheaded felons of Germany and Scandinavia were very clearly identifiable, and only very recently dead. And, if certain aged Europeans did really suck blood from the arms of young men, then the contact with such donors was very intimate indeed. In other cases, distance offered its own forms of alienation. As the Wars of Religion raged between Protestants and Catholics, the enemy who fell before your sword might be physically very close, and yet ideologically quite as other as the savages of Canada or Brazil. There is also evidence, however, to show that the Europeans were 'cannibalising' the savages of South America – a habit which is consistent with both the otherness of native Indians in the minds of the Spanish, and with the other cruelties inflicted on them.

Since the discovery of the Americas by Europeans, cannibalism has been used as a potent form of colonial propaganda. Partly for this reason, chapter four begins by clarifying the often misconstrued cannibalism of those few New World tribes for whom this was a habitual practice. Drawing on the research of anthropologist Beth Conklin among the Brazilian Wari', it looks in detail at the religious and social significance of consensual (or endo-) cannibalism. For the Wari', this was a vital form of bereavement therapy. For all its spectacular violence, even the aggressive cannibalism of the Huron or Tupinamba was at bottom highly ritualised – an essentially religious practice shaped by ideas of honour, courage, and social harmony. Moreover, the ambiguous victims of these rites were not 'violated' in the way that a European might be when transformed into medicine. Although they could undergo almost inconceivable torments before death and consumption, they would co-operate in the whole ritual, in the belief that their courage was being tested and witnessed by the sun god prior to death.

These opening sections give us some idea of what cannibalism meant to those practising it in the New World. On the surface, its meanings for most educated Europeans were plainly negative. Yet during some of the worst excesses of essentially tribal violence – from the Wars of Religion through to the French Revolution – spontaneous incidents of exo-cannibalism did occur on Christian soil.

Whilst such incidents are themselves now largely forgotten, perhaps still more obscure is the ability of certain Europeans to explicitly or implicitly subdivide New World cannibalism into hierarchical categories. Broadly following Lévi-Strauss's division of the raw and the cooked, Frank Lestringant has shown how European observers imposed this distinction on the tribal man-eaters of the Americas. The raw form was more savage, because more animalistic, unable to distance itself from the realm of unmediated nature. Cooking, meanwhile, could be literal or symbolic: in either case it elevated cannibalism (and tribal life per se) by using various levels of cultural mediation. These forms of human intervention and processing recur in following chapters, when we seek to understand just how Europeans psychologically distanced their own habitual cannibalism from that of tribal savagery.

When told about medicinal cannibalism, many modern individuals are startled, horrified, or disgusted. There again, they are sometimes more startled, horrified, or disgusted when told that men such as Robert Boyle recommended rubbing dried excrement into the eyes as a cure for cataracts. Chapter five begins to address the seeming puzzle of corpse medicine by exploring the highly distinctive economy of disgust which characterised life in early modern Europe. Firstly: as the above example implies, many non-cannibalistic animal substances were used in medicine. Along with numerous kinds of offal, there were also the excrement of dogs, goats, geese, and pigeons; the urine of a boar; crushed body-lice; and animal blood drunk warm. Set against these agents, some well-processed mummy flesh, lost amidst several other ingredients, may have seemed relatively untroubling. As well as emphasising the greater vulnerability of early modern individuals to sickness, pain or violence, the chapter sets the seemingly disgusting cures of the day within a more general social economy of disgust. Although historians still debate exact levels of dirt and correspondent attitudes to it, it is clear that, in relative terms, early modern life stank. The rich and the poor frequently had sharp olfactory, tactile, or visual contact with the excrement and urine of humans and animals, and with the putrescence and slime of decaying corpses. In a world where everything was so disgusting, could you really afford to be disgusted? Drawing on work such as William Miller's *Anatomy of Disgust*, this section argues that seemingly instinctive, universal attitudes towards hygiene, defecation and modesty have been learned by Europeans only relatively recently.

Chapter five deals substantially with the way in which mental attitudes condition what might (mistakenly) be thought of as gut reactions. Chapter six turns to the most powerful and widespread mental attitude of the sixteenth and seventeenth centuries. In a number of important ways, Christian piety conditioned responses to medicinal cannibalism. Some writers quite unequivocally used mummy as a symbol for the triumph of spirit over matter. At one level such habits can be linked to the more general power of piety: for the most fervent Christians, everything was part of God's creation. The raw matter of earthly life was already saturated with religious significance or power.

But there were also very precise physiological reasons why the human body could inspire pious belief in its healing powers. Consumption of blood remedies; Paracelsian corpse flesh (derived from freshly killed felons); and even skull medicines were often underpinned by a desire to consume the basic vitality of youthful, healthy corpses. Motivated in part by beliefs in the 'animate corpse' (whose biological potency smouldered on for months after legal death), such therapies also aimed at imbibing those vital spirits of the blood which often blurred ambiguously into the soul itself. The Brazilian Wari' at times forced down human flesh so putrid that it made them nauseous. They did so through pious respect for their dead kin and for the web of religious ideas which generated funerary cannibalism. Similarly, Christians swallowed the substance and the idea of corpse medicine because, for some, it was validated and elevated by the highly animated nature of the Christian body.

Chapter six concludes by returning to the European distinction between raw and cooked varieties of New World cannibalism. In various ways, European medicine successfully raised corpse medicine above the raw animal necessity of mere appetite or consumption. In doing so it also raised it (for most) above the level of American cannibalism. Whilst older medical traditions achieved this through the ancient theoretical authority of European medicine, Paracelsian physicians elevated corpse matter by the painstaking cookery of their essentially alchemical processes. Here we see a new version of the phenomena described by Charles Webster, in which a kind of pious alchemy and ideology slowly blur into the beginnings of modern scientific chemistry.

The final two chapters examine various phases and levels of opposition to corpse medicine. There are just a very few overt attacks on corpse medicine prior to the eighteenth century. A range of uneasy or derisive attitudes, however, are expressed in coded form by writers of the Stuart era. The broad thrust of these references is toward a progressive demystification of mummy and associated substances. Whilst early Stuart drama has some telling quips about people being 'sold for mummy', Restoration playwrights give such jibes a sharply irreverent twist via numerous instances of people 'beaten' to mummy. Come the time of Charles II, mummy seems to be ever more often figured as a degraded or disreputable commodity. But for much of the century, ambivalence toward corpse medicines is the more characteristic attitude. This kind of wavering position is brought out with especial clarity through a detailed case study of several references to mummy by one author, the minister Thomas Fuller.

Chapter eight brings us to the eighteenth century. From around the middle of this period we encounter some characteristically Enlightenment attitudes towards past 'superstition'. We also find certain doctors attempting to distance themselves from corpse medicines in the more general process of reforming and defining a new kind of 'medical profession'. Yet even in this era, attitudes to corpse medicines are far from straightforward. One very successful practitioner continued to recommend human skull in the 1790s, and even those who turn against the bulk of human therapies still vigorously advocate the use of human fat in this period. From another angle, examination of the first stage character to be labelled 'Dr Mummy' suggests that some early medical opponents of corpse medicine may have been shamed into their new stance by the jibes of the dramatist James Miller. Final sections look at how the distinctively Enlightenment attitudes of certain authors persist into the works of twentieth-century medical historians. Why did it take so long for corpse medicines to be accurately described by academic authors, and what were the distortions consequent on the long decades of neglect?

The book's conclusion examines the various afterlives of corpse medicine. It can be plausibly argued that new attitudes to medicine, to science, and to disgust and propriety helped banish such remedies from privileged society by the end of the eighteenth century. Yet in a sense the more interesting question is not: why did it end? so much as: where did it go? In the popular culture which formed the bulk of human lives prior to the twentieth century, most medicine was 'folk medicine', and cannibal or corpse therapies persisted well into the late Victorian period. More-over, alongside the enduring medical use of body parts, we find various levels of magic. Blood is used as a love potion; people are murdered for their fat, so as to produce candles which will render the bearer invisible. In the latter case, fear of such murders survives as I write, encoded in the figures of the South American pishtaco and kharisiri. In the former, we find an uncertain but intriguing link with that most successful demon of postmodern culture, the vampire.

A good deal will be said in chapter four about the explicit and implicit meanings of the word 'cannibal' for early modern Europeans. A brief note on my own use is probably helpful before we begin. The *OED* defines 'cannibal' as 'a man (*esp.* a savage) that eats human flesh; a man-eater, an anthropophagite'. Some tend to limit cannibalism solely to the eating of human flesh. Although the *OED* might seem at first glance to take this line, 'man-eater' is clearly far more comprehensive (and we can plausibly argue that someone who ate a *whole* person (flesh, bones, and organs) might be seen as more cannibalistic than someone who ate *only* human flesh). Moreover, in its definition of 'cannibalism', the *OED* cites Edmund Burke, who in 1796 wrote, 'by cannibalism, I mean their devouring, as a nutriment of their ferocity, *some part of the bodies* of those they have murdered' (italics mine).

An academic book such as this can hardly give an absolutely rigid, canonical definition of a word which it is deliberately aiming to problematise. (There would be little point in the book if it could.) My primary working definition of 'cannibalism', however, is this: consumption by mouth of those body parts or fluids which a donor cannot very easily do without. Perhaps most obviously, this excludes hair and nail cuttings, and could reasonably be held to exclude saliva, mucus, semen, sweat, milk, urine, excrement, and so forth. Blood could also conceivably be excluded from that primary definition. Because of the taboos surrounding it, however, I will include blood in that first, more rigid sense of 'cannibalism'.

Many anthropologists would hardly pause to argue about whether or not the consumption of bones is cannibalism. In the context of tribal man-eating, the motives and behaviour involved are clearly very similar, whether participants are swallowing roasted meat or powdered skull. It is when we come to seemingly 'disposable' parts and fluids that matters become more problematic. My own choice is to include these amongst bodily substances which can be considered cannibalistic. Those readers who (like myself as I type) have been absent-mindedly chewing their fingers as they peruse this, may object vigorously to the (potential) inclusion of nails as cannibal food (or, more precisely, auto-cannibalism). Recently delivered mothers may also protest at the inclusion of human milk. It will become clear in chapters two and seven why I have been broad-minded about milk. Here I will briefly give three examples which show how less obviously cannibalistic substances or acts can prompt discussions of cannibalism, or even the kind of horror which early modern Christians expressed toward the Huron, Tupinamba, and Caribs of the New World.

First: the early Church father Tertullian thought fellatio to be cannibalistic. (Those women who protest about the calorific excesses of semen may be pleased to hear that they have another weapon on their side.) Second: in 2007 various press stories claimed that Keith Richards had snorted his father's ashes. A quick Internet search on this subject will show that many individuals at least asked whether such an act was cannibalistic, and Richards himself notes that 'there were op-eds on cannibalism' in the wake of the story.[8] Thirdly: let us ask the savages … The authors of a 2001 book on cannibalism describe an ironic moment recorded by the Australian anthropologist Alfred Gell. In the 1970s, Gell was living with the Umeda in Papua New Guinea. Having cut his finger while peeling sugar cane, he instinctively slipped it into his mouth. The watching Umeda were aghast. For a people who would never dream of even chewing their own nails, this was a significant act of auto-cannibalism.[9] Blood, as I have said, is not so obviously disposable as mucus or hair or sweat. But surely few of us would think twice before doing what Gell did. And for the Umeda, nail-biting would have been hardly less abhorrent.

Bracketing off these wider debates for a moment, it should also be admitted that terms such as 'corpse medicine' and 'medicinal cannibalism' can generate their own problems. In what follows I will at times use these terms broadly, in order to vary the otherwise inevitable repetition of a single phrase. I am aware that 'corpse medicine' does not strictly cover the bodily fluids of the living, and that certain substances (such as topically applied fat or moss from human skulls) are not necessarily cannibalistic. But there is much ground to cover here, and the very least the reader deserves is some reasonably elegant prose. One other caveat concerns primary material, rather than my own comments on it. Only after signing my contract with Routledge a few days ago did I notice the potentially alarming clause 4.1e: 'any recipe, formula or instruction in the Work will not, if followed correctly, cause physical injury or damage to any person'. Frankly, I would hesitate to defend this statement in the present case. *Caveat lector*, then, must be our wary motto; or, in plain English: do not try any of this at home. Let us begin.

1

CORPSE MEDICINE FROM THE MIDDLE AGES TO CAROLINE ENGLAND

My first three chapters will deal chiefly with the sixteenth and seventeenth centuries, and with western European countries (England, Ireland, Scandinavia, Germanic states, the Netherlands, France, Italy, Spain, and Portugal). Naturally enough, however, classical precedents are important for much of this period. Those medieval cases founded on alchemical practices are particularly relevant to the seventeenth-century habits of Paracelsians which we will meet in chapters two and seven, and may also give us a better understanding of the alleged treatment of Pope Innocent VIII, in 1492.

Classical and non-Christian uses

A patient is receiving treatment. The date is some time around 25 AD; the site is the Roman Colosseum. A gladiator lies crumpled on the sand at the side of the arena. Behind him a dark trail leads back to the spot from which he has just been dragged. Looking closer, we notice something slightly odd about the figure crouching over the wounded man. His posture does not suggest a doctor attempting to staunch bleeding, or even to check heartbeat or pulse. Look a little closer still, and you may be inclined to suddenly reel back or to close your eyes. The man sprawled at such an odd angle beside the injured fighter has his face pressed against a gaping tear in the gladiator's throat. He is drinking blood fresh from the wound. Why? As you may now realise, it is in fact he who is the patient. He suffers from epilepsy, and is using a widely known cure for his mysterious affliction.[1] He and other sufferers, we are told, were wont to drink from gladiators' bodies 'as though from living cups'.[2]

What was the opinion of medical authorities on such treatment? One historian tells us that 'a remedy for epilepsy involving the blood of a dead gladiator, warrior, or street brawler, although disdained by Scribonius Largus, Celsus, and Galen, nevertheless was singled out as an "excellent and well proven remedy of Marsinius the Thracian" by Alexander of Tralles, writing around 570'.[3] While this statement identifies two educated and relatively influential supporters, it is in fact a little misleading. 'Disdained' implies scorn – possibly even disbelief. But the eminent physician Celsus (*c*.25 BC–*c*.50 AD), though considering such therapy repugnant, did not deny its efficacy.[4] In their survey of epileptic blood remedies, Ferdinand Moog and Axel Karenburg cite Pliny the Elder (d.79 AD), who told in his *Natural History* of how '"the blood of gladiators is drunk by epileptics as though it were the draught of life"'. This caused Pliny himself to '"shudder with horror"'. But, around 300 AD, 'a somewhat uncritical summary called *Medicina Plinii*' skewed his initial attitude when it stated simply, '"human blood is also effective against [epilepsy]"'.[5] We can add that those who refused to drink the blood of others could, according to Largus, '"swallow blood drawn from their own veins"'.[6]

It was also around this time that a physician could recommend a more prolonged cannibalistic therapy for 'the sacred disease'. A related treatment involved nine doses of human liver, again derived from a gladiator.[7] Guido Majno cites Largus on those Roman spectators who would 'step forward and snatch a piece of liver from a gladiator lying gutted in the dust'.[8] There were probably many potential sources of both blood and liver available in this era. But there is good reason to believe that a gladiator was a quite deliberate and precise choice. He was young and strong, and he died healthy. He was also, we can fairly imagine, courageous, and the liver was at this point (and through the Renaissance itself) thought to be a seat of physical courage. Hence, by contrast, those with bloodless livers, or with blood of poor quality, were cowards, being white or 'lily-livered', or (more enduringly) 'yellow'.

Much later, the Paracelsian physician Thomas Moffett was unequivocally hostile to this classical therapy: 'yea in Rome (the seat and nurse of all inhumanity) physicians did prescribe their patients the blood of wrestlers, causing them to suck it warm breathing and spinning out of their veins, drawing into their corrupt bodies a sound man's life, and sucking that in with both lips, which a dog is not suffered to lick with his tongue'. At the same time, he also reveals other cannibalistic treatments: 'they were not ashamed', he adds, 'to prescribe them a meat made of man's marrow and infants' brains'. The Grecians, meanwhile,

> were as bold and impious as the Romans, tasting of every inward and outward part of man's body, not leaving the nails unprosecuted … Let Democritus dream and comment, that some diseases are best cured with anointing the blood of strangers and malefactors, others with the blood of our friends and kinsfolks; let Miletus cure sore eyes with men's galls; Artemon the falling sickness with dead men's skulls; Antheus convulsions with pills made of dead men's brains; Apollonius bad gums with dead men's teeth … [9]

Less hostile was the French encyclopedist, Pierre Boaistuau: 'many ancient physicians of Graecia and Arabia have used the marrow of our bones, the brains of men, and their bowels, yea even the dust and ashes of men's bones, for to drink them and cause them to serve with marvellous effects to the usage of physic'.[10]

We also know that various parts of the body were considered therapeutic by 'Mesopotamian, Egyptian, Greek, Chinese, Talmudic ... [and] Indian' medicine, as well as by the Romans.[11] Corpse medicine was advocated to some extent by one of Europe's most important medical authorities, the physician Claudius Galen (*c.*120–200 AD), while 'ancient Hippocratic medical texts' prescribed 'pollutant therapy – the use of bodily pollutants, such as the "polluted blood of violence," menstrual blood, and "corpse-food" – to fight impurity or disease'. So states Louise Noble, who adds other human body fluids with a long history of use as medicines, such as 'milk ... urine, menses, and dung'.[12] The historian Owsei Temkin, meanwhile, points out that while it was chiefly midwives who were known to rouse epileptics from their seizures by rubbing menstrual blood on their feet, it 'can by no means be objected that these practices were believed in only by superstitious Romans or midwives'.[13] Later on, 'in the Byzantine Empire, the blood of executed criminals was used as a substitute' for that of gladiators.[14]

A closer look at Galen's remarks is subtly revealing. He concedes that '"some of our people have cured epilepsy and arthritis ... by prescribing a drink of burned (human) bones, the patients not knowing what they drank lest they should be nauseated"'.[15] It is possible that this statement reflects his own discomfort, and certainly significant that physicians did not expect patients to easily acquiesce to the therapy. Others were more overt in their hostility. The Greek physician Aretaeus of Cappadocia, for example, openly condemned the drinking of blood and the eating of human liver.[16] And, circa 400 AD, the physician Caelius Aurelianus cited human blood among various anti-epileptic treatments which he regarded as '"detestable, barbarous and inhuman"'.[17] Although there is insufficient data on classical corpse medicine to permit a thorough comparison with early modern habits, there is some reason for thinking that it was Christianity which made such therapies more acceptable in later centuries. At very least, Moffett's indignation at classical habits looks more than a touch ironic when one compares the unease of Pliny and others with the numerous Christian blood therapies of later centuries.

The Middle Ages

Reaching the medieval period, we find ourselves at a crucial watershed in the history of corpse medicine. As the seminal research of Karl Dannenfeldt has shown, it was around this time that both the term and the agent known as 'mummy' underwent a curious transformation. In early Arabic medicine a natural mineral pitch, found solidified on mountainsides in Darábjerd in Persia, had been used therapeutically, and was given the name 'mumiya' (from 'mum', meaning 'wax'). The word which we now generally assume to refer to embalmed Egyptian bodies has, then, a medical origin. Whilst the mineral substance, often known as pissasphaltum, was used in classical Europe, it was in the eleventh century that the term began to be associated with the corpses of the ancient Egyptians. Constantinus Africanus rendered the definition of the Baghdad physician Rhazes (d.923) as 'the substance found in the land where bodies are buried with aloes by which the liquid of the dead, mixed with the aloes, is transformed, and it is similar to marine pitch', with Gerard of Cremona compounding this new identity in the following century. Around the same time, Simon Cordo made a Latin translation of the Arab physician Ibn Serapion the younger (*fl.* 1070).[18] Cordo's version described 'the mumia of the sepulchres' as a substance made of 'aloes and myrrh mixed with the liquid of the human body'. Here the essentially cannibalistic component of the agent is explicitly identified.[19]

Nevertheless, Dannenfeldt's research indicates that – at least in earlier centuries – mummies were exploited for medicine precisely because they were thought to be an alternative source of mineral pitch – something which was now held to be available within the head and gut cavities of embalmed bodies.[20] We can only speculate cautiously as to what role this earlier belief played in promoting corpse medicine. It may indicate that the route to full-blown medicinal cannibalism was initially smoothed (or blurred), involving a path which began with legitimate desire for a mineral agent, and ultimately led to the widespread use of human body matter. Come the early modern era, this possible motivation had largely faded from view. It may still have been convenient for early modern users that the dry and friable substance of ancient mummies was far from visceral. For all that, we know that at least some figures explicitly identified its use as cannibalistic during the sixteenth century.

Surviving evidence suggests that there was not a particularly strong European demand for Egyptian mummy until the fifteenth century.[21] In the thirteenth, the Baghdad physician Abd Allatif had been able to purchase 'three heads filled' with mummy for 'half a dirhem' – an amount which he explicitly describes as 'a trifle'.[22] But come 1424 certain merchants were engaged in a more systematic trade, plundering the tombs to an extent which proved reckless: 'the authorities in Cairo discovered persons who had amassed a considerable number of cadavers', and who confessed under torture that they 'were removing bodies from the tombs, boiling them in hot water, and collecting the oil which rose to the surface. This was sold to the Europeans for 25 gold pieces per hundredweight. The men were imprisoned'.[23] A hundredweight was then 112 pounds, or eight stone, and although three heads were unlikely to weigh more than about two stone, we can clearly see that prices rose sharply between the time of Abd Allatif and 1424.

The alchemy of blood

A brief survey of medicinal cannibalism in medieval Europe takes us away from mummy itself. The influential surgeon Lanfranc of Milan (*c.*1250–1306) cited a medicine for broken bones which contained (among other things) gum arabic and mummy; and Pandolphus Collenucius notes the use of human skulls in the fifteenth century.[24] Both before and after this, however, blood seems to have been the most common medical agent derived from human bodies. In the sixteenth century, a work credited to the Swiss physician and herbalist Conrad Gesner (1516–65) refers to 'a most precious water of Albertus Magnus, as I found it in a certain written book'. To make this you should 'distil the blood of a healthful man, by a glass, as men do rose water'. With this, any disease of the body, if it be anointed therewith, is made whole, and all inward diseases by the drinking thereof. A small quantity thereof received, restoreth them that have lost all their strength: it cureth the palsy effectuously, and preserveth the body from all sickness. To be short it healeth all kinds of diseases.

This statement itself tells us a good deal. The blood should be taken from a live and healthy male, and thereafter processed. It could then be applied externally or swallowed, and was clearly viewed as something like an elixir of life.[25] Given the status of St Albertus Magnus (c.1206–80) as perhaps the greatest scientist of his day, we can well imagine that the recipe was widely used.

Magnus' contemporary and fellow scientist Roger Bacon (d.1294) referred in *The Cure of Old Age and Preservation of Youth* to 'certain wise men' who 'have tacitly made mention of some medicine, which is likened to that which goes out of the mine of the noble animal. They affirm that in it there is a force and virtue, which restores and increases the natural heat'. This agent was, indeed, said to be 'like youth it self'. Bacon himself was sceptical about this substance, and his seventeenth-century translator, the physician Richard Browne, also doubted that the medicine referred to was any kind of quintessence. For all that, Browne did note that 'some would have this to be quintessence of man's blood'.[26]

The Spanish alchemist, astrologer, and physician Arnold of Villanova (c.1238–c.1310) described various oils 'made from human bones, against epilepsy, gout' – and, indeed, 'all griefs'.[27] Arnold was also believed to have given quite detailed directions for the preparation of blood around this time. A letter thought to have been written by Arnold, addressed to his 'dearly beloved friend' Master Jacobus of Toledo, answered this latter's request 'that I would open to you my secret of man's blood'.[28] Jacobus was instructed, accordingly, to use the blood 'of healthful men, about thirty years of age, out of which draw according to art, the four elements, as you well have learned and know by the rules of alchemy, and diligently stop each element apart, that no air breathe forth'. This water of blood, the letter claimed, had power against 'all sicknesses'. It was especially effective at restoring 'the spiritual members' (presumably the liver, heart and brain, then thought to contain a vaporous spirit of blood and air). It expelled poison from the heart, enlarged the arteries, cleared phlegm from the lungs, healed ulcers, cleansed the blood, and cured diarrhoea or cysts. Air of blood, particularly well-suited to the young, was recommended for apoplexy, epilepsy, eye problems, migraine and dizziness.

Most remarkable of all, however, was the distilled fire of human blood. Given to one 'in the hour of death', in

the quantity of a wheat grain, distempered or mixed with wine, in such manner entered down, that it be past the throat, it shall forthwith cause the person to revive again, and shall at the instant enter to the heart it self, in expelling the superfluous humours, and with this reviveth the natural heat of his liver, and quickneth so all the parts, that it moveth the patient and very weak person, as it were within an hour to speak, and to dispose and utter his will.

The author further asserts that he had indeed seen 'a miracle wrought' by this agent 'on the noble Earl and deputy of Paris, which before lay in a manner as dead, and immediately after he had received this down, became again to himself somewhat, and within an hour after died'. If this miracle appears somewhat limited, we will find the author's claims echoed and amplified in following centuries.[29] He adds, moreover, that, 'if old men also use of this fire every day, in a little quantity, it maketh old age lusty, and to continue in like estate a long time, in that this cheereth their hearts, in such manner that they will think themselves to possess juvenile hearts and courages. And for that cause this fire, is named the elixir vitae'.[30]

These last lines in particular prompt some intriguing questions. Is it worse to take another's blood as a kind of habitual health supplement (or indeed elixir of youth and life) than it is to take it for specific medical ills or emergencies? (The question still applies in our own time, given that certain jaded rock stars are supposed to have themselves replenished with someone else's healthy blood at specific intervals). However we might quibble about this at the level of scientifically based physiology (blood – unlike the proverbial 'arm and a leg' – will after all replenish itself) it is clear that the general wisdom enshrined in phrases such as 'sucking their lifeblood' feels otherwise.[31] More importantly, this routine elixir now swiftly conjures both the demonised spectre of the vampire, and all those numerous metaphors of social, economic or psychological vampirism to which he would give rise.[32]

At one level, then, we here confront an intriguing possibility: the first vampires known to western Europe were social, rather than supernatural predators, and were sustained not by spirit forces, but by the labours of a proto-scientific chemistry. Whoever wrote Arnold's letter clearly took this matter seriously. He had treated a French earl, and his epistle managed to survive for some centuries after it was written. There seem, then, to have been medically authorised vampires abroad in Italy and Spain (and perhaps England) in the thirteenth century – men (possibly also women) who habitually consumed the life forces of their fellow human beings in order to stave off both the rigours of age, and the final hand of Death itself.

At another level, it is possible that the medieval alchemy of blood comprised a tradition of medical cannibalism which was more or less independent of the tradition centred on Egyptian mummy. If this is so, it is clearly significant, both from a social and an anthropological viewpoint. It suggests that European Christians were effectively able to surmount the nominally very basic taboo against cannibalism not once, but twice. As we will see, once this prohibition was broken, it was broken with a vengeance, and for many centuries to come.

Corpse medicine from Renaissance to Civil War

Chief substances and uses

The basic picture of early modern usage is as follows. Flesh of various sorts was used chiefly against internal or external bruising and bleeding. It was usually powdered, and applied externally in the form of plasters, and internally in liquid mixtures. In both cases it was one of several ingredients (though, as we will see, a relatively costly one). It could also be swallowed for gout or other inflammations, as an antidote to poison, and as a treatment for various fevers or diarrhoea.[33] Mixed with unguents or ointments, it was applied to haemorrhoids and ulcers. Mummy plasters could further be used against venomous bites, joint pain, and the nodes or tubercles on the bones (then held to be a result of syphilis).[34]

Powdered skull (often from the rear part of the head) was particularly popular in recipes to combat epilepsy and other diseases of the head.[35] In distilled form it was also used against convulsions, and by some (not least Charles II) could be regarded as something of a basic cure-all. Usually applied externally, the oil of human fat treated rheumatism, nervous complaints, gout, wounds, cancer of the breast, cramp, aches and pains, and melancholy. It was also believed by some to be a sarcotic agent, able to promote the growth of flesh.[36]

We have already seen that certain preparations of blood could be regarded as either panaceas, or veritable elixirs of life itself. Fresh blood was especially popular as a cure for epilepsy. Powdered, blood could be sprinkled into wounds, or snuffed up the nostrils – in both cases, to staunch bleeding. It could be used in a plaster against ruptures; and the physician George Thomson held that 'the saline spirit of blood, bones, and urine well rectified, are of admirable use' against the plague.[37] The moss of the skull (as seen in Tradescant's portrait) was perhaps most typically used in powdered form against nosebleeds, inserted directly into the nostrils, and into bleeding cuts or wounds in cases of accident, violence or warfare. (Sphagnum moss, which is mildly antiseptic and highly absorbent, has been used 'as a wound dressing as long ago as the battle of Clontarf in 1014 and as recently as World War I and World War II'.[38]) The herbalist John Gerard noted that it was thought highly effective against epilepsy, as well as 'the chin-cough in children, if it be powdered, and given in sweet wine for certain days together'.[39] In Germany in particular it was used as one key ingredient (along with human skull and fat) in the wound salve – the ointment held to cure injury if rubbed on the offending implement or weapon, rather than the patient.

Across the early modern period, there are four broad types of 'mummy' (excepting, for now, the outrightly counterfeit forms to be examined in chapter three). One is mineral pitch; the second the matter derived from embalmed Egyptian corpses; the third, the relatively recent bodies of travellers, drowned by sandstorms in the Arabian deserts; and the fourth, flesh taken from fresh corpses (usually those of executed felons, and ideally within about three days) and then treated and dried by Paracelsian practitioners.[40]

The unwary reader should be warned that names for these different types can be misleading, sometimes reflecting the medical preferences of a particular author. Most straightforwardly, mineral pitch can be known as bitumen, bitumen indaicum, pissasphaltum, 'natural mummy', or 'transmarine mummy'.[41] The Egyptian variety can be described as 'true mummy', or 'mumia sincere', though these terms are also quite frequently used by Paracelsians.[42] Less ambiguous names for this category are 'foreign mummy' and 'mumia sepulchorum'.[43] The most common description for the drowned corpses of the deserts seems to be 'Arabian mummy' (after the desert region itself). There again, that term can be used to denote Egyptian mummy, probably because it is often known – by a shorthand for the actual or perceived authority of Arabian physicians – as 'the mummy of the Arabians'.[44]

As the surgeon John Hall rightly notes in the early Elizabethan period, 'there is an uncertain variety of opinions' on what exactly is 'mumia'.[45] For Wilhelm Adolf Scribonius in the late sixteenth century, 'pissasphaltus is asphaltus, smelling of pitch, mingled with bitumen', and 'is called mummy'.[46] Authors can accept more than one type as authentic or efficacious, this being the case most commonly with mineral pitch and Egyptian mummy.[47] As the seventeenth century progresses, Paracelsian mummy becomes an especially strong rival to the Egyptian version – a shift promoted partly by the general rise of Paracelsianism, and partly by the decreasing availability of Egyptian mummies. Natural pitch is still used across this whole period, but the term 'mummy' is increasingly likely to refer to some kind of corpse material.[48]

Continental Europe

After the medieval period, the evidence for early use (or at least advocacy) of corpse medicine comes chiefly from the continent. Piero Camporesi has noted that the influential anatomist and medical writer Berengario da Carpi (1460–1530) made frequent use of mummy as an ingredient in medical plasters. Carpi himself was only the most recent member of his family to employ mummy. The recipe for the plaster was a kind of proud family secret, going back several decades. So highly valued was it that the Carpi clan kept mummified heads in the house, thus ensuring that this vital ingredient was always to hand.[49] The Carpi family's use of mummy in the fifteenth century quite closely matches the Egyptian prosecutions of mummy-dealers in 1424.

Around the same time, Bartholomew Montagna, professor of medicine at Padua from 1422–60, was using distillations of human blood.[50] In his influential work on surgery in 1497, the German medical author Jerome of Brunswick (c.1450–c.1512) frequently cited mummy as part of recipes against wounds and bleeding, congealed blood, and several different kinds of fractured, broken or dislocated bones, from jaw and fingers through to the skull, neck or back.[51] For many authors (and presumably patients), corpse medicine could be validated by various more or less abstracting factors (Paracelsianism, alchemy, pious belief in the human body as the apex of creation, and so on). By contrast, Brunswick – a practising surgeon – can at times be strikingly empirical. In addition to illustrations of various surgical machines for treating broken bones, he very precisely commends mummy, not just against congealed blood, but against just that sort resultant upon 'a fall or stricken with a blunt weapon as with a club or staff or other instrument not edged nor cutting.' Similarly, it can be used on those particular 'dents of the brain-pan like as a kettle is dented when they fall upon a hard stone'.[52]

It is also notable that, having cited pills made of mummy, rhubarb, barleycorn and wine for congealed blood, Jerome adds, 'if ye have not this, or if he be a poor man, then give him black coals of elm wood, eyes of crayfish', and 'leaves of chervil dried', powdered and taken in vinegar. As it seems unlikely that barleycorn or rhubarb were very expensive (though we should note that wine evidently was, given the vinegar substitute) it is possible that this gives us some sense of the relative cost of mummy, toward the close of the fifteenth century.[53]

Innocent VIII

In July 1492 Pope Innocent VIII lay dying. We can well imagine that such a figure was offered an impressive – and costly – range of medical treatments. Perhaps never was a physician's motivation to save a human life so keen; the gain in custom, revenue and reputation would be incalculable. One of the alleged cures attempted at Innocent's deathbed is particularly memorable. Three healthy youths were bribed by the pope's physician, with the promise of a ducat apiece. The youths were then cut and bled. Bloodletting was of course a routine medical procedure of the period. The three youths, however, were bled to death. The pope drank their blood, still fresh and hot, in an attempt to revive his failing powers. The attempt was not successful. Innocent himself also died soon after, on 25 July.[54]

So runs the account of the pope's contemporary, Stefano Infessura. Infessura was a lawyer and a fierce critic of Innocent VIII. Can his claims be trusted? There is no easy answer to this question. Here I will examine how far the claim was plausible, by addressing three different areas: was the tale credible ethically, socially, or medically? The first category can be dealt with relatively quickly. The historical whitewash achieved by the modern Catholic Church vastly exceeds the strange amnesia surrounding medicinal cannibalism. Taken as a whole, the Renaissance popes were some of the most corrupt, worldly, scheming and violent men who ever lived. Fourteen years before Innocent's death, Sixtus IV had occupied the papal chair. Sixtus was the most eminent participant in the Pazzi Conspiracy of 1478. In April of this year, the Pazzi family attempted to murder two members of Florence's powerful Medici clan, Giuliano and Lorenzo. If the Pazzi were successful, control of the city would then pass to the pope's 'nephew', Girolamo Riario. (This detail is significant: in this period 'nephew' was very frequently a coded label for one of the pope's many illegitimate sons.) The Pazzi's murderous attempt was partially successful. Giuliano was killed. The blows were struck on Sunday in the Duomo cathedral, just as the Medici brothers were kneeling to receive the sacrament.[55]

Innocent VIII's successor, Alexander VI, has often been referred to as 'the Nero among popes'. He was supposed to have committed his first murder at the age of twelve.[56] Not surprisingly, such a career attracted some criticism. One especially vocal opponent was the Florentine monk, Girolamo Savonarola. After besieging and storming the monastery where he was sheltered, Alexander captured Savonarola in 1498. He was tortured for sixteen days. On one particular day he was racked fourteen times. His 'trial' was so ruthlessly manipulated by the pope that, according to one contemporary, the papal agents were determined to 'put Savonarola to death were he even another St John the Baptist'. On 23 May 1498 Savonarola was hanged and burned.[57]

We should not judge Innocent VIII too harshly if he did not quite manage to live down to the standards of Alexander or Sixtus. But various historians have noted that he made quite a commendable effort. Perhaps most famously, by giving a stamp of papal authority to the witch-hunting obsessions of Henrich Kramer and Jacob Sprenger, Innocent not only helped to catalyse the German witch persecutions of the late fifteenth century, but arguably also contributed to many later ones, given the enduring status of Kramer and Sprenger's *Malleus Maleficarum* as a witch-hunter's bible.[58]

Innocent has also been linked to an early instance of slavery, and is noted for his ignoble attitude to the Crusades, being the first pope to bargain with the Ottoman Empire instead of fighting it.[59] To these achievements, along with his sixteen illegitimate children, one can add the fact that Innocent (like Pius II and Sixtus IV) was bent on installing his nephews and sons in the newly conquered territories of the papal states; that he banned the theses of the celebrated philosopher Pico della Mirandola; and that, 'irresolute [and] lax', he oversaw a reign in which there 'could be no question of church reform' and which, at his death 'left the papal states in anarchy'.[60]

We can hardly say, then, that this piece of medical vampirism seems inconceivable by the ethical standards of the papacy. What of the ethical codes of Innocent's physician? Here matters become slightly complicated, given that this figure was in fact supposedly Jewish. Jews themselves were expressly forbidden, by passages from Leviticus and Deuteronomy, to consume blood. They were also accused, by Christians, of ritually consuming the blood of Christian children.[61] If Infessura took the Jewish blood taboos seriously, then he may simply have been assuming that a Jewish physician could give blood to Christians; or that a sufficiently dedicated or ambitious doctor would temporarily suspend his religious codes in such a case. There again, the Blood Libel itself shows that Christians were habitually able to ignore the inconsistency posed by Old Testament blood laws. It is also therefore possible that Infessura, well aware of how seriously many took Blood Libel stories, felt that his peers would more readily believe such actions if they were credited to a Jewish physician. Such a view would imply that Infessura was merely inventing the story; but this possibility does not put the tale itself wholly beyond our concern.

Two other possibilities are worth considering. First: it is quite possible that the youths died accidentally (although, if so, a doctor could hardly escape a charge of negligence). Secondly, there is the possibility that the physician himself, aware of how high profile the whole case was, actually chose the bleeding of the youths as a strategy which was at least as much politic as simply medical: namely, to show that he was prepared to be suitably ruthless in the pursuit of a cure. Such a stance would partially correspond to what the physician William Hunter, circa 1780, explicitly identified as a kind of 'necessary inhumanity'.[62]

The social and medical issues surrounding the claim can be treated together. Here we should note at once that one recent author, Tony Thorne, while believing Innocent himself to have refused the treatment, does not dispute the fact that his physician had already bled the three 'donors' to death.[63] Although Thorne seems too confident on the issue of Innocent's refusal, it is notable that even he accepts the physician's attempt. If Thorne were correct, it would mean that the treatment was considered practically valid, although not ethically so by the pope himself.[64]

We also know that it had been socially acceptable for Albertus Magnus to use and record a broadly similar treatment. (Although Magnus was not canonised until the 1930s, he was clearly revered by Innocent's time, and would be beatified in 1622).[65] It was socially acceptable for Arnold of Villanova to treat an Earl with such a remedy. By the late fifteenth century, both figures had substantial medical authority. We might object that the preparations used by these men were far less raw than the warm blood swallowed by Innocent. The objection has some weight. But it also brings us to a contemporary of Innocent's who had considerable intellectual and social cachet. Marsilio Ficino (1433–99) was one of the most highly respected figures of Renaissance Europe. And he too believed that the aged could rejuvenate themselves if they would 'suck the blood of an adolescent' who was 'clean, happy, temperate, and whose blood is excellent but perhaps a little excessive'. Although Ficino proposes this, rather than recording actual occurrences, he also makes it quite clear that blood was indeed used as a medicine by 'good doctors' at just this time.[66] Ficino's own father had been a medical doctor, and *The Book of Life*, in which this suggestion appears, is full of similarly practical ideas or details. Notice too that Ficino on one hand treats blood therapy as a routine form of rejuvenation (thus echoing Arnold), and that on the other he is quite happy to have recipients suck the blood directly from the donor's arm.

And Ficino had another remedy for those who, being past seventy, needed to be 'irrigated with a human and youthful fluid'. Such people should 'select a clean girl, one who is beautiful, cheerful, and calm, and, being ravishingly hungry … and with the moon rising, proceed to suck her milk'.[67] The consumption of human milk is said to have been one of the chief treatments of the ailing pope, in the days before his illness became critical. Like those aged men (or women?) who followed Ficino's advice, the pope probably sucked directly from the breast. (Compare, for example, the physician John Caius, who did so during his last sickness in 1573.[68]) For us, this does not make him a cannibal or a vampire. But it does suggest that his desperate physicians wished him to imbibe the essence of human vitality. In Renaissance medical theory, milk and blood were merely variants of the same bodily fluid.[69] According to the ideas of Ficino and others, the drinking of human blood was a slightly more drastic, but perfectly logical, extension of the breastfeeding remedy.[70]

Other evidence shows that Ficino's views would not have been considered wildly eccentric. As Camporesi points out, the Paduan physician, Giovanni Michele Savonarola (d.1464?), had stated that "'the quintessence of human blood" was often utilised "against hopeless diseases"'.[71] In 1512 Jerome of Brunswick described a water distilled from the blood of a thirty-year-old man, 'of nature rejoicing, of mind fair, clear, and wholesome from all sickness'. The blood should be drawn when superfluous, about the middle of May, and its water could be rubbed on 'a consumed member' or on fistulas, or drunk for consumptive fever and 'the consuming of the body'. It was also supposed to make hair grow.[72] Well into the sixteenth century the barber-surgeon Leonardo Fioravanti (1517–88) was making yet greater claims for this "'fifth essence of human blood, with which, rectified and spun, I have as good as raised the dead, giving it as a drink to persons who had all but given up the ghost"'.[73]

Nor should we forget the following recipe for making jam. First, you should 'let it dry into a sticky mass'. Then:

> Place it upon a flat, smooth table of soft wood, and cut it into thin little slices, allowing its watery part to drip away. When it is no longer dripping, place it on a stove on the same table, and stir it to a batter with a knife ... When it is absolutely dry, place it immediately in a very warm bronze mortar, and pound it, forcing it through a sieve of finest silk. When it has all been sieved, seal it in a glass jar. Renew it in the spring of every year.

Although this formula is rather old – dating from 1679 – it should be reliable, as it was given by a Franciscan apothecary. For all that, you may not want to try it at home. For the fruit involved is somewhat exotic. Let us run back a little to the source of the sole ingredient. Our apothecary advises us to '"draw blood ... from persons of warm, moist temperament, such as those of a blotchy, red complexion and rather plump of build. Their blood will be perfect, even if they have not red hair ... Let it dry ... "'. Our source for this strange recipe, Piero Camporesi, rightly notes that we have here a kind of blood jam or marmalade.[74] Almost a hundred years after the supposed transfusion given by Infessura, we find that human blood has a status which for some may blur into the most homely steams and aromas of a well-stocked kitchen.

Returning to the general history of corpse medicine, we find the German magus Henricus Cornelius Agrippa inveighing in 1526 against various 'strange and uncouth medicaments', and lamenting the use of 'human fat, and flesh of men embalmed in spices, which they call mummy'.[75] The phrasing of these last words may imply that mummy was still relatively novel at this point. While Agrippa was referring in part to the Egyptian form of corpse medicine, the herbalist Leonhard Fuchs evidently had much fresher ingredients in mind when, in 1535, he denounced the 'gory matter of cadavers ... sold for medicine' in German pharmacies, going on to describe these latter as 'the very offices of hangmen and shops of vultures'.[76] 'Gory matter' associated with 'hangmen' probably means, at this time, either Paracelsian mummy, human fat, or both. The latter substance had been mentioned by Agrippa almost ten years earlier, and in 1534 the Italian medical author Antonius Musa Brasavola (b.1500) argued in favour of its medical use.[77] A few years later, *The New Jewel of Health* would cite Paracelsus on 'the grease of mumia', while the Paracelsian compendium of Leo Suavius recommended human blood and mummy in 1567.[78]

Paracelsians undoubtedly favoured the freshest kind of corpse as a source of human flesh. The great polymath and medical iconoclast (1491–1541?) Paracelsus was supposed to have asserted that, 'if physicians or any other body understood but the right use of this mummy, or what it is good for, not any malefactors would be left three days on the gallows, or continue on the wheel', but would be swiftly 'stolen away; for they would run any hazard for procuring of these bodies'.[79] Paracelsus' conditional phrasing clearly implies that few (if any) doctors *were* aware of the medical powers of newly dead corpses when he wrote.[80] By the time that it was processed into its medically viable form, Paracelsian mummy was no longer 'gory'. But it is hard to easily equate Fuchs' adjective with human fat. What he could be referring to is the human flesh which apothecaries had acquired from hangman or gibbet, and which could be found in their shops before it was treated. Given that later Paracelsian recipes have strips of flesh hung up to be smoked and cured, this would also more broadly match Fuchs' angry contempt for 'shops of vultures'. Whilst these possibilities are far from conclusive, they do suggest that Paracelsus' non-Egyptian mummy may have been produced by certain practitioners at least a few years before he died (and some decades before his recipes were published).

Over the French border, Fuchs' contemporary Francis I (1494–1547) had no such qualms. An especially keen believer in the efficacy of mummy as a treatment for bruising, Francis 'always carried it in his purse, fearing no accident, if he had but a little of that by him'.[81] In 1555 the Italian humanist Girolamo Ruscelli first published his *Book of Secrets*. This work would become immensely popular, running through innumerable editions and at least seven languages.[82] Ruscelli recommends mummy against flux or spitting of blood, ulcers and tumours, and both mummy and boiled human blood (mixed with pomegranate flowers, coral, red wax and mineral pitch) against ruptures.[83] If someone suffers a nosebleed, the blood should be burned on a plate of iron, made into fine powder, and blown into the sufferer's nostrils. Man's blood dried in the sun and powdered will staunch bleeding.[84]

When Pierre Boaistuau's encyclopaedic *Theatre du Monde* appeared in 1558, it emphasised that 'the flesh embalmed is very sovereign in many usages of physic', and around the same time we find *The New Jewel of Health* prescribing mummy against head pains, gout, wounds, ulcers, eye problems, plague, poisoning, and worms, whilst a Paracelsian mixture for wounds of the joints which contains mummy is known as 'Christ's balm'.[85] While some of these mummy recipes were topical, others, such as a water to combat 'the canker, the fistula ... the falling sickness, the ring worm, the serpigo, the joint sickness, the gout, and any pain of the sinews' clearly had to be swallowed.[86]

The French royal surgeon Ambroise Paré (1510–90) ultimately became one of the most vocal and emphatic opponents of corpse medicine. Yet Paré, for all his own antipathy, confirms the continuing popularity of corpse medicine even as he attacks it. In 1585 he admits that mummy is 'the very first and last medicine of almost all our practitioners' against bruising.[87] In 1580 Paré treated a Moniseur Christophe des Ursins for a fall from his horse. In keeping with his hostility to mummy, Paré used his own particular ingredients against des Ursins' injuries. It has been noted for some time now that more privileged early modern individuals especially were often reluctant to defer to medical authority, whilst certain physicians were equally keen to pamper the whims of affluent clients.[88] (In our own day, when a scientifically based medical authority has become far more powerful, the modern demand for antibiotics, and the potentially bad image of doctors who will not dish them out with lavish recklessness, offers some broad comparison.[89]) On recovering consciousness, des Ursins, rather than thanking Paré for his enlightened stance, indignantly demanded to know why mummy had *not* been applied to the wound.[90] Not long after Paré's death, the Danish King Christian IV (1577–1648) suffered from epilepsy, and accordingly took 'powders partly composed of the skulls of criminals as a cure'.[91]

The continental picture which emerges here seems to be notably slanted toward Italy, Germany, France and Switzerland.[92] In the first case, this may be in part because of the rise of anatomical dissections (in Italy the first recorded public dissection took place in Rome in 1512), which made corpse material a little more readily available for certain surgeons and physicians.[93] As we will see, however, this factor should not be over-emphasised, given that executioners could and did sell any parts of a felon's body to various practitioners or patients. In Switzerland, France and Germany the influence of Paracelsus was probably important.[94] In Italy, there was evidently some demand for mummy from the early sixteenth century; da Carpi, for example, had seen the '"nearly intact bodies"' of Ancient Egyptians in Venice some time before 1518.[95]

Elizabethan England

In terms of medical authority and published prescriptions, corpse medicines seem to have had a relatively marginal status in England until the seventeenth century. In his 1565 edition of Lanfranc, the surgeon John Hall noted, under 'Mumia', the mineral pitch of Serapion, along with 'Mumia sepulchorum' ('that which the most of the Arabians do mention … [the] result of the embalming or spicery of dead bodies at their burials, as aloe, myrrha and balsamo, being coagulated and grown together (with the fat and moisture of the corpse) into a body'); and the sand mummy of the deserts. He was uncertain as to whether bodies could be preserved in this latter way, but stated quite explicitly that the mummy 'which is now among our apothecaries extant' was neither mineral pitch nor 'mumia sepulchorum', but rather 'the very flesh of man's body, as it were burned to a coal; for both whole arms and whole legs, have been here not rarely seen, being dried as black as a coal. Wherefore it must needs be thought, that either the merchants bring from thence whole buried bodies, or very parts of the same; or else that it becometh so, by that means that divers merchants make report of (if it be worthy credit)'. These reports are those of supposedly mummified sandstorm victims (which must mean that 'buried bodies' refers to those normally interred, whether embalmed or not). Having wondered if such a kind of mummification is possible, Hall presently shifts from speculation to certainty, concluding, 'but certainly it is man's flesh, either thus or otherwise dried into a coal'.[96]

The phrase 'man's flesh' arguably tilts nearer to the question of cannibalism than (say) 'dead bodies' (which might be better suited to the transfigured flesh of ancient Egyptians). So too does Hall's unambiguous assertion that the mummy used by London apothecaries at this time was that of the recent dead ('the very flesh … '). We will see in chapter three that his brief glance at alternative methods of mummification ('either thus or otherwise dried … ') leads in a direction very different from the revered necropoles of the pharaohs. What concerns us here is that Hall not only confirms the general use of recently dead mummies by apothecaries, but also very precisely supports this by reference to 'whole arms and whole legs ... not rarely seen' in early Elizabethan London, 'dried as black as a coal'. Those dealing in or handling Egyptian mummy for medicine were often quite exact about its correct texture and appearance, and it seems unlikely that a working surgeon such as Hall would have confused the limbs of ancient Egyptians with those of contemporary desert travellers.[97]

In 1562 the physician William Bullein published *Bullein's Bulwark of Defence Against all Sickness* – a work which may have been composed as early as 1560.[98] This deliberately popularising book recommended mummy as one of several ingredients in 'Theriaca Galeni'. This Galenic treacle featured mummy, along with wild fennel, juice of black poppy, gentian, honey and wild yellow carrots, to treat 'the falling sickness ... and convulsions', as well as headache, stomach pain, migraine, 'spitting of blood' and 'yellow jaundice'.[99] Elsewhere in this work we are told that mummy comes 'from Arabia, and is made of dead bodies, of some of the noble people: because the said dead are richly embalmed with precious ointments and spices, chiefly myrrh, saffron, and aloes'. It 'hath virtue to staunch blood, to incarnate wounds', and, when 'tempered with cassiafistula and drunk with plantain water, it is very good against bruises'.[100] Human blood was also included in plasters against ruptures and dysentery.[101]

The brief words on the derivation of mummy suggest that the substance still needed explaining in England at this time. They show too that Bullein appeared to be comfortable with an agent which he explicitly described as coming 'from dead bodies'; and that much of its virtue was attributed to the embalming materials and process ('because the said dead...'). Bullein also quite precisely notes that, 'to help the falling sickness', mummy should be 'beaten into powder and squirted ... with mariarum water into the nostrils'.[102] In Bullein, then, we find both some of the earliest English medical references to mummy and blood-medicines, and (tellingly) 'some of the earliest printed references to Paracelsus ... in English medical writing'. Given what we will hear later about blood medicines, it is also interesting to find Bullein noting, in a marginal aside, that the 'blood of man is to be had at [the] barber's or blood-letter's' – after which it must be 'dried in the oven'.

In 1575 the queen's surgeon John Banister describes a water of rhubarb and mummy drunk for ulcers of the breast, and a mummy plaster for a tumorous ulcer.[103] Come Banister's 1589 *Antidotary Chyrurgical*, these two references have flourished into numerous balms, plasters, drinks, powders and oils – chiefly aimed at wounds, fractures, ruptures and surgical haemorrhaging, but also for ulcers and inflammations.[104] This change may have resulted partly from Banister's friendship with fellow royal surgeon William Clowes, whose surgical textbook of 1588 cited mummy in recipes against the bleeding from amputation and against wounds.[105] But chief credit is probably due to Banister himself. He has been noted, for example, for his efforts to promote a closer union between surgeons and the then more narrowly theoretical physicians.[106] Hence in 1578 he published an important anatomical textbook, *The History of Man*, with Vesalian illustrations and text from the influential Italian anatomy professor Realdo Columbo. This in turn may have helped to coax (or shame) the physicians into establishing the new Lumleian anatomy lectures, founded in 1582.[107]

Banister's interest in recent medical developments on the continent is a fairly accurate reflection of the profile of mummy in England up to 1600. At this stage continental influence was particularly important. A search for 'mumia', 'mummia', 'mummy' and 'mummiae' on the *Early English Books Online* database (inclusive of 1600) yields only those English authors already cited, with two additions.[108] One – aptly enough – is the travel writer Richard Hakluyt, and the second is the poet and translator George Turberville.[109] Other citations come from English translations of Duchesne, Ruscelli, Cornelius Shilander, Paracelsus, and the German surgeon Johann Jacob Wecker (translated by Banister).[110] In addition to its early mentions of Paracelsus, Bullein's work relies to some extent on Leonhard Fuchs and Gesner. He may also have studied for some time in Germany in the 1550s.[111] Hall cites continental sources such as Brasavola and Matthiolus, and Banister's 1589 work includes Paracelsian recipes and ingredients.[112]

As well as relying on continental authors at this time, English corpse medicine is also notable for being promoted by surgeons, rather than physicians. (Whilst Bullein is described as a physician by his biographer, Patrick Wallis, his educational background is obscure; he is not known to have gained an MD, and he was never a member of the Royal College of Physicians (although his ability to escape their censure is no small achievement).) As well as the influence of Hall, Banister and Clowes, we should also note that the 1576 translation of Gesner was partly the work of the London surgeon George Baker.[113] Gustav Ungerer in the DNB notes that 'Baker considered himself a Galenist who thought it opportune to warn against the harm done by empirics and Paracelsians, but he none the less kept an open mind about chemical medicine'. It was another surgeon, George Barrough, who in his highly popular medical work of 1583 recommended various powders for epileptics, including one from 'the skull of a man burned'.[114] In Scotland, the influential surgeon Peter Lowe (b. *c.*1550) broadly echoed (and surpassed) Banister's efforts to unite surgery and élite physic, and spent perhaps thirty years of his early career in France. In 1597 Lowe notes 'sanguis humanus ustus' (human skull burned) amongst various 'medicaments which stay the flux of blood'.[115]

At one level, this bias tells us something about the relatively open-minded qualities of surgeons as opposed to physicians. It is also possible that it tells us something particular about the nature of earlier English interest in corpse medicine. The surgeons were clearly less heavily burdened than their condescending medical 'superiors' by antiquated Galenic theories. Paracelsus himself was hardly short of theories, but was also in many ways an empiricist. And, by their very nature, surgeons were typically dealing with the most practically physical (as opposed to psychological or partly psychosomatic) class of medical problems. Some of these were not only very real, but highly urgent. We must therefore take seriously the possibility that at this early stage corpse medicines were used because they were seen or thought to work, and that this belief was held by some of the more carefully empirical practitioners of the day.

We should also bear in mind that surviving printed references to corpse medicine do not tell us much about the illicit, but immensely popular medical services offered by numerous unlicensed practitioners in Elizabethan England. Deborah E. Harkness has shown that Baker and Clowes in particular played an important role in mediating between these street mountebanks and the conservative physicians.[116] In doing so she not only confirms the surgeons' relative openness to Paracelsian treatments, but also makes it clear that itinerant healers were making 'Paracelsian therapies … wildly popular among consumers'.[117] We can reasonably assume that, if corpse or blood medicines were being offered by the opportunistic street medics of the day, medical consumers were open-minded about them. Given the greater likelihood of personal violence in this period, it would be surprising if cures for bruising and bleeding were not beginning to circulate amongst Londoners via oral as well as printed sources.[118]

One particularly successful street doctor was the German Valentine Russwurin. Russwurin – writes Harkness – treated William Cecil himself for gout, and was accordingly made a 'denizen' of the country by Elizabeth in winter 1574. By this point Russwurin was already ·famous among Londoners for 'his treatment of eye complaints, bladder stones, and skin ailments'. We have seen that human fat was known as a medical agent in Germany from at least the 1520s, and from this time until the eighteenth century its chief use was in cases of rheumatism or gout. If Russwurin was able to obtain it, he may well have been using it on Cecil. Russwurin also stressed, when complaining of the habitually hostile behaviour of the physicians toward him, that he had been 'esteemed by such highly regarded continental physicians as Pier Andrea Mattioli and Rembert Dodoens'. Lynn Thorndike notes that by 1561 Mattioli had distilled salt from two human skulls, and given Russwurin's mastery of Paracelsian chemical theories, such practices might also have been of interest to him.[119] Come August 1602 the unlicensed practitioner Francis Anthony was defying the strictures of the Royal College of Physicians, insisting that it 'had no power to examine him' and openly admitting that he had 'made use of an extraordinary purging remedy, and was master of another for fevers made out of mummy, communicated to him by [the agricultural writer and inventor] Hugo Plat'.[120] Another practitioner who was at once highly successful and not strictly orthodox was the astrologer Simon Forman. As Lauren Kassell points out, a casebook of 1607–10 lists various human ingredients, including 'urine, hair, blood, menstrual blood, turds' and semen.[121]

The apparently partial impact of corpse medicine at this earlier stage is broadly reinforced by the relatively small number of literary references to mummy before 1600. In 1594, the exuberantly witty Thomas Nashe stated that, while 'mummy is somewhat obscure' (presumably to the general public), it is 'to physicians and their confectioners … as familiar as mumchance [a card game] amongst pages'.[122] Nashe was answering critics who accused him of using, or coining, highly obscure words in his 1593 book, *Christ's Tears over Jerusalem*. Overall, the charge is certainly true. *Christ's Tears* – an extravagant and fantastical response to the supposedly heaven-sent plague of that year – is at times almost Joycean, or indeed hallucinatory, in its linguistic invention and excess. Among Nashe's many coinages is the word 'mummianized'. At one level, criticism of his term reflects the relative novelty of corpse medicine at this time. And Nashe's exact word choice supports this impression. He uses 'mummia-nized' to mean 'mummified', thereby implying that the word is too novel to have acquired one generally accepted verb form. In 1593 the first version is as good a choice as the second.[123]

Nashe also implies a split between patients and practitioners. This – as chapter seven will show – persisted to some extent throughout the seventeenth century. Nashe himself may have gained his knowledge of mummy from the 1579 edition of Bullein, whose work he acknowledges as inspiration for the formal structure of *Have With You to Saffron Walden* (1596). It would also have been typical of Nashe to have seized on whatever was novel and startling, and the same can be said of Donne, whose poem 'Love's Alchemy', featuring an unflattering comparison between women and mummy, probably predates 1600 (and will be considered at some length in a few moments). In around 1596 Shakespeare joins this élite handful, when he has Falstaff lamenting his ducking in the Thames, and observing what a momentous figure he would have cut as a drowned corpse: 'the water swells a man; and what a thing should I have been, when I had been swell'd? I should have been a mountain of mummy'.[124] This seems to be a modishly alliterative way of saying 'mountain of flesh'. Modish or not, however, it does seem to assume that at least some (if not most) members of the audience in 1596 will know what Falstaff means. Some of them must surely have noted the implication of the phrase, which effectively glosses mummy as 'flesh', ancient or otherwise.

Hawk medicines and fish bait

In the midst of this period there appears an interest in mummy which is at once non-cannibalistic, yet arguably more disturbing than routine human consumption. 1575 saw the appearance of George Turberville's *The Book of Falconry or Hawking*. This work shows that the serious falconer should treat mummy rather as did Francis I: 'he must always be assured to have mummy in powder in his bag in a readiness ... for that it may so fall out, as his hawk may receive a bruise at the encounter of a fowl'.[125] If mummy really was healing wounded hawks (and it was certainly thought to do so) then any opponents of corpse medicine who suggested its efficacy to be the result of psychological suggestion would be conveniently stumped.[126] Whilst citing various bird medicines, Turberville also makes it clear that mummy was the primary treat-ment for injured hawks, singling it out as intimately associated with hawking in his opening poetical outline of the sport:

> When hawks are hurt and bruised, by rash encounter in the skies,
> What better skill, than for their harms a powder to devise,
> To dry the blood within the bulk, and make his mummy so,
> As no physician greater art, on patients can bestow?[127]

The book goes on to offer precise guidelines for monitoring a hawk's physical condition. Of vital importance is inspection of the bird's excrement (possibly because hawk's urine was hard to find or collect). Attention to this substance rivals that of the most obsessive parent to a sickly infant's nappies: 'if so it be black, and stinking ... the more the hawk is in evil case and state', and has probably been 'foul fed, and with corrupt flesh'. There again, when 'the casting happeneth to be yellowish black, and very moist and slimy, it argueth your hawk to be stuffed with evil humours, proceeding of too great heat, or of immoderate and overgreat flights, or too much baiting'. You should therefore restore good feeding, cool the bird by washing its meat in good fresh water, and 'allow ... her besides, one or two, or more castings of cotton: into which you must convey very excellent good mummy beaten into powder'.[128] This kind of advice is repeated with variations, dependent on the state of the excrement, and implied health problems.[129]

Whilst the tenant families of great estates often languished in squalor and hunger in damp cottages, the aristocrats of early modern Europe were rigorously scrutinising the excrement of their sporting pets, feeding them beef and veal, and dosing them with medicines or appetite stimulants, with the most vital active ingredient having been carefully matured for perhaps twenty centuries, before being shipped from Egypt to the pharmacies of Rome, Paris and London.[130] In 1575, such habits may have been far more common in Italy and France than in England. Turberville's title page openly advertises his book as 'collected out of the best authors, as well Italians as Frenchmen, and some English practises'. This seems at once designed to sell the work to those keen to keep abreast of continental innovations, and to notably marginalise the status of 'some English practises'.[131] One mummy recipe is credited to the Marburg professor Jerome Cornarus (1500–558), and another to a 'Messer Manoli ... the falconer to the renowned Signor Bartholomew Alviano'. Another remedy seems (phrasing is ambiguous) to be attributed to a Master Amé Cassian.[132]

If we assume for the moment that such habits were, circa 1575, far more common in France or Italy, we can already note two interesting points. One is that these practices were fairly well established there (rather than being purely theoretical novelties); for, when advising that a bird with a suspect liver should be given 'meat all powdered with mummy prepared', the book adds, 'if she will take it with her flesh, as divers hawks will do of themselves'. This last phrase shows that this medicine was widely used – sufficiently so that one could give a generalised picture of how birds would respond to it. Elsewhere, the reader is given a detailed guide to the preparation of hawk mummy, involving cloves, ginger, cinnamon, nutmeg and saffron. And he is told that he should 'take mummy three ounces, or four, or so much as shall content you, beating it to powder, and putting it into a linen cloth'.[133] Whether the recipe was mixed by a leisured aristocrat or his servant, it is clear that the mummy is supposed to be processed (i.e., powdered) on one's estate. This implies a desire to be sure of getting authentic mummy, as well as a familiarity with the appearance of the genuine article.

Hawk mummy may have been relatively novel in England in 1575 (though one might add that, novel or not, Turberville's book has more references to mummy than any other work published in England and in English up to 1600). But there is some evidence that it caught on.[134] In 1678 John Ray published *The Ornithology of Francis*

Willoughby of Middleton … Fellow of the Royal Society. This too advised that the competent falconer 'ought to carry into the field with him mummy in powder, with other medicines', and repeats the advice about bad excrement and consequent mummy dosing.[135] A little later, in 1686, the publisher Nicholas Cox drew on Turberville for the same kind of advice to genteel sportsmen.[136] Turberville's work was itself republished in 1611, and by the 1670s his advice had the new authority of the Royal Society.

If the dosing of hawks with Egyptian mummy may disturb some, other uses of the human body offer further food for thought. In 1616 an expanded version of *Maison Rustique* (a work originally credited to the eminent French anatomist Charles Estienne (1504–*c*.1564)) tells us that 'in some countries' rabbit breeders feed their animals 'with man's blood, such as is to be come by when sick persons are let blood'.[137] On the subject of sport, we should also note that mummy was held by some, from about the mid-seventeenth century, to be an excellent fish bait.[138] A 1686 sporting manual credited to the bookseller Richard Blome repeats this advice, describing two pastes which serve as bait.[139] One involves a heron, plucked, chopped, and minced very small, and kept in a dunghill in a strong glass bottle for three weeks. The second is, Blome admits, more expensive, but worth twice the price nonetheless. It is made from hempseed, along with either 'two ounces of mummy', or 'the fat of a man, which may be had at the apothecaries'.[140]

Such a recipe may have struck those who were given to musing upon the curious cycles of growth, decay, and consumption. Donne, for example, talks in a 1623 resurrection sermon of the alleged problems posed for heavenly bodies 'when a fish eats a man, and another man eats that fish'.[141] Donne here is probably referring to the bodies of drowned men. But if he had heard of fish swallowing human fat, and men swallowing those fish, he may well have perceived such a dilemma as similarly metaphysical, rather than moral. Elsewhere in the same sermon, evoking the fall of human eloquence with dark mastery, he asks his listeners to imagine 'that brain that produced means to becalm gusts at council tables, storms in parliaments, tempests in popular commotions', finally reduced, in death, to generating 'nothing but swarms of worms and no proclamation to disperse them'.[142] What, we might wonder, would such a rhetorician have made of Blome's further suggestion for anglers, that 'a dead man's skull beaten to powder for worms to scour in, is excellent'?[143] Whilst 'scour' seems here to have the sense of 'to move about hastily or energetically' (*OED*, 1a), we cannot rule out feeding. For in the same breath the author also explains that worms may be kept in moss, into which one should drop 'a spoonful of cream' every three or four days.[144] We now face a densely ravelled nexus of life, death and consumption which even Donne might find hard to restitch into a satisfying or meaningful pattern.

Corpse cosmetics

In the middle years of James I we encounter another use of corpse materials which is not strictly medical. In 1615 the preacher Thomas Adams, attacking both general pride and feminine vanity, refers to 'powders, liquors, unguents ... derived from the living [and] from the dead'.[145] Among other things, Adams was probably alluding to the use of human fat as a cosmetic. We know that survivors of smallpox around this time took trouble to mask scars, with the white lead pastes of Elizabeth I being only the most famous example. Well into the eighteenth century, one recipe specifically identifies a mixture of turpentine, human fat and beeswax as an 'unguent' to fill the facial pits left by smallpox.[146]

In Philip Massinger's 1623 play *The Bond-Man*, a character called Timagoras scornfully derides a woman whose age is no longer hidden even by the most artful cosmetic devices:

> You are grown thrifty, smell like other women;
> The College of Physicians have not sat,
> As they were us'd, in counsel how to fill
> The crannies in your cheeks, or raise a rampire,
> With mummy, ceruses, or infants' fat,
> To keep off age, and time.

> (4.4, 30–35)

The opening of this sally, with its burlesque image of the College 'sat in council' on so grave a problem, colours our sense of the later lines to some degree. Similarly, 'infants' fat' seems in part to be used as a structural opposition to the literal and moral corruption of age. For all that, it would be rash to too quickly write this off as an extravagant piece of misogyny (or ageism). Whilst infants' fat was commonly thought of at this time as an ingredient used by witches (allegedly to assist the aerodynamic properties of the common broomstick), we need to remind ourselves that, for men such as Donne and Jonson (to say nothing of James I, Scottish witch-hunter and author of the 1597 *Demonology*) witches were real.[147] In his 1609 *Masque of Queens*, Jonson had a witch state: 'I had a dagger: what did I with that?/Kill'd an infant, to have his fat'; and in the annotated version of the masque in his 1616 *Works*, he makes it very clear that this was founded on personal belief.[148] At the level of the realistic detail of Timagoras' speech, we must also note that mummy was far less arcane (or ethically dubious) than infants' fat, whilst ceruses were commonly used to cover smallpox scars – this being the white lead paste favoured by Elizabeth.[149] There may also be an implication (serious or otherwise) that infants are a particularly suitable choice for those desiring a youthful appearance.

Divine and human cannibalism

On 4 September 1612, the fervent Protestant minister Daniel Featley engaged in a debate on the Eucharist with the Catholic convert Richard Smith (later to become Bishop of Chalcedon). Excluding discussions of the New World, it was the supposedly literal swallowing of Christ which generated the most frequent accusations of cannibalism from Protestants.[150] In the era of corpse medicine, however, such polemic was not as straightforward as Protestants would have wished. We enter the debate at the point when Featley has just cited St Augustine's belief, that 'if the scripture seem to command a sin, or an horrible wickedness ... [then] the speech is figurative', emphasising that Augustine had given the words 'unless you eat the flesh of the Son of man ... ' as a prime example of such a figure. Smith answered 'that it was no horrible, nor wicked thing to eat man's flesh, since we usually eat it in mummy'. 'What', asks Featley, 'not the flesh of a live man?' Smith then gives the compressed, slightly cryptic response: 'Not ... under another shape or form'. He seems here to be implicitly conceding the point about dead versus live flesh, but trying to score his own point by alluding to the Protestant claim that the Eucharist really involves consumption of Christ's body 'under another shape or form' than that of actual flesh and blood. Mummy, he implies, *is* man's flesh, nothing more nor less. It is not 'under another shape or form'. Here, just six years before one of the worst religious conflicts of all history commenced in the shape of the Thirty Years War, Featley and Smith find themselves bizarrely united as joint participants in medicinal cannibalism (*'we* usually eat it ... ').[151]

In 1628 the same tactic was used upon Featley by the Jesuit priest Thomas Everard. Featley cites 'the doctrine of concomitancy' as holding 'that the flesh and bones of Christ are in the consecrated chalice'. 'What', asks Everard, 'if I grant you that also?' Featley: 'then you do more than Christ commands: for Christ commands you to eat his flesh, and drink his blood; and he no where commands you to drink his flesh and bones. Who ever heard of flesh and bones to be drunk, and that properly, without any figure?' Everard responds simply: 'in mummy the flesh of man may be drunk'. Featley replies: 'peradventure the flesh of man may be so handled, and altered, and the bones also grounded to so small a powder, that in some liquor they may be drunk: but the flesh of man and bones, without an alteration of quality, or quantity, cannot be drunk. And', he concludes, 'I hope you will not say, that the flesh and bones of Christ in the Sacrament receive any alteration at all'. We can only guess as to whether or not Everard felt this sufficient answer. For, 'at these words, Doctor Featley and Master Everard were entreated to desist from any further dispute, till after supper. And so this point was not further pursued'.[152]

At one level, this exchange shows yet more clearly that Featley is unable to dispute the commonplace use of mummy itself. He does not (as we might expect him to) claim that Egyptian mummy is somehow different from ordinary flesh. Given that he uses the phrase 'man's flesh', it is possible that he is actually referring here to Paracelsian rather than Egyptian mummy. He clearly is referring to another form of corpse medicine when, echoing the point about Christ's bones, he admits that bones also may be ground up and drunk as medicine. At another level, the argument of 1628 suggests that Everard, like Smith, thought corpse medicine to be a useful polemical weapon in such an area. This may have been because he knew of the earlier exchange, and felt that Featley had been wrong-footed. Or it may have been just because corpse medicine was so widely practised, and so little criticised. If we turn to Featley himself, we can well suspect that the 1612 reference to mummy had stuck with him, given that he seems notably better prepared in 1628.

Indeed, the topic was still evidently a live and troubling presence in his mind come 1638, when he published a letter to Smith concerning the debate of 1612. It is, Featley now insists, 'an horrible thing to eat man's flesh, and drink his blood *though in another shape*'. For 'it is not the disregard of the countenance of man, or the disfiguring his shape, which makes anthropophagy or man eating so horrible a sin: but the making the flesh of one man the food of another, and the belly a sepulchre'. He offers five illustrations, two of which are of particular interest. First, he asks Smith to suppose that 'at Rome or Venice on the day of your carnivals when many murders are committed by men in disguised habits ... one of the masquers or mummers slain, should be boiled or roasted, and served in at table, in the habit of a whiffler, or masquer'. Were it not 'a horrible wickedness think you to eat of this man's flesh, his head for example though with a vizard upon it'? 'And so', Featley concludes triumphantly, 'I return you a mummer for your mumme'. He presently turns to 'the argument you take ... from the apothecary's shop'. As to this, 'I wish you some better drug of theirs, I mean some strong confection of helleborum to purge your brain. For our question is not of the *medicinal* use of man's flesh, altered by art, but whether it be not a sin, and that a horrible one, to eat with the mouth and teeth the flesh of a known man, nay of the Son of God'.[153]

The first of these examples seems designed to defamiliarise and vivify the act of cannibalism (implicitly over-familiarised by Catholic Mass rites) as sharply as possible. It can also be argued that, coming just a few lines before the reference to mummy, the startling carnival passage effectively softens the (again familiar) cannibalism of European medicine. If we then take the second passage alone, we find two important qualifications. First, Featley emphasises that 'our question is not of the *medicinal* use of man's flesh, altered by art' (his italic). There is something intriguingly axiomatic about the added emphasis on 'medicinal', with its acid implication that Smith is raising a question which is so obviously understood by their peers as a special case. The phrase 'altered by art' is also clearly meant to carry a lot of weight without further gloss. Potentially, it could be taken to mean that after such artful processing, man's flesh is indeed *not* man's flesh any longer. Finally, we have the glancing but eloquent attack on those Catholics who, by contrast, 'eat with the mouth and teeth the flesh of a known man' – namely, Christ. Again, cannibalism is implicitly vivified, made more repellent by the concrete evocation of 'mouth and teeth'. But most important of all for us is the phrase 'a known man'. Tacit though it may be, the corollary seems unambiguous: corpse medicine is somehow better, somehow less cannibalistic, because it very typically involves the body of an *unknown* person. Beyond all these individual points, Featley's two debates remind us that, whilst early modern Christians seem very little concerned about the habitual cannibalism of medicine, many of them were already cannibals. If this point seems at first to apply most obviously to Catholics, we will see that the medicinal status of the human body could in fact be sharply spiritualised by certain Protestants.

In 1616 Estienne's popular compendium, *Maison Rustique,* gives several recipes for distilling animal blood. That of a goat, it recommends, should be drawn in mid-flow (that is, ignore the first flow of liquid, and the last). After being treated with salt and stored in horse dung forty days, it should be distilled and then kept in dung a further forty days. The author goes on to explain that, 'the blood of a young man is distilled in the same sort, but the man must be of a good complexion, and sound body, of the age of twenty years or thereabouts, of a well fed and fleshy body'. The resulting agent 'serveth instead of restoratives unto those which are in a consumption', and 'is good likewise against rheumes and distillations falling upon the joints, if the diseased places be fomented therewithal'. The author then admits: 'I do not greatly approve the distilling of man's blood for any such end, seeing it is an unworthy and heinous thing, and not beseeming Christians, and a thing likewise which in the middest of so many other helps may easily be spared'.[154] This explicit unease is at once rare in early modern medicine, and also oddly ambiguous. There is a subtle disjuncture between the very precise instructions, and the following note of opposition. The recipe itself again implies that youth is integral (the donor being around twenty); and the author seems in no doubt that the treatment is effective. Given the formidable popularity of this book, we can imagine that others may well have treated the formula with less scruple.[155]

Maison Rustique also proposes to those suffering from gout a 'sovereign ointment' made from roots, rye flowers, butter, and 'man's grease'. Repeating the popular epilepsy cure of powdered skull, taken for forty days (and commending especially 'that part of the skull which is nearest unto the seam of the crown'), the book further suggests wearing a piece of skull around the neck, and adds that 'you shall deliver them that are in that fit, if you tickle them and pinch their great toe, or rub their lips with man's blood'.[156]

In 1623, with Shakespeare's first folio being propped up to catch the eyes of browsers at London bookstalls, the Bard's son-in-law, the physician John Hall, was called to treat William Fortescue, an eminent Worcestershire landowner and sufferer from epilepsy. Using neither skull nor blood, Hall instead burned 'a mixture of the aromatic resin benzoin, powdered mummy, black pitch and juice of rue', the resultant fumes being inhaled by Fortescue as a soporific.[157]

Some time before his death in 1626, Francis Bacon echoed the widespread belief that 'mummy has great force in staunching of blood'.[158] Bacon also cites a recipe for the wound salve. While sceptical as to the particular formula which he quotes, Bacon is not flatly dismissive. Listing some key ingredients, he states that 'the strangest and hardest to come by, are the moss upon the skull of a dead man, unburied; and the fats of a bear, and a bear, killed in the act of generation'. Many authorities recommended that moss, or *usnea*, should be derived from the skull of a young man, perished by a violent death, and this itself preferably hanging or drowning. Hanged corpses were not so hard to come by, but the problem of scarcity at which Bacon gestures was probably a result of the need for the skull to be left alone unburied, and for the moss to grow, which would take time, if it did occur at all. This difficulty of supply seems to have vanished in later decades. Typically practical, Bacon himself also suggests a possible Jacobean source for usnea. There are, he observes, 'heaps of slain bodies' lying unburied over in Ireland.[159]

For whom the bell tolls: John Donne and the king's physician

The poem 'Love's Alchemy' (probably written in the 1590s) contains what appears to be Donne's earliest reference to corpse medicine. This fiercely unsentimental attack on idealising notions of romantic love concludes with the warning,

> Hope not for mind in women; at their best
> Sweetness and wit, they are but mummy, possessed.

As A.J. Smith noted some time ago, these very last words could mean either that, when one possesses them, women yield not a marriage of minds, but only 'mummy', that is, mindless or soul-less flesh; or that they are 'mummy possessed' in the sense of soul-less flesh, possessed and therefore animated by a demon spirit.[160]

Whilst both of these options are plausible, W.A. Murray has offered further evidence in support of the first view, whilst also nuancing and elaborating its implications. Arguing that much of the style of the poem echoes Paracelsian theories about men and women, Murray goes on to claim that the final lines are based upon the Paracelsian sense of 'mummy' as 'an actual sweet balsam or healing fluid of the body'. For 'Paracelsus had observed that open wounds grew new flesh from the inside outwards, and he attributed this process to the operation of "mumia", which he visualized as a sweet, penetrating combining form of "quicksilver"'.[161] Murray's belief, that Donne precisely alludes to the Paracelsian 'sweetness' of mummy as physiological balsam, is one which broadly fits the often highly compressed multiple meanings of a line or word in Donne's poems, as well as his sly vaunting of personal erudition.

It also seems to fit Donne's lifelong interest in Paracelsus and Paracelsian balsam. In an undated letter to Henry Goodyer, he remarks that, according to 'the later physicians, when our natural inborn preservative is corrupted or wasted, and must be restored by a like extracted from other bodies ... the chief care is that the mummy have in it no excelling quality, but an equally digested temper'.[162] Here 'the later physicians' are almost certainly Paracelsus and his followers. The phrase 'corrupted or wasted' seems to imply first illness, and then age, with the latter word broadly echoing Ficino's belief about ageing and the restorative powers of youthful blood. The reference to the 'equally digested temper' is again precise; and taken together, these two conceptions of mummy seem to indicate two things. One: it was mummy as balsam which most interested Donne; two: it was Paracelsus' idea of balsam which Donne found of particular interest in that author. (It is also telling that Goodyer is given no basic explanation as to the more general nature of mummy; whenever the letter was written, Donne's relatively coded reference to 'other bodies' must have been known to indicate human ones.)

In the 1611 poem *An Anatomy of the World*, Donne attributes the putrefaction of the world to the loss of Elizabeth Drury, who represented its 'intrinsic balm, and ... preservative'.[163] An especially close echo of Murray's definition of Paracelsian mummy is found in a Whitehall sermon, where a comparison between Protestants and Catholics involves reference to 'that *balsamum natural,* which Paracelsus speaks of, that natural balm which is in every body, and would cure any wound, if that wound were kept clean, and recover any body, if that body were purged, as that natural balm is in that body, how diseased soever that body be'.[164] Still more precisely, in another sermon he talks of how, 'if a man do but prick a finger, and bind it above that part, so that the spirits, or that which they call the balsamum of the body, cannot descend, by reason of that ligature, to that part, it will gangrene'.[165]

At one level, Donne's interest in Paracelsian mummy or balsam seems to match his interest in the concrete and vibrant nature of the living body.[166] At another, it shows that what he valued most about Paracelsus was his empiricism. That last example in particular is a result of careful observation. Although Donne – following the general physiology of his day – blames spirits instead of blood for the resultant gangrene, the idea is clearly derived from experience, and is broadly accurate. Donne's overall attitude to Paracelsus is by no means straightforward. There are several negative and sardonic references in poetry and prose.[167] Some of the criticisms made in *Ignatius his Conclave*, where Paracelsus is commended to Lucifer in hell, look merely opportunistic, and are more or less contradicted elsewhere.[168] One, however, is echoed in a private letter, where Donne suggests that 'new physic' has arisen just because the older, Galenic version was so inadequate in certain areas, rather than because its new rival is wholly superior. Here he also adds that Paracelsus' part in this shift has been overstated.[169]

Despite some degree of ambivalence, it is clear that certain of Paracelsus' ideas appealed to Donne's imagination. More precisely, whilst Donne was evidently impatient with some of the grander cosmic theories of Paracelsus and his followers, his respect for the empirical talents of the great iconoclast is evident on several occasions. Another sermon approvingly cites Paracelsus' maxim 'practise is a physician's study', and his assertion that 'he that professes himself a physician, without experience, *chronica de futuro scribit*, he undertakes to write a chronicle of things before they are done, which is an irregular, and a perverse way'.[170] Similarly, in *Biathanatos* Donne talks of 'one excellent chirurgian', who is identified in a marginal note as Paracelsus. Here and elsewhere Donne specifically refers to Paracelsus' book on surgery, *Chirurgia Magna* – a work which he owned, and had evidently read.[171]

In 1623 Donne fell seriously ill. Taking a typically religious approach to his sickness, he composed a set of pious reflections and prayers as he lay sweating and trembling, continually in fear of death. Published in 1624 as *Devotions on Emergent Occasions*, these ruminations are now best remembered for the assertion that 'no man is an island', and for Donne's response to the tolling of a funeral bell in a neighbouring church ('never send to know for whom the bell tolls'). Less well known is a passage from his twenty-second Meditation, on the material corruption of the human body. Here Donne reflects that even the medical utility of this entity arises only after death: 'if my body may have any physic, any medicine from another body, one man from the flesh of another man (as by mummy, or any such composition) it must be from a man that is dead'. This too seems to refer to Paracelsian mummy, rather than the Egyptian variety; Donne twice talks about a 'man', and even the phrase 'from a man that is dead' seems to imply a recently dead person, rather than an ancient and partially dehumanised Egyptian relic.

It is at this point that Sir Theodore Turquet de Mayerne enters our story. The eighth Meditation bears the title, 'The king sends his own physician'. It is now generally agreed that this physician was Mayerne.[172] A few words on his career up to that point are necessary. Although Mayerne was probably not the most fervently Paracelsian physician of his day, he is notable for combining a significant degree of Paracelsianism with a high degree of success, prestige and influence. His openness to Paracelsian theory, indeed, was sufficient to get him banned from medical practice, in 1603, by the Parisian medical faculty.[173] It has also been argued that it was largely Mayerne, along with Thomas Moffett, who was responsible for ensuring that Paracelsian remedies were included in the first ever *Pharmacopeia*.[174] Issued in Latin in 1618, this (in varying incarnations) was to be the standard prescriptive bible for decades to come.[175] As Moffett was in fact hostile to corpse medicine, it seems likely that the several listings of mummy plasters in this work were due to Mayerne.[176]

In terms of prestige, we find that Mayerne's patients included Henri IV, Robert Cecil, James I, Charles I, Charles II, and Oliver Cromwell.[177] Especially notable among these is James. As Hugh Trevor-Roper's biography of Mayerne reminds us, James had been notoriously unhealthy since birth. In his very first year he was entrusted to 'a tipsy Scottish nurse whose alcoholic milk made him so weak that he was six years old before he could walk'.[178] Among other things, James suffered from gout from 1616 on, and Mayerne was treating him for this in 1623. Trevor-Roper cites a letter written by Mayerne for the benefit of James's other doctors, and including advice on James's health and his habits.[179] Because James could not be relied upon to follow a sensible regimen, Mayerne proposed medicine for his gout, including 'an arthritic powder composed of scrapings of an unburied human skull, herbs, white wine', and whey, 'to be taken at full moon'.[180] But, remarks Trevor-Roper, 'since the king hates eating human bodies, an ox's head can be substituted' in his case.[181]

James's refusal of corpse medicine is interesting, giving a wry twist on Webster's 'physicians are like kings/They brook no contradiction'.[182] We have no other evidence of patients declining such treatment around this time, and Mayerne himself was clearly making fairly regular use of various body parts. A version of the skull powder for gout is listed in his *Treatise of the Gout*, and in the same work he recommends a painkilling plaster composed of opium, hemlock, and human fat.[183] In various other works Mayerne cites powdered skull against epilepsy and haemorrhoids, and mummy as a sarcotic, or in a balsam against bruises.[184] Standard as these cures are, Mayerne is also notable for preferring mummy specifically derived from the lungs of a man who had suffered a violent death, as well as the placenta of a woman who had borne a male child.[185]

We are presented, then, with a question: does Donne mention corpse medicine in *Devotions* because he was given it by Mayerne, during his near-fatal illness? Whilst this question cannot be conclusively answered, it is a little surprising that it seems not to have been raised before.[186] Over thirty years ago, Kate Frost wrote about the sickbed encounter of Donne and Mayerne, and painstakingly identified the latter's likely treatments for what was almost certainly typhus fever (then known as the purple or spotted fever). 'The typhus epidemic of 1623/4 in England was' (she emphasises) 'a severe one', with the death toll estimated at 8,000.[187] Clearly, if Mayerne had thought that pulverised lungs or powdered skull would help Donne, then he would not have hesitated to use them. (In terms of agents which would now startle modern doctors, indeed, he very probably did apply oil of scorpions – made, as Frost points out, from thirty live scorpions, caught when the sun was in Leo – as well as unicorn's horn and bezoar stone.)[188]

Frost derived these and Mayerne's other therapies from a Latin prescription written later in 1624. Although this document was intended for possible future treatment of James I, Frost suspected (perhaps rightly) that it drew on Donne's case history.[189] Whilst corpse ingredients are not explicitly cited, they may have been contained in one or other of the preparations (such as diascordia) which included a large number of potentially variable substances.[190] Moreover, we cannot simply assume that what Mayerne wrote listed everything which he tried on Donne. He may have tried corpse medicine, felt that it was not effective, and therefore omitted it from the later prescription. Given that human skull was used for convulsions, it is possible that it was employed in this case, whose chief symptom was a dangerously high fever.[191] Frost also notes that Mayerne recommended opening the haemorrhoidal veins – if engorged – in such cases, and we know that Mayerne used powdered skull to treat haemorrhoids.[192]

Turning back to Donne himself, it could be argued that his words alone, in Meditation 22, would be enough to make us wonder about his treatment, even if Mayerne were not known to have been at his bedside. Although the reference to corpse medicine could be mere coincidence (and suits the rhetorical aims of the passage fairly well), the general circumstances and structure of *Devotions* give us some cause to suspect that, in a relatively spontaneous composition, mummy could have intruded here just because it was fresh in Donne's memory (and, indeed, fresh in his body). Given that powdered skull would have been a particularly likely agent for Donne's case, it may also be significant that Donne carefully opens out the initial reference to mummy ('or any such composition') in a way that is probably meant to include substances such as skull or fat. This hypothesis necessarily assumes that Donne knew he had been given some form of corpse medicine. It seems reasonable to assume that both Mayerne and Donne's other doctor, Simeon Foxe, would have informed their patient as to what they were doing whenever possible.[193] Foxe was himself a friend of Donne's, and may have been particularly well aware of Donne's more general interest in medicine.[194] Both men, we can safely infer, would have wanted to keep a figure of Donne's social and intellectual standing as well informed as they could, quite aside from any humane desire to allay his personal fears. It is also probable that anything Donne was not told during the illness could have been discussed in following weeks.

Finally, this question must remain a question. But it is an intriguing one, and one which perhaps merits further research. Do we owe the surviving sermons of the last seven years of Donne's life to the cannibalistic habits of early modern doctors? At very least, he and his contemporaries may have believed that this was the case.

It should by now be clear that during the continental Renaissance and the Tudor and early Stuart eras, corpse medicine was far from being the preserve of quacks or superstitious peasants. But at this stage, medical use of the human body was arguably tentative by comparison with following decades. Come the English Revolution, and the so-called Scientific Revolution, it seems only to have grown more extensive and more respectable.

2

CORPSE MEDICINE FROM THE CIVIL WAR TO THE EIGHTEENTH CENTURY

In 1649 the apothecary and astrologer Nicholas Culpeper first published his English translation of the *Pharmacopeia*. We have seen that this had included certain mummy recipes back in 1618. But Culpeper's vernacular edition of this standard directory was a very different affair from the élite Latin bible of the physicians. As Patrick Curry points out, the original version had been 'difficult even for some apothecaries, and impossible for the barely literate'. The political or social ramifications of Culpeper's move were certainly clear to the Royalists and the physicians of the day. As Curry adds, 'the royalist newsheet Mercurius Pragmaticus' accused Culpeper, that September, of 'mixing every receipt endeavouring "to bring into obloquy the famous societies of apothecaries and chyrurgeons"'; while 'William Johnson, the college's chemist, asked whether the result was "fit to wipe one's breeches withal"'.[1]

The basic historical circumstances which permitted Culpeper's translation to appear were of course the Civil War and attendant collapse of print censorship. But it is clear from just the briefest glance at this work that the collapse of Royalist political authority also had powerful psychological effects upon authority in general in the years after 1642.[2] Culpeper is gleefully ebullient in his irreverent swipes at the ignorance and corruption of the old Royal College of Physicians. Noting the numerous kinds of animal excrement listed by the Latin *Pharmacopeia*, he briskly distances himself from such substances: 'I have here inserted the living creatures, and excrements, etc. in the order the College left them, (for impose them they could not for want of authority; alack! alack! the king is dead, and the College of Physicians want power to impose the turds upon men)'.[3]

More will be said about these seemingly arcane ingredients in chapter five. Here we can emphasise that, sharply critical as Culpeper often was, he did not take issue with mummy recipes. The *Physical Directory* features several, especially those involving plasters.[4] In his own *Directory for Midwives* Culpeper also repeats the enduring powder (peony seeds, oak mistletoe, human skull) for epilepsy, adding specifically that this is 'a great disease, and kills for the most part young children', and also presenting a version of the medicine which is intriguingly akin to a kind of blanket vaccination. For one should, he states, 'give this powder to prevent it, to a child as soon as it is born'.[5] Given Culpeper's frequent disdain of the 'outlandish' remedies of the physicians, it is telling that even in his *English Physician* – a popular health manual 'whereby ... a man may ... cure himself being sick for three pence charge, with such things only as grow in England' – his medicine for clotted blood and internal ruptures includes not only the homely powder of rhubarb, but also 'a little mummia'.[6]

These individual recipes, however, are only a minute part of the new climate of post-revolutionary medicine. Culpeper's own books were highly influential, with many being reprinted several times, and his *Directory for Midwives* appearing in 1651. Perhaps no less important were Culpeper's attacks on the greed of the old physicians. Claiming that in Italy any doctor will go to a patient for a fee of eighteen pence, he contrasts this with the London physicians: 'send for them to a poor man's house, who is not able to give them their fee, then they will not come, and the poor creature for whom Christ died must forfeit his life for want of money'.[7] Set against that kind of medical culture, we have not only Culpeper's works, but such books as Richard Elkes' *Approved Medicines of Little Cost*, which in 1652 commends 'man's blood dried into powder' against severe arterial haemorrhaging.[8] Whilst it seems likely that human blood was relatively cheap in an age of habitual bloodletting, we also find a similarly styled work of 1652 echoing the familiar belief that 'the skull of a man is good against the falling sickness', and proposing that female convulsions be treated with a cordial made from pearl, burnt ivory, the hoof of an elk, and 'the skull of a man newly dead of some violent death'.[9] Although none of these notably match the titular advertisement of remedies 'cheap in the price', the work as a whole probably was responding to the new market conditions which favoured 'democratic', vernacular medical textbooks.[10]

If the more democratic and egalitarian qualities of Interregnum medicine make us feel closer to the England of 1650, we may need to remind ourselves that in many ways the beliefs of this era can now seem far more alien to us than might those of 1600. This period saw the worst excesses of English witch-hunting. In the areas of medicine and science, it has long been accepted that some of the most important advances in chemistry were bound up not only with alchemical pursuits, but with varying degrees of what can loosely be termed the occult. As Charles Webster famously emphasised, much of the scientific work of the day was conducted by men not only fiercely pious, but often passionately committed to the imminent coming of Christ, and the end of all ordinary human history.[11]

We have seen that the great medical iconoclast Paracelsus was a crucial figure in the history of corpse medicine. Paracelsianism flourished during Civil War and Interregnum, congenial to many of those who – like Culpeper – practised iconoclasm at various levels. Similarly influential was Paracelsus' sometime follower, the Belgian chemist Jean Baptiste van Helmont (d.1644). The two figures are partially united by their interest in chemical medicines and their mysticism. But they are also importantly distinct, insofar as van Helmont found favour with thinkers who would not readily follow

Paracelsus, and so probably allowed the chemico-mystical tradition a broader sweep of influence. In van Helmont, we have a kind of bridge between the followers of Paracelsus and the chemistry of Robert Boyle. Moreover, whilst Paracelsians have often been associated with the revolutionary left wing, van Helmont was translated by the Royalist (and royal physician) Walter Charleton, whose first edition of Helmont's writings included commendatory poems by fellow Royalists Alexander Ross and Thomas Philipott (d.1682).[12] Similarly, it was in 1665, well inside the Restoration, that the Helmontians conceived of 'a college of chemical physicians to challenge the [Royal] college's monopoly'.[13]

Whilst the mysticism and faction of different individuals and groups can offer a daunting prospect to those first encountering the science of this era, the key points to bear in mind for our purposes are these: from around 1649 to the end of the century, the chemical and alchemical sides of corpse medicine become stronger and more widespread; the meaning of 'mummy' acquires important new senses (and attendant powers); and for some thinkers, a far wider range of body parts and fluids become legitimate medicines. Excepting bone, and the moss of the skull, these agents are now far more frequently derived from fresh corpses or living bodies. Given that it is still not unknown for corpse medicine to be seen as a 'medieval' phenomenon, it is well worth emphasising that the zenith of English medicinal cannibalism in fact appears to have occurred in the later seventeenth century, during what has often been seen as the birth of modern science. Whereas, in 1623, James I refused the powdered skull offered by Mayerne, his grandson, Charles II, had no such qualms, and busily distilled such powder himself.

Jean Baptiste van Helmont

Perhaps the simplest forms of corpse medicine recommended by van Helmont are the skull and the moss of the skull. Even here, however, there are notable twists on general theory. It was fairly widely accepted that both powdered skull and usnea should be derived from those who had suffered violent deaths. These deaths themselves should be ones which did not involve haemorrhaging. The German professor Rudolph Goclenius (*fl. c.*1618) had held that the victim should have been hung, arguing that, in those who were strangled, the vital spirits were forced up into the skull, remaining trapped there for as long as seven years. (The 'vital spirits' were a mixture of blood and air closely associated with the soul, and held responsible for most physiological operations. We will hear much more of them in chapter six.)

Van Helmont disdained Goclenius' insistence on hanging, claiming that a body broken on the wheel would do just as well.[14] Van Helmont proceeds to explain why, among all the human bones, *only* the skull has such efficacy. For, after death, 'all the brain is consumed and dissolved in the skull'. It is, he believes, by 'the continual … imbibing of [this] precious liquor' of dissolved brains that 'the skull acquires such virtues'.[15] The skull seems here to have been all but marinaded in its own brains. Steeped in the 'precious liquor' which refines and improves with time like some rare old wine, the brain-sodden skull acts as a kind of natural laboratory or alchemical vessel.

Extolling usnea as 'the noble issue of celestial seed', van Helmont goes on to explain that this moss has a quite literally celestial origin.[16] It can be produced only when a special influence from the stars properly 'fertilises' the exposed skull. It is this mysterious insemination, from 'the celestial spheres, distilled upon the skull' which gives the moss its vital power. For van Helmont and his followers, corpse medicine – far from being associated solely with the low, rawly material putrescence of death and decay – is part of an invisible yet potent cosmic web, all but literally spun between heaven and earth. Blessed with 'the seminary excretions of the stars', such growths are indeed called, 'by hermetical philosophers, the flowers or fruits of the celestial orbs'.[17] Similarly, that potentially spiritual life force which others felt they could derive from warm blood is also recognised by van Helmont. The human corpse, he insists, harbours 'an obscure vitality' – at least, that is, if it has suffered a violent death.[18]

Van Helmont not only has a distinctive idea of the origin of skull-moss, but also very particular uses for it. He tells, for example, of 'a certain soldier of a noble extraction', who 'wore a little lock of the moss of a man's skull, finely enclosed betwixt the skin and flesh of his head'. On one occasion, 'interceding betwixt two brothers, that were fighting a mortal duel', this nobleman 'unfortunately received so violent a blow with a sword on his head, that he immediately fell to the earth'. The blow was so strong that 'his hat, and hair were cut through, as with an incision knife, even to the skin'. Nevertheless, 'he escaped without the smallest wound, or pene-tration of the skin'.[19] If the inference being made here now appears fantastical to us, we should bear in mind that many besides van Helmont and Charleton believed it. For them, this had something of the quality of an experimental proof in science. It is also hard not to be struck by the conviction of this (presumably educated) noble-man.[20] So great was this that he appears to have actually had the moss *sewn inside* his skin ('enclosed betwixt the skin and flesh of his head') – a procedure which was surely painful to accomplish, and may have been somewhat uncomfortable upon healing.[21]

Van Helmont's other chief use for skull moss is no less intriguing. We have briefly glimpsed the wound salve, as cited by the undecided Father of Science, Francis Bacon. Our chief concern with the cure at present is this: it involves what we might call action at a distance. Invisible vapours (the 'vital spirits' noted above) can travel between certain objects, and these spirits are particularly prevalent in human blood. As we will see in chapter six, it was certainly accepted by many that the spirits of a human body could leave it, and cause significant effects.

In the case of the wound salve, there was believed to be a kind of 'sympathy' between the blood on a weapon (or other object, such as a handkerchief) and the blood of the injured person. Hence the apparent success of smearing ointment on the bloodied object. Recipes for this ointment varied, and were never less than challen-ging. One cited by van Helmont (and attributed to Gianbattista della Porta) involves 'the moss of an unburied cranium; the fat of man, each two ounces; mummy, human blood each half an ounce', and 'oil of linseed, and turpentine, each one ounce'.[22]

Van Helmont's belief in the active and mobile nature of vital spirits can be seen in various other areas of his thought. He tells, for example, of 'a noble matron, of my acquaintance' who suffered badly from gout. Having recovered temporarily, this woman 'reposed her self in a chair, wherein a brother of hers, many years past, and in another city, cruelly tortured with the gout, was wont to sit'. Although the brother himself was now dead, 'she instantly found that from thence the disease did awake, and afresh invade her'. This was because 'the mummy of her dead brother deservedly rendered the chair suspected of contagion, which penetrating through all her clothes' sparked a relapse in the sister. Van Helmont further emphasises that their kinship aided this transfer – anyone else, it was noticed, could occupy the tainted chair with impunity.[23]

One vital element of this tale (again, considered carefully empirical by those involved) is the seemingly odd transfer of spirits from the dead to the living. For many, this was a key part of the logic of corpse medicine. The tale also reminds us that, by this period, certain thinkers could use 'mummy' in new and quite specialised ways. In the above passage the word means something like 'principle of vitality', and is again broadly interchangeable with spirits. (Compare also Charleton, who in his preface talks about the 'mummy of the blood', meaning roughly 'spirit' or 'life'.[24]) In this sense, 'mummy' is about as far as one could imagine from the dry remains of ancient Egyptians. Similarly, van Helmont talks elsewhere about the medical power of 'the mumial blood'; explains how usnea acquires its force from 'the mumial virtue of the bones, and the seminal influence of celestial orbs'; and notes the active role of 'mumial effluviums, shot from' spilled blood 'back to [the] vital fountain' of the living body.[25] Here as elsewhere, the line between the occult and the scientific is not an easy one to draw. Since its revival in the early seventeenth century, the classical theory of atomism had been seen by many Christians as dangerously materialistic (if not atheistical); yet van Helmont also uses the term 'mumial atoms' to refer to spiritual action at a distance.[26]

English chemists

Before turning to individual figures, we should first look in some detail at the distinctive Paracelsian recipe for mummy. We have heard Paracelsus recommending the very freshest corpse that one could obtain. Although the recipes of his followers sometimes varied slightly, a formula credited to the German physician Oswald Croll seems to have been particularly influential. One should 'choose the carcass of a red man, whole, clear without blemish, of the age of twenty four years, that hath been hanged, broke upon a wheel, or thrust-through, having been for one day and night exposed to the open air, in a serene time'. This flesh should be cut into small pieces or slices, and sprinkled with powder of myrrh and aloes, before being repeatedly macerated in spirit of wine. It should then be 'hung up to dry in the air', after which 'it will be like flesh hardened in smoke' and 'without stink'. Although this recipe was probably known by various English Paracelsians not long after its first appearance on the continent in 1609, it would have become especially prominent in England following translations of 1670 and 1672.[27] We should also bear in mind that, whilst the preparation of the formula would have made vegetarians quail, the final result may well have seemed to patients far less noisome than the animal guts and excrement which they were frequently asked to swallow. For, Croll concludes, the chemist must lastly 'with spirit of wine, or spirit of elderflowers ... extract a most red tincture' from the flesh itself.[28] In some cases this liquid may well have been administered in a conveniently unnamed form.[29]

1653 sees the first English-language book wholly and explicitly devoted to mummy, when a translation of a work by the German Andreas Tentzel appears as *Medicina Diastatica, or Sympathetical Mummy*. As Lynn Thorndike rightly states, Tentzel notably 'enlarged the scope and definition' of mummy.[30] The English version of his work includes prefaces by the astrologer John Lily and one Roger Ellis, both of which typify the pious zeal of many Interregnum Paracelsians. The former claims that the author's subject is 'sublime and high (if not the greatest mystery known to mortal man)', and the latter implies a miraculous revolution in medicine when he writes: 'physicians need no more their trade advance,/By tedious, fulsome long receipts and chance'.[31] A good deal more will be said about the work's newly extended sense of mummy below, when dealing with Christopher Irvine's ideas of transplantation. But a brief idea of this new range can be gained if we consider Tentzel's method of reconciling 'private or public enemies'. To do this, mummy 'must be extracted from both parties'. (By this Tentzel seems to mean the letting of blood from a particular part of the body.[32]) This mummy should next be 'intermingled with some kind of fertile earth and implanted into' a suitable herb. The herb should then be 'indifferently administered' to both parties.[33] Rivalling this suggestion is a non-cannibalistic use of 'mummy' (here evidently meaning power or vitality). To 'transmit or infuse' the strength of a horse into a man, one should 'mingle the sperm of the strongest horses with pure earth, implant it into the black thistles', and when these are well grown, hang one around the neck of your chosen recipient. The 'strong horses' will soon languish and 'the party will strengthen'.[34]

Daniel Border

Acknowledging the influence of the Italian Leonardo Fioravanti, the journalist and sometime Paracelsian physician Daniel Border states, in 1651, that, 'I have made the quintessence of man's blood, rectified and circulated, with the which I have done most wonderful cures, for if you give thereof one dram it will restore those that lie at the point of death'.[35] Border also extends our impression of how routinely human blood might have been consumed in this period when he adds of this quintessence that 'if you put a little of it into an hogshead of wine it will purify it, and preserve it a long time more than any other thing whatsoever'.[36]

The quintessence is prepared with the typically painstaking care of the era's chemistry and alchemy. Taking fresh blood, you must let it stand, skim away the watery part, and then 'paste and bake it with ten parts of common salt'. You must then 'put it in horse dung' for around ten days, 'til it be rotted and putrified all the blood into water'. Next, 'put it in a limbec and distil it by a good fire, and take thereof the water as much as thou may, and grind the dregs that it leaveth on a marble stone, and put all the water thereto and grind it again together, and then distil it, and so continue grinding and distilling as before, many times until thou have a noble water of blood'. At this point much further stilling is required to gain the quintessence itself, which will be of a 'great sweetness, and marvellous odour'.[37] Border also cites the common belief that 'the blood of a man dried' is good 'for the staying of blood at the nose, and in a wound'. Although he adds that the herb geranium will work the same effect, he gives no impression of preferring a purely herbal alternative.[38]

By 1651, Border is able to assume that the medical virtues of human fat are more or less universally familiar: 'the fat of a man is (as every man knoweth) hot and penetrative, and mollifying if you anoint the parts therewith (where the sinews be hard) and drawn together, or contracted; therefore it will quickly resolve them'.[39] From human liver, there can be 'drawn by distillation a water and an oil. If the water be drunk every morning together, by the space of a month, in the quantity of one dram, with two ounces of liverwort', it will recover 'such as are half rotten through diseases of the liver'. (The modern-day persistence of liver transplants for alcoholics and others suggests that this may have worked; it also reminds us how arbitrarily we draw the lines as to what is 'cannibalistic' and what not.) Liver medicines were relatively uncommon. And Border is similarly unusual in claiming that 'from the flesh of man distilled, there will come forth a stinking water and an oil, which is most excellent to anoint wounds withal, when they are badly healed'. This water also 'mollifieth and softeneth all hardness of tumour'.[40]

John French

In 1651 John French published a book titled *The Art of Distillation*.[41] French, notes Peter Elmer, was not only an energetic promoter of the ideas of Paracelsus and van Helmont, but also 'well respected by many, including Robert Boyle, for his expertise in the practical side of chemistry and mineralogy'. As physician to the Savoy Hospital, French 'encouraged the implementation of various new approaches to medical training and practice, including the use of spa water treatments for maimed soldiers ... and anatomical dissection'.[42] The hospital – remarks Charles Webster – offered unusually comfortable conditions and food (even clay smoking pipes) at the expense of the state.[43] Whilst all this fits quite well into a standard history of science, some of French's other interests are harder for the modern reader to swallow. Offering his own recipes for oil and water of blood, and for 'magistery' (or quintessence) 'of blood', he asserts that this latter 'being taken inwardly and applied outwardly, cureth most diseases, and easeth pain'.[44] Like Border and other Paracelsians, French also believes in distilling (rather than merely curing) human flesh. One should 'take of mummy (i.e., man's flesh hardened) cut small, four ounces', add spirit of wine, and set the two in a large glazed vessel in horse dung for one month. Finally, 'that which remains in the bottom' will 'be like an oil, which is the true elixir of mummy' and is 'a wonderful preservative against all infections'.[45]

French has two different formulae to prepare human skull into spirit. For the first, 'take of *cranium humanum* as much as you please, break it into small pieces', and put them 'into a glass retort'. (Note that these directions imply the ready availability of entire human skulls.) Heating this with a strong fire will eventually yield 'a yellowish spirit, a red oil, and a volatile salt'. The salt and spirit must then be processed a further two or three months to produce 'a most excellent spirit'. This, French states, is more or less identical to 'that famous spirit of Dr. Goddard's in Holborn', thus revealing that the expensive recipe supposedly bought by Charles II was already celebrated several years before the Restoration.[46] The spirit of skull not only 'helps the falling sickness, gout, dropsy' and infirm stomachs, but is indeed 'a kind of panacea'.[47] A second recipe adds hartshorn and ivory, and boils these, along with small pieces of skull, in a kind of mesh for three days and nights, until both bones and horn 'will be as soft as cheese'. This is then pounded, and mixed with spirit of wine into a paste; after much distillation, the resultant spirit will treat 'epilepsy, convulsions, all fevers putrid or pestilential, passions of the heart, and is a very excellent sudorific' (i.e., an agent which promotes or causes perspiration).[48]

Certain of French's other ingredients could be taken from the living. A mixture of woman's milk and processed zinc, for example, was distilled in ashes to produce the 'compound water of milk', with which inflamed eyes should be 'washed three or four times … a day'. It may seem merely a quibble to argue that, in finding this kind of recipe less repellent than the use of human blood, we are again making arbitrary distinctions as to what is cannibalistic (or what is 'unnatural'). But the point had a peculiar edge to it in French's day, if we recall that milk was indeed seen as a variant of blood. As Robert Boyle noted a few years later, it seemed unfair to count the American cannibals 'so barbarous merely upon the score of feeding on man's flesh and blood', given that 'woman's milk, by which alone we feed our sucking children, is, according to the received opinion, but blanched blood'.[49]

A formula for spirit of urine, meanwhile, involved 'the urine of a young man drinking much wine', stood in 'glass vessels in putrefaction forty days', and then carefully distilled. Not only would this ease the pains of the gout, and 'quicken any part that is benumbed', but such was its potency that it would 'burn as fire, and dissolve gold and precious stones'. A second spirit of urine seems to have required the physician to procure some unadulterated child's urine ('a boy that is healthy'). The resultant spirit was swallowed to great effect by sufferers from epilepsy, gout, dropsy, and convulsions.[50] Alongside this, French's 'water and oil made out of hair' may look relatively innocuous. Its production was also fairly straightforward, as one merely had to 'fill an earthen retort with hair cut small, set it over the fire, and fit a receiver to it, and there will come over a very stinking water and oil'. French explains that 'this water and oil is used in Germany to be sprinkled upon fences and hedges to keep wild and hurtful cattle from coming to do harm in any place'; for 'such is the stink of this liquor that it doth affright them from coming to any place near it'.[51] It is perhaps not insignificant that human chemists are able to tolerate the stench of this formidable agent, whilst animals are not. Here as elsewhere, the power of ideas seems to overcome the force of brute instinct.

One final medicine for epilepsy is particularly memorable. The practitioner should 'take the brains of a young man that hath died a violent death, together with the membranes, arteries, veins, nerves, [and] all the pith of the back', and 'bruise these in a stone mortar til they become a kind of pap'. Over this cerebral pâté you should then pour 'as much of the spirit of wine, as will cover it three or four fingers breadth', convey the whole into a large glass, and allow it to 'digest … half a year in horse dung' before distillation.[52] We have seen that French was a keen anatomist, and his biographer Peter Elmer notes that dissections were carried out at the Savoy Hospital.[53] He would therefore have had little trouble obtaining fresh human heads and similar ingredients, and it would also appear that he was preparing such confections on the hospital premises. There was perhaps a good chance, then, that a colleague may well have wandered in on French, elbow deep in gore, carefully mashing up brains and spinal marrow into his medicinal paste.

Christopher Irvine

Matters are only about to get stranger as we enter the company of the Paracelsian physician Christopher Irvine (c.1620–93).[54] It is, indeed, probably just as well to start off with those biographical details which may prejudice some readers in Irvine's favour. His father was a barrister, and his brother, Sir Gerard Irvine, a baronet. Christopher gained his first degree at Edinburgh, and later an MD 'from an unknown university abroad'. Although Paracelsian, he was originally also 'an ardent Royalist' (attending the camp of Charles II at Atholl in June 1651), and after the Restoration was for some years surgeon to the Royal Horse Guards.[55]

Three things about Irvine are particularly interesting. One is that he proposed the use of a lamp filled with human blood. The state of the blood in this vessel – often known as 'the lamp of life' – was supposed to reflect the health of the person who had produced it. Irvine indeed stated quite plainly that, 'this lamp burneth so long as he liveth of whose blood it is made, and expireth with him. If it burn clearly and quietly, it sheweth his condition to be such; if sparkling, dim, and cloudy, it sheweth his griefs and languishings'.[56] The second is that he was an especially strong believer in the idea of curing disease by the transfer of spirits. Like van Helmont (who also subscribed to this notion), Irvine thought of these spirits as a kind of 'mummy'. The third is that Irvine believed that, to be most effective, human medical materials should ideally be derived from a *living* body.

The lamp of life was closely associated with the chemist and Paracelsian John Ernest Burgravius, who described it in his *Biolychnium* of 1611.[57] Whilst Irvine's instructions for the preparation of the Lamp are brief and in places cryptic, it does appear that he had indeed assembled at least one such piece of lighting apparatus. For his descriptions of blood as it separates out into different layers ('vile … white … phlegmatic … golden') form an accurate picture of the variously coloured strata which modern doctors will often have seen in a test tube.[58]

The lamp of life already hints at Irvine's idea of spiritual transfer, given the implicit need for action-at-a-distance between lamp and donor. Another example of Irvine's notion of transfer of spirits broadly resembles that of the 'gouty chair' described by van Helmont. Irvine begins by outlining a theory of the 'infusion' of disease, stating that it is transferred by an 'insensible transpiration and sweat' – this latter being 'impregnate with much spirit'.[59] We should, therefore, 'take heed we be not partakers of the sweat or exhalation of an unsound body', and 'that we touch not the sheets so impregnate, nor put on [their] shoes or stockings, or gloves' – particularly, he adds, 'that we be no bedfellows with them'.[60] It is now obvious to us that Irvine is describing the routine spread of germs. There was of course no concept of these, however, until many decades later; Irvine here gives a typical example of someone carefully observing the phenomena of disease, without having fully realised the scientific laws which underlie such events. For all that, his warnings are based in an empiricism which is itself scientifically valid.

Having further explained that Adam and Eve lived so long through sleeping on herbs, and that in summer people should sleep naked, 'covered over with wholesome herbs' to absorb their virtues, Irvine goes on to argue that those of 'a weak body' should wear the clothes of 'strong and sound men', so as to draw 'from thence … such spirits as will fortify weak nature'.[61] Similarly, the enfeebled should give their own clothes to 'them that are lusty and healthful' to wear for some time before they put them on. This kind of transfer, Irvine adds, is the result of 'a great deal of invisible mummy [which] lieth hid' in all garments.[62]

This notion of transferring spirits (or 'mummy') brings us to a therapy which involves a peculiar twist on previous ideas of corpse or blood medicine. Irvine believes not that you should give blood to a patient to drink, but that the patient's blood should be consumed by an animal. Anyone afflicted by jaundice, rabies or leprosy should have blood drawn in the month of May from the median vein in the right arm. Before doing this, the practitioner will have prepared two or three eggshells, emptying out all the yolk and white through two small holes, and gluing up one hole before pouring the blood into the other, which is then also carefully sealed. The eggs are now 'put under a hen that bringeth forth young ones' for between fourteen to twenty days. On removing them, you should 'lay them apart for a day' before opening them, upon which 'thou shalt find the blood of the sick-man by that digestion become monstrous, and of a most vile smell'. As with the cattle and the water of hair, no sensible animal would eat this. Hence, mixing it with bread or suchlike, you must give it to a pig or dog 'which hath been kept up from meat two or three days'. You will now 'perceive … the disease to leave the man, and infect the beast'. The animal should then be killed, 'lest if it get loose, it hurt other men'. By this, which Irvine calls the 'true mumia of Paracelsus', one can cure not only jaundice, leprosy and rabies, but also gout, consumption, and cancers.[63]

One obvious point about this treatment (aside from its somewhat shaky conception of animal rights) is that it is again highly painstaking. It too has something of the mentality of the scientist, driven to persist with slow and arduous tasks in hope of discovery. In this sense, the seemingly whimsical idea of using warm brooding hens is motivated (like the related use of horse dung) by a broadly scientific desire to produce invariant thermal conditions for 'digestion' of the blood. The idea makes very good sense in a period when it would have been extremely expensive and difficult to have obtained this kind of continuous heat by any other means. We can also add that this cure throws the habitual cannibalism of the era's medicine into a slightly different light. Afflicted by disease and discomfort throughout their life, how might any given patient feel about these two alternatives? Was it worse to have animals eating your blood than to drink the blood of a fellow human being?

Two points should be made about Irvine's theories of disease transfer. One is that versions of the idea were reasonably commonplace in the period. Simon Forman, who died in 1611, had a recipe for curing frenzy which involved feeding the patient's blood to an animal and then killing it.[64] In his dangerous sickness of 1623 Donne, attended by the king's own physicians, had dead pigeons split open and placed at his feet to draw out malign vapours. That treatment was still current in Irvine's time, as he himself notes: 'doves cloven in the midst, and applied hot to the soles of the feet, do by attraction, rectify the preternatural heat'. He adds that if cucumbers are laid 'by an infant that hath a fever, when he is asleep, the cucumbers will wither, and the child be cured'; whilst some would also lay puppies 'to the feet of young children in their cradles' for similar reasons. Again, 'the arse of a hen plucked bare, and applied to the biting of a viper, freeth the body from venom'.[65] In Irvine's own time, Robert Boyle seems to have credited a number of accounts by which human illnesses were transferred to animals.[66]

Such comparisons give us a clearer idea of the context in which Irvine was working, and prevent us from too hastily marginalising him as a mystical eccentric. The second point about such notions of disease transfer is rather different. For we need also to be aware that, in using these cures, Irvine, living less than four centuries ago, had more in common with the world of the New Testament than he did with us. The most famous version of human–animal transfer, after all, was Christ's cure of lunatics, whose evil spirits were conjured out into the Gadarene swine.[67] As with the dying chickens, the swine showed proof of this, as they ran mad and plunged from a cliff into a lake. Although the biblical incident is complicated by popular tendencies to see all illness as the result of demonic forces, Irvine's belief that the dog should be killed to prevent spread of the disease broadly parallels the Gadarene story. In each case, there is a definite sense that spirit forces are mobile, enduring and potent. Christ's transfer of them into the swine, and the subsequent drowning, are two forms of containment; and the killing of the dog is another.[68] Again: when the sick woman furtively touches the hem of Christ's garment in a throng of people, it is very likely that she is trying to covertly transfer her affliction, rather than get something from him.[69] Around the same time, Christ's partial contemporary, Pliny the Elder (23–79 AD), believed that '"a heavy cold clears up if the sufferer kisses a mule's muzzle"'.[70] A line runs, here, for over 1,500 years between Christ and Pliny, and the age of Cromwell, Newton and Boyle. To us this implies an odd mixture of nascent science and outright magic. For Irvine and Boyle, it did not feel that way.[71]

We now come, finally, to Irvine's third distinctive quality. Irvine generally prefers to work with human blood rather than human flesh. This is evidently because blood most closely matches the qualities of a living body. Such a body has the most active spirits, and it is these (as with the dog or pig) which draw off the spirits of disease. Naturally enough, dead flesh is less suitable.[72] So Irvine advises that 'the medicines taken from men' should be gathered 'as soon as they come out of the living body'. In particular, if you wish to use mummy (which for Irvine is the dried flesh of a man, slain by a violent death) you should 'take it possibly from a body living, or next to life, (otherwise it will not do so much good as the warm blood)'. You should then dice it into small pieces, 'set it to dry in the shade' and try to heighten its spirit powers by adding warm blood to it. Lest we should be in any doubt, Irvine makes the point again: 'if thou canst not have it from a living, or from a warm body, it either must be often anointed with warm blood, or steeped in it, and left there for a time, and cautiously dried; for so it is fortified with the spirits, drawn from the blood'. Underlining the importance of living (or recently dead) organic tissue, Irvine also points out that different cures require body substances to be kept in different vessels. To treat vomiting, for example, you should use the stomach of a swine as a medical vessel.[73]

Irvine's book is called *Medicina Magnetica* because these kinds of cures were broadly inspired by observation of magnets. This reminds us, again, how real spirit forces were being associated with the mysterious yet clearly very definite powers of the magnet. As the above examples of transfer show, all living things have this magnetic power to some extent; humans, animals and plant forms all have spirits of various kinds. Irvine accordingly refers to medicines composed of human materials as 'magnets'. Having explained that 'this magnet is nothing else, but dried man's flesh, which [it] is certain, hath a mighty attractive power' he again emphasises that this 'must be taken, if it be possible, from the body of a man that dies a violent death, and yet while it is warm'.[74] Irvine admits, however, that this magnet would be very difficult to obtain – presumably because one would have to get hold of a corpse very soon after death. Irvine therefore proposes an alternative, 'better magnet ... not gotten with so much cruelty. Take ... the blood of a sound young man, drawn in the spring ... as much as thou canst get'. Then mix together 'a great quantity of man's dung' (again, of a sound man), with wine and human sweat (gathered on linen cloths). The resultant paste is dried, and the fresh blood is then added, the whole being kept in a tightly sealed vessel. One now has 'a magnet, the compendium of all man's body, gotten without any horror or cruelty' – which, Irvine stresses, 'we altogether detest'.[75]

What exactly does Irvine mean by 'horror or cruelty'? Although the latter word could just imply the process of execution, the association with Irvine's magnet would be rather loose, given that the cruelty of that act was independent of his requirements.[76] 'Horror' could appear to mean the general horror prompted by use of human body parts. But this was evidently very rare in the period. All in all, taking this phrase along with the clear reference to 'a living ... body', we seem to find that the idea of cutting flesh from a living donor was at least entertained by Irvine. This was in fact done at least twice for medical reasons in the early modern period, in a pioneering 'nose transplant', in which a severed nose was replaced by a graft of flesh from the arms of two donors (one being the patient).[77] As chapter four will show, in

Chinese medicine living bodies yielded up some impressive medical agents well into the twentieth century.

Distinctive as Irvine may be in some ways, he was by no means alone. 1656 saw the publication of both Irvine's *Medicina Magnetica*, and Samuel Boulton's *Medicina Magica Tamen Physica*. Most of this latter work is wholly identical to the text of Irvine's book (although Boulton's is shorter). Boulton's preface is signed May 1656, and Irvine's June. Whilst this could well indicate that the books were published within less than a month of one another, we also know that Boulton's was printed in London, and Irvine's in Edinburgh. Boulton published nothing else that we know of, but Irvine produced several other books, and in none of these does he appear to accuse Boulton of plagiarism. In his DNB article on Boulton, John Henry points out that the author himself acknowledges the unoriginal character of part of his book: "'I ingenuously confess it is not all from mine own Minerva, I was beholding for some part thereof … to a worthy gentleman of Kent, one Mr M.B. a dear friend of mine who had some loose papers of an unknown Mr but by us supposed to proceed from that late worthy and reverend chemist Dr Everard" (A4v)'.[78] Henry has further shown that almost all of Boulton's work is identical with an anonymous manuscript (now in the British Library). Henry's suspicion that this MS was not Boulton's work, and that he copied from it, is confirmed by clues found at the opening of Irvine's book. In his dedication to General George Monck, he writes: 'it is the law of this and other nations, that whatsoever treasure is found, straight to be carried to the Supreme of that people. Wherefore falling on this, no little … treasure, that I might not be guilty of concealment, I present it to your Lordship'.[79] Irvine's full title also describes the work as something 'preserved and published, as a master-piece in this skill'. This clearly implies that Irvine has 'preserved' a manuscript by publishing it, this itself echoing the admission of his 'falling on' a 'treasure' not his own, and thus rendered unto the 'Supreme of the people'. Aside from the fact that Irvine, in Edinburgh in June 1656, could scarcely have obtained Boulton's book in time to copy and print it, it would have been highly impolitic to dedicate to Monck something plagiarised from a newly published work.

It seems, then, that both Boulton and Irvine either used the same manuscript, or that there were two or more copies of this document.[80] Henry rightly notes that Boulton gives no cause for attributing the manuscript to Dr Everard (identified by Henry as 'John Everard (*c*.1575–*c*.1650), the first English translator of the Hermetic *Poemander*'), and the reference to 'an unknown Mr' indeed tallies with further evidence. Whoever this person was, the manuscript is heavily indebted to Burgravius. An expanded, 1800 version of Robert Burton's *Anatomy of Melancholy* says that Burgravius published not only 'a discourse in which he specifies a lamp to be made of man's blood' but also 'another tract of mumia … by which he will cure most diseases, and transfer them from a man to a beast, by drawing blood from one, and applying it to the other'.[81] It is evident, therefore, that these beliefs were circulating in both Germany and Britain, and it is possible that the manuscript used by Boulton and Irvine may well have passed through other hands in the decades before and after the Interregnum.

Edward Bolnest

In his *Aurora Chymica* of 1672, the Paracelsian physician Edward Bolnest makes it very clear that certain doctors were both using Croll's recipe, and employing their own variations in the early Restoration period.[82] Bolnest describes a 'mumial quintessence' made from 'the flesh of a sound young man dying a violent death, about the middle of August'. Three or four pounds of flesh should 'be taken from his thighs or other fleshy parts', and put into a suitable glass, into which must be poured 'highly rectified spirit of wine', covering the flesh by several inches. After letting this stand three or four days, you then 'take out the flesh and put it upon a glass plate', frequently covering it with 'well rectified spirit of salt'. The plate should stand uncovered in the shade for some time, away from dirt (and, presumably, hungry animals), being often soaked with spirit of salt, and turned occasionally. Once it is well dried, 'you may put it up into a fit glass and keep it for use'. This presumably implies that you would scrape off some of the flesh in form of powder. But, Bolnest adds, if you are 'willing to have it yet a more efficacious medicine', you should take a pound of the cured flesh, 'beat or grind it to a most subtle powder' and then prepare it chemically for a long period of time until you have a tincture broadly similar to that described by Croll.[83]

Bolnest's instructions for distillation cover some thirty odd lines, and have the painstaking rigour and obsessiveness of alchemical directions. Bolnest seems also to have taken some initiative in deciding that the body should be 'harvested' (as it were) in August, and that precisely three or four pounds of flesh should be taken from the thighs. Such details (along with the flesh beaten or ground into powder) strongly imply that Bolnest himself had followed this recipe. The same can be said of his quintessence of man's blood, taken in 'a large quantity' from 'healthy young men, in the springtime', when Mercury is in conjunction with the sun; and of his quintessence of man's bones. With quasi-scientific exactitude Bolnest specifies that one should use 'the bones of a man which hath not been buried fully a year', making sure 'to cleanse them well from the earth and dry them'. These last words in particular make it almost certain that Bolnest was writing from his own experience, throwing up before the reader's eye a sudden vision of him scraping clean the anonymous bones of some unwilling donor. The resultant oil, he adds, should be applied with lint to patients suffering arthritic pains.[84]

At one level, Bolnest looks typical of the more fervent proponents of Charles Webster's 'great instauration' (not least in the title of his earlier book, *Medicina Instaurata*). Not only did he see medicine as a pious social duty, but he claims that the 'only intent and design of noble chemia' is to prepare medicines that will 'cure diseases, and … restore to absolute and perfect health', so as to 'perfect imperfect things'.[85] This in particular sounds like the kind of millenarian natural philosophy which Webster discusses: for such thinkers, the (perhaps imminent) coming of Christ will be preceded by a return to the earthly purity (and corresponding freedom from sickness) once found in Eden before the Fall.[86] Bolnest seems also to have believed that the central goal of alchemy – the production of gold from base metals – was still possible, given his apparent attempts to learn the secret of the philosopher's stone from the philosopher and alchemist Thomas Vaughan.[87]

At the same time, Bolnest's alchemical interests would also fit quite nicely into a conservative history of science or medicine. His obsessive sense that medical materials were being insufficiently analysed and prepared must have made some contribution to a more thorough and scientific chemistry. Moreover, Bolnest could be very happily located in a heroic history of medical bravery and altruism, given that – unlike various élite physicians – he did not flee from London during the plague epidemics of 1665 and 66. Not only does he sign his 1665 *Medicina Instaurata* from 'my house in Jewen Street near Cripplegate, April 14, 1665', but his name features in a broadsheet advertisement issued in late June 1665 by the 'Society of Chemical Physicians'.[88] The Society declares itself 'deeply moved with commiseration of the calamity befallen this great city by the pestilence' and lists the houses of various doctors (including Bolnest) as places where 'all persons concerned may repair and be furnished with the antidotes so by us prepared, at reasonable rates, with directions how to use them in order to preservation, and in case of cure'. The advertisement also stresses that the plague has so far resisted 'common Galenical medicines', and that the Society will accordingly be offering chemically prepared alternatives, 'not borrowed out of former authors, but agreeably devised and fitted to the nature of the present pest'.[89]

Bolnest's quintessence of mummy was supposed to produce 'wonderful effects both in preserving and restoring health'. If this tincture were relatively affordable, it seems very likely that some of those terrified citizens flocking to Bolnest's house in Jewen Street would have been keen to try it by way of either prevention or cure. The same would hold for the quintessence of blood, which Bolnest specifically describes as 'a potent preservative in time of pestilence'.[90] Although the *Aurora* was published only in 1672, it evidently existed in 1665, for in April of that year Bolnest states that he soon hopes to publish it in English.[91] We can therefore infer that Bolnest had known and used these recipes in 1665, and perhaps earlier.

George Thomson

Any readers who feel that these figures were not fully exploiting the medical resources offered by the human body may be pleased to meet the physician George Thomson. Despite having impressive medical training (in Edinburgh and Leiden) Thomson was kept out of the Royal College of Physicians due to his inability to pay the member's fee.[92] This did not stop Thomson from practising (from 1651) at Rochford in Essex, nor from performing the first experimental splenectomy on a dog (which subsequently survived for over two years).[93] Thomson also seems to have followed Culpeper's lead in treating the poor, as in February 1655 he spent considerable time with a serving woman, Anne Taylor of Romford, who was suffering severely from stones.[94] Like Bolnest (whom he must have known), Thomson was among the brave cluster of chemical physicians who stayed in plague-struck London in 1665.[95]

Ironically, about the only thing Thomson would not use was mummy. Although he was a follower of van Helmont, he did not adhere to the use of recent corpse flesh, and thought that it was now impossible to obtain Egyptian mummy.[96] But little else was allowed to go to waste. Among the usual suspects, Thomson prescribes spirit of blood and powdered skull for epilepsy.[97] 'The saline spirit of blood, bones, and urine well rectified, are of admirable use against' plague.[98] (Given that this advice appeared in a work published in 1666, one can again imagine that even the squeamish may have been tempted to follow it.) Less typically, Thomson believes that the falling sickness will respond to spirit of human brain.[99] His use for human fat is also unusual, as he holds that it can remove 'weak, troublesome, tormenting marks made on certain parts of the body'.[100] An alkali made 'out of man's bones' is 'an admirable medicine ... both for inward and outward griefs of the body, if construed by a philosophical hand'.[101] Anyone threatened by the plague should drink their own urine, while women suffering from abnormally heavy menstrual bleeding should swallow the afterbirth of a newly delivered mother. At the same time, this patient might want to keep hold of her own copious quantities of monthly blood, which was itself a valuable therapeutic agent. For – so long as she was a virgin – this fluid could be used against erysipelas.[102] Human gall cures deafness, and the spirit of hair (whose stench is not mentioned by Thomson) 'causeth hair to grow'. The sweat of a dying man reduces the swelling of piles ('and other excrescences'); and any sufferer who had not managed to collect this fluid in time could later use 'a dead-man's hand, caused to stroke the same' for this purpose.[103] Although these cures were published only in 1675, we can assume that Thomson was using them in his medical practice throughout the fifties and sixties.[104]

Household medicines

In certain ways, then, several of these Paracelsian or Helmontian authors fit well into any standard history of medical and scientific progress.[105] Nor were they the only eminent or educated figures using or recommending corpse medicine in the decades between the Civil War and the century's end. In 1653 there appeared a book entitled *A Choice Manual, or Rare Secrets in Physic and Chirurgery*. This work includes a painstaking recipe for a Paracelsian plaster, and a water for overheated feet: 'take a quantity of snails of the garden and boil them in stale urine, then let the patient bathe and set his feet therein, and using that often, he shall be cured'.[106] It also offers an unusual twist on the otherwise familiar use of human skull against epilepsy. Along with 'a pennyweight of the powder of gold, six pennyweight of pearl, 6 pennyweight of amber, 6 pennyweight of coral, 8 grains of bezoar, half an ounce of peony seed, also you must put some powder of a dead man's skull that hath been an anatomy, for a woman, and the powder of a woman for a man'. You should then 'compound all these together, and take as much of the powder ... as will lie upon a two-pence, for 9 mornings together in endive water, and drink a good draught of endive water after it'.[107]

The specific use of opposite genders is rare. The reference to anatomy probably means that the source should have died a violent death – something which was usually the case with anatomical specimens gained by the physicians from executions. Women were far less rarely executed, though when they were the physicians seem to have been especially keen to dissect them.[108] Unless one was well-trained in medicine oneself, it would have been hard to know the sex of a human skull. The recipe therefore implies that one must buy from a trusted source. Perhaps for this reason, perhaps because the skulls of dissected women were very rare, and certainly given the quantities of gold, pearl, coral and bezoar, such a formula must have been expensive. This is worth bearing in mind, given that an alternative cure for epilepsy simply involved drinking blood – something which was evidently cheaper, at least in Germany and parts of Scandinavia.

It is also particularly relevant, given that the author of this recipe is supposed to have been Elizabeth Grey, Countess of Kent. Elizabeth must have been reasonably wealthy from 1601, when she married Henry Grey (heir to the Kentish earldom); and from 1636 she was also able to enjoy a long-delayed and substantial inheritance.[109] The full title of the *Choice Manual* emphasises that its recipes were 'collected, and practised by the Right Honourable the Countess of Kent'. Although we lack information about their use, there is good reason for thinking that Grey was making these and other medicines herself on her estate in Bedfordshire, where she lived on as a widow from 1639–51.

Research carried out by Elaine Leong has shown that there were a great number of such household medical works in manuscript; and that a widow such as Elizabeth Freke (1641–1714) was making large quantities of her own medicines in the early eighteenth century.[110] Leong situates Grey and Freke in a wider tradition of female medicine, stating that books such as Gervase Markham's *The English Housewife* (1623) 'presented medical knowledge as essential to any early modern housewife', whilst 'the papers of gentlewomen like Mary Hoby [later Mary Vere], Grace Mildmay and Alice Thornton attest that these views were not only prescribed but also followed'.[111] Like Freke, Grace Mildmay prepared her medicines in large quantities, and (notes Linda A. Pollock) was relatively scientific in doing so.[112] Leong believes that Mildmay (who died in 1620) began her written collection of recipes in the late sixteenth century, and in this manuscript we find 'mummia' listed in a formula for an opiate ('laudanum').[113] Leong's ongoing research shows that human body parts feature in several other manuscript collections of the early modern period. Mummy, human skull, and skull-moss appear frequently in these works, with blood and fat also being cited occasionally.[114] These manuscripts not only extend our sense of how widespread medicinal cannibalism was, but also add a new note of empiricism to the ingredients found among various surgeons and physicians. One tells, for example, of how human milk combats inflammation of the eyes, and was accordingly used 'upon my own child Arthur Stanhope upon such an occasion'; and another of how milk was successfully 'tried by Mrs Ayscough of Nutthald' for an 'impostume in the head'.[115]

Indeed, for those who are rigorous about the definition of cannibalism (and unashamed about their own shady infantile activities) it is interesting to find that by far the most popular ingredient extracted from that portable medicine chest, the human body, was milk. This was used for a vast range of purposes. Especially popular as an eye balm (for problems as minor as sore eyes, or as major as cataracts) it was also commended 'to procure speedy deliverance to a woman in labour', to dissolve a cancer, 'to comfort the brains and procure sleep'; and for burns, deafness, gout, headache, piles, and consumption.[116] The recipe book of the aristocratic Fairfax family claims that human milk had been given to Queen Mary by Vesalius himself. Moreover, when we hear another manuscript prescribing it for one who 'shall live or die that lieth sick and is not wounded' we quickly recall the breast-milk treatment offered to Innocent VIII on his deathbed in 1492.[117] Similarly, the Chesterfield manuscript features 'a receipt of man's blood for the renewing the blood throughout the whole body … good in a dropsy and other disease proceeding from the corruption of the blood', as well as a chemically prepared 'spirit of man's blood to renew and restore strength of the body'.[118] This both echoes the more radical treatment allegedly given to the pope, and quite specifically parallels what we will hear from Robert Boyle about blood medicines.

Although we have no definite indication as to how human milk was obtained, we seem here to glimpse another of the numerous relationships between rich and poor in an age of radical inequality. Almost no privileged woman of this era breastfed her own children. This would mean that privileged mothers probably could not produce milk, even a few weeks after childbirth. It thus appears that the considerable demand for human milk had to be met by the wet nurses of the early modern era.[119] In addition to feeding perhaps two or more children, such a woman could also have been required to somehow express milk for medical purposes. It is arresting to think of the life of a wet nurse on a seventeenth-century English estate: perhaps she had a particular (relatively privileged) diet. At any rate, like the cows or goats of this property, she too could expect to be milked fairly routinely, for the benefit of her employers and their servants. Bear in mind, too, that at least one of Leong's manuscripts recommends human milk to keep the skin 'white and clear'. Hence, if you were a poor wet nurse, you might, circa 1600, be milked into a glass, so that the essence of your maternal body could be rubbed into the cheeks of a Lady, thus rendering her sufficiently attractive to become a wife and mother in her turn.[120]

Country estates were generally remote from surgeons or physicians, and given the quantities of remedies prepared by Freke and Mildmay, it seems likely that more altruistic landowners were at times treating their tenants as well as themselves.[121] Emphasising that 'a particularly important medical role was assumed by gentlewomen and clergymen, who would dispense medicine for their neighbours as an expression of charity', Charles Webster indeed cites Grey as an especially 'celebrated aristocratic practitioner'.[122] One can well imagine that even the most fiercely independent-minded labourer or servant would have hesitated to refuse the human skull or flesh offered to them by their well-meaning master or mistress.[123] Whilst numerous of these collections existed only in manuscript, John Considine notes that the (perhaps opportunistic) publication of Grey's recipes sparked a number of imitations, such as *The Queen's Closet Opened* (1656) and *The Closet of the Eminently Learned Sir Kenelm Digby Kt. Opened,* in 1669. Grey's work alone, described as 'bestselling' by Mary Fissell, went through at least twenty editions.[124]

In 1655 the poet Henry Vaughan, who seems to have practised medicine in his native Brecknockshire, cited Croll's 'theriac of mummy' as an antidote against poison in his translation of the German chemist, Heinrich Nolle (*fl.* 1612–19).[125] If Vaughan is now remembered for his pious mysticism, the prolific writings of the Puritan minister Richard Baxter were to appeal to more conservative Christians long after his death in 1691. Readers of George Eliot's *The Mill on the Floss* may recall that the self-righteous Aunt Glegg is still an avid fan of his, some time in the earlier nineteenth century. Aunt Glegg and other Victorian readers of Baxter would no doubt have been surprised to hear of his recovery from a 'fit of bleeding' suffered around 1659. He was, he tells us, not only 'restored by the mercy of God', but – more directly – by 'the moss of a dead man's skull which I had from Dr. Micklethwait'.[126] Like various other users of this cure, Baxter would probably have inserted the powdered moss directly into his nostrils.

Skull-moss does seem to have worked for Baxter and others. The Dutch physician Ysbrand van Diemerbroeck (1609–74) implies that this was because pretty much anything thrust up the nostrils could stem bleeding. He states that he has always found a piece of chalk effective, and also recommends cotton dipped in ink. He adds that he knew of 'a noble German, cured of a desperate bleeding at the nose' by the insertion of warm hog's dung. Also commending dried human blood, he notes that 'an old woman that had bled for three days' was relieved by 'thrusting up mint into her nostrils'.[127] This evidence suggests that patients using errhines (as the various nostril plugs were termed) may have recovered because the plug stopped the flow of air into the nose, or perhaps simply because they held their heads back during the treatment.

In 1659 there appeared an English version of *Zoologia* – a work first published by the German Paracelsian chemist Johann Schroeder. Although tellingly subtitled 'the history of *animals* as they are useful in physic and chirurgery', this book has a great deal to say about the medical virtues of the human body. In addition to numerous more familiar preparations, Schroeder proposes liquor of hair to promote hair growth, powdered hair for jaundice, and burned hair with sheep's suet for bleeding wounds.[128] The 'urine of a boy (twelve years old, who drinks good wine)' can be distilled into spirit form and drunk to expel the stone – although (admits Schroeder) 'it stinks grievously'. Those sufficiently repelled by its odour may or may not have preferred an alternative method of delivery, which was to inject the medicine into the bladder with a syringe.[129] Noting the general belief that blood, 'fresh and drunk hot is said to avail against the epilepsy', Schroeder also adds quite precisely that 'the drinking of the blood requires great caution, because it not only brings a truculency' but also (ironically) 'the epilepsy'.[130] This alleged 'truculency' is interesting: it would seem to correspond to the heightened degree of aggression that one might expect from a dose of concentrated chemical energy – even if this energy is metabolised, rather than directly taken into the veins. This in turn suggests that Schroeder or others had seen what happened to those who drank blood. Following lines give several different procedures for distillation of blood, which in various forms can treat consumption, pleurisy, apoplexy, gout and epilepsy, as well as providing a general tonic for the sick.[131] 'The marrow of the bones', meanwhile, is 'commended against the shrinking of members' (and may well have been expensive, given the difficulty of extracting it). Dried human heart is another cure for epilepsy, and this disease will also respond to an infusion made from water of lily, lavender, malmsey, and three pounds of human brain.[132]

Last but not least, Schroeder twice implies that he and other practitioners were producing medicines from the pulverised matter of entire human corpses. He first states that 'the whole carcass or flesh in shops comes under the name of mummy'. This cannot refer to whole Egyptian mummies, as Schroeder presently doubts that this kind 'is brought to us' any longer – a doubt which would scarcely have arisen if he had seen an entire mummy in an apothecary's shop. Moreover, he then goes on to imply that those serious about such therapies needed to use a whole corpse just so as to avoid 'the danger which Renodeus intimates, affirming the mummy of the shops to be nothing but the juice of a rotten carcass pressed out and thickened, and therefore sold to the great hurt of mankind'.[133] Schroeder himself was presumably able to judge (by smell or otherwise) how fresh a corpse was. For he was evidently using whole ones to prepare his 'divine water'. If you are ever offered any of this pleasant-sounding drink, you should bear in mind that a Paracelsian will have prepared it by taking 'a whole carcass with the bone, flesh, bowels (of one killed by a violent death)' cutting it into very small pieces, and mashing it up until the whole pulverised mass is indistinguishable. It is then distilled, and is used in the manner of Irvine, to take disease away from a patient, by mixing some of the patient's blood with it.[134] If anyone did actually drink it, we can assume that it would also have been a valuable source of protein.

Now celebrated in the history of science for his experiments in embryology, the amateur natural philosopher Sir Kenelm Digby listed both usnea and powdered skull in various remedies in his *Choice and Experimented Receipts in Physic and Surgery*.[135] He recommends that for epilepsy you should take not only 'the skull of a man that died of a violent death' but also 'parings of nails of man, of each two ounces' and powder them together with various kinds of mistletoe and peony root. As Digby's title implies, he and others had tested this kind of remedy. Digby's steward, George Hartman, stated that in Frankfurt in 1659 he had personally witnessed an epileptic, the son of a church minister, Mr Lichtenstein, cured by Digby with a recipe of this kind.[136] Around the same time, the pioneer of microscopy, Robert Hooke, was dosing himself with powdered skull.[137] We have seen that Goddard's 'famous recipe' for spirit of skull was circulating before the Restoration; that Charles II was supposed to have paid £6,000 for this secret, and that, in later life, Charles would prepare this remedy in his own laboratory. In 1684 (the year before Charles was heavily plied with spirit of skull on his deathbed) one of his surgeons, John Browne, recommended human fat as an agent to soften tumours.[138]

Thomas Willis

A modern GP who prescribed chocolate would perhaps not be entirely unpopular (and could of course respond to any critics that cocoa is a source of magnesium). In the 1660s, one doctor was recommending for apoplexy a chocolate mixture which was also rich in calcium. It contained 'the powder of the root of the male peony' mixed with human skull, ambergris and musk. To this one should add 'of the kernels of the cocoa nuts one pound', and 'of sugar what will suffice'; and 'of this make chocolate', taking 'half an ounce or six drams every morning in a draught of the decoction of sage or of the flowers of peony'.[139]

It was by no means unknown for the then novel import 'chocalata' to be prescribed by eminent doctors.[140] Whilst this recipe seems slightly unusual, it had considerable authority behind it. The doctor in question was Thomas Willis. Now remembered particularly as a pioneer of brain research, in a time when this organ was strikingly little known and under-appreciated, the 'father of neuroscience' was also a vigorous anatomist, and (by 1667) the highest paid man in Oxford. His income of £300 per year came from a thriving medical practice. Before his death in 1675, Willis was able (notes his biographer, Robert Martensen) 'to buy a 3,000 acre country estate from the Duke of Buckinghamshire', and was thought by his peers to be the richest doctor in England.[141]

Although a pious Christian, Willis is notable for taking a relatively avant-garde attitude to the study of the brain, cautiously but definitely shifting away from typical discussions of the soul to consider structure, pathology and physiology.[142] Admittedly, Willis's scepticism also extended to the prevalent belief that moss of the skull could stop bleeding if held in the hand or inserted into the nostrils. Yet even in that discussion Willis referred to this moss as a 'famous medicine'.[143] Elsewhere, he prescribed spirit of human blood against pleurisy, scorbutic gout, and 'excessive pissing'.[144] Willis also credited human skull as a medicine for vertigo, epilepsy, apoplectic fits, and even for those afflicted by 'stupidity [and] slow and torpid spirits'.[145] Not only that, but he was evidently making fairly regular use of it in his medical visits, particularly when treating a number of young women suffering from convulsions.

In one case, around 1657, he attended a nobleman's daughter, aged sixteen, who at the winter solstice was suddenly taken with headaches and giddiness. Violent contractions in her arms followed, and the day after this, she suddenly leapt without warning from her chair, fetching 'one or two jumps, and many others successively, with wonderful agility, at the distance of many feet'. She now 'stood leaping a great while in the same place, and every time to a great height' until exhausted, at which point she fell down, presently being compelled to beat the floor or walls violently with hands and feet. Willis – again taking a relatively scientific attitude, given that some observers thought the girl to be possessed by an evil spirit – prescribed emetics, drew ten ounces of blood, and dosed the girl twice daily with 'powders of precious stones ... human skull, and the root of the male peony'. Although the case was a difficult one, characterised by relapse, the girl at this point did gain relief for some two weeks. There is no indication in the case history that the girl or her family had any objection (either to the powdered skull, or to a subsequent draught of 'white wine, dilated with the water of black cherries, with sows or hog-lice bruised and infused therein'[146]).

Noble as she was, this girl was in fact not Willis's most eminent patient. He tells elsewhere of his various experiences of 'apoplectical persons ... of some who were once or twice touched, and yet living; and of others who have died at the first assault, or in the second or third fit'. ('Apoplexy' was at this time rather loosely used to indicate severe attacks; in some of these cases it probably refers to a stroke.) Among those who survived was Gilbert Sheldon, benefactor of Wren's Oxford theatre, and Archbishop of Canterbury from 1663–77. Sheldon was treated by Willis in around 1666, after suffering 'a grievous apoplectical fit'.[147] With 'God prospering our medicinal help', Sheldon recovered, and 'from that time, though he sometimes suffered some light skirmishes of the disease, yet he never fell, or became speechless or senseless'.[148] We have seen that Willis recommended human skull as an ingredient to be swallowed by apoplectics; and it is also significant that, even when casting doubt on skull-moss as a cure for bleeding, he nevertheless adds that, when such remedies 'may be administered without trouble or cost, we make no refusal' of them, as 'in a dangerous case every thing is to be attempted; and applications of that sort do help sometimes in respect that they fortify the imagination of the patient'.[149] Given that the apoplexy of Gilbert Sheldon would clearly have been considered a 'dangerous case', it seems almost certain that one of the agents used by Willis in his treatment would indeed have been human skull.

Robert Boyle

Among Willis's associates and fellow scientists, Boyle has some particularly interesting things to say about corpse medicine. Boyle's own recipe for convulsions describes a medicine which had 'cured very many, especially children, and young boys and girls, of ... fits'. One should 'take of the powder (whether made by filing, rasping, or, otherwise) of the sound skull of a dead man, and give of it about as much as will lie upon a groat, made up into a bolus with conserve of rosemary-flowers'. For adults one should double this dose. Human skull also features in a plaster 'to prevent corns'. Interestingly, these recipes appear in collections of remedies compiled from Boyle's manuscripts and published after his death as 'Medicinal experiments, or, A collection of choice and safe remedies, for the most part simple and easily prepared' and 'very useful in families and fitted for the service of country people'.[150] Thus we find that Boyle, in addition to his considerable influence on eighteenth-century scientists, also helped to spread a cannibalistic recipe in the same way as did Elizabeth Grey and other authors or compilers of popular medical self-help books.

In 1665 Boyle notes that 'mummy is one of the usual medicines commended and given by our physicians for falls and bruises, and in other cases too'.[151] We will see later that the context of this reference is unusual. It can be stated here that Boyle does not seem sceptical of the benefits of mummy, or clearly hostile about it in ethical terms. The agents in which Boyle was most interested, however, were the moss of the skull, and various distillations of human blood.

Although Boyle seems to have been unusually pious (even by the standards of his time) he was also essentially sceptical in his approach to natural phenomena.[152] For the author of the carefully titled *Sceptical Chemist*, claims must be proved. Similarly, his attitude to usnea is notably balanced and empirical: 'the true moss growing upon a human skull, though I do not find experience warrant all the strange things some chemical writers attribute to it for the staunching of blood, yet I deny not, but in some bodies it does it wonderful enough', writes Boyle in 1663. He proceeds to tell of an 'eminent virtuoso' who 'finds the effects of this moss so considerable upon himself, that after having been let blood, his arm falling to bleed again, and he apprehending the consequences of it, his physician, who chanced to be present, put a little of the above-mentioned moss into his hand'. The moss, being 'barely held there, did, to the patient's wonder, staunch his blood, and gave him the curiosity to lay it out of his hand, to try whether that moss were the cause of the blood's so oddly stopping its course'; upon which 'his arm after a little while, beginning to bleed afresh, he took the moss again into his hand, and thereby presently staunched his bleeding the second time'. And, adds Boyle, 'if I misremember not, he added, that he repeated the experiment once more with the like success'.[153]

Recounting this tale again in 1685, Boyle emphasises that the story was 'not only solemnly averred to me by' the patient himself ('one of the eminentest members of the Royal Society') but also 'confirmed to me by his ingenious physician, with both whom I had a particular acquaintance'; adding that the event was one 'which other-wise I should have thought scarce credible, unless imagination, a faculty very strong in that gentleman, contributed to the strange effect of the remedy'.[154] This report tells us that, despite his scepticism about the possibility of such a cure, Boyle felt himself obliged to believe empirical evidence. His last words, on the 'very strong' imagination of the gentleman, also suggest that such cures might well have worked in those whose temperaments (or physiology) predisposed them to psychosomatic responses.

True to the new science's credo of personal experience, Boyle also used usnea himself. He tells of how, particularly afflicted by nosebleeds one summer, he tried various remedies, most of which succeeded, albeit 'not ... with quick success'. Presently,

> falling once unexpectedly into a fit, whose violence somewhat alarmed me, I resolved to try an unusual remedy: and having easily obtained of my sister, in whose house this accident happened, some true moss of a dead man's skull, which had been sent her, by a great person, for a present out of Ireland, in which country, I found it less rare and more esteemed than elsewhere: I was going to employ it after the usual manner, which is to put it up into the patient's nostrils, but before I did it, I had the curiosity to try, notwithstanding the briskness of my haemorrhage, whether the medicine would produce its effect by being only held in my hand, and therefore covering a piece of the moss with my fist, that the warmth might a little actuate the medicine, I found, to the wonder of the by-standers, that the blood speedily stopped, nor thanks be to God have I been troubled with a haemorrhage for some years from that very time.[155]

Here, a cure which would later be construed as the nadir of pre-Enlightenment superstition appears as an exemplary case of proto-scientific empiricism. If the 'magnetic' cures of Irvine and others, with their theories of invisible action-at-a-distance, may at times seem occult in their expression and associations, Boyle's use of the moss in his hand, rather than nostrils, threatens to set such beliefs in a quite different light.[156] Boyle's characteristic scepticism is again implied when he describes the remedy as 'unusual'. But if this predisposed him against it in any way, he was clearly unable to deny the evidence of his own senses. Moreover, despite the impromptu nature of the incident, the bystanders might well have been deliberately called in as witnesses, to strengthen the experimental value of the cure. Recalling Bacon, we find that his suggestion about Ireland as a good source of unburied skulls and skull-moss could indeed have been taken up after his death. It is certainly notable that – perhaps in the manner of Elizabeth Grey and the Fairfaxes – Boyle's sister has the ingredient to hand; and that the 'great person' in Ireland not only owned some, but credited its powers sufficiently to send it to Boyle's sister.[157]

The moss of the human skull clearly impressed Boyle and certain of his eminent peers. But most of his attention was concentrated on the nature and powers of human blood. As Kenneth Dewhurst has pointed out, Boyle was encouraging John Locke (a physician as well as philosopher) to make experiments on human blood in the 1660s, with the two men meeting at the start of the decade, and Locke's first experiment occurring in June 1666.[158] (It is worth emphasising that Locke's taking the trouble to obtain '"some good man's blood"' in the summer of this notorious plague year suggests no small keenness).[159] Boyle himself would publish his own *Memoirs for the History of Humane Blood* in 1683. But, as Dewhurst again notes, this was based on manuscript papers which Boyle had had since the 1660s, and of these a great number had in fact been lost.[160] Even in their incomplete, published form, the accounts of Boyle's researches and interests are impressively thorough and painstaking. Along with numerous careful types of analysis and distillation, we find Boyle using both human blood and urine as invisible inks, and not infrequently tasting various preparations of blood.[161]

Here as elsewhere, Boyle's ultimate belief in the medical powers of blood is won through what he considers rigorously persuasive evidence, derived both from his own experiments, and reliable associates. The absence of any initial beliefs in favour of blood as a medicine (or physical agent per se) is sharply asserted when he states in the *Memoirs*: 'I ignore not that there are extant in Burgravius, Beguinus, and divers other chemical authors, very pompous and promising processes of the essence of men's blood, to which they ascribe such stupendous faculties as I should not only wonder to find true, but admire that they can hope the reader should believe them so'. Very probably referring to Burgravius' sanguinary 'lamp of life' when he cites the 'very mystical and unlikely' claims of this author, he nevertheless goes on with typical openness to assert that he 'shall be very forward to acknowledge their excellency, if any man shall vouchsafe me an experimental conviction of it'.[162] By contrast, Boyle thinks it likely that spirit of blood can be used against asthma, epilepsy, acute fevers, pleurisy, consumption, hysteria, convulsions, certain types of headache, palsy, 'incipient apoplexies', distempers and jaundice. He believes it to be a good cordial, and 'probably against some poisons an antidote'.[163]

Whilst part of Boyle's faith in the medical powers of blood was derived from his experiments with it, he also had access to the case histories of those friends and associates who worked as practising physicians.[164] In *Some Considerations* he writes of 'a recent account brought me by a physician, whom I had entrusted with some spirit of blood' and who 'represents it as so very good a medicine'; and of 'a very ingenious friend of ours Dr N. N.' who has 'lately practised yet a more easy and preferable way of preparing medicines of this nature'.[165] In the same work he also refers to 'a friend of mine, an excellent chemist, whose rare cures first gave me a value for remedies made of blood'.[166] This friend may well have been John French. We have seen that Boyle did indeed have great respect for French's chemistry, and that French was a relatively early advocate of chemically prepared blood medicines (such as spirit and oil). French died in 1657, and *Some Considerations* was published in 1663. But Michael Hunter points out that Boyle 'wrote the bulk' of the work in the late 1650s, so that Boyle's reference to a living 'friend' could plausibly date from 1656 or 1657.[167] Whoever the friend was, this and the other references to work with physicians shows us a new alliance between practical medicine and the most advanced chemistry of the day. Once again, medicinal cannibalism here aligns itself with the most progressive elements of any standard history of Interregnum or Restoration science.[168]

Having talked of 'the recent account' from the unnamed physician, Boyle quite explicitly proceeds to assert that it is this report which prompts him to set down his particular recipe (evidently for the general benefit of patients). He advises one to 'take of the blood of an healthy young man as much as you please, and whilst it is yet warm, add to it twice its weight of good spirit of wine, and incorporating them well together, shut them carefully up in a convenient glass vessel'. After digesting six weeks in horse dung, the resultant matter should be carefully distilled in a retort kept in sand.[169] He further emphasises the medical value of spirit of blood when giving a kind of emergency recipe for it: 'because you may sometimes not have the leisure to wait six weeks for the preparation of blood; and because oftentimes the occasion of using the medicines we have been describing, may be so hasty and urgent, that unless some speedy course to relieve them be taken before the physic can be prepared, the patients will be dead', it is permissible to immediately distil out a salt and spirit, both of which are only slightly inferior to the fully prepared versions.[170]

Boyle underlines his belief that this remedy could be life-saving when stressing that 'with exceedingly piercing essence or spirit of man's blood, I have known … strange things performed even in a deplorable and hereditary consumption'.[171] This claim appears to refer to a case history given much more fully in the *Memoirs*. 'A young Lady, in whose family the consumption was an hereditary disease, was molested with a violent and stubborn cough, that was judged consumptive, and looked upon by those that gave her physic, as not to be cured by any other way, than a seasonable remove from London into the French air'. As it was winter, and too dangerous for her to travel until spring, Boyle was 'solicited by some friends of hers and mine, to try what I could do to preserve her'. He accordingly 'sent her some spirit of human blood very carefully prepared and rectified, (to which I gave some name that I do not well remember) upon the use of which she manifestly mended, notwithstanding the unfriendliness of the season' – so much so that 'about the end of February, she had gained relief and strength enough to venture to cross the seas, and make a journey to Montpellier, whence in autumn she brought home good looks and recovery'.[172] Whatever the exact cause of the woman's dramatic recovery, it was clearly not because she herself had a strong belief in the power of spirit of blood. For Boyle admits that the medicine was given to her under a false name; a precaution no doubt suggested to him by the 'strong aversion', or even 'insuperable ... abhorrency', which some patients felt towards 'medicines made of man's blood'.[173]

Elsewhere Boyle tells of giving to 'a friend of mine some pure yellow oil of man's blood, dissolved in spirit of wine', for a patient 'sick of a hectic fever (in which disease I had seen the spirit of blood very successful)', and of how the friend 'within a few days ... brought me word of the unexpected recovery of his patient'.[174] The same medicine also worked wonders on a tailor, apparently afflicted by migraines or something similar ('this man was frequently obnoxious to such violent and tormenting fits of the head-ache, that he could not endure the light, and was offended with almost every noise or motion that reached his ears; insomuch that he was forced to give over his profession'). Despite having previously 'baffled the endeavours' of several 'eminent doctors', the tailor, following 'constant use of ... spirit of blood' was soon able, 'with great joy and thankfulness', to 'return to the exercise of his trade'. This case history is valuable, in part, because it suggests that from around mid-seventeenth century, human blood gained its medical reputation for practical as much as theoretical reasons. It is also valuable because it supplies one further level of vividly empirical 'proof', and one which impressed itself on a surgeon rather than a physician. For the patient, 'having by our famous Harvey's advice, been used to bleed once in two or three months, the physician counselled him, notwithstanding his recovery, not abruptly to break off his ancient custom'. The tailor 'thereupon sent for the same surgeon that had been formerly wont to let him blood', and who had (with notably empirical scrutiny) been wont 'to complain of the great badness of his blood'. Not knowing anything of the patient's recent treatment, the surgeon opened a vein, and, seeing 'what kind of blood it afforded, he was so surprised, that he stopped the operation, and asked the man with wonder, how he came by such florid blood', adding, that 'twas pity to deprive him of so well conditioned a liquor'.[175]

It is accepted by many that Boyle was the 'acknowledged leading intellect' of the Royal Society, a man whom 'even Newton addressed' with uncharacteristic humility.[176] And Boyle's influence stretched well beyond his own lifetime. Versions of his *Medicinal Experiments* appeared down to 1731, and in 1747 he featured in the popular domestic and medical handbook, *The Family Magazine*.[177] Perhaps more importantly, the monumental eighteenth-century editions of his works gave him something of a canonical status in the Enlightenment era, and in these imposing volumes various of his claims about corpse medicine reappear, from 1725 through to 1772, as well as being cited by other authors down to the close of the eighteenth century.[178] In 1792 the physician Benjamin Moseley refers to him with a sense of patriotic ownership as 'our great Boyle'.

The King's Drops

Although less weighty than that of Boyle, the influence of Charles II is also of interest. In paying an impressive amount to Goddard for his recipe, Charles effectively achieved a curious transfer of intellectual ownership. From then on, many people seem to have viewed 'Goddard's Drops' as 'the King's Drops'.[179] The medicine clearly had a high status before Charles took it over. As we saw, John French could already refer to it as 'famous' in 1653; and in a letter of 1677 John Locke recommended 'Goddard's drops' as a routine tonic for an ailing female patient of Dr John Mapletoft.[180]

In such an age, however, it seems likely that some consumers would certainly have been more swayed by the royal seal of quality than by a scientific one. And the drops were evidently being fairly widely used for some time after Charles's own death. In 1686 the unhappily married Anne Dormer wrote to her sister, Lady Anne Trumbull, stating: 'I apply myself to tend my crazy health, and keep up my weak shattered carcass, broken with restless nights and unquiet days. I take the king's drops and drink chocolate, and when my soul is sad to death I run and play with the children'.[181] Whatever the exact nature of these health problems (which sound at least partly emotional or mental), it is interesting to note that Dormer's dosings broadly echo Willis's use of human skull and chocolate against apoplexy.

And the drops were clearly also considered effective in far more urgent cases (despite their failure on Charles's deathbed). On 16 January 1687, for example, William Cartwright, the bishop of Chester, 'sent the King's drops to Mr Alford'.[182] Alford was evidently very ill at this time, as he died before the end of the month. A few years on we find a partial re-enactment of the scenes at Charles's deathbed, when Queen Mary II lies dying on Thursday 27 December 1694. By this time the queen is 'ill to extremity, having a little before taken some of the late King Charles's Drops, being a high cordial, and the last refuge of the physicians'.[183] Although the drops again failed (with Mary dying around 1.15 that morning) their reputation against the falling sickness was still high in élite circles across the channel toward the close of the century. C.J.S. Thompson notes that, 'when in Paris in 1698', the English physician Martin Lister 'was summoned by the Prince de Conti to see his son, and was requested to bring with him some of "King Charles' Drops"', for the Prince's evidently epileptic son.[184]

The wealthy peers of Charles and Mary clearly set some store by this famous distillation of human skull. They may have known cases in which it did indeed seem to recover those at death's door (and we should add that even Alford may have appeared temporarily rallied by them). And there is in fact some evidence that these drops could have a powerful chemical effect. In his unfinished autobiography, the lawyer and politician Roger North (1651–1734) recalled some of his worst experiences of drunkenness. One of these was induced by William Chiffinch (c.1602–91), a courtier and royal official who carried immense influence as the effectual private secretary of Charles II.[185] Chiffinch, writes North,

> delighted to send his guests away foxed; and to finish me, who was not easily drawn to any degree of good fellowship, he put the king's drops (an extract of bone) in our wine. I had not very much, but found it heavy, and that I must have some care to carry it off steadily as I did, I think, over the tarras into the park, and then to the side of the cliff among the bushes, I laid me down and lay on the ground for six hours. If any saw me or not I know not. My brother jested and said he with the king had walked that way, and found his learned counsel drunk in a bush.[186]

If this visit to Windsor was perhaps not among North's happiest memories (and his memory of it was clearly slight in itself) he perhaps got off relatively lightly. For, as North notes elsewhere, it seems to have been Chiffinch's habit to use the drops as a means of extracting secrets from those under their influence: '"he was a most impetuous drinker, and, in that capacity, an admirable spy; for he let none part from him sober, if it were possible to get them drunk ... Nor, to make sure work, would he scruple to put his master's salutiferous drops (which were called the king's, of the nature of Goddard's), into the glasses ... he thus fished out many secrets, which the king could never have obtained ... by other means'".[187] According to Christopher Hibbert, Charles himself was also known to have used the drops for this purpose.[188]

If it is difficult to be sure just what ingredient of the drops produced such an effect on North, it seems quite clear that the effect itself was potent in the extreme. This may have resulted from unusually heavy dosing. There again, if it was the mixing with alcohol which was the problem, we would have to assume that such an effect was by no means uncommon. To write 'do not take with alcohol' on your medicine circa 1680 was rather like saying 'do not take at all'. At very least, if you were washing it down with anything, the drink would probably be wine, if not something stronger. As we will see in the Conclusion, the king's drops survived, at least in name, almost until the Victorian era.

A brief word on comparable usage in France takes us up close to the end of the seventeenth century. In 1694 Pierre Pomet, chief apothecary to the French king Louis XIV, published his *Complete History of Drugs*.[189] Advising buyers on the risk of being defrauded, Pomet recommends that Egyptian mummy should be a kind 'of fine shining black ... of a good smell, and which, being burnt, does not stink of pitch'. Pomet seems slightly ambivalent about its virtue. He acknowledges that it is 'reckoned proper' for contusions, and to stop blood coagulating in the body (probably in cases of internal bleeding). But, he adds (echoing various sporting authorities of the day), 'its greatest use is for catching fish'.[190] This ambivalence is interesting, as it compounds the impression that Pomet – like the English chemists examined above – accepts only those body substances which have undergone some degree of chemical processing. Noting, for example, that in France 'human fat or grease' is sold for the medical treatment of rheumatism, he admits that the bulk of this trade is monopolised by the Parisian executioner, before commending the professional version – 'prepared with aromatical herbs' – as far better. 'Besides the fat', he continues, 'we sell the fixed and volatile salts of the blood, skull, hair and urine' – all these substances being listed, as he says, in the *Pharmacopeia* of 'Monsieur Charas'.[191]

We will hear much more about the chemical preferences of Pomet and others in chapter six. We need now, however, to complete the present survey of early modern medicinal cannibalism by shifting to the question of supply. Just where did all these diverse materials come from? This question takes us through graveyards, hospitals, and battlefields, and to the side of anatomy slabs and execution scaffolds. We begin, however, with a world which, for Shakespeare or Pepys, was perhaps as strange as their world is to us. It is time to pay a visit to Egypt.

3

THE BLOODY HARVEST

Sources of human body parts

Egypt

Cairo, c.2000 BC

On a table carved into the shape of a lion lies a corpse, surrounded by four men. The masks on their faces have beaks like those of sparrowhawks. One now raises a sharpened stone and cuts into the side of the body. In keeping with the ritual of embalming he then flees, bystanders pursuing him angrily and hurling stones. With this fundamental violation accomplished and acknowledged, the remaining embalmers draw out the brains and the organs of the trunk.[1] Cavities are washed in Phoenician wine and treated with cinnamon, myrrh and cassia. In all the process lasts several weeks. Finally the body, wrapped in gum-soaked linen bandages, is returned to relatives, who presently inter it in a tomb around twelve miles from Cairo. Time passes. Homer, Plato, and Alexander the Great come and go. The Roman Empire rises and falls. Some time in the early sixteenth century money changes hands, and Arab guides begin to dig away the sand blocking the entrance to the burial chambers.[2] A shaft of sunlight knifes cleanly through the soft accumulated shadows of time and death. Men slide down on ropes. Tapers flare. The crack of hatchets echoes down the tunnels as first coffins, then bodies themselves are broken open.

At this point the dead man escapes the plunder. In fact, guarded by a particularly large and nasty set of bats who happen to have made their home nearby, he survives undisturbed until 1581. To be fair, he is soon settled back in the darkness once again. Immured in the hold of an English merchant ship he is of no interest to the grey tomcat padding softly over his coffin, its nostrils diverted by the far stronger smell of pepper and ginger which pierces through nearby canvas sacking. On deck the captain raises his spyglass one last time, tilting it beyond the teeming babel of the quayside and back toward Cairo, that great mercantile whirlpool of Christians, Armenians,

Abexins, Turks, Moors, Jews, Indians, Medians, Persians, and Arabians. He glances briefly at a crocodile sunning itself along the river bank, and at two half-naked men wrestling before a small crowd, their oiled bodies shining in the dry glitter of Egyptian light. A few vital words with the first mate establish that all the appropriate parties have been bribed, and that no rice has been allowed on board.[3] It is now late afternoon, and time to leave, as none but the most inexperienced smuggler would ever seek to steal away in darkness. Ropes slither; sails pucker and tighten. The captain closes his eyes on the bright confusion of tongues and clothing, and with a supreme effort of will summons up a momentary vision that soothes his eyes and anoints his sun-cracked brain: England ... cool, damp, and – above all – green.[4]

The ship reaches home in good time to fulfil this yearning. Sliding between the hills and meadows of Gloucestershire that spring, its crew finds that the pyramids, mummies, and even the wondrous dancing dogs and camels of Cairo fade to a dry unreal speck in a corner of the memory. By 15 May the coffin sits on a dock beside the Thames. At 5.45 p.m. on Wednesday 20 May, a stray pig darts from an alleyway onto the street known as Bucklersbury. A horse rears up, and a man is hurled down onto the unforgiving flint of the road. He has picked the right place to do this, as Bucklersbury is lined with the shops of apothecaries and grocers.[5] The accident is a minor one, and the job is soon done. A few crumbled particles of the body of a mummified Egyptian (just that week dismembered and dispersed among the numerous chemists along the street) are mixed with earth of Lemnos, dragon's blood, rhubarb and spermaceti, and applied to a linen plaster.[6] With this clamped to his hip, the rider also swallows a fluid preparation of mummy in order to prevent internal coagulation of blood.

Such, we might reasonably imagine, was the long journey of an Egyptian corpse in the earlier years of the English mummy trade. In examining the various sources of human body parts, we will again find that the social presence of corpse medicine spanned a network at once broad and intricate. In the case of most of these sources, it is also important to know what that particular area of supply *meant* to the peers of Marlowe or Milton.

What did ancient Egypt mean to Renaissance or early modern observers? The original land of the pharaohs and the pyramids must have seemed fabulously distant to the men and women of the sixteenth century. And in one crucial sense it was far *more* historically remote than for ourselves, some 400 years on. For the Christians of the later seventeenth century in particular were convinced that the world had been created just 5,000 years before Christ – or, to be more precise, on 23 October 4004 BC. In the early 1650s the Church of Ireland archbishop, James Ussher, worked obsessively through the Bible to derive this chronology (managing, indeed, to show that God accomplished his task in good businesslike fashion at 9 a.m. one morning).[7] Even had there been any fossil analysis or carbon dating which might suggest otherwise, it seems unlikely that the Christian scriptures, the supreme historical authority of the age, would have been seriously challenged. Some mummies were thought to have lasted almost four millennia.[8] The ancient Egyptians, therefore, were more than half as old as Time itself.[9]

And to this strange fact we must add the Renaissance attitude to the past in general. The whole concept of a 're-naissance', or rebirth, was of course founded on a more or less unquestioned reverence for the culture of the ancient and classical worlds. The thought, literature, architecture and art of early modern Europe were saturated with ideas or styles imitated from Greece and Rome. In terms of secular literature this necessarily ran back only as far as Homer. But the Egyptians had left two highly impressive phenomena which substantially predated the epic deeds of Achilles and Odysseus.

On one hand there were those unmistakable and durable artefacts such as the pyramids, the Great Sphinx, and the monument of Cheops. Anyone who has spent just a few moments among the most fragmentary relics of Egypt in the British Museum cannot help but wonder breathlessly at the sheer scale of a single severed arm or disembodied head. Egyptian architecture alone was enough to make some Europeans feel half-consciously insecure about their own technological powers – as when the pioneering Egyptologist John Greaves made a peculiarly tortuous effort to prove that even the greatest of the pyramids was in fact not as tall as the spire of St Paul's (which had itself been destroyed by lightning in 1561).[10] Rather less grudgingly, the French baron Jean Dumont, writing from Cairo in February 1691, spoke of those 'stately monuments' which pronounced the 'ancient kings of Egypt … the most powerful monarchs in the universe'. By comparison with 'these magnificent sepulchres', which seemed to be 'copies of the tower of Babel', 'how vastly inferior are the pantheon, coliseum' and the capitol.[11]

Less monumental in size, but colossal in their evocation of time (and far more portable), were the curiously immaculate bodies of the Egyptians themselves. No other culture had achieved anything like this. At this point most Europeans had little or no knowledge of bog mummies (and would not have guessed their true age even if they had.[12]) Occasionally in Europe bodies would fail to decompose: thus one had saintly mummies in Italy, and demonic ones in the territory of the vampire.[13] In London, after the Great Fire of 1666 destroyed much of St Paul's Cathedral, Samuel Pepys and others saw the exposed remains of Robert Braybrooke, Bishop of London (d.1404), being 'his skeleton with the flesh on; but all tough and dry like a spongy dry leather'. Many, Pepys added, were 'flocking to see it'.[14] In 1701 a man's body was found trapped in a Piccadilly chimney, its flesh wasted away, and skin 'extreme hard and dry as shoe leather'; and in 1774 a mummified husband and wife appeared in a vault in St Martin's-in-the-Fields, their coffins having evidently mouldered away.[15] In Protestant England such oddities seem, however, to have been more a source of curiosity than of either wonder or terror. And they were, of course, seen to be the work of chance rather than of art.[16]

Time and again, by contrast, seventeenth-century commentators marvelled at the vanished art of Egyptian embalmers. Around 1672, down in the darkness of an Egyptian burial cavern, one European traveller gazed in wonder at 'that balm which is now quite lost'. It was, he noted, looking into the broken mummy which he and his assistants had just violated, 'black, hard, and shines like pitch, having much such a smell, but more pleasant'.[17] There was certainly pressure to imitate the art of the ancient Egyptians. But, as Pierre Pomet ruefully confessed in 1694, all the best and most costly efforts on the bodies of the honoured dead had never staved off decay for longer than a mere two or three centuries – a bare fraction of the 4,000 years which some Egyptian mummies were thought to have endured.[18] Even the legendary conqueror Alexander the Great, embalmed after his early death in the summer of 323 BC, began to weather badly after 300 or so years. By the time that the Roman Emperor Augustus came to view Alexander's body – a few years before the birth of Christ – it was (remarks Francis Bacon) 'so tender, as Caesar touching but the nose of it, defaced it'.[19] The difference between modern and ancient embalmers could not be explained simply by the proverbially arid climate of North Africa. Here were real human beings whose flesh, transmuted into a hard shining brown or black, 'like stone pitch', and having 'a good smell', offered an extraordinary suspended fragment of remotest antiquity.

Such uncannily preserved relics invested the Egypt of the sixteenth century with a semi-mythic status in the minds of many Europeans.[20] Those who could afford to make such a journey might well have heeded the commonplace advice that travel per se was dangerous and foolhardy – a notion underlying (and amply proved by) Thomas Nashe's *The Unfortunate Traveller* of 1594. Others, who just barely knew the region as part of Old Testament history and could never have funded even a quarter of the voyage, may have found it effectively as distant as the moon.

This situation must have changed as explorers and academics became increasingly interested in the area, and returned home with both reports and relics. A memorable example is that of the German Jesuit, Father Johann Michael Vansleb. At a casual glance Vansleb looks like a kind of seventeenth-century Indiana Jones. Some time between 1672 and 1676, Vansleb could be found dauntlessly probing the darkest and most morbid caverns of the Egyptian desert.[21] He tells of French explorers scaling the great Sphinx with rope ladders, and finding its head to be hollow (though predictably filled up with sand); and of the stark plains of death spread out across the desert:

> think upon a boundless champagne, even and covered over with sand, where neither trees, nor grass, nor houses, nor any such thing is to be seen … [and] full of dry bones of arms, legs, feet, and heads … of scattered pieces of wood of coffins, [and] of little idols … marked before and behind with hieroglyphic letters.

Even the intrepid Jesuit admits that these 'mournful signs of man's mortality' are, on first sight, 'able to dash a person newly arrived out of countenance, and to affright him'.[22]

Despite this, and despite suffering intermittently from a quite severe fever, Vansleb more than once has himself lowered down on a rope into the mummy pits or 'wells' of Saccara (now usually Saqqara), the great necropolis located north-west of Memphis, and some twelve miles from modern Cairo. Sometimes wriggling on his belly along a tunnel half buried in sand, he peers by the wavering light of candles and matches at sarcophagi of sycamore wood or stone; breaks open coffins; unwraps bodies. Mummies themselves are rifled in search of the funerary idols sometimes lodged within their eviscerated trunks. Vansleb and his comrades are undeterred by either the shadows of death, the occasional foetid air which snuffs their candles, or even the ugly bats – 'exceeding a foot in length' – which we met earlier.[23] He is rewarded not only by his detailed observations, but by assorted pieces of plunder, including one stone coffin of about 800 weight, and another 'made of above forty cloths glued or pasted together in thickness, which are not in the least rotten'. In a neat emblem of the relations between Time and Vanity, a mummy's head bandage 'on which the countenance of that person was represented in gold' is removed to reveal 'nothing of the face remaining, which is commonly reduced to ashes'.[24]

Clearly European reverence for Egypt could have ironic consequences. It did not guard these relics against vandalism or theft. At the same time, it was significant that they were thought *worth* stealing. Similarly, for some it was only this 'true mummy' of the pharaohs which was worth eating. Vansleb himself was of this opinion, and others, including Samuel Purchas, the compiler of Renaissance travel narratives, agreed with him.

This 'true mummy' was not only a costly and effective medical agent. In certain literary passages of the seventeenth century it indeed assumes that general aura of the sacred (or magical) more usually reserved for the saintly relics of Catholicism. Shakespeare's Othello, for example, seems to suffer from epilepsy, falling into a fit in act four, scene one, at the peak of his jealous rage. It may be for this reason that he so highly values the handkerchief mislaid by the luckless Desdemona. This, he tells her, had been given to his grandmother by an Egyptian sorceress. Although its exact date of origin is not specified, we know that 'the worms were hallowed that did breed the silk', and that it had been 'dyed in mummy, which the skilful/Conserved of maidens' hearts'. Medical use of the heart was rare, though not unknown.[25] It seems to have been more definitely agreed that mummy made from the bodies of virgins, or maidens, was indeed specially potent, and commanded an unusually high price for that reason.[26] The possible association with epilepsy may here be purely accidental. What is interesting is the way that Egypt is drawn in as a loose but (we may assume) swiftly recognisable source of magical power. The aim of the passage is to steep the handkerchief in the most mystical and revered atmosphere, and in this sense Egypt is a shrewd choice.

For many Renaissance Christians the great hypnotising expanses of time, lying like deserts of vast eternity between themselves and the pharaohs, considerably mitigated the potential taboos of Egyptian corpse medicine. Perhaps equally important was the fact that these ancient bodies had nothing like the smell or texture of ordinary dead flesh. Even their stylised shapes and decorations served to abstract them from those ordinary human beings strolling down Bucklersbury at the time of Shakespeare or Marvell. If mummy had, in an unadmitted psychological sense, always to come from somewhere else, and from some*one* else, then this was a highly suitable choice. Is it, then, a mere oddity of phrasing when the Italian anatomist and advocate of corpse medicine, Berengario da Carpi, says of his medicinal plaster that 'a notable part of human, *or rather mummy* substance enters into its composition'?[27]

As Philip Schwyzer has pointed out, supply from Egypt probably became increasingly difficult as the seventeenth century wore on.[28] Come 1652 Alexander Ross was already highly sceptical about the availability of 'true', Egyptian mummy, and by 1691 Dumont was able to report from Saccara that 'the curiosity of the Franks has at last exhausted' the ancient mummies of this site.[29] Although there were allegedly some coffins 'that were never opened', the Moors 'who only know where they are ... keep the price of such rarities very high'. Managing (perhaps by bribery) to be let down into these burial pits, Dumont saw 'some pieces of mummy, but so spoiled, that 'twas impossible to preserve any of 'em'.[30] One further indication of the difficulty of obtaining Egyptian mummies is offered by W.R. Dawson, who points out that 'Guanche mummies from the Canary Islands were also exported to Europe for the apothecaries'.[31]

Arabian mummy

In 1609 the traveller Robert Cottington explained how intrepid Arabian merchants could tramp for up to two months 'thorough the sandy deserts, where no people dwell, neither any road way', directed only by observing 'the courses of sun, moon, and stars, for fear of missing their way'. So perilous were these regions that travellers, 'not meeting with water in twelve or fifteen days' space' would sometimes 'to save their own lives ... kill their camels, and drink the blood'. When this did not avail, Cottington adds, their 'dead carcasses consume not, but maketh munna', or mummy, 'every way as physical or medicinable, as that which cometh from Alexandria'.[32] Not everyone agreed on the virtue of this distinct, Arabian mummy. But the source itself seems clear. On occasion, even those with adequate water supplies might simply be overwhelmed by 'hurricanes of sand ... driven with the wind', which – as Samuel Wesley reports in 1693 – could sometimes 'make mummy of whole armies'.[33] Vansleb, similarly, told of how, in the Arabian deserts, 'the dead bodies of men and dogs are found entire, who falling asleep, and staying behind the caravans, are covered over with an ocean of sand driven by the high winds'.[34]

Vansleb himself did not believe that these sand corpses could be 'termed true mummy', and over in England in mid-century, the reactionary thinker Alexander Ross was in agreement.[35] The mummy from 'the tombs of the Egyptian kings' had been, he believed, 'spent long ago', and that from the desert sandstorms had 'no more virtue to staunch blood' than did 'a stick'.[36] Others were uncertain not just about the power of this alternative source, but as to the basic claim of preservation itself. In 1565 John Hall was open-minded but cautiously undecided, able only to note that 'baked or dried sand, hath been proved to preserve fruits longtime unputrefied', and to hope that someone else would presently offer a more conclusive view.[37] Some time before 1594, the Dutch cartographer Petrus Plancius was more emphatic, deriding those 'great palpable lies, whereby fools are persuaded, that the mummy proceedeth of those bodies which do perish in the sands that be in the deserts of Arabia, as though it were possible that those bodies could be preserved in those sands without stench or putrefaction'.[38] The Frenchman Vincent Leblanc claimed to have set out on some remarkably lengthy journeys through the east in 1567, when he was about thirteen or fourteen, and in the English translation of these traveller's tales we hear of how, from 'the sands of Egypt ... the greatest part of mummy or flesh buried and roasted in the sand is gotten, which the wind uncovering, the next passenger brings to town for trade, it being very medicinable'. Either Leblanc had a sharp change of heart, or his work was edited at some point, for on the same page we are told that this sand mummy is indeed 'a mere fable, since there is nothing but bones to be found there, the rest being eaten by the worms'.[39] Toward the close of the seventeenth century, an anonymous author seemed no more certain than Hall, including among 'imperfect relations of many things' the question 'whether mummies be found in the sands of Arabia, that are the dried flesh of men, buried in those sandy deserts in travelling; and how they differ in their virtue from the embalmed ones'.[40]

Some may have connected the natural sand mummies of the deserts with those of Peru (or even Poland).[41] In the former case, Garcilaso de la Vega, a sometime inhabitant of Peru, told of how 'the air of Cozco being rather cold and dry, than hot and moist, is not subject to corruption; so that flesh being hanged up in a room where the windows are open on all sides, will keep eight, or fifteen, or thirty, nay to a hundred days without being mortified, until it is become dried like mummy'. He had, he added, not only seen this himself, but also 'tried and experimented' such natural mummification 'with the flesh of cattle of that country'.[42]

For others, it may not have been only the powers of climate which were involved. Whilst Ross had no time for the alleged medicinal qualities of such corpses, he did take seriously the idea that 'diet ... is a great help to further or retard putrefaction; for they that feed plentifully on flesh, fish, or other humid meats, which breed much blood and humours, are apter to putrify than those who feed sparingly on hard and dry meats'. Hence, 'in the siege of Amida, by Sapor the Persian king, this difference was found; for the European bodies, who lay four days unburied, did in that time so putrefy, that they could scarce be known: but the Persian bodies were grown hard and dry, because of their hard and dry food'.[43] Those who did believe in the 'sand mummies' of Arabia might have felt this to be useful evidence, given the broadly eastern character of the merchants crossing these desert wastes.

For those who did credit it, this type of mummy seems to have been softened and made acceptable not by time, but by the strange alchemy of the climate. At least potentially, European travellers in the region might have recognised that the merchant they saw in a bazaar one day could be the curative which they or their peers swallowed down just a few months later. For all this, Cottington's 'munna' was occasionally used as a (perhaps archaic) form of 'manna'. In that case, then, mummy is not only accepted, but associated with the heavenly food which God sent to the Israelites during their wanderings through the desert.[44]

For those who flatly refused to believe in the sandstorms themselves, there was also yet one more variant of the sand mummy. In 1694 Pomet wrote of those bodies 'which are called white mummies, and are nothing else but the bodies of those that are drowned in the sea, which being cast upon the African coast, are buried and dried in the sands, which are very hot'. These corpses, 'though they have been lusty men in their lives, after they have lain some time there, they weigh not above thirty pounds, and are then in a condition of keeping forever'. Pomet goes on to put the existence of this type of mummy beyond doubt when he adds that, 'there is one in Paris, in the cabinet of Mr Boudet, nephew to Mr Boudet, the king's physician'. Although Pomet himself asserts that these bodies 'have little or no virtue in them', he tells us several things here. One: the Egyptian sands were thought so potent in their preservative qualities that they could mummify not only those overwhelmed in sand mountains, but those who had been well-sodden by drowning. Two: having cast a quasi-scientific eye over one specimen (perhaps in Boudet's cabinet) Pomet had been struck by the lightness and dryness of the body. And three: for all his disdain of this variety, Pomet further admits that such bodies are in fact 'dear' to buyers.[45] They too, it would seem, were in demand.

One last point on the commercial value of human bodies is especially intriguing. For Pomet also stated that 'the same druggists [of London] send to foreign countries, especially Germany, these skulls covered with moss, to put into the composition of the sympathetic ointment, which Crollius describes in his *Royal Chemist*', and which Pomet himself felt to be very effective in the cure of the falling sickness.[46] There is no ambiguity here. Pomet makes it quite clear that Britain was actively exporting human skulls to the continent – in particular, to Germany. As strong supporters of Paracelsianism, German practitioners were themselves likely importers. But why was Britain in particular such an active exporter of these moss–clad skulls? The answer to this has been hinted at by Francis Bacon, and will be discussed below, in the context of European warfare.

Trade

In 1565 one Johann Helffrich of Leipzig was searching fruitlessly for Egyptian mummies in the sands outside Cairo. 'The natives, he wrote, "seek these with all energy, for they sell them to the merchants of Cairo by whom they are further sold. Some of the Arabs eat them out of curiosity"'.[47] As well as implying that mummy was not a routine medical agent for the Arabs at this point, Hellfrich clearly shows us that it was being vigorously plundered and exported to Europe. We have seen that the surgeon John Hall was able to prescribe it in this same year, and some time before 1582 one intrepid traveller witnessed the determined grave-robbing activities which secured supplies for European apothecaries and their customers. An anonymous Elizabethan tells of seeing 'the bodies of ancient men, not rotten but all whole', being daily unearthed from a Cairo pyramid. This kind of trade was still flourishing in 1586, when a British merchant apprentice, John Sanderson, illicitly obtained a mummy shipment of over 600 pounds in weight.[48] In France, some time in or before 1584, the influential Huguenot poet Guillaume du Bartas wrote a stanza on global trade:

So come our sugars from Canary isles:
From Candy, currans, muscadels, and oils:

From the Moluques, spices: balsamum
From Egypt: odours from Arabia come:
From India, drugs, rich gems, and ivory:
From Syria, mummy: black-red ebony,
From burning Chus: from Peru, pearl and gold.

Interestingly, this seems to refer to both Egyptian and sand mummies (the former being 'balsamum' and the latter that from Syria).[49] If so, then it would appear that by the 1580s both these substances were well-known items of trade in France, and were more or less as synonymous with Egypt and Syria as sugar was with the Canaries.

In his 1601 satire *Poetaster*, Jonson had the merchant Albius assert his commercial creed with the words: 'He that respects to get, must relish all commodities alike; and admit no difference betwixt oade, and frankincense; or the most precious balsamum, and a tar-barrel'. A few lines on, Albius' endearments to his wife Chloe include 'my dear mummia, my balsamum', thus confirming that his 'precious balsamum' is indeed mummy.[50] Again, mummy seems here to be synonymous with trade, and to require no gloss. But there is some possibility that Jonson (like Shakespeare and Donne in the 1590s) was being a little modish. Come 1605, the sometime archbishop of Canterbury George Abbot could write in his *Brief Description of the Whole World* of those mummies known 'plentifully at this day, by the whole bodies, hands, or other parts, which by merchants are now brought from thence, and doth make the mummia which the apothecaries use'.[51] Notably, Abbot had not included any reference to mummy (or mummies) in the section on 'Afric and Egypt' in the book's first edition of 1599. Given that he was (as Kenneth Fincham points out) a man of 'broad intellectual tastes' with a fondness for expanding his work, it seems that he had become aware of this new commodity only some time after 1599 (rather than merely being too slapdash to mention it in his first edition). By contrast, mummy appears to have been both more common and more conspicuous by the time Abbot did come to discuss it. For when he refers to 'the colour being very black, and the flesh clung unto the bones' he seems to be describing something which he himself has seen.[52]

By the time of Cromwell, in 1650, mummy was still a sufficiently popular commodity to be included in a list of items subject to import duty, attracting a tax of one shilling per pound.[53] The association between mummy and trade seems only to have grown stronger after the Restoration: when Samuel Pepys saw a mummy it was not in a collector's cabinet, but in a merchant's warehouse.[54] Much later, in 1793, a government select committee discussed a proposal to trade with Japan. This would involve a ship of 800 tons, carrying £7,000 worth of merchandise from Europe. Mummy features here in a prospective list of only eight commodities.[55] Whilst it is just possible that the 'mumia' of this document refers to mineral pitch, we would be wrong to assume that human mummy was itself not a significant commodity at the close of the eighteenth century. In 1799 Philipp Andreas Nemnich's trade dictionary cites words for 'mumia' in German, Dutch, Danish, Swedish, French, Italian, Spanish, Portuguese, Russian, and Polish. Tellingly, the Spanish and Portuguese term, 'carnemomia', is conspicuously fleshly.[56]

A further indication of the trade value of mummy comes from the alleged manu-facture of fraudulent substitutes. In 1564 the French royal physician, Guy de la Fontaine, visited Alexandria. Fontaine claimed that he there met a Jew who traded in mum-mies. After much persuasion, Fontaine succeeded in being shown the merchant's storehouse. Here he saw 'several bodies piled one upon another'. He then asked the merchant 'what sort of drugs he made use of? and what sort of bodies were fit for his service? The Jew answered him, that as to the dead, he took such bodies as he could get, whether they died of a common disease, or of some contagion; and as to the drugs, that they were nothing but a heap of several old drugs mixed together'. He then dried the bodies in an oven and exported them to Europe. He himself, he added, 'was amazed to see that the Christians were lovers of such filthiness'.[57]

We will find what looks like a peculiarly warped version of this story resurfacing in the eighteenth century. Even in the form given here, the tale must prompt some suspicion. Why would a Jewish merchant endanger his allegedly thriving trade by so candidly laughing in the face of one of France's most influential customers? Yet, whilst we must be cautious as to just who was producing such counterfeits, these do indeed seem to have existed. And, if they really did exist in the year of Shakespeare's birth, then we can infer that demand was already strong from certain quarters at this point. For fraud made more sense once the supply of Egyptian mummies was becom-ing genuinely scarcer or more difficult to plunder. Yet in the 1580s Britain had received a shipment of 800 pounds' weight of mummy, and this itself was evidently genuine, given the busy excavations which Hakluyt's voyager saw around 1582. From a very early stage, then, European demand for mummy seems to have been great enough to prompt commercial opportunism – a habit which might stand as an ironic precedent for the adulteration of leisure drugs such as cocaine and heroine in the twentieth century.

Some time before 1626, the play *The Fair Maid of the Inn* could use the insult 'Out thou concealment of tallow, and counterfeit mummy' without further gloss.[58] In his geographical work of 1635, John Swan was aware of a variant of Fontaine's story (which had itself been emphatically repeated by Ambroise Paré in 1582). Whilst he disbelieved such tales ('most ridiculously (in my opinion) do they err who say it is made of man's flesh boiled in pitch') Swan did suspect a form of 'counterfeit mummy' to be on the market. For Swan, this was 'a corrupted humour taken out of old tombs, which there droppeth from embalmed bodies' – the problem being that these bodies were not the most noble and costly mummies of the region, but instead those of 'poor men ... merely dressed and stuffed up with bitumen'.[59]

Karen Gordon-Grube has argued that 'the abuses of mummy dealers in selling inferior wares' were especially widespread and notorious by the end of the seventeenth century, and in 1694 this problem was forcefully lamented by Pomet.[60] As well as repeating the story of Fontaine and the Jewish merchant, Pomet goes to some trouble to emphasise the painstaking nature of the best Egyptian embalming. He seems to do this just because it is difficult to persuade many agents or customers that they *are* being defrauded; for he then goes on to stress that a people who took such trouble would not easily allow these bodies to be plundered for export. Echoing the tale of

1564, he proceeds to assert that 'we may daily see the Jews carrying on their rogueries, as to these mummies, and after them the Christians'. For 'the mummies that are brought from Alexandria, Egypt, Venice and Lyons, are nothing else but the bodies of people that die several ways, whether buried or unburied'. Well over a century after Fontaine's visit, these are still being disembowelled, filled with 'myrrh, aloes, bitumen, pitch and other gums', baked in an oven, wrapped in cerecloth, and dried, to be 'sold here for true Egyptian mummies to those who know no better'. Underscoring the futility of trying to halt this practice, Pomet adds, 'as I am not able to stop the abuses committed by those who sell this commodity, I shall only advise such as buy' to choose carefully, before going on to describe in detail just what authentic mummy should look, feel and smell like.[61]

It seems clear that, for at least 130 odd years, the web of the corpse trade threw its strands out not just to the deserts of Cairo and Syria, but to obscure backstreet dealers in North Africa. Dead bodies were actively scavenged. For all we know, they may have been actively produced, just as they would be for anatomy teaching, in Edinburgh several decades later, or in Colombia in 1992.[62] Amidst the heat and flies of Alexandria, now forgotten men kept company with heaps of anonymous dead, busily seeking to roast and process them before they putrefied. We have seen that Francis I was a specially avid user of mummy in the earlier sixteenth century. Such a client was probably better able than most to fill his purse with the true mummy of the noble burial chambers of Cairo (and, dying in 1547, Francis may also have met his end before fraud became more widespread). There again, we have also seen that the patients of Theodore Turquet de Mayerne included Henri IV, Charles I, and Charles II, figures who lived during the peaks of the counterfeit trade. It is just possible, then, that when Hamlet explained how 'a king might go a progress through the guts of a beggar' he had in fact got this sobering journey the wrong way round.

Europe

If the dry sunlight and dry bodies of modern Arabia and of ancient Egypt might somehow cleanse corpse medicine of its more abhorrent connotations, the same can hardly be said for that which was harvested from the bloody and brutal killing sites of Britain and the neighbouring continent. Europe had four chief sources of direct supply for human body parts. These were the gallows; the anatomists; the grave; and the battlefield.

The executioner

Germanic and Scandinavian countries

In the winter of 1668–69 the English traveller Edward Browne was touring Vienna. Although it was a particularly hard winter – with even the majestic Danube now as frozen as the Thames would be in 1684 – Browne took himself around the sights energetically, admiring the Prater gardens, the menagerie with its lions and tigers, and the usual curiosities and churches. He also had the good fortune to be present at more than one execution:

> in treason and high crimes they cut off the right hand of the malefactor, and his head immediately after. I saw a woman beheaded sitting in a chair, the executioner striking off her head with a foreblow; she behaved her self well, and was accompanied unto the market place by the Confraternity of the Dead, who have a charitable care of such persons, and are not of any religious order, but lay-men.

On what seems to be the same occasion, Browne saw a man 'executed after the same manner'. 'As soon as his head fell to the ground, while the body was in the chair', and even as the corpse was shooting jets of blood and steam into the frosty Viennese air, Browne saw 'a man run speedily with a pot in his hand, and filling it with the blood, yet spouting out of his neck, he presently drank it off, and ran away'. It seems that Brown did not have to have this action explained to him: 'this he did as a remedy against the falling-sickness. I have read of some who have approved the same medicine; and heard of others who have done the like in Germany'. He admits that he did not 'stay afterwards so long as to know the effect thereof, as to the intended cure', adding, 'but most men looked upon it as of great uncertainty'.[63]

These few lines tell us a good deal about the popular treatment of epilepsy in Germanic countries of the early modern era. First: it seems that a woman's blood was not considered suitable medicine by the patient in question. Second: the man drank the blood and then ran. This could at first look like the action of someone afraid of capture, ashamed of his behaviour, or both. It could also imply that he was seeking to escape the executioner, who might well have expected payment for the blood. As for the payment, it is likely that this had been arranged beforehand. And, in running away after he had gulped down the hot blood, the patient was almost certainly following a standard medical prescription.[64]

On 6 June 1755 in Dresden a man named Johann Geord Wiedemann took the blood cure and then '"ran away"'.[65] In 1812 in Hanover, one Louis Stromeyer (aged eight, we might note) 'was taken by the family servant to see a beheading, and observed how women dipped handkerchiefs in the decapitated malefactor's blood to use as a cure for epilepsy. The epileptics then ran off through the crowd, accompanied by those administering the cure, and were supposed to keep running until they dropped'. Meanwhile, 'after a beheading in Stralsund in 1814' one witness wrote of '"a remarkable phenomenon"': '"two riders … led a poor sick man, probably an epileptic, and filled a moderately large jug to the brim with the executed person's blood. After the invalid had drained the ghastly contents right to the bottom, he was bound fast between the horses with strong reins and pulled away at a breakneck gallop"'.[66]

Comparing these two accounts, we can see that the perhaps initially ambiguous phrasing of the second means just what is clearly stated in the first. After drinking the blood, the patient must be made physically exhausted, and as quickly as possible.

Hence, in 1814, the sick man indeed seems to have been forced to gallop with the horses until he, too, 'dropped' from fatigue. There may well have been various reasons for this custom. One has already been hinted to us by the German chemist Johann Schroeder: 'the drinking of the blood requires great caution, because it … brings a truculency' upon those who imbibe it. Schroeder too advised that those epileptics taking the blood cure should afterwards vigorously exercise until 'there is a free perspiration', and this warning was still being given by an Irish author in the eighteenth century.[67] It is clear, then, that the effects of blood-drinking were sufficiently well-known for onlookers to realise that patients (and perhaps especially men) could become extremely aggressive after swallowing such a concentrated shot of human energy.[68] In some, this 'truculency' might only have registered as intense physical agitation. But in either case the remedy was the same: burn off some energy quickly, before the blood dose takes effect.

Yet this was probably not the only (or even chief) reason behind the sudden breakneck dash of the epileptic vampire. Richard J. Evans, the scholar who has given us those valuable accounts from Germany, also shrewdly notes that, for many people from the Middle Ages on, epilepsy was at least partly attributed to the malfunction or temporary absence of the human soul. As the soul at this time was the core of vitality and energy (as well as a spiritual idea), epileptics sought to consume the vitality of executed criminals by drinking the blood in which the soul (at least partly) resided. While we will have much more to say about this reasoning in chapter six, we can here emphasise one interesting point. In forcing this sudden hectic sprint of the blood-gorged epileptic, medical advisers were not just hoping to burn away unwanted aggression, and were certainly not merely following a traditional habit for custom's sake. Their motivation was not vague and magical, but precise and medical. The life force that had just been imbibed needed to be circulated around the body as briskly and thoroughly as possible. Hence a state of maximum physiological agitation was required, in order to fully absorb the vital powers of the criminal.

Linking the eyewitness of 1814 back to Browne, we can elaborate two further points from the English traveller's report. Browne was himself a physician (as was his father, the celebrated writer Sir Thomas Browne).[69] Stating that 'many physicians have, in all times, abominated' such medicine, he both distances himself from it, and implies that it was unfamiliar in England. Browne also seems to have questioned onlookers in the execution crowd about the therapy: 'most men looked upon it as of great uncertainty'. He would almost certainly have inquired of gentlemen, not commoners. What we seem to find, then, is that many of the educated Viennese viewed the practice with scepticism or bemusement: hence the 1814 reference to 'a most remarkable phenomenon'. But that latter phrase (along with the revulsion at 'the ghastly contents' of the jug) may in part be the product not just of educated society, but of the post-Enlightenment world per se. We know that a number of highly learned men (including Robert Boyle, c.1685) took blood therapies seriously.

Nor is this the only important point we should make about the (perceived) division between literate and popular culture. Perched far above such habits, in the safe and sanitised twenty-first century, we are in danger of forgetting something quite basic.

Even if blood-drinking had been merely the preserve of the illiterate, this would not permit us to automatically sweep it away, with a dismissive gesture, into the shadowy netherlands of popular magic and superstition. To put the point one way: *most* people were illiterate and uneducated, and this was the way in which most people saw the world. To put it another way: most of *our* ancestors were illiterate, and believed these kinds of things. If *we* were transported back there, we would believe them, and we would be likely to try and drink human blood if we suffered from the then frightening and highly tabooed condition known as the falling-sickness or 'sacred disease'.[70]

And – whatever the observer of 1814 may have felt – we would have been attempting it until quite late on in the nineteenth century. The practice certainly went back some way. Kathy Stuart details a scene from 'an early sixteenth-century execution in Swabia', where 'a vagrant grabbed the beheaded body "before it had fallen, and drank the blood from him, and they say he was cured of the falling sickness from it"'. (This account, incidentally, shows no obvious sign of revulsion, and derives from an aristocratic family chronicle.)[71] Evans, meanwhile, cites just a few of the 'numerous reports of this practice', starting with Nuremberg in 1674, where 'the blood of executed criminals was caught in a cup as it spurted from the severed neck', and which fluid was indeed reported (by an obviously literate observer) to have made various epileptics '"healthy and healed"'. There, as in Dresden in 1731 and 1755, Evans rightly infers that the blood was sold by the executioner, confirming this when he finds that, in Mainz in 1802, eyewitnesses saw 'the executioner's servants' catching 'the blood in a beaker' before 'some of the onlookers drank it as a cure for epilepsy'.[72]

Whilst the custom was still common throughout the 1820s in Germany, an interesting variation appears during a Stockhausen execution of 1843. 'Six epileptics, equipped with drinking-mugs, had gathered round the scaffold, but the officials refused them access to the blood on the advice of a medical specialist, who told them it had no effect on the disease'. But a court official, by contrast, 'took pity on them and secured a certification from two professors at the nearby University of Gottingen that drinking the blood could have a beneficial psychological effect'. This incident is interesting because it suggests that – whether due to suggestion or otherwise – epileptics *were* sometimes cured by drinking blood. It also shows that, around mid-century, there was by no means a general revulsion at such habits on the part of educated and powerful authorities – something confirmed by trouble-free instances in Franconia in 1854, and Göttingen in 1858. In the latter case, epileptics stood close by the scaffold, having '"handed the [executioner's] assistants glass vessels in which the assistants caught the blood as it bubbled over"' before giving it to the patients, '"who drank it immediately"'. The educated or powerful were still co-operating with the practice come 1861, when workhouse governors in Hanau 'gave an epileptic inmate permission to attend a nearby execution', actively 'advising her to drink three mouthfuls of warm blood from the dead malefactor's corpse'. In Berlin in 1864 the executioner's assistants were allegedly selling blood-soaked handkerchiefs, whilst actual drinking was recorded at a Marburg execution of 1865.[73]

Leo Kanner has shown that, occasionally, a woman's blood might also be considered effective. In 1859, a student called Woytasch 'witnessed the execution of a woman poisoner' who was 'beheaded with a sword. When the head was severed from the body and a blood fountain whizzed up as high as one foot and a half, the mob broke through the chain of soldiers, rushed to the scaffold and caught the blood in vessels or dipped white towels in it'.[74]

It is worth emphasising that, whatever the gulf between rich and poor, the blood-drinking of the scaffold (along with the spectacular races of people usually unlikely to desire vigorous exercise) was occurring in the same Germany, or the same Austria, which we are more accustomed to see as the lands and eras of Leibniz, Goethe, Kant or Schiller; of J.S. Bach, Haydn, Mozart, or Beethoven. While the polished violins of the great concerti, string quartets, and monumental symphonies flashed in stately harmony in the salons and palaces and concert halls of Hanover and Salzburg and Vienna, a now forgotten (and perhaps often more pious) ritual was occurring time and again, from north to south of the German-speaking states, as the sick raised steaming cups to their lips and bloodied handkerchiefs were handed down from the spattered scaffold. It continued to do so as the sound of Beethoven gave way to that of Chopin, and as Chopin faded beneath that of Strauss the younger.

It is also worth emphasising that the last recorded occurrence may not have been the last actual occurrence. The Marburg blood-sale of 1865 was paralleled by Danish incidents: in 1823 the Danish storyteller Hans Christian Andersen saw '"a pitiful poor person made to drink by his superstitious parents a cup of the blood of an executed person, in an attempt to cure him from epilepsy"'.[75] Writing in 1860, Horace Marryat tells of how, 'even in the present century, either in the island of Amak or Møen' in Denmark, 'the epileptics stand around the scaffolds in crowds, cup in hand, ready to quaff the red blood as it flows from the still quivering body'. Marryat sounds surprised; but he also sounds as if he is speaking about an ongoing practice. L. Lloyd's 1870 account of Swedish peasant culture similarly states that, in Denmark and Sweden, blood '*is* invaluable for the treatment of a variety of disorders, if the culprit has granted the sick person leave to drink it while yet warm' (italic mine). Mabel Peacock, the folklorist who listed these references in 1896, further added that, in the 1860s, 'human blood was' still 'a well known remedy for epilepsy in Switzerland'.[76]

These diverse accounts offer us certain regional variations: in the Danish islands the patients themselves hold the cups to catch the blood, whilst in Denmark and Sweden we find an intriguing detail which might give pause to legal philosophers: 'if the culprit has granted the sick person leave … '. Do you own your own blood after your head has been severed? In these countries you evidently did, as you (the felon) gave permission, rather than the executioner or legal authorities. (It does not appear that felons in these cases ever *sold* their own blood; although, in Britain in the early eighteenth century (notes Ruth Richardson), some condemned prisoners did respond to the invitation of dissecting surgeons 'to barter their own corpses for money'.[77])

Certain other tales related to blood and epilepsy are also instructive. In 1592 an earlier traveller, Fynes Moryson, was in Germany, and wrote a good deal about what he heard or saw concerning justice, punishment and executions. Emphasising that, typically, the executioners of this country, 'having most sharp swords ... commonly show great dexterity in beheading many at one time', Moryson goes on to recount what he had heard of a rather less virtuosic performance in Bremen. Charged with the daunting task of beheading 'forty freebooting soldiers ... at one time', the 'hangman ... failed in giving a foul wound to the first man executed'. In such cases the executioner could well be stoned by a hostile crowd. Here, having completed the execution, and 'having with much difficulty appeased the people's anger', the headsman presently drank 'some of the man's blood that was dead, and after he had fetched a frisk or two, beheaded all the rest with strange dexterity (as it were) in a moment'.[78] If the spectacle of the dancing executioner is not central to our tale, it certainly helps vivify an event which now risks seeming wholly mythical. The blood drinking is curiously opaque in its meaning or motivation. Was it a form of distraction or appeasement? Or a gesture of bravado? Whatever the case, it implies that the executioner's behaviour was a twist on a familiar practice; not least because it seems that he or an assistant had a cup to hand at that moment.[79]

Secondly, we have the strange case of the German cat-woman. For decades in Europe there circulated various versions of this event, dating back to at least 1544, which was sometimes said to have occurred in Breslau. In the account given in 1664, Margaret Cavendish, Duchess of Newcastle, told of 'a wench who being struck into an epilepsy, upon the seeing of a malefactor's head cut off, was advised to drink cat's-blood; which being done, she not long after degenerated into the nature and property of that animal, cried and jumped like a cat, and hunted mice with the same silence and watchfulness as they do'.[80] Cavendish took this story seriously – as did Robert Boyle, writing a little later of how the girl came to 'imitate cats in her voice, motion and actions, when the fit was coming upon her', as well as 'watching silently at little mouse-holes'.[81]

Useful as this talent may have been in an age of overpopulated wainscot, Boyle's version implies that the girl had not been cured. What he further suggests about the psychology of the tale is also interesting (the girl became most catlike just before fits took her); but more relevant for us is what this incident says about the medical value of blood at the time. It is already useful to know that this girl was at an execution before 1544, given that most accounts of blood-drinking come from the seventeenth century or after. She seems to have been there to gain such a cure, but (ironically) was so traumatised by the spectacle (or merely unlucky in the timing of a fit) that she was unable to take it.[82] She then resorted to the drinking of cat's blood (the gentle reader, however resilient they have been thus far, should prepare to learn that these animals were often hated in the early modern period) as a substitute. Cures involving animal blood were by no means uncommon at this time, as we will see in chapter five.[83] But what is most notable here is the impression that, for many epileptics, blood therapy was the first choice; if you could not attend an execution to get the blood fresh, then you must, nevertheless, have fresh blood of some kind. (For some, we may add, this may also have been a cheaper remedy than payments to the executioner, who at times could be accused of overcharging for the felon's blood.)[84]

Very occasionally, a more drastic alternative to the ordinary blood sales of the scaffold might be sought out. 'So widespread indeed was the belief in the healing powers of a malefactor's blood that, on one occasion at least, a sick person even committed murder to obtain it. In 1824, a young, mentally ill rural labourer, Johann Georg Sörgel' was 'arrested for the murder of an elderly peasant, and confessed: "I've killed him, so that I can get a poor sinner's blood to drink; the man has horns on."' The accused, Evans adds, 'heard voices ... and was liable to bouts of violence, and evidently thought that he could cure himself in this way'.[85]

For those who were not prepared to drink blood from cups or jugs, there were a number of intermediate forms of consumption. Some time before his death in 1535, the German magus Henricus Cornelius Agrippa cited the belief (which he himself seemed to credit) that 'if any man shall dip a sword, wherewith men were beheaded, in wine; and the sick drink thereof, he shall be cured of his quartain [ague]'.[86] This suggests that certain forms of blood therapy were practised several decades before the examples which Evans records, and also shows that epilepsy was not the only condition held to respond to human blood. Evans notes that handkerchiefs were frequently used as a means of absorbing and transferring the felon's blood, and cites one eyewitness report of an 1854 execution in Franconia, after which '"a number of people, mainly women, hurried eagerly to the scaffold to dip their aprons, handkerchiefs and whips in the poor sinner's blood"'.[87] Although in such cases the use of blood was not always medical, it seems likely that all these media could be employed in the same way as the sword mentioned by Agrippa. Drawing on Nicholas Dennys' *Folklore of China* (1876), Peacock further points out that, '"after an execution at Peking, certain large pith-balls are steeped in the blood of the defunct criminal, and under the name of 'blood-bread' are sold as a medicine for consumption"'.[88]

In emphasising the highly popular medical services of the executioner in Germanic countries, Stuart also makes it very clear that these hangmen rigorously exploited the bodies of condemned felons for flesh, skin, and bone, among other things. Most of all, they seem to have been keen to supply themselves with human fat, and in Munich 'the executioner delivered human fat to the city's apothecaries by the pound until the mid-eighteenth century'.[89] There seem to have been various reasons why, for wounds, sores and breakages especially, the hangman was a far more effective healer than surgeons or physicians. But his use of human fat is particularly striking. Stuart tells, for example, of how 'Lorenz Seitz ... a journeyman brewer in Nuremburg, was rescued from knife-happy barber-surgeons by ... Johann Michael Schmidt, the local executioner. Schmidt saved Seitz's wounded leg, which the barber-surgeons had threatened to amputate, by visiting him in his home and applying new bandages twice a day'. Adding that Seitz and others are 'frustratingly vague' as to the use of human fat in this treatment, Stuart wonders: 'should we interpret this silence to mean that the use of human fat on external injuries was so obvious as to need no mention ... ?'[90] As preceding and following pages should make clear, the answer to that question is almost certainly a resounding yes.

France, Italy, and Britain

In other parts of the continent, executioners were also the chief suppliers of human fat. In 1694 Pomet notes that the Parisian apothecaries 'sell human fat or grease, which is brought us from several parts'. But, he adds, 'as everybody knows in Paris, the public executioner sells it to those that want it, so that the druggists and apothecaries sell very little'.[91] The phrase 'brought us from several parts' is tantalisingly cryptic. It could indicate battlefields, or it could refer to the anatomists, who gained certain criminal bodies for dissection. More broadly, Pomet's vagueness could reflect a reluctance to specify dubious sources. But the reference to the executioner is certainly clear enough. As with the sale of blood, this particular supplier would have had a number of attractions. Although there was less need to obtain the fat quite so swiftly, customers may have bought it at point of sale, so that they could be assured of the quality of the product. They would probably know the dead man's age, and have some idea of his state of health. Most basically (and ironically, from our point of view), they would be quite sure that they were getting *human* fat, and not an inferior animal substitute. Clearly the executioner could provide almost any body part or substance (excepting usnea, which needed time to grow). 'The skulls of criminals newly hanged, stripped of the fleshy membrane, and the brains taken out, being well washed and dried, and separated with a saw from the lower part, is what the druggists sell by the name of human skull'.[92] Pomet's derisive phrase, 'by the name of', implies that this product is inferior. But we must assume that it had a market. The executioner (or the apothecary) would hardly have gone to such trouble with knife and bone-saw otherwise.

Writing about the value of executed corpses in early-modern Italy, Giovanni Ferrari emphasises that 'what was sought after above all was the fat, but also blood, teeth, hair, burnt skull' and the navel. Human fat, later to be '"purified and liquefied, like that of other animals", was generally extracted from the bodies of convicts by the executioner'; sometimes, Ferrari adds, 'as the last act of execution'. It was surely no small irony that this scarcely imaginable torment – the scooping of fat from a still just living body – would then result in a medicine 'sold as a pain-killer'.[93]

Pomet's remarks make it clear that the French executioner would not only sell whatever he could, but would also effectively undercut the apothecaries, so that they were able to sell 'very little' human fat themselves. Similarly, the Parisian hangman's commercial acuity led him to produce a rival type of human skull. He was, it seems, keen not to waste anything. We have no evidence that the English executioner was trying to compete with apothecaries and physicians as a retailer of corpse materials. Indeed, unless his victim was peculiarly alone in the world, this would have been hard, as in England the felon's body was usually handed over to family or friends for burial.[94] If he was very occasionally selling bodies (or body parts) to medical practitioners, then we would not expect to hear about it as easily as we would in the case of Germany's public blood sales.

In early modern France, Italy and England the commonest form of capital punishment was hanging (although we should note one interesting regional variation: Halifax was said to be the 'most famous' town in Yorkshire because of 'that rare law, by which any one found in open theft, is without delay beheaded').[95] Beheadings were typically reserved for the relatively infrequent executions of gentility and nobility. It seems likely that in some of these cases, friends or relatives of the condemned used various means (from political influence to bribery) to secure the corpse from the hangman. In cases where a head or other body parts were ritually displayed on city walls or gates, this would not have been possible. Nor could the executioner have sold such parts of the body. But he may, like the Italian executioner, have sold hair and teeth. And, if it suited the state to have the traitor's corpse publically degraded on the scaffold, he could also have sold blood.

Whether or not it was sold, it was indeed consumed in Italy in the eighteenth century. In 1741 there appeared a book of anonymous travel writings, apparently penned by 'two young persons who went hither to improve' their painting skills. In Florence, shortly before 1741, these aspiring artists saw a man hanged for murdering his wife. The felon was accompanied to the gallows by the Company of Mercy, whose members administered religious rites and comfort moments before death. Having derided this Catholic ceremony, the English author relates how, as soon as the hanged man 'was taken down, they opened his veins, received his blood into several vessels, and the Fraternity distributed it in large glassfuls, to such as were afraid of apoplectic fits, or any other sudden or violent death, who drank it up greedily, from a superstitious presumption that this would preserve them from such accidents'.

What is particularly notable about this case is that the dead man's blood (perhaps all of it) was drunk *despite* the fact that he was hanged, not beheaded. The medical or magical powers of blood were considered important not only by those who drank, but by the state authorities who permitted this. These authorities had presumably given permission, also, for the deliberate opening of the veins – something which further suggests a concern to facilitate the drinking, as the condemned in this case was actually cut into pieces anyway. Yet, rather than merely allowing people to consume the blood that would have flowed at that point, someone in charge tried to ensure that the process of drinking went on in a reasonably orderly fashion (perhaps being concerned, also, that no blood should be wasted). This implies that the practice was by no means unknown. There was a formula for its conduct; and this formula itself may have been prompted by earlier problems of people jostling or fighting for precedence. Again, the Company of Mercy was obviously acquiescent, handing around the glasses as it did – and our author notes, in detailing the procession of this company before the hanging, that the brotherhood was a large one.[96] Note, too, that in Italy the blood was drunk not by those who were either desperate or stigmatised (namely, epileptics) but by people who wished to *prevent* death. This implies something distinctive about the perceived powers of human blood, and about readiness to drink it when not actually sick.[97]

Whilst the corpses of many French and English nobles were probably protected after beheadings, the very highest were not always immune. Evans notes that, when Louis XVI was guillotined during the French Revolution, spectators dipped into his blood 'handkerchiefs, paper, linen, and even a couple of dice'.[98] Why? The beheading of Charles I in January 1649 gives us some idea. One moment Charles, mistaking a gesture of the headsman for a too hasty swing of the axe, was imperiously commanding his killer to wait while he fully composed himself (and, as Patricia Fumerton emphasises, effectively stage-managing his own death with remarkable dexterity). The next the executioner was selling tiny scraps of the king's hair, along with parcels of the blood-soaked sand strewn upon the chopping-block.[99] From demi-god to commodity in a bare few seconds ... Later, one of Charles's Royalist hagiographers claimed that some bystanders 'washed their hands in the royal blood', while others 'dipt their staves in it; and that they might indulge their insatiate covetousness as well as their boundless inhumanity, they sold the chips of the block, and the sands that were discoloured with his blood, and exposed his very hairs to sale'. These, the author notes, were 'purchased for different uses. Some did it to preserve the relics of so glorious a Prince, whom they so dearly loved. Others hoped that they would be as means of cure for that disease which our English kings ... by their touch did usually heal: and it was reported that these relics experienced failed not of the effect. And some out of a brutish malice would have them as spoils and trophies of their hatred to their lawful sovereign'.[100] Whatever the motivations involved, there seems no doubt as to the basic actions described here. For in the same year the artist John Weesop showed such people mopping up blood in his painting 'An Eyewitness Representation of the Execution of King Charles I'.

Needless to say, there undoubtedly was an unusually wide range of motives present at this rather famous beheading. (Even the author's psychology seems ironically convoluted: he probably did not approve of commoners swabbing up Charles's blood, but nevertheless felt compelled to boast that those seeking cures were indeed healed by the divinely touched person of the king.) An obvious division in the above account is that of positive and negative, or Royalists and Republicans. But it is also interesting to consider that, if some of the bystanders were indeed epileptics seeking a time-honoured cure, they may have treated Charles rather as certain ordinary people treated Christ in the Gospels.[101] He was not valued in any moral sense, but simply because his body was seen as useful or powerful.[102]

From other angles, we find that Charles's execution precisely matches features of routine executions. For a long time in England the executioner's rope was held by many to have absorbed a similar potency to the execution stool or chopping block. Accordingly, the executioner might sell it, cut into the smallest possible pieces, to satisfy demand and maximise personal profit.[103] In Germany, blood-soaked sand was routinely sold, and on at least one occasion (in 1820) a crowd stormed the scaffold in order to break up the stool of the condemned and distribute the pieces – a rough echo of the chopping block sold off piecemeal in 1649.[104] Whilst some wanted Charles's hair as a pious relic, others may have been merely following the habits of those Italians who routinely demanded hair from the executioner in Rome or Milan.[105]

The political context of Charles's beheading naturally does imply that the actions of the Royalists around the scaffold had at least quasi-Catholic overtones. At the execution of the Jesuit martyr Robert Southwell in 1595, 'the crowd clamoured for

mementoes of the dead man, and "dipped handkerchiefs in the sprayed blood"'.[106]
Later, when Cornelius O'Deveny, bishop of Down and Connor, was beheaded in
Dublin in 1611, the Catholic hunger for relics was yet more pronounced (if the
account by Barnabe Rich is to be trusted).[107] We hear that 'the executioner had no
sooner taken off the bishop's head, but that the townsmen of Dublin began to flock
about him: some taking up the head with piteous aspect, accompanied with sobs and
sighs', while 'some cut away all the hair from the head, which lousy commodity, they
religiously reserved, for a lousy relic'. The head itself, Rich insists, would have been
stolen if not for the executioner's vigilance. Meanwhile, when the headsman

> began to quarter the body, the women thronged about him as fast, and happy
> was she that could get but her handkerchief dipped in the blood of the traitor.
> And the body being once dissevered into four quarters, they neither left finger
> nor toe, but they cut them off, and carried them away. And to shew their
> Catholic zeal, they tore his garments into tatters, and some others that could
> get no holy monuments that appertained to his person, with their knives they
> shaved off chips from the hallowed gallows: neither would they so much as
> omit the halter wherewith he was hanged, but it was gathered up to be
> reserved for holy uses.[108]

The Bishop's breeches were supposedly sold by the executioner for five shillings, and
by way of poetic justice the executioner's cloak was stolen, allegedly under the
assumption that it was that of the Bishop. 'Catholic' as this may have been, some of it
was probably also magical; and it is certainly clear that many of these supposedly
papist excesses were being echoed by German Protestants well into the nineteenth
century.

Infamy and magic

In certain countries, the executioner was regarded with intense superstition by many
of those around him. The 'infamy' which tainted this figure seems indeed to have
resembled a kind of leprosy: it could infect those who came into contact with the
executioner himself, his possessions, or even his family. So powerful was the taboo
surrounding this figure in the island of Corsica that, as James Boswell noted in
October 1765, the hangman of that nation was *always* a foreigner, despite the fact
that any condemned Corsican could have saved his life by taking up the post.[109] For
the Corsicans, administering death was worse than suffering it.

   In northern Europe, the infamy of the headsman seems to have been most powerfully
felt in Germanic countries. After visiting in the early 1590s, Moryson wrote:

> the Germans are so superstitious, as they think it a great reproach to touch the
> head or body of any put to death, and think it most ridiculous for any man to
> salute the hangman, or speak courteously to him, and esteem it a foul fault to
> eat or drink with them, or any of his family. Therefore the hang-man and

those of their family, who help them in their office (and succeed them having no children) do all wear a green cap, or some apparent mark, by which they may be known … when they come into any company, lest any man should offend in the former kinds. And in public taverns they have tables proper to them, at which the basest body will not sit for any reward.[110]

This sketch is emphatically confirmed by Evans, who stresses that 'the most dishonouring element of all in a German execution was the touch of the executioner'. He adds numerous details on the tabooed status of this figure: he could often marry no one except another executioner's daughter; his children 'could still find it difficult to get employment even in the late eighteenth century'; and in some cases he was barred from the local inn altogether, separate table or not.[111]

But this negative side of the executioner's aura was inseparable from a range of more positive powers. He could, Evans adds, 'earn money by performing small surgical operations on people, or by supplying them with magical cures for illnesses'.[112] Stuart's research on Germany indeed suggests that his popularity as a healer was greater than Evans' brief words imply, and that in many cases he was remarkably effective.[113] Pieter Spierenburg reports 'numerous cases of hangmen practicing medicine … in the Dutch Republic from the 1590s to the 1790s'.[114] Even in France it was believed that the hangman could cure 'certain forms of illness by touching the sick with his hand when returning from carrying out an execution'.[115] Like other highly charged vehicles of superstition, the executioner was never simply positive or negative in the eyes of those who feared him. Rather, he and the corpse he dealt with were, at bottom, powerful. Both had an unstable potency which could easily slide from good to bad.[116] The crucial point to realise is that, ambiguous as it was, this dense supernatural aura could in fact have deflected those feelings of distaste or revulsion which might, to us, seem the most natural ones in such an area. For many, superstitious wonder overcame visceral repugnance.

Although we are chiefly concerned with the bodies the executioner handled, and the crowds who made use of these, the peculiarly dualistic status of the axeman offers us a useful model for the similarly paradoxical qualities of the felon.[117] Moreover, as can often be the case with broadly magical beliefs, it is difficult to easily draw a line between the powers of the corpse and of the man who had dispatched him. Just where, for example, did the power of the shattered stool come from in 1820, or the chopped rope, or that of the splintered chopping block, in 1649? If we could ask those who sought to obtain these fragments, we may have had different answers from different people. But what does seem clear on surviving evidence is that the body, like the executioner, had an unstable and transferable power. Again, Germany abounds in examples: bits of the criminal body or clothing could bring possessors good luck; a finger could ward off lice; it could also attract money, or indeed customers, if suspended in a beer barrel by an innkeeper; while 'pieces of skin … were used in amulets'. Blood, in particular, kept "'witches from house and stable'" and protected them "'from the danger of lightning'". In 1858 one peasant woman "'took some blood away with her in a little bottle'", saying, ""I'm going to paint the front door

with it, it's good against the danger of fire'"". In 1893, the biographer of the celebrated German executioner Julius Krautz stated that, though his subject had been
retired some four years, '"not a week passes … without Krautz receiving … requests
to 'remove curses' from cattle, or to provide pieces of rope and shards from the
scaffold or handkerchiefs dipped in the blood of the beheaded'".[118]

Many of these uses serve to sharply underline the highly animate status of the
corpse and the things surrounding it. Though the body died, its powers lived on.
This impression is confirmed by the frequency of those thefts which occurred some
time after the execution itself.

The gibbet and the wheel

Late one night in April 1635 a London butcher passed the corpse of Tom Shearwood,
a notorious robber and murderer, recently executed and now hung in chains as an
example outside Pancras Church. The butcher remarked soberly to himself that it were
no bad thing if all such rogues should be served so. Ironically, he was just at this point set
on by a gang of lurking villains. Finding little money on him, they stripped his clothes,
gagged him, and bound him to the gibbet, wryly bidding him 'watch the corpse'.

Even for hardened criminals, the proximity of a decaying corpse must have offered
some deterrent. But it seems that these lurking robbers had good reason to wait in
that particular spot. Shearwood's corpse was an immensely popular spectacle in
1635 – so much so that civic authorities had ultimately to respond to the trampling of
the 'growing fields' around the site by moving the body further out, 'to the ring-
cross beyond Islington'. (This itself had to be done at night, just so as to avoid further
'confusion of spectators'.[119]) Some of these wondering onlookers were probably just
fascinated by the spectacle, or by the special notoriety clinging to Shearwood, who
had carried out his crimes with the aid of a female accomplice, Elizabeth Evans. But
some would almost certainly have been seeking relics or cures from the corpse – the
simplest of these being the touch of the dead hand or body. We should add that
Pancras Church was conveniently near to Bucklersbury, the street of London apothecaries, who may have occasionally taken some of their more fearless clients there
to touch the corpse.

Chained or gibbeted bodies such as these might often be left exposed for at least
several months. Clearly this was the idea in the case of Shearwood, who could
otherwise have been buried with less trouble than it took to move him. In his 1609
Masque of Queens, Jonson has a witch tell of 'a murderer … hung in chains' so long that
'the sun and wind had shrunk his veins'.[120] Back in 1591 Jonson himself may have seen
such a body, after Arnold Cosby was hung on Wednesday, 27 January for the murder of
Lord Burke. Carted to a high hill at Wandsworth town end, Cosby made a penitent end,
pouring forth prayers before he was turned off the ladder, 'still calling upon God to
forgive him even to the last gasp'. He was then left in this prominent spot, 'hanged up in
chains' for all to see.[121] A similar fate fell to William Anderson Horner in 1708, suspended in chains between Edinburgh and Leith after his execution for the murder of
a Mrs Blyth.[122] In Britain gibbets were abolished by law only in 1834.[123]

For those who wanted to merely touch a corpse, a single body would have gone a long way. In Germany, Evans notes, one corpse rotted patiently on the gallows outside Munich from 1697 to 1702; another was supposed to have endured from 1776 to 1784; and 'the doctor Louis Stromeyer ... remembered seeing "the blackish remains" of an executed malefactor on the gallows near Hanover over a period of at least ten years' in the early nineteenth century.[124] Moryson seemed to be struck by the number of such bodies, as well as by the frequency of executions, and the range of crimes for which one might suffer death.[125] He also remarked on the torments and methods of execution peculiar to the continent: 'he that kills a man of set malice, and like heinous murtherers, have all their bones broken upon a wheel, and in some cases their flesh is pinched off, with hot burning pincers'. Meanwhile, 'after the execution, the bones and members of the malefactor are gathered together, and laid upon the wheel, which is set up in the place of execution ... for eternal memory of his wickedness, with so many bones hanging on the sides of the wheel, as he committed murthers or like crimes; and my self have numbered sometimes eighteen, often fourteen bones thus hanging for memory of so many murthers'.[126]

Whilst Moryson describes 'these marks' as 'long remaining', Evans shows that this was frequently not the case. 'In 1770 the fingers were cut off and removed from the body of a criminal hanged in Memmingen', and similar thefts were reported some way into the nineteenth century, with one of the bones described by Moryson being stolen from a wheel in Pollnow around 1811. In Rochlitz in 1837 'the head of a decapitated murderer disappeared without trace the night after the execution', and in Hamburg in 1801 one doctor 'complained that the corpses of executed criminals were "completely ransacked in a moment for the purposes of anti-epileptic pharmacology"'.[127] It seems likely that the doctor was complaining specifically because people were managing to mutilate criminal corpses before physicians could procure them for anatomy.[128] If this kind of theft was swift and enterprising, the removal of bones from the wheel may also have required some skill and determination, given that the wheel itself was usually set upon a pole some twelve feet from the ground.[129]

Although we know less about such thefts in other countries, we do know that bodies would have been displayed in a similar way in France (Robert Perceval, a visiting Irish medical student, was shocked by such a spectacle in 1781).[130] And we know from Pomet's remarks that body parts were in much demand in that country in the late seventeenth century. Over in Louvain in around 1536, in an ironic reversal of the plundering which the German doctor complained of, the celebrated anatomist Vesalius had stolen the bones of an exposed criminal in order to construct a skeleton.[131] On the European continent especially, Paracelsus' suggestion about gibbeted bodies was evidently a quite practical one.

Anatomists

Our discussion of the early stages of English corpse medicine showed surgeons, rather than physicians, playing an especially active role. For much of Elizabeth's reign, it was surgeons who were left to undertake the still lowly and demeaning task of dissection for medical training. Even in the first year of the Lumleian lecture there were complaints about the poor attendance of the physicians.[132] We can well imagine, then, that the surgeons would also probably be left to dispose of the bodies used as anatomy specimens once lectures were over.[133] Given their early advocacy of corpse medicine, it would be surprising if figures such as Banister and Hall did not take advantage of this source of supply. Surgeons and physicians were permitted just six convicts' bodies per year (from 1584), so that in England such commodities would have been especially precious, given the difficulty of buying materials from the executioner.[134]

And there is certainly evidence to suggest that both physicians and barber-surgeons were not always overscrupulous about final disposal of criminal corpses. The historian Sidney Young records an edict from the Annals of the barber-surgeons for 1578, forbidding its members to remove parts of criminal bodies from its Hall – and specifically prohibiting them from removing skins in order to 'tan [them] like leather'. Young argues that this ruling reflected a 'mania for the relics of notorious criminals' in late-sixteenth-century England.[135] It is hard to say if this mania rivalled that of Germany: but we do know that in that country skin was highly valued by midwives and pregnant women. An executioner named Johann Georg Trenkler told in 1747 of how 'he had "given pregnant women very valuable help by applying human skin"', and Stuart shows that it was indeed probably tanned first, then being 'cut into straps, which women wore as belts during labour'.[136] The English ruling tells us two things. One: there was a strong demand for human body parts which were thought to have both supernatural and medical powers. Two: at least some barber-surgeons were prepared to smuggle corpse materials out of Surgeons' Hall. As they were almost certainly doing this for financial gain, they may well have been ready to supply other substances, such as human fat or bone. Although his reasons might have been different, a Scottish surgeon, John Bell, was accused of smuggling body parts from Surgeons' Hall in Edinburgh in 1794.[137]

Were the physicians also involved in this kind of trade? In Jonson's 1605 comedy *Volpone*, the eponymous protagonist at one point imitates a mountebank, or quack doctor, under the assumed name of 'Scoto of Mantua'. His fictitious panacea – modestly labelled 'Oglio del Scoto' – is an oil which includes 'six hundred several simples' along with 'some quantity of human fat, for the conglutination, which we buy of the/anatomists'.[138] By this stage, 'anatomists' may well indicate physicians rather than surgeons.

One story in particular suggests that the physicians had certain attractions for more genteel patients. We know that the physician and anatomist Robert Fludd was an especially keen advocate of corpse medicine. Fludd was able to obtain the flesh of 'a man strangled in the air' for use as medicine. This would almost certainly have been derived from one of the six criminal corpses permitted annually for the physicians' public anatomy lectures. Fludd was probably sharing the role of lecturer (with William Harvey and others) from the mid-1620s onwards. In a posthumously published book he reveals that it was customary for lecturers to prepare for the public events by practising privately on a separate criminal corpse.[139]

Having this body in his house on such an occasion, 'I was', he tells us, 'solicited by Mr Kellet the apothecary, to permit a gentlewoman, who had a schirrous tumour in her belly, to be touched and stroked with the dead man's hand, because experience had taught it to be very efficacious, for the abolishing of the like horrid protuberation in others'. Fludd agreed, and shortly afterwards the woman's husband came to thank him, explaining that she was now cured.[140] The incident shows us that such therapies were sought after by the educated; that apothecaries might act as intermediaries, and that a sympathetic physician would be ready to co-operate. (In later decades, Boyle 'highly recommended' this remedy for those suffering from goitre.[141]) It also shows us that there was a conveniently discreet alternative to the distasteful mêlée of the public scaffold. In this case, unusually, nothing was eaten. But we cannot rule out cannibalistic uses of anatomy specimens. If a physician genuinely believed in the power of corpse medicine, they could indeed assist in this practice, and perhaps chiefly for the good of their patients.

Despite the surgeons' ruling about the illegitimate use of dissection specimens, it seems that someone was still doing odd things with dead bodies many decades after Fludd's time. In the spring of 1684, some children knocked their ball into a pond on Gray's Inn Lane in London. Attempting to retrieve it, they spied what they at first thought to be a periwig floating on the water. They presently discovered that this was in fact human hair. The hair was brown, and it was attached to an entire human skin – one which still showed distinct marks of its nose, lips, eyelids and ears. There were several potential murder victims at this time. The London merchant, Edmund Hally, for example, had been missing for some three weeks. Yet the skin never seems to have been definitely identified, despite being subsequently displayed to 'many hundreds of people'. Amazed as the public were, 'diverse surgeons who saw it' also affirmed that 'who ever performed the exploit, must have [had] more than ordinary dexterity, to effect' its removal 'so completely in every part'.[142] We can add that, dexterous or not, whoever did the flaying went to a lot of trouble. We might wonder if the unknown knife-wielder had intended to tan this skin like leather, and to sell it for the kind of uses Evans details in Germany from the seventeenth century onwards.[143]

Bodysnatching

Imagine that you are out walking your dog one evening, in the countryside around Avebury in 1678. As you approach the ancient stone circles on Overton Hill the animal suddenly emits a wary growl. Restraining her, you take a few cautious steps and then freeze. Through the dusk some yards ahead you gradually perceive two men, vigorously plying spades. Before them a third figure is stooped intently over what seems to be a heap of white sticks, shining with an oddly ghostly pallor through the deepening twilight. Still oblivious of your presence, he now lifts up something which is clearly *not* a stick. As he shifts the lantern in his other hand and the shadows flicker across his face, you have momentarily the strange illusion that he is speaking, perhaps whimsically interrogating the skull which sits staring up at him from his outstretched palm. Behind him the spades continue to rhythmically dip and scrape through dirt and stones. The substantial rents already gouged from the burial mound, and the dangling skeletal hand which one man has just uncovered put the matter beyond all doubt ...

If you had confronted this dubious figure you would have been yet more surprised. He would probably have greeted you with all the well-bred, well-spoken bonhomie and charm of any Restoration gentleman, praising the fine evening air, and behaving for all the world as though he was some amateur naturalist out netting butterflies on a spring afternoon. He would then begin explaining – still in his best graveside manner – about the great success of the 'noble medicine' he had recently made from human bones. All of which was reasonable and natural enough – as he was in fact your local GP, the well-known and much esteemed Dr Toope of Marlborough.

Toope was remarkably keen to acquire human bones. The archaeologist Jonathan Trigg, who is currently working on Toope, suspects that the doctor dug successfully for bones in both 1678 and 1685 (and given the fairly long gap between these two dates, we can well imagine that he also did so in intervening years).[144] Moreover, Toope not only dug bones from 'what may have been a Saxon cemetery near The Sanctuary' circle, but also made vigorous inroads on the ancient burial mound known as West Kennet Long Barrow. Although he here failed to reach any bones (owing to the distinctive formation of the mound, and the depth of the burial chambers) the mutilations of the enterprising doctor were visible long after his death.[145] Toope – or Took, as he was also known – became notorious among archaeologists for having '"miserably defaced south long barrow by digging half the length of it"'.[146] But Toope himself was far from apologetic or embarrassed about his necropolis-cum-laboratory. In a letter of 1 December 1685 he explained to the gentleman diarist John Aubrey how he had 'stored myself with many bushels' of these bones, 'of which I made a noble medicine that relieved many of my distressed neighbours'. The bones themselves, he adds, 'are large and nearly rotten, but the teeth extreme and wonderfully white, hard and sound' (noting in an aside that 'no tobacco' was 'taken in those days').[147]

What are we to make of Dr Toope's 'noble medicine'? One obvious point strikes us at once. He chose convenient sources of supply, as the skeletons of the Saxon cemetery and West Kennet were both distant and anonymous. No one need feel concerned that in curing their gout they were swallowing down their own grandmother. Once again, the force of time was able to soften the potentially raw exploitation and cannibalism of the dead. We can also reasonably assume that Dr Toope was making some profit from this abundant supply of cheap pharmaceutical materials. (Aubrey confirms that Toope certainly dug at Overton Hill more than once, noting drily, '"Dr Toope was lately at the Golgotha again to supply a defect of medicine he had from hence"').[148] There again, we should not too readily deny his claim that he had indeed 'relieved many of my distressed neighbours'. If they *thought* they had been relieved, then they had been treated quite as successfully as any modern recipients of placebo drugs. Whatever the ethics of the situation, both potential motives – of profit and professional duty – suggest that in rural areas, far from the busiest scaffolds of London or Edinburgh, other more or less qualified practitioners may well have shown a similar initiative to that of Dr Toope.

Toope probably drew the line at robbing individual marked graves, whether of the recently or long dead. But bones and skulls were clearly in considerable demand around this time, and not everyone had the luck to live so close to an anonymous burial mound. We have seen a sporting manual of Toope's day recommending powdered human skull as a food for the worms that in turn baited one's fish; and Thomas Willis, among others, was using skull as medicine in the 1660s. In 1694 Pomet commented on how 'English druggists, especially those of London, sell the heads or skulls of the dead, upon which there is a little greenish moss' like that on oaks.[149] Pomet's colleague Charas had seen these on a visit to England, and had also noticed how some heads were 'entirely covered with moss, and some … only have the moss growing on some parts'. Charas seems here to imply that these were displayed openly in apothecaries' shops – perhaps in the windows to attract buyers – and his attention to detail also suggests that such spectacles were not common in France. Skulls in particular seem to have been very readily available – so much so that anglers were advised to obtain them as worm-food, and that the writer in question did not trouble to say where one might get them. As the royal surgeon Gideon Harvey informs us in 1678, 'a dead man's skull, if sound', would fetch between eight and eleven shillings.[150] At this time an unskilled labourer might earn perhaps ten pence a day. If he happened to see a skull, he might well feel great delight, rather than great terror, the object standing for him as the image of luck and money, rather than decay and death. Over in Italy, a medical work of 1726 cited by Camporesi refers to the theft of skulls from cemeteries in a way which suggests the practice to be both routine and unproblematic.[151] If skulls were so available and so profitable, and if they could be sold or displayed without anyone asking difficult questions about their origins, then bones (probably perceived as more anonymous) must have been treated in a similar way.[152]

We should recall, too, Johann Schroeder's discussion of mummy, in which he states that 'the whole carcass or flesh in shops comes under the name of mummy'. A whole carcass may have been a rare commodity, and it may not have been as openly sold in England or France as it was in Schroeder's Germany. Yet we know that from the 1650s onwards people such as John French and George Thomson would have looked on virtually the whole body as medical material, thus raising the value of that commodity accordingly, and perhaps giving extra incentive to gravediggers and sextons (neither of whom were highly paid). Moreover, given the popularity of corpse ingredients with certain aristocratic families, we must wonder about how these estates gained their supply. They could certainly have afforded to pay for skulls. But, given their distance from likely suppliers, it is possible that they simply excavated the humbler graves of estate servants a few months or years after burial.

As is now well known, the worst excesses of systematic and commercial grave-robbing occurred in the late eighteenth and early nineteenth centuries.[153] Around 3 a.m. one Friday morning in March 1798, for example, a London watchman saw men in a

Hackney coach coming from Tottenham Court Road burial ground. Police presently discovered the body of an infant in the coach, and eight other corpses were later found in sacks in a ditch near the burial ground. Both the sexton and the cab driver were suspected of conniving in this theft. Most of the bodies 'had been interred the preceding evening'.[154] This last detail is especially telling, given that the anatomy schools who paid for these bodies obviously wanted relatively fresh corpses. Such precision had already been noted by an author of 1777, who wrote a fictional but evidently plausible tale of grave-robbing, in which both the sexton and the local apothecary assisted bodysnatchers, advising not only on the freshest graves, but on the exact type of death that occupants had met.[155] In this climate, graveyards became not so much places of rest as well-run shops of death.

Writing some time before his death in 1743, the poet and playwright Richard Savage linked grave-robbing with both corpse medicines and dissection. Satirising an unscrupulous parson as someone who was highly selective about his attendance at deathbeds, the poet tells of how

> Poor folks he'll shun; but pray by rich, if ill,
> And watch, and watch – to slide into their will;
> Then pop, perchance, in consecrated wine,
> What speeds the soul, he fits for realms divine.
> Why could not London this good parson gain?
> Before him sepulchres had rent in twain.
> Then had he learned with sextons to invade,
> And strip with sacrilegious hands the dead;
> To tear off rings, e'er yet the finger rots;
> To part 'em, for the vesture-shroud cast lots;
> Had made dead skulls for coin the chymist's share,
> The female corpse the surgeon's purchas'd ware … [156]

By the time of the Tottenham Court Road incident bodysnatching was already so commonplace that *The Times* could wryly propose a new method 'to prevent grave robbing, and to supply the anatomical schools, without shocking vulgar prejudices' – namely 'to dissect the bodies of medical persons, who profess to be above such prejudices'.[157] Similarly, come 1817 the practice was so familiar as to provoke a rather more dramatic form of black humour, when, on Saturday night, 18 October, 'some wags stripped a drunken man quite naked, put him into a sack, head and ears, and carried him in a coach to a celebrated anatomist in Blenheim St, where they obtained the usual fee as for a dead subject'. Only when the sack was about to be tumbled down some stone steps did its occupant, 'now roused from his stupor, thrust his head and arms out, to the horror and astonishment of the surgeon and his attendant, and begged for mercy'.[158]

We have seen that Germanic countries had an especially strong and enduring tradition of corpse medicine. Given this, it is interesting to find that in Vienna, a shift in the location of the cemeteries after 1784 (writes Tatjana Buklijas) 'created favourable conditions for gravediggers to trade in bodies and body parts'. Although the bulk of such trade may have been prompted by medical schools, it was just around this time that the celebrated (and usually more privileged) dead became the target of another kind of theft.

The quasi-scientific 'Gall system' (proposed in the late-eighteenth century by Franz Joseph Gall) with its theory of intelligence or genius correspondent to the shape of the skull, now meant that not only fresh bodies, but bare skulls were also a valuable commodity. At least, that was, if you had been particularly intelligent or talented in your lifetime. This new wave of grave-robbing claimed the skulls of Haydn, Beethoven, the artist Francisco Goya, and the English doctor and author Sir Thomas Browne.[159] This latter case was especially ironic, Browne having famously wondered, 'who knows the fate of his bones, or how often he is to be buried? ... To be gnawed out of our graves, to have our skulls made drinking-bowls, and our bones turned into pipes to delight and sport our enemies, are tragical abominations'.[160] Elsewhere he made the intriguing admission, 'I am not so much afraid of death, as ashamed thereof'.[161] Buklijas adds that 'skulls acquired at Viennese suburban cemeteries became the basis' of 'Gall's famous collection', and it would seem that in this region especially the humble remains of the poorer classes would have stood little chance of resting in peace if apothecaries were prepared to pay for them.[162] In terms of such local variations, we should also note that, as late as the 1880s, the bodies of the poor (including children) were quite frequently being dissected without permission by Oxford University's medical school.[163]

These combined assaults on the privacy of the quiet grave occurred after the zenith of European medicinal cannibalism (particularly as regards England). But we should bear in mind two things about this later wave of attacks upon the dead. First, it is no small irony that medical science, a field founded on the sanctity of human life and its general physical improvement, should have been responsible for over 300 years worth of corpse violation, human indignity, and mental trauma. Second: if grave-robbing could thrive so long and so widely (and penetrate so deep into the most revered of tombs) in those later eras, it seems very likely that it did so in the sixteenth and seventeenth centuries.

It does seem unlikely that grave-robbing occurred on the scale of the late-Georgian period back in the time of Milton or Willis. It is probably partly for this reason that it is so much harder to come upon direct accounts of it. Instead, we have to work from small clues. Looking again, for example, at the words of Paracelsus on the value of fresh bodies, we notice that he says, quite precisely, 'if physicians or any other body understood but the right use of this mummy', no corpse 'would be left three days on the gallows'.[164] The phrase 'any other body' could perhaps mean an apothecary or surgeon; but there must also be a strong chance it refers to a bodysnatcher – an intermediary motivated by personal profit. While Paracelsus was here talking overtly just about criminal corpses, any enterprising supplier in this area would of course have used as many sources as were required to meet medical demand. Looking at similar clues from the early-modern period, we find that, in terms of burial, there were evidently three broad classes of body available.

First, there were those who were simply not properly buried at all. Even outside of warfare and massacre, this seems to have occurred more often than it later would. In autumn 1736 in Dublin 'a large old mastiff scraped open a grave in the churchyard, broke a coffin, pulled out of it the corpse, and was eating it, when one of the parishioners came into the church yard'. Although the man and his neighbours quickly seized and hanged the offending animal, they came to realise that it had probably also unearthed and mangled the body of a child in the same place a few days earlier. The reporter who told this story specifically blamed shallow and poorly-dug graves, noting that the dog could probably smell the bodies just a few inches below the surface of the ground.[165]

We have seen that John French, physician at London's Savoy Hospital in the late 1640s and 1650s, could probably rely on a fair supply of corpse material from some of those who died on site (and who were then first dissected).[166] Those paupers who died in hospitals must often have undergone very crude burials, even if they did escape the anatomist's knife. At a convent hospital just outside Paris around 1750, the English traveller Sacheverell Stevens 'saw three men, who died the preceding night', buried 'in a most unChristian manner' – each being put naked into a sack, taken in a wheelbarrow to the side of a bank, and having some earth briefly flattened over him with a pickaxe.[167] Here, as in the Dublin cases, graves were shallow, and there was no question of even the flimsiest coffin. Nor can we be certain that the bodies enjoyed the luxury of these rudimentary homes for very long: as Mary Roach points out, around this time the anatomy schools of Paris were using as specimens the 'unclaimed corpses of the poor who died at city hospitals'.[168]

Secondly, we must remind ourselves that, in another sense, the graves of the privileged were also often less tightly sealed in the early modern era. The supposed epitaph of Shakespeare, for example, read: 'Blest be ye man that spares these stones, and curst be he that moves my bones'. Probably writing in the 1590s, Donne opened his poem 'The Relic' with the lines, 'When my grave is broke up again,/Some second guest to entertain'; and anyone who saw *Hamlet* at the close of that decade would have been reminded of how irreverently grave workers might treat the bones of the dead.[169] Perhaps partly because of the very high death rate, cemeteries were often overcrowded, and older graves would have to be disturbed for the sake of newcomers.[170] The most famous example of this comes from Sedlice, outside Prague, where a burial site became immensely popular after an abbot sprinkled earth from Golgotha over it around 1278. The cemetery accordingly grew so crowded that in the fifteenth century monks unearthed older skulls and bones, and used them to build the now famous bells, chandelier, and monstrance of the church erected over the cemetery in about 1400.[171] Novel as this might have been, it has been claimed that in the early modern period 'no burial was secure against further disturbance, usually for further burial on the same site'.[172] It has been pointed out that bones can often be seen lying scattered around in pictures of the era's graveyards, and in the sixteenth century Rabelais claimed that beggars sometimes used them as fuel for fires.[173]

Thirdly: if your bones survived such disturbances unmolested, then there was still a good chance that they might be shifted to a more general and anonymous home – namely, one of the charnel houses used for the storage of older human remains. In 1633, commenting on the medically valued moss of the human skull, one writer noted that, 'this kind of moss is found upon the skulls or bare scalps of men and women, lying long in charnel houses or other places, where the bones of men and women are kept together'.[174] Although these were less common in some places after the Middle Ages, in France (notes Philippe Ariès) 'probably until the seventeenth century or so, the skulls came right up to ground level, where they were mixed with bones and pebbles'. Even in the early nineteenth century Gabriel Le Bras could still see, in Brittany, 'behind the railing of the clerestory ... bones piled in heaps', while 'outside the church one walks by rows of moss-covered skulls that follow the ... passerby with empty eyes'.[175] In London there was 'an ossuary and chapel in the churchyard of old St Paul's and in St Bride's in Fleet Street'.[176]

In later decades, as we have seen, usnea continued to be taken seriously as a stiptic by Boyle and others. Indeed, it was so much in demand that as late as 1758 a visitor to the Chelsea physic garden of the apothecaries could have seen 'laid ... in a mossy corner ... pieces of human skulls, that the moss from the ground may creep over' them.[177] Although the writer who tells us this was sharply disdainful of usnea, he clearly implies that at around this time either an apothecary or physician was trying to artificially encourage the growth of skull-moss.

In this kind of environment, many of those wanting bones or skulls may have found that there was no need to resort to the plundering of actual graves and coffins. But it seems that some did. For Edward Bolnest, the Paracelsian physician we met in chapter two, stated very candidly in 1672 that for his oil of bones you should use 'the bones of a man which hath not been buried fully a year', making sure 'to cleanse them well from the earth and dry them'.[178] In these few quite unembarrassed words there is a good deal of implicit detail. To know that the bones were from a corpse less than one year old, Bolnest or his supplier must have robbed a marked grave.[179] Once obtained, these bones were damp and dirty. They had come from the earth, and it seems that they had come from someone too poor to have a coffin (or at least any very durable coffin).

Warfare and massacres

If you asked one historian, they might tell you that in Europe the seventeenth century was the century of the scientific revolution. For another, it might be the century of political reinvention; for yet another, the era of the witch craze. But perhaps most of all, on the European continent this was a century of almost perpetual war. That categorisation indeed runs back through much of the sixteenth century, from the Protestant Reformation which sparked and sustained almost all of the major conflicts and slaughters after 1530, through to the persecution of Protestant minorities shortly after the Edict of Fontainebleau in 1685. The bulk of these conflicts naturally occurred on the continent, with France, the Netherlands, and Germanic states feeling the force of religious strife most severely.

What did this mean for the supply of human bodies? In France in 1558 (writes Penny Roberts) a Huguenot man was beaten to death by Catholics while in prison. The jailor thrust him into a shallow grave in an area used for disposing of rubbish. With his feet visibly sticking out of the earth, the dead man fell prey to other Catholics, who repeatedly stabbed and slashed at his legs. After an unsuccessful attempt of friends to re-bury him, this man's corpse was presently reburied by Catholics, '"in a place where everyone was accustomed to urinate and defecate"'.[180]

Ironically, even efforts to bring peace to the two embittered Christian factions could produce monumental slaughter. In August 1572 there was an attempt to unite French Protestants and Catholics by the strategic royal marriage of the Protestant Henri de Navarre with the Catholic Marguerite de Valois. With an unusual number of Protestants assembled in Paris to celebrate the wedding, political and religious tensions broke loose. In the early morning of 24 August the slaughter of the French Protestants began. The event known as the St Bartholomew's Day Massacre probably claimed over 5,000 Protestant lives, with the violence lasting several days, and being spontaneously repeated in the provinces as the news spilled out of the capital.[181] Ambroise Paré, the royal surgeon who was thought by some to be Protestant, is said to have survived the slaughter only by the intervention of his patron, Charles IX, who locked him in a wardrobe during the massacre. It may be, then, that one of the most strident opponents of corpse medicine only narrowly escaped being pounded up in an apothecary's mortar himself.

In July 1601, the new century quickly marked out its identity when the Spanish began the siege of Ostend. This became known as one of the bloodiest battles of the Dutch revolt against the Spanish, and was one of the longest sieges in history by the time the town finally gave way in September 1604. A contemporary account translated in that same year by the English Protestant Edward Grimeston tells of how, on 17 October 1601, 'the enemies shot very furiously with their fiery bullets and stones into the town'. That night, entering a space called 'the half moon, which is beyond the gullet before the bridge', the Spanish ran into a trap. Bombarded with cannon fire and musket shot, all the besiegers in this sally were quickly slain. And it was at this point that 'the surgeons of the town went thither ... and brought away sacks full of man's grease which they had drawn out of their bodies'.

There is little doubt that part of the motivation for this impromptu liposuction was pure hatred. As we will see in chapter four, the inhumanity of the two Christian factions could run to worse excesses than this. Even as the surgeons dragged back their wobbling sacks, other townsfolk were rummaging amidst the debris of sundered 'arms, legs and hands', where they found 'much money upon the dead men, and garments of good price', along with 'perfumed gloves'.[182] We will also learn in a few moments that some of the surgeons or onlookers may have felt a keenly precise sense of poetic justice as they saw the fat carved out of the still warm bodies on the ground. Yet, whatever basic ideological fury simmered through this surgical assault, it was also underpinned by one very simple pragmatic rationale: the Ostenders were besieged by the most powerful nation in the world, and human fat was held to be a prime agent for the treatment of wounds.[183] In this sense, practical utility and moral justice dovetailed with seamless ease.

The practical impetus for this attack suggests that it may well have been standard practice in such conflicts both before and after Ostend. In the Netherlands alone there was no shortage of these. The period from 1568 to 1648, in which the Dutch rebelled against the invading Spanish, was known as the Eighty Years War. In November and December 1572, with the St Bartholomew's Day Massacre fresh in the minds of Protestants, all the citizens of Zutphen and Naarden were slaughtered by the Spanish. From 11 December that year the city of Haarlem was besieged, holding out for seven months until 13 July 1573.

In October 1576 the English poet George Gascoigne was in Antwerp when its siege ended, marked again by mass murder of civilians and by looting. The 'heaps of dead carcasses which lay at every trench' were so commonplace a sight that Gascoigne barely troubled to describe them (just briefly mentioning that in many places they were piled up beyond the height of a man). The same went for 'the huge numbers, drowned in the new town, where a man might behold as many sundry shapes and forms of man's motion at time of death, as ever Michelangelo did portray in his tables of Doomsday'. On the Thursday following the Spanish entry, a count of Antwerp's dead ran to 17,000 men, women and children.[184]

On 29 June 1579 the Spanish finally ended another siege, outside Maastricht, entering whilst the ravaged town's defenders were briefly sleeping. To say that only around 400 of an original population of some 30,000 survived, and that the looting went on for three days gives us just the most cursory sense of the sufferings endured by the citizens.[185] We get a more vivid idea of the hatred and ferocity at stake when we hear of the Dutch pouring boiling water into the tunnels used by the encroaching Spanish. In this case many Spaniards were also slain during the siege, with 500 alone killed in one moment, when one of their own mines exploded prematurely by the city walls.

Within the struggle fought by the Dutch, perhaps the most bitter European war of all time occurred. From 1618 to 1648, the Thirty Years War between Protestants and Catholics produced a proportionally higher loss of population than World War Two.[186] Although estimates vary, even a conservative view puts the German death toll at 25 per cent of its pre-war population. Some go as high as 35 or even 40 per cent: a drop from around 18 million to 12 million inhabitants.[187] In one district in Thüringen, only 627 of the original 1,717 houses were still standing by 1649, and only 316 families could be found to occupy them.[188] In 1635, just over halfway through this conflict, we hear of how, in Bavaria, 'the living were nothing near able to bury the dead', whilst 'rats and mice devoured their carcasses, most horrible to behold'.[189] Even those who were buried could be easily disinterred – possibly to feed starving citizens, possibly by animals, or by looting soldiers.[190] In the following year the Englishman William Crowne was travelling through Germany with the Earl of Arundel in early May, passing 'a poor little village called Neunkirchen', now deserted and with one house still burning. Early next morning they found the church plundered and desecrated, and 'a dead body scraped out of the grave'.[191]

Whilst British Protestants waited avidly for news of these struggles to reach them, they remained relatively isolated from the direct sufferings of the Wars of Religion. The Civil War changed all this for around five years, and at times the degree of hatred between the two sides (again sharply inflected by religious divisions) must have rivalled that seen on the continent. It was certainly believed by some Royalists in later decades that Charles I had been dissected after his execution, and we can imagine that the thousands of bodies lying on the battlefields of Naseby and Marston Moor may have undergone broadly similar indignities.[192] There was clearly no shortage of unburied corpses for any who were ready to trade in them. After the Battle of Edgehill on 23 October 1642, Richard Baxter, 'being at Alcester, went to see the ground and some unburied bodies'.[193] The Battle of Marston Moor on 2 July 1644 was the worst conflict of the Civil War, and the largest ever to occur on British soil – an apocalyptic clash which left some 8,000 soldiers dead. Bodies were so hastily and thinly covered with earth that their stench (according to a writer of 1676) 'almost poisoned them that passed over the moor'; while 'at Kendal, a place near adjacent, the bell for six weeks together never ceased tolling for the inhabitants who were poisoned and infected with the smell'.[194]

Ireland

The relatively peaceable character of life on English soil in the early modern period seems to have thrown especially great importance on one nearby source of corpse materials. We have seen that skulls and bones were probably not so hard to come by, and the writings of Paracelsians suggest that human flesh could also be obtained by those who wanted it. But there was one other substance evidently much less common in England. This was the moss of the human skull – something much prized by Boyle and certain colleagues in the 1670s and 80s, and perhaps generally acceptable to those who would baulk at using more obviously cannibalistic medicines. Skull-moss could – as one author implied – be obtained from charnel houses. But the most popular source indeed seems to have been a skull which had lain unburied – and which, for many authors, had also suffered a violent death. We might imagine that, after 1649, there were a fair number of such skulls strewn about, particularly in more remote areas of the north and Scotland. Yet it appears that these themselves were either unsuitable, or insufficient to meet overall demand.

We have heard Francis Bacon, some time before his own death in 1626, suggesting that usnea could be obtained from the 'heaps of slain bodies' lying unburied in Ireland. Bacon's high profile in social and political life leads us to think that he would have known if moss-covered skulls were already being imported when he wrote. What we have here, then, is a suggestion, and clear evidence that Ireland already contained many unburied corpses in the earlier seventeenth century. Although Bacon himself does not seem to have been to Ireland, he was a close friend of the Earl of Essex (who was fighting the Irish in 1599) and in 1608 he wrote a treatise on the settlement of the country.[195] Knowing Bacon's respect for reliable evidence, we can assume that his knowledge of these heaps of corpses came from Essex. I have argued throughout this chapter that corpse medicines were often derived from bodies alienated, in various ways, from ordinary humanity – distant, most of all, from *you* (whether you were merchant, thief, apothecary, physician or patient). In many ways, the Irish perfectly fulfilled this criterion in the minds of the English.

Both mental attitudes and physical treatment of these supposed rebels (whose country had in reality been invaded and settled by their more powerful neighbours) amply confirm this. The Irish were intrinsically backward, degenerate, and inferior. In 1610 the poet and lawyer Sir John Davies could be heard asserting in a letter that if the Irish '"were suffered to possess the whole country … they would never (to the end of the world) build houses, make townships or villages, or improve the land as it ought to be"'.[196] This perennial excuse for oppression and colonisation was rather ironically countered by the fact that during the sixteenth century men such as the governor Sir Henry Sidney could be found vigorously burning up to twenty-four miles of Irish corn in one go.[197] In the minds of certain other Englishmen, their Celtic neighbours were not so much substandard as subhuman.[198] The historian Keith Thomas tells of a mid-seventeenth-century English captain whose soldiers slaughtered an Irish garrison. Having inspected the enemy casualties, the captain went on to claim that several of the Irish dead had tails a quarter of a yard long. This being doubted, forty soldiers came forward to confirm the story on oath.[199] Come the mid-nineteenth century, the Irish may have shed their tails; but the writer Charles Kingsley could still describe them, after a brief visit, as 'human chimpanzees'.[200]

Recalling the frequent savagery of the continental wars of religion at this time, we must also recall that, however confused and impressionistic English prejudice might have been in many respects, there was one very clear and definite basis for such hostility. To the geographical distance of Ireland we must add the cultural distance which thrust the country into a still more remote corner of the Protestant imagination. For most Englishmen, the native Irish were not only generally alien, but quite specifically Catholic. It must surely have been this which was uppermost in the mind of the Quaker George Fox when he visited the country in 1669. The moment he landed, Fox was struck by the impression that '"the earth and the very air, smelt with the corruption of the nation"'.[201]

In many cases this kind of social or religious prejudice must have been responsible for the inhumanity with which the Irish were treated.[202] From the opening of the sixteenth century, the corpses described by Bacon were piling up across the Irish countryside. On 19 August 1504, at the Hill of the Axes near Knockdoe, eight out of nine of the Irish battalions of Ulick Burke were killed by Gerald Fitzgerald (then governor of Ireland).[203] By the time of Sir Henry Sidney, the Irish may have been looking back with wistful nostalgia to those days of honest manly warfare. In 1566 – writes Rory Rapple – one Humphrey Gilbert was sent out 'to assist … Sidney, the lord deputy of Ireland, in the campaign to defeat Shane O'Neill'.[204] On 2 June 1567 O'Neill was treacherously murdered by the McDonnells (who were themselves prompted by English offers of reward). After an initial burial O'Neill's body was exhumed, and his severed head preserved in salt so that it could be thrust on a pole outside Dublin castle.[205]

The English soldier Thomas Churchyard, who served under Gilbert, left a particularly memorable account of Gilbert's dealings with the Irish.[206] He told of how Gilbert ordered 'that the heads of all those which were killed in the day, should be cut off from their bodies, and brought to the place where he incamped at night'. There, they were 'laid on the ground, by each side of the way leading into his own tent: so that none could come into his tent for any cause, but commonly he must pass through a lane of heads'. By this means, Churchyard explained, Gilbert aimed to 'bring great terror to the people, when they saw the heads of their dead fathers, brothers, children, kinsfolk, and friends, lie on the ground before their faces, as they came to speak with the said Colonel'. Although Churchyard perceived that some would think this cruel, he unembarrassedly praised Gilbert's rule as one which brought unprecedented order to the country.[207]

Other tactics used by Gilbert were cited with seeming approval. Whenever he 'made any … inroad, into the enemy's country' he unfailingly 'killed man, woman, and child, and spoiled, wasted, and burned' to 'the ground all that he might'. This, Gilbert stated, was done so that no remaining family would be able to assist or support the rebels, even by anything so much as tending farms or milking cattle.[208] Whilst we can already well imagine that the most grief-stricken relative never tried to bury anything from the highway of heads outside Gilbert's tent, we can now also further see just how so many bones and skulls came to lie untouched in the hills and fields of Munster. All too often in Gilbert's time, there was not a soul left to bury them.

If Gilbert (who was knighted for his troubles in 1570) used his powers of martial law with particular savagery, there seemed to be little greater humanity by the time that he left that same year. In October 1573, for example, 'an Irish servant shot and killed' the son of English settler Sir Thomas Smith. The servant's body 'was subsequently boiled and fed to the dogs'.[209] Individual attitudes aside, the general picture itself notably deteriorated in the last decade of Elizabeth's reign. From 1594–1603 England and Ireland were openly at war, with the Battle of Kinsale on the Cork Coast, on 24 December 1601, claiming between 1,000 and 2,000 Irish lives.[210]

The Irish Massacre

We must take seriously the possibility that Ireland became a reservoir of profitable corpse materials. We have heard Robert Boyle telling of how usnea had been sent to his sister 'by a great person, for a present out of Ireland' – 'in which country' Boyle adds, 'I found it less rare and more esteemed than elsewhere'. Citing Boyle's cure in 1694, the physician John Pechey noted again that such moss is 'common in Ireland'.[211] It was also in 1694 that Pomet described the English export of moss-covered skulls 'to foreign countries, especially Germany' – where they were used in the wound salve, as well as to stop bleeding. And, Pomet adds, 'the English druggists generally bring these heads from Ireland; that country having been remarkable for them ever since the Irish massacre'.[212]

The Irish Massacre occurred in 1641. Given what Bacon had said before 1626, Pomet's statement may be slightly misleading. Unburied bodies had been available before 1641, and moss of the skull known and used before that date. Yet Pomet's phrasing ('having been remarkable for them') could just mean that the export trade had particularly flourished since the massacre. This would match the relatively large number of surviving references to a specifically Irish moss in the later seventeenth century. There is also some evidence that demand for corpse medicines per se was growing in Germany from about the 1660s. Discussing the German cities of Lüneburg and Brunswick, a geographical work of 1689 states, 'from this place the true mum[my] is brought over'. In the 1657 edition of that book we find a similar passage on Lüneburg and Brunswick, but no mention of their role in the mummy trade.[213]

There seems, then, to be no doubt that English ships were ferrying skulls back across the Irish Sea in the time of Cromwell and Charles II. These would then be driven over to various eastern seaports in order to be further shipped across to north Germany. But a further question now arises. Just whose were these moss-covered skulls, stoically rocking in eyeless penumbra in the chill holds of English cargo vessels? For, as any Englishman or woman could have told you, just for once the massacre of 1641 was largely not of the Irish themselves. In 1638 the Scots had rebelled against England after high-handed attempts to impose new religious practices on them. In 1639 and 1640 English armies were twice defeated by Scottish forces. Inspired by this example, a substantial number of Irish now also revolted against the unjust rule of the Stuarts. After a failed attempt to seize Dublin castle on 23 October 1641 there was a general rising across Ulster. Perhaps as many as 10,000 Protestant settlers were killed in this outbreak of violence. Predictably, English accounts seriously exaggerated the number of Protestant dead.[214] The massacre became, in every sense, legendary. Questions of truth and rumour aside, however, we can be quite certain that an event so fiercely denounced by religious polemicists would indeed have earned the title of '*the* Irish massacre'.

Ironically, then, Bacon's conveniently *alien* source of supply could only have endured, in its purest form, until autumn 1641. After this, it must have been increasingly difficult to know whether you were using the moss or cranial bone of an Irish Catholic or of an Anglo-Irish Protestant.[215] Although the rebellion suffered a notable blow in early March 1642, when Colonel Monck arrived in Dublin with 1,500 foot soldiers, the conflict dragged on until the peace talks of November 1642.[216] Given that the English Civil War had begun across the water in August, it would be surprising if the English now had sufficient man-power to bury all of their dead countrymen. Before long, it would have been impossible (especially so long before the Gall system) to tell an English skull from an Irish one. And so, once again, as with the strange Eucharistic sparring of Daniel Featley and his Romish adversaries, we find Protestants and Catholics bizarrely united by corpse medicine – perhaps literally so, via the sale, shipping, processing and consumption of the dead. Murdered by Catholics, moss clad under Irish skies, shipped home by English Protestants, a skull within which the most fervently anti-papist thoughts had flickered now travelled back to the heart of the Reformation, to be swallowed by a man or a woman who would never for a moment have dreamed of eating the body of Christ.[217]

To anyone just casually familiar with the length and extent of oppression Ireland has suffered at English hands, the wholesale cannibalisation-for-profit of Irish dead might well appear just one more peculiarly dark irony among many. Those English-men deputed to mediate possession of Ireland certainly varied in their harshness or humanity. But in general terms it is hard to deny that for many privileged English settlers the country was just one great material resource. Given that the idea of 'cannibal oppression' was current in the Renaissance and after, we might well ima-gine the English both literally and metaphorically feeding off the body of Ireland and its people.

Human fat

On 20 November 2009 bizarre tales from Peru suddenly hit the global press. General Felix Murga, head of the national police's criminal-investigation division, and Colonel Jorge Mejia (in charge of an anti-kidnapping unit) stated that they had arrested four men for murder. The murders had been committed solely so as to obtain the victims' fat. The corpses were decapitated, the police claimed, and hung upside down over candles so that the fat could drip out into basins. A press conference showed a severed head, and plastic bottles filled with a yellowish viscous fluid. A litre of this fat was said to be worth $15,000 (more than £9,000). The buyers were Italian nationals, working as intermediaries in a global black market, which itself was ultimately linked to Eur-opean cosmetics firms, using the fat as an ingredient in skin creams. Perhaps as many as sixty people had been killed by this gang – nicknamed 'the Pishtacos' – which lured victims to remote country roads with offers of employment. Only two weeks after these revelations first startled the world a further twist occurred. The story was said to have been largely fabricated, the sole murder victim the product of a drug feud, and Murga was suspended from duty. It was claimed that the police had con-cocted the tale in order to distract attention from various of their own failings and crimes, including possible involvement in an illicit death squad.

Reporting for the BBC, Dan Collyns cited anthropologists who believed that 'the police's story deliberately played on an old Peruvian myth to explain crimes which the police had failed to investigate fully'. The myth in question was that of the Pishtaco. Usually mounted on horseback, wearing high boots, a leather jacket and a felt hat, this nocturnal figure was held to murder Indians chiefly to gain their fat, which would then be sold to industries to lubricate machines, or to pharmacies to cure certain diseases. From a European viewpoint, this strange semi-mythical figure looks very much like a variation of the vampire. But in both Peru and Bolivia, the key element was always fat rather than blood. Writing of the Bolivian version (known as the kharisiri) in 2000, anthropologist Andrew Canessa made it very clear that, to the indigenous people he worked with in Bolivia, this fat-sucking demon was still a live and real danger. Two of the local Andean people were convinced that the recent death of their friend, Alfredo, was the work of a kharisiri, and accordingly begged Canessa not to risk his planned journey down the mountains into La Paz.[218]

Such beliefs may now look fantastic to most European readers. Ironically, however, some modern anthropologists think that they originated from the activities of Spanish Christian invaders in the sixteenth and seventeenth centuries. According to two Spanish authors of the day, the New World conquerors were not only using the fat of those Indians who had died in battle, but also actively murdering them for this reason. "'See how many were roasted and burned alive'" (wrote Antonio Herrera), "'how many were thrown to the wild dogs to be eaten alive, how many were killed because they were fat in order to extract their grease to heal the sores of the Castilians'". Herrera's contemporary Cristóbal de Molina further asserted that fat was used to cure a disease for which there was no other cure. This made the substance especially valuable, and before long many Indians were terrified to bring firewood or food to the invaders, convinced that they would be murdered upon entering a Spaniard's house.[219] In around 1520 Hernando Cortez, the conqueror of Mexico, was supposed to have used the fat of slain Indians to caulk his army's boats, in the absence of ordinary tallow.[220]

Were these claims true? To this question we can give various answers. These contemporary accounts were written by Spanish authors. In the longer term, we know not only that Peru and Bolivia became home to the distinctive fat-sucking vampires of south America, but that (as native Peruvian anthropologist Efrain Morote Best could write in the early 1950s) 'the fatty tissues of human bodies are still valued in the region for their therapeutic effect on wounds, rheumatism', and smallpox scars.[221] This twentieth-century echo of European corpse medicines brings us to the two most central questions of all. First: did human fat work as a medicine? Second: were the Spanish capable of treating the native Americans in the way alleged by Molina and Herrera?

If we address that first question from the viewpoint of early modern Europe, we already have quite a lot of evidence that it was effective in certain areas. In William Baldwin's intriguing novelistic tale, *Beware the Cat* (published in 1561, but probably composed in 1553), the narrator catches a cat which is 'exceeding fat' and then takes 'some of the grease [from] the inwards and the head' to make 'a medicine for the gout'.[222] Although this alleged usage actually masks other interests in fat, what becomes clear is that animal fat was already known, by this stage, as an agent against gout. As we have seen, in Italy it was 'above all the fat' which was sought from the bodies of executed criminals. In 1631 Fludd insisted that

> the oil of man's fat is a great appeaser of the gout and other dolours, and a healer of wounds, and a present drier up of all manner of excoriations; often experience hath taught, as well my Masters as my self. Do we not see, that the dropping of a candle will in one night heal up an excoriation? And every ostler will certify you, that a horse's heel being wounded or cut with a stone or shoe [healeth?], with the anointing of a candle's end; that hogs'-grease, deer-suet, are esteemed good and necessary ingredients for a healing salve, there is not a chirurgion but will confess.[223]

Fludd could almost certainly have obtained human fat from the anatomy specimens used by the physicians for lectures. But more important than that detail are the phrases 'experience hath taught' and 'every ostler will certify you'. Human or animal fat was seen to work (especially on wounds and sores) by those used to relying not on abstruse theories, but on homely empirical evidence.[224] This impression is supported with particular weight by the continuing use of fat in popular south American medicine in the twentieth century, where successful results probably counted for more than medical theories.[225]

In the eighteenth century, as other corpse medicines were gradually abandoned, human fat was repeatedly recommended by the European medical élite – it may, indeed, have even grown more popular at this time. With so many older medical ideas and substances now being attacked or discarded, it is surely not insignificant that human fat continued to thrive. It must have done so, again, because the self-consciously rational and 'enlightened' physicians of the day believed it to work. At this stage, its practical utility still fought off all the theoretical and cultural artillery likely to be aimed against it. And for the chief group of complaints with which it was associated (namely gout, rheumatism, wounds, and skin problems) it probably worked at least as well as animal fat. It was naturally lubricating and soothing, and was an ideal substance with which to apply the gentle friction that eighteenth-century doctors so often recommended for gout. In North American popular medicine 'goose grease has been rubbed into muscles to make them supple', whilst the fat of 'a buzzard, goat, or black dog has been used as a rheumatism treatment'.[226] Come 1889, the German settlers of Pennsylvania were still using dog-fat, skunk-fat, and bacon fat for certain types of wounds.[227] Moving into our own era, we find that tiger balm, still used against muscular aches and sprains, is a mixture of various oils, whilst the sheep fat lanolin has been an enduring central ingredient of skin creams.

Spanish soldiers who had sailed across the world and ventured through some of the most alien and dangerous territories then known to man were nothing if not practical and hard-headed. Like the ostlers cited by Fludd, the surgeons of Ostend, and the executioner-healers of early modern Germany, they used fat because it worked. We might further add that, in regions bristling with unknown diseases, poisons, and alien flora and fauna, they may well have valued human fat precisely *because* it was human, and therefore more or less universally familiar and reliable.[228]

To answer our second question, we need to compress decades of oppression and atrocity into a bare few words. However much Protestants may have exaggerated such accounts, it now seems clear that the first Spanish invaders and settlers inflicted habitual cruelties upon the native inhabitants of central and south America. Slaughtered in colossal numbers, tricked and betrayed, roasted alive on slow fires, the Americans had their children brained and murdered before their eyes. These arguably genocidal slaughters, and the seemingly incredible tortures inflicted by the Spanish, are described above by Herrera, and they were initially reported by an evidently reliable witness, who had nothing to gain from his accounts. This figure was the Spanish Jesuit Bartolomé de las Casas (1474–1566), a man who spent much time in South America, and who championed native rights in a remarkably enlightened way.[229] In this kind of context, native fear of the Spanish (including fears about human fat murders) was highly rational, rather than superstitious. European Protestants were all very familiar with the 'Black Legend' of New World atrocities by the mid-sixteenth century, and the tale of Cortez and his cannibalised boats also lingered on in Protestant writings.[230] It may well have been that this story was especially prominent in the minds of those Ostenders who so swiftly drained the fat from their Catholic besiegers in the autumn of 1601, and who felt a keen sense of poetic justice as they did so.

It looks, then, as if the real pishtacos were in fact Spanish soldiers and settlers – men from a country which was then by far the most powerful in the Western, nominally civilised Christian world. Certain of the details of the Bolivian kharisiri fit this ironic derivation with wry precision. For this spectre, explains Canessa, would first put you to sleep with prayers and powder, and then, with a sharp and fiendishly clever instrument would make a cut down your side in order to extract the fat. On waking you would neither recall nor realise what had happened (or recollect the kharisiri). But ever after, you would feel weak and tired, and would slowly waste away and die.[231]

At one level, this displays certain universal elements of supernatural folklore. It tames the unknown by localising and explaining otherwise inexplicable and unpredictable sickness and death – thus partially matching the vampires of Greece, or the fairies and changelings of Britain.[232] At another, it quite neatly mythicises the early behaviour and longer term effects of European colonisers. These men literally drained out your fat to heal themselves. They plundered vast shiploads of natural resources in the form of gold. They left your land nominally intact, but forever changed and sickening – not least by European diseases such as smallpox, into whose scars human fat was still rubbed centuries later. We might further add that, in many tales, both kharisiri and pishtaco were white men.[233]

This blend of myth and reality resurfaced in the Peruvian hoax over human fat and cosmetics. The officials involved shrewdly picked on a distracting lie about a global black market in human fat not just because of the local legends of pishtacos and kharisiri, but because it so neatly united the European colonial oppressions of past and present. Peruvians who recalled the stories of atrocities committed by the Spanish, when that nation first initiated the age of global capitalism, would perceive a grim but familiar logic here. Among the European corporate heirs of that legacy were those plutocratic cosmetics firms who were prepared to connive in murder so that the privileged citizens of France or Britain or North America could smear the guts of the poor upon their ageing skins.

We will see in the conclusion that human fat continued to occupy a peculiar space between reality and fantasy to the very end of the nineteenth century. Here we can say just a few more words about the possible lengths to which those in other parts of Europe might go to obtain human fat in later decades. In Scotland human fat was being sold and used in the earlier seventeenth century. An enterprising Aberdeen apothecary named Gordon advertised medical ingredients available at a shop in 'Robert Farquhar's high lodging', offering 'human fat at 12s Scots per ounce', and 'mumia of Egypt at 2s per dram'.[234] The sources were presumably local, and could possibly have included anatomy specimens, as well as executed criminals.

What other sources of supply were available? As late as 1856 a rough (and indeed more startling) forerunner of the Peruvian fabrications was circulating in the Swiss press. A peasant of the mountains had, it was claimed, 'killed his little girl seven years of age, in order to boil the body and procure human fat, which he had been told would cure him of a severe rheumatism'. The crime was said to have been committed with the aid of his wife. This may have been merely a peculiar blend of village feuding and folklore, a kind of nineteenth-century version of witchcraft accusations. (It does not appear, for example, that the case ever came to trial.) But it is certainly telling that such accusations could still take that particular form in 1856. They could be invented and believed at that stage, in a way that they never could a hundred years later, by even the most vindictive or twisted neighbour. They also, at this stage, held sufficient credibility to make it into cold print.[235]

Moreover, in England eighty years earlier, there was an evidently genuine case which showed a similarly harsh state of family relations. In October 1736 various papers and magazines told of how, a few days since, at Rushall in Norfolk, after a man and his wife had 'had some words', the husband suddenly 'went out and hanged himself'. An inquest ruled that, as this was suicide, the man must be buried at the crossroads. But, eschewing funeral or burial, 'his wife sent for a surgeon, and sold the body for half a guinea'. While the surgeon was carefully 'feeling about the body' the woman assured him: '"he is fit for your purpose, he is as fat as butter"'; after which the deceased 'was put naked into a sack, with his legs hanging out, thrown upon a cart, and conveyed to the surgeon's'.[236] Even in that form, this tale was quite well detailed, and was something which the readers of *The Gentleman's Magazine* were expected to take seriously. And, in certain other versions, the details were yet more grimly convincing. For it was also said that, following the argument, the husband 'went out and cut some brambles, with which he hanged himself upon a tree, and was found with one knee upon the ground'. With these words, the misty outlines of rumour leap into cruelly sharp focus: a man so unhinged that he seizes the first impromptu rope he can find, and a suicide so hastily organised that death comes just before the weight of the body yanks it to earth.[237]

By 1736 we cannot automatically assume that the surgeon could make use of the entire body. It is therefore possible that he paid half a guinea just for the fat (as the wife's remark implies), and that this quite high price matches the relative scarcity of human fat in an era when it was nevertheless still in high demand. In 1764, for example, Domenico Cotugno's *Treatise on the Nervous Sciatica* describes human fat as 'a thing whose scarcity will recommend it' (presumably to the patient).[238] And just four years after the Rushall incident there occurred a peculiar London murder. One Saturday morning in early June 1740 a man's body was discovered in an uninhabited house in Sword-bearer's Alley ('commonly called the Devil's Nursery'), in Chiswell Street. The man had apparently been murdered about a fortnight before. His head was separated from his body, and the body itself had been ripped from the throat to the lower belly, so that his entrails were hanging out. The flayed carcass of a dog (supposed to be that of the victim) was also found in the sack.[239] Why had the body been mutilated in this way? Severing the head was of course an obvious and traditional way to disguise its identity. But the laceration of the trunk looks far more like the work of someone who wanted to extract human fat quickly, before selling it on to a suitable buyer.

The first vampires

A final word remains to be said about those medicines which could be taken from the living body. For some, these could include hair, nails, lice, sperm, saliva, milk, sweat, tapeworms, stones, urine, and excrement (much more of which in chapter five). But evidently the most popular fluid was blood. A number of physicians clearly considered this to be effective against many conditions besides epilepsy. We have heard Boyle commending it for asthma, acute fevers, pleurisy, consumption, hysteria, convulsions, certain types of headache, palsy, 'incipient apoplexies', distempers and jaundice; and it was also an antidote against certain poisons.[240] Some decades earlier Fludd had stated: 'man's blood and bones do contain an admirable deal of volatile salt, in which there is so excellent a balsamic disposition, that it doth ... appease dolours of the gout, and intolerable aches'; it 'cureth wounds, healeth such as are affected with the mother and falling-sickness', whilst 'experience hath made manifest, that the volatile salt and oil of the blood, is an excellent cordial'.

Notably, Fludd attributes these discoveries to those 'who have applied themselves unto the art of distilling'.[241] For those who may have been repelled by the drinking of hot blood at the scaffold, the various distillations of blood (produced since at least the thirteenth century) offered a very different form of medicine. Occasionally, we find someone recommending both versions, as when Ficino (himself the son of a doctor) proposed that the elderly should suck blood 'the way leeches do, an ounce or two from a vein on the left arm barely opened'. He adds, too, that 'good doctors try, with human blood distilled in fire, to restore those whom old age has eaten away'.[242] Around two centuries later, Moise Charas asserts, 'I am not of their opinion, that the blood of man, gulped down warm as it runs out of the veins, is a specific remedy against the epilepsy' – a statement which could refer either to the blood sales of the scaffold, or to the more private bloodsucking advocated by Ficino. Although Charas denounces such a 'cruel beverage' as both unethical and medically useless, he too believes that blood is a valid medicine if it is first painstakingly distilled by a chemist – finding it effective against diseases of the brain, for purifying the blood, and (aptly) for improving circulation. He also cites van Helmont's opinion, 'that the use of it cures persons that are grown in years'.[243]

There may also have been a relatively general habit of bloodsucking in France among the elderly. In 1777 one Thomas Mortimer claimed that, 'towards the close of the fifteenth century, an idle opinion prevailed, that the declining strength and vigour of old people might be repaired by transfusing the blood of young persons'.[244] He adds that some 'drank the warm blood of young persons' and that the practice was suppressed in France after 'some of the principal nobility ... turned raving mad' as a result.[245] Mortimer does not say exactly when this practice was stamped out; but if there is any truth in his claims (which certainly match the late fifteenth-century arguments of Ficino) then it is telling that the chief culprits were 'the nobility' – people who could no doubt easily afford to pay healthy young men to stab their veins and let out youthful blood.

All in all, the basic question as regards medical vampirism was not: should you do it? but rather, how should you do it? Despite his opposition to the 'cruel beverage' taken directly from the body, Charas was quite happy to specify blood from 'healthy young men' (without red hair, in this case) for chemical processing. Boyle, similarly, was able to obtain not just fresh blood, but that of quite definite physical types. On the whole, it seems that, in an age of habitual bloodletting, this was usually one of the easier substances to get hold of. In barbers' shops jars of blood could sometimes be seen advertising phlebotomy, and its familiarity is encoded in the seemingly pro-verbial phrase, 'every man's blood in a basin looks of one colour'.[246] One potential problem in this area was that those undergoing bloodletting would often themselves be sick. Ficino seems to recognise this when he proposes that the donor should be someone 'whose blood is excellent but perhaps a little excessive'. Here blood is let merely to remove superfluity. In such cases, the 'blood donor' may well have been happy to have had blood drawn for free by those taking it for medical use.

This inference assumes that the practitioner was himself drawing the blood, rather than relying on a separate surgeon. Although phrasing is not conclusive, Irvine and Schroeder do seem to imply as much, with the latter stating, 'take the blood of a healthful young man drawn from a vein in May', and again, 'take man's blood, while it is hot'.[247] Irvine writes: 'take therefore the blood of a sound young man, drawn in the spring (there are every where fools enow) as much as thou canst get'. What are we to make of this intriguing parenthetical aside? At very least, it seems clear that Irvine himself felt such fluid to be easily available (and the contemptuous tone may even imply that his donors were indeed paying him, rather than vice versa). The Paracelsian physician Daniel Border makes it quite clear that he simply uses the bar-bers as a routine supplier, and also that he can easily choose a very precise type of donor: 'take the blood of a young sanguine man and choleric man at the barbers' shops as thou mayest have it, and namely of such men as use good wines'.[248] Boyle at one point remarks that 'because it is difficult to get the blood of healthy men, and perhaps not so safe to use that of unsound persons' he has been accordingly experi-menting with certain types of animal blood.[249] But elsewhere he routinely specifies the blood of both healthy men and women without further comment.[250] His refer-ence to supply problems may reflect the large number of trials he undertook, and the correspondingly large volumes of blood required. Certainly his sometime partner, Locke, had registered no such difficulties when he wrote in his notebook, '"human blood from a living body 2 lbs. Let it congeal … "'.[251]

On the whole, it seems that for much of the early modern era, people were likely to welcome rather than fear the sensation of a hollow arm. (One thing which probably commended bloodletting to the empirically minded was just that one did definitely *feel* different afterwards).[252] In a world as sharply unequal as this, some healthy young men must have been tempted by payment (as they are even now, in the case of phar-maceutical drug trials). It was financial incentive, after all, which allowed Jean-Baptiste

Denis – physician to Louis XIV – to secure a volunteer for a comprehensive (and daunting) experiment in blood transfusion in 1667.[253] On a broader ethical note, we find the Dutch physician H.M. Herwig referring quite plainly to 'those things that may be taken away without any hurt or prejudice, as the seed, blood and stone'.[254] In the present day, donation of the first two substances is indeed routine and virtuous (and in some cases is paid). Comfortable as most are with modern blood transfusion, early modern habits again present us with an uncertain ethical question: should one person's lifeblood be another person's health tonic? How much urgency is required to legitimise the transfer of blood? Some might respond that blood donors had more choice than the slaughtered inhabitants of Ireland or South America, or the casualties of warfare. Marxists might respond that the starkly poor have few choices, and many of them hard ones.

We have now established in some detail that medicinal cannibalism was attractive to patients of all social classes, as well as to physicians, apothecaries, and a variety of financially motivated intermediaries, from merchants to executioners. Indeed, so many types of people seem to have been involved in this phenomenon that it must have been quite hard, circa 1650, to remain unaware of its existence. In the following chapter we turn to forms of cannibalism traditionally associated with the tribes of the New World. What did the eating of human flesh mean, not only to the Europeans who so often (and so hypocritically) condemned it, but to those engaged in it, in the thinly charted regions of Canada and Brazil?

4

THE OTHER CANNIBALS

Man-eaters of the New World

In an age which prides itself on challenging taboos, cannibalism retains a remarkably potent charge of horror. It is the ultimate form of violence or dominance, the most extreme possible aggravation of corporeal terrorism. Even at the habitual, everyday level of seemingly casual speech, certain basic fears or fantasies about anthropophagy seem to be revealed: an experience or a personality, for example, might be 'all-consuming' or 'devouring'. As these examples suggest, cannibalism can be seen as an especially severe form of invasion. If someone steps into our personal space, stares too long or too aggressively at us, or even simply addresses us in an unacceptable way, we register their behaviour as invasive. Fundamental boundaries are being violated. Cannibalism shifts this kind of attack into a whole new dimension. The boundary line is not simply crossed, but utterly annihilated, as two individuals are collapsed together by the act of consumption.

Given the enduring, arguably mythic power of cannibalism in the human imagination, we need to realise at once that there is some well-documented reality behind the myths and the slurs. Anthropologists have often been uneasy about identifying cannibalistic communities, because of the long-standing use of 'cannibal' as a convenient propaganda weapon. Once labelled in this way, and effectively dehumanised, tribal peoples in the Americas, Africa and Australasia could be 'legitimately' civilised, colonised, or outrightly destroyed. There is little doubt that cannibalism was both a political tool and a dangerously unstable fantasy in the minds of European Christians during the decades that followed Christopher Columbus' momentous landing. Cannibals were deliberately invented or imagined without justification. But they did exist. The (perhaps well-meaning) attempt of the anthropologist William Arens, in 1979, to deny that cannibalism had ever taken place as a general custom has now been substantially discredited.[1] For some years, accumulated evidence from archaeological finds, from historians, and from anthropologists, has put this basic question beyond all doubt.

One especially compelling reason for accepting the reality of habitual, communal cannibalism is the sheer wealth of complex detail found in so many accounts. In numerous different cultures, the eating of human beings was quite as densely ritualistic, quite as religiously solemn as any Catholic Mass. Cannibalism was anything but senseless violence. Indeed, as Beth A. Conklin in particular has emphasised, it was often the absolute opposite of violence, functioning as an intensely compassionate mourning ritual for one's dead kin.[2]

Perhaps the most basic division in the realm of man-eating is that between ritual and famine cannibalism. The first is highly meaningful for those who practise it. The second kind is usually seen as a desperate last resort, imposed by extreme circumstances. The cannibalism of the psychopathic killer, although highly specialised in its own right (and almost always eminently *anti*social) can be allied with ritual anthropophagy more easily than with cases of famine.[3]

Like corpse medicine, ritual cannibalism is emphatically not a question of hunger or of food. Accordingly, it is ritual forms of man-eating which will concern us here. Ritual cannibalism itself splits into two broadly distinct forms. Exo-cannibalism (from the Greek for 'outside') is emphatically directed against outsiders. It is a deliberately terrifying and appalling aggravation of tribal warfare. By extension, such assaults on alien communities usually help to define the acceptable, legitimate identity of the aggressors. If exo-cannibalism is very much a question of 'us and them', the variety known as 'endo-cannibalism' is by contrast a purely internal matter ('endo' is Greek for 'inside'). It is usually a kind of funeral rite, and is entirely consensual. A dying person will expect to be eaten after death, and will indeed *want* this to happen. Similarly, the relatives who consume the deceased will feel not merely that the custom is acceptable and natural, but that it has immense religious and social importance.

If we look closely at these tribal practices we can begin to see just what it was that European society opposed and attacked so vigorously in the eras of Columbus, Michelangelo, Shakespeare and Milton. A second aim is perhaps more important. As well as emphasising the reality of cannibalism – dissolving its heavy mythic aura – we will also be able to see a number of striking parallels to the practice in Old World society. For all their very different forms of technology, dress and language, the London or Rome of the sixteenth century were in many ways quite as fiercely tribal as the isolated world of the Tupinamba Indians. In terms of social identity, violence, and religion, the Old World and the New had far more in common than any pope or archbishop would have cared to admit. Let us begin with the least familiar form of cannibalism: the funeral rites in which communities ate their own relatives or tribe members.

The New World cannibals

Funerary cannibalism

> [A]s I took the lid off of the box, a fine spray of his ashes blew out onto the table. I couldn't just brush him off, so I wiped my finger over it and snorted

the residue. Ashes to ashes, father to son … John Humphrys on prime-time radio was heard to ask, 'Do you think Keith Richards has gone too far this time?' … There were also articles saying this is a perfectly normal thing, it goes back to ancient times, the ingestion of your ancestor. So there were two schools of thought.[4]

It is 1964. In London, the streets of Soho are bright with Carnaby Street fashions. Cafés (and the very few nightclubs then grudgingly tolerated by the police) pulse to the accelerated beat of amphetamines and amplified rock music. Parents, the BBC, the *Daily Telegraph* and the *Daily Mail* are all near-hysterical about the threat to society posed by that drug-crazed, sexually liberated, guitar-wielding monster, the teenager. They cannot understand what Mick Jagger is singing, and so assume that it must be something very nasty indeed.[5] Meanwhile, over in Brazil, somewhere between the mountain range known as the Serra dos Pacaas Novos and the Madeira River adjacent to Bolivia, the tribal people called the Wari' are preparing for the funeral of a recently deceased man.[6]

It is late afternoon. The corpse lies on a mat, naked and bloated. It has been painted with stripes of red annatto, and is already suffering the effects of rigor mortis. Three men form a triangle around it. One holds its legs straight; opposite, behind the head, another bears a mat. The third man, at the apex of the triangle, now moves in, lowers a bamboo arrow tip, and makes a vertical cut along the abdominal area. Pungent gases flood out of the body, which collapses back to something like its normal dimensions. The mat bearer waves his mat like a fan in order to try and dissipate the overwhelming stench of death and putrefaction.

Vibrating around this central scene, a crescendo of human wailing marks the separation of the body from its kin, aiming also to frighten evil spirits away from the corpse. Dusk is now hovering in the air. Separate body parts are washed and placed on a nearby roasting rack. Beneath it the bundle of firewood has been carefully decorated with the feathers of vultures and scarlet macaws. Genitals and intestines are burned in the fire. The heart and liver, which cook most quickly, are wrapped in leaves. Occasionally a distraught relative will attempt to throw themself onto the blaze, being prevented only by a guard specially appointed to stand by the fire.

Presently a male official cuts up the heart and liver, and blood relatives begin to eat them. They do this slowly and very respectfully. Later, other flesh is eaten with corn bread. In a familiar ritual, non-related tribe members are begged to join in with the eating. They at first refuse, and finally give way after repeated pleading from the deceased's kin. It is important for mourners' hands not to touch the flesh, and so thin splinters of wood are used as cutlery. As the dead man is a tribal elder, mourning has been prolonged. His flesh is particularly putrid, and no amount of cooking can disguise this. From time to time, participants will leave the gathering in order to vomit. Nevertheless, no one will refuse to eat. Those tribe members who are not intended to consume flesh cry continually around the central mourners while the ceremony proceeds. By the time that the body has been eaten it is nearly dawn. The prevailing chill and semi-darkness are soon dissipated as the house of the dead man is set alight and ritually burned to ashes. Back in London, parents tremble over the latest tabloid editorial, wondering if the rock–mad teenager really will 'devour the very heart of our society' or simply consume themself in the heat of their own wild dancing.

We owe the above account to the anthropologist Beth A. Conklin.[7] Conklin carried out initial fieldwork among the South American Wari' in the 1980s, some twenty years after the tribe had been forced to abandon its ancient, cannibalistic funeral practices by the interference of government officials and Christian missionaries. Accordingly, she never witnessed the original ceremonies, instead gathering details from older tribe members.

As well as providing accounts of what occurred at Wari' funerals, the informants also explained why. There were three fundamental reasons. First, the cannibalism was compassionate: the body was eaten because the dead person's spirit wished this to happen. No mourner ever *wanted* to eat human flesh in any kind of purely animal, appetitive way. Indeed, as we have just seen, they at times forced down putrid flesh simply because they felt that they must satisfy the spirit of the dead. Secondly, the Wari' were horrified at the notion of imprisoning a corpse in cold, dank earth – something which they considered to be polluting. They suffered genuine distress when forced to adopt this alien, essentially taboo practice, and may well have found it quite as revolting as a Londoner would to eat their dead mother or father. Thirdly, the body was eaten in order to soften the trauma of bereavement. As one Wari' man, Jimon Maram, told Conklin: "'when the others ate the body, we did not think longingly about the ones who died; we were not so sad'".[8]

Maram's explanation reminds us how much funeral rites can vary across time or continents. Where most of us are in many ways trying to *increase* the distance between ourselves and a dead friend or relative, the Wari' were quite literally closing that distance. And cannibalistic funeral rituals also seem to have varied considerably. As Conklin points out, most South American tribes probably did not engage in this practice at all. Those which did might consume bones, rather than flesh, grinding them down into a powder which could be mixed into honey or drinks. One obvious universal feature of such ceremonies is that they are thoroughly consensual; all those involved, including the deceased as living person or as spirit, agree not simply that the corpse may be eaten, but that it *must* be. This general agreement offers a knotty problem to opponents of cannibalism (at least, that is, if they are intelligent or thoughtful.) The prohibition imposed in the 1960s was a typically Christian attack on what is often called 'victimless crime' (compare, most notably, religious attitudes to sex, and particularly to homosexuality). Interestingly, it was just this vexed issue of consent which made the recent trial of Armin Meiwes such a complicated legal affair. As readers may recall, in March 2001, Meiwes killed and ate a fellow German, Bernd Jürgen Brandes, who willingly agreed to the whole arrangement, conscientiously taking a day off work and making his will before he kept the appointment.[9]

While the psychology of the Meiwes–Brandes case was clearly very complex, sexual desire of some kind was evidently a strong element. By contrast, tribal cannibalism was an intensely solemn and religious affair. (It lacked the selfishness, we might say, of either lust or greed.) Hence the carefully observed nuances of ritual involved: the firewood bundle must be ornately decorated; the wood itself must come from the village houses, 'leaving the thatched roofs sagging in tangible evidence of death's violation'. The seriousness of all these details was underlined when one Wari' man complained to Conklin that both missionaries and anthropologists were overly obsessed with the tribe's cannibalism, and thus neglected other elements of the mourning rites: '"eating was not all that we did! We cried, we sang, we burned the house, we burned all their things ... Write about all of this, not just the eating!"'[10] This criticism might well be likened to that of a Christian, who found that a bemused observer of the High Mass was obsessed only with the participants eating and drinking their God.

Funerary cannibalism was often closely tied to the spirit world. The Wari' themselves ate the corpse to please the spirit of the dead; they did not believe that the flesh *contained* any spiritual potency at all. But other tribes seem to have believed that they were indeed eating the souls of their deceased. They were quite literally 'incorporating' (re-embodying) the vital principle of the dead, in order that it should not be lost to the community.[11] Compare the South American Yanomami, as studied in the late twentieth century: '"when a child dies they consume it so thoroughly, even pulverizing the bones and drinking them down in plantain soup, that there is nothing left"'. (In a pre-industrial environment, pulverising an entire skeleton was probably much more difficult than digging a grave, and this alone gives some idea of the importance attached to such a practice.) Similarly, in the 1970s the Guiaca people of the upper Orinoco would cremate bodies, grind the half-burned bones, and mix these into plantain soup to be drunk, being '"very careful not to spill any of it"'.[12]

Given how strange such rituals may be to us, it is useful to offer another broad comparison. It has been claimed that – perhaps partly because of a history of unusually common famine cannibalism – China has evolved a particularly strong tradition of medicinal cannibalism. A medical compendium of 1578 cites thirty-five different human body parts or substances as remedies, and includes 'nail, hair, skin, milk, urine, urine sediments, gall, placenta and ... flesh'.[13] These cures look relatively bland, however, when we come to the treatments known as 'ko ku' and 'ko kan'. Drawing on the work of the Chinese scholar Yu Chun-Fang, Daniel Korn, Mark Radice and Charlie Hawes show that 'ko ku' was rooted in traditions of filial piety, deriving from the Tang Dynasty of the seventh to tenth century AD. Most reported cases of this practice in fact involved not a blood relation, but the daughter-in-law of an aged and sick man or woman. 'Typically, the devoted daughter-in-law would tie her arm or thigh very tightly with a piece of clothing'. Using a sharp knife, she would then 'quickly slice off a piece from her upper arm or upper thigh'. After this the flesh would be mixed with soup or gruel, and (according to folklore) a miraculous recovery would follow. An incidence of ko ku was recorded as late as 1987 – by which time, admittedly, the practice was no longer an accepted custom.[14]

In the unlikely event that you are ever asked to offer ko ku or ko kan to your ailing mother- or father-in-law, you would be well advised to choose the former. The latter involves not just self-mutilation of one's arm or thigh, but the self-accomplished removal of one's own liver. Incredible as this might seem, there are innumerable accounts of the practice, with the latest occurring as recently as the nineteenth century. Moreover: as Korn, Radice and Hawes rightly emphasise, surviving descriptions can be horribly convincing by their very detail:

> after bathing and worshipping, he took up the knife and aimed at the place where his liver and lung were located. Blood gushed out after one cut. The ribcage was exposed after the second cut. After the third and fourth cuts there was a resounding sound, and after the sixth cut the heart leaped out. Following the heart he groped for the lung and after the lung he groped for the liver. By then he nearly fainted because of the extreme pain. After a moment's rest he called his wife and told her quickly to cook the liver to serve his mother [probably a piece of liver, although the text didn't indicate so]. Not knowing what it really was, the mother ate it happily and soon became well.[15]

In many cases this was not *wholly* consensual, given the ignorance of the recipient (although, as this was a quite widespread tradition, one might imagine that the elderly would come to expect a very special kind of soup during times of illness). But it is surely hard to equate such behaviour with stereotyped negative images of the savage cannibal. It is difficult, indeed, to imagine a more striking instance of human courage and filial devotion. Modern organ donation, for example, seems rather like cutting off a lock of hair by comparison.

European awareness

The contemporaries of Elizabeth I or John Milton clearly knew nothing about Chinese cannibalism. As regards the Americas, most were evidently far more interested in the warlike, supposedly savage cannibal (whose subjects were thought to be very reluctant supper guests) than in consensual man-eating. But literate Europeans were aware of the existence of funerary cannibalism. They had heard the ancient Greek historian Herodotus (living in the middle of the fifth century BC) tell of the Essedones. This Scythian people, straddling the borders of Europe and Asia, were supposed to mix the flesh of a dead father with that of a sheep. This was served at a funeral banquet, while his skull was framed in gold and brought out once a year, at a festival held in the dead man's honour.[16] Some centuries later, the Roman encyclopedist Pliny the Elder (23–79 AD) embroidered this account, claiming that the skulls were not merely ornamental, but were also used as drinking bowls (presumably at the annual memorials).[17]

A similar tale concerned the Calatians (or Calantians), a people living in Asia Minor at the time of the Persian Emperor Darius (522–486 BC).[18] As the bishop Jeremy Taylor observes in 1660, Darius had 'asked the Indians upon what conditions they would be induced to burn the bodies of their fathers, and not to eat them'. The Calatians 'desired him not to speak to them of any such horrid impiety as to burn their fathers' carcasses, and to deny to them the honour of a natural burial in the bowels of their dear children'.[19] Note the crucial phrase here: 'a *natural* burial' …

This powerful horror of cremation already recalls the Wari' taboo concerning burial. And the resemblance grows when Taylor himself explains that 'custom is the genius or spirit of a man's actions … Custom is as nature'. As Conklin notes, when asked why they ate their dead, the Wari' would most frequently respond, 'thus was our custom'.[20] One commentator of 1665 describes endo-cannibalism as 'absolutely inhumane'.[21] But neither Taylor, nor the Scot, David Person, writing in 1635 of this form of 'honourable sepulchre', appear at all condemnatory.[22]

Were Renaissance Europeans also aware of endo-cannibalism in the newly discovered Americas? If they wanted to know, they had certainly stumbled on the right continents in 1492. Endo-cannibalism seems to have been more common in South America than in any other region (with Conklin noting reliably documented cases in Peru, Paraguay and southern Venezuela). The French writer André Thevet observed Brazilian cannibalism personally, when living there in the later sixteenth century. Thevet noted that the Tapuia people 'ate their own dead relatives to spare them the indignity of rotting in the earth'.[23] Again, this statement very closely echoes the attitude to burial found among the Wari' just a few decades ago. Thevet's remark, however, occurs in a work which was not published. His other writings, which were well known, tended to dwell on cases of violent, aggressive cannibalism.[24]

A few years later, in 1595, that great Renaissance adventurer, Sir Walter Raleigh, made his own pioneering journey down the Orinoco River in search of the fabled mountains of gold in El Dorado. In his account of the expedition, Raleigh tells of the people called the Arwacas, dwelling south of the Orinoco, who at their funerals, 'do … beat the bones of their Lords into powder', after which 'their wives and friends drink it all in their several sorts of drinks'.[25] It is difficult to detect any trace of hostility or revulsion in this plain statement. (Admittedly, Raleigh seems to have been unusually open-minded in his attitude to the Amazonian tribes he encountered, and often talks with respect or admiration of their vigour and nobility of bearing.[26])

A particularly striking case of consensual cannibalism occurred in New England in 1675. A letter sent from the colony to London in November tells of how a native Indian was executed by the colonists. While the condemned man was as yet 'half alive and half dead, there came an Indian, a friend of his, and with his knife made a hole in his breast to his heart, and sucked out his heart's blood. Being asked his reason therefore, his answer was: " … me be stronger as I was before, me be so strong as he and me too [i.e. as two men], he be very strong man before he die"'.[27] The Indian's response gives a particularly clear sense of one feature of tribal or magical cannibalism. Like Ficino, or those doctors and apothecaries using blood to restore the aged, this man believed that the most basic stuff of life could be sucked out of one human body and absorbed by another.

Occasionally, the contemporaries of Shakespeare could observe this kind of practice very close to home. As we have seen, Anglo-Irish relations were often far from easy around this time. In 1577, the poet Edmund Spenser watched the Irish rebel, Murrogh O'Brien, hung, drawn and quartered at Limerick. And he also saw 'an old woman which was his foster mother take up his head while he was quartered and sucked up all the blood running thereout, saying that the earth was not worthy to drink it, and therewith also steeped her face, and breast … crying and shrieking out most terrible'.[28]

Aggressive cannibalism

3 August 1492. The sun is rising over the European continent. From the harbour of Palos de Frontera in Spain, an enterprising Italian, Christopher Columbus, has just begun one of the most momentous voyages of history. Down in Rome, Innocent VIII, the alleged medical vampire of Infessura's reports, has been dead little more than a week. Meanwhile, over in an area which will presently receive the name of Brazil, a war party of the Tupinamba is re-entering its home village, following just one of its numerous conflicts with a neighbouring tribe. The procession is headed by a bold-looking, even haughty man, decorated with feathers from thigh to shoulder. He and the accompanying warriors have just paid a solemn visit to the cemetery outside the village, honouring the tribe's dead ancestors. The plumed man is taken to the house of a recently dead tribe's member, and given the bow and arrows of the deceased. He is also given the dead man's widow by way of a wife. He feasts on the finest meats available. Weeks pass. Columbus sails on. In Rome, the new pope, Alexander VI, is busy instating two of his 'nephews' as cardinals. The honoured warrior goes fishing and hunting with the other men of the tribe. He assists in its farming, and enjoys the company of his adopted wife. In April of 1493 they have a child. The man wears a necklace of shells, and at each new moon, one of the shells is removed.

In May, Alexander VI draws a line on a new world map. With breathtaking arrogance, this notorious stroke of the papal pen grants American territories on the west of it to Spain, and those on the east to Portugal. (Learning that most of the Portuguese territories happen to be mere expanses of seawater, the sharp-witted reader will rightly guess that Alexander himself was Spanish.) By this stage, the situation of the plumed man has shifted dramatically. He is surrounded by a vast formal assembly, comprising the entire tribe. The last of the shells around his neck has vanished. He is tightly bound with cords, held by two men some distance away. As they watch him, tribal elders gulp down millet beer in great quantities. The prisoner defies his captors with a volley of aggressive taunts. He is unafraid; they will suffer in their turn. Suddenly, two simultaneous actions seal his fate. In front of him one man lights a specially prepared fire. Beside him another raises a club. It swings down. Dead at the first stroke, the victim collapses just as the dry flames leap into the air. In a few hours' time, nothing remains of him but a cleanly picked skeleton. Every one of the vast gathering (numbering perhaps thousands) has had at least a tiny fragment of his flesh or organs. Women have consumed his entrails and his genitals. The child born to him by his new wife has also been eaten.

We have just witnessed a religious ceremony performed by the Brazilian Tupinamba. It was originally recorded by Thevet in the 1560s, and has been reproduced here from Frank Lestringant's invaluable study of cannibalism.[29] Despite appearances, the plumed man was not a Tupinamba leader. He may in a strange sense be described as an honoured guest. But he was also very definitely a prisoner of war. On his first entry to the village, and through all the long months which followed, he was in fact a captive. Why, then, was he allowed such a remarkable degree of freedom? As we saw, he entered the tribe at a very specific point, taking both the weapons and the widow of a recently dead man. And it does indeed seem that his chief role was to fill the gap left by the deceased. This, of course, does not easily explain the oddly prolonged captivity, and the way in which he engaged so thoroughly in all the activities of the host tribe.

One vital word helps us to pull these disparate scraps of the puzzle together: incorporation. As Lestringant has pointed out, the prisoner was, in every sense, incorporated into the tribe. He not only replaced the dead man in certain obvious ways, but was progressively absorbed into the community by leading its normal life and contributing to it, both practically and socially. Finally, he was quite literally incorporated into the tribe during the cannibalistic feast in which all participated.[30] As Lestringant further notes, among the Guarani of Paraguay this comprehensive ingestion was so important that even suckling infants would have a small amount of cannibal broth put into their mouths.[31]

We are now able to see both how and why this whole affair was organised. It was so systematic, patient, precise, and eminently social just because it was so meaningful for those involved. That impression is confirmed by a slightly earlier contemporary account. In 1550 the German adventurer Hans Staden was captured by the Tupinamba whilst hiring out his services as a gunner to the Portuguese. Although held for nine months by the tribe, Staden had the luck to survive his ordeal, and later wrote about it, sketching in numerous details about the ritual cannibalism of the Tupinamba in the process. Their prisoners would be deliberately mocked and beaten by women and children, in a way evidently designed to maximise a male warrior's sense of shame and dishonour.[32] There were ritual paintings and dances, and even the club which struck down the sacrificial victim was very carefully designed and painted.[33]

The same kind of respect for detail and order could be seen in broadly similar cannibalistic ceremonies, practised many miles north of the Tupinamba by tribes such as the Iroquois and Huron, in what would later become the Canadian province of Ontario. These tribes, observed with some care by Jesuit missionaries during the seventeenth century, also sacrificed and ate prisoners of war. As Peggy Reeves Sanday has shown, their fate was often far less easy than that of the Tupinambas' victim. The prisoner would be horribly tortured by his captors. Yet, at the same time, he too was being carefully 'incorporated'. Even as they tortured him, the Huron would refer to their victim as 'uncle'. Moreover, as Sanday points out, some prisoners of war 'were allowed to live and assume the rights and duties of the family members lost in war … In a fundamental sense it did not matter whether the victim was allowed to live or was tortured to death, because in either case the victim was physically incorporated into the community'.[34]

The social and religious character of the ritual is evident from the way that the aggressive participants might at one stage be '"howling at the tops of their voices … their eyes flashing with rage and fury"', while at another the watching Jesuits 'were struck by the fact that' the torturers' faces clearly expressed 'gentleness and humanity' toward their tormented captive.[35] Equally, the ceremony was very carefully controlled and prolonged, with the victim being intermittently revived so that he should not die before the appointed time. Despite suffering pain and exhaustion seemingly beyond the limits of human endurance, he himself would essentially co-operate in the whole proceeding because he shared certain basic religious beliefs with his tormentors. He must, for example, show extraordinary courage, knowing as he did that, at the conclusion of the tortures at daybreak, he was being watched by the sun god. The Iroquois, similarly, prized his valour because in eating him (and in particular his heart) they would gain his strength and courage.[36]

In such rituals qualities which we might see as at least partially abstract (strength and courage) can be transferred and physically absorbed – recycled within a kind of spiritual ecology. In the case of Fijian cannibals this notion was remarkably precise. They 'believed that the spirit of a body clung to a corpse for four days after death. Sacrificing and eating the body annihilated the spirit and prevented it from ascending to the spirit world and becoming a source of power and guidance to your enemies'.[37] Similarly, for the Orokaiva of the Pacific, cannibal victims were 'intended to compensate for the spirit of an Orokaiva man' killed during intertribal conflict.[38]

For certain cannibal tribes (including the Brazilian Wari'), it was possible to tyrannise one's enemies 'body and soul' in an entirely literal way. We find, then, that the religious side of aggressive cannibalism has a very precise focus. Once more, to eat the body is to eat the soul. But there is one further, crucial aspect of hostile cannibalism which we have not yet explored in detail. A wealth of evidence from different periods and different communities (including, as we will see, Renaissance Europe itself) shows that these practices were motivated by a fundamental antagonism towards outsiders. The degree of hostility involved here is so extreme that it is certainly tempting to use the word hatred. But, given the highly controlled, systematic nature of the Tupinamba, Iroquois and Huron sacrifices, it certainly cannot always be said that this involves wild or unthinking rage. It is very far from the behaviour of animals.[39] Rather, for the Tupinamba, the highly alien qualities of the outsider-victim mean that he must be treated very carefully. His oddly prolonged captivity and his inclusion in ordinary life reflect the difficulty of *successfully* absorbing someone who is initially very alien to the group he enters.

Hostility to alien communities is so fundamental just because it is vital to a tribe's sense of identity. To really know who you are, you must be vigorously aware of who you are not. This kind of oppositional identity is one of the chief sources of violence throughout history. Christians vs Jews; Catholic vs Protestant; white vs black; east vs west; sunnis against shias … The billions of lives that have been claimed by these tragic divisions have been murders founded not simply on practical competition for resources, but on fiercely ideological schisms. Thevet, the sixteenth-century Frenchman who observed the Tupinamba at first hand, gives a slightly skewed version of such psychology when he says that, despite abundance of natural goods, American tribes continually kill and devour one another due to 'a desire of vengeance'. This, he asserts, they have 'without any other reason or cause, but even like brute beasts, that cannot agree one with another by no honest means'. As tribesmen supposedly told him, 'they have been always their mortal enemies ... say they ... we have eaten your parents, also we will eat you, with many other threatenings ... The greatest vengeance that these wild men use, and that seemeth to them most cruel, is to eat their enemies'.[40]

Thevet's account of aggressive cannibalism is slightly distorting. It over-emphasises the irrationality of aggressive cannibalism ('like brute beasts'), and gives no thought to its religious dimension. (Animals do not eat one another for psychological reasons.) But the simple statement 'they have always been [our] mortal enemies' has a familiar ring. Why did the Wari' eat their dead? 'Thus was our custom'. It was always this way. This seemed natural and inevitable to those involved in it. And many anthropologists would probably agree that this kind of fiercely narrow-minded attitude to outsiders is indeed very common among small, closed, isolated communities – whether the Tupinamba of the fifteenth century, or an Oxford college in the twentieth. We will see in a few moments how such antagonism could flourish all too vigorously among the supposedly civilised Europeans of Christendom. In our own era cannibalism has been credibly recorded as a deliberate aggravation of violence in Liberia and Rwanda. In the latter case, the extremes of hatred hardly need emphasising: in 1994, perhaps as many as 500,000 Tutsis were slaughtered by extremist Hutus, in an ethnic conflict which had a fundamentally tribal basis. Let us briefly examine one other remarkable case of aggressive cannibalism before we turn to the question of European attitudes to the New World.

Some time in the later 1960s, not long after the end of Wari' cannibalism, and while the Beatles and the Stones were gaining an even more terrifying grip on the heart of 'all that we hold dear' in Western civilisation, China was in the throes of its own Cultural Revolution – something which went far beyond music, sex and drugs. Here the ideology was that of communism, and the source of hatred derived from notions of class. All across the country, 'class enemies' were being denounced and often slaughtered. But, as the authors of *Cannibal* rightly note, this was a time when 'just killing the class enemy was not enough to express class hatred'. At a school in Wuxuan Province, students turned against their teachers. The Head of the Chinese Department, Wu Shufang, was condemned as a class enemy and beaten to death. Another teacher was forced to cut out Shufang's liver, which was cooked in strips over a fire in the school yard. Before long the cannibalism had spread, until "'the school yard was full of the smell of students cooking their teachers'". In another incident a young man was attacked and tortured because he was the son of an ex-landlord. While still just alive, he was bound to a telegraph pole and taken down to the river. The attackers cut open his stomach and removed his liver; the cavity was still so hot that they had to pour river water in to cool it. Once again, the 'liver of the landlord's son made a revolutionary feast for the villagers involved'. In all, some 10,000 people are thought to have taken part in cannibalism in these episodes, with up to 100 victims being eaten.[41] These fiercely guarded internal secrets were revealed by Zheng Yi, a former Red Guard member, now in permanent exile as a result.[42]

These episodes show that, while aggressive cannibalism almost invariably stems from violent antagonism to alien groups, such hatred does not have to be religious or even typically tribal in nature. Moreover, while for the Tupinamba cannibalism was an age-old custom, here the powerful boundary lines between opposing groups had been drawn only quite recently. The 'class enemy' was a relatively new outsider. This novelty may lead us to wonder if such attacks were not motivated simply by a desire to preserve revolutionary identity, but to actively recreate and reassert it in a highly tangible way. Sometimes, those who are most insecure about their identities can seek to defend them with the greatest ferocity.[43]

We have now gone a considerable way toward demythicising the legendary spectre of the cannibal. Without necessarily wanting to practise exo-cannibalism ourselves, we can begin to recognise that some degree of hostility to others is present in all of us. At certain moments, even if only unconsciously, all of us will probably feel a sense of bewilderment or anger toward alien people or groups whose behaviour is in some ways unacceptable or incomprehensible. Such divisions criss-cross every society like a kind of tense psychological grid, more or less visible, more or less vibrant, at certain flashpoints of conflict. Muslims and Christians; Socialists and Tories; young and old; men and women; drivers and cyclists; rival football supporters ... I myself am occasionally aware that I have had this kind of attitude toward George Bush and the strange assemblage of creatures who once voted him back into power. I did not want to eat them (I am a vegetarian, and mindful of my health) but I did have considerable difficulty in persuading myself that they were quite real – that they were complex, three-dimensional beings who believed in themselves quite as vigorously as I do. Having acknowledged this, we may perhaps be less surprised at the often ferociously maintained divisions and antipathies of Renaissance Europe – a realm in which the psychology of the cannibal was in fact dimly recognisable.

The cannibal in Europe

If by some strange chance we happened to have lost all purely factual records on early European contacts with the Americas, we would still be able to form a very clear idea of what the cannibal meant to the Christians of the Old World. Fascinating as he was, the cannibal made his home in numerous other forms of literature. Time and again this mythical demon flashes its teeth in moments of literary polemic. Whenever a writer or preacher wishes to conjure up the worst excesses of human behaviour, the word 'cannibal' is hurled like a kind of verbal hand grenade, producing an effect which is not always precise, but which certainly never lacks force. The cannibal is associated, either literally or metaphorically, with incest, witchcraft and the most lurid extremes of cruelty, violence or murder.[44] Even when used purely in isolation, the mere word itself must, in the time of Shakespeare and Milton, have had an impact which future generations could never quite appreciate. For, while the Renaissance had for some time known of those classical 'anthropophagi' such as the Essedones, the man-eater of the New World was to be honoured with a brand new name. 'Cannibal' was derived from 'Carib'. In native American languages, the letters *l*, *n* and *r* interchange across different dialects: hence it was perhaps only by a slight chance that English came to speak of the 'Caribbean' rather than 'Cannibean' islands (and hence, perhaps, Shakespeare's 'Caliban').[45] For various reasons the Caribbean in particular was thought to be the home of especially savage peoples. And so, in the earliest published accounts of this brave new world in the mid-sixteenth century, the very word 'cannibal' was peculiarly fused with these strange unexpected continents, almost as if it were a distinct species of flora, thriving only in the exotic rich soils of the Americas.[46]

Those mere three syllables, then, must for some time have had a special sonic and social vibration (perhaps not unlike the effect of the word 'punk' in seventies Britain). True, some European men may have had a grudging admiration for the sheer masculine skill and courage of warlike cannibal tribes (as the Spanish chronicler of the Indies, Gonzalo Fernández de Oviedo, pointed out, '*caribe* signifies "brave and daring"').[47] But on the whole, the cannibal's status was emphatically negative. Nor was he redeemed by the company he kept. In a court sermon of 10 March 1634, the bishop of Exeter, Joseph Hall, heaps together 'bloody Turks, man-eating cannibals', and 'mongrel Troglodites feeding upon buried carcasses' – throwing in for good measure those notorious Patavians who were supposed to habitually prostitute their own daughters. A few years before, in 1631, the preacher William Twisse had attacked the supposedly heretical notion that Christ died for *all* humanity, rather than for Christians alone, demanding rhetorically, 'even for Turks and Saracens, for Tartars and cannibals, not one of them excepted?'[48] In 1661, some twelve years after Charles I had been executed by Cromwell and the Parliamentarians, the Royalist John Gauden fuses religious, political and ethnic prejudices when he denounces the regicides as those 'ravening wolves' and eulogises his dead sovereign: 'this was the man, this the Christian, this the King, this the Saint, this the martyr, whom these Judases have betrayed, these Jews destroyed, these cannibals devoured'.[49]

Occasionally this negative association would appear as part of a kind of grudging complement. In 1674 Aunt Glegg's beloved Richard Baxter attacked a Catholic idolatry which outdid 'even cannibals and the most barbarous nations upon earth'.[50] In 1609, just four years after the Catholic plot to blow up both James I and the Houses of Parliament, the Lancashire minister William Leigh asserted that this infamous scheme had backfired not only because of its failure, but equally in terms of public relations: 'for instead of blowing up us, they have blown up themselves, and their religion … being blotted with one of the horriblest treasons … such as God and nature could never brook to be amongst the cruellest cannibals, Turks, or Scythians … '.[51] Similarly, the preacher John Scott claimed that the Gunpowder Plot was 'a villainy so foul and monstrous' that 'had the most barbarous cannibal in America been hired to act it', even he 'could not but have relented'.[52]

Needless to say, rhetoric of this kind was a pretty backhanded complement. The writer relied on the shared assumption that to be worse than a cannibal was a very bad thing indeed. Just now and then, the man-eater would be briefly allowed into the company of legitimate human beings. In 1599, for example, the poet Sir John Davies insisted that not only the Christians, Turks and Jews, but even 'the cannibal and tartar' recognised the immortality of the soul.[53] Still more surprisingly, in 1643 Roger Williams (the founder of Providence, New England) lamented that his neighbours, 'the Mauquaûogs, or men-eaters' favoured 'a delicious monstrous dish of the head and brains of their enemies'; yet still believed that this was 'yet ... no bar against God's call, and their repentance'.[54]

Clearly, however, Williams's attitude was an unusually charitable one. On the whole cannibals were deeply taboo for the Old World. Not only that, but at times they acted as a kind of magnet for some equally powerful taboos. In 1688 we hear of the Chirihuana, a Peruvian people who sought to outdo even the archetypal man-eaters of the Caribbean. Besides devouring their enemies, this nation exhibited a similar rapacity toward its own kin: 'they went naked, and promiscuously used coition without regard either to sisters, daughters or mothers'. Interestingly, the Spanish author retailing this claim briefly glances at the magical or religious significance of Chirihuana practices. Hearing that the tribe would cut the throats of their enemies and drink their blood, we find ourselves in familiar psychological territory. This is not merely savage terrorism, but that common tribal desire to consume an essence or quality (a spirit, strength, courage). Again, we are told of how the Chirihuana ate not just their enemies, but also 'the flesh ... of their own people, when they died'; after which, 'they lamented over their bones', which were carefully arranged and then 'buried ... in rocks, or caves, and the hollow of trees'. We can quickly recognise this as funerary, consensual cannibalism. The Spanish author of 1688, however, blurs the practice in with the tribe's other 'barbaric' habits, automatically assuming that his readers will share his own revulsion. Moving on to recount how the Chirihuana stubbornly resisted all outside attempts at moral improvement, he tells of the thwarted Spanish viceroy Francisco de Toledo, forced to abandon the region in despair. Carried in a litter by Spaniards and Indians, Toledo departed with the Chirihuana shouting 'curses and reproaches, saying, "throw down that old woman from her basket, that we may eat her alive"'.[55]

Perhaps surprisingly, there was yet one more cannibal horror which might claim to rival murder, witchcraft, incest or blood-drinking. In 1494 French armies celebrated their successful conquest of Naples in the city's brothels. Shortly afterwards, they returned to France carrying not just plunder and glory, but a peculiarly terrible new disease. In following decades and centuries, syphilis, or the pox, had an impact on Europe which can be justifiably compared to that of AIDs. Syphilis was terminal, hereditary, and disfiguring. Victims (among the more famous were William Davenant and Pope Julius II) were branded with painful sores and scars – hence 'pox', as in 'pock-marked'. If they were lucky, they lost only their hair. The disease could also devour their hands and feet, as well as their noses. Syphilis was the more horrific because of its novelty and its uncertain origins. It is an old joke that it was known as 'the French, Italian, or English disease' depending on one's nationality. But it was probably no accident that people were always determined to foist the cause of this sexual plague on outsiders, in a kind of negative tribute to the terror and incomprehension which it inspired.

At some point in the earlier history of syphilis, a particularly sensational rumour gave a further twist to its alien character. As Francis Bacon records, the French, in blaming the Italians for the disease, cited a report that 'at the siege of Naples, there were certain wicked merchants, that barrelled up man's flesh (of some that had been lately slain in Barbary) and sold it for tuna'. What better proof that cannibalism violated the most basic laws of nature? This tale is strikingly like the more recent urban myths as to the origin of AIDs, a disease allegedly produced by sexual intercourse with monkeys. Bacon himself took seriously the idea that 'upon that foul and high nourishment, was the original of that disease'. This, he admitted, 'may well be; for that it is certain, that the cannibals in the West Indies, eat man's flesh; and the West Indies were full of the pox when they were first discovered'.[56] With syphilis hitting Europe in the 1490s, people were not slow to point to the Americas as a source. But Bacon seems to go a little further, blaming not just the exotic new lands, but that which was thought to be one of their strangest and most definitive features. For some, syphilis was a result of cannibalism. An Italian amateur scientist, Giovanni Fiorevanti, even went so far as to test the theory by experiment. Having fed a dog on the flesh of another dog, he indeed found that the creature lost its hair, and soon had 'most filthy sores breaking forth' all over its body.[57]

For many Europeans cannibalism seems to have acted like a kind of imaginative black hole. It sucked in a variety of other transgressions or taboos and formed the boundary marker of a realm into which good Christians dare not enter. At this point the ordinary laws of society broke down so radically that one could only keep back at a safe distance, terrified and secretly fascinated, faintly sensing the pulse of unstable energy given off from within. Cannibalism was sufficiently dense and potent to take on a rhetorical life of its own. It encompassed murderers, witches, traitors and regicides – even, occasionally, moneylenders, or oppressive creditors, the latter being held, memorably, to boast that they would 'make dice from the bones' of their imprisoned debtors.[58] If Shylock's seemingly irrational hunger for the heart of Antonio in *The Merchant of Venice* is now the most famous example of such Christian paranoia, it was by no means the only one.

Savage Europe

The violence of social hierarchy

At this point we need to consider one of the most important ironies in the European image of the cannibal. As I suggested at the outset, the Old World and the New had far more in common than the former would like to admit. First: if we define tribalism as a social system which obsessively values a set of pervasive, intricate and minutely subtle rules, then there were many tribal features in European life. These could be found across and within distinct classes, at times involving bewilderingly detailed laws and codes. Secondly: at certain moments the underlying class antagonisms of these tribal, quasi-feudal worlds could produce some memorable instances of exo-cannibalism.

In Hungary in 1514, after the defeat of a serious popular uprising, the notoriously oppressive Hungarian nobility decided to make an example of the rebellion's leader, George Dósza:

while they had an iron throne and crown made for Dósza, his imprisoned footsoldiers were not given anything to eat for two weeks. Many perished. But some were still alive, half-mad with hunger when, on July 20 1514, our nobles instructed the gypsy executioners to make a big fire under the iron throne until it was white-hot. They had the white-hot iron crown for the Peasant King ready also. Then they placed our leader on the white-hot iron throne, put the white-hot iron crown on his head and forced his soldiers to eat his roasted flesh.[59]

Fabulous as this account may seem, it yet shares certain features with other well-documented modes of execution or cannibalistic terrorism. It has been claimed, for example, that the use of a white-hot (or at least red-hot) crown was a known mode of capital punishment during the Renaissance.[60]

Elsewhere, personal (rather than state) violence seems to have been at its very worst among the rich and titled – those who had the greatest stake in the obsessive tribal laws of the day. So, in Renaissance Italy, we find aristocratic revenge feuds erupting into a savagery that might appear sharply opposed to the surviving beauties of Rome or Florence. Piero Camporesi tells of a case in which one Andrea Orsi was 'dragged three times round the square by a horse' – a tactic still occasionally used (now by cars) in cases of racial murder in North America. Other victims of these Italian feuds were castrated, or had their severed penises thrust into their mouths. One man was reduced to a skeleton in the course of just a single sustained assault. And it is here that the tribal violence of the Old World most obviously begins to blur into that of the New. For, as Camporesi further explains, in one attack a disentrailed heart is bitten, while in another, "'lucky was the man who might grind the entrails between his teeth'". Finally, after gnawing Orsi's intestines his enemies proceeded to "'cut him up into small pieces to remove his fat because he was young, being probably twenty-eight years of age, tall and slim in build'". If Camporesi is right in assuming that the fat would be sold to doctors to cure 'nervous ailments' then we here witness not just gestures at cannibalism (grinding between the teeth) but a direct link between violence and the cannibalism of European medicine.[61]

Come the eighteenth century, the etiquette of Versailles seems to have involved more distinctions amongst the courtly initiate than Britain now acknowledges across all social classes.[62] Small wonder that, once this obscenely unjust society broke down, its violence should at times foreshadow the exo-cannibalism of 1960s China. In September 1789 the English press tells of a 'brave young officer', Monsieur De Belzunce, recently murdered in 'an excess of blind fury' at Caen. Various of his attackers are said to have been arrested, including a number of people, 'chiefly women … who ate his flesh and drank his blood'.[63] Recalling this in the nineteenth century, François-René de Chateaubriand wrote of how the crowd at Caen 'had their fill of slaughter and ate the heart of Monsieur de Belzunce'. In the light of more well-documented incidents, this claim is not improbable (and Chateaubriand's editor confirms that Belzunce's body was indeed 'torn apart' by his attackers).[64]

In August 1791 the aristocrat Guillin de Montet, a figure who seems to have been justly hated by the common people of Lyons, was killed when his castle was stormed and burned. A local butcher then cut up his body, and at least two people either ate or chewed parts of it. Reporting this in September 1792, the London *Evening Mail* presents De Montet as devoured entirely, claiming also that his attackers 'drank his blood'.[65] Whilst these details may have been invented, the scholar Paolo Viola has verified the occurrence of cannibalism through legal records of the affair.[66] A few weeks later, the *Evening Mail* insisted that the French had 'made pies of the flesh of the Swiss troops murdered on the 2nd of September'. A reliable eyewitness had confirmed this, adding that 'some of the mob drank their blood out of a can, and declared it was the best wine they had ever tasted'.[67]

The violence of religion

Typically, the tribal violence of the Renaissance (as opposed to the late eighteenth century) tended to be religious rather than overtly political. No cannibal tribe ever displayed more intolerance toward its neighbouring enemies than the two chief factions of Christianity toward one another. At the broadest level of religious politics, Protestant–Catholic relations in the mid–sixteenth century mirror the psychology of exo-cannibalism with uncanny precision. The implicit message of cannibal violence was this: we deny your identity; we deny your reality as human beings; and we will prove this by the way in which we treat you.[68]

In Europe such treatment often stretched the imaginable limits of violence. And, just occasionally, it also ran to outright cannibalism. In his famously enlightened essay of 1580, 'On Cannibals', the remarkable French thinker Michel de Montaigne argued that the cannibalism of the New World was in fact less horrific than the religious savagery of the Old. There was, Montaigne insisted, 'more barbarity in eating a man alive, than when he is dead'. Montaigne first glosses this by implying that victims of religious hatred have been effectively devoured by their torturers and executioners. He then adds that 'we have not only read, but lately seen' people roasted by degrees, and 'bit and worried by dogs and swine'. This was done while the victim was 'in perfect sense' – that is, alive and conscious – and indeed performed 'not amongst inveterate and mortal enemies, but neighbours, and fellow citizens, and which is worse, under colour of piety and religion'.[69]

Although Montaigne gives no further detail of these atrocities, it is clear that he refers to the Wars of Religion. Moreover, Lestringant informs us of a specific incident which closely echoes Montaigne's claims. The witness was Jean de Léry, a French traveller who had lived for some time with the Tupinamba in Brazil. If Léry was at first relieved to be home, he may soon have felt differently. Around the time of the St Bartholomew's Day Massacre, Léry saw a French Protestant executed by Catholics in Auxerre. Just as with the class hatred of the revolutionary Chinese students, mere killing was not enough to exhaust the profound hostility aroused by this heretic. He was not only ritually executed, but also had his heart 'plucked out, chopped in pieces, auctioned off, cooked on a grill and finally eaten with much enjoyment'.[70] In this extraordinary incident even the detail of the 'auctioning' seems to offer a distorted echo of New World ritual, both drawing out the whole process of cannibalism, and replacing a familiar habit of the Tupinamba or Iroquois with the accepted system of European monetary values. The victim is at once literally devoured by his enemies, and impersonally consumed in a process of exchange, effectively commodified into a piece of property.

In April 1655 the Protestants of the Piedmontese valleys were massacred by Catholic troops. At a glance, reports of associated atrocities can appear mythical. Yet these stories were substantiated by a high-ranking French soldier, Monsieur du Petit Bourg. In a lengthy English account, the clergyman Samuel Clarke tells of soldiers eating boiled human brains; tricking their comrades into consuming 'tripe' (in fact the breasts and genitals of one of the Protestant victims); and roasting a young girl alive on a pike. In this latter case, the flesh proved too poorly roasted to eat. But the soldiers who killed 'Daniel Cardon of Roccappiata' readily ate his brains, records Clarke, after 'frying them in a pan'; and having taken out his heart, would have fried this also, had they not been 'frighted by some of the poor peoples' troops ... coming that way'.[71]

In making comparisons, it is easy to push them too far. Finally, we have to preserve the differences between cultures as well as drawing out similarities. Habitual cannibalism of a ritual kind was not practised in the Old World. And yet, certain shrewd contemporary thinkers admitted that the parallels were indeed strong. Perhaps still more discomforting was the feeling of shrewder observers that, if New World tribes were at times more savagely transgressive, they yet remained utopias of social justice by comparison with London, Paris and Madrid. Such contrasts were underlined with memorable irony when missionaries brought a small party of Tupinamba tribesmen to France in 1562. Already bewildered by the reigning monarch, the then twelve-year-old Charles IX, the Tupinamba were probably also struck by the general devastation of their host city: Rouen had, after all, just been forcibly wrested from Protestant soldiers by royal armies. But most of all, the Brazilians were 'taken aback by the juxtaposition of rich and poor, and wondered how the latter "could endure such injustice without taking the others by the throat and setting fire to their houses"'.[72]

Meanwhile, a form of cannibalism was being practised all across Europe. It was supported by patients, physicians, apothecaries and merchants. How was this possible? Given how heavily tabooed cannibalism was for Europeans and how they treated many native peoples (in the Americas and elsewhere), the stance of the Old World, around 1600 or 1700, must rank as one of the biggest, most impressive acts of hypocrisy in world history. We have already begun to close the gap between the supposedly 'civilised' realms of Florence, Madrid, Wittenberg and London, and the nominally savage worlds of Peru or Brazil. Another piece in the puzzle facing us can be fitted into place if we now look more closely at European attitudes to New World cannibalism.

The raw and the cooked

The distinction between 'the raw and the cooked' was first coined by the French anthropologist Claude Lévi-Strauss.[73] The opposition is one which can work literally (raw food versus cooked food) and symbolically. In the second case, another way of seeing the idea is this: the raw is associated with nature, and the cooked with culture. Given that this last word is often used rather loosely, referring to what is broadly 'high culture', it is useful to appreciate that Lévi-Strauss had a far more democratic idea of 'culture'. In one sense, Lévi-Strauss's culture is simply all the things which humans do with the raw materials of nature. Here, the definition given by the composer and musician Brian Eno offers us a fairly snappy formula. Culture, for Eno, 'is everything we do which we don't have to do'. We need to eat, but not nouvelle cuisine. We need to dress, but not in designer clothes.[74] Culture puts a distance between us and nature. Certain animals probably have more culture than we might at first suspect; but it still seems fair to say that on the whole it is a distinctively human thing.

There again: once we have stopped deferring to familiar cultural hierarchies (Shakespeare is better than Woody Allen, Bach is better than the Beatles) we are likely to start noticing that culture is nothing if not arbitrary. We do it this way, they do it that way. Even within modern Europe, for example, an English person visiting Greece can be surprised at a number of basic differences: not least the fact that, when another car flashes its headlights at a narrow bridge it doesn't mean 'come through', but rather, 'Wait – *I'm* coming through'. How does this relate to Old World and New World relations? We can well imagine that European Christians could be tempted to take the attitude of the frustrated English motorist (or the frustrated Greek motorist in England). The strange cultural habits of the New World are not just different and interesting. Rather, they are in the end different and *wrong*. In many cases, Shakespeare's contemporaries evidently did take this stance. The grim tales of European inhumanity post-Columbus already show us where such an attitude could lead. Once you start denying someone's humanity, then it becomes much easier to do all sorts of bad things to them. To put this another way: if culture is a distinctively human thing, and yet highly varied across different human groups and eras, then it can sometimes be all too easy to deny that a particular group *has* culture. In the same breath, the observer has then necessarily begun to deny their humanity.

In reality, of course, ritual cannibalism, is clearly, emphatically *un*necessary from a practical, animal, merely nutritional viewpoint. And it is, therefore, eminently cultural. Some recent authors indeed go so far as to state that, in Fiji, 'the origin of cannibalism was ... the origin of culture'.[75] The point becomes still clearer if we contrast ritual and famine cannibalism. For much of history the latter has been a grim, if sporadic reality, and one not merely limited to shipwrecks or plane crashes. In an Italian famine of 450 AD parents supposedly ate their children.[76] In a Restoration sermon William Barton recalled the English famine of 1316, when 'men did eat one another, and thieves newly brought into the jail were torn in pieces and eaten half alive, by them that had been longer in'.[77] In 1594, during the siege of Paris by Henri IV, an emergency famine committee agreed that bread should be made from bones from the charnel house of the Holy Innocents. (It was available by mid-August, but those eating it apparently died).[78] In 1641 the preacher Stephen Marshall laments the horrors of the Thirty Years War then still in progress, claiming that in Germany, 'a field of blood', people again ate their dead children in sheer desperation.[79] On one occasion, moreover, in late 1636, in the village of Steinhaus near Hornebach, a woman allegedly lured a girl of twelve and a boy of five into her house, 'killed them both, and devoured them with her neighbour'. In Heidelberg around this time men were said to 'have digged out of the graves dead bodies, and ... eaten them', while one woman 'was found dead, having a man's head roasted by her, and the rib of a man in her mouth'.[80] In Picardy during this conflict, the Jesuit G.S. Menochio saw '"several inhabitants"' so crazed with hunger that they '"ate their own arms and hands and died in despair"'.[81] In 1761, in what was then still the cannibal territory of Canada, three Anglo-Americans were killed by Indians 'in revenge for an Indian boy that the famished trio had killed and eaten'.[82]

Nothing could have been more grimly, brutally necessary than famine cannibalism. It was the triumph of nature over culture. It had no particular meaning, and in warfare it was more generally the product of social chaos and disintegration – an archetypal case of the extremes brought about by the excesses of 'civilised' societies. (The 1594 incident, for example, occurred during conflict between Protestants and Catholics in the same country.) Clearly, this was very much 'raw cannibalism'.

And it was in fact too raw for even the most hardened New World traveller to swallow. Lestringant tells of how Léry – that veteran of cannibal society – adjusted himself to the man-eating of the Tupinamba, but came down to earth (again) with a vicious bump on returning to Europe. With Protestant–Catholic wars now raging across the continent, the French town of Sancerre suffered an especially prolonged siege in 1573. In one starving family, a small girl died. Soon after, the elderly grandmother persuaded the child's parents to eat her. The grandmother was later condemned and executed. Having seen a good deal of cannibalism in Brazil, Léry found himself confronted with the dead girl's butchered carcass. At this point, his whole body made its own judgement. For him, this was very different from the meaningful rituals of the Tupinamba, and he spontaneously vomited at the sight.[83]

Famine cannibalism was not the only type which one might contrast with that of the carefully systematic Tupinamba or Huron. Those Christians who wished to familiarise the Americans tended to divide potentially redeemable tribes from those who were allegedly beyond help or salvation. This was sometimes practically convenient, for purposes of trade. Its ideological convenience lay in the way that 'good Americans' could then be rescued from especially warlike or cannibal neighbours. But European observers went further. New World cannibalism itself was internally divided. The cooked version, as we have seen, was well regulated, controlled, and culturally meaningful.

What exactly was 'raw cannibalism'? In one sense, it was quite literally that: something practised by those tribes who devoured raw human flesh. Emphasising how some Europeans at least tacitly admitted the cultural status of ritual cannibalism, Lestringant offers the Brazilian tribe known as the Ouetecas as a particularly notorious contrast. Its members ate humans raw, and essentially treated them *only* as food.[84] There was no symbolic or social meaning involved. Other cases were also known. In 1666 a French *History of the Caribby Islands* was translated into English. It claimed that 'the inhabitants of the Country of Antis' in South America, were 'more cruel than tigers'. The Antis would eat a lowly prisoner of war in a quite ordinary way, or 'sell them in the shambles'. But,

> if he be a person of quality, the chiefest among them meet together, with their wives and children, to be present at his death. Then these unmerciful people having stripped him, fasten him stark naked to a post, and cut and slash him all over the body with a sort of knives and razors made of a certain stone, such as may be flint ... In this cruel execution they do not presently dismember him, but they only take the flesh from the parts which have most, as the calf of the leg, the thighs, the buttocks, and the arms; that done, they all pell-mell, men, women, and children, dye themselves with the blood of that wretched person; and not staying for the roasting or boiling of the flesh they had taken away, they devour it like so many cormorants, or rather swallow it down without any chewing ... Thus the wretch sees himself eaten alive, and buried in the bellies of his enemies ... The women adding yet somewhat to the cruelty of the men, though excessively barbarous and inhumane, rub the ends of their breasts with the blood of the patient, that so their children may suck it in with their milk.

The utterly raw savagery of the Antis region has been partly imposed or constructed by the French author César Rochefort. He fails to note that the status of the victim is important, or that the rite broadly parallels that of the Iroquois, which tested the courage of the condemned man. For, 'if these inhumane executioners have observed, that amidst all the torments' the prisoner had 'expressed the least sense of pain' they would then 'break his bones ... and cast them into some nasty place, or into a river, with an extreme contempt'.[85]

Clearly, though, the affair is too raw for most people's taste. The victim is not only uncooked, but alive (again, the way he must watch himself consumed matches the European traitor's death, and thus gives the custom some symbolic status).[86] Participants, including women and children, appear to spontaneously bathe themselves in his blood.[87] Even the way in which they (allegedly) gulp flesh without chewing seems to intensify the quality of raw, animalistic appetite. The consumption lacks not only the mediation of culture, but even that of the teeth.[88]

In 1691 the poet Thomas Heyrick evoked the 'barbarous cannibals' of the Amazon, people who were supposed to lay their 'bloody teeth ... on men's entrails' and to devour the 'yet-quaking members' of living victims.[89] And raw cannibalism might sometimes be found (or claimed) beyond the Americas. So the geographer Samuel Clarke, in 1657, condemns the habits of those Africans dwelling on the Cape of Good Hope because they, too, 'eat men alive, or dead'. Here the issue of cooking is unclear, but Clarke adds that they indeed eat the 'raw puddings' or guts of animals, and do not even hunt, merely consuming the dead whales or penguins which they find by chance.[90]

The idea of raw meat as food was evidently a potent one. A dictionary of 1598 quite precisely distinguishes 'antropophago ... a devourer or eater of men', from the 'cannibal ... a man that eats man's flesh or raw flesh'. The implication is clear: raw flesh of *animals* can be as bad as cooked human flesh. So, in the 1611 edition of the dictionary, 'antropophago' is 'an eater of men' and the cannibal has become 'a feeder' solely 'on man's raw flesh'.[91] In 1634 the writer Francis Meres went further, implying that the eating of raw meat was worse (or more fundamental) than consumption of human flesh: 'those barbarous people called cannibals feed only upon raw flesh, especially of men' – this diet being so habitual that 'if they happen to eat a piece of roasted meat, commonly they surfeit of it and die'.[92]

We have already caught a glimpse of how such tribes might effectively degrade themselves, not only by *lacking* culture, but by violating other basic, near universal cultural norms. So Rochefort finds incest to be rife among the Chirihuana, who are equally raw in their utter nakedness. Similarly, the raw bestiality of the Africans extends, for Clarke, to all aspects of their lifestyle: 'they have no spark of devotion, no knowledge of God, heaven, hell, or immortality; no place of worship, no day of rest, no order in nature, no shame, no truth, no ceremony in births, or burials'.[93] The Ouetecas, for Léry, are no better. They not only lack society and culture, and eat flesh raw 'like dogs and wolves'; they are also fundamentally opposed to culture in general, refusing to trade with the Europeans or even their neighbours. And – neatly symbolising the profound gulf of incomprehension across which Léry views them – we find that, for all the Europeans' impressive ability with other American languages, that of the Ouetecas stubbornly defies all translation.[94]

In the New World, the raw cannibal could act as the furthest point of strangeness or repugnance, along a line which ranged from 'civilised' Protestant Christendom through various stages of increasing wildness. In doing so, this figure helped to soften and even familiarise other cannibals, as well as American tribes in general. With this in mind, we can now readdress a central question of this story: just how was medicinal cannibalism able to thrive for so long in Christian Europe? The mummies of Egypt, wrapped in the long dry glow of time, were not so raw as any ordinary corpses. The mummies of Arabia (those luckless travellers drowned in sandstorms) were at least physically distant in their origins. But the fresh blood, the liquefied fat or flesh of criminals must seem pretty raw to us. To put it another way: they seem, quite simply, disgusting. Most of us would never touch these substances, let alone swallow them. We, however, have come a long way from the days of Donne or even of Dr Johnson. Before modern medical science, few people could afford to be so easily disgusted. All too often, it must have been a case of: swallow this, or death will swallow you. Thus far, the present history may not have been entirely pleasant. But the reader should be warned that it is now about to become wholly filthy.

5

DIRTY HISTORY, FILTHY MEDICINE

What does corpse medicine look like when set against the typical medical ingredients, and the experiences of illness, pain, and death found in the early modern era? What does it look like when compared to people's experiences of what many of us would now find intolerably disgusting? By exploring these questions we are able to get a clearer sense of why corpse medicine needed to exist, and how it was able to endure for so many decades.

Medicine before science

An apprentice's life in early modern London was typically not an easy one. And yet, if you were a youthful assistant at one of the apothecaries, there is a good chance that matters were a little different. However dark and cold the morning on which you entered to begin sweeping out and re-laying the fire, you would never fail to experience a certain subtle thrill. Something like religious wonder warmed your chilly bones as the unmistakable atmosphere of the Bucklersbury shop enfolded you. Of what was this atmosphere composed? On innumerable shelves and in assorted jars, detectable by smell, sight, labelling, or merely through long memory of physical position, there could be found

> the fat, grease, or suet of a duck, goose, eel, bear, heron, thymallos ... dog, capon, beaver, wild cat, stork, coney, horse, hedgehog, hen, man, lion, hare, pike ... wolf, mouse of the mountains ... hog, serpent, badger ... bear, fox, vulture ... a dog's turd, the hucklebone of a hare and a hog, East and West bezoar ... stone taken out of a man's bladder, vipers' flesh ... white, yellow, and virgin's wax, the brains of hares and sparrows, crabs' claws, the rennet of a lamb, kid, a hare, and a calf ... the heart of a bullock, a stag, a hog, and a wether; the horn of an elk, a hart, a rhinoceros, an unicorn; the skull of a man,

killed by a violent death ... the tooth of a boar, an elephant, and a sea-horse, ivory, or elephant's tooth, the skin a snake hath cast off, the gall of a hawk, bullock, a she goat, a hare, a kite, a hog, a bull, a bear, the cases of silk-worms, the liver of a wolf, an otter, a frog ... the guts of a wolf, and a fox, the milk of a she ass, a she goat, a woman, an ewe, a heifer ... pearls, the marrow of the leg of a sheep, ox, goat, stag, calf, common and virgin honey, musk, mummy, a swallow's nest, crab's eyes, the omentum or caul of a lamb, ram, wether, calf, the whites, yolks, and shells of hens' eggs, emmets' eggs, bone of a stag's heart, an ox leg ... the inner skin of a hen's gizzard ... the pizzle of a stag, of a bull, fox lungs, fasting spittle, the blood of a pigeon, of a cat, of a he goat, of a hare, of a partridge, of a sow, of a bull, of a badger, of a snail, silk, whey, the suet of a bullock, of a stag, of a he goat, of a sheep, of a heifer, spermaceti, a bullock's spleen ... the turds of a goose, of a dog, of a goat, of pigeons, of a stone-horse, of a hen, of swallows, of men, of women, of mice, of peacocks, of a hog, of a heifer, the ankle of a hare, of a sow, cobwebs, water shells ... the hoof of an elk, of an ass, of a bullock, of a horse, of a lion, the piss of a boar, of a she goat, of a man or woman that is a maid, and that is not a maid, the moss on a man's skull,

and, finally, 'zibeth'.[1] We will hear more about some of these substances below. A few of the more puzzling can be briefly glossed here. The thymallos is a kind of fish. The bezoar stone was a fabled antidote against poison. It was thought to be formed out of poisonous fluids which dripped from the eyes of a male deer, before solidifying into a petrified state.[2] Spermaceti was the fat of the sperm whale. The zibeth was the civet cat, from whose anal glands chemists would make the perfume known as musk.[3] (Hence the plea of the deranged King Lear, following a particularly wild outburst against womankind: 'give me an ounce of civet, good apothecary, to sweeten my imagination'.[4]) Readers happy about using the anal glands of a cat should perhaps be warned, however, that 'zibethum occidentale' could also sometimes refer to human excrement.[5]

This list (taken, we should note, from the élite *Pharmacopeia* of the physicians) is far from exhaustive. What might you do with these or other ingredients of the day? A brief survey is no less arresting than the list seen above. At the end of the century, for example, the lawyer and physician John Jones speculated that the sperm of male animals was a reputed opiate.[6] (If we wonder how he obtained this, we might be no less baffled at how apothecaries obtained the teeth of sea horses, or 'the piss of a boar'.) Although in France in 1617 'René Moreau [d.1656] ruled out of court' as medicines 'not just ... gold and rubies but ... the palpitating heart of the turtle', we can imagine that he did not persuade everyone.[7] In the same country in the previous century, the highly esteemed physician Jean Fernel credited the apparently quite general belief that 'eating the still palpitating heart of a swallow confers memory and intelligence'.[8] Edward Topsell's 1607 encyclopedia of animal life had its own sub-section on 'The Medicines of a Wolf', noting among other things that 'a wolf being sodden alive until the bones do only remain, is very much commended for the pains of the gout', whilst 'a live wolf steeped in oil and covered with wax, is also good for the same disease'.[9]

The blood of numerous animals was prescribed for a range of complaints. For erysipelas (inflammation of the skin) you should 'take the blood of a hare ('tis best if killed by hunting in March)' and apply it to the patient with a linen cloth.[10] For poor eyesight John Banister recommended bathing the eyes with fennel water and pigeon's blood. For 'any bloody suffusion in the eye' he also suggested a mixture of several ingredients, two of which were hen's blood and human breast milk.[11] Some of these eyebaths may have worked. In 1547 the Italian sculptor Benvenuto Cellini had a shard of metal fly into his eye while he was working. A surgeon presently laid Cellini down flat, cut the veins of two live pigeons, and dripped blood into the affected eye. In two days the chip had loosened and was removed, and the eye was saved.[12]

Epilepsy

We have seen that blood featured in some quite memorable cures for the falling sickness. Those studying the history of this disease have indeed noted that there is very little which epileptics, at one time or another, have not been required to swallow. The twelfth century mystic Hildegard of Bingen (1098–1179) cited a curative recipe which included four parts of mole's blood. This was because the mole 'sometimes shows himself and sometimes hides' – just like epilepsy ... [13] You could eat the heart of a wolf. Your doctor could 'take a frog and split him down the back with a knife'. You would then 'extract his liver and wrap it up in a cabbage leaf, and reduce it to a powder in a sealed pot, and give it to the epileptic to drink with the best wine'.[14] (Sceptics should note that Frederick IV, elector Palatinate, was cured by a remedy made from green frogs).[15] Rather more exotically, you might consume the liver of a vulture, pulverised and drunk with the creature's blood for nine days. You could hang a dog's hairs round your neck, or eat 'the gall still warm from a dog who should have been killed the moment the epileptic fell in the fit'.[16] Equally, 'the brain of a weasel dried, and drunk with vinegar, doth help them that have the falling sickness'.

You could wear an amulet (basically almost anything, hung around the neck or under the armpit, or elsewhere against the skin).[17] As Keith Thomas points out, Elias Ashmole 'wore three spiders to counteract the ague'; while Pepys hung a hare's foot around his neck against cholic.[18] One amulet involved 'the right hind hoof of an elk, worn in a ring so that it touches the skin'.[19] Another required wood from the elder tree. The elder in question must, though, have been 'growing above a willow' (this seems to mean roughly 'out of'). This kind of elder, according to some, had itself been produced by 'the putrefied corpse of an epileptic sparrow' – so that the cure had a certain logic to it.[20] If you were an epileptic man, you could get yourself castrated (something still being reported around 1850, and recommended by the pioneering surgeon Lawson Tait in 1880). You could eat the testicles of a bear, pulverised camel's brain, a young dog, maggots from a rotting sheep's nose, or earthworms during coitus (yours, not theirs). You could (as we have seen) drink the blood of a cat, as well as the urine of a black horse, the blood of your father or mother, or wine with woodlice in it. Leo Kanner, compiler of these last few remedies (and many more besides) notes that a German innkeeper's wife was still selling this last beverage as a remedy in 1925.[21]

For epileptics in particular, corpse medicine may have seemed a reasonable and quite readily available choice of cure. The hearts of wolves and the livers of vultures may indeed be tasty, but in England even the most resourceful butcher or poacher would surely name you a high price at most times of year. Dogs would have been less scarce. But we can well imagine that they developed a shrewd instinct for trouble if they ever sensed someone on the verge of an epileptic fit. (The trick would be, presumably, to run and avoid the doctor, rather than running to fetch him.) Some of these cures date back well into the Middle Ages. But many clearly survived into the seventeenth century (and probably longer among the rural poor). Some way into the age of Dr Johnson and George II epileptics were advised by the educated to take human afterbirth and navel string, or dried menstrual blood.[22]

However misguided in detail some of these cures might be, the general principle behind them made a certain sense 300 or 400 years ago. You were trying to get nature on your side. All too often, nature seemed to be out of control, and to really bear you some serious grudges. 'Nature' did not mean a blissful release from urban pressure and dirt. It was not something which you must protect from the toxic wastes of modern industry. Frequently, nature stank, and it was trying to kill you.

Plague

Shakespeare was born in a plague year. As Park Honan points out, the epidemic reached Stratford by 11 June, when the playwright was just a bare few weeks old. Come September, one in fifteen of his parish was infected.[23] Perhaps the infant genius was particularly tough. Perhaps there was a specially alert and protective cat darting about the Shakespeare household, cracking the necks of brown rats before they could get very close to that sacred cradle. We will never know for certain if we owe this remarkable collection of plays to such an animal. But Shakespeare certainly survived some horrific plagues in later life. In the years 1592 and 1593, around 20,000 Londoners died during the worst outbreaks of the late sixteenth century. In 1603, by the time that he had written *Romeo and Juliet*, *Hamlet* and *Twelfth Night*, the plague struck again with still greater savagery. Over 30,000 perished in all, and September alone saw 3,000 deaths.[24] After a surprisingly unseasonal outbreak in January 1609 the plague slumbered for some time, returning with a vengeance in 1625, when over 35,000 died of it. 1636 was also a bad year, with more than 10,000 fatalities. There was again a merciful lull in the years of the Civil War and Cromwell's protectorate, before the notorious visitation of 1665 – this itself of course being purged in part by the Great Fire of 1666.[25]

It may be fair to say that the sheer lack of medical progress in this area was reflected in one of the most enduring and successful responses to plague outbreaks. If you could afford to, you simply fled London altogether. In 1603 the Royal Court, far from stoically honouring a communal early modern 'spirit of the blitz', merely ran and kept running, galloping from Oatlands to Richmond, to Woodstock, South-ampton, Winchester, and finally to Wilton, some eighty miles from London.[26] As F.P. Wilson vividly records, the city was eerily silent during the bleak summer of this terrible year. A survivor recalled how, at one point in August, there suddenly appeared one single ghostly coach. It was covered entirely with the medicinal herb rue ('to keep the leather and nails from infection'); and the horses' nostrils were 'stopped with herb-grace'.[27]

If you could not leave, nominal remedies were certainly plentiful. For the rich, there was unicorn's horn, taken as powder (an entire horn, owned by Queen Elizabeth, was supposed to be worth £10,000). If you were poorer you could make a plaster from onion, butter, mallows and garlic, and lay it warm against a sore. Onions were especially popular because they were absorbent, and so would soak up poisonous vapours. Garlic, meanwhile, was powerful in this and many other ways (partly because of its potent smell). Long before it became standard protection against vampires, it was widely held to cancel the force of a magnet (and thus to interfere with mariners' compasses).

In chapter two we heard Christopher Irvine stating that 'the arse of a hen plucked bare, and applied to the biting of a viper, freeth the body from venom'.[28] This last cure echoes plague therapies going back at least some decades. Plucking feathers from a live chicken, you held the bare part to your plague sore until the bird died. You then used another live bird (and possibly a third) until you reached one which sur-vived. This bird's deliverance indicated that the plague spirits had been fully drawn out of you.[29] Some time around 1612 Bosola in *The Duchess of Malfi* gets his point across forcefully by assuring an old lady: 'I would sooner eat a dead pigeon taken from the soles of the feet of one sick of the plague, than kiss one of you fasting'.[30] With Irvine asserting various uses of spiritual transfer in 1656, we can imagine that such cures would have been frequently attempted in the notorious plagues of 1665 and '66. Yet even before this, the sheer range of therapies aimed to cure or prevent plague strongly suggests that, for some, there was nothing which was not worth trying.[31]

So, along with numerous roots, flowers, seeds or spices, you might take 'the flesh of vipers, mummy … quails, thrushes, hart's-horn, unicorn's-horn, bezoar … ivory … emerald, ruby, carbuncle, pearls, coral', or gold or silver. For pains of the belly incited by plague, you could apply a plaster which included frankincense, dragon's blood, mummy, and nutmeg oil.[32] Clearly, these various gems, and unicorn's horn, would have been very much more expensive than mummy. There again, if you were rich and believed in the unicorn, then your sense of wonder very probably extended to the curative potency of the human body. And finally, given that all ultimately rested in the hands of God, why not try whatever came to hand, and hope that the Almighty would assist the cure? If God left a physician such as Edward Bolnest in London in 1665, after most doctors had fled, he surely meant you to take advantage of the corpse medicines which this brave altruist could supply.[33]

The sweating sickness

It is hard now to really imagine the social chaos and trauma of severe plague outbreaks. Perhaps the best modern fictional resemblance occurs in Danny Boyle's 2002 film *28 Days Later*, with its bleak apocalyptic scenarios and violent social disintegration. But the plague at least gave many people some bare chance of preparing remedies, or of simply composing themselves for a good pious death. In 1485, just before the coronation of Henry VII, England was hit by an entirely unfamiliar disease whose combined ferocity and speed of attack are comparable to a widespread epidemic of SARS or Ebola. Its horrors still seem fresh decades later, as recalled in 1552 by the physician John Caius. Where the plague might take between four and fourteen days to decisively claim its victims, the sweating sickness

> immediately killed some in opening their windows, some in playing with children in their street doors, some in one hour, many in two it destroyed, and at the longest, to them that merrily dined, it gave a sorrowful supper. As it found them so it took them … and in one house sometime three sometime five … sometime more sometime all, of the which, if the half in every town escaped, it was thought great favour.[34]

Unlike syphilis, 'Sudor Anglicus', or 'the English Sweat', was acknowledged as a peculiarly Anglo-Saxon affliction. First recorded in Shrewsbury in mid-April 1485, the sweating sickness spread through Chester, Coventry and Oxford, and reached London by 7 July, moving east and north in August and September. As Roy Porter notes, the English sweat returned in 1507, 1528, 1551, and 1578. According to the physician Thomas Cogan, during that penultimate recurrence of mid-century 'there died … within six days space … eight hundred persons, and most of them men in their best years'.[35] And this, incidentally, was merely in London and its immediate neighbourhood.[36]

The hand of death

To plague and the English Sweat we must add tuberculosis, smallpox, and the all too frequent cot or infant deaths which have come down to us in the bare outlines of baptismal and burial records. For centuries smallpox hit rich and poor, young and old, with either fatal or permanently disfiguring results. As we have seen, Elizabeth I was scarred after contracting the disease in 1562, while in September 1660 smallpox claimed the life of Charles II's youngest brother, Henry, and his sister Mary.[37] It has been claimed that by the Restoration the disease 'had overtaken the Plague, leprosy and syphilis' as the greatest killer within Europe.[38] Right up until Edward Jenner introduced vaccination in 1798, medicine remained largely powerless against this durable scourge. There were especially severe outbreaks in 1641, 1695, 1718–19, 1733–39, 1749, and 1764–65. When Europeans took this disease to the New World, the biologically defenceless native inhabitants were mowed down in staggering numbers. The Huron, for example, lost 'one half to two-thirds of their population' to smallpox and other diseases in just six years. By the 1760s, the devastating power of smallpox in the New World was so well recognised that the British commander-in-chief of North America, Sir Geoffrey Amherst, deliberately gave infected blankets to rebellious Canadian tribes as a tactic of early germ warfare.[39]

If we had only data on plague and sweating sickness, we would still retain a powerful impression of Renaissance disease and mortality. The first excelled in its sheer persistence and the bewildering scale of casualties. Although population estimates for this period are notoriously uncertain, the London plague toll of 1625, exceeding 35,000, could have been as much as a fifth of the capital's population.[40] Scaling this up to population levels of 2011, we find that perhaps as many as one and a half million would have perished. In general terms, such statistics were not that great an anomaly. The historians E.A. Wrigley and Roger Schofield estimate that of the twenty-three worst years for overall mortality between 1541 and 1871, eighteen occurred in the sixteenth and seventeenth centuries.[41]

If plague had the upper hand statistically, the sweating sickness took the prize for sheer speed of attack. One moment you were alive, seething with all the vitality, hope and possibility you or I feel now. The next you were hurtling breathlessly into the depths of an undecided eternity. As Donne put it from his sickbed of 1623: 'variable, and therefore miserable condition of man; this minute I was well, and am ill, this minute. I am surprised with a sudden change, and alteration to worse, and can impute it to no cause, nor call it by any name'.[42]

Ultimately, Donne survived not only his relapsing fever of 1623, but several plagues, including the epic outbreak just a few months later, in 1625. Yet Donne and his family were equally familiar with sudden deaths in the earlier years of James I. Between early 1603 and August 1617, Donne's wife, Ann, had twelve children. Two were stillborn; two died before age five; one before age ten, and one before the age of twenty. When she herself finally perished in August 1617, five days after the especially difficult birth of a stillborn child, Ann was less than thirty-five years old.[43] When Donne himself told his audience, in a sermon preached at Lincoln's Inn, that 'thy flesh is but dust held together by plasters ... dissolution and putrefaction is gone over thee alive', he captured the essentially porous division between life and death with grim accuracy.[44]

For most people in this era, death really did stalk unchecked through the midst of human life. Recalling the popular image of the hand of death, laid in skeletal chill on an unwary shoulder, we might rather imagine that for the Renaissance life was lived perpetually within the half-closed fist of death. It was just a question of when it might suddenly snap to, a matter of sensing its putrid muscles as they tightened over the frail shell of the defenceless human body. From any mournful pulpit or any creaking gibbet, from the busy gallows of Tyburn to the spiked heads and quarters of London Bridge and the city gates, death stared you hard in the face, calm and unblinking. And the response of many was probably to stare back with similar composure. Take, for example, the Swiss visitor Thomas Platter, who in 1599 saw 'more than thirty skulls of noble men ... executed and beheaded for treason', stuck on pikes at the south side of London Bridge. With some surprise Platter further notes that the descendants of these traitors would often eagerly point out a family skull (perhaps incorrectly?), taking pride in the fact that 'their antecedents were of such high descent that they could even covet the crown'.[45] In August 1661 the Dutch visitor William Schellinks saw on the bridge 'all the heads on stakes, nineteen or twenty in number, amongst them the head of Hugh Peters the preacher', who had suffered hanging, drawing and quartering the year before in revenge for the execution of Charles I. The following day, passing out of the city at Moorgate, Schellinks was greeted by 'many limbs of traitors or accomplices of Oliver Cromwell ... displayed on stakes'.[46]

We can never be absolutely sure just how this kind of environment affected the contemporaries of Marlowe or Rochester. But we can confidently say that the average privileged European is now far more terrified of dying than were Donne, Cromwell or Milton. Fervent belief in the possibility of salvation dominated the minds and hearts of these three men and of all their millions of fellow Christians. Any schoolboy could tell you the cause of the plague: it was God's anger. And any schoolboy could use the most popular and democratic remedy of the age for this and all other diseases. You would, simply, kneel down and pray – sometimes alone, sometimes collectively. In the sixteenth century and after, plague and other sudden calamities typically prompted national fasts and prayer days.[47] In the late seventeenth century the clergyman Richard Allestree (d.1681) estimated over 4,000 deaths in one week in 1624, and over 7,000 in a week in 1665. For all that, he readily insisted of God, 'it was his tender mercy, that he spared any alive', for He 'wounds, that he may heal; and in wounding, heals us; for his compassions fails not to us sinners'.[48]

We must accept that most people in this era did not die in the way that agnostics or atheists do now. (And we might add that there are very few Christian martyrs in our own time.) And yet there must, for all that, have remained certain basic instincts: in the young, especially, a brute love of life or will to survive; in the old or middle-aged, a stubborn lingering fear of the unknown. As the forty-year-old Earl of Perth admitted, waiting uncertainly in prison on 29 December 1688: 'the rabble curse and would tear me to pieces' and 'the prospect of approaching death cannot but be uneasy to flesh and blood'.[49]

It was not, then, that most people actively wanted to die. (Your end, after all, was in God's hands, not your own.) Most would resort to medicine (and, as we shall see, often go to startling lengths in search of cures). But there was simply no hiding from the presence of death. Since the nineteenth century, this presence has been increasingly shut out of the general consciousness of Western Europe.[50] It is worth bearing in mind that certain men and women of 1600 or 1700 would have found this separation as puzzling or offensive as we now find the idea of medicinal cannibalism. And this kind of distinction is crucial if we are to fully understand just how numerous sick people were able to eat, drink, or deliberately touch the bones and bodies of the dead in hope of cure. In doing so, they were not having to wrench themselves across the same fundamental divide as that which we now (mistakenly) perceive as a natural and universal barrier between the living and the dead. It may indeed have seemed to them more as if they were entering a kind of transitional zone, the space between the stoically endured pains of earthly life, and those shimmering expanses of blissful eternity which were the only true goal of all human existence. Let us now shift from the realm of death, to some of the particularly striking hardships of life and sickness in the early modern world.

Surgery

In late November 1526 Giovanni de Medici was struck by a cannonball in a battle against German troops. A few days later, on 10 December, that distinctive Renaissance man Pietro Aretino described the amputation of Giovanni's gangrened leg. The patient was given 'a soporific draught', and Aretino was asked to fetch 'eight or ten people … to hold him during the pain of the sawing'. Joking valiantly that 'not even twenty would be enough', Giovanni then 'sat up with face as resolute as could be, and took in his own hands the candle that was to give light for the operation'.

Aretino, who at this point 'fled from the room, and thrust my hands into my ears', claims that he heard 'only two groans' as the saw ground and rasped through flesh and bone.[51] For all his courage, Giovanni's only reward was to be remembered in Aretino's account. Like many others in such situations, he died just a few hours afterwards – apparently of blood poisoning, which may itself have been caused by the use of unsterilised instruments.[52]

Matters had not changed much in England, almost 150 years later. On 24 March 1672, John Evelyn watched 'my surgeon cut off a poor creature's leg, a little under the knee, first cutting the living and untainted flesh above the gangrene with a sharp knife, and then sawing off the bone in an instant'. The surgeon then staunched the blood ('which issued abundantly') by cauterising the wound. Meanwhile, 'the stout and gallant man' endured all 'with incredible patience, and that without being bound to his chair, as is usual in such painful operations, or hardly making a face or crying oh'. Evelyn himself admits that he 'had hardly courage enough to be present', and 'nor could I endure to see any more such cruel operations'. Once again, all this was in vain. The leg had been cut too low down, and gangrene remained further up. And so, Evelyn adds, 'a second amputation of the thigh, cost the poor creature his life'.[53]

If you did survive, the mental trauma may well have been considerable. In 1580 the surgeon William Clowes explains how those performing such operations would need 'a good strong form and a steady' to lay the patient on, whilst bestriding 'the form behind him' must be 'a man that is able to hold him fast by both his arms'. A second strong man was needed to 'bestride the leg that is to be taken off, and he must hold fast the member above the place where the incision is to be made' – not least because, if he had 'a large hand and a good grip', he could 'the better stay the bleeding'. Having next 'cut the flesh round about to the bones', the surgeon must then 'with a light hand speedily saw … off' the leg. If you (the patient) had not already fainted after this, one doubts that you would refuse the 'restrictive powder to stay the flux of blood' which Clowes and others employed. His version included aloes and mummy, whilst his colleague John Banister used mummy and dragon's blood, along with 'the whites of eggs and hares' hairs clipped so short as is possible'.[54]

You would probably think yourself similarly lucky if a surgeon such as Paul Barbette had managed successfully to stitch up your wounded guts – for which 'you must … take a needle, thread it with a waxen thread, thrust it from without through the skin and muscles unto the very peritoneum … pierce it through, and the muscles and the skin also, drawing the lips together'; and, 'seeing that by reason of the continual motion of the belly, your stitches may be easily undone, the rather, because the haste, sometimes here to be used, will not permit to make them with exactness, it is always necessary to apply to the wound a sticking-plaster'. Whether Barbette used the plaster, or his powdered mixture of aloes, mastic, frankincense, mummy, and dragon's blood, there cannot have been many patients ready to begin neurotic arguments about the medical ethics of cannibalism at such a moment.[55]

Few things divide us so powerfully from the pre-clinical past as the torments of live surgery. In modern times, after all, the oblivion of anaesthetic is so complete that patients will not suffer so much as a nightmare. Seeing someone bound to a chair in a modern film, we will automatically assume that they are going to be tortured. And this was more or less what must have happened, on a routine basis, to thousands of men, women and children before medical science bestowed on the world those great chemical gifts of temporary oblivion, from ether and chloroform through to tiletamine–zolazepam.[56]

We must also remind ourselves that, if amputations were not common, they were far more so than in later centuries. First, gangrene was obviously a greater hazard than it would be now, which meant that relatively mild injuries could quickly become life-threatening. Moreover, to the colossal death tolls and maimings of continental wars, we must add the general violence of everyday life. Tellingly, some especially startling instances of this come from the casebook of the seventeenth-century surgeon Joseph Binns. In 1638, for example, Mr Robert Peyton received a fractured skull after being struck with a pottle pot by a Captain Nayle. In 1643 the lutenist Mr Ashberry had over an inch of his cheek bitten off by a French lutenist, M Gottier; and in that same year an eighty-year-old man begging alms was stabbed in the stomach by a Sergeant Major Jenkins.[57] Nor was such aggression a purely adult monopoly. In 1731, for example, one Eton schoolboy, Dalton, stabbed and killed a boy named Cockram. Both were aged around twelve.[58] Notice that these assaults were all committed by people of at least relatively high status – something which is consistent with the tendency to fight for points of honour, which in themselves so often came down to a mere matter of words.

Then there were accidents. Among children in particular, these were clearly far more common and more perilous than in privileged countries of our own day. A medical book of 1594 tells of 'a little boy' fallen from a horse, and of how a seven-year-old was treated for 'a puncture in the eye, with a knife'.[59] As various historians have argued, such incidents probably stemmed in part from a relatively fatalistic attitude, among parents who were almost certain to lose some children in infancy or soon after. (Montaigne (who was hardly callous) stated vaguely, 'I have lost two or three children … ').[60] The Elizabethan astrologer, navigator, mathematician and occultist John Dee loved his children enough to record their accidents, but not quite enough to prevent their causes. For example: on 3 July 1582 'Arthur Dee fell from the top of Watergate stairs down to the foot ... and cut his forehead on the right eyebrow. Sir Richard brought the rent'. On 1 January 1588 'about nine of the clock afternoon, Michael, going childishly with a sharp stick of eight inches long and a little wax candle light on the top of it, did fall upon the plain boards in Marie's chamber, and the sharp point of the stick entered through the lid of his left eye ... '; while on 27 June 1591 Arthur was 'wounded on his head by his own wanton throwing of a brick-bat upright, and not well avoiding the fall of it again, at Mr Herbert's about sun-setting'. (Arthur survived (deservedly or not) even though 'the half-brick weighed two and a half pounds'.)[61]

For adults, there were riding accidents. Robert Boyle recalled a man of around twenty-four who, after falling from his horse, 'had his skull broken in several places'. Although the man was rich enough to have a number of surgeons attend to him ('during which he was divers times trepanned, and had several pieces of his skull taken off') he did not recover easily. About three days after the fall he suffered a loss of sense in his right side, while his arm and head became completely paralysed. Having endured this state for almost six months, he was saved by just one of the surgeons, who refused to let the others close up the skull. With the patient's agreement 'his head was further laid open; and at length, under a piece of proud flesh, they found, with much ado, a splinter, or rather flake, of a bone'. This, Boyle adds 'was not pulled out without a great haemorrhage, and such a stretch of the parts, as made the patient think his brain itself was tearing out'. Despite living on without an entire skull, the man went on to become 'strong [and] healthy', saving that he was 'a little obnoxious to take cold in his head'.[62]

If you survived your childhood, kept out of wars, deferred obsequiously to every man who bandied words with you, and were not thrashed by your employers, you still had a fair chance of being cut open at some point in your life. Men of all ages seem to have been frequently afflicted with urinary stones of sometimes startling size. After his death in 1622, the Puritan minister Nicholas Byfield underwent an autopsy which yielded a bladder stone of thirty-three ounces in weight (compare a good-sized red cabbage).[63] In February 1602 the lawyer John Manningham pictures lithotomy as a kind of surgical Russian roulette. After cutting open the scrotum, the surgeons would 'grope for the stone with ... a tool which they call a duck's bill'; but, 'if the stone be greater than may be drawn forth at the hole made by the seam, the party dies for it'. This fate had indeed recently befallen one 'Burneham of London', Manningham tells us, after he resorted to the procedure out of desperation.[64]

Samuel Pepys was cut for the stone on 26 March 1658. In May 1669 John Evelyn's brother seems to have been suffering from a bladder stone for some time. Because he was resistant to the idea of an operation, Evelyn took Pepys along in an effort to persuade him. Although we are not told precisely what Pepys said, we know that he was brandishing a proud trophy on his visit: his own bladder stone, which, Evelyn states, was 'as big as a tennis ball'.[65] Evelyn himself must have had a good idea of what was in store for his brother. Back in May 1650, during his French visit, he had seen five different patients undergo lithotomies in a Paris hospital:

there was one person of forty years old had a stone taken out of him, bigger than a turkey's egg: the manner thus: the sick creature was stripped to his shirt, and bound arms and thighs to an high chair, two men holding his shoulders fast down: then the surgeon with a crooked instrument probed til he hit on the stone … he made incision through the scrotum about an inch in length, then he put in his forefingers to get the stone as near the orifice of the wound as he could, then with another instrument like a crane's neck he pulled it out with incredible torture to the patient …

Adding laconically that 'the effusion of blood is great', Evelyn further notes that there is a common danger of fever or gangrene, and that some wounds will never close. We can only hope that the next victim Evelyn saw was happily oblivious of these dangers. He certainly seems to have been surprisingly little perturbed at his ordeal – showing 'much cheerfulness' and 'going through the operation with extraordinary patience, and expressing great joy, when he saw the stone was drawn'. All this is impressive in its own right – but still more so when we learn that the subject was a child, just eight or nine years old.[66]

We have seen that those undergoing surgery would rarely be in any state to quibble about cannibalistic medicines. And we can also assume that most would have taken such treatments as an *alternative* to surgery if they could. The list of ingredients cited at the start of this chapter includes a 'stone taken out of a man's bladder'. Perhaps shrewd patients sold these after their own lithotomies. At any rate, they were commonly held to cure the stone, being recommended as late as 1739 by an Irish clergyman. For ruptures Barbette advised pills made of mummy, myrrh, filings of steel, dried hare's dung and powdered earthworms.[67] The royal surgeon John Browne proposes that scrofulous tumours be 'softened and dissipated' with 'resolving and discussive medicines' such as 'hen's fat, man's fat, oil of sweet almonds' and so on; whilst Banister holds that a wound drink of herbs and mummy is better for bones fractured by gunshot 'than all those splints wherewith some are sore tormented'.[68] As we saw in chapter three, the case of Lorenz Seitz, the 'journeyman brewer in Nuremberg … rescued from knife-happy barber-surgeons by … Johann Michael Schmidt, the local executioner' offers a particularly sharp contrast between the horrors of amputation and the simple use of bandages – these latter almost certainly being steeped in human fat.[69]

Some degree of anaesthetic relief was in fact available in the early modern period. In October 1602 John Manningham writes of 'a certain kind of compound called *laudanum*'. Available 'at Dr Turner's, apothecary, in Bishopgate St', this was 'very sovereign to mitigate any pain' and 'will for a time lay a man in a sweet trance'. But laudanum, or opium, was clearly novel at that point; and even later on seems to have been used far less than we might expect. Unlike the numerous genteel opium addicts of the nineteenth century, good Christians of Milton's time suffered their pain stoically.[70] Indeed, in the sixteenth century the Puritan City Fathers of Zurich had banned even the primitive anaesthesia of the day, insisting that '"pain is a natural and intended curse of the primal sin"', and that '"any attempt to do away with it must be wrong'".[71] Although Mayerne noted the use of opium (and human fat) as painkillers in his treatise on gout, Barbette stated, tellingly, that pain 'must of necessity be eased, because it creates watchings, and dejects the spirits, and is cause of the flux of humours to the party affected' – that is, only because it makes the patient yet more sick.[72]

Illness

If much of the above is all too vivid, it is perhaps also (at this distance) a little impersonal. Let us therefore focus our attention for a moment by returning to that pious devotee of skull-moss, the clergyman and popular religious author Richard Baxter (b.1615). 'Poor health was a permanent feature of Baxter's life', according to his biographer, N.H. Keeble: 'as a child he suffered from catarrh, colds, and a prolonged cough. In the early 1630s he was', by his own admission, '"in expectation of death, by a violent cough, with spitting of blood, etc, of two years continuance"'. '"From the age of twenty one till near twenty three"', Baxter adds, '"my weakness was so great, that I expected not to live above a year"'. When Baxter's book *The Saints' Everlasting Rest* appeared in 1650, it was, Keeble tells us, 'addressed to its reader as the legacy of a dying man'. Perhaps to his own disappointment, Baxter in fact limped on through a quite long but incessantly painful life (dying only in 1691). He 'suffered chronically'

> from flatulency and gastric problems, 'incredible inflammations of stomach, bowels, back, sides, head, thighs, as if I had been daily filled with wind'; from scurvy and from repeated haemorrhaging from 'eyes, and teeth, and jaws, and joints, so that I had scarce rest night or day'; he was prone to catch colds and chills, and he suffered regularly from headaches, from 'terrible toothache', and from gallstones, in later life the severity of the pain leaving 'scarce any part or hour … free'.[73]

The impressive volume of Baxter's writings looks little short of miraculous in view of this extraordinary suffering. As Keeble concludes, 'physical indisposition at best, pain at worst, were his constant experience'.

Keeble also notes that 'the thirty or more different physicians Baxter was to consult during his life were unable to prescribe any sustained relief'. Little wonder, then, that Baxter would gladly insert the moss of a dead man's skull into his nostrils (although nosebleeds may have been a mild complaint by comparison with haemorrhages from the eyes and joints). Baxter's case seems to have been an extreme one. He himself described his symptoms as those usually experienced only by men 'about fourscore years of age'.[74] Nowadays, anyone under sixty who suffered even a fifth of this pain and discomfort would consider themselves immensely unlucky – especially if medical science offered them almost no help whatsoever.

Baxter himself undoubtedly took a very Christian attitude toward his sufferings. As an intensely fervent Protestant, he not only often believed that he was about to die, but very possibly wanted to. Few people so vividly exemplify that porous boundary between heaven and earth, or life and death, which we noted above. Baxter was, for example, an avid believer in ghosts, poltergeists and demonic possession.[75] And Baxter's experience suggests another distinctive feature of early modern illness. Whether passionately religious or not, many people must have endured frequent pain or severe discomfort as a more or less *normal* feature of their lives. Did they really always consider themselves to be 'ill'? For most of us, the psychology of occasional illness is relative to long periods of being well. But such psychology must be very different if you are almost never fully healthy in the first place. Even if they were not especially tough or stoical, most men and women would probably have minimised their response to degrees of sickness or pain just because it was so familiar. Thus, in the time of Charles I and Cromwell, the gentleman Walter Powell of Llantilio is brisk and seemingly stoical when he records in his diary, 'I fell sick of the small pocks for six days', 'my gout began in ye joint of my great toe', 'I fell on my stairs and break my rib' – and even when 'my right eye began to fail and I fell sick shortly and was like to die at Christmas'.[76] (This seemed to hold for the deaths of others, with Powell noting sparely on 7 and 13 January 1654, 'John Rawlins died drowned', and 'my son Charles his messenger came to tell us that my son Richard was like to die'.[77])

Teeth

In the case of his toothache, wretched Baxter was at least far from alone. It has often been claimed that this was an especially pervasive problem of the pre-modern world. Although most people could not possibly have consumed a fraction of the extrinsic sugar easily available to European children nowadays, they also seem to have had very rudimentary methods of tooth care.[78] As Honan notes, in Shakespeare's boyhood reasonably affluent children usually cleaned their teeth 'with a cloth and a sweetish paste'.[79] This may have been more effective than the plain 'cold water' recommended by a writer of 1547 – but probably not much.[80] To 'go to the dentist' meant simply to have your rotten tooth yanked from your head by a surgeon – an experience which could hardly have been much more pleasant than being cut for the stone.[81] By the time she was sixty-five, Elizabeth I was supposed to have black teeth, and she would go on to lose even these some time before she died in 1603.

If surviving records offered us not one direct complaint about toothache, we could still infer the seriousness of this problem from the number and range of medical remedies directed against it. A relatively palatable option was burnt deer horn. If you were a dog, meanwhile, you were likely to have your own peculiar dental problems. In addition to not brushing your teeth, you might find that people were trying to get them off you, healthy or not, as another popular cure was a powder made from canine molars.[82] Cavities, we are told, 'may be filled with the brain of a partridge or crow's dung'. And the terrors of surgical tooth extraction are obliquely visible to us in the belief that, alternatively, 'a tooth may be easily extracted by touching it with dog's milk' (although you should avoid touching healthy teeth, as these would fall out also if you did[83]). It is certainly no small matter trying to find a National Health

Service dentist amidst the wreckage left by the legacy of Margaret Thatcher and her monstrous offspring, Mr Blair. But even now, that may just be slightly easier than trying to milk a dog. Small wonder, then, that you might resort to a form of corpse medicine to avoid losing teeth if you could help it. You could, it was thought, cure an ailing tooth by touching it with one taken from a dead body.[84]

Food for worms

Most of us could happily forget the frequent or continual tooth pain experienced by men and women through the ages of Marlowe, Pepys and Boswell. But there is one other ailment of the period of which we are still more thoroughly (and mercifully) oblivious. As Piero Camporesi in particular has emphasised, when Christians of the sixteenth and seventeenth centuries insisted on the fundamental vileness, putrescence and corruption of human flesh, they had far better cause than we might ever guess. Why? Close your eyes a moment, and imagine that you have acquired the doubtful gift of X-ray vision. You are looking at the contents of a live intestine: large amounts of half-digested meat and fish are patiently dissolving in a mist of stomach acid and ale fumes. But in the midst of this peaceful scene, things are moving. Long, hairy, squirming and densely entangled as they coil in a writhing greedy maze around one another, intestinal worms are busily finishing off the meal that this well-fed Elizabethan has not yet digested. For yes, this is not an animal, but a human stomach.

For reasons which are not entirely clear, numerous people seem to have been horribly afflicted by intestinal worms in this period. Camporesi tells of various cases, from those causing emaciation, to others marked by horrible convulsions and torments, and a handful considered life-threatening. There was, for example, "'a five-year-old child in whom worms had gnawed through the belly and come out of the navel'"; while another sufferer recovered after he had "'thrown up a worm, four inches in length'" with "'a small, round head'".[85] In summer 1655 a London inn-keeper, Mr Parry, fell ill. On the thirtieth of July, when 'going to stool' he voided a total of twelve 'serpents' – one having a head like a horse, another 'headed like a toad', and a third 'like a greyhound'. Admittedly, the apocalyptic overtones of the pamphlet ('before the destruction of Sodom and Gomorrah, sundry strange prodigies … were seen') were in this case probably inspired by the recent civil war, and the execution of Charles I, six years previous.[86]

But more sober observers were still finding broadly similar creatures come the Restoration. Writing in 1668, the physician William Ramsey laments the 'several species of worms macerating and direfully cruciating every part of the bodies of mankind', asserting that they had indeed killed 'more than either sword or plague'.[87] Infants less than a year old could, Ramsey claims, be 'molested with worms'; one child at Delph, for example, having been 'miserably macerated' by them. In Montpellier a man voided a flatworm seven foot long. Innumerable other victims expelled creatures of remarkable lengths and shapes through their mouths, anuses or ears, as well as in urine. More dramatically, one forty-year-old man had a swelling in his groin which finally split to release three huge worms.[88]

And these patients of course had to think themselves lucky that they had managed to *eject* the worms, however painfully. 'Infinite numbers of people', Ramsey insists, 'die by these vermin under the notion of other maladies', with both patient and doctor remaining oblivious.[89] Ramsey's explanation of these creatures looks to us partly religious and partly scientific. One cause was gluttony, and another simply the wrong kinds of meat. We can only guess at what it felt like to be inhabited by this teeming voracity of serpentine life forms. Anyone still doubtful about their existence might want to inspect the breathtaking variety of worms which Ramsey has had drawn in his book – some twenty-five assorted creatures which are, he adds, just a few specimens found 'among millions of others' in the dank cellars of the guts.[90] Anyone looking at these drawings would be inclined to imagine the human digestive tracts not as quiet, private regions of gustatory pleasure, but as busy entomological landscapes in their own right – the material, indeed, of a whole televised nature programme, had anyone been able to insert a modern surgical camera into these penumbrous bristling depths.

Eaten alive

For many of the early modern poor, it was clearly hard enough getting food into your body in the first place. But even once you had, it seems that someone (or something) was still likely to steal it. Anyone who has found this especially difficult to stomach may now want to skip to the following section. For matters are about to deteriorate. In this case, you need only imagine that you are looking at the outside of your body. You will need, however, to picture a small boil on (say) your upper arm. Then imagine that it is itching. On inspecting it curiously, you can further discern that it is – albeit very faintly – moving. Finally galvanised by mingled discomfort, fear and curiosity, you allow a surgeon to thrust a lancet into this alien entity. The pain is mild by comparison with what follows. The boil proves to be oddly dry, with little or no pus secreted beneath the skin. Instead, a closely packed swarm of innumerable minute insects comes bursting forth.

This description may now seem to have something of the flavour of an urban myth. But it does indeed appear to be an accurate representation of the medical condition known as phthiriasis – a disease which afflicted people at all levels of society, from antiquity until the later nineteenth century. The twentieth century physician Jan Bondeson has explained how phthiriasis was traditionally said to be a divine punishment against evil rulers (or, occasionally, just one's political enemies). Emphasising that cases afflicting the powerful must accordingly be treated with caution, Bondeson nevertheless goes on to describe a large number of apparently authentic instances. In this period most educated people believed in spontaneous generation – the production of smaller creatures, such as worms, birds, eels, and toads, from otherwise inanimate matter or fluid (wood, mud, and water). In this sense, the internal production of human lice was readily comprehensible (though there was debate as to just what the precise cause might be.) Bondeson argues for various reasons that the creatures were probably in fact mites – rather than lice, as was then thought. But he otherwise accepts the general validity of the medical reports, finally stating that, 'it is impossible to reach any other conclusion than that a disease of these characteristics really existed' in the early modern period.

In the sixteenth century we find the physician Thomas Moffet telling of how a noblewoman, Lady Penruddoc, 'developed hundreds of small insect-filled boils and perished in phthiriasis'. Around the same time, in 1556, 'the Portuguese physician Amatus Lusitanus described the death of the nobleman Tabora, who had many swellings all over his body, from which small insects streamed out incessantly; two of his Ethiopian slaves were employed in emptying small baskets of them into the sea'. In just a few weeks Tabora died, devoured alive 'by these "lice" engendered under his own skin'. When the celebrated parliamentarian John Pym died in 1643, his Royalist detractors claimed that he too had been brought to his grave by just such an infestation. The tale was probably untrue. Yet Pym's supporters felt the need to have the body autopsied in order to counter these claims. In general terms, the notion was clearly still a plausible one at this time. Much later, in 1808, a Prussian military surgeon, Professor Rust, examined 'a thirteen-year-old Jewish boy with a large head tumour'. Eight days on, the boy 'seemed to be dying, and the tumour was enormous'. On cutting it open, he and the onlookers saw 'a mass of solidly packed insects, but not a droplet of pus or moisture. After the insects had been scraped out' the boy was treated with ointment and the cavity 'injected with mercury', and he presently made a complete recovery.

Phthiriasis is striking for a number of reasons. It seems that issues of wealth, diet or personal hygiene were not responsible for this condition, which was evidently a matter of physiological ill luck. While the above accounts have probably made its peculiar nature all too clear, it is worth re-emphasising how strange and appalling this disease was. A sufferer could be afflicted with as many as hundreds of boils, and therefore effectively colonised by thousands of hungry and ever-multiplying insects, vigorously feeding in their warm nests beneath the epidermis. These not only produced intolerable itching, but did actually eat victims alive. As Bondeson plainly states, the biological economy of phthiriasis was horribly simple: the host's flesh was steadily transformed into ever more devouring insects. While the condition mysteriously (and mercifully) vanished in the late nineteenth century, Bondeson has shrewdly noted that twentieth-century mite infestations of birds very much 'resemble the classical reports of phthiriasis'.[91]

The potential hazards of injury, death and sickness which the average person faced at this time must have strongly influenced their attitude to medicines which most of us would consider unacceptable, bizarre, or even horrific. It is now time to turn to another area of early modern life which powerfully conditioned people in their response to the myriad animal and human guts, dungs, organs and fluids of the apothecary's shop.

Filth

The preceding sections on medicine already offer us several glimpses of how revolting (to the modern mind) both diseases and cures could be, some 300 or 400 years ago.

In many cases, we can see why patients would have readily used corpse medicines where available. The last two sections do not fall under that heading. But they are included, in part, to emphasise just how fraught the battle against nature could be in this era. The second half of this chapter aims to broaden out the medical context of corpse medicine by linking it to a particular area of social context. Reasonable as this might sound in cool, abstract terms, the sensitive reader should be warned that what follows is rather like the explosion of a non-lethal hand grenade across succeeding pages.

Giving the nose a very brief moment of grace, we can start with the eyes. Modern cataract operations are one of the many blessings of scientific medicine: quick, cheap, and remarkably effective. True, they can be a little painful. But compare these other options: in the seventeenth century, you could apply preparations made from the marrow of a goose wing, or the ashes of a burnt snail. Or, you could use a more readily available ingredient. Take some human excrement; dry it into powder; and then blow it into the eye. As Lawrence Stone reminds us, this was yet another colourful remedy proposed by that pioneering chemist Robert Boyle.[92]

In the late 1650s, Thomas Willis treated a large number of people (usually young women, as we saw in chapter two) who were suffering from severe convulsions. During one case, a local country woman intervened, dosing the patient with 'six spoonfuls of blood, taken from the ear of an ass'. Willis does not seem to have regarded this as the foolish interference of a mere layperson – noting, indeed, that for some time the young woman seemed to be cured. And Willis would certainly not have been squeamish about such a cure. For another sufferer he prescribed not only powdered skull, but a draught of 'white wine, dilated with the water of black cherries, with sow's or hog-lice bruised and infused therein'. A third patient, though cured of convulsions, suffered 'extreme sourness' in her throat, upon which Willis instructed her to drink her own urine (while still warm) each morning.[93]

Over in the Puritan settlements of North America, meanwhile, the New England minister Cotton Mather (d.1728) followed Willis's lead, using crushed sow bugs and crushed body lice as medicine.[94] As we know, Willis's clients were unlikely to be found indignantly brandishing their Patient's Charters in protest at such treatment – in his day, he represented the very best care that money could buy. As for Mather – he was not only a model of Christian piety, but sufficiently proto-scientific to risk his life by proposing some of the very earliest Western experiments in smallpox inoculation.[95]

It is surely no exaggeration to say that many modern patients would find such therapies quite as repugnant as medicinal cannibalism. When told of these cures, people often react with the kind of involuntary physical gestures and expressions which border on outright fear. They might, for example, blink rapidly, grimace, or shake their head. They might sweep their hands before their face. In each case, they are trying to somehow shake off the almost physical presence of pollution. To put it another way: the very idea of such things can seem like an immediate physical threat. As such, these substances at least partly spark quite basic animal instincts: something is threatening us, so we must fight it or flee it; attack or escape. (Virginia Smith notes that many animals indeed show very similar physical reactions in comparable cases, 'averting the eyes, shaking the paws or wrinkling the nose'.[96]) Yet, as William Miller points out, in his book *The Anatomy of Disgust*, disgust severely problematises such evolutionary reactions. The object of disgust is at once quasi-physical, and invasively mental – somehow at once abstract and concrete. Hence, it is already inside us, and we cannot easily escape it or destroy it.[97]

Feelings of disgust are therefore complex and subjective. They are not merely a question of animal instinct. Our modern attitude to such contamination is one which arose in Europe around the middle of the eighteenth century. This will become all too clear in just a moment. But consider, here, those last two distinctive afflictions of the pre-modern world, the mites and worms which devoured you or your food. Disgusting things were *inside* you. Central to the modern sense of disgust is the notion that (as with cannibalism) fundamental boundaries are being violated. Something repellent is invading us. But the strength of our response to that attack must depend upon just how strong or well-defined those boundaries (of the self, cleanliness, privacy) actually are. If worms or lice or mites (disgusting things, rather than just ideas) are already inside you, then those boundaries themselves simply cannot be so definite or solid. Even fleas, in their way, must have helped to keep such personal limits frail or porous, and the most privileged were exposed to their attacks, especially if they were travelling.[98] Little surprise, then, to find Miller emphasising that the very word 'disgust' was simply not used in English until the seventeenth century.[99] Like so many other things, the seemingly instinctual, seemingly animalistic response to filth had to be *learned*.[100]

By now this lesson has been so thoroughly absorbed that it does indeed seem wholly natural. Ironically, however, certain sections of affluent Western society have refined their growing obsession with cleanliness and hygiene to such an extent that it threatens to become outrightly *un*natural and unhealthy. In North America in particular, germs are reviled and attacked with the kind of vigilant disgust and aggression which older eras reserved for their religious or racial enemies.[101] The children of middle-class parents will have their mouths habitually swabbed with antiseptic wipes, or be forcibly prevented from sharing drinking cups. So thoroughly oversanitised is the general environment of many modern infants that they lack even the bare minimum of dirt needed to develop an efficient immune system. With their basic bodily defence systems eroded by this well-meaning germ warfare, such children will be far more likely to develop allergies or asthma in later life.

These paradoxical afflictions would have seemed a blessing in disguise to the average contemporary of Henry VIII or Charles II. Even in the earlier years of Queen Victoria, as England spread 'civilisation' across the globe, the streets and slums of London and Birmingham were often little more than open cauldrons of disease, with smallpox, cholera and tuberculosis patiently simmering in innumerable corners.[102] In London in 1858, and in Paris in 1880, there were summers of such intolerable stench that the accompanying outrage and media coverage threatened to rival modern attention to terrorist atrocities.[103] The London underground sewers were established only in the early 1860s, with the Parisian versions lagging notably.

For all its glamour, the French capital (notes Alain Corbin) stank habitually every summer until the eve of the First World War.[104]

The stench and the filth of the past have been forgotten with remarkable completeness – perhaps quite as thoroughly as the existence of medicinal cannibalism itself. In one sense, of course, this is understandable and unavoidable. Smell is at once primal and fragile. Scholars working on this and other senses emphasise that we cannot remember even the smells of our own experience in the way that we can recall images or emotions.[105] A smell is physically there, or it is nowhere. What we recollect is merely our *reaction* to a particular odour. Naturally enough, the distinctive scents of early modern London are equally irrecoverable, long since evaporated from the frozen, exquisitely coloured and varnished images of affluent men and women, now hanging in cool dustless galleries. (It is an especially nice irony that, sub-consciously, we perhaps feel the past to smell of the clean wood and expensive polish which surrounds these little fragments of it.)

As Roland Barthes neatly put it, '"when written, shit does not smell"'.[106] With this in mind, I make no apology for what follows. Much of this book, after all, is a kind of 'Dirty History' – a recovery of habits and beliefs which have been effectively whitewashed from so many history books. In particular, I make no apology for what might at first seem to be quite unscholarly vocabulary. Some seventeen years ago, taking a course on swear words with the Old Norse specialist Rory McTurk, I learned of how the terms denoting tabooed human activities have come to be those of 'the nursery, the laboratory, or the gutter'. Matters have, admittedly, changed a little as the general level of social discourse has grown more informal. But the statement still rings true in broad terms, and perhaps nowhere more so than in the area of human bodily waste. How often do we say to someone, 'Hang on a minute, I've just got to urinate'? Terms such as 'excrement' and 'defecate', while perhaps not ultra-clinical, hardly capture the potential for revulsion which human shit and piss still harbour for most adults. It is almost as if, in times when foul smells were pervasive and more or less unavoidable, language itself was used as a subtle means of mentally deodorising tabooed substances and activities.[107] Precisely because none of the habitual terms seem adequate or neutral, I will in what follows aim for some level of balance by employing a representative mixture of them. (If this should offend the kind of people who are especially devoted to euphemisms such as 'washroom' and 'restroom' – well, so much the better.)

Let us begin with the heady atmosphere of eighteenth-century Paris: 'the streets stank of manure, the courtyards of urine, the stairwells of mouldering wood and rat droppings, the kitchens of spoiled cabbage and mutton fat; the unaired parlours stank of stale dust, the bedrooms of greasy sheets, damp featherbeds, and the pungently sweet aroma of chamber-pots'. People, meanwhile, 'stank of sweat and unwashed clothes; from their mouths came the stench of rotting teeth, from their bellies that of onions, and from their bodies, if they were no longer very young, came the stench of rancid cheese and sour milk and tumorous disease … The peasant stank as did the priest … the whole of the aristocracy stank, even the King himself stank, stank like a rank lion, and the Queen like an old goat, summer and winter'.[108]

These last lines are no exaggeration. Certain monarchs, such as Louis XIV, were relatively fastidious.[109] There again, one's own body never smells as bad to us as to others. Pity the courtiers, then, who must violently and efficiently stifle their revulsion toward the ageing Henry VIII, a man afflicted by leg sores which in turn afflicted all around with an almost intolerable stink. Queen Elizabeth's mouth must have stunk impressively as her teeth rotted. James I, meanwhile, seems to have been quite literally as dirty as any London beggar (who were at least occasionally rinsed by a shower of rain). One seventeenth-century writer noted that James 'never washed his hands, only rubbed his fingers' ends slightly with the wet end of a napkin'.[110] Elizabeth Lane Furdell reminds us that James 'detested water as a beverage or a bath. Because he never washed, he itched constantly; because he did not change clothes until they wore out, he reeked of body odor ... one lady at court complained that she and her companions got "lousy by sitting in [a councillor's] chamber that James frequented"'.[111] Out of doors, James was so addicted to hunting that he would urinate in the saddle to save the labour of dismounting. (One can well imagine that such a habit would considerably diminish the personal charms of a man who did not change his clothes until they wore out.) Charles II, John Evelyn tells us, 'took delight to have a number of little spaniels follow him, and lie in his bed-chamber, where often times he suffered the bitches to puppy and give suck'. These dogs – and presumably the untrained puppies in particular – rendered the room 'very offensive, and indeed made the whole Court nasty and stinking'.[112]

A visit to the average stately home would provide scant relief. Given the number of overfed dogs that aristocrats liked to keep, the situation there was in some ways notably worse. Keith Thomas cites the instance of Henry Hastings, son of the 4th Earl of Huntingdon in the earlier seventeenth century. This noble gentleman had a great hall which 'was strewn with marrow bones' and which 'swarmed with hawks, hounds, spaniels and terriers', whilst his walls were hung with the skins of 'recently-killed foxes and polecats'. For a long time, dogs were used to turn a meat-spit by the fire. Only in 1723 did the northern landowner William Cotesworth order 'the dog-wheel to be moved "on purpose to keep the dog from the fire, the wheel out of the way and the dog prevented [from] shitting upon anything it could"'.[113] This kind of environment would have been particularly unsavoury in the earlier decades of our period, when rushes were a common floor covering. Not only would these, harbouring 'spittle, vomit, scraps of food and the leakage of dogs', offer a partial disguise for dirt, but instead of being swept out they would for some time simply be re-covered with another, 'fresh' layer of cut stalks, while veritable strata of accumulated debris proliferated and festered beneath one's feet.[114]

Civic and personal hygiene

Although some affluent London streets were evidently better swept and tended than the poorer quarters of the city, this was an age in which filth was not merely synonymous with poverty. The 'great unwashed' meant everybody. Life stank. Modern psychology concerning body wastes is crucially shaped by a fundamental event in the long pungent history of sanitation.[115] Almost magically, seamlessly, human urine and excrement are banished *under*ground.[116] A great gulf divides this privileged era from those in which piss and shit were habitually stagnating over-ground (or, at best, relatively near its surface, as Pepys discovered on 20 October 1660, when, 'going down into my cellar … I stepped into a great heap of turds, by which I found that Mr Turner's house of office is full and comes into my cellar, which do trouble me … '). Excrement could be sealed off in partial, minimal ways, beneath the lids of close stools or chamber pots.[117] But surviving evidence suggests that even these basic coverings were often neglected by both rich and poor. There were almost no public lavatories. The few which did exist, such as the quite sizeable one on London Bridge, evidently stank much of the time, as house buyers were warned to avoid living near such places.[118]

Here is the typical morning routine of a French schoolboy in 1568: '"I woke up, got out of bed, put on my shirt, stockings, and shoes, buckled my belt, urinated against the courtyard wall, took fresh water from the bucket, washed my hands and face … "'.[119] The historian who relates this, Norbert Elias, has many other examples of the period's distinctive toilet habits. An instance uncertainly attributed to the fif-teenth century warns the reader: 'before you sit down, make sure your seat has not been fouled'. This might look like fairly obvious, universal advice for anyone a little wary of public lavatories. But the warning in fact derives from a guide to table manners. The seat in question seems to have been not a lavatory, but an ordinary dining chair. Who fouled it? Perhaps a cat or dog. But – as the case of James I reminds us – it may well have just been a guest who was too drunk or too lazy to get up and loose their urine somewhere more suitable.

No less startling is the opinion of the early sixteenth-century scholar and educational reformer, Desiderius Erasmus: 'it is impolite to greet someone who is urinating or defecating'. (This advice did not stop Madame de Prie receiving the Marquis De Argenson whilst sat on her new bidet in 1710.[120]) Similarly, a German book of manners from 1570 advises that 'one should not, like rustics … relieve oneself with-out shame or reserve in front of ladies, or before the doors or windows of court chambers'. Note the implications of the phrasing here: it seems that one *can* relieve oneself 'in front of ladies', provided one does it *with* 'shame and reserve' (presumably, with one's back turned). In some contexts, it was not merely rustics who were forced to behave without shame or reserve: '"you are indeed fortunate to shit whenever you please and to do so to your heart's content! … We are not so lucky here. I have to hold on to my turd until evening; the houses next to the forest are not equipped with facilities. I have the misfortune of inhabiting one and consequently the dis-pleasure of having to shit outside, which gravely perturbs me because I like to shit at my ease with my ass fully bared. *Item* all manner of people can see us shitting; there are men who walk by, women, girls, boys, abbeys, Swiss Guards … "'. So complained the Duchess of Orléans from Fontainebleau in October 1694.[121]

An Italian work of 1589 warns, '"let no one, whoever he may be, before, at, or after meals, early or late, foul the staircases, corridors, or closets with urine or other filth, but go to suitable, prescribed places for such relief"'.[122] (Note the phrase 'whoever he may be'. This seems to imply status, as if the highest born are especially likely to piss or shit wherever they please.) Even when people did use 'prescribed places', many were in the habit of standing on or over the toilet – and, perhaps, often aiming poorly. As eighteenth-century French schoolmasters increasingly sought to stamp out this habit it was arranged that they should, accordingly, be able to see the floor and ceiling of the lavatory cubicles from their chairs ... [123]

Perhaps most remarkable of all is a guide to manners dating from 1558. 'It does not', admonishes the author, 'befit a modest, honourable man to prepare to relieve nature in the presence of other people, nor to do up his clothes afterward in their presence'. And

> for the same reason it is not a refined habit when coming across something disgusting in the street ... to turn at once to one's companion and point it out to him. It is far less proper to hold out the stinking thing for the other to smell, as some are wont, who even urge the other to do so, lifting the foul-smelling thing to his nostrils and saying, "I should like to know how much that stinks" ... [124]

Even assuming that the waggish gentleman here is gloved, the scenario is arresting. It seems almost certain that the disgusting 'something' is either human or animal faeces. The joker is ready to pick it up, and his companion is – evidently – prepared to show considerable tolerance as it is thrust into his face. How much, then, did the Renaissance city stink during a long dry summer? Imagine the foulest urine-soaked alleyway, one hot Sunday morning. Garnish it with a dead cat, some rats, and perhaps even a mule.[125] Stir in the contents of human and animal bladders and bowels, and heat until vomiting point ... you are now just beginning to uncover a few threads of the richly coloured tapestry of urban smells, circa 1600.

For all the Duchess's complaint, we have perhaps already begun to sense that for many the habits described above were not simply a matter of brute necessity. True, the lack of complex underground sewers and of effective antibacterial agents were basic facts of life. The fumes of animal blood and offal, smoking out into the neighbouring air around the shambles, or slaughterhouse, were equally inescapable. But in many other areas people lived in filth as a matter of routine tolerance, or of active and rational choice. Soap did exist. Yet, while people washed small areas of their bodies (most often, those which would be seen) almost no one ever bathed.[126] This was thought to be positively harmful. Francis Bacon marvels at the habitual bathing of the Romans, and notes that the Turks, similarly addicted to this vice, could escape its effects only because their diet of rice specially toughened their bodies against the invasion of the water.[127] Around 1671, John Burbury marvelled, similarly, at the excessive 'cleanliness of the Turks, who, as they had occasion to make urine ... afterwards washed their hands, as they do still before and after their eating, which with them is as often as their prayers, four or five times a day'.[128]

Queen Elizabeth, notes Lawrence Wright, had very fine 'bathing-rooms', but took a bath just once a month, '"whether she need it or no"'.[129] Keith Thomas, noting that in 1653 'the diarist John Evelyn resolved' to wash his head 'once a year', goes on to cite a popular proverb of the day: "'Wash thy hands often, thy face seldom, but thy head never'".[130] Smith notes how the 1648 attempt of Dr Peter Chamberlen to introduce London public baths was contemptuously scotched by Cromwell's administration, which feared the consequent "'physical prejudice, effeminating bodies and procuring infirmities'", and the expected moral "'debauching ... of the people'".[131] In the eighteenth century, French doctors still 'condemned the harmful effects of thoughtless use of water. Overfrequent ablutions and ... baths', they believed, 'weakened animalization and therefore sexual desire'.[132]

While the affluent or rich might in some cases change their clothes now and then, the poorer sort would retain the same set for weeks on end. Perfume was used by some members of both sexes. But it was intended chiefly to 'protect oneself and to purify the surrounding air' – that is, to ward off disease, and to secure one's own olfactory comfort, rather than that of others. And, if you ever did travel in Dr Who's TARDIS to Renaissance London, you might want to know a bit more about its choices of perfumes before using them yourself. There was, for example, a 'long-lived fashion for animal perfumes with an odour of excrement'. (Hence the use of secretions from the anal glands of the zibeth, or civet cat, which we met above.) Add to this the fact that musk, 'a waste product originating in the putrid guts of the musk deer' was especially popular; that, if your musk had lost its scent, you should refresh it by hanging it over "'a humid floor ... particularly near a privy'"; and that the promisingly named 'Eau de Mille Fleurs' included human excrement as a key ingredient, and you begin to realise that perfume may have been part of the problem, rather than its solution.[133] As Michael Stoddart notes, 'at the time of her death the walls of the Empress Josephine's rooms were so heavily impregnated with the sexual lure of the Himalayan musk deer' that men working there suffered nausea and fainting spells.[134]

The dead, the sick, and the jail

So much, then, for the living and the relatively healthy. Let us imagine for a moment that a smell is a sound. How loud was the stench of the past? We can estimate modern olfactory environments as a kind of background hum or whispering, punctuated by a few harsher percussions. In a rich man's house circa 1600, your nose could barely hear itself think. In a one-room hovel, shared with several children, chickens and cattle, the din rose to a mind-shattering cacophony. Meanwhile, the dead contributed their own special flavours to this complex and gamey olfactory recipe. They rotted on gibbets, as we saw in chapter three (with the bad trick played on the honest butcher in fact being an updated version of a punishment supposedly practised by certain Roman emperors – in that latter case you could be tied to a corpse until you perished). They stared down sightlessly from city gates.

Beneath them, dead dogs, cats, and mules were left rotting in streets, alleyways and courtyards. Rats, which often lived within the relatively porous walls of pre-modern houses, died there on occasion, decaying pungently out of reach.[135] In Paris, the notoriously ill-designed and overcrowded cemetery of Les Innocentes overpowered its neighbours so violently by the late eighteenth century that (as Patrick Suskind puts it) the citizens arose to 'actual insurrection' and forced its closure.[136] In 1839, whilst making a survey of London burials, George Walker described the private London burial chamber of Enon Chapel in Clement's Lane. This was 'separated from the chapel above only by floorboards', and Walker 'graphically described repellent black flies living off the putrefaction of the bodies ... in the summer ... the stench was simply intolerable'.[137]

We have heard how, after the Battle of Marston Moor the stench of corpses 'almost poisoned them that passed over the moor'.[138] In that case the author uses 'poisoned' quite literally, reflecting the general belief that such smells were contagious – hence the tolling funeral bell in the weeks following the battle. In other cases the reek of death became a deliberate military weapon in its own right. Back in the early centuries of Christianity, Vandal hordes besieging castles would heap up corpses beneath the walls, 'that by the stench thereof they might force them to surrender'.[139] In the fourteenth century one army was supposed to have actually catapulted corpses over the walls in order to compel the submission of those within. Such tactics no doubt continued as the Wars of Religion ravaged Europe after the Reformation.[140] In keeping with this theory of contagion, it was believed that plague could be caught via smell alone. One author wrote that, in 1635 (a particular nadir of the Thirty Years War) 'such an infection happened through the stench of the dead unburied bodies, that in the Bishopric of Metz alone there died of this and hunger twenty four thousand people'.[141] Only in the 1880s would the scientific authorities of France emphatically abandon belief in olfactory contagion: '"we can repeat that everything that stinks does not kill, and everything that kills does not stink"'.[142]

Somewhere in between these two relatively well-defined zones of the living and dead there lay shadowy and fertile limbos. Hospitals, sickrooms and prisons had smells all their own. If the reek of disease was not always deadly, it was often hardly less overpowering. In the fourteenth century Catherine of Siena (c. 1370) was treating a sick nun. This woman (notes William Miller) 'had a cancer on her breast that put forth such an awful smell that no one would attend her in her sickness'. Catherine was the only volunteer. And even she, we are told, more than once vomited spontaneously at the extremity of this stench.[143] Nature itself must have multiplied similar cases such as this across Europe up to and through the nineteenth century. But some doctors also tried their best to add to the overwhelming aromas of disease. For precise medical reasons, the eminent Dutch physician Ysbrand van Diemerbroeck warned that a sufferer from smallpox should be left unmoved and unchanged for up to fourteen days: 'far better it is to suffer the shifts of the patient, moist with sweat, to dry of themselves with the heat of the bed, and for the patient for some days to bear with the stench of the sweat, and the pustles coming forth, than to change his linen and be the cause of his own death'. If 'there be an urgent necessity for the patient to change his linen', they should then 'have the same foul linen' which they had discarded just before their sickness. Newly washed linen is most dangerous of all, van Diemerbroeck warns. Why? Well – naturally enough – because of the lingering smell of soap.[144]

Dead pigeons must have also become quite aromatic after remaining some time by a patient's body. On 22 September 1689 a Dr Cotton applied these not to the feet but to the head of one Mrs Patty, a woman who was suffering from violent convulsions. We have no idea what she felt about this. But we do know that the birds were there on her pillow for almost five days. If a week is a long time in politics, five days is a pretty fair while to be intimate with rotting pigeons. We can at least rest assured that this affluent woman was attended by the finest doctors, as one of her consultants was in fact Thomas Willis. The treatment would have been thought successful, as the birds were removed only when the patient 'appeared somewhat better in her senses' on the morning of the 26th.[145] At times the human body, afflicted with a putrescent living death, could outdo the stench of mere dead birds. Just before he died, the amputation victim seen by John Evelyn had gangrene so severe that one could have 'run a straw through' the rotted leg. And, Evelyn adds, 'I do not remember that ever in my life I smelt so intolerable a stink' as that of this man's sundered leg – consequently ordering that it should 'immediately be buried in the garden'.[146]

If the sick, in some of these cases, began to hope for death, they were not alone. In 1686 Louis XIV coerced the Duke of Savoy into assisting with the persecution of the Waldenses, a heretical sect whose members dwelt in the valleys of Piedmont. After refusing to abandon their faith, 3,000 of the Waldenses were killed, and the remaining 12,000 thrown into prison. When their historian, Gilbert Burnet, stated that the imprisoned survivors were hardly more fortunate than the slain, he was scarcely exaggerating:

> corruption … had engendered abundance of lice that would not let the prisoners sleep night nor day … there were several sick persons … that were … eaten up alive with worms; for by continual lying, as not being able to rise or lift themselves up, these poor people were become so mangy, that their very skin being already putrified, parted from their flesh and mouldered away in pieces: they left them thus flayed and miserably languishing till death put a period to all their sufferings.[147]

This kind of environment may have been a little harder for the genteel than it was for 'ordinary criminals' – a point worth noting, given that the imprisonment of eminent men (Donne and Cellini are just two examples) was a fairly routine hazard of the era. Not all such figures complained openly about their temporarily degraded living conditions. But one response is particularly memorable. In the eighteenth century, 'the comte de Struensee, taken out of his dungeon to be beheaded, cried out: "Oh, the happiness of breathing fresh air!"'.[148]

The conditions of many early modern prisons do indeed seem to have amounted to a kind of living hell. To the abundance of rats, lice and spiders we must add not only darkness, but severe extremes of heat and cold. If you had no immediate friends or relatives nearby you stood to go without food (which was not the jail's responsibility) or a change of clothing. If it was summer, plague and dysentery bristled through the mire of piss and shit like electricity down wires. If it was winter, matters may not be much more pleasant. On one occasion, the French magistrate, Dr Cottu, visited a dungeon in Reims prison:

> I felt I was being stifled by the horrible stench that hit me as soon as I entered ... At the sound of my voice, which I tried to make soft and consoling, I saw a woman's head emerge from the dung; as it was barely raised, it presented the image of a severed head thrown onto the dung; all the rest of this wretched woman's body was sunk in excrement ... Lack of clothing had forced her to shelter from the stringencies of the weather in her dung.[149]

This incident is so extraordinary as to challenge the capacities of the modern imagination. A few decades ago, admittedly, farm workers would often deliberately stand in fresh cow pats on chill mornings. But – to make a kind of impromptu blanket out of around five cubic feet of human shit ... ? Cottu's vivid image – a severed head perched on a dung heap – forces us to realise not only that the woman was more *comfortable* in this situation, but that it was possible for a prison to achieve this level of degradation: a mound of excrement so large that it could cocoon an entire human body.

Sensory invasion

If we remained in any doubt, the above example should persuade us that the inhabitants of pre-modern Europe generally had a considerably higher stink threshold than most of us. (Even Cottu, after all, had to endure this for some time, and it is not merely whimsical to emphasise that it was not *his* excrement.) To some extent, this tolerance must have been a matter of sheer brute necessity. As Louis-Sébastien Mercier put it, in his attack on eighteenth-century Paris:

> If I am asked how anyone can stay in this filthy haunt of all the vices ... amid an air poisoned by a thousand putrid vapours, among butchers' shops, cemeteries, hospitals, drains, streams of urine, heaps of excrement ... in the midst of the arsenic, bituminous, and sulphurous parts that are ceaselessly exhaled by workshops ... I would say that familiarity accustoms the Parisians to humid fogs, maleficent vapours, and foul-smelling ooze.[150]

Doubtless some people suffered more than others. And perhaps each person had their own catalogue of most intolerable odours. We will see in a moment that mere physical familiarity was by no means the only factor involved. But let us pause just briefly to consider the special qualities of smell as a whole.

Like noise, smell invades us. Other senses do not involve the same aggressive penetration: we can avoid tasting, touching or looking at things that repel us. But sound and smell cannot very easily be shut out (although in the latter case we seem sometimes to try, as when our bodies noticeably shrink or stiffen under intense olfactory pressures). At least in relative terms, the way in which most of us routinely experience unwanted noise is quite similar to pre-modern exposure to bad smells. Yet, while it is thought that noise pollution – and amplification in general – tends to deaden aural sensitivity, the reverse seems to have been true in the rich, almost canine environment of the pre-modern world.

Smell invades us. But at times it seems that, where now we just cautiously dip our toes within the great sea of odours, much of early modern humanity took an oblique revenge, effectively invading the world of smell, plunging vigorously into the chaotic stinking melée of any large European city as it fermented in the odours of life and death, animal and vegetable, old and young. Returning to that striking case of faeces jokingly proffered to the human nose ('I should like to know how much that stinks') we might begin to wonder if this seemingly bizarre action was in fact unintentionally symbolic. Was this kind of person (of whom there seem to have been more than one) actually confronting, and thereby partially taming, something which was at once offensive and unavoidable? To put it another way: when everything was so disgusting, it was not really possible to be disgusted.

Once immersed in this invasive sensory experience, people in general could not only tolerate it, but actively exploit it.[151] The average person seems indeed to have been relatively doglike in their precise use of smell. They monitored their own personal scents in order to watch for the possible onset of illness.[152] (Is this why, secretly, we never find our own bad smells as bad as those from other people? Has evolution conditioned us to be tolerant, even interested?) In this same sphere, qualified medical practitioners could '"tell the odour that emanates from ulcers complicated by gangrene ... dysentery, malign putrid fevers, and that odour of mice which is part of hospital and jail fevers"'.[153] Angry people had a particular scent on their breath, and the gluttonous their own special odour. The Italian saint, Philip Neri, could supposedly recognise the stench of sinners destined for hell.[154] Prostitutes were held to suffer from putrescence of their internal fluids, due to their excessive sexual activity. Accordingly, one could recognise them by their allegedly intolerable stink. The belief is still encoded in the French word for whore: 'putain', from the Latin 'putris', means 'rotten'. A Prague monk writing in 1684 claimed that he could detect the telltale odour of adulterous women (a skill which he no doubt put only to virtuous uses[155]). Small wonder that, circa 1599, the poet Sir John Davies should insist that 'they smell best, that do of nothing smell'.[156]

In November 1602 Manningham related a joke then current among his circle of friends: '"his mouth were good to make a mouse trap"' it was said 'of one that smells of cheese-eating'.[157] Notice how exact this is. The precise identification of a person's recent meal (rather than simply 'bad breath') seems to imply a special olfactory refinement. And such skill was evident elsewhere. We ourselves still attempt to gauge the quality of some foods (milk or cheese, for instance) by smell. But in the seventeenth century those buying rabbits would rely on their noses to ascertain not just basic edibility, but whether or not the animal had been recently killed.[158] Before sell-by dates simplified such problems, you trusted your own nose to calculate grades of freshness. What use is a sell-by date, after all, when most people (including the servants who buy food) are more or less illiterate? In such a context, smell could sometimes be a peculiarly useful (and democratic) kind of gift. Once again, the basic rule was to get nature on your side as far as possible.

Mind over matter

What do such attitudes to smell and to dirt suggest about people's broader attitudes to organic life in general? The average stink threshold was clearly much higher. Was there also a much higher threshold of disgust? Imagine for a moment that you have a new puppy. Delightful as the creature is, it has not yet learned about dirt and disgust (something which already implies that such feelings are not purely 'natural' or evolutionary). Finding one morning that it has left shit on the kitchen floor, you will probably be impelled to clean this up immediately, despite an urgent desire for coffee and breakfast. You could of course consume these in another room. But you probably will not. Why? Disgust pervades your consciousness, and by extension the whole house, until you have eliminated the source of pollution. To put it another way: the idea of neglecting this mess is somehow *morally* distasteful or offensive.[159]

Consider, by contrast, Keith Thomas's comments on the changing attitudes of 'polite society' in the later seventeenth century. The interior-decorating style of a Henry Hastings was, it seems, slowly going out of fashion. Certain people were now 'coming to despise this old way of housekeeping, "with dogs' turds and marrow-bones as ornaments in the hall"'.[160] There is one crucial word in that contemporary quotation: 'ornaments' … Ironic as it is, it clearly implies that the rich (for 'hall' means 'great hall' rather than merely 'entrance hall') would tolerate – perhaps for hours, perhaps for days – what we would feel compelled to eradicate in a matter of minutes. Bear in mind, too, that for these people it was only a question of instructing one's *servants*, rather than handling the problem in person.

We have now begun to relocate corpse medicine – to see it within medical and social worlds since mercifully faded from our eyes, noses and skins. If people could tolerate the everyday filth and irritation we have encountered here, then their toler-ance of medicinal cannibalism must have been moulded accordingly. If they were so ferociously attacked by death and disease, they may have been more ready to accept remedies which we would feel able to shun. Linking these arguments back to our discussion of sources in chapter three, we might add another practical issue. Although (as we will see in a few moments) corpse medicine was recommended by some very convincing abstract reasons, we should not forget that, in an age with far more basic industrial technologies, you frequently needed to use *everything* you could get. This applied to all areas of life. When we now look at the quaint old pink cot-tages of country villages and hamlets, we all too easily forget that this colour was originally derived from pigs' blood. In 1698 a Dorset farmer wrote of how '"my old dog Quon was killed … and baked for his grease, of which he yielded 11 pounds"'.[161] Fat was indeed an essential commodity. Most candles were made not of expensive beeswax, but of tallow. Hence the job of 'grease-dealer' – a person who made their living by collecting the grease of domestic kitchens, scraping it into a tub, and presently reselling it.[162]

Urine was highly valued, offering as it did a cheap source of ammonia. As Boyle notes, it was 'made much use of, not only by dyers', but by 'several other trades-men in divers operations', including cloth-workers (fullers) and leather workers, who used it to soak animal hides. Dominique Laporte notes that 'it was common practice in the fifteenth century ... to use urine for the cleansing of draperies and clothes'. Although, 'in 1493, Parisian haberdashers ... appealed to the King himself on the grounds that "bonnets ... cleansed by means of piss are neither proper nor appropriate nor healthful to place on one's head"', the habit was reintroduced some fifty years later.[163]

Even now, older people may well recall how quickly fresh horse dung would be seized from the street by the fastest gardener of the area. Around 400 years ago, manure was considered so valuable that it might be left to friends or kin in one's Will. Leonard Holme, for example 'died in 1610 leaving "dung" worth 8s', and John Brown died in 1667 leaving 'manure or dung' worth 2s.[164] In Inverness in 1564, James Duff took James Kar to court, prosecuting him for '28 loads of muck' which Kar had borrowed and failed to return (different muck, but roughly same quantity, it seems).[165] Human excrement, meanwhile, was also sometimes used as fertiliser. As Laporte points out, in France 'all the treatises of the day concurred on the eminent status of human manure'; although, interestingly, some thought that '"three-to-four-year-old dung is best because the passage of time will have dissipated its stench and whatever was bad in it will have softened"'.[166] Here we seem to meet a strange alchemy of shit, maturing and refining like vintage cheese or wine. Human excrement was still being routinely collected for this purpose in certain Spanish towns in the nineteenth century.[167]

In those days, to be left a load of old shit in someone's will was no bad thing. And, for all the profusion of organic muck in any city, there was certainly far less inorganic litter than we now find in our own streets. Centuries before Green politics were dreamed of, recycling was a hard-headed, common-sense practice. In so brutally unequal a society, someone would always want someone else's cast-offs, however ragged. Well into the nineteenth century, street criers could be heard calling out for 'Ogh Clo' (or old clothes).[168] The smallest scraps of metal could be sold to a suitable dealer. A certain type of brick was made in part out of 'grit and ashes riddled from the street sweepings'.[169] Within this kind of organic economy of waste disposal that now rare wild bird, the kite, was so familiar that it was known to occasionally snatch bread and butter from children's hands. Adept at ridding the city of animal waste, these birds were accordingly protected by law in the early modern period. Those Spanish peasants gathering human faeces in the nineteenth century were, similarly, part of a vital mutual economy which aided city hygiene as well as country farming.[170]

A particularly vivid instance of this kind of mentality can be found in the nineteenth century in the west Highlands, where 'a cure for blindness ... was to dry and powder human excrement and blow it in the eyes of the afflicted person'. This practice at once amplifies and historically extends the cure recommended by Boyle for cataracts. Moreover, the informant who related this to Mary Beith explained it in a way which broadly echoes the general early modern need to exploit all available resources: "'they were very poor people. They had nothing, nothing, and they tried anything'".[171]

In the early modern period, however, people would probably have been far less likely to apologise for such cures in that way. Corpse medicines could be seen as not just acceptable, but as the most desirable apex of those powers lodged within Nature as a whole by the Almighty. For all his naughtiness, after all, man was still the paragon of animals. Almost everything was there to be used, if you only knew how … Lest we doubt this, let us look briefly at two forms of medicinal cannibalism which are at once less obviously cannibalistic, and (for most of us) probably far more disgusting.

Pliny had advised urine for the treatment of 'sores, burns, affections of the anus, chaps, and scorpion stings', while old urine mixed with the ash of burnt oyster shells could be rubbed on your baby for the Roman equivalent of nappy rash.[172] In the thirteenth century, Arnold of Villanova had commended not just oils of human blood and bones, but 'an oil drawn out of the excrements of children, that availeth in the foul mattery scabs of the head'. Having distilled the shit thoroughly, you should then apply the oil 'hot on the grieved place'. Oils drawn 'out of man's ordure' would 'cure the cancer, and mortifieth the fistula'. Although details are lacking, these latter sound as if they may have been taken orally.[173] Later, Estienne's *Maison Rustique* spoke of the distillation of 'all juices and liquors, as man's blood, urine, vinegar, the dew, milk … man's dung, or beast's dung'.[174] Christopher Irvine had his own distinctive uses for the spirit of human dung, and asserted that the 'excrements of the backdoor' would cure 'all diseases of the intestines'.[175] To stop the bleeding of a wound, you should 'take a hound's turd and lay it on a hot coal, and bind it' to the injured area. So said the popular medical compilation of Elizabeth Grey, Countess of Kent.[176]

The French physician Moise Charas was convinced that urine was an effective medicine, and Boyle, meanwhile, had innumerable uses for the spirit of human urine – asserting at one point that as a medicine it could be employed against jaundice, pleurisy, fevers and asthma.[177] At another he refers to the experimental use of undistilled urine, which is well-suited for certain ends, provided (of course) that 'it be stale and rank enough'.[178] For 'obstructions' he prescribes that the patient should drink every morning 'a moderate draught of his own urine', preferably while 'tis yet warm' and 'forbearing food for an hour or two after it'.[179] Over in France in 1671, Matte la Faveur (a chemist at the University of Montpellier) described a volatile salt of urine which required no small patience in the collection alone. The diligent practitioner needed to obtain 'about sixty pints of the urine of little children who drink very little wine'.[180] Madame de Sévigné, writing 'to her daughter on June 13th 1685', remarked that "'for my vapours I take eight drops of essence of urine'".[181] Some time before his death in 1674, van Diemerbroeck suggested a number of things to be thrust into the nostrils against nosebleeds. Options included 'green horsetail or shave grass, or pimpernel or plantain bruised, or hog's or ass's dung'. All these, he insisted, were 'found by experience to have wrought great cures'.[182] In 1739 it was claimed that two drams of 'the dung of an infant pulverized … taken … for several days, quite eradicates the epilepsy'.[183]

Willis, meanwhile, confirms with a vengeance the old adage 'where there's muck there's brass'. The richest doctor in the country remarks that inflammation of the lungs can respond to 'powders of shell-fish, the tooth of a boar, and the jaws of a pike', adding that 'the infusion of horse-dung' is 'a common remedy' which 'affords oftentimes singular help'. Pleurisy can be treated with distillations from the shit of horses, cocks, oxen or pigeons. Willis thinks dog shit equally effective in this area, either taken orally or as part of an ointment containing oils of marshmallow and of almond. For jaundice one should use the dung of sheep and geese, or swallow nine live lice each day. (Willis also adds that merely 'pissing upon horse-dung while it is hot' has helped many jaundiced patients.) 'The whitest dung of a peacock' could combat vertigo and apoplexy: we hear of a sixty-year-old gentleman afflicted with the former who made a particularly difficult patient until given a powder of peony roots and flowers, peacock dung and white sugar. 'It is scarce credible', Willis writes, 'how much help he received from this remedy; visiting me after a month, he seemed a new and another man'.[184]

Whatever we may think about these therapies (or of 'a poultice of fresh cow dung applied warm' to the gouty), we can hardly claim that they look merely like just any load of old shit.[185] You must carefully choose the right animal or bird, mix in the correct ingredients, and distil effectively. We seem, indeed, to have here a veritable science of shit, of nature's most contemptible by-products probed, tamed, classified and swallowed. Come the eighteenth century, it was still believed that rat-droppings were 'a surefire remedy for constipation' – and also (if mixed with honey and onion juices) a cure for baldness.[186]

If distilled medicines were not affordable by all, it was some consolation to know that '"the dirt to be found around the neck of a man's penis"' could be spread on scorpion stings (again, in the circumstances, you'd probably try it – especially if you were a man).[187] And there was also a similarly impromptu use of human urine in this period. In some modern films, when a person is badly beaten by one or more men, it is not uncommon to see the victim urinated on as a concluding gesture of humiliation. What is less predictable is that a doctor or surgeon should then rush up, carefully inspect the patient, and do exactly the same thing – aiming carefully, of course, for the worst of the victim's wounds. In the early modern period this was clearly considered an effective method of treating injuries. The Italian doctor Leonardo Fioravanti tells in 1580 of working in Africa when a Spanish gentleman, Andreas Gutiero, 'walked in the field, and fell at words with a soldier'. Seeing Gutiero draw his weapon, the soldier quickly struck a left-handed blow with his own sword 'and cut off his nose'. When this 'fell down in the sand' Fioravanti picked it up 'and pissed thereon to wash away the sand' before stitching it on again and dressing it with his 'balsamo artificiato'. After being bound up for eight days, the nose was found 'fast conglutinated' and Gutiero was soon 'perfectly whole, so that all Naples did marvel thereat'.[188]

Tragically, early modern doctors and surgeons had no concept of sterilisation – something which Fioravanti seems to reflect when he talks merely of washing off the sand. But he may well have had some sense that urine seemed to be effective in cases of surgery and later healing. As Beith points out, the chemical urea is still used in modern medicine in 'treatments for ulcers and infected wounds'.[189] Moreover, given that it is sterile when it leaves the body, it was probably safer than the kind of water generally available. In 1551 he treated a young sailor, Francisco di Giovanni Raguseo, who during combat had had his liver badly cut. We glimpse the hazards of early modern surgery when we hear that the first surgeon botched the repairs, leaving Fioravanti to find, next day, that 'the wound [was] not well stitched, the which I ripped up again, and found the belly full of blood ... when I saw that, I caused divers to make water, and there-with I washed him'. Here the surgeon goes to some trouble to get a considerable quantity of urine, echoing all those of his peers who so often turned to that portable and ever-renewable medicine cabinet, the human body. Despite losing a piece of his liver, in three weeks' time Raguseo had completely recovered.[190]

Thomas Vicary (d.1561), sometime surgeon to Henry VIII, had also stated that a surgeon should immediately wash all types of battle wounds 'very clean with urine' before putting in quintessence of wine.[191] Similarly, when a French sea captain and his men were blown out of the water by an English ship in 1695, the captain first washed his bleeding head with urine and then quickly bound the wound with linen torn from his shirt – adding that 'the same thing was done to the rest that had been wounded'.[192] For itching eyelids (wrote Ambroise Paré), 'some wish that the patient's urine be kept all night in a barber's basin', and his 'eye-lids ... washed therewith'.[193] The Dutch physician Giles Everard, moreover, explicitly claimed that falling hair, and 'old corrupt ulcers of the arms, legs, and other parts' which were otherwise 'ready to gangrene', could be 'brought to cicatrize if they be first washed in white wine or urine, and wiped with a wet cloth, with one or two green leaves of tobacco bruised'.[194] Again, when Stephen Bredwell, in 1633, states that venomous stings or bites should be washed with urine, or salt water, or vinegar, or white wine, it is clear enough which fluid would be cheapest and most easily available.[195] In 1675 we read of 'a gentlewoman [who] had three great white excrescences in one of her eyes after the smallpox', and who was cured in part by 'washing the eye ... with a drop of spirit of urine'.[196] Barbette advised that anyone suffering from 'old sores ... in their legs especially ... must above all things be careful to keep them clean, and to that end wash them, at least once a day, with your own urine'.[197] (Henry VIII take note.)

In many of those cases, medical urgency or desperation might seem to offer some explanation for what is otherwise baffling to the modern mind. But the same clearly does not hold for some of the beauty tips found in the 1675 work *The Accomplish'd Lady's Delight in Preserving, Physic, Beautifying, and Cookery*. Against falling hair, the discerning Restoration lady might wash her head with 'the ashes of pigeon's-dung in lye'; whilst to thicken it she could employ the ashes of burned frogs or 'the ashes of goat's-dung mingled with oil'. One's own urine, meanwhile, was 'very good to wash the face withal, to make it fair'.[198] A reputable beauty journal such as the above makes us more inclined to trust a mere man (the surgeon William Bullein), when he claims that those 'whose faces be unclean' should wash their skin with distilled water of honey, mixed with 'strong vinegar, milk, and the urine of a boy'.[199] (Writing in

1995 Beith emphasises that, 'today, urea remains an important ingredient in medicinal skin creams', and recalls 'babies having their faces wiped with their own wet nappies in the belief that this practice would give them good complexions. A friend of mine with four boys made a virtual religion' of this, 'and not one of those boys became a spotty teenager'.[200]) No less popular amongst self-respecting ladies was fresh blood. After a hart was killed in the park of Sir Arnold Braems in Kent on 10 August 1661, 'everybody, especially the ladies, washed their hands in the warm blood, to get white hands'.[201]

These and similar habits went back a very long way. Laporte discusses at some length 'the cosmetic properties of shit, which was once used on ladies' faces and hair'. St Jerome, 'advisor to the ladies of Rome from 382 to 385', had 'warned against the practice of smearing one's face with shit to preserve a youthful complexion'. 'Numerous distillations destined for cosmetic use and an array of beauty potions purporting to whiten the skin were generated from fecal matter', along with a host of urine-based products designed to beautify the complexion and heal scars. Most intriguingly of all, a rarefied elixir of youth might be anointed upon the cheeks of privileged women. 'The shit of athletic youths', Laporte writes, 'was prized above all', while 'in some instances, custom went so far as to exact … the "discharge of just born infants"'.

In the later eighteenth century, the French physician M. Geoffroy knew of one '"lady of high standing, who relied on stercorary fluid to keep her complexion the most beautiful in the world until a very advanced age. She retained a healthy young man in her service whose sole duty was to answer nature's call in a special basin of tin-plated copper with a very tight lid"'. This was covered so that none of the contents could evaporate. When the shit had cooled, the young man collected the moisture which had formed under the lid of the basin. '"This precious elixir was then poured into a flask that was kept on Madame's dressing table. Every day, without fail, this lady would wash her hands and face in the fragrant liquid; she had uncovered the secret to being beautiful for an entire lifetime"'.[202] Here we once again encounter a kind of alchemy of excrement, tinged in this case with the quasi-vampiric desire to absorb the powers of the young and vigorous (compare Ficino's idea about youthful blood for the elderly). For this woman, there was clearly no question of painting one's face with anything as lowly (or disgusting) as mere dog shit.

How did people tolerate the uncertainty, the fear, discomfort, and potential disgust of a world wriggling with unwanted life forms, steaming with the rank perfumes of human waste, and shadowed beneath the cold, ever-present eye of Death? There are two very simple answers: words, and ideas.[203] Reality is made out of words, quite as much as it is out of brute matter. It is filtered by ideas which change significantly across different nations and eras. (Why else is the constellation known in Britain as 'the plough' referred to as 'the cooking pot' by the French, and as 'the big dipper' by the North Americans?) Even as the body's five senses were assailed by heat, cold, pain, shock and revulsion, a sixth sense was busily reworking all these stimuli. This sense was the brain. At a very basic level, the human mind filtered and reordered surrounding chaos. To do so, it used a shield made up of long-established intellectual and religious beliefs. In the early modern period, the pungent ooze of the animal and vegetable worlds was animated not simply by the dance of atoms or the pulse of microbes, but by the resilient pressure of human ideas. So, when Donne stated on his sickbed that 'I am surprised with a sudden change, and alteration to worse, *and can impute it to no cause, nor call it by any name*', he was at once registering the peculiar fear inspired by the unknown, and taming this anxiety through the very act of ordered speech and writing. As we will see at the start of the following chapter, the whole of the *Devotions* can indeed be viewed as an attempt to make such uncertainty not only comprehensible, but religiously meaningful.

At times the apogee of holiness and the apparent dregs of base matter could indeed be indissolubly fused by early modern healers. Kathy Stuart, for example, notes an immensely popular German work, 'the *Salutary Apothecary of Filth, wherein almost all diseases are cured with Excrement and Urine*, first published in 1696 by the physician and professor of medicine Christian Franz Paulani'. Paulani, who prescribed 'skull, powdered blood, peacock's dung, and human sweat, ear wax, nails, spit, afterbirth, semen, and menstrual blood', stated quite unequivocally: '"God and nature lie in excrement and urine"'.[204]

Ultimately, it is difficult to know just how reality *felt* in such circumstances. For some people, perhaps no amount of religious intensity was sufficient to fully drug or trick the body's basic animal responses to stench or horror. Yet for Richard Baxter, Christian piety was surely the greatest and most effective medicine. For others, it may have been precisely the inescapable squalor of ordinary life which inspired such transcendent feats of musical, artistic and literary skill. In such a world, it was all the more vital to assert the power of the human mind over the brute facts of organic disorder. At the same time, there seems often to be a certain distinctive smell of raw earth about the art of this era. At its best it has an immediacy, a visual or phonetic punch which may indeed have arisen from perpetual exposure to the uncertain flux of harsh life and sudden death. Nothing could be at once more airily deft and more practically robust than the work of Shakespeare, a writer who could have Hamlet talk both of 'this brave o'erhanging firmament, this majestical roof fretted with golden fire', and of his mother 'in the rank sweat of an enseamèd bed,/ ... honeying and making love/Over the nasty sty'.[205]

To fully grasp the power of words over things in this period, we need to see that Western medical authority was – for a scientific observer – a seemingly paradoxical creation. For centuries, knowledge and practice were based not on practical experience, but on the bizarrely antiquated writings of long-dead physicians and philosophers. Personally, if Aristotle or Galen told me that it was a nice day, I'd look out the window. And if one of their intellectual followers told me to drink blood, I'd want some reliable case histories ...

Those older authorities began to be attacked or discarded as the early stages of a self-conscious empirical science got under way in the Restoration. But in many ways this later period only confirms the power of ideas over raw matter or human emotions. Scientists used the idea of progress, for example, to harden themselves to the potential traumas of vivisecting innumerable animals.[206] We have seen that Charles II both produced and consumed corpse medicine. If this already jolts traditional perceptions of such a figure, there is another story about him which makes his accepted image more or less unrecognisable.

On 11 May 1663 Pepys talked to a Mr Pierce, a surgeon, who told Samuel that 'the other day Dr Clerke and he did dissect two bodies, a man and a woman ... before the king, with which the king was highly pleased'. A few weeks earlier, on 17 February, Pepys relates a seemingly authentic story of how a baby was stillborn during a court entertainment that January. This incident itself – in which the mother may well have been taken by surprise – is striking enough.[207] But Pepys further adds that 'the king had [the baby] in his closet a week after, and did dissect it'.[208] (When I told this story to one academic colleague, his immediate response was, 'that's disgusting'.) Nor was this the strangest part of the tale. For the child's mother was reliably thought to be Winifred Wells, one of the Queen's Maids of Honour, and yet another of Charles's innumerable mistresses. If the account is accurate, Charles therefore seems to have been dissecting his own son. To set this seemingly incredible claim in context, we should add that William Harvey had dissected his own father and sister a few decades since.[209] We can also add that, whatever the final truth of the tale, Pepys and others clearly believed it. They probably believed, in part, that Charles, like many of his peers, could use the idea of scientific and medical progress to overcome any basic emotional qualms about the dissection of his own baby.

If we may not want to defend this strange mental world, we can at least begin to understand its attractions in the realm of medicine. The power of words had a certain viable logic in the days before modern science. The natural world – especially from our point of view – was chaotic. It could be tamed not simply by language, but by languages sufficiently far removed from the grubby mundanity of the urban present. Ancient languages (Latin and Greek) and ancient traditions had sufficient weight to anchor the human mind, liable otherwise to be engulfed by the natural forces surging so perilously around it. We should not underestimate the importance of this mental stability. Studies of people with severe memory loss – recall Christopher Nolan's 2000 drama, *Memento* – show us how terrifying life can be without the fullest defences of language and mental habit. Even when they are wrong, ideas can protect us. It is partly for this reason that children are frightened so much more easily than adults. (A popping champagne cork, for example, will gladden the heart of most adults, but can easily make a small child cry.)

Back then, words mattered. Human belief and human language caught the world in a web and held it still – made it at once manageable and meaningful. For the illiterate this sense may have been all the more powerful just because written knowledge was so far beyond their reach. And, more precisely, we need to wrench our imaginations for a moment and see that for a young apprentice apothecary, that strange catalogue of ingredients found in the Bucklersbury shop had not simply the airy fancy of quaint exotica, but the powerful weight of medical *technology*. For every potent variety of natural disease, humanity had a substance which buffered the mind against fear and helplessness.

We have now made some profitable journeys through the streets and alleyways of London. These gamey diversions may cause us to suspect that the arguably over-developed sense of disgust found in much of modern Europe and North America is something of an idle luxury – the kind of concern that one can afford when the outright terrors and agonies of pre-modern society have receded far over the historical horizon. Having got our boots dirty in the pursuit of a rawer, more pungent side of history, and having simultaneously begun to sense the precarious ferment of life and decay amidst which humanity lived in these times, we need now to plunge into a region of formidable interior darkness and uncertainty. In this new journey, we will descend to the minutest cavities and fibres of the heart and brain, and into a space as deep and wide as eternity itself. Our final key to the seeming riddle of corpse medicine lies not just in the human body, but in the human soul.

6

EATING THE SOUL

In our second chapter we saw John Donne, by then Dean of St Paul's, lying in a perilous condition with dead pigeons at his feet. How, a modern observer might ask, could the Dean of St Paul's tolerate this? We have already begun to see that he and his contemporaries could tolerate a great deal of seemingly overwhelming stench, filth and discomfort. But the picture sketched there was necessarily incomplete. The point was that Donne could tolerate these dead – and possibly quite pungent – birds precisely *because* he was the Dean of St Paul's.

Rather than recoiling from these creatures, Donne effectively embraces them. He proceeds to transform the potentially revolting dead matter into a symbol of the most exalted holiness. In a prayer (which we can reasonably assume was made as the birds lay soaking up harmful vapours at the bed's end) Donne first asks that God should 'prosper, I humbly beseech thee, this means of bodily assistance in this thy ordinary creature' – something which He has made 'to conduce medicinally to our bodily health'. In following lines, the pigeons seamlessly transform into the doves of the Bible: first, that which brought leaves back to Noah's ark; and second, that which, with 'thy Spirit in it', was 'a witness of thy Son's baptism'. In this last reference the slowly decaying pigeon at the Dean's feet has effectively become the Almighty himself. For, according to Luke 3.22, the Holy Ghost appeared in the shape of a dove just as Christ was being baptised by John. So, Donne finally hopes, God may carry the bird 'and the qualities of it, home to my soul, and imprint there that simplicity, that mildness, that harmlessness, which thou hast imprinted by nature in this creature'.[1] If ever words could seem to control reality, surely it was here. In a few brisk turns of the mind, a dead, gamily aromatic pigeon becomes momentarily equivalent to the Christian God.

In doing this, Donne was not being merely whimsical or fanciful.[2] Rather, he was pushing his way through the surface appearance of the crude material world, to the ultimate reality beneath (and, in a sense, doing so with the same conviction that a modern physicist would feel, piercing the outer skin of an object to reveal its atomic and subatomic structure). For Donne and almost all his European contemporaries, the ultimate reality of life was spiritual. It came from God. Whilst this held for medicine in general, it seems to have applied with special force to corpse medicine. The human body, after all, represented the pinnacle of natural creation, God's finest piece of artistry. Hence the belief of a French author in the 1660s, that mummy had 'received, not only while it was animated, but afterwards, all the influences whereof the human body is susceptible' – thus becoming 'the abstract of all the celestial powers', and accordingly able to 'communicate ... the same to him that uses it'. Such was the special potency of 'man ... the abridgement of the world'.[3] Similarly, defending the wound salve against charges of 'superstition', van Helmont demanded rhetorically whether this was 'because it is compounded of the moss, blood, mummy, and fat of man?' before responding, 'alas! the physician uses these inoffensively, and to this purpose the apothecary is licensed to sell them'. (Notice how this answer is, in its effective tautology, remarkably like the Wari' man who stated, 'thus was our custom'.) Adding that the cure was used 'only to a good and charitable end', van Helmont further insists that 'the remedies themselves are all mere natural means', whose power was ultimately 'given by God himself'.[4]

In such a context it is perhaps little surprise to find a Paracelsian author asserting that either human blood or urine could provide 'a most precious balsam of life'. The latter was 'more noble than the urine of any beast', and 'its salt hath not its like in the whole universal nature'.[5] Arguably rather more startling, however, is the implicit attitude of Pierre Pomet to the different substances classified under the term 'mummy'. Although he himself seems not to have credited mummy's therapeutic force, he was very far from disconcerted by the consumption of human flesh. Noting that some have given the 'name of mummy to several natural bitumens' from Judaea and the mountains of Arabia, Pomet suddenly bursts out: 'those appellations are very improper, they being fat, stinking, viscous humours that breed in the entrails of the earth'. Bizarrely, to our ears, Pomet seems to find a mineral substance far more repulsive than a human, cannibalised one.[6] This statement (made just after he has described at length the arguably more disgusting techniques of counterfeit-mummy dealers) seems to be rooted in a general attitude toward the hierarchy of God's creation – for Pomet, these mineral substances fall very low down in that chain.

If such beliefs could be expressed in relatively general terms, they were finally rooted in quite precise notions of human physiology. To fully understand the logic and attraction of corpse medicine, we need to realise, first, how densely and precisely the Christian soul pervaded the human body. By doing so, we are able to grasp one of the more startling aspects of European corpse medicine: certain Christian practitioners seem to have believed that it was possible to consume the powers of the human soul. Secondly, we need to look at how an increasingly scientific medicine sought to make use of the force of the soul, alchemically processing and transforming the raw material of the body. Thirdly, we will find that for much of Northern Europe, medicinal cannibalism was not only a deeply religious practice, but a quite emphatically Protestant one.

Body, soul, and spirits

At a casual glance, the human body seems to be a conveniently transhistorical entity, always with us, both then and now. Once seen in any detail, however, the early modern, pre-scientific body can appear bizarrely unfamiliar to the modern eye. To grasp what it then was and how it worked, we need to retain its organs, nerves and blood, but to empty it of later ideas. We need, as it were, to drain modern science out of it. Most importantly of all, we need to appreciate the relationship between body and soul. In the seventeenth century, the soul was very definitely *inside* the body. Where? Some thought the heart, some the brain. Others broadly followed Thomas Aquinas, who had stated that 'the whole soul is in the whole body and in each part thereof' – effectively, in good theological fashion, 'everywhere and nowhere' in the body.[7] But, in one sense, the exact location did not matter. Especially before the Restoration, few people felt the need to *prove* that the soul was in the body: if it had not been, it would simply not have been possible to explain all those bodily processes which the soul was understood to mediate or control. There was no idea, for example, of electrical impulses in the brain. More basically still, blood did not circulate of its own accord. Even after William Harvey published his radical new theory in 1628, many peers fiercely opposed him. For a long time, it was the soul which moved the body. The belief is still with us. If we take the word 'animation', wipe off its historic dust, and break it open, we find nestled inside the Latin word for soul: 'anima'. To be 'animated' was, by definition, to have a soul.

Just how did the soul and body interact? In the time of Shakespeare or Harvey, there was a crucial third level between body and soul. This intermediate zone was occupied by the spirits of the body. Imagine cutting your finger outside on a cold day. As well as blood, you would also see steam. If Shakespeare had cut his finger out at the Globe Theatre in January, he would not have seen steam, but spirits. Similarly, when he and his peers watched Dr Faustus writing that diabolic contract in his own blood, they would have realised that Faustus was using his soul to sign away his soul – which may have been precisely why the blood then congealed and temporarily denied him any more ink.[8] Spirits were a mixture of air and blood. As blood in its most rarefied state, spirits were at once material, yet sufficiently refined to actually join body and soul. Because they were at once fine and hot (as vapour naturally is) they were able to flash like lightning through the body, doing all that the pumping blood or electrical impulses would later do. If you wanted to raise your arm, spirits flitted from the brain and accomplished this. If you were stabbed, spirits flitted from the wound into the brain, transmitting the sense of pain.

Modern scientific medicine has so successfully rewritten the body that it is remarkably hard for us to *believe* that Donne and Milton and others really believed in this now outdated system. A few further details may help persuade us. Take, first, the realm of anatomy. Until some way into the seventeenth century, it was generally agreed that the human brain had a distinct organ, 'the wonderful net', dedicated to the zone between body and soul. A specially twisted labyrinth of veins and arteries at the base of the brain was believed to help refine the coarser spirits of the body into those of the soul itself.[9] This idea was no airy fantasy, but something linked to basic notions of physiology. When you ate or drank, food or liquid was processed into blood by the liver. 'Meat digested', explained the preacher Thomas Adams, 'turns to juice in the stomach, to blood in the liver, to spirits in the heart'.[10] Following the traditional 'rule of threes', blood or spirits rose to greater levels of refinement in the three key organs, liver, heart, and brain. In the net and in the brain itself, the spirits were 'boiled and laboured' with a quasi-alchemical vigour.[11]

Like the occasional steam of blood, spirits were not necessarily always invisible. Notoriously, the pioneering anatomist Andreas Vesalius (1514–60) had been accused of vivisecting live criminals, precisely so that he could watch the spirits fleeting off their bodies. More mundanely, Francis Bacon thought that the discolouring of a bruise was chiefly due to congealed *spirits*, rather than congealed blood.[12] And numerous writers make it quite clear that they were continually feeling the movement of spirits, just as we now feel chemical changes within our bodies. In Sonnet 129, Shakespeare describes male ejaculation as 'th'expense of spirits in a waste of shame'. At one level, this captures a familiar feeling of male sexual experience: after orgasm, you have lost something, and you *feel* emphatically different. As this implies, spirits were the active agent in semen (they needed, after all, to transmit a soul to an embryo). They were also the active force behind the erection of the penis, and so were felt in that familiar hydraulic mechanism too. And, as in love, so in war. If you were angry, spirits could flood dangerously from heart to head: hence the danger of the 'hot-headed' losing their reason and lashing out violently at the source of their rage.

But there were far greater dangers than this. The eyes have often been described as 'the windows of the soul'. In Shakespeare's time this phrase was as much literal as figurative. When Hamlet sees his father's ghost in act three scene four, the spectre remains invisible to Hamlet's mother, Gertrude. Yet she is terrified by Hamlet's own terror. She states that not only does his hair stand on end, but that 'forth at your eyes your spirits wildly peep'. Again, this is not figurative. When Hamlet's eyes flash, Gertrude sees his over-agitated spirits flashing out of them. Spirits could also leave the eyes quite naturally. Vision itself was understood in terms of spirits entering or leaving the optic nerves to transmit objects to the brain. In such a climate, catching someone's eye could mean catching their disease. In times of plague the spirits of the diseased might be shot out of their eyes. Their spirits could pass the infection into your pupils, and from there into the rest of your body. Similarly, spirit-based optics explained the dangers of a witch's gaze, or the perilous 'sideways glance' of an envious person. In the former case, dangerous spirits entered the victim's eyes, fused with their blood, and on reaching their heart could kill them.[13] In the latter, a sideways glance was not merely a sign of covert malice, but a way of actively transmitting it. Bacon, again, took this idea seriously, explaining that 'envy ... emitteth some malign and poison spirit, which taketh hold of the spirit of another; and is likewise of the greatest force, when the cast of the eye is oblique'.[14]

We have already glimpsed similar notions in Irvine's theories of disease transfer, and in van Helmont's claims about the inspirited chair. Similar notions of the transfer of spirits underpinned belief in the wound salve, with its occult sympathy between the besmeared weapon and the injured body. Around 1652, Alexander Ross went so far as to claim that, when he was standing by his father's deathbed, the sympathy between their spirits was so great that those of the younger man kept those of the older one agitated and mobile, and therefore alive. Ross senior, staring intently at his son, 'could not die till I went aside', and only then 'he departed'.[15]

In all areas of mind–body unity, from ordinary movement through to extreme states of fear, anger, sadness or love, spirits were busily leaping and sparking through nerves and organs. It was spirits which explained gooseflesh, and hair standing on end – even the rarer event of hair turned white by extreme terror.[16] As Bacon rightly insisted, sometime before 1626, the spirits did indeed 'do all' the physiological work of the body.[17]

In this light, medicinal cannibalism begins to look rather different. Medical vampires, for example, were trying to swallow not just blood, but those vital spirits nestled within the blood. They were trying, at times, to gulp down the very force of life itself. For spirits had a distinctive, highly ambiguous relationship with the soul – something which was not only powerful, but finally indestructible. As the minister Thomas Walkington put it in 1607, 'in the body the blood, in the blood the spirits, in the spirits soul'. In theory, this formula implied a hierarchy. In practice, it was not always easy to clearly separate spirits and soul. Around 1580, one influential French author, Pierre de La Primaudaye, felt it necessary to attack those thinkers who had claimed 'the soul of man' to be 'nothing else but natural heat, or else the vital spirit that is in the blood'. While La Primaudaye himself is emphatic that the spirits 'are only instruments of the soul, and not the soul it self', his need to reassert this is telling.[18]

Meanwhile, over in England, Donne pondered that popular Christian notion of the soul as 'everywhere and nowhere in the body'. For Donne, this was a physical reality as much as an abstract idea. Accordingly, while 'our souls are truly said to be in every part of our bodies', yet 'if any part of the body be cut off, no part of the soul perishes, but is sucked into that soul that remains'.[19] Here as elsewhere, your soul was a matter of precise physical concern. For all we know, Donne may have even imagined the extra scrap of soul leaping the gap (like a kind of precious electrical current) between a severed arm and hand. Whatever the case, it is hard not to notice how this picture of the soul looks especially like that of the spirits – agents which were subtle yet real, which pervaded the whole body, and which were known at times to pass out of it.

We should by now have a better sense of how vigorously and exactly the soul was felt and perceived within the body, whether in sickness or in health. But of course much of corpse medicine was based on the use of dead bodies. How, then, could the soul or spirits be tapped from these spent shells of humanity? Having just effortfully adjusted our minds to grasp the oddities of the living Renaissance body, we must now twist the imaginative screw yet harder and tighter. For some Christians of this era, it seems that even the corpse itself continued to be 'animated' by the lingering presence of the soul.

The animate corpse

We have seen that Germany was a specially keen importer of human skulls. And Moise Charas also states, in 1676, that a powder containing 'shavings of a man's skull that died a violent death' is 'very much used in the north-parts, especially in Germany, where it is used in malignant fevers, and all epidemic distempers, and against all sorts of poisons'.[20] It appears that human skull, the moss of the skull, and mummy obtained from recently dead corpses were all particularly popular in northern Europe. Why was this? The intriguing research of the American scholar Katharine Park has shown that 'while Italians envisaged physical death as a quick and radical separation of body and soul, northern Europeans saw it as an extended and gradual process, corresponding to the slow decomposition of the corpse and its reduction to the skeleton and hard tissues, which was thought to last about a year'.[21] For the Italians, life cut off absolutely, as if at the flick of a switch. For the French, the Germans and the English (and probably also for the Danes) it smouldered into extinction gradually, like the coals of a dying fire. Accordingly, the Italians (Park points out) preferred mummy 'to come from embalmed and long-dead corpses', rather than the relatively fresh ones used by the Paracelsians.[22]

The recently dead were somehow not fully dead. What can this mean? Park offers several pieces of evidence in support of this extraordinary theory. One is the widely credited idea that a homicide victim would bleed spontaneously in the presence of their killer. 'Well into the seventeenth century ... northern European law admitted the Germanic principle of "bier-right", which held that the body of a recent murder victim would bleed or exhibit other physical changes in the presence of its murderer'.[23] In the mid-century English translation of van Helmont's work that notion is firmly asserted in a way which even seems to invest the corpse's blood with memory or will.[24] In 1654 Thomas Fuller, though apparently not inclined to give the phenomenon secure legal status, does also admit that 'this sometimes happeneth'.[25] In 1673 the preacher and poet Nathaniel Wanley cites an instance which occurred in Denmark, and goes on to explain that 'hereupon arose that practice (which is now ordinary in many places) of finding out unknown murders, which by the admirable power of God, are for the most part revealed, either by the bleeding of the corpse, or the opening of its eye, or some other extraordinary sign, as daily experience teaches'.[26] But in Italy, Park emphasises, this notion was treated with scepticism.[27]

For northern Europeans, a corpse could even possess some degree of personality. Accordingly, northern tomb monuments often featured something known as a 'transi'. This was a sculpted replica, not of the dead person, or of the skeleton, but of the partially decayed body. The transi depicted the deceased as they looked 'during the crucial liminal period of decomposition when the corpse was most sensitive and vital, and when the person was still in the corpse'.[28] Moreover, it was believed that 'the person ... was continuing in some sense to suffer as the body itself decayed'.[29] From slightly different angles, we find the same idea surfacing in English attitudes to dissection. Well into the eighteenth century, fierce popular riots displayed protest at this treatment of the most lowly criminal corpse.[30] Hence we might even wonder just how literally we should take the physician Edward May when, in 1639, he accuses the common people of seeing anatomy as a kind of 'murder after death'.[31]

We have seen that tribal cannibals sometimes sought to consume the strength or spiritual force of those they devoured. And this, it seems, was in part the logic behind medicinal cannibalism. One has to say 'in part', because Europeans ate the soul for reasons of health or (more indirectly) of profit. Whatever one's exact personal motivation, however, the underlying religious theory was essentially the same.

Eating the soul

There seems to have been some general awareness that certain chemists were actively probing the basic core of human vitality. In 1643 the zealous Protestant John Spencer talks with some precision of that 'fat aerial oily substance inplanted, inbred and inherent in the body from the conformation thereof', known as 'radical moisture, or natural balsam'. Synonymous with this is 'an inbred and innate heat' – which is 'the instrument of the soul and is likened to the flame wasting the candle'. Adding that 'the coexistence of these two in the heart chiefly is the beginning and continuation of life', Spencer further emphasises that 'this perpetual fire' of the human body is something 'which hitherto the chemics have in vain laboured to imitate and blow up or kindle'.[32] Spencer here implies that chemists were attempting to somehow synthesise the vital spirits of the human organism. They had, he also states, failed in their attempts thus far. But, if the basic essence of human life could not be reproduced, could it instead be harvested?

On the surface, of course, no one admitted that patients were actually eating another person's soul. Both Protestants and Catholics were united in the unshakeable belief that this, the property of God, was unalterably bound for heaven or hell.[33] But, as even the intensely pious Donne was forced to admit, theology itself was ultimately far from clear or consistent on the details of the human soul.[34] And, as I have already implied, a central reason for using human organic matter was precisely that it had that spiritual virtue which animals lacked. As van Helmont put it, 'truly from animals there is not drawn the quint essence', as in beasts 'the principal, and paramount essence perisheth, together with the influent spirit, and life' at death.[35] Finally, we are obliged to take a deep breath and confront this remarkable, long-forgotten secret, neatly filed away in the dusty archives of European religious and medical history. Until perhaps as late as the mid-eighteenth century, Christians were effectively seeking to consume the powers of the immortal soul.

Egyptian mummy

Such attempts usually involved the body parts of those who were alive or recently dead. But the same kind of ideas may also have underpinned the use of the most ancient, Egyptian mummy. Although we do not have explicit Christian statements on the presence of the soul in these entities, the Egyptians themselves were held to have believed this. Where Christians repeated time and again that the soul was joyously liberated from the prison of its material shell at death, the Egyptians seem to have felt that the dissolution of the body either caused, or signalled, the destruction of the soul. It was for this reason that embalming was so vital to Egyptian conceptions of the afterlife.[36] As the seventeenth-century Egyptologist John Greaves explains, they 'believed that as long as the body endured, so long the soul continued with it'. For this reason they would 'keep their dead embalmed so much the longer, to the end that the soul may for a long while continue' there, rather than escaping to be reincarnated in some other body'.[37] Similarly, the French traveller Leblanc stated: 'if any [mummy], through fatness, which causes humidity, and by consequence putrefaction' might 'chance to be consumed by worms, they hold the soul that left this body lost, and condemned to darkness amongst the devils'.[38]

The life forces of early modern corpse medicine

In the time of Marlowe or Dryden, various non-medical writers acknowledge the availability of biological life forces after legal death. In 1669 one John Reynolds referred to the 'potential heat more or less in all human bodies' as something also 'remaining when we are dead and key-cold'. With quasi-scientific precision he compared this to 'the heat of sulphur, arsenic, etc' and cited as evidence the kind of 'chemical operations on man's blood' which Boyle and Locke were performing around that time. And, he added, 'it must be granted, that there is an actual heat abiding in us whilst we live, and somewhile after death'.[39] Just over twenty years later, the author Whitelocke Bulstrode talked of how 'bodies, after the sensitive spirit has left them, and before their resolution into dust, have a sort of vegetable life remaining in them; as appears by the growth of hair and nails, that may be perceived in dead bodies'. Along with these traditional marks of the central European vampire corpse, one could detect, also, 'a weak animal [life] that lurks in the moisture; whence in putrefaction, worms and divers sorts of insects may be generated'.[40] Bulstrode went on to claim that 'the radical moisture of bodies, that lies in the bones' strongly implied the 'eternal duration' of such life forces – citing 'bones that are found entire after a thousand years burial', as well as 'the bodies of Egyptian mummies, preserved whole for several thousand years'. Hence, he concluded, 'there is in the bones a radical moisture, that is fixed and permanent'.[41]

Although Bulstrode was quite particularly arguing in favour of the Pythagorean transmigration of souls, it is clear how versions of his beliefs could underpin corpse medicine. As we have seen, various practitioners used bones for medicine. Those favoured by Dr Toope were hundreds of years old, whilst Edward Bolnest falls in much more closely with Park's span of 'up to a year' when he prescribes those 'of a man which hath not been buried fully a year'.[42]

Reynolds was certainly quite careful to distinguish lower (vegetable and animal) forms of life from the immortal soul itself – only these lower spirits, for him, could remain after legal death. But it must again be stressed how prone the different kinds of spirits were to blur together. All were in the blood, and all were part of a dynamic physiological circulation. Moreover, the most pious Christian could on occasion imply that this hierarchy was potentially unstable. In a sermon of 1602, for example, the preacher Thomas Mountford opined: 'the glutton eats like a dog, and lives like a hog, having his soul as salt only to keep his body from stinking'.[43] Here the soul seems to be a purely biological entity.

We have seen that, in Germany in particular, there was a widespread and enduring tradition of blood-drinking by epileptics. Given the social status of some of these patients, it is clear that such habits were by no means limited to self-conscious (educated) Paracelsians. Rather, as Richard Evans argues, this cure seems to have once again been rooted in the distinctive powers and qualities of a soul which was located in the blood. Epilepsy had traditionally been seen as either a result of demonic possession (most notably in the New Testament) or a kind of '"quasi-death"'.

> By the Middle Ages, writers were combining these two ideas of possession and 'quasi-death' by arguing that in an epileptic fit the soul was driven out of the body by a demon. Thus St Hildegard of Bingen, writing in the twelfth century, argued that epilepsy was a symptom of the withdrawal of the soul from the body, which then fell down and remained still until the soul returned. St Thomas Aquinas argued that the disease rendered its victims 'quasi-dead'. ... The practice of using blood and body parts of executed criminals to treat epilepsy thus reflected a popular belief that the life-force which resided in them could be transferred to the sufferers from the disease in order to prevent them succumbing to these bouts of temporary 'quasi-death'. Sudden death cut off people before their time, and lent potency to those parts of their body – the fingernails and toenails and hair – that appeared to carry on growing after death, as well as to the blood itself, the life-force which continued to flow for some time after the execution had taken place ... [44]

Here we find another version of that distinctive vampirism of the soul which Ficino had advised for the elderly, and which the Pope's physician may have relied on in 1492.[45]

This in turn reminds us of the similar logic which lay beneath the use of blood or mummy, not simply as particular cures (for epilepsy or for rheumatism), but as universal panaceas or elixirs of life. As we saw, this idea was followed by Albertus Magnus, Arnold of Villanova, Leonardo Fioravanti and Giambattista della Porta – men who all talked of the life-saving, quasi-miraculous powers of various bodily quintessences. Porta indeed states quite specifically that an 'elixir' containing mummy is effective 'against poisons, and pestilential contagions; especially, those that are apt to *seize on the spirits*', going on to explain that, 'a drop of it, being anointed on the lips or nostrils, *reviveth the soul*, and keepeth it in perfect senses at least six hours'.[46]

Come the age of the first blood transfusions, the clergyman and natural philosopher John Beale could present to Boyle a yet more striking collision of Christian and proto-scientific beliefs:

> in what I represented for you by Mr Oldenburg for the immediate conveyance of the superabounding blood of healthful young people into the veins of the

aged and decayed (if such a way could be devised) I had special regard to the vital spirits, and congenial heat, which may possibly have in some respects a more indulgent virtue, than mummy, or salt of human blood. And the mighty power of imagination may be advanced by the choice of the person. This I called transanimation in allusion to the Scripture-expression, The life or soul is in the blood.[47]

Here Ficino's hopes are explicitly articulated in connection with both corpse medicine and the vital spirits of the blood. Most intriguingly of all: Beale seems to believe it possible that the most essential core of human vitality can be transferred from one person to another, without any fundamental harm being done to the youthful donor. Exactly what weight Beale places on the term 'transanimation' is hard to say. But he does quite explicitly link it with the very plain Scriptural declaration about soul and blood. He would therefore seem to imply that natural philosophers are potentially able to transfer *some* of the soul of the donor to an aged recipient.[48]

Paracelsian life forces

In preceding chapters we have glimpsed those distinctive Paracelsian recipes which required either fresh corpses, or the skull or skull-moss of a man slain by a violent death. Let us now recall the basic recipe for Paracelsian mummy, cited by disciples such as Croll and Schroeder. One should take 'the cadaver of a reddish man (because in such a man the blood is believed lighter and so the flesh is better), whole, fresh without blemish, of around twenty-four years of age, dead of a violent death (not of illness), exposed to the moon's rays for one day and night, but with a clear sky'. One should then 'cut the muscular flesh of this man and sprinkle it with powder of myrrh and at least a little bit of aloe, then soak it, making it tender, finally hanging the pieces in a very dry and shady place until they dry out. Then it comes to resemble smoke-cured meat, without any stench'.[49] As we saw in chapter two, the chemist should finally extract 'a most red tincture' from this cured flesh.

Seemingly bizarre as this recipe may appear on first glance, it combines a kind of scientific precision with the fervent Christian piety of the day. A red-haired man was most suitable precisely because he was held to have a particular type of blood (the primal agent of the cure) which in turn conditioned his flesh.[50] Not only that, but at twenty-four he was in a state of optimum physical vitality, the power of his spirits being still undimmed by age (the average age of death in this era, we should bear in mind, was less than forty). It was partly for this reason that the subject should have died a violent death. He would therefore have expired in a state of full health, without illness or age having wasted his spiritual vigour. And there was a further intriguing reason behind this choice of specimen. The subject should be young, healthy, and prematurely killed because 'all living beings have a foreordained life span', and the remainder of that span can therefore effectively be drawn from their corpse.[51] Or, as the Merton College fellow, Henry Cuff, put it in 1607, 'man hath an appointed time of being, which he cannot pass'.[52] Cuff evidently had Paracelsus in mind. For he goes on to tell us that, 'I have read of a late living learned physician, Paracelsus by name, who had such confidence in the absolute perfection of his skill, that he doubted not to profess himself able by physic to preserve a man in so perfect a temperature, that he should never die by sickness'.[53]

It was not only Paracelsians who were open to this belief. Bacon, for example, wrote of those 'writers of natural magic' who attributed 'much to the virtues that come from the parts of living creatures'. These must, he adds, 'be taken from them [while] the creatures remain … still alive … as if the creature still living did infuse some immateriate virtue, and vigour, into the part severed. So much', he admits 'may be true; that any part, taken from a living creature, newly slain, may be of greater force, than if it were taken from the like creature dying of it self, because it is fuller of spirit'.[54] Here we have reference to spirit, and to an 'immateriate virtue' or power – the latter term being an accurate label for the soul itself. These statements look, indeed, rather like a revised version of Donne's ideas about the soul and amputation – Bacon implies that the vital powers do not escape back into the remainder of the body, but stay in 'the part severed'. Phrasing seems ambiguous in one sense: it is not wholly clear whether such authors recommend a part of the body from a creature which survives this amputation ('the part severed'), or part from a creature 'newly slain'. But it certainly is clear that the creature in question must die a violent, not a natural death.

These points were echoed by Christopher Irvine, whose curative 'magnet' should have been taken 'if it be possible, from the body of a man that dies a violent death, and yet while it is warm'. Irvine had admitted that this would be very hard to obtain, and thus proposed fresh blood as an alternative source of human vitality. The German Paracelsian Andreas Tentzel had another solution to this difficulty. As Thorndike points out, Tentzel actually advocated 'extraction of the mumia of the aerial body by interception of the dying breath'.[55] In doing so he allied himself with those Ancient Romans who had employed a peculiarly positive 'kiss of death'. As a person died, the nearest male kin put their mouth to that of the dying, in order to receive their departing spirit.[56] As E.B. Tylor notes, this practice was itself broadly echoed by the Seminole Indians of Florida: 'when a woman died in childbirth, the infant was held over her face to receive her parting spirit, and thus acquire strength and knowledge for its future use'.[57] (Notice how, for that culture, the soul combines 'strength and knowledge', as it did in Donne's time; and how, too, the familial limits of the custom again contrast with the far more impersonal exploitations of Christian corpse medicine.) We should note, also, that when Tentzel cites Ficino's suggestion about the elderly sucking youthful blood, he is quite clear that the active part of this treatment is 'the instauration of … youthful spirits into [the] old man'.[58]

Among Paracelsians, the most popular method of extracting human vitality was one based on the notion of the animate corpse. We have heard Paracelsus stating that, 'if physicians … understood but the right use of this mummy' no 'malefactors would be left three days on the gallows, or continue on the wheel'.[59] It seems that Paracelsian mummy could be prepared in *less* than three days after the subject's death. But the crucial point here is that three days is represented as an outer limit. That time span is highly significant. It corresponds exactly with religious attitudes to the corpse which are otherwise separated by many hundreds of years, and many thousands of miles.

Take, first of all, the New Testament. There were clearly varying degrees of death in this culture. Notably, when Christ resurrected Lazarus, he had been dead for longer than three days, and stank. It was partly for this reason that the miracle was found so impressive.[60] Christ here raised not just the dead, but the *very* dead. And biblical corpses in general seem to have been relatively animated in the very first stages of death.[61] Only after three days would the soul leave a corpse. As Frederick Paxton explains: 'the soul lingered near the corpse for three days after death, hoping to re-enter the body. Only when the soul observed the face of the corpse begin to change in the process of decay did it give up hope and go on its way'.[62] We have glimpsed a similar idea among the cannibal tribes of Fiji. Recall their belief that 'the spirit of a body clung to a corpse for four days after death' and that 'sacrificing and eating the body annihilated the spirit and prevented it from ascending to the spirit world and becoming a source of power and guidance to your enemies'.[63] Here as elsewhere, spiritual potency can be tapped and absorbed, but only for a relatively short time.

In small rural communities, the transitional period between death and full death has been acknowledged well into the twentieth century – sometimes in quite surprising ways. Elizabeth Warner tells of how, in Russia's Vologda Province in the 1970s, ritual keening or lamentation must not begin too soon after death. For it was actually possible to '"howl back" … the deceased'. Villagers recounted 'terrible instances of how, when this rule was broken, the dead man was "called back" … and thrashed about in convulsions for days afterwards'.[64] In parts of Rumania around 1919, a dead body was usually taken out for burial only 'after three days'; whilst the recently dead could even attend their own funerals: 'the dead person is either carried uncovered to church, or holes are made in the coffin, so that he may see and hear what is going on'.[65] In Russian, meanwhile, 'the word for corpse (*pokoinik*)' is in fact 'an animate noun'.[66]

As with many universal beliefs, certain universal phenomena underlie that of transitional death. As the case of Lazarus makes clear, the newly dead do not smell – or, at least, do not smell nearly so bad as the very dead. And the very dead also look different. Signs of decay are apparent. (Given the Paracelsian requirement for the body of a healthy young man it is therefore interesting to note that the bodies of those dying in good health are said to decompose less quickly than others.[67]) For the Egyptians, as cited by Greaves, and for Near Eastern mourners in the time of Christ, there was a clear reason for this. The soul had left.

Many of the above beliefs or customs mingle religious elements with a kind of quasi-scientific attention to empirical details. In early modern corpse medicine there is a similarly precise attitude not just to death itself, but to the presence or behaviour of the spirits in those either dying or dead.

Consider, for example, the beliefs of Harvey's colleague Robert Fludd. In a work of 1631 Fludd very firmly roots the potency of blood and spirits in Scripture:

'"whosoever sheddeth the blood of man, by man let his blood be shed, because God made him after his own image"; whereby is argued, that by reason of the divine spirit, which dwelleth in man's blood ... we are fashioned after the image of God'. And, again: 'the text saith: "He giveth life, breath, and all things"'. Next, he hath made all mankind of one blood and spirit: and therefore he operateth all in all in man's blood in general, as well to life as health'. Referring here to the processes underpinning the wound salve, Fludd goes so far as to claim that 'the spirit of the dead man's bones ... which issued originally out of man's blood, in the which in part lurketh God's spirit of life', therefore naturally sympathises with 'the lively blood of man' – going on to cite as proof Job 12.10, which (in Fludd's reading) states that '"all mankind is made of one blood only"'.[68] Again: the medical practitioner and astrologer Simon Forman effortlessly blended divinity and chemistry in his theory of the physiology of disease. To Forman, 'air was the breath of God, source of blood and life, vitalizer of the soul', so that, 'if fumes and vapours corrupted the air, it infected the blood, spreading to the heart and brain and disrupting the ... three principal spirits of man'.[69]

If such notions are hardly going to chime favourably with modern scientists, we must bear in mind that they could at times have quite concrete empirical underpinnings. In chapter three we saw Fludd using 'the flesh of a man strangled in the air' to cure a gentlewoman of a tumour. And his related experiments in this area must have persuaded him that his success was no lucky coincidence. In one case, Fludd took some of the hanged man's flesh and 'applied it ... unto the part of my body, which was nearest unto it in natural position'.[70] The spirits which still remained in this dead flesh were presently agitated by the presence of Fludd's living body. Accordingly, Fludd noticed that 'they drew off my mumial and vivifying spirits greedily, and at some times ... I felt them ... sensibly ... to tug and pull some adjacent parts'. The corpse, Fludd tells us, greedily sucked at the forces of life with a kind of spongelike vampirism. Moreover, when the corpse flesh was removed from his body, Fludd found the former to be 'much altered in smell and view, by reason of the quantity of my spirits ... attracted' into it. Finally, he proceeded to extract these spirits, which he 'prepared after my manner, for the use of my own body'.[71] In this there are two striking moments, both (to us) very different from the general and absolute authority of the Bible. One: Fludd believes himself to actually *feel* these invisible spirits, magnetically tugging at his flesh. Two: he also sees how his own spirits have visibly changed the piece of dead flesh. Whatever we may think about the strangeness of the beliefs involved, both of those points clearly echo one basic habit of a full-blown hard science: they pay close attention to matter and to material processes.

The corpse used by Fludd had suffered a violent death. Time and again, authors insisted on this kind of source material. We have seen part of the reason for this – the basic desire to harvest an unspent human vitality. But there are also other reasons, rooted in the period's more or less universal physiology of spirits. At one level, there was a general early modern notion of how spirits behaved in moments of fear: 'if the heart be in fear or danger, all the blood and spirits in the body will forsake the outward parts, and run to preserve and succour it'.[72] This idea was a commonplace of the period. Nor was it purely a matter of abstract theory. On one hand, the swift rush of spirits and blood to the heart would explain the heightened activity of that organ. On the other, it also accounted for additional symptoms of terror. Bacon tells us that 'fear causeth paleness; trembling ... starting; and screeching', and explains that 'the paleness is caused, for that the blood runneth inward, to succour the heart. The trembling is caused, for that through the flight of the spirits inward, the outward parts are destituted, and not sustained', while 'starting ... is an erection of the spirits to attend'.[73] The heightened alertness of this state ('starting') clearly foreshadows modern notions of evolutionary conditioning – the sudden spurting adrenalin of a body being prompted for fight or flight.

What did this imply about the hanged men so often used for various forms of corpse medicine? One answer in fact comes from discussion of the sand mummies of the deserts. Like hanged felons, these people were suffocated. And, it was believed, '"this sudden suffocation doth concentrate the spirits by reason of the fear and sudden surprisal which seizes on the travellers'".[74] So said the noted French chemist Nicasius Lefebvre – the man employed by that dilettante enthusiast of distilled skull, Charles II, and someone who was in fact also Protestant.[75] Tentzel, meanwhile, asserted that 'a body dying by the interception of air ... remaineth wholly undestroyed, and is less subject to ... elementary resolution or putrefaction'. In such a case the 'mumial spirits ... are drawn and retired into their chiefest ripeness and perfection'.[76] Again, in judicial hangings it would be assumed that there was a similar level of fear, and that the bulk of the victim's spirits had remained trapped within the body – not just because there was no haemorrhage, but because spirits which fled in toward the heart were less likely to escape via eyes or mouth.

Although medical use of the heart was rare, the assumed physiology of hanging gives us cause to wonder about Mayerne's specific use of a kind of mummy derived from the lungs, which could reasonably be inferred to be a potent source of spirit in such cases.[77] On the whole, however, the clearest attempt to exploit such corpses is found in uses of the skull and the moss of the skull. According to the German Professor, Rudolph Goclenius, the spirits of a strangled corpse would remain in the skull for up to *seven* years. This meant that those skulls used for usnea, the curative moss, were still convincingly potent, despite the relatively long period following the death of the subject. As we have seen, authors such as van Helmont indeed believed that this moss was a hybrid creation, the soil of the in-spirited skull being fertilised by a seed which streamed down from the stars. This would also explain why these skulls should be left unburied, exposed to the emanations of the heavens (compare the influence of the 'moon's rays', in the recipe cited above). Come the eighteenth century, one Italian medical work still commended the skull of a man violently killed, because '"none of its innate spirit ... has been dissipated in ... disease'", and cited usnea as a proof of this lingering potency.[78] Similarly, the influ-ential German physician Daniel Beckher thought that usnea was 'coagulated animal spirit coalesced with vital and natural spirits, which are carried upward as a man is strangled and burst forth to the circumference of the cranium'.[79] In this case, a seemingly humble growth of moss becomes, in effect, the distillation of all the body's life forces.

Not everyone accepted such theories. Yet, for all that, anyone who had seen a hanging knew that the male body could behave in a very striking way at the moments of its death. So powerful is such physiology that it can produce not only erection of the penis, but even an orgasm worth dying for. Hence, in 1994 and 1997 respectively the Conservative MP Stephen Milligan and the rock star Michael Hutchence killed themselves whilst playing a dangerous sex game: semi-strangulation, in order to achieve a heightened form of orgasm. Jeffrey Meyers cites Shearon Lowery and Charles Wetli on the use of temporary strangulation "'to control the flow of oxygen to the brain'", as well as H.L.P. Resnik on the 'physiological con-nection between self-suspension and orgasm: "the lumbar cord reflex center, which mediates both erection and ejaculation, is under the influence of ... the cerebral cortex. This would explain erections immediately following a hanging when inhibitory impulses have been suddenly severed"'.[80]

In the days when hanging was a grim fact of life rather than a risky thrill, crowds were evidently well aware that the victim could experience not only erection but ejaculation in his final moments. For early modern medicine, this meant two things. First, the hydraulics of erection were caused by the force of spirits elevating the penis. Second: the spirits and blood were effectively boiled into their most highly agitated and concentrated form in order to produce and then release semen. We might at once note, therefore, that some spirits *were* routinely lost from such a body. But this did not necessarily mean that they were lost entirely. The not uncommon belief that mandrakes grew where the semen of the hanged man fell offers another tangible (and magical) product of the hyper-agitated spirits of the dying felon.[81] However far one's beliefs extended, it is in interesting to consider that, for all careful observers, public hangings offered a kind of democratic open-air laboratory, in which the inner processes of spirit-based physiology could be seen in violent action.

Given how radically orgasm affects not just physiology but consciousness, we can well imagine that some linked this violent agitation of the body and spirits to the soul itself. (Compare the 'quasi-death' of epileptics to the 'little death' of erotic fulfil-ment.) At a more purely empirical level, there must also have been a sense that hanging, or other violent, highly stressful deaths not only helped trap the spirits, but actually, precisely *conditioned* them. This logic lay behind the use of certain animal ingredients. In chapter one we heard Bacon briefly citing a recipe for the wound salve. Among other things this formula involved the moss of the skull, and the fat of two bears, 'killed in the act of generation'.

One can well imagine that this fetched a high price. Someone has to roam bear-infested woods during mating season. He perhaps strews about some pieces of meat laced with aphrodisiacs. He has the luck to spy two bears growing amorous. Even at this point it is not simply a case of shooting them cleanly. Rather, he will need a keen and expert eye to judge their ursine countenances and growlings, ensuring that the final pitch of ecstasy is occurring just as he raises his rifle. For this, it seems, is precisely what 'in the act of generation' means: not simply copulation, but actual *conception* – something which, in Renaissance medical theory, required not just insemination, but mutual orgasm.[82] To put this point beyond doubt, we can turn to Tentzel, who quite explicitly recommends 'mummy' (i.e., spiritual power) extracted from 'the nut of a stag's pizzle, transfixed in the act of copulation'.[83] (Yes – that is what he means.)

Did these recipes also aim to capture the inner heat of the soul? Although animal souls were not immortal, Beckher definitely believed that *all* forms of spirit played their part in producing the moss of the human skull. In the case of the amorous bears and the unlucky stag, the carefully exact moment of death seems designed to capture that very moment when the creatures' vital spirits were most vigorously agitated within the generative fluids.

We might further compare these scrupulous Christian recipes to the fantastically prolonged ritual cruelties of certain 'savage', exo-cannibalistic ceremonies. In those cases, were the tormentors indeed seeking to *physically* condition the heart which they would presently eat, saturated with the effects of suffering and courage quite as tangibly as with the modern permeation of adrenalin or endorphins? In each case, such attempts at manipulating both spirit and flesh would be just as concrete (and hardly more cruel) than the deliberately slow bleeding of animal corpses, or certain early modern culinary practices, such as the roasting of a live goose.[84] Once again, we might add that New World cannibalism accords more *respect* to the victim, whose personal courage is acknowledged, while the Old World subject should merely conform to certain physical characteristics, uninflected by moral values.

Two final, related points in this area concern those anatomists who so often had the chance to use criminal corpses for medical purposes. Modern medical science indicates that any form of violent death can have a very distinctive physiological effect. As Tony Thorne explains: 'when a victim undergoes a sudden and violent death, the extreme stress experienced just before dying may trigger an over-production of fibrinolysin, a powerful anticoagulant agent. The result is that, even hours after death, the blood in the victim's cadaver remains perfectly liquid, so much so that it has been possible to transfuse blood taken from a corpse successfully into a living patient'.[85] Anatomists in particular must have noticed this phenomenon at times, especially in cases where they were keen to dissect a corpse quickly, during relatively warm weather.[86] And it may also have been that the general public did so, given the alleged bleeding of murder victims – people who had, by definition, usually suffered violent deaths.

A second, darker possibility concerns the powers of those anatomists who were known to have influenced the mode of death of felons, so as to procure the most suitable specimens for dissection. Hanging or drowning or suffocation, for example, were sometimes chosen because of the relatively slight damage inflicted on the body as the subject of anatomy.[87] If anatomists could exert such surprising powers for broadly scientific ends, it is possible that they could also sometimes choose a mode of death which best suited the demands of corpse medicine. For most practitioners, indeed, the two areas would have dovetailed neatly, as suffocation was usually required in both cases. Moreover, in early modern Germany drowning was in fact an accepted method of capital punishment – one usually reserved for women, as when a mother found guilty of infanticide was submerged by the Nuremberg hangman, Franz Schmidt, on 13 July 1579.[88]

We find, then, that Paracelsian mummy presents a distinctive mixture of science and religion. The standard Paracelsian recipe for mummy is scrupulously detailed and exact. And Paracelsians display an unflinchingly hard-headed, neutral attitude toward human bodies, depersonalised into so much organic raw matter. Again, a kind of scientific observation is used to decide when a body is becoming too old to be of use (what does it look like? what does it smell like?). But these scientific traits might be said to form the mere surface layer of a belief whose final core is emphatically religious. The most integral ingredient is not actually the raw meat of human flesh, but the vital, quasi-divine spirits which permeate the dead body. It cannot be emphasised too strongly that these were at once physiological and 'spiritual' (in the now more familiar, religious sense of the word). Similarly, someone such as John French can be narrowly, locally irreverent towards particular bodies (pounding and mashing them into a kind of medicinal paste) just because his general reverence for God's natural resources is itself so powerful. We have now seen how sudden death or judicial decree might condition human bodies. Following pages look at how human corpses could be processed in more deliberately scientific ways; and at what such processing might mean for those involved in corpse medicine.

Processing

The alchemy of the corpse

Our exploration of New World cannibalism has shown that Europeans were particularly hostile to what they saw as 'raw cannibalism' – that which was the closest to animal behaviour, the least mediated by those distinctive human interventions which make up culture. It has been suggested already that Egyptian mummies were especially well suited to those who wanted the raw matter of the body transformed – both by the human art of the embalmers, and the long alchemy of time. Some time between 1517 and 1557, a formal religious ruling explicitly codified what was perhaps often a more tacit and unanalysed feeling about the Egyptian form of mummy. Interestingly, this was not a Christian decree. Sceptical as we might be of the anti-Semitic smokescreen around such fake mummy dealers as the one supposedly encountered by Fontaine, it *does* seem that some Jews actually used mummy. For once, we can be certain of this, because there now survives a question put to the Egyptian chief rabbi David ben Zimra around the mid-sixteenth century: "'on what basis do people use the flesh of dead persons, called *mumia*, as a drug, even when there is no mortal danger involved, and by swallowing it'"? The question also refers to the fact of mummy's "'being traded'" (evidently by Jews) "'even though it is *our* established law that it is forbidden to eat the flesh of a dead person'" (italic mine).

Raphael Patai, the scholar who unearthed this in an examination of the use of mumia in Sephardic folk medicine, goes on to note – tellingly – that 'David ben Zimra's answer is very lengthy' – adding that 'its gist ... is contained in these sentences: it is allowed, because its form has changed, and it has reverted to dust. "For the *mumia* is the flesh of embalmed bodies which had been embalmed with all kinds of spices"'. But by the time of consumption, such a body '"has become again similar to bitumen, and it is not forbidden to eat it ... Moreover, it is taken not for the sake of the flesh, but of the spices that are in it, for it is well known that the flesh of the other dead, which are not embalmed, has no medicinal value at all"'.[89] These last words suggest that there were few Paracelsians in the Jewish community. But, as regards Egyptian mummy, ben Zimra's response clearly bridges the Jewish–Christian divide. Compare, again, the Italian anatomist Carpi, stating of his medicinal plaster that 'a notable part of human, *or rather mummy* substance enters into its composition'.[90] Compare, still more precisely, the Protestant polemicist Daniel Featley: 'our question is not of the *medicinal* use of man's flesh, altered by art, but whether it be not a sin, and that a horrible one, to eat with the mouth and teeth the flesh of a known man, nay of the Son of God'.[91] It is probably significant that Featley needed to formalise this answer in the quiet of his study. He could not make it on the spot to either of his Catholic opponents, precisely because for many mummy was a tacitly accepted medical custom, rather than the subject of religious or legal analysis. For all that, one central point closely echoes ben Zimra: mummy, Featley says, has been 'altered by art'. Although it is not certain whether Featley is thinking of Egyptian or Paracelsian mummy, we now find that not only Catholics and Protestants, but also Christians and Jews were effectively united in the practice of medicinal cannibalism.

Moreover, Featley's second main point is captured in that emphatic use of '*medicinal*'. And this itself was echoed in 1647 by the prolific religious author and biographer, Thomas Fuller. For Fuller, mummy was 'good physic' even though it was 'bad food'.[92] Just what did Fuller mean? He seems to imply that the tactics of learned medicine somehow deflected the threat of cannibalism. They could, at least, deflect the very rawest kind of cannibalism – something which, as we have seen, was associated *only* with uncooked food and brute appetite.

On one hand, medicine was a regrettable necessity – not, like food, something to be enjoyed. On the other, Fuller's opposition between food and medicine neatly echoes that basic opposition between culture and nature. Animals have food, but little medicine. Most of all, animals do not have *theories* about medicine. In that seemingly small phrase, 'good physic', a mass of powerful human ideas is compressed – the weight of antiquity, tradition and religious belief, all compacted into a brief three syllables. All this helps to put cannibalism (or 'raw cannibalism') at a reasonably safe distance. Once again, it is unclear if Fuller has Egyptian or Paracelsian mummy in mind: his phrase could apply to either. In what follows I want to use his words as a key to Paracelsian attitudes, and in particular to the reverent, painstaking forms of processing which Paracelsians employed in order to 'alter by art' the raw stuff of the human body.

Alchemy as chemistry

Those using relatively new corpses clearly felt that it was necessary to condition the body, and then to process it. They were concerned in various ways with the chemistry of the human organism. They were very far, of course, from being modern biochemists. But the Paracelsians were in fact far more interested in chemistry than were most other physicians. Looking back at the mid- to late seventeenth century, it is particularly difficult to draw a hard line between 'magical' and relatively scientific forms of chemistry. Famously, Isaac Newton himself was still practising alchemy. And, by comparison with some of the aims outlined above, the artificial production of gold was perhaps a fairly realistic dream.

It is probably no accident that in the medieval period, when Europe lacked a widespread culture of medicinal cannibalism, the chief exponents of corpse medicine were alchemists such as Arnold of Villanova and Albertus Magnus. For these men, with their artful and secretive distillations of blood and bone, the pious transformation of human organic materials may well have felt like the ultimate challenge. If anything could hold at bay the very basic taboo of cannibalism, it was the reverent art of the Christian alchemist.

But matters were different come the seventeenth century. What we must understand at once is that, however much old-fashioned histories of science present chemistry triumphantly emerging from the mystical swamps of alchemy, it did not feel that way to men like Irvine or Boyle. As the seventeenth century wore on, both alchemy and chemistry were able to become (from our viewpoint) more 'scientific' whilst at the same still feeling intensely pious to many of those involved. Like modern scientists, Paracelsian chemists were extremely patient, painstaking, and exact. As Charles Webster emphasises, Paracelsian chemists after Francis Bacon were continually and vigorously revising the design of furnaces and the kind of fuels used.[93] We also need to remember that shortly after the Restoration we enter the first age of the microscope.[94] Here science and religion might be seen to merge in a peculiarly unexpected way. The word 'occult', though generally associated with mystical forms of religion, literally means 'hidden'. The microscope showed that certain things clearly *were* hidden from the unaided human eye. Once experimenters started peering down at levels of material composition previously invisible or unknown, it was arguably very scientific – rather than rashly mystical – to take the idea of hidden forces and substances quite seriously. Webster has also shown that a great deal of British scientific endeavour was galvanised by a specifically Protestant religious fervour. It is worth wondering just how subtly the strenuous ethics of Puritans in particular influenced their attitude to the chemistry of medicinal cannibalism. For some, it may have seemed that the raw use of blood (for example) was in fact just too *easy*, compared with the attractively arduous labours of alchemy and chemistry.

Alchemising blood

The microscope also made it possible to refine the processes of chemical analysis. Paracelsians were noted for their attempts to separate out the 'oils', 'salts' and 'spirits' of different substances. Such efforts extended to the human body, with blood in particular being distilled by various chemists and physicians. We have heard Leonardo Fioravanti claiming that his "'fifth essence of human blood'" had "'as good as raised the dead'".[95] And Fioravanti clearly believed distillation to be crucial to the success of this panacea. Moise Charas insists, meanwhile, that blood cannot be treated like food. If it is drunk, it will simply be metabolised in the stomach. And, he adds, it will already have been significantly altered the moment it leaves the veins of the donor. 'But', Charas goes on, 'by the way of distillation, and separation of the pure parts of human blood, most effectual remedies may be prepared'. He then proceeds to give very precise instructions for this distillation. 'In the month of May take a considerable quantity of healthy young men's blood … who are not red hairs'. You should then

> put this blood … into one or more cucurbits [alchemical vessels] of earth, of which three quarters must be empty, and having fitted to them their heads and their small recipients, draw off all the watery part in an ember-bath with a moderate fire, till that which remains in the cucurbit be quite dry, but not burnt. To which purpose you must have great care of the fire, especially at the end. Then having cooled the vessels and put up the distilled water, put into a great glass cucurbit the dry blood in the other cucurbits, and having set the retort in a close furnace of reverberation, and fitted and luted to it a large recipient, make a new distillation with a gradual fire, soft at first, but afterwards very violent, and by that means you shall have a new water with the oil, and the volatile salt will presently follow and accompany, issuing out of the cucurbit in white clouds, and dissolving themselves into the recipient.[96]

As well as typifying the arduous care involved in such processes in the pre-industrial world, these instructions clearly have psychological as well as practical value. They help to cook the raw matter of blood into something far less merely cannibalistic. Tentzel, similarly, is more than comfortable with medical use of the body, if suitably processed, but asserts in no uncertain terms that it is 'detestable, improfitable and noxious' for a person 'to receive human blood into the body' merely by way of nutrition.[97]

From a rather different angle, the psychological importance of this artful processing is made clear by John Locke in 1690. Denouncing the habits of certain Peruvians, Locke indignantly cites Garcilasso de la Vega: 'in some provinces, says he, they were so liquorish after man's flesh, that they would not have the patience to stay till the breath was out of the body, but would suck the blood as it ran from the wounds of the dying man'. Locke does not seem to be aware how closely this mirrors the habits of epileptics in classical Rome, or those in Germany and elsewhere in his own life-time. But in the present context what matters most is the strikingly clear opposition between such raw consumption, and the wholly unproblematic experiments on blood made by Locke in the 1660s. Given Boyle's involvement with these, and his interest in prepared blood as medicine, Locke (who was himself a physician) must have been open to the possibility that some of the resultant substances could be consumed by medical patients. Whilst Locke's own work already represented a highly cooked use of blood, the distance between his activities and those of the Peruvians was made still greater by the fact that the latter were (allegedly) using blood and flesh purely as food: 'they had public shambles of man's flesh, and ... they spared not their own children which they had begot on strangers, taken in war'.[98]

Some years earlier, Christopher Irvine had discussed the importance of chemical processing in a way which touched with especial precision on the relationship between spirits of blood and the soul. Emphasising, like Fludd, how 'the Scriptures say, and teach us, that blood is the principal chariot of the spirits, by placing the soul in the blood', he goes on to argue that 'if the spirit is the bond, by which the soul is tied to the body, then where the spirit most resideth, there shall the soul most powerfully work'. In these few words Irvine makes explicit what is so often implied about corpse medicine, and especially by Paracelsians: finally, the most potent ingredient in this strange therapy is indeed the soul itself.[99] It is a source of power, and this power somehow leaks out into the blood, ready to be tapped by the industrious chemist. Accordingly, 'the blood ... which so plentifully possesseth the spirits, and communicates them to the body, is surely the fittest instrument to cure diseases'. Adding that the spirit is most easily available in human blood, Irvine yet warns: 'we must not immediately conclude, that it may be taken and used presently, without any fermentation or putrefaction'. Stressing how carefully the fermentation process must be handled, Irvine then proceeds to expound a 'secret' use of blood which is notably tinged with the hermetic flavour of so much alchemical literature.[100]

Across the channel a few years later, the oil of human blood featured amidst yet greater occult wonders. A letter of 24 March 1678, sent to Boyle by the French natural philosopher Georges Pierre Des Clozets, told of a gathering of alchemical adepts near Nice, at which 'the Chinese gentleman, Pursafeda, exhibited a homunculus which was about seven months old, which he fed in the matrass with balsam of blood, that is to say, the oil of human blood'.[101]

Alchemising the corpse: the laboratory of the soul

The widely used Paracelsian recipe of Croll and Schroeder already offers us a clear example of how the newest and most degraded (criminal) flesh could be elevated above raw cannibalism. It was carefully treated with myrrh and aloes, and macerated in spirit of wine. It was left out under the moon at 'a serene time', thus being automatically interfused with the whole cosmic web of astrological and lunar influences. Finally, from the viscerally raw fibres of the slaughtered corpse, there came 'a most red tincture' – the highly abstracted distillation of the human body, which not even the most unredeemed cannibal could have chewed if they had wished.

Although not everyone subscribed to this very precise recipe, the quasi-alchemical principles underlying it may well have inspired broadly similar uses of the human body. Take, for example, the formula given in a 1611 history of Ethiopia:

> they take a captive Moor, of the best complexion; and after long dieting and medicining of him, cut off his head in his sleep, and gashing his body full of

wounds, put therein all the best spices, and then wrap him up in hay, being before covered with a sear-cloth; after which they bury him in a moist place, covering the body with earth. Five days being passed, they take him up again, and removing the sear-cloth and hay, hang him up in the sun, whereby the body resolveth and droppeth a substance like pure balm, which liquor is of great price: the fragrant scent is such, while it hangeth in the sun, that it may be smelt ... a league off.[102]

Again the victim (who is 'of the best complexion') dies a violent death, presumably while still young and healthy. But what is most striking is that – partly by using the natural power of the sun as a version of the heat employed by chemists – this formula has essentially alchemised the purest gold from the human organism, in the form of a balm whose delightful perfume echoes that 'odour of sanctity' associated with both living and dead Catholic saints. By contrast, the Paracelsian curing process, merely neutralising the flesh into something 'without stink', looks decidedly inferior.

It is possible that this account is one version of what would now be called an urban legend. For Robert Fludd claimed to have heard of a very similar incident, recounted to him by a sailor just returned from Barbary: 'a certain Jew after he had beheld an English mariner in the ship, who had a red head, and feigning himself to be much taken with the love of him, wrought so with him, that for three hundred pound' the sailor agreed 'to sell himself unto him for his slave, thinking in time to come to give his Jewish master the slip, and run away'. Presently, 'the ship being ready to return, and the mariners going to take their leave of their captive fellow, they resorted unto the Jew's house, who after they had demanded for their fellow, led them into a back court, where they found the red-headed captive, his back being broke, and a gag in his mouth and chops and throat swollen'. This – the Jew was supposed to have confessed, with surprising candour – had been 'caused by the stinging of vipers, which were forced into his mouth'. From this victim, 'hung up and exposed unto the hot sun, with a silver basin under his mouth, to receive that which dropped from' it, the Jew allegedly 'made a kind of poison so deadly, that it did surely kill where it touched'.[103]

Here, as in the case of the Jewish mummy dealer, the supposed culprit is remarkably unguarded about his darkest secrets ('your red-headed friend? of course! he's being tortured as we speak ... '). A lamentable abundance of fantastic tales about Jewish poisoners, and about murders committed by Jews upon Christians, leaves us in no doubt that this report is yet one more anti-Semitic myth (although we can be equally confident that Fludd and others quite genuinely believed it).[104] Yet as fantasies go, it is remarkably exact. Once more the body becomes a kind of alchemical still – in this case, more horrifyingly, while it is still alive. As with standard Paracelsian recipes, the subject is not only young and healthy, but red-headed (hence the distinctive quality and value of his blood).

We can be rather less certain that the Ethiopian recipe was purely fictitious – it was, after all, no more strange than certain Paracelsian formulae, such as John French's mashing of the human organism into pâté. But ultimately, what matters most about both of these cases is that they *made sense* to many European adherents of corpse medicine. Both tales confirm the spiritual or chemical power seen as lying dormant within the human organism. Admittedly, in the second instance this power has been modified in some way by the poison of the vipers. But the 'recipe' is clearly an inverted version of corpse medicine. It was a general principle of the day that poison could be rendered into medicine (and vice versa) by those sufficiently skilled.[105] Fuller, for example, explains that 'good physic may be made of poison well corrected'.[106]

Fludd himself admits that: 'as out of a wholesome man, there may be had a spiritual mummy, which is wondrous healthful and salutiferous unto mankind ... so also there may be attracted out of man, after a strange manner of corruption of his spiritual mummy, a venom, than the which there cannot be found a more pernicious or malignant one to mankind in the world'.[107] This seems to imply that while the effect of the mummy has been radically altered, its essential *potency* remains the same. Such an unsurpassable poison neatly matches the Paracelsian idea of mummy as a universal panacea or elixir of life. Moreover, while the breaking of the victim's back is not found in mummy recipes, it broadly matches the broken necks of hanged felons. More precisely, it is consistent with the frequently implied desire to somehow condition the spirits into the most medically viable state. The spinal marrow was thought to be a central conduit of spirits, transmitted in a rarefied form from the brain down through the nerves, veins and arteries.[108] It appears that the general aim of the alleged Jewish recipe is to somehow divert or relocalise these spirits by disrupting ordinary physiology. If they cannot circulate, then they will ferment or putrefy in the 'strange manner of corruption' which Fludd describes.

What do these two stories tell us about the religious and scientific status of Paracelsian mummy? Potentially, the innate vitality of the body (whether positive or negative) might be taken as a material index of God's power. Compare, for example, a medicine 'distilled' from the pulverised mass of an entire corpse, and known as '*aqua divina*'.[109] For all that, both tales also seem to encode European anxieties about the correct limits of 'godly science'. For the Ethiopian and Jewish agents involved are not merely a general reflection of racism, xenophobia or religious bigotry. At the same time, they reflect the notion that *only* these alien or outrightly demonised peoples would seek to manipulate natural powers with such extreme Faustian daring.[110] At first glance, we might want to see this anti-Semitic version of corpse chemistry as a twist on that most savage 'raw cannibalism' of the Ouetecas or the Antis. The victim is effectively devoured – or drained – while he is still alive. Yet, as often happens, this anti-Semitic fantasy is a densely contradictory one. It seems also to grudgingly *admire* someone who would attempt to so rigorously utilise the forces of human vitality. Irvine, after all, was a man very much influenced by the kind of ideas about spirits and spirit transfer which Fludd entertained. And he, as we saw, outlined quite precisely the desirability of a therapeutic 'magnet' obtained from the living human body.

We can well imagine that devout Protestant alchemists or chemists did not explicitly praise such experiments. Paracelsians, indeed, often made a self-conscious point of the necessary piety of the physician, thus hoping to set themselves apart from other, more worldly doctors.[111] Such figures would have seen themselves as reverently drawing forth some divine inner essence of the body, rather than impiously tampering with natural forces. To understand this more fully, we need to realise the basic (now generally forgotten) logic behind mineral alchemy. Early modern chemists did not fully recognise the later distinction between organic plant life and inorganic minerals. When authors of this era talk about the 'womb' or 'bowels' of the earth, they are being more or less literal. For, in the time of Shakespeare or Dryden, even metals were held to 'grow' underground. This idea, of their slowly ripening within the earth, extended to a general belief that gold was in fact not a particular metal, but the natural, most perfect end state of all metallic ore, with even lead being able to mature into gold over sufficient time. The notion would only have been strengthened by European experience of South America, where the legendary stores of gold would be understood to have resulted, in part, from the fierce heat of the Guianan or Peruvian sun.

Seen in this light, alchemy looks less like a quaint fantasy, and more like a logical process of acceleration. And various forms of corpse medicine also look quite different, when set against that central model of diverse lower metals, all slowly aspiring to their natural end state of gold. As we have seen, Egyptian mummy might be viewed as the natural alchemy of time, with these bodies having exhaled off their cruder material qualities, leaving them both purified and densely inspirited. Again, if we recall van Helmont's notion of the human brain as 'consumed and dissolved in the skull' after death, we find that the latter seems to have absorbed chemical powers quite naturally, without any artificial assistance. Others took the hint offered by the body's natural chemical powers, and sought to actively improve on them. For the French physician Nicolas Lémery, it was possible to distil a spirit, oil, and volatile salt, from a fresh human head with the brain in it.[112]

Devout alchemists (rather than conscious tricksters) clearly saw themselves as engaged in a deeply holy enterprise. And this aura of spirituality was not just derived from the idea of assisting natural processes (as opposed to devilishly tampering with God's secrets). Many alchemists also genuinely believed that they *themselves* were undergoing a similar (and inextricable) process of spiritual purification. In this sense they were wholly unlike the modern scientist, who typically seeks to erase personal qualities in favour of a suitably neutral, almost machine-like attitude. For the true alchemist, success or failure was quite definitely bound up with one's own moral state.

Nor did one have to be a self-conscious alchemist to partake in such pious attitudes to the material world. Charas, for example, was at once scientific in his emphasis on the processing of blood, and emphatically reverent in his general attitude to medicine and nature. Dividing medicine into 'the internal which is the true knowledge, and tends to the perfect preparation of medicaments; and the external, which is the health of man' he made it clear that the former 'requires much more skill and experience' than the latter. 'Nor can it be obtained but by preparation, and by making an exact dissolution of all the parts, which cannot be accomplished without the help of chemical pharmacy'. Charas made these remarks in a passage which asserted that 'the body of man ... affords parts which are in truth medicaments, as the brains, the blood, the fat, the hair, etc, which a student in pharmacy ought to consider, and understand how to prepare'. But he prefaced it all with these words: 'thus great is the benignity of the good Creator, who hath not suffered man to be destitute of excellent remedies contained in his own body, for the mitigation ... of the sad calamities [which] he hath, and doth daily bring upon himself through his exorbitant, lustful fancy'.[113] Nothing could be more perfectly devout or religiously humble. Here the source of sickness is essentially humanity's fault, and the generous resources to be aimed against it are all the gift of God, the font and architect of nature itself.

Catholic saints versus Protestant science

What did the distinctively spiritual status of corpse medicine mean to those Christians beyond the realms of chemistry and pharmacy? Here I want briefly to consider some of the more remarkable pious literary uses of mummy and related substances. Without over-emphasising any general stance (which would be especially rash in post-Reformation or post-revolutionary Britain) it can confidently be said that the attitudes of both Catholics and Protestants toward nature and the human body were far more reverent than those of the post-Enlightenment world. Within this general reverence, it is also possible to discriminate between Protestant and Catholic responses to the various numinous qualities of human bodies.

Certain rhetorical uses of mummy, whilst not overtly Catholic or Protestant, are undoubtedly surprising to the modern eye. So, in 1614, among various authors praising the moralising poem, *The Labyrinth of Man's Life*, by John Norden, an admirer signed as 'R.J.' claims that

> While vulgar heads are stilling Venus' rose,
> Norden thy lembec drops the purest balm:
> Thy nectar to the pensive shed in prose,
> With this thy mummy mingled for each qualm,
> Shall give thee life ... [114]

That is, unlike the profane love poetry of 'Venus' rose', Norden's work has a quasi-divine status, being alchemised from the most fundamental essences of Christian life. As in the laboratories of those preparing corpse medicines, alchemy, piety, and the human body all combine in an intensely reverent fusion.

In 1646 the prolific author James Howell writes sycophantically in praise of Charles I's wife, Queen Henrietta-Maria, then in exile over in Jersey. Not only is she that 'immortal queen, great arbitress of time', but, Howell insists, she is a kind of general moral exemplar – one

> Which dost brave men embalm, and them conserve
> Longer than can Arabian gums or spice,

And of their memory dost mummy make,
More firm than that hot Lybia's sands do cake.[115]

Although Henrietta-Maria is not herself compared to mummy, she is exalted because of her power to produce it (albeit at a rhetorical level). It is not quite clear whether Howell refers to Egyptian or to sand mummy ('Lybia's sands' could imply sandstorm corpses, but it could also merely allude to the proverbially arid nature of the North African climate). But it is notable that he is not afraid to give a certain sensuous edge to his lines, via the phrase 'more firm' – here we have precise texture, rather than merely abstract metaphor.

Elsewhere, the rhetoric of mummy becomes unashamedly Protestant. In 1691 the Paracelsian Edward Taylor ponders that long-standing theological conundrum: just what *are* communicants eating and drinking during the Protestant ceremony of the Eucharist? As any good Protestant would know, this ritual was no longer held to produce, in real time, an actual metamorphosis into Christ's body and blood. Good Protestants also knew, of course, that it was best to turn to the Scriptures themselves when in doubt. Taylor accordingly shifts the whole question back to Christ's Last Supper. He then goes on to make a remarkable claim. When the disciples ate and drank Christ's flesh and blood, he states, they consumed 'not the palpable fleshly humanity, but the spiritual humanity', namely, 'the virtue and power of his body and blood, his own mumia in which was the divine and human power'.[116]

Mummy (or 'mumia') could hardly appear in a more reverent and sacred context than this. For a rough gloss of 'Christ's mumia', one could do far worse than 'Christ's soul'. Extraordinary as the idea is, we might see Taylor as simply pushing the spiritual dimension of corpse medicine to its logical conclusion. And for a writer who wishes to do that, Christ's body is a perfectly exact match for corpse medicine. The whole doctrine of the Incarnation, after all (Christ was, paradoxically, both divine and human) echoes the ability of any ordinary human body to yield ultimately divine powers. As well as effectively exalting mummy in this way, Taylor also adds a remarkable eulogy of 'the virtue of … usnea':

> I compare the arabian odours, oriental gems, palms of Asia, wine of pomegranates, the American pine-apple, and what else is most desirable, in comparison of the paradisical productions, to the obscure vitality surviving in men's dead bodies; generating some as it were fibres of gold amongst the decaying teeth, and the usnea on the skulls of persons strangled.[117]

At a general level, this strange passage, broadly resembling the tone of the Old Testament Song of Solomon, clearly asserts the 'obscure vitality' of the animate corpse. More precisely, it even seems to obliquely hint at the alchemical powers of this body, in its mysterious reference to 'fibres of gold amongst the decaying teeth'.[118]

Did other Protestants secretly harbour such feelings about mummy? Certainly Taylor was by no means the only one to exalt corpse medicine in this way. On the surface, more ardent Protestants saw the rejection of the Catholic Mass as a liberation from superstitious darkness and error. But secretly, some must have felt the need to recreate that lost sensual communion. They could do this by effectively displacing such sensuality into other areas.[119] We have already seen at some length how mummy was well-suited to this role. In particular, it combined the sensuous consumption of spiritual forces with a typically democratic redistribution of spiritual power. The hierarchical, and allegedly corrupt and superstitious Mass priest was replaced by the altruistic, industrious and rational experimenters in chemistry – men whose position could to a far greater extent depend on personal merit.

Similarly, this Protestant version of the Eucharist was democratic insofar as it insisted that these spiritual powers were to be found throughout the natural world, lodged within the most sinful flesh of any healthy criminal corpse. At one level, this idea stemmed from the allegedly north European attachment to the animate corpse. At the same time, nature as a whole was far more definitely animated in this era. And there is some reason to believe that this was more the case for Protestants than for Catholics. The reformed Church was particularly opposed to Catholic belief in miracles. When a seemingly inexplicable, extraordinary event occurred, Catholic believers would interpret it as not merely supernatural, but as miraculous – that is, as something which God had very precisely and deliberately performed, perhaps at that very moment. Regarding miracles as superstitious or fraudulent, Protestants would often see such events as the product of a more general animism – of diffused supernatural forces, rather than one overt act. In this sense, the Catholic Mass was a kind of routine miracle, while the Protestant one simply involved divine presences which were there already, rather than being effectively created at that moment by a priest. Equally, the bleeding of a murdered corpse was not a miracle, but the behaviour of the animate corpse under a certain natural stimulus.

To appreciate such contrasts more fully, it is helpful to look at some precise examples of how Catholicism tended to exalt the bodies of the most devout of believers. Here there is again a powerful element of mind (or soul) over matter. (Those readers whose minds or souls are less robust may want to read the following on an empty stomach.) The most directly relevant example from Catholic culture is that of those saints who were themselves mummified after death. In traditional Catholic belief, an undecayed corpse could be a strong indication of sanctity.[120] Similarly, the 'odour of sanctity' referred to the allegedly sweet-smelling cadavers of especially pious, privileged Christians: a quite recent example is that of Padre Pio, the Franciscan friar canonised as St Pius in 2002. This figure was claimed by certain of his numerous followers to have possessed '"the odour of sanctity", a fragrance like roses'.[121] As Camporesi notes, the thirteenth-century saint, Beatrice II, of Este in Ferrara, exhibited both these traits. As we have seen, modern science suggests corpse preservation to be a natural, if uncommon occurrence: certain bodies develop a condition known as 'adipocere' and do not decay. From a religious viewpoint, this defiance of ordinary natural laws was perhaps the more impressive, in that it was so spontaneous and effortless. The saint's unusual piety had pervaded their whole being so thoroughly that their soul's preservative action (recall Mountford and his salt) carried over even into death.

Camporesi also introduces us to other ways in which the holiest Catholics might defy nature. Well into the seventeenth century such figures would mortify the flesh not simply by fasting, but by living on food and drink which relatively discerning beggars might have rejected. As Camporesi points out, Joseph Copertino (1603–63) ate a herb 'so bitter and disgusting that if only touched with the tip of the tongue it caused nauseous feelings for several days'. Carlo Severoli (1641–1712), meanwhile, would eat his bread only after soaking it in 'stagnant and verminous water'. Intriguingly, it seems as if these acts were an implicit gesture of faith in God's ultimate power over all of Nature, including what would later be seen as inviolable laws of science. In the case of Copertino, for example, the triumph of spirit over matter involved more than just the ability to overcome revulsion or nausea. Unlike any ordinary beggar or lunatic, this saint did not slowly putrefy in the lowest ebbs of filth, but broke through into some purified realm beyond. For he could, Camporesi adds, levitate and even fly.[122]

In certain cases, the triumph of piety over disgust did indeed slide into outright cannibalism. The twelfth-century Bishop, Hugh of Lincoln (c.1140–1200), was 'accused of biting off a piece of the bone of Mary Magdalene while venerating it at Fécamp' in northern France. Hugh was unabashed. He argued, quite unrepentantly, that 'if he could touch Christ's body in the Mass, he could certainly chew the Magdalene's arm'.[123] Here we find a mingling of sacred ideas and emotions producing behaviour which we might now associate with the world of Neanderthal man. (Some Protestants, we should bear in mind, would have said that the Catholic Mass was no less cannibalistic than the crunching of Mary's bones.[124])

We saw in chapter five that Catherine of Siena was similarly able to stifle her disgust, when tending a cancerous nun whose odour overpowered all others in the order. Yet there is a little more to that story. Catherine seems to have outdone even Hugh's crunching of hallowed bone. Not content with simply treating the sick woman, and consciously absorbing the smell of her tumour, Catherine 'twice forced herself to overcome nausea by thrusting her mouth into the putrifying breast of a dying woman or by drinking pus'.[125] Had we but world enough and time we might dwell on these remarkable acts at greater length. They clearly have strong elements of psychotic compulsion (much later, for example, we find the Marquis de Sade delighting in the eating of human excrement). More precisely, they are arguably egotistical, given that they could hardly help the suffering nun in any very tangible way.[126] And for some Catherine's act would indeed have counted as cannibalism. For some of us, her behaviour is surely more disgusting than cannibalism (especially if mere nail or finger chewing is seen as cannibalistic).[127]

Without attempting to do full justice to the evidently very dense and murky psychology of this tale, we can again view it as an exemplary case of the power of spirit over matter.[128] Like the fairy-tale princess who kisses the frog, Catherine seems implicitly to make a daring magical bargain with the limits of disgust, and (at least in her own mind) to then break through this lowest strata of abjection into a transfigured world of matter redeemed. Nor was she alone. Catherine of Genoa, for example, 'ate lice'. Angela of Foligno 'drank water that came from washing the sores of lepers'. When one of the sores stuck in her throat, she remarked that it 'tasted "as sweet as communion'''. Whatever we now think of such characters, we cannot deny that they and their peers felt them to be intensely holy. All of them – along with Donne and his effortlessly rarefied dead pigeons – might draw the same biblical motto: 'to the pure, all things are pure'.[129]

Where does this leave the Paracelsian chemists or mummy-physicians? In 1628, musing on that distinctively Protestant issue of individual conscience, the outspoken and courageous Puritan minister Henry Burton exclaims: 'blessed be God, who hath provided such treacle, made of the mummy of his dead saints, to cure his living ones of the serpent's mortal sting'.[130] Burton is clearly thinking of corpse medicine – hence the reference to 'cure', and to 'treacle', then often a medical term. Any Catholic readers who saw this line, by contrast, could not have avoided thinking of their mummified saint, Beatrice of Este. What is the difference? Obviously enough, Burton is being figurative. But what probably matters most in his image is this: whether figurative or literal, Protestant mummy is *useful*. In its medical form it can cure diseases. In its spiritual form (roughly, the examples of saintly lives) it can cure problems of sin or conscience.

Some Catholics may well have felt that they could make use of the examples of Catherine, or Severoli, or Copertino. Yet there was probably less active emphasis on the practical 'usefulness' of such figures. In the Catholic spiritual hierarchy, lowly believers were more likely to look up with wondering awe. They were unlikely to imagine that they themselves could attain such status. If we compare certain Catholic saints with the Protestant attitude to mummy, we find ourselves looking at something like the opposition between pre-modern religion and post-Enlightenment science. Saints are special, élitist even in their nominal humility. In such a sphere, humanity looks up with grateful passivity, perceiving divinely bestowed miracles in the case of the mummified Beatrice or the levitating Copertino. Protestant physicians and chemists, by contrast, believe that any young and healthy corpse (that of the most sinful murderer, perhaps) has an innate *natural* power, if it is properly tapped by the industrious chemist or doctor. And this power is practically useful. As time went on, moreover, science would grow increasingly co-operative, shifting it still further from the spiritual élitism and egocentricity of Catholic sainthood.

Having said this, we can conclude by looking at a spiritual rapture so unusual that it seems to finally defy easy categorisation into either 'Protestant' or 'Catholic'. In 1628 the prophetic writer and ardent Republican George Wither wrote a long poem in which he meditated on the best way to fulfil his cherished religious vocation. Wither contrasts his possible membership of 'some communion/Of Saints on earth' with the benefits of pious isolation:

> ... I could bide
> Shut up, until my flesh were mummy-fied;
> And (though the world should woo me) would disdain
> (For ever) to unclose my door again.

Just what can this mean? It is broadly clear that this mummification is essentially pious and desirable. We have seen that most literal cases of undecayed corpses as spiritually exalted occur in Catholic countries. Yet Wither believes that he will somehow be mummified while still alive. At a broad level this could be seen to echo those Catholic saints who defied the ordinary laws of the material world during life: Copertino, as we saw, represents a similar triumph of spirit over matter. At the same time, we must also consider that the lines typify a very Protestant conception of the devout individual, whose isolation is in some senses greater than that of Catholic mystics, given the high value placed on personal conscience by the reformed faith. This seems confirmed when Wither adds that

> ... when I come forth ... I lose again
> My raptures; and have thoughts like other men;
> Because my natural frailties, and the fog
> Of earthly vanities, my soul doth clog.

It is hard to convey the immensely powerful sense of spiritual interiority which the most deeply religious Protestants could feel in this era. In some cases it led negatively to bouts of self-harm and madness, in others to outpourings of prophecy which had pervasive influence in both religious and political spheres.[131] In Wither's case, its potency is attested by a strong edge of sensuality. For in the same passage he also imagines how

> I might with Lot,
> Upon the daughters of my brain begot,
> Commit some spiritual incest, had I none
> To spend the seed of my full soul upon.[132]

These brief lines are both dense and allusive. Where the biblical Lot committed incest with his daughters, Wither bizarrely imagines a kind of spiritual copulation, in which his soul spurts out semen ('spend the seed') and fertilises his own religious ideas ('daughters of my brain'). To us this is so strange that we might be inclined to think of it as merely whimsical. But this would do a severe injustice to Wither's well-attested religious passion. In one sense, the idea of his soul as emitting semen matches the distinctively tight fusion of human matter and spiritual power associated with Paracelsian corpse medicine. And these lines also suggest a still more fascinating possibility. Some believed that, ultimately, mummy derived its power from the human soul. In orthodox medical terms, the moral state of that soul clearly did not matter, given that the gallows was so common a source for this drug. But Wither may feel, consciously or unconsciously, that the sheer claustrophobic intensity of his very inward, Protestant soul causes it to spontaneously saturate his flesh with spirits to such a degree that he is indeed 'mummy-fied' in some obscurely holy way.

This is at once a mental, spiritual, and finally *physical* process. As with the body of the Ethiopian recipe, of the mythical sailor, of the suffocated corpses of sandstorms and gallows, flesh and spirits were being quite precisely conditioned by the pious physiological intensity of Wither's spiritual withdrawal. And, as with certain hangings, that fiercely pious introspection catalyses a kind of overwhelming spiritual orgasm. Ironically, we cannot quite describe the condition as 'ecstatic'. At this time 'ec-stasy' was an *out*-of-body experience, known especially to Catholic mystics such as Copertino. Is it perhaps significant that, as a typically introspective Protestant, Wither cannot escape his body, but rather seeks to flood his soul out through its minutest pores, precisely as someone might feel the effects of sexual climax vibrating out through their finest nerves, or to the tips of their toes?

It seems, then, that the most fervent Protestants could at times all but join hands, intentionally or not, with their Catholic counterparts. At least rhetorically, Wither can sublimate sexuality in the same way that Catherine or Angela could exalt the stinking pus and sores of the suffering human body. We have explored at some length the distinctive cosmology which helped corpse medicine survive for so long in Christian Europe. We now turn, at last, to its longer term decline. Even here, however, it was to prove almost as impressively stubborn and vital as the animate corpse itself.

7

OPPOSITION AND AMBIVALENCE

Pre-eighteenth century

For well over 200 years European Christians ate or drank human flesh, bone, brains and blood. They rubbed the oil of human fat onto rheumatic or gouty joints, onto cancers, and into the facial scars left by smallpox. Some ate or drank human shit and urine. A shadowy network of suppliers, sea captains, grave robbers, executioners and anatomists oversaw the acquisition of bodies, blood, bones and fat. Whilst English soldiers and settlers seized Irish land, others discreetly foraged for moss-crowned skulls (prizes which, admittedly, may sometimes have been those of the invaders rather than the natives). Doctors and chemists and hangmen chopped, sawed, filed, dissected and pulverised human bones, skull, tissue, brains and nerves into the various forms required for practitioners and clients. How could the small-scale communal rituals of the Huron, the Tupinamba or the Wari' ever begin to approach the systematic, quasi-scientific determination of these educated Christian man-eaters? By now we are surely in little doubt as to who, for some two and more centuries, were the real cannibals of the early modern world. They read and wrote in Latin, dressed in silks, debated theology, painted many of the greatest Western artworks, threw up some of Christendom's most astonishing palaces and cathedrals and churches.

When and why did this end? Neither of these are easy questions. In these final chapters I aim to set out a good deal of evidence, but refrain from drawing rash or totalising conclusions. Treating these divisions themselves with some caution, I will split this survey of opposition and decline into pre-Restoration, post-Restoration, and eighteenth-century periods. The present chapter handles the first two of those phases, which are generally marked by ambivalence rather than outright opposition. But, as we will see, the eighteenth century itself has to be internally divided. This is in part because it is so difficult to say when corpse medicine was abandoned, even by the educated or literate.

Early opposition

Open hostility

We saw in chapter one that both the herbalist Leonhard Fuchs and the magus, Henricus Cornelius Agrippa, denounced corpse medicines in the earlier sixteenth century. Fuchs himself falls into a particularly élite minority of opponents when he actually goes on to wonder 'who, unless he approves of cannibalism, would not loathe this remedy?'[1] Obvious as the label may now seem to us, it was surprisingly rare at that time. If Fuchs' hostility is pretty much unqualified, Agrippa's is slightly less straightforward. At one level, we should bear in mind that Agrippa was in many ways an unusual figure in his own time – not least for his remarkable defence of women in an age of pervasive misogyny.[2] Moreover, the fuller context of Agrippa's remarks is instructive. What he precisely says is this:

> but there are some robbing empirics that persuade us that none but strange and uncouth medicaments are most available, without which there can be no health; trying their experiments at the expenses of the miserable; mingling the most hurtful insects and reptiles in their medicaments; and as if all other remedies were defective, using human fat, and flesh of men embalmed in spices, which they call mummy, which they cause men to eat, as it were to atone nature.

Agrippa seems here to single out fat and mummy as some of the worst examples of 'strange ... medicaments', rather than merely attacking corpse medicines alone. His antipathy to such agents is so great that, a few lines before, he states: 'it would be better for the general health of men, and for the Commonwealth, to forbid the use of all exotic medicaments, which are brought in by piratical merchants, at such miraculous prices, to the bane of the inhabitants'.[3]

In 1538 the Italian philosopher and physician, Aloysius Mundella of Brescia, asserted very plainly that medical use of corpses was '"abominable and detestable"'.[4] Yet many others were less forceful or single-minded than this. Take, for example, Gesner's *Treasure of Euonymus*. The 1559 translation cites Albertus Magnus' recipe for distilling blood. Our author (let us presume Gesner, and not an editor) then adds: 'I can neither allow the making of medicines for men of man's blood, which although reason and experience would move us unto it, yet religion seemeth to forbid it, namely when there is [sic] so many other medicines'.[5] It is, first, at least slightly odd that Gesner cites this recipe in some detail, and only then voices his unease. Someone more fiercely antagonistic would probably have begun by stating their hostility, and also refrained from giving much space to such cannibal formulae. More subtly, it is perhaps also telling that Gesner sets 'reason and experience' against 'religion'. Whilst we should not underestimate the weight of the latter, some readers could perhaps feel that Gesner is almost faintly apologising for his inability to follow the dictates of reason and experience. A broadly similar pattern of equivocation appears a few lines on, when he cites three other authors on medical use of blood, and devotes some seven lines to instructions for distilling the blood of 'sanguine young men'. He then notes that the surgeon Hieronymus Brunswick has known 'marvellous things' accomplished by 'the water of man's excrements and ordure ... mixed together'. Only at this point does he suddenly burst out: 'my heart riseth against such medicines and abhorreth them'.[6] There seems little doubt that, for all his strength of feeling (exhibited in the visceral revulsion of those three opening words) Gesner feels himself in something of a minority – hence the sense of obligation to cite the formulae he so much detests. We should also note that, whilst 'such medicines' must mean all of the above, he certainly does not trouble to establish any clear hierarchy of revulsion. The water of excrement and urine seems, implicitly, just as unacceptable as the use of blood.

In his 1580 essay 'Of Cannibals' Montaigne attacked European hypocrisy by comparing New World cannibalism with European corpse medicine. Having cited the arguably far worse violence of the Wars of Religion, he then added: 'physicans fear not, in all kinds of compositions availful to our health, to make use of [the human body], be it for outward or inward applications'.[7] The phrase 'all kinds of compositions' clearly implies at least one substance beyond human flesh, and could indicate several. While already atypical in many ways, Montaigne is clearly more interested in European double standards than in mounting a direct attack on corpse medicine itself. And at this stage, any such attempt would clearly have been unsuccessful. For it was just around this time that another unusually clear-sighted Frenchman emphatically lamented that 'we are ... compelled both foolishly and cruelly to devour the mangled and putrid particles of the carcasses of the basest people of Egypt, or such as are hanged, as though there were no other way to recover one bruised'.[8]

Despite overwhelming support for mummy from practitioners and patients alike, Ambroise Paré was convinced that other remedies were both more humane and more effective. A weaker figure might well have succumbed to popular pressure when, 'on June 7, 1582, the twenty-six-month-old son of Mathurin le Beau, merchant milliner' was run over in the street by 'the wheels of a coach loaded with five gentlemen'. (Only a modern parent, we must now realise, would be so naive as to ask why a two-year-old boy was crawling along the middle of the road.) Onlookers, Paré tells us:

> cried to the coachman, who stopped his horses, pulled them back and the wheel again went over the baby's body. He was carried into his father's house, thought to be dead and eviscerated. I was called immediately to treat the child. When I examined him very carefully I could find no fracture nor dislocation anywhere in his body. I immediately sent to the Paris gate to get a sheep. I had it skinned, and after rubbing the infant's body with oil of rose and myrtle, I wrapped him naked in the hot sheepskin. Then I gave him oxycrate to drink instead of mummy to prevent the blood from curdling and congealing in the body. In addition, I told the mother to keep him from sleeping as much as possible for at least four to five hours, so the blood would not run so much to

the interior of the body (which she did). Moreover I applied fomentations of resolving herbs and plasters proper for contusions, to dissolve the bruised blood.[9]

'Oxycrate' was a humble mixture of vinegar and water. Paré's use of it is telling: rigorously empirical, he was concerned simply with what might actually *work* against a given disease or injury. And mummy, he insisted, did not. He is sure of this because, as he asserts in 1585, he himself has tried mummy 'an hundred times' without success. By contrast, the two year-old babe in sheep's clothing made a miraculous recovery.

Paré is notable as an early medical opponent of mummy: not least because, in one part of his attack on it he strikingly undermines the implicit distinction between 'good physic' and 'bad food', emphasising that the Egyptians had not embalmed their dead in order for them to '"serve as food and drink for the living"'.[10] Yet Paré did concede that, *if* mummy was effective, then its advocates 'might perhaps have some pretence, for this their more than barbarous inhumanity'.[11] This statement, along with his repeated trials, implies that he would have accepted corpse medicine, notwithstanding his abhorrence of it. We have seen Monsieur Christophe des Ursins all but demanding mummy from the reluctant Paré after a fall in 1580. And we should also recall how long it took for Paré's opposition to fully crystallise. Just a few years earlier, in his *Works* of 1575, he was still unequivocally referring to '*cranium humanum*, fat, blood, flesh' and marrow, as 'useful in physic'.[12]

Sometime before his death in 1604, the physician Thomas Moffett attacked not just those classical forms of corpse medicine met in chapter one, but also the more recent advice of Ficino. 'No doubt (saith he) the milk of a young and sound woman is very restorative for old men, but the liquor of man's blood is far better ... what law, what reason, nay what conjecture found out this cannibals' diet? well, let it proceed from the Americans and barbarians ... but far be it from any humane or Christian heart ... to suck away one another's life in the blood of young men'. Going on to refer to 'Charles IX King of France' who, 'being but outwardly bathed for his leprosy, died therefore ... a most bloody death', Moffett unequivocally sets the seal of divine judgement upon such transgressions.[13] He also sets the rare label of 'cannibal' upon Ficino's blood therapy – and it is notable that he does *not* do so in order to score points for Protestantism, emphatically lamenting that he had understood the Italian to be not only 'a most famous scholar' but 'accounted for a good Catholic'. Had Moffett lived a little longer, he might have found something to admire in his own monarch, James I, who stands out as one of the very few patients of the day known to have refused corpse medicine, when in 1623 Mayerne prescribed it for his gout.[14]

If Moffett was unswayed, here, by his own Paracelsian leanings, the Spanish writer, Francisco de Quevedo (1580–1645) was similarly unimpressed by alchemy. In one of his *Visions* (penned sometime between 1606 and 1622) he wrote of 'a great hall, smelling abundantly of sulphur; wherein were alchemists, whom devils examined with much trouble, for they could not understand their gibberish', their talk being 'altogether of metallic substances, which they named after the seven planets', and whose furnaces and crucibles 'were all charged with … minerals, dungs, man's blood, and alembic powder'. Although this itself is chiefly an attack on alchemy (one of the few areas beyond medicine where human blood had been historically used as an ingredient), there is no doubt about Quevedo's stance on medicinal cannibalism. Elsewhere in the same work he quite plainly condemns those physicians who come 'armed with a drug made of man's grease … though disguised under the name of mummy, to take off the horror and disgust of it'.[15] If Quevedo stops short of mentioning cannibals, he quite clearly identifies physicians; and he or his translator also – unusually – employs the then novel term 'disgust'. In France, Vincent Leblanc (writing sometime before 1640) had no strong personal opinions on Egyptian mummy, but did note that 'some approve not of the physic'.[16]

Back in England in the early 1630s, Fludd's arch-opponent, the clergyman William Foster, and the physician James Hart both hurled abuse at the cannibalistic ingredients of the wound salve: 'moss taken from the skull of a thief that hath been hanged … man's fat … man's blood warm … as it is taken from his body, collected and composed with a great deal of superstition'. Foster – who is quoted there – compounded the charge of 'superstition' by wondering 'if these weapon curing mediciners' did not indeed 'make … a god of their unguent, and commit not idolatry in attributing that to a little smearing ointment of their own making, which is proper to God only'. Going on to claim that the Devil ('usually delighting in such things') actually effects these cures, Foster is echoed by Hart, who warns of how 'Satan hath from the beginning thirsted after man's blood'.[17] Hence it was, Hart insists, that the Devil 'suggested to his ministers so many remedies composed not only of the blood, but of divers other parts of the body of man, and as our magicians still teach their too too credulous disciples'.[18] Fierce as these attacks are, we have to wonder if these authors would have troubled to attack corpse medicine without the motivation of their more general opposition to the wound salve, and (in Foster's case) its imputedly Faustian hubris.

Ambivalence

At the start of this story we heard Nashe defending his allegedly bizarre neologism, 'mummianized'. Writing in 1594, he asserted that, while 'mummy is somewhat obscure' (presumably to the general public), it is 'to physicians and their confectioners … as familiar as mumchance amongst pages'.[19] A decade or so earlier an English traveller in Egypt was watching the excavation of mummies from a Cairo pyramid. 'These dead bodies', he wrote later, 'are the mummy which the physicians and apothecaries do against our wills make us to swallow'.[20] For this author, the Egyptian mummies were not redeemed by their antiquity, and it seems that the rabbi ben Zimra could not have convinced him that they had been transformed into some new state beyond the human. They were, simply, 'dead bodies'. For all this, the anonymous voyager seems ultimately to be cowed by medical authority. Mummy is something which 'the physicians and apothecaries do *against our wills* make us to swallow'. Nowhere is Nashe's imputed gap between public and physicians more starkly clear. These words must mean that patients know what they are taking. If they meant that mummy was given secretly, then the issue of the 'will' would seem not to apply. The point is precisely that the will of the patient is subordinated to that of the physician. And, if a physician had to justify his charges, it would be all the more necessary to make clear that an exotic and quite costly drug had been employed.[21]

This blunt statement seems to be unique among surviving references to mummy. It makes us look again, however, at James I's refusal of skull medicine: was it only monarchs or aristocrats who would express their unease by outright defiance in this way? The traveller makes us wonder, too, if mummy and related treatments were still arcane for some around the time of James's unwanted prescription. In 1630 William Basse's *Help to Memory and Discourse* implied that the origin and nature of mummy still needed explaining. Amongst its numerous question and answer formulae we find a query on the location of 'that wilderness through which the children of Israel wandered forty years'. Readily answering, 'the desert of Arabia, from whom is brought the excellentest mummia', the imagined respondent is then asked what this is, and what is its use. Basse replies: 'it is a thing like pitch, some say it is made of man's flesh boiled in pitch, others, that it is taken out of old tombs, being a corrupted humour, that droppeth from embalmed bodies: or those there buried in the hotter sands'. Confirming the impression about medicine's ability to cook poison into medicine, he adds that 'it is the principal of poisons, which physic in some kinds maketh use of'.[22]

Elsewhere in the early Stuart period, the gap implied by Nashe and Hakluyt's traveller is obliquely glanced at in a range of negative references to mummy. In 1606 Dekker satirises an ancient suitor, imagined as preying on a sixteen-year-old virgin; this worthy is derided as one 'into whose bosom threescore winters have thrust their frozen fingers … his breath … ranker then a muck-hill, his body more dry than mummy, and his mind more lame than ignorance it self'.[23] This early reference to the mummified desiccation of the elderly anticipates an immensely popular jibe of the Restoration. Dekker himself had been narrowly beaten in this respect by Jonson, who in *Volpone* (1605) has two particularly greedy and unscrupulous characters, Mosca and Corvino, relentlessly trick all around them, including an equally disreputable (and aged) advocate, Voltore. Mosca suggests that, once this legal vulture has been fully exploited, he and Corvino might 'sell him for mummia' as he is 'half dust already'.[24] If we are hardly meant to feel much sympathy for Voltore, we are probably also intended to realise that this nominally flippant quip neatly captures the extremes of ruthless opportunism found in Mosca and Corvino (and, by extension, mummy suppliers themselves).

Jonson was especially alert in combining these two popular figurings of mummy so early on. In 1613, in Field and Fletcher's play *The Honest Man's Fortune*, a character fears that the merchant, Mallicorne, will 'sell us all to the Moors to/make mummy'.[25] Fifteen years later, in Robert Daborne's 1628 drama *A Christian Turned Turk*, Rabshake, servant of a stereotypically Machiavellian Jewish master, insists that 'If you gull me now, I'll give you leave to make mummy/Of me'.[26] That kind of shift (from selling someone, or fearing such a fate, to rhetorically exploiting it by way of defiance) reappears in 1633 in Shirley's *Bird in a Cage*.[27] The disguised lover Philenzo seeks to persuade the Duke of his skill and resolution by swearing, 'let me have freedom, and money enough ... and if I do not conjure up a spirit hot enough to inflame a frozen Lucrece bosom, make mummy of my flesh, and sell me to the apothecaries'.[28]

To make sense of these kind of uses, we need to see anxiety about mummy as a peculiarly mobile and amorphous phenomenon. Precisely because people so rarely confront its cannibalistic status openly, their discomfort tends to take a range of different shapes, with blame being effectively shifted away from mainstream Christian Europe to other parties. Notice that these references all to some extent highlight the middlemen, rather than doctors or patients. (Even Shirley only goes as far as the apothecaries, rather than the physicians.) This could imply that mummy itself is seen as valid for its medical benefits, while those who profit from the sale of human bodies are regarded with hostility. But the hostility is yet more precise than that. In 1613 the character imagines himself and others being sold to 'the *Moors*' – a destination which probably implies the counterfeit-mummy trade associated with Alexandria. Comparing this to Rabshake's quip, we notice that it is part of a broader tendency to deflect guilt about medicinal cannibalism by projecting it onto some of the more alien scapegoats of Christian culture. For Daborne's audiences, it would be an easy and natural step to see a Jewish character ignoring all scruples in the relentless pursuit of profit – especially given the tendency to see Jews as monopolising trade in genuine or fake mummy. In each case, corpse medicine is neatly shifted into the doubtful company of those habitually demonised for their religion and race.[29]

If such references as these tend to point up the commercial opportunism (rather than human benefits) of mummy, others from the period probe still more narrowly at the crucial distinction between raw and cooked, food and physic. When John Webster's tragedy *The White Devil* was first performed in 1612, audiences could hear the enraged Isabella swear of Vittoria that she hoped

> To dig the strumpet's eyes out, let her lie
> Some twenty months a dying, to cut off
> Her nose and lips, pull out her rotten teeth,
> Preserve her flesh like mummia, for trophies
> Of my just anger.[30]

In 1612, those last lines must necessarily waver ambiguously between the wondrous antiquity of the mummy tombs, and the potentially degraded commodity now pounded up in the shops of Bucklersbury. Whilst this of course suits the passage in question, there is another moment in the play which twists that sense of degradation yet further. At the very opening of the tragedy, Gasparo pitilessly dissects the friendless web of sycophancy in which his associate, Lodovico, is caught. Devoured alive by human parasites, the latter is told that

> Your followers
> Have swallowed you, like mummia, and being sick

> With such unnatural and horrid physic
> Vomit you up i'th' kennel.[31]

Quite literally dragging corpse medicine into the gutter (denoted by the Jacobean 'kennel'), Webster here briskly undoes all the laborious work of those who had somehow temporarily cooked human flesh into a state beyond that of mere food. In this intriguingly nuanced speech mummy is neither food nor physic, but vomit. At one level, it is interesting that nobody has benefited from this illegitimate act of consumption. Lodovico, implicitly depersonalised into a medico-financial commodity, is subjected to a ruthless utilitarianism, while those attempting to swallow him find that their own bodies rebel against the attempt. And it is this vomiting which most perfectly captures Webster's attitude. On one hand, we are offered an ironic reversal of the whole logic of medical culture over raw nature. The body spontaneously, *naturally* rejects something which remains fundamentally unnatural, whether processed, theorised, or otherwise. On the other, the result is vomit: the epitome of raw matter, entropic, low, repellent and largely useless (excepting the purgation itself). The apt outcome of this tabooed therapy is that nature not only spontaneously rejects it, but also spontaneously reprocesses medicine down into food, and then into something still rawer than food itself.[32]

In *The Duchess of Malfi*, meanwhile, Bosola tells the eponymous heroine, moments before the death he brings her, that 'thou art a box of worm-seed at best, but a salvatory/ Of green mummy: what's this flesh? a little cruded milk,/phantastical puff-paste … '.[33] The phrase 'green mummy' offers a sharply pithy glance at the medical exploitation of human beings, presenting them not as holistic individuals, but as medicine-in-waiting, a kind of generalised crop, ripening suitably only in death. But what points that criticism the more finely is the word 'salvatory' – a specialised term almost wholly limited to medicine and surgery. Glossing the word as 'a box for holding ointment' (1a obsolete) the *OED* gives Webster's line as one example.[34] Used in English in this way (rather than Latin, in predictably devotional contexts) the word indeed seems to have been quite rare even within medicine, so that Webster's phrase must have gained a yet more potent charge of vivid and arcane ugliness, as the minds of readers or viewers flickered uneasily between a living human being and this silver box filled with cannibalistic unguent. In these perceptive lines the alienating powers of corpse medicine are brilliantly encapsulated: a live woman is boiled down into this usable essence, and relocated within a specialised medical container, the walls of flesh replaced by the cold limits of metal.

Given Webster's genius for the grotesque or horrific, it is striking to find that mummy is something which even he cannot stomach. From another angle, ambivalence about corpse medicine comes across with special clarity in those writers who make two or more quite different uses of it. We glanced at John Norden's 1611 poem, *The Labyrinth of Man's Life*, when considering rhetoric which exalted or sacralised mummy. Although the strongest case of that was from an admirer of Norden's work, Norden himself had very probably seen and accepted this compliment, and his poem also contained a similarly positive usage.[35] But in 1626, denouncing the avarice of certain creditors, Norden wrote:

who hath not heard ... some cruel man say, he would make dice of his debtor's
bones? he were as good to say, he would eat his flesh like a cannibal: and what
less do they, that enforce a poor debtor to perish in prison, there to leave his
bones, and flesh too, for the satisfaction of the creditor, to make use of both his
bones for dice, and his flesh for mummy, fit relics for cruel creditors, sweet
odours for their consciences, and wholesome physic for their hearts?[36]

Whilst this could be seen as a twist on the more general quips about selling people
for mummy, the most obvious feature of it is the association between savage and
medicinal cannibalism. It is a little more difficult to be sure if – or how – this association implies criticism of corpse medicine. One possibility is that Norden was at
ease with the idea of Egyptian mummy, but not with that derived from people he
might pass in the London streets. Another way of saying this is to argue that he may
have been less troubled by use of recent corpses, so long as he had no idea of their
origins. Thirdly, it can be argued that this does not clearly attack the mummy trade,
but uses it to attack those tyrannically oppressing debtors. In doing so it ironically
insinuates that such cruelty is finally fruitless – whereas mummy is useful, there is no
benefit to be gained from having someone rot in prison out of malice. Yet even if we
accept this last view, we find that Norden again points at the precarious legitimacy of
mummy: its status, for some, is so dualistic that it will serve at one moment for
eulogies of refinement, at another for metaphors of un-Christian transgression and
cruelty.

By far the strongest case of ambivalence, however, is found in Thomas Fuller. This
is particularly intriguing, given that it was Fuller who at one point offered one of the
neatest formulae to explain just how mummy achieved some degree of legitimacy. It
was, he stated in 1647, 'good physic but bad food'. We need first to look at the
context in which this phrase occurs.

Attacking parliamentary land seizures, Fuller demands: 'can their pelf prosper? not
got by valour or industry, but deceit; surely it cannot be wholesome, when every
morsel of their meat is mummy (good physic but bad food) made of the corpse of
men's estates. Nor will it prove happy, it being to be feared, that such who have been
enriched with other men's ruins, will be ruined by their own riches'.[37] At first glance
one might just compare this to Norden, who uses mummy to make an attack on
something else. But with Fuller the close tie between mummy and 'meat' seems
more problematic. Why not say (for example) that their meat is *cannibalism*? Fuller
appears here to tacitly concede how easily mummy may slide from the level of physic
to that of food, stating not just that this plundered meat is mummy, but that mummy
itself is still, finally, meat. If his lines as a whole broadly mean, 'it is illegitimate to use
Royalists for gain in this way', then the coded attitude toward mummy may also be:
'it is illegitimate to use human beings for profit in that way'.

It is probably also significant that the key phrase of these lines occurs in brackets.
Although this superficially fits the rhythm of the prose, we feel, nevertheless, as
though we can all but sense the deeper rhythm of Fuller's mental processes through
this aside. He is writing quite quickly (note, more generally, the impressive volume of

his writings) and a neat phrase leaps to his pen, already pre-bracketed in his mind. The point is that he does not think hard about it, does not painstakingly formulate it, and certainly does not analyse it. Conjectural as this view might seem, it fits the impression that what Fuller is actually doing is merely accepting – temporarily – the partly successful propaganda image conveyed by physicians or apothecaries. In this light, even Fuller's last sentence, warning that such men might be 'ruined by their own riches' perhaps carries a faint echo of Webster, similarly asserting that those who feed on others will have their stomachs spontaneously purged in response to such unnatural practices.

Comparison of New and Old World cannibalism has shown that good or bad forms of anthropophagy depended to at least some extent on social context: were the cannibals 'savage' or 'civilised' in other ways? In the social entropy of civil war, Fuller's whole attitude may well have been generally skewed toward a sense of low cannibalism. Fuller himself had particular cause to lament parliamentary exactions. As W.B. Patterson points out, he lost his own Dorset property in 1646, and thereafter stayed with various friends or patrons, as well as at the clerical foundation of Sion College. *Good Thoughts in Worse Times* – the work from which the 'good physic' passage comes – has, Patterson adds, 'a doubting mood approaching despair'.[38]

But these cannot be the only reasons for Fuller's coded unease about mummy. For he had already made two rhetorical uses of it by 1642. In a series of moral aphorisms about 'jesting', he tells readers: 'seeing we are civilized English men, let us not be naked salvages in our talk … Let not thy jests like mummy be made of dead men's flesh. Abuse not any that are departed; for to wrong their memories is to rob their ghosts of their winding-sheets'.[39] There must here be some kind of unconscious association between those 'naked salvages' who sometimes practised cannibalism, and those 'civilised Englishmen' who routinely did so for medical purposes. Indeed, it is not otherwise obvious why these 'salvages' are in the passage at all; there were innumerable other ways to condemn those who spoke ill of the dead. The chief thrust of the similes used here seems to be: keep your distance from the dead. To jest about them is to close that distance, to invade the sanctity of the grave – or, rather, to more or less chew them up, thus closing the gap in that most absolute and invasive way, usually reserved for one's very worst tribal enemies.[40] By implication, mummy itself becomes a violation of fundamental boundaries, a breaking of a basic taboo worsened by the drive for profit. Similarly, that 'good physic' which was tacitly agreed to be necessary for the public good, and founded on the weighty theories and ethics of authorised medicine, appears to be brought down to the level of a jest – something whose necessity is questionable at very least.[41]

In this same work of 1642 – *The Holy State* – Fuller has a chapter on the various qualities of 'The Tyrant'. This figure, he writes, is someone who 'leaves nothing that his poor subjects can call their own but their miseries. And as in the West-Indies thousands of kine are killed for their tallow alone, and their flesh cast away: so many men are murdered merely for their wealth, that other men may make mummy of the fat of their estates'.[42] Taken on its own this offers a markedly pre-utilitarian view of the use of nature. Although they were created by God for humanity's use, animals are not to be so narrowly, wastefully exploited and slaughtered in this way. Equally, people are more than just a source of material gain. Whilst this passage shows that even in 1642 land seizures were able to attract Fuller's criticism, its main value is the way it sharply alters our reading of the broadly similar lines from 1647. In the earlier case there is no redeeming afterthought in brackets, no discrimination between physic and food. The lines are essentially about illegitimate profit, a selfish, opportunistic gain as far removed from medical notions of the public good as one could imagine.[43] Instead of the cannibalistic plunder occurring as a side effect of war, men are here figured as deliberately 'murdered' *in order that* 'other men may make mummy of the fat of their estates'. Moreover, given that this plainly hostile stance occurs before the more equivocal passage, we must suspect that Fuller's ambivalence was not simply a matter of changing opinions over time, of an ongoing rational debate with himself about the status or legitimacy of mummy. Rather, a basic level of unease and uncertainty was always there, operating at an unconscious or subconscious level.

That impression is confirmed when we find Fuller swinging violently away from the fragile truce of 1647 just three years later. In a general description of Egypt he notes that, amongst its various distinctive phenomena, 'mummy must not be forgotten, being man's flesh, at the first embalmed for forty days together, and afterward for many years buried, in that hot and sandy country'. And yet, he emphasises, 'such cost and curiosity used for their preservation, accidentally occasioneth their speedier destruction' given that such bodies are 'taken up out of their graves' and 'bought and brought into foreign countries for medicinal uses'. Then, without any bridge, Fuller suddenly bursts out: 'What, is there such a dearth of drugs? such a famine of physic in nature that (as in the siege of Samaria) one man must feed on another?'[44] The sharp drop down to famine cannibalism is deliberately ironic, contrasting the desperate necessity of Samaria with the very different world of medicine in ordinary society. And this ironically imagined 'famine of physic in nature' could also be a way of more forcibly underlining how corpse medicine effectively – and needlessly – goes *beyond* nature in its quest for cures. Even without these points of detail, the passage is plainly, all but viscerally hostile. Indeed, the sudden dramatic change of tone very neatly captures the sense of something long but only partially suppressed, now bursting violently up from the unconscious to the conscious mind.[45]

If we remained in any doubt about Fuller's very basic disquiet in this area, we would only need to turn to an undated funeral sermon, 'Death's Prerogative', preached on Genesis 3.19 ('For dust thou art, and unto dust thou shalt return'). Here we find several of the above phrases repeated verbatim, but mingled with some important variations. In order to emphasise the levelling power of death over all human wishes and arts, Fuller imagines an 'experiment' in which all the greatest skills of surgeons and embalmers attempt to defy the natural forces of decay. After detailing the processes involved, he warns that

> such prodigious cost of embalming bestowed on bodies, hath accidentally occasioned their speedier corruption. Many a poor man's body hath slept quietly in his grave without any disturbance, whilst the corpse of some

> Egyptian princes might justly complain with [seeming] Samuel to Saul, 1 Sam.
> 28.15. Why hast thou disquieted me, to bring me up, their fingers, and hands,
> and arms, toes, feet, and legs, and thighs, and all their body, tugged and torn
> out of their tombs, tumbled and tossed many hundred miles by sea and land,
> bought and brought by druggists for mummy, and buried in the bellies of other
> men, they it seems being cannibals, who feed on man's flesh for food, though
> not for physic, all which may seem a just judgement of God, on the immo-
> derate cost and curiosity in their embalming, as if endeavouring thereby to
> defeat and frustrate Gods sentence, and to confute the truth in my text. Dust
> thou art, and unto dust thou shalt return.[46]

Despite the lack of dating, it looks very much as if this version of the unquiet grave
came later than that of 1650. This is partly because it is so notably expanded (running
back several paragraphs before the one quoted), but most of all just because it so
deliberately and emphatically heightens the irreverence of the mummy traders. In this
case, time does seem to have changed Fuller's mind. Rather than glancing at those
merely generalised bodies which were 'taken up out of their graves', now we are
obliged to move in close through the particular 'fingers, and hands, and arms, toes,
feet, and legs, and thighs' which are themselves 'torn out of their tombs, tumbled and
tossed many hundred miles by sea and land … and buried in the bellies of other
men'. It is hard to overstate the significance of these words. Where so often there is a
conveniently empty space between the plunderings of Egypt and the swallowed
drugs of London or Paris, we now find ourselves forced to ride the pitching waves
which bear these ancient body parts across that often misty gap between the grave
and the patient. It is almost as if the physicians had somehow fenced off the details of
this therapy, keeping the public back at a certain habitual distance. In the above lines,
Fuller defiantly leaps that fence and irreverently tears up the fragile web of mystification
which had otherwise kept critics at bay.

Another way of viewing the passage is to see Fuller as angry with himself for
having so long been kept at bay, having been taken in sufficiently to write, in 1647, a
neat piece of propaganda for the whole dubious phenomenon. Hence, when he now
states, with heavy irony, 'they it seems being cannibals, who feed on man's flesh for
food, though not for physic' he more or less entirely reverses his earlier formula,
pouring sarcasm upon it like a kind of corrosive acid of derision. We might sum up
Fuller's various dealings with mummy by imagining his temporary elevation of
medicinal cannibalism as a kind of strenuous effort, almost as if he were physically
lifting a heavy weight. Sooner or later, the gravity of disgust would confound his
attempt.[47]

A few months before the Restoration, Sir Thomas Browne published his archaeological
discussion of urn burials, *Hydriotaphia* (1658). Ranging across various attitudes to
human mortality, from Pythagoreanism to those who were 'content to recede into
the common Being, and make one particle of the public soul of all things' Browne
presently comes to the art of the Egyptian embalmers, 'contriving their bodies in
sweet consistences to attend the return of their souls. But', he admits, here too 'all

was vanity, feeding the wind, and folly. The Egyptian mummies, which Cambyses or Time hath spared, avarice now consumeth. Mummy is become merchandise, Mizraim cures wounds, and Pharaoh is sold for balsams'. Here there is no sense of the public good, of the regrettable necessities of effective medical care. The basic driving force is 'avarice'. Like Fuller, Browne also shifts that bit closer to these ransacked men and women of antiquity. Admittedly, his rhetoric here is itself generalised and to some degree abstract – Mizraim and Pharoah are themselves remote and semi-mythical figures to the readers of the 1650s or 60s. But the basic aim is clear: Browne is trying to force home the sharp contrast between those ancient glories, ancient arts, and their modern degradation. Rhetorical this may be, but it cannot be wholly accidental that Browne singles out real names.

The Restoration

Open hostility

We can assume that, by the time he wrote of his experiences in Vienna, Thomas Browne's son, Edward, had read *Hydriotaphia*. For all that, even when confronted with the startling spectacle of a man gulping blood from a body in the throes of death, Browne the younger does not directly attack this therapy. Rather, having noted how, 'I have read of some who have approved the same medicine; and heard of others who have done the like in Germany', he then adds, 'but many physicians have, in all times, abominated that medicine'. Perhaps so: but what does Browne *himself* think? We are not told. The hint may be subtle, but it is consistent with what had gone before in attitudes to corpse medicine. Implicitly, Browne seems to defer to medical authority, even when seeking condemnation; it is what physicians think about this that matters most. Edward himself was to become a fully fledged physician; we can only assume that, in his youth, he imagines himself to lack sufficient experience or training to make his own clear judgement.

If Edward Browne is at once uneasy and yet equivocal, he is nevertheless about as openly hostile as any British author between 1660 and 1700. Boyle, in his 1683 *Memoires for the Natural History of Human Blood*, admits that 'many have a strong aversion, and some an insuperable, though groundless abhorrency, from medicines made of man's blood'. Groundless though this may be, it is sufficiently potent and widespread to prompt Boyle to experiment with deer's blood as a possible alternative.[48] Without letting us know who these patients might be, Boyle confirms the persistent gap between practitioners and certain of their clients, underlining the divide quite nicely via his own airy dismissal of such qualms ('groundless abhorrency'). As we saw in chapter two, the woman who had seemed to respond so well to blood therapy had had this remedy given her under a false name.[49] Given the apparently spectacular results in that case, we can well imagine that Boyle could easily square the duplicity with his conscience.

Similarly, the Lichfield physician Sir John Floyer has no ethical qualms himself about 'mummy, or other putrid parts of animals' (such as skulls), being merely concerned, at a technical level, to warn readers that 'all putrid things are very unwholesome in our diet'. At another level, he recognises the opinion of Theophrastus, that 'the foetor gives us an aversion' to such treatments; hence, one 'should always avoid giving mummy, or other putrid parts of animals ... to those who have a violent aversion, especially if we smell their putrid ... odour'.[50] Besides having some concern about the material effects of mummy, Floyer here is notably just humouring the delicacy of certain patients in a similar way to Boyle. There is no outright objection to medicinal cannibalism as a phenomenon.[51]

Ambivalence

> Trade makes all things common ... [52]

If we compare this neat little aphorism from Du Bartas with Thomas Browne's pithy summation ('mummy is become merchandise') we have a very useful key with which to approach the coded but consistent literary references to mummy found after 1660. In a sense, one of the most interesting things about Browne's phrase is this: it was only in 1658 that a writer could so plainly say something which had arguably been very obvious for at least several decades. In the ambivalent literary references before the Restoration, one recurrent factor was an implied gap between the attitudes of physicians, and those of patients or other members of the public. At times this gap is a matter of discomfort for non-medical personnel; at others it more basically involves the sense that mummy is arcane or unfamiliar for some members of the public. As the Restoration period progresses, mummy increasingly becomes markedly *over*-familiar (especially to ardent playgoers). And in most literary usages, this is a familiarity which is marked by varying degrees of contempt.

There must be a number of reasons for this new status. First, we should not underestimate the general demystifying effects of the English Revolution and the regicide – events which radically subverted the old aura around monarchy, for example, and the power of religion to hold back the advances of nascent science. Secondly, mummy was necessarily bound to become at least slightly more familiar over time, however it was treated by those involved in its use. But the fact remains that one of the chief ways in which mummy was familiarised was through its status as a valuable commodity. When du Bartas remarks that 'trade makes all things common' he implies two possible effects on a substance such as mummy. On one hand, the normalising, levelling powers of the mercantile world could initially work to defuse the charge of strangeness or taboo which hovered about corpse medicine. At one level mummy was just another commodity, no more offensive than molasses or myrrh. But in the longer term, as mummy was levelled down to the point of degradation, we reach the stage where more coded jibes about profit and commerce ('sell us for mummy' and so forth) crystallise into Browne's unequivocal four words. And it perhaps is not going too far to hear a subtle emphasis on the word 'become'. It is not just that mummy has 'become merchandise' since the trade became especially viable in the sixteenth century. Rather, in a more oblique but real sense, the several decades of this commerce mean that mummy has *become* merchandise in a quite special way by 1658. It has been turned into merchandise, by this stage, in a way that it was not in (say) 1590. For some decades it was both a commodity and a partly separate entity, an object of wonder and admiration. But when Browne writes *Hydriotaphia*, mummy has become, for some observers, nothing *but* merchandise. Where once the long alchemy of time had elevated human flesh into something faintly numinous, the corrosive acids of trade have now reversed the process.

Jonson had captured the early stages of that process particularly well back in *Poetaster* in 1601. In chapter three we heard the merchant Albius criticised by his wife Chloe for a narrow focus on trade. Albius responds: 'upbraid me not with that: "Gain savours sweetly from any thing; he that respects to get, must relish all commodities alike; and admit no difference betwixt oade, and frankincense; or the most precious balsamum, and a tar-barrel"'. By 'balsamum' Albius almost certainly means mummy; and in juxtaposing this with the lowly 'tar-barrel' he is not merely offering a general contrast, but very probably inviting the reader to suspect of him readily making or dealing in counterfeit mummy, prepared with ordinary pitch. Whilst in du Bartas' phrase, 'common' perhaps carries a relatively neutral tone (as in 'shared' or 'general'), we can well imagine that Jonson, like Chloe, had a certain disdain for 'common little men' such as Albius.

Albius's real-life counterparts do indeed seem to have made mummy quite negatively common by the time of Charles II. Occasionally, we hear of an intact mummy, a wondrous artefact with some status as an individual. The king himself had 'an entire Egyptian mummy with all the hieroglyphics and scutcheons upon it' presented to him on Friday 20 December 1661 'at Whitehall by Captain Hurst, who lately brought it into England from the Libyan sands'. And this artefact, supposedly 'the body of a princely young Lady' preserved at least 2,500 years, could also be seen 'by any person of quality, who is delighted in such curiosities, at the sign of the Hand and Comb near Essex house in the Strand'.[53] But, if you were a playwright or a playgoer, your attitude was likely to be far less reverent or wondering than this advertisement might imply. Even without recalling that Pepys saw his first mummy in a warehouse, we can infer from dramatic references that mummies now were, almost overwhelmingly, the stuff of derisive wit and low comedy.

Mummy in Restoration literature and drama

We have seen that pre-Restoration literature could show considerable ambivalence towards corpse medicine. But from 1660, references in non-medical texts display a particularly clear shift of attitude. All the uses of mummy which we encounter in plays, poems, and fictional prose are negative ones. It is probably also significant that most are comic.[54] Instances generally fall into one of two groups. First: while dramatic characters had previously imagined themselves or their victims being made into mummy or sold for it, it seems to be only from the start of the Restoration that people risk being '*beaten* into mummy'. The phrase presently grows so common as to be more or less proverbial, and seems to have been a good deal more popular than the now familiar 'beat to a jelly'. It probably implies a victim beaten to the colour of mummy; possibly also the texture too – and evidently with a more general sense of human flesh in its most radically altered form.[55]

Why else was this particular threat so popular in this period? Firstly, we find that four instances of beating or threatened beating explicitly involve master–servant relations, with a fifth concerning a threat from a 'gentleman' to a 'foolish citizen', and a sixth involving the poor in general. The implicit sense of ownership and commodification thus conferred on mummy is especially clear when a character in John Dryden's 1668 play *Sir Martin Mar-All* remarks of his servant, 'An' I had a mind to beat him to mummy, he's my own, I hope'.[56] In a different but related way, it would have been taken for granted by many readers or viewers that this was a spontaneous, dishonourable form of violence, at the furthest remove from the ritualised, honourable combat of duelling. In Mary Pix's 1697 comedy, *The Innocent Mistress*, an irate master underlines this point, proposing to his servant to 'kick thee into mummy, for though my sword's drawn, I scorn to hurt thee that way'.[57] Despite this ostensible condescension, the trend ultimately indicates a need to reassert status boundaries which had been fatally damaged by the revolution.

Popular as such threats are in Restoration plays, they often vary so little as to provide scant clue as to other possible implications of this new expression. It must be significant in some way that particular living people (other than criminals) are now so frequently imagined as potential material for medicine. This shift may in part reflect the spread of Paracelsian mummy recipes from the forties onwards, given that in those cases the unwilling donors were indeed the recently dead. But most basic of all to this new rhetoric is one particular trait. To beat somebody into mummy is, in effect, to get much *closer* to them than one would by merely threatening to sell them. It is here especially that we see the indirect effects of that 'trade' which 'makes all things common'. People in general now feel much closer to mummy than did those who, like Greaves, wondered reverently at the culture of the ancient Egyptians. The actors of the Restoration stage are very far from being stunned into a reverent dream of times past, or time suspended. Another way of saying this is to see that, after 1660, *anyone* can make mummy; just kick your servant or your enemy hard enough, and you have in a few moments what once alchemised itself across centuries into a drily statuesque artefact.

One further way of glossing all the mummy beatings of the era is to imagine that – not unlike Fuller – such authors have jumped the fence of authority behind which corpse physicians had previously sheltered. In this latter case, it is not so much that they rip up the veil of mystification, as that (like good Restoration virtuosi) they break into the laboratory and begin pounding up Egyptian imports in the mortar themselves. Even Egyptian mummy, after all, had to be beaten or at least crumbled if it was to be spread on plasters or swallowed in liquids. Occasionally an author comes unintentionally close to the precise mechanics of processing, as when Sir Peregrine Bubble ('credulous fond cuckold' and eponymous spouse of Thomas D'Urfey's *The Fond Husband*) ironically swears: 'My bed! my bed is my castle; and, by the Lord Harry, he that violates it but with a look, my fist shall crush him into mummy'.[58] Here the verb more realistically offers us, not a mere bruising, but something much nearer the behaviour of mummy when powdered or crumbled into the constituent atoms which allow it to be mixed and drunk.

The second popular usage compares the old or prematurely aged with 'mummy' or 'a mummy'.[59] We have seen that the dryness of mummy had been proverbial for some time. Yet interestingly, in past decades it did not often prompt this kind of rhetorical twist. As I have argued, it may indeed have helped to distance mummified bodies from the repellently viscous corruption of ordinary decaying corpses. What we seem to find with this new category is that it implicitly degrades both the person abused, and the mummified body itself. In this way, it contrasts sharply with that Paracelsian thought which in fact elevated the medical potency of *any* corpse into something semi-divine. (Indeed, just thirty odd years since, George Wither had managed, without the influence of Paracelsianism, to equate self-mummification with the most potent spiritual ephiphanies.) To put it another way: in popular theatre mummies are now negatively, rather than positively ancient.[60]

Restoration comedy being what it is, such rhetoric lends itself especially well to the horror of young women faced with ancient suitors. In *The Loving Enemies* in 1680, the young Lucinda rebels against the prospect of a husband no more than 'an history incarnate, true annals writ upon a skeleton', demanding of her father, 'and what then, go to bed with this rotten chronicle? no he shall lie covered with cobwebs first. I don't intend to embalm matrimonial mummy, to spoil the apothecary's trade, and fill my closet with gally-pots'.[61] In 1696 even a lowly serving girl, Ansilva, recoils at Gerardo, 'a lover of threescore' who will come to her arms 'all wrapt up in sear-cloth like a mummy – my imagination sickens at it ... '.[62] In Elkanah Settle's opera *The World in the Moon* Jacintha tells the aged alderman Sir Dottrel Fondlove in no uncertain terms that he is 'a scarecrow to flesh and blood; an antidote to love', one who 'hast been dead to womankind these fifty years' and 'buried in searcloth and flannel threescore', before demanding:

> Does thy cozening lawyer want a memento mori?
> The scrivener dried parchment for thy mortgages?
> Thy surgeon want a skeleton? thy 'pothecary a mummy?
> And thy brother Belzebub a broker's shop?
> Thy lumber-house of antiquity would furnish 'em all.[63]

But this extra charge of (intra-generational) antipathy is by no means de rigeur for such abuse. In 1674 a servant, Sanco-Panco, is derided as 'some Egyptian mummy preserv'd/By a petrifying vapour' – one who moves 'as if he/Had no soul'; while Sanco-Panco's aged and deformed mistress, Strega, is described as 'Arabian mummy'.[64] By the later seventeenth century we can hear in a private letter of how, 'on Tuesday last, that walking piece of English mummy, that Sybil incarnate, I mean my Lady Courtall, who has not had one tooth in her head, since King Charles's Restoration, and looks old enough to pass for Venerable Bede's grandmother, was married – could you believe it? – to young Lisanio ... '.[65] As well as redressing the gender balance a little as regards such marriages, these lines suggest that this rhetoric began to pass from stage wit into more or less common speech as the century neared its end.

Not only that, but the joke had become so oft repeated as to be itself a venerable piece of antiquity. Whilst that letter writer effectively signals this in his briskness of phrasing, by 1689 Thomas Shadwell had already flung a jibe at the stale habits of weak playwrights, having the aptly named Oldwit rail at his wife and daughter for 'out-painting all the Christian Jezebels in England'. 'Pox on't', he adds specifically to his wife, 'you would by art appear a beauty, and are by nature a mere mummy. There's wit for you again. Gad, I'll pepper you with wit'.[66] In those last two sentences we can clearly perceive Shadwell establishing an ironic distance between himself and the tired quips of certain peers. We might add that, for all his lack of wit, Oldwit here points up a certain truth of his day. When he says, 'you would by art appear a beauty, and are by nature a mere mummy' he oddly reverses the way in which the 'art' of Egyptian embalmers had been so often perceived to miraculously defy 'nature'. Yet this seeming oddity is apt – at least as regards the degraded stage mummies of the Restoration. Implicitly, these hybrid entities (part living Europeans, part ancient Egyptians) are now merely the result of *natural* ageing and decay. In the age of over-familiarised wonders, they are increasingly ordinary.

A variant on that ironic inversion is found in 1677 in Wycherley's *The Plain Dealer,* where a widow tells Major Oldfox, 'you Major, my walking hospital of an ancient foundation, thou bag of mummy ... wouldst fall asunder, if 'twere not for thy sear-cloths'.[67] Here we meet an almost complete inversion of the perennial endurance and firmness of mummy (recall Howell: 'More firm than that hot Lybia's sands do cake'[68]). This may be just an accidental result of the great popularity of such jibes. Yet it is also hard not to feel that it again says something about the growing lack of reverence for mummy, or mummies. At least in the English imagination, these durable artefacts are somehow becoming less substantial, even putrefying, some 2,000 years after their deaths. This imaginative decay could not be achieved by just one physical act of violation, or even several. But almost 20 years after Browne, it has begun to occur as a result of an accumulated irreverence. What time could not do, avarice has.[69]

We can put this another way if we view such rhetoric in terms not just of its irreverence for long-dead Egyptians, but for those Europeans loosely imagined as dried and ancient mummies whilst still alive. Are such quips, finally, rather more than just a modish (and presently hackneyed) way of sniping at the aged? It is certainly no accident that several of these jibes are aimed at those who (effectively) refuse to lie down and die in the winter of their years. Aspiring to youthful brides or lovers, they acquire just the faintest edge of those uncanny qualities which accrued around the mummy more fully in later eras, doggedly haunting a world which they should really have left long ago. But if we turn back to the medical side of mummy, we also find another coded message bound up in the ravelled sear-cloths and gums of these ancient reprobates. At a quite basic level, this rhetoric *identifies* living Europeans and dead mummies. Arguably, it does so in a way that was very rarely seen in the earlier decades of a thriving mummy trade. Throughout that period, patients were, in the simplest physiological sense, literally, chemically identified with the mummy which they swallowed, and which became, at least temporarily, part of them. Yet almost no one (including the most vocal critics) overtly stated this. Come the Restoration, that identity is figuratively asserted, time and again, in well-worn jokes about the elderly.

As with that slow process of trade and familiarity which, in Browne's words, caused mummy to *become* merchandise, the identity of patient and drug comes about only after an unusually long period of digestion and assimilation. Even then the merging of the two is portrayed obliquely, with criticism or blame being shifted onto those who are either fading to the edge of society through sheer physical age, or who fail to quite follow tacit laws about just how the elderly should behave. Yet the identity is now there, in a way that it rarely was before. The long habit of swallowing human flesh has finally produced a definite physiological effect – as if the patient and the source material have begun to blur or fuse together. Mummy has, in more senses than one, finally come of age.

In the cases of both beating and age, mummy rhetoric must have been finely balanced between cause and effect. That is: mummy was now sufficiently familiar, sufficiently demystified, to lend itself to the first wave of these quips, from the late 1660s and onwards. As time went on, such rhetoric – not only read, but heard upon the stage – must necessarily have conditioned attitudes to mummy, and probably to corpse medicine more generally, thus cementing the irreverence which had given rise to the earliest of these jokes from the likes of Duffett and Dryden.

In saying this, however, one has to discriminate to some extent between mummy and mummies. If mummy itself, as relatively anonymous material used for hard-headed practical ends, now grew more degraded in literary and dramatic uses, mummies were perhaps slowly beginning to enjoy rather more dignity than in previous decades. (Even in quips about aged 'human mummies', the mummy does at least occasionally cease to be a mere collective noun, moving some way from commodity to artefact, or even person.) They were, as suggested above, starting to shift from typically being something to some*one*. And the novelty of this new status could be quite precisely registered. In Duffett's 1678 comedy *Psyche Debauched*, for example, a character vaunting whoredom over matrimony vows, 'I will revive the Sect of Adamites, renew the Family of Love, and make the slavery of marriage so out of fashion, that a man and wife shall be showed about, and wondered at as much as an hermaphrodite, an entire Egyptian mummy, or a cat with two tails'.[70] Here the cause of wonder is not mummy, but 'an *entire* Egyptian mummy' – something still sufficiently unusual, at this point, to be worth gaping at.

Come the mid-1680s, the dilettante playwright Sir Francis Fane also thought that this was the case. In 1686 Fane published a tragedy called *The Sacrifice*. This play, set in China, features not only a decidedly lame incarnation of Tamburlaine, but a whole chamber full of mummies. Plotting to murder Tamburlaine, a character called Ragalzan seeks the aid of 'a mummy-priest' – an eastern religious official whom Ragalzan himself derides as an essentially fraudulent guardian of mysteries. The would-be assassin is disguised as a mummy, and then hides in 'an amphitheatre of crowned mummies'. This itself is part of a temple, and is disclosed only some way into the scene, presumably with an attempt at dramatic effect. With the audience aware that Ragalzan is lurking there disguised, Tamburlaine, his daughter Irene, and his general Axalla stand alone viewing these wonders. Irene, seemingly as well travelled as her restless father, remarks that 'These mummies are more curious and magnificent/Than those we saw at Cairo', to which Axalla:

> And much more numerous:
> Which answers not amiss, to the prodigious space
> Of time, supposed by their chronology.

There follow some tedious speeches on fame, glory, and mortality, after which, 'Enter mummy priest, habited like a conjurer'. Elaborating on the 'prodigious ... chronology', this worthy begs:

> Greatest of emperors, draw near, and see
> The richest wardrobe of mortality
> The world affords: Here stand time-daring mummies
> Of China monarchs for ten thousand years.

Although less than reverent of these artefacts and their alleged age, Tamburlaine and Axalla sound rather more like doubtful Western Christians than the impatient men of action invented by Marlowe:

> Tam.
> What a canting tone,
> And what a monstrous tale!
> Ax.
> They've long traditions;
> And lie by old records as well as hear-says.
> Tam.
> No, no. Printing has been here in use some thousand
> of years, no wonder they have so many lies.

For pious Christians, 'ten thousand years' *had* to be a lie. Some years after Ussher's calculation of the age of the world and the date of Creation, Fane very probably knew that, whether Chinese or Egyptian, mummies were simply not allowed to be more than 6,000 years old. The priest goes on to describe these various princely mummies: one built a university, one invented printing, another gunpowder, and so on. When Tamburlaine asks, 'Are all your princes then philosophers?', the priest responds:

> No. But whosoever finds an admirable art,
> Is straight made governor of some wealthy province,
> And his invention is ascribed unto
> The king, whose reign he lived in.

This tour and associated explanations are prolonged for some time – presumably so as to build up suspense, as the audience is at once expecting one of the mummies to pounce on Tamburlaine, yet also evidently unsure which of them is actually the disguised assassin, Ragalzan.

Finally, with the priest pointing out 'the great Tzionzon, builder of the Wall', Irene remarks, 'He stares, and turns about his head. Oh horrid!'. ''Tis strange!' agrees Tamburlaine (perhaps rather mildly, in the circumstances). With no less improbability the mummy priest responds

> Marvel not, sir; 'tis usual with him:
> He seems offended at your conquests here

after which, 'Ragalzan leaps down, stabs at Tamerlane: Irene interposes. He and the priest leap down the trap-door' (Stage Direction).[71]

At one level, it is surely no small irony that, after having been so rudely plundered in order to treat wounds all those decades, the mummy should now take his revenge by seeking to inflict one. In this case treatment is not required, however, as by remarkable luck the blow has merely struck Irene's bracelet, thus averting injury to either father or daughter. At another level, we can add that we here encounter perhaps the first English dramatisation of the uncanny qualities of the mummy – ones which were to be exploited vigorously in later epochs, and which even now arguably take second place only to the vampire. True, the key mummy here is a human impostor. But in Fane's imagination this quality must have been offset by the audience's uncertainty as to just who or what was going to suddenly jolt out of the frozen shadows of Time to strike the blow. In this sense, then, the play effectively foreshadows the uncanny shiver generated by those later fantasy mummies, who somehow cheated not only decay but death itself, rising when it suited them to avenge their violated tombs.

At this point, the present author must reveal his own dramatic sleight of hand. Whilst I have deliberately invited the reader to imagine the staging of Fane's play, it was in fact never acted. This may indeed have been just because the presentation of this formidable chamber of mummies was considered prohibitively troublesome or expensive. There again, it may have just been due to Fane's '"having long since devoted himself to a country life, and wanting patience to attend the leisure of the stage"'.[72] But there seems to be no doubt that Fane had at some point intended the play to be acted (as his comedy, *Love in the Dark*, had been in 1675). When writing, he took the unusual step of placing a mummy (whether mentioned or seen) in a tragedy rather than a comedy, thus clearly assuming that the sight of *a* mummy could generate awe and terror, even if the reference to *some* mummy was now typically the stuff of abusive low comedy.

Three quite distinctive references to corpse medicine take us up to the eighteenth century. First, we have a long poem by the Royalist clergyman Robert Dixon. In Dixon's *Canidia, or, The Witches*, the eponymous women of darkness boast of how

> In laboratories' zealous fire,
> The chymists' limbics we inspire,
> To firk up salts, fixed or volatil,
> Spirits of silver, gold and steel,
> Sulphur and mercury dance in a wheel;
> Egyptian mummies, and the moss
> Of dead-men's skulls purged from dross;
> Elixirs, quintessential draughts,
> Raising sallets, and such like crafts.[73]

Taken alone, these lines look like a sharply critical inversion of those Paracelsian chemists who in fact usually prided themselves on their piety, and for whom chemistry and alchemy were tightly bound up with the numinous essences that God had locked up within ordinary earthly matter. The tone is at one level satirical, whilst at another it is the witches (and thus also the Devil) who are responsible for any successes which these chemists have.[74] That impression seems to be reinforced when Dixon elsewhere cites the old rumour that syphilis had been caused by cannibalism:

> Is the pox an American disease,
> Or came it rather from the Genovese?
> Who barrelled up Venetian mummy
> And sold it to them again for tunny?
> And so they got both pox and money.[75]

Overall, the poem's several references to mummy are more negative than positive (as when one group of witches has 'lank breasts, lean arms, with wrizzled flanks,/And mummy hips, and shrunk up shanks').[76] But when the speaker asks the witches to explain various perennial mysteries, such as 'Why carcasses buried in the sand,/Never corrupt in mummy land', when 'whole caravans' stuff, flesh and bone/Of man and beast', are 'turned into stone' he is more or less neutral, and nowhere in the poem is there an overt attack on corpse medicine, or any closer association with cannibalism than that seen above.

This association is made unusually plain by Robert Boyle. In 1665 Boyle published a set of philosophical dialogues between two characters, named Eugenius and Lindamor. Partially dramatised in the manner of Plato, these featured a conversation sparked when the two sat amongst a group eating oysters. Wondering why Lindamor alone is not partaking of these, Eugenius is told: 'whilst I saw such persons so gustfully swallow these extolled fishes, the sight lead me to take more notice than perhaps you have done of the strange power of education and custom'. Lindamor has been prompted, he further explains, to consider 'how forward we are to think other nations absurd or barbarous for such practices, that either the same, or little better, may be found unscrupled at among our selves'. Because of his travels, he adds, 'I am not forward to deride ... the practice of any people for being new, and am not apt to think, their customs must be therefore worse than ours, because they widely differ from them'.

He then turns to the notoriously raw behaviour of American tribes such as the Ouetecas: 'we impute it for a barbarous custom to many nations of the Indians, that like beasts they eat raw flesh. And pray, how much is that worse than our eating raw fish, as we do in eating these oysters?' Nor, he emphasises, 'is this a practice of the rude vulgar only, but of the politest and nicest persons among us, such as physicians, divines, and even ladies. And our way of eating seems much more barbarous than theirs, since they are wont to kill before they eat, but we scruple not to devour oysters alive'.

Presently this essay in cultural relativism reaches that most glaring blindspot of early modern Christendom: 'among the savagest barbarians', notes Lindamor, 'we count the cannibals'. Admitting that, 'as for those among them that kill men to eat them, their inhumane cruelty cannot be too much detested', he adds, 'but to count them so barbarous merely upon the score of feeding on man's flesh and blood, is to forget that woman's milk, by which alone we feed our sucking children, is, according to the received opinion, but blanched blood; and that mummy is one of the usual medicines commended and given by our physicians for falls and bruises, and in other cases too'. Moreover, 'if we plead that we use not mummy for food, but physic, the Indians may easily answer, that by our way of using man's flesh, we do oftentimes but protract sickness and pain, whereas they by theirs maintain their health and vigour'.

Just what are we to make of this rare moment of European candour? Although a very few critics had, before this, explicitly described corpse medicines as cannibalistic, the closest precise parallel with Boyle's reflections seems to be Montaigne − a fore-runner who is indeed a very good match for the enlightened relativism of the dialo-gue as a whole. At the time Boyle writes, he and Montaigne seem to be alone in having overtly attacked European hypocrisy on the issue of cannibalism.[77] Although we could split the details of this criticism in various ways, I will here divide it into the categories of blood and flesh.

In the first case, we find Boyle ingeniously raising the question of 'blood-cannibalism' long before routine blood transfusions had made the subject a matter of occasional debate.[78] As noted in chapter one, the charge regarding milk made more sense in a medical world where all bodily fluids were finally variants of blood. If it may seem whimsical for all that, we should recall, too, the outrage prompted by Alfred Gell in Papua New Guinea, when the Umeda saw him unthinkingly thrust his cut finger into his mouth. For a people who would never dream of even chewing their own nails, this was a significant act of auto-cannibalism.[79]

Within the context of corpse medicine, however, Boyle's remarks on blood and milk are not merely *avant-garde*, but oddly puzzling. He himself, after all, was fre-quently using blood for experiments of various kinds. Given the broad reflectiveness of the oyster dialogue, these trials alone could well have fallen under Lindamor's critical eye. But clearly more pertinent still were those preparations of blood used for medicine − something which, as Boyle himself confessed, bred 'insuperable aversion' in certain clients. Why then pick on milk, rather than blood medicines? The two are remarkably similar, even down to the fact that both are essentially *processed* forms of blood: the one altered by nature, the other by the chemist's art. Hence, having questioned the drinking of human milk, Boyle could not very easily defend blood medicine by claiming that it was cooked, as opposed to raw, cannibalism. In this light, we might begin to wonder if his defence of the 'barbarous Indian custom' of eating 'raw flesh' is an unconscious form of apology for a European hypocrisy which is not merely general, but very closely associated with himself in particular. This might explain why he once again turns back to raw feeding after discussion of mummy, noting that 'as the highest degree of brutishness, our travellers mention the practice of the Soldanians at the Cape of Good Hope, who not only eat raw meat, but, if they be hungry, eat the guts and all of their cattle, with the dung in them'. To this Lindamor answers (among other things) that 'I know several among us, (and perhaps some fair Ladies too) that to prevent the scurvy and the gout, drink their own or boy's urine', whilst peacocks' and dogs' dung are 'commonly given to patients of all sorts and qualities against sore throats'.

Boyle's handling of mummy seems more straightforward. It reinforces our impression that the distinction between physic and food was an important one, and that (Fuller notwithstanding) it remained a viable one in the 1660s. For Boyle does not – like Fuller – question that distinction itself. Rather, he tries to argue that physic is no *better* than food, and perhaps worse ('by our way of using man's flesh, we do oftentimes but protract sickness and pain, whereas they by theirs maintain their health and vigour'). It is probably significant that Boyle makes these impressively shrewd and enlightened remarks in a work which is generically distinct from his medical or chemical writings. Such a criticism notably arises in a book specially devoted to probing what is *not* normally discussed by educated Christians. It does not naturally, automatically arise when Boyle is talking about medicinal cannibalism in scientific contexts. It also seems important that the tone of the *Occasional Reflections* is largely just that – reflective, and gently provocative, rather than violently indignant or in any way prescriptive. It seems on the whole designed to make a few people think differently, not to make everyone act differently. For all that, we cannot help but be impressed by a mode of thought so like that of a late twentieth-century anthropologist; one which freely admits that 'most nations in styling one another's manners extravagant and absurd, are guided more by education and partiality than reason', and that 'we laugh at many customs of strangers only because we never were bred to them, and prize many of our own only because we never considered them'.[80] Here, at last, was an early modern author who could nod with genuine understanding if the Wari' had replied to him, 'thus was our custom'.

Our third case takes us close to the end of the seventeenth century. Around its midst, we found the ambivalent Thomas Fuller ready to fill in some of the typically blank space which lay between the plunderings of Cairo and the wounded or bruised bodies of European mummy patients. He imagined various fragments of the mummy ransacked from the quiet tomb, and presently 'tumbled and tossed' upon the waves before being 'buried in the bellies of other men'. Around 1693, the baronet Sir Samuel Morland probed that space in yet more obsessive and lurid detail. Morland deliberately chose three cases of complex bodily dispersal, so as to insist that no such problems could finally obstruct the omnipotence of God in the process of Resurrection. He talked of a man eaten by fishes, and another devoured in a forest by animals, in both cases mingling these initial acts of consumption with further levels of the food chain. Thirdly, he asked his readers to

> suppose a man-child born into the world, and (as 'tis believed) the flesh of that infant, in a few years, to be evaporated, and new flesh grown up in the room of the other; and let us suppose this body to live and change for the space of threescore or fourscore years, and then be buried in the sands, (as is practised in some very hot countries) and there remain a thousand or fifteen hundred years, till such time, as it is grown perfectly dry, and fit to be made use of for mummy; and this mummy to be distributed into the hands of several hundreds of apothecaries, and each of these apothecaries to make use of it in their physical doses, potions, or otherwise, and to administer it to as many hundreds of their patients, and each of those patients to void the same, or any part of it, by stool and those stools to be carried away by the scavengers, into some common place, and there mingled with the ordures of ten thousand other persons, and from that place taken up by the salt-petre men and converted into gun-powder, and that powder shot away into the air.[81]

What interests us here is not Morland's subsequent assertion that 'the Almighty God, and maker of heaven and earth, is able to recall every particle, dust or atom of a human body, in any of the aforesaid instances to its original and proper mass' (although we may briefly note both that Morland had been an amateur scientist in earlier life, and was now expecting fairly imminent death).[82] What matters is just how precisely, relentlessly familiarising this passage is. All the familiar detail works, of course, to Morland's general aim – like a good scientist, he seeks the hardest level of falsifiability for his spiritual hypothesis. But from our point of view what stands out is not so much divine omnipotence, as the sad mutability of the most honoured dead. Someone raised in a culture of habitual embalming dies imagining that they will join their kin in a state of material suspension, with their soul protected accordingly. Fifteen hundred years later they are reduced to more fragments than an anatomy specimen. These pieces pass through the hands of hundreds of apothecaries and are presently defecated, flung into dung heaps and mingled with 10,000 other pieces of shit, being finally recycled into an ingredient for gunpowder, and thus blasted up into a sky which is yet very far from that imagined heaven of past millennia. Here the fence of professional mystification is not only vaulted but obliterated. Morland takes Browne's bare four words of lament and rewrites them into a mini-essay upon the vagaries of the human corpse, pursuing its picaresque meanderings through a labyrinth of details and a myriad lowly orifices. Over eighty years after Webster's Gasparo was vomited out by greedy followers, we find the effectual processing of Time undone with cruelly scientific skill. The end of all that natural alchemy is, again, the basest, most entropic state of human matter. Mummy has become, not just merchandise, but faeces. Where once Arnold of Villanova had promised to distil excrement into medicine, medicine has here been reprocessed into the raw filth and stench of the London muckheaps – food for flies, until carted away by the capital's scavengers.

8

THE EIGHTEENTH CENTURY

On the surface, the period from the mid-eighteenth century onwards shows some of the plainest shifts of attitude towards corpse medicines. Yet further probing in this era indicates that these hostile attitudes are far from being unanimous. In order to set them in context, I will look first at the impressive persistence of corpse medicine through this century, before turning to some suggestive uses of mummy in Georgian literature and drama. A third section examines overt and mainstream attacks on mummy, human skull, and skull-moss. Finally 'The Great Whitewash' relates those distinctively Enlightenment responses to some of the more misleading references found in twentieth-century medical history, showing how, for a long period, the history of corpse medicine remained either unwritten, or effectively rewritten.

The persistence of Corpse medicine in the eighteenth century

Smuggling William III (d.1702) over the centurial border, we find Leo Kanner noting that 'a preparation of earthworms and human skull was prescribed as a remedy' by the physician of this epileptic monarch sometime before the latter's death.[1] A little further down the social scale there was the art connoisseur Lord Leominster, who was not only sick, but dangerously close to death on 30 August 1711. Leominster rallied in following days, and on 13 September the Northamptonshire physician James Keill treated him with spirit of skull (here referred to as 'Goddard's drops'). Leominster survived some weeks longer, finally dying on 7 December that year.[2] In 1712 one Henry Curzon advised that spirits of human skull or human blood be inhaled by those afflicted with 'swoonings and faintings', and in 1721 an English *Pharmacopeia* recommended 'three drams' of human skull in a recipe against epilepsy, and two ounces of mummy in a 'plaster against ruptures'.[3] Human skull is listed in a 1738 reprint of a late seventeenth-century work, and again (without comment) in an apparently standard catalogue of medicines published by the physician and theologian Robert Poole in 1741.[4]

Whether described as 'Goddard's drops' or 'the King's drops', spirit of skull was recommended fairly frequently for much of the century. In 1709 the recipe was associated with the eminent physician and surgeon Sir Edmund King. Although King himself died in this year, Londoners could still have King's formulae 'faithfully prepared by Nath. Rokeby, apothecary, at the Unicorn at Holborn Bride', including 'King's Drops, famous against apoplectic fits, and all nervous complaints, being the medicine King Charles the Second received so much benefit from'. Come 1743 the 'gentlemen and ladies' of the capital were advised of a similar transfer: 'the famous Imperial honey-water and King's Drops, formerly prepared by Mrs Prothers' could now be had at various London shops (none apparently druggists), the recipe having been left to a Mrs Malcolm.[5]

As late as 1792 the physician Benjamin Moseley continued to recommend powdered human skull against dysentery – 'particularly if it be from the skull of one who has been hanged, or broken on the wheel, or any other way received a sudden death'.[6] As Deborah Brunton notes, Moseley had a good practice among the London upper classes, and from the late 1780s was physician to the Royal Hospital at Chelsea. Moreover, Moseley cites powdered skull on the authority of 'the great Boyle' – thus reminding us of the chemist's continued influence well into the late eighteenth century.[7] Eighteenth-century editions of Boyle's own works were still recommending moss of the skull through to 1772.[8]

Indeed, usnea was being used around 1719 not just against wounds and nosebleeds, but against excessive menstrual flux.[9] As we saw in chapter three, circa 1758 someone was even attempting to artificially cultivate this medical staple, for around this time 'there are now laid, in a mossy corner, in the physic garden at Chelsea, pieces of human skulls, that the moss from the ground may creep over' them. Although John Hill (the author who states this) openly attacks mummy, and appears to distance skull-moss from his own time with the words 'it *was believed* that it had thence great virtue' we might wonder, on one hand, if these skull fragments had been placed there recently, and – on the other – why no one had removed them if such a therapy was by then considered wholly illegitimate.[10] Indeed, Hill elsewhere admits that skulls are sometimes 'laid on purpose' in places where common ground moss might grow over them.[11] In 1771, John Cruso's *A Treasure of Easy Medicines* was still advising that 'moss of the human skull, held in the hands, or hung from the neck of infants, stops bleeding'.[12] The historian Karen Gordon-Grube states, moreover, that English Pharmacopeias were recommending usnea until the nineteenth century.[13]

Mummy is prescribed in 1714 for rheumatism, and in 1733 for bruising and ruptures.[14] Although the physician and surgeon Daniel Turner argues against giving it internally for syphilis come 1737, he clearly implies that the practice was common enough to need opposing – perhaps not surprisingly, given the desperation which that disease must have prompted in some sufferers.[15] Turner's objection, moreover, was presumably a particular, technical one, given that he *did* advise the use of mummy against bruising and congealed blood.[16] Before his death in 1748, Noel Broxholme (or Bloxam) was topically applying a balsam of mummy, hog's lard, olive oil and yellow wax to those suffering wounds and ulcers, pains, gout, or cramps – possibly to the patients he served as physician at St George's hospital, among others.[17] The *Dispensatory* of the Royal College of Physicians was still listing, under 'man and woman', 'the blood, urine, fat, milk, skull and mummy' in 1747, and in this same year human blood, drunk '"recent and hot"' was being prescribed for epilepsy in England.[18] Women suffering prolapse of the womb around 1760 could have sprinkled on the offending organ a powder containing mummy, frankincense, and pomegranate flowers.[19]

Occasionally, negative or ambiguous references to corpse medicine also give us hints as to its continuing popularity with some. Commenting on remedies for difficult labour in 1728, the physician Peter Shaw reluctantly admitted that 'those who have credulous women to deal with, advise the wearing of a lodestone, eaglestone, the cranium humanum, or the like; and this sometimes to the great consolation of the patient'. Where 'such assistances are not highly prized', he adds, 'the following may be substituted to advantage' – going on to cite myrrh and various other alternatives.[20] Shaw clearly implies a new version of the older, occasionally glimpsed split between patients and practitioners. Where previously various clients had refused or been disturbed by corpse medicines, some patients are now clinging onto them, even as outright opposition rises amongst certain physicians.

In 1730 a course of lectures, apparently read to Cambridge medical students by the botanist and fellow of the Royal Society, Richard Bradley, noted that mummy was 'brought to us from Egypt', being 'the flesh of bodies that have been embalmed'. Adding that 'we have it every year brought over in large quantities, though at present it is not so much in use as it has been formerly', Bradley registers no unease or opposition about the drug.[21] He also tells us that as a commodity (genuine or otherwise) it was still profitable in the time of George II. He may further imply that medical interest is now outweighed by the financial motives of merchants, given that 'large quantities' are being shipped at a time of slackened usage.[22] For all that, when the 'man-midwife' and surgeon William Rowley attacked the continuing business of counterfeit mummy in 1794, he necessarily suggested that there was still sufficient demand to make such fraud worthwhile.[23]

Just three years before that, indeed, the physician George Motherby had a surprising amount to say about legitimate versions of mummy. Motherby discriminated between Egyptian and sand mummies (or, as he termed the latter, 'white mummies … of the consistence of horn, and light'); referred to 'mumia medullae' (the marrow of the bones); cited Paracelsus on mummy as balsam; and also described as 'mumia' that 'water … which is collected in a phial from the breath of a man received therein after washing his mouth with water'. This last category strongly recalls the role played by soul and spirits for some adherents of corpse medicine, and Motherby cements that association by still subscribing, at this late stage, to the notion of the animate corpse: mumia is also, he writes, 'a subtle, spirituous, ethereal substance, innate in every body, and remaining therein in some measure after death'.[24]

In France, Jean-Louis Petit, master surgeon and member of the Academy of Sciences, commended the volatile salts of human skull against infant tapeworms (stating that they could be given both to the child and its nurse); whilst Noel Chomel advised a decoction made from cucumber seeds, white poppies and mummy for 'phthisicky persons and consumptives'.[25] In Germany Matthias Gottfried Purmann cited mummy in a wound powder and a plaster for fractures, and the 1768 edition of Lorenz Heister's popular work on surgery repeated the well-worn advice about its powers against internal bruising.[26] (These references, it should be added, all derive from English translations, whose advice presumably found favour with some in the Georgian era.)

In 1795, in his play *Poverty and Nobleness of Mind*, August von Kotzebue introduced corpse medicine in a dialogue between a housekeeper and her daughter, Louisa. The latter, concerned about the wounded naval Lieutenant, von Cederström, begs her mother, 'O dear mother! go up and ask him how he does, and if he wants any thing?' With her mother concerned about the impropriety of such contact, Louisa insists, 'Why not? I know you have many fine receipts, balsams for wounds, and such like. Carry them to him'. The mother now relents, admitting: 'it is very true, I have many very fine medicines, vegetables, and roots, to which our good God has given many virtues. I possess also among others, an arcanum: it is prepared from men's skulls and Egyptian mummy'.[27] This use of 'arcanum' seems to fall under the *OED*'s second definition, 'one of the supposed great secrets of nature which the alchemists aimed at discovering; *hence*, a marvellous remedy, an elixir'. There is, then, probably something a little recondite about such a treatment. Yet, as the pious allusion to God-given virtues attests, this is a positive sense of strangeness. Louisa's response – 'make haste then' – has no touch of surprise or horror; and, most importantly, she requires no explanation of the nature or value of these substances. In such a context it is evidently rare to possess such recipes, but by no means incomprehensible. Throughout this scene there is clearly more concern about potential 'impropriety' and scandal than there is about the possible associations of corpse medicine.

Recalling what was said in chapter one about the doubtful ethics of using mummy as fish bait, or to physic hawks, we find that in 1790 one Charles Bowlker was telling his readers that they 'cannot set too high a value on' a fish baiting ointment made from cat's fat, heron's fat, cumin seed, and mummy finely powdered (and this despite the fact that 'fresh horse dung thrown into the water has the same effect').[28] In summer 1761 Londoners were much diverted with a member of the cat family which General Clive had brought back to the capital from India. This creature was exotic enough to lack a name, but sounds something like a lynx, and was sufficiently tame to let one Thomas Birch examine its teeth.[29] Walter Charleton, writing on the keeping of these creatures in India, remarked that, when the beasts were sick from overeating 'their keepers steep a piece of tender meat in human urine, and feed them with it, and being bruised or tired by over-hunting, they give them some mummy, wrapped up in their meat, and a warm place to rest in til they recover'.[30] Such medicine would evidently have been available to this new London citizen had he or she required it.

Human fat

In summer 1788 the London *Morning Chronicle* reported with some indignation on medical treatments recently used in the Vatican. For once, the Pope (then Pius VI) was not swallowing human blood. The patient was in fact his infant grand-nephew, and initial therapy involved 'the image called Bambino (superstitiously imagined to have the power of curing all maladies by its presence)'. This was accordingly 'brought in great processional pomp to the sick chamber'. The infant may have been a closet Protestant, as this holiest of pharmaceuticals had no effect upon him. Next, 'upon the advice of some ignorant enthusiasts in quackery', the Pope had, we learn, 'ordered a piece of human fat, cut from the body of a deceased person, before the corpse was cold, to be given the sick child to suck'. While the infant (perhaps also an early vegetarian) was taking this cure, it sickened further and died. 'Would any man imagine' wondered the *Chronicle*'s reporter, 'that such monstrous credulity and folly could exist in the eighteenth century?'[31]

If this hypothetical man had been a doctor, or someone suffering from sciatica, gout, rheumatism, rickets, or tumours, then he would not merely have responded 'yes' to this indignant question.[32] Rather, he would have found it distinctly puzzling, if not incomprehensible. From beginning to end of the eighteenth century, human fat remained one of the most enduring corpse medicines in England, Germany and France. It was advocated by physicians, as well as in the kind of general medical works which probably formed a staple of any self-reliant household. Enlightenment chemists analysed it and experimented on it, quantifying its behaviour and its yields of different substances.

In the very same year in which this popish hocus-pocus was afoot, the popular *Ladies' Friend and Family Physical Library* cited the general opinion 'of most practitioners at present, that there is no possibility of dispersing a schirrous' tumour, save by 'cutting it out: but that I religiously deny!'. The author went on to describe various external applications, such as 'Venice soap dissolved in milk, fresh cow's dung boiled in milk, warm sea sand', and human fat.[33] Had he known it, this writer might also have appealed to Richard Guy's 1759 work on tumours, which itself cited the influential surgeon Richard Wiseman (d.1676).[34] Wiseman, Guy records, 'imputes the cure of a lady, whose legs were swelled and become schirrous … chiefly to the parts being embrocated twice a day with clarified human fat'.[35] Nor did ailments have to be that severe to warrant similar treatments. In 1780 Thomas Goulard wrote of a Lady who had suffered pains in the arm after being bled. These persisted for some time, finally clearing up twelve days after the application of a plaster made of wax, human fat, a little camphor and vegeto-mineral water.[36]

Human fat was also frequently cited as a specially potent agent against rabies. In this area, the opinion of the successful London physician Robert James is particularly interesting. In 1747 James attacked the use of both human skull and skull-moss.[37] Yet James was still ready to publish the virtues of human fat for a number of purposes. In his *Medicinal Dictionary* of 1743 he noted its powers as a painkiller, an emollient, an anti-paralytic, and against gout and contracted nerves. As T.A.B. Corley points out, this book was a derivative work – a status confirmed by the way that James quotes verbatim from Pomet on human fat without acknowledging his predecessor.[38] Even so, James was in that case prepared to associate his name with the medical benefits of human fat; whilst in two other works he more actively asserted its powers to combat rabies. It was also in 1743 that he published a book on rabies which described itself as having been 'laid before the Royal Society in February 1741'. Here James has the grace to acknowledge the influence of a London surgeon, John Douglas, who brought to his attention the methods and writings of the French surgeon J.P. Desault. James goes on to quote Desault at length, including the remedy which the Frenchman had '"tried with constant success, and which I propose to prevent and cure the hydrophobia … the ointment made of one third part of mercury revived from cinnabar, one third part of human fat, and as much of hog's lard"'.[39]

Desault's claims for this ointment were backed up by numerous precise case histories – such as the one James cites, where it cured a lady who had rashly picked up a highly-spirited stray dog during a coach journey from Bordeaux to Medoc.[40] Desault himself had been emphatic that his belief in the ointment was the product of personal experience: 'I think I am the first who made this trial, and have no reason to repent it, since all those who have followed this process have been preserved from the hydrophobia'.[41] Quoting Desault again in a work of 1760, James echoes this stress on empirical findings by the words with which he prefaces his citations: 'as Desault's theory seems but indifferent, I shall confine myself … entirely to his practice, as much more worthy of notice'.[42]

Whilst human fat was frequently recommended by physicians, the involvement of eighteenth-century surgeons broadly recalls the early uses of corpse medicine in Elizabethan England, when it was chiefly promoted by men such as Banister, Clowes and Hall. For many of those advising its use, fat worked. It was commended by its practical utility in sometimes urgent or perilous situations, and was clearly far from being the quasi-magical nonsense it appeared in the *Morning Chronicle* in 1788. Indeed, for some it was very much the object of a rigorous proto-scientific chemistry. The German chemist, Lorenz Crell, used it to obtain phosphoric acids, and his French counterpart, Comte Antoine-François de Fourcroy, explained very precisely how a chemist could 'prepare fat for pharmaceutical purposes'.[43] It must 'be cut in pieces, and the membranes and vessels separated; it is afterwards to be washed with much water, and melted in a new earthen vessel, with the addition of a small quantity of water; when this fluid is dissipated, and the ebullition ceases, it must be poured into a glazed earthen vessel, where it fixes, and becomes solid'. At the end of his instructions, Fourcroy cites Crell's own calculation, that 'twenty eight ounces of human fat afforded … twenty ounces, five drams [and] forty grains of fluid oil'.[44] Robert James himself also implied that he had experimented with it, stating in 1747: 'all expressed oils and fats, when distilled with alkaline substances, become highly penetrating, as is obvious from distilled human fat … and the oil of soap'.[45]

Not everyone used human fat because of its supposedly obvious chemical efficacy. Writing on sciatica in 1764, the celebrated Italian physician Domenico Cotugno recommended using oil to apply a gentle friction to affected areas. He added: 'I use oil of olives or melted suet, which the patient imagines is the great remedy, and the thing that frees him from his disorder'. Although clearly keen to distinguish between actual causes and the (possibly psychosomatic) role of imagination, Cotugno was ready to let the latter work if possible. So, 'to such as mete out health under the appearance of remedies, I recommend … vipers' oil; or a thing whose scarcity will recommend it, human fat. It is for this reason', he explains, 'that patients choose this or that oil for the friction. The more oil is poured on, the less apt the flesh is to be inflamed'.[46] Here Cotugno implies both that any oil will work for this purpose, and that the scarcity of human fat will appeal to those patients swayed by various 'imaginative' factors.

Cotugno also points up two other important aspects of this therapy, circa 1764. In Italy, where human fat had once been routinely derived from execution victims, it was now known for its 'scarcity'. The strange case of the Norfolk husband sold by his wife in 1736 suggests that this may also have been the case in England for some time – at least in those areas distant from the public anatomies of the capital. Although executions were occurring across the country, relatives would probably often have been keen to bury felons intact if they could. The Norfolk incident implies that a body full of human fat was ultimately worth more than half a guinea, if a canny surgeon would pay that much for it.[47] (Recall that, in Aberdeen in 1625, human fat bought from an apothecary cost twelve Scots shillings per ounce.[48]) It also implies that, even in a relatively remote part of the country, an ordinary woman was aware of the demand for this commodity. As we have just seen, for decades after the 1730s physicians, surgeons and chemists in England, Germany and France all took the trouble to obtain human fat, difficult as this may have been.[49]

If human fat was getting increasingly hard to find, it seems likely that not everyone could afford such a treatment. We have seen above that some of its known beneficiaries were indeed 'ladies'. We might at first imagine that these genteel women had the exact nature of their cure carefully shielded from them by their physicians. But if this was sometimes the case, we must recall, on one hand, that the wealthy would often have wanted to know what ingredients made up the cost of their bill, especially in an age when patients were relatively assertive toward their doctors. On the other hand, Cotugno makes it clear that he *deliberately* told certain patients what was being used, precisely because this was important to their expectations of cure. It may well have been that many physicians and clients were relatively at ease with a corpse remedy which seems rarely to have been swallowed. There again, if it was not (obviously) cannibalistic (both Boyle and the Umeda tribe might have felt otherwise, given that it could be absorbed by the body) it was far from having the proverbial dryness of mummy, or the natural dryness of human skull.[50] In the case of the Pope's grand-nephew, the aim *was* evidently to swallow the powers of human fat (and it seems likely that the child may have been persuaded to eat it, had he had any teeth). Given that the corpse used in 1788 was 'still warm', it is hard not to suspect that we here meet an altered version of those various uses of fresh human blood. The cure was based on the idea that one could suck the very forces of life itself from fat as well as from blood. If at one level this links back to Pope Innocent VIII, we will see in the Conclusion that the vital density of human fat was also attested by some still more surprising uses throughout the nineteenth century.

The cannibal priest

Evidence derived from what we would now consider orthodox medical sources shows that corpse medicines were fairly widespread in the eighteenth century. Indeed, given how late was their uptake in Elizabethan England, it is very likely that eighteenth-century usage outstrips that of the sixteenth century. By now it should be clear that what passed for 'orthodox' (or simply acceptable) medical sources to some could be – for the modern eye – remarkable, if not startling. There was the violently spurting blood of a decapitated felon, for example, to say nothing of the whole complex science of shit pursued by respectable patients and practitioners. And, along with various unlicensed healers, wise women, and benevolent aristocrats, there was also the common natural recourse to one's religious minister.[51] If you lived in or around Mitchelstown, County Cork, in the earlier eighteenth century, there is a good chance that in sickness you would, at some time or other, have been grateful to John Keogh the younger (*c.*1680–1754).

Modern readers who are nervous about meeting a cannibal priest might be reassured to know that Keogh had more or less impeccable social credentials. Although he did not, like Richard Baxter, cover hundreds of miles worth of paper with pious reflections, he generally looks like the sort of person that Aunt Glegg would have respected. As James O'Hara explains, preaching was in the Keogh blood.[52] John Keogh the elder (*c.*1650–1725) and his sons, John and Michael, were all clergymen. Given that the elder Keogh also had a considerable reputation as a scientist, it seems likely that the family in general would have been looked to in this respect even before its numerous children grew up. The younger John's wife was a cousin of the Duchess of Marlborough, and the pair had three sons and three daughters. John Keogh junior was a keen amateur naturalist, and wrote extensively on the birds, beasts, fishes and insects peculiar to Ireland. All in all, this would seem to be a model clerical family of the era – socially well-connected, and marked by a colourful and well-rounded portfolio of extra-ministerial interests. At the same time, it seems hard to imagine that, circa 1739, anyone could have been a more fervent advocate of corpse medicine than John Keogh of County Cork.

For the falling sickness, he recommends blood drunk warm, 'using exercise after it until there is a free perspiration'. He believes that water, oil, salt and spirit can be distilled from blood, and used to treat gout, palsy or vertigo. The 'volatile spirit extracted from urine is good', he tells us, 'against the stone, gout, gravel, asthma, pleurisies, stitches, coughs' and colds. 'An oil distilled from the hair' eases pain and cures baldness. Keogh holds mummy to be effective against green wounds or any kind of haemorrhage, and recommends human fat or grease to those suffering from paralysis, gout, or contracted nerves. If you were afflicted by stone in the bladder or kidneys you should procure a stone (or 'gravel') voided from someone else's urinary system. And, if you objected to this, you might be comforted to hear that 'the oil which is extracted from the tartareous matter, which sticketh to the chamber pot, is an excellent remedy to dissolve' bladder or kidney stones.

Keogh also elaborates on cosmetic uses of the human corpse. To fill 'the pits or holes' left by smallpox you could employ an unguent made from two pounds of 'man's grease' and a pound each of beeswax and turpentine. Dried menstrual blood could be 'given inwardly' against the stone or epilepsy. Powder of skull, taken 'one dram every morning fasting, or at night going to bed' would combat epilepsy and 'most other diseases of the head'. Powder scraped from the *inside* of a man's skull 'is a very excellent styptic' which 'instantly stops any flux of blood'. Epilepsy should also respond to an oil distilled from human brains, while extract of man's gall, taken with spirit of wine, cures deafness if dropped into the ears. Pulverised human heart can be taken 'a dram in the morning fasting' for epilepsy, apoplexy, vertigo and other diseases of the head. Human shit could be 'applied outwardly … against scald heads, gouts, cancers' and quinsy. The dung of an infant could be swallowed by epileptics, and urine could be dropped into the ears for deafness, or into the eyes for poor sight. It could be swallowed to ease obstructions of the liver, spleen and gall; and, like various surgeons before him, Keogh also held that it could be used to clean wounds. Add to these the time-honoured moss of the skull against bleeding; marrow against contraction of the nerves or sinews; oil of bones against gout; and a triangular bone from the temples as one more agent to fight epilepsy, and you have some idea of the medicine chest of a highly respected man of God, circa 1739.[53]

One other cure, however, may have had to be made to order. If suffering from 'blastings' (flatulence) or 'contractions of the joints', you were advised to make sure you put your gloves on. These should, however, be made of human skin. While Keogh does not state how these were produced, we can assume that the skin was tanned and handled like animal leather.[54] We know that in the Renaissance books were occasionally bound in human skin, and such bindings have weathered well. (Readers may recall that in late 2007 a 1606 work on the Gunpowder Plot was auctioned in Yorkshire. This was thought to have been bound in the skin of one of the executed plotters, the Jesuit Henry Garnet). In the case of the mummified corpse found in a London chimney in 1701, the skin had naturally become 'so much like leather that one of the bricklayers cut a piece of it, supposing it had been one of his pockets in hope to find some money'.[55] The modern author Mary Roach, on finding that wallets had been made from the skin of the anatomy murderer, William Burke, learned from the secretary of the Royal College of Surgeons that one of these 'looked like any other brown leather wallet' and that '"you would not know it is made from human skin"'.[56]

If the practical manufacture of these gloves was relatively straightforward, the thinking behind the remedy is another matter again. Both the barber-surgeons' 1578 ruling against those allowing skins to be tanned and the findings of Richard Evans and Kathy Stuart about the use of criminals' skin in Germany suggest that Keogh is here part of a significant tradition of his age. For all that, modern readers are likely to feel a particularly strong friction between the genteel and proto-scientific ambience of the Keogh family, and this seemingly magical use of human skin. Ironically, we are probably more likely to believe that swallowing cannibalistic medicines at least offers the chance of a basic chemical effect. These gloves, by contrast, seem to be based more in older notions of occult sympathy or spiritual transfer – the stuff of the wound salve and similar cures. Indeed, a good deal of Keogh's remedies derive from a broadly Paracelsian tradition (and may have been directly sourced from the work of Johann Schroeder).[57]

But many of those relying on Keogh's medical knowledge would not have been able to frame or rationalise his ingredients in that way. Evidence from the case histories of Thomas Willis suggests that few would have complained about such therapies. Those who were tempted to do so may have just felt obliged to grimace and swallow (as patients often still do, for a variety of reasons). Twenty-first-century Mitchelstown has a population of just 4,500. Around 1739, when distances and times of travel between a physician and potential patients would have been vastly greater, even townsfolk must often have been grateful for Keogh's services. Those living in the surrounding countryside must have been still more so – especially if they chanced to see their minister out seeking local birds and butterflies at a time of sickness.

Trade

One thing Keogh could probably obtain with relative ease was human skull and the moss which sometimes came with it. If so, he had some reason to be grateful. The evidence of customs' charges from this period shows that the international trade in human skulls was sufficiently notable to attract a number of government taxes. As we saw, in 1799 a trade dictionary featured words for 'mumia' in ten European languages.[58] In 1755, Dr Johnson, though not acquiescent in the practice, noted that human skull remained on sale in London apothecaries' shops.[59] For most of the eighteenth century, skulls would have attracted a basic import duty of one shilling per head (the moss, it seems, came tax-free).[60]

Although there may have been more than one source for 'cranium humanum', it seems certain that Ireland was still a key area of supply as far as England was concerned. There would, after all, have been little point in an import duty on a commodity exclusively derived from home soil. Moreover, it also appears that England was still acting as a middleman for the further export of skulls to German and Scandinavian countries. For there were also additional duties (of just over three pence) payable on commodities carried 'in foreign built ships' and which were 'not from the place of their growth' – that is, brought from outside Britain to be sold on in other countries.[61] Skulls fell under these taxes, which strongly suggests that they were being shipped from Ireland and then (once domestic needs were met) on into the northern continent. Once again, it seems likely that the trade in human skulls was actually more vigorous in England in the time of Johnson and Boswell than it had been in the days of Shakespeare and Marlowe.

Moreover, it may well have grown between the Restoration and the time of George I and George II. For records show that there was no duty imposed on skulls by the customs Act of 1672. The initial one shilling duty was levied only from 1725.[62] Again, when Jean Jacob Berlu published his *Treasury of Drugs Unlocked* in 1690, he made no mention of 'cranium humanum'. But in later editions in 1733 and 1738, both this commodity and skull-moss are listed. In the former case, 'the skull of a man ought to be of such an one as dieth a violent death (as war, or criminal execution) and never buried: therefore those of Ireland are here best esteemed, being very clean and white, and often covered over with moss'.[63] The word 'therefore' implies that Ireland is noted for its relatively high number of unburied bodies. Moreover, the fact that 'cranium humanum' appears only in eighteenth century editions of the *Treasury* seems to reflect not so much increased use of skulls, as increased trade in them.[64] For Berlu's work specifically commends itself to those practising the 'trade of druggist', and Berlu styles himself as 'merchant in drugs'.[65] In 1751, meanwhile, the physician John Hill writes of how moss-covered skulls are still being 'sent from Ireland, and other places ... into all parts of Europe'.[66]

Corpse medicines and mummies in literature and drama

In eighteenth century literature and drama the well-worn jests about age and beating still persist (in much diminished quantity) for some time.[67] (Indeed, come 1756, the phrase 'to beat to a mummy' ('to beat soundly') features as an instance of word usage, under 'mummy', in Johnson's dictionary).[68] There are also other signs that corpse medicine is, at least for some, slowly changing its status. In Samuel Garth's 1714 poem *The Dispensary* we hear of an apothecary's shop in which 'mummies lay most reverendly stale,/And there, the tortoise hung her coat o'mail', whilst 'in this place, drugs in musty heaps decayed,/In that, dried bladders, and drawn teeth were laid'. Although Garth is generally satirical of this ambience – marked out, also, by 'some huge shark's devouring head' and 'a scaly alligator' – the phrase 'reverendly stale' does offer us a nice epigram for the over-familiarised, relatively debased nature of mummy and mummies around this time. Here as elsewhere, age is not something to be merely proud of any more.[69]

A little differently, Samuel Bowden's poem 'The Earth' has nothing explicitly negative to say about mummy, but does seem to associate it specially with Germany:

> In rapture raised I view the trav'lling sphere,
> Clime after clime successively appear.
> See polisht China in the East advance,
> And savage Tartary lead on the dance;
> Here Russia clad in ignorance and snows,
> Here o'er their mummy-pots dull Germans dose.[70]

Some time before his death in 1769, the poet William Falconer refers to a political adversary as 'some soft mummy of a peer, who stains/His rank, some sodden lump of ass's brains ... '.[71] In these lines the opponent's imputed age is again a broadly negative thing, in which moral and physical corruption uncertainly fuse. Moreover, whilst any reader can see that 'soft' is clearly part of this peer's degeneracy, the term is for us especially ironic. For decades, everyone knew that mummy, proverbially dry as it might be, was notably firm. Pomet said as much when advising on how to know the genuine article from counterfeits, and when Howell wrote, in 1635, of a memorial 'more firm than that hot Lybia's sands do cake' he assumed that the firmness of mummy was sufficiently well-known to make his lines comprehensible.[72] Yet Falconer seems equally to feel that what he implies needs little gloss. In his lines, mummy is soft (and apparently 'sodden'). Once again, it seems as if mummy has been bruised, damaged and softened not by time, but by the irreverent handling it has suffered in well over a century of medical trade.

The mummy as artefact

As I have suggested, at the same time as the medical version of mummy grew increasingly debased in popular representations, this long-suffering entity also began to acquire another status. In yet one more irony worthy of the pen of Thomas Browne, we find that the ancient Egyptians had gone to immeasurable trouble to preserve individual bodies, only to have the matter of these bodies ruthlessly *de*personalised. For decades, merchants and apothecaries dealt in *some* mummy, not *a* mummy. If they were at all concerned about genealogy, it was only because the rich were held to have been embalmed with materials more conducive to medical use. But from the Restoration period on, the mummy began slowly to re-possess the full outlines and markings of a body which had for so long been forgotten by European traders. Mummies were collected and displayed as artefacts by the wealthy. They were given as presents to monarchs.[73] In October 1742 the property of one Mrs Garnier of Pall Mall went on sale, offering richer Londoners the chance to acquire not just tapestry hangings, curtains, and carpets, but also 'a most perfect mummy of a daughter of Ptolomy', whose authenticity 'will plainly appear to the curious by the Egyptian hieroglyphics'. At this point the expected curiosity about this wonder was such that only 'gentlemen and ladies' were permitted to view it, and even they had to confirm their interest by obtaining free tickets, so as 'to prevent the curious from being obstructed in their observations' by overly large crowds.[74]

There again, come 1767 in Paris, the traffic in collectors' mummies had grown sufficiently common to prompt a mildly farcical incident, after an officer forgetfully 'left in the public stage[coach] a small mummy which he brought from Egypt'. When this box was opened by Customs' officers it was thought to contain the body of a murdered child. A commissary and a surgeon had been called in, the body transferred to the morgue, and a death certificate was about to be signed when the officer returned to claim the twice-dead Egyptian.[75] Back in England, as early as 1754 the trade in collectible mummies had swelled so much that these new plunderers began to gain something of the negative reputation of the older merchants and druggists of the medical realm. One author proposed that, 'as common malefactors are delivered to the surgeons to be anatomized, I would propose that a Connoisseur should be made into a mummy, and preserved in the Hall of the Royal Society, for the terror and admiration of his brethren'.[76]

Literary references to these exotic showpieces could imply a similar criticism of the collector's irreverence. In the first case, a poetic epistle of 1781 laments these new violations of the mummy's unquiet grave:

Whole ages though secure they rest,
Hid in their hieroglyphic chest,
Yet, time the pyramid decays,
And opens all its secret ways,
Excites th'exploring trav'ler's wonder,
Or the wild pilf'ring Arab's plunder,
Who tear the mummy from its tomb
To grace some virtuoso's room,
Divide with bart'ring Jews the prize,
And sell the race of Ptolomies![77]

If this satirised the vulgarity of plunder acquired by the mediation of 'bart'ring Jews', other popular uses glanced wryly at the doubtful claims made for the age and status of various collectors' mummies. Hannah Cowley's popular comedy *The Belle's Stratagem* (also published in 1781) featured the auctioning of 'an Egyptian mummy', once 'confidant to a maid of honour, the third wife of king Sesostris, and the toast of Grand Cairo'. When one gentleman ventures some doubt about this impressively precise identification, the auctioneer answers briskly, 'nothing so easy; we get at the genealogy of a mummy as easy as that of a horse', before rapidly shifting the bidding from twelve to eighteen guineas.[78]

In Phanuel Bacon's 1757 play *The Trial of the Time Killers*, this kind of satire is set within the broader context of a more general rage for collectible exotica.[79] A conspirator called Methusalem Rust is found to have in his house 'one large stone taken from the ruins of Troy ... one tooth of an elephant killed by Alexander the Great in his expedition against Darius ... a complete collection of the Hydra's heads killed by Hercules' (buyer beware, here, as 'the skulls and jaw-bones [are] greatly fractured') as well as 'the body of the famous Cleopatra preserved – with a genuine receipt to make the true mummy'.[80] Here the artefact and the drug appear side by side. Whilst Bacon clearly expects some acquiescent laughter from his audience at the expense of those selling doubtfully authenticated mummies for display, the medical side of this skit seems also to hinge on negative perceptions of mummy as a therapy. There is a hint that this is now increasingly recondite, given the implied rarity of Rust's 'true receipt'; and the implication that Cleopatra herself might be brayed up in a mortar offers a deliberately farcical wrench of Browne's earlier lament for Cambyses and his like. Come William Beckford's novel *Vathek*, in 1786, mummies clearly lend themselves to a new strain of uncanny horror.[81] But that kind of usage, undoubtedly interesting in its own right, is clearly far from representative of the eighteenth century as a whole.

In general, those attacking mummy dealers or collectors all have one thing in common in the Georgian era. Whatever the reasons, the effect is almost always the same: mummy and mummies are the stuff of comedy. In the period of transition in which mummy as medicine and mummies as artefacts temporarily coexist, this comic status is important, even where it is only *a* mummy which is being represented to readers or audience. For at this time, the two versions are clearly still linked in the minds of most writers. Two dramatic uses of 'mummy' and 'the mummy' are particularly notable.

Mummies on stage

Married just three hours, and your wife is already trying to have sex with the ancient dead … It could, we might feel, easily be the Restoration that spawned John Gay's 1717 comedy, *Three Hours after Marriage*, rather than the early years of George I. Yet we must recall that, around 1687, the first mummy to appear on the stage might easily have been a figure of uncanny menace – the disguised would-be assassin of Tamburlaine who featured in Francis Fane's play *The Sacrifice*. Instead, come 1717, that entity which would later be the stuff of mystic curses and cinematic horror enjoyed his first public outing in the realm of the very lowest crowd-pleasing slap-stick. His appearance involved four characters: the just-married Fossile and his wife Townley, and her two would-be lovers, Plotwell and Underplot. Amongst the various intended or inferred pieces of satire in Gay's quickly notorious play, Fossile is especially notable as a skit on the physician, natural scientist and antiquary John Woodward (1665/1668–1728). (The stage name, it should be added, was prompted largely by Woodward's scientific interest in fossils, rather than by a desire to emphasise his personal antiquity.[82])

If Gay is somewhat awry in his mockery of Fossile's fear of cuckolding (the real Woodward was unmarried, and said to be 'notoriously homosexual') he is broadly accurate in his parody of Woodward's mania for collecting. Thus act three opens with an exotic delivery. Upon the stage direction 'enter two porters bearing a mummy' Fossile responds, 'Oh! here's my mummy. Set him down. I am in haste. Tell Captain Bantam, I'll talk with him at the coffee-house'. This rather brisk offhand welcome for the son or daughter of Ptolemy implies that, even by 1717, such imports are sufficiently common to be treated fairly lightly. The porters, having exited, return immediately 'bearing an alligator' – thus depositing two pieces of exotica which also happen to be closely associated with apothecaries or physicians. Briefly exclaiming 'a most stupendous animal! set him down', Fossile quickly shifts to anxieties of a professional and (more importantly) personal nature:

> Poor Lady Hippokekoana's convulsions! I believe there is a fatality in it, that I can never get to her. Who can I trust my house to in my absence? Were my wife as chaste as Lucretia, who knows what an unlucky minute may bring forth! In cuckoldom, the art of attack is prodigiously improved beyond the art of defence. So far it is manifest, Underplot has a design upon my honour. For the ease of my mind, I will lock up my wife in this my museum, 'till my return.

Townley enters, seems to grudgingly acquiesce to the arcane and mute company of the new specimens, and is swiftly deserted by Fossile, clutching the key as he hastes to his patient.

With Townley now commenting wryly, 'since he has locked me in, to be even with him, I'll bolt him out', 'Plotwell, dressed like a mummy, comes forward':

> Plot.
> Thus trav'ling far from his Egyptian tomb,
> Thy Antony salutes his Cleopatra.
> Townley.
> Thus Cleopatra, in desiring arms
> Receives her Antony – But prithee dear pickled hieroglyphic, who so suddenly could assist thee with this shape?
> Plot.
> The play-house can dress mummies, bears, lions, crocodiles, and all the monsters of Lybia. My arms, Madam, are ready to break their paste-board prison to embrace you.

This embrace is temporarily delayed by some further witticisms, with Townley averring to her mummified lover, 'here may'st thou remain the ornament of his study, and the support of his old age. Thou shalt divert his company, and be a father to his children. I will bring thee legs of pullets, remnants of tarts, and fragments of desserts'. Just as Plotwell has vowed to 'slip off this habit of death' and display 'some symptoms of life', a fresh stage direction reads: 'Underplot in the alligator crawls forward, then rises up and embraces her':

> Underplot.
> Thus Jove within the serpent's scaly folds,
> Twined round the Macedonian queen.
> Townley.
> Ah!
> [shrieks].
> Plot.
> Fear not, Madam. This is my evil genius Underplot that still haunts me. How the Devil got you here?
> Underplot.
> Why should not the play-house lend me a crocodile as well as you a mummy?

Why not indeed? In this case the props certainly seem to have been a shrewd investment. The scene, as one might imagine, went down a storm with many of those who packed the Drury Lane theatre for the play's seven-night run. Noting an additional delight in the fact that 'Plotwell, played by Colley Cibber, didn't realize that the part ridiculed himself', David Nokes adds that 'Penkethman, in the role of the crocodile, caused a riot of hilarity'.[83] Although Dr Johnson was perhaps right in thinking that 'Dr. Woodward the Fossilist [was] a man not really or justly contemptible' he may have been less accurate in his belief that 'the scene in which Woodward was directly and apparently ridiculed, by the introduction of a mummy and a crocodile, disgusted the audience, and the performance was driven off the stage with general condemnation'.[84] As Nokes further explains, the potentially long-running comedy was arguably damned before it began, largely because of its place in the literary infighting of the day: 'ten days before it opened the rumour was that "Pope is coming out with a play in which every one of our modern poets are ridiculed"'. The comedy does indeed seem to have involved the collaboration of Pope and Arbuthnot.[85] It seems to have been partly for this reason that it was both briefly very popular, and (because of the pamphlet attacks on it in following weeks) notorious for some time after its actual run. For an uncertain mixture of reasons, the first comic mummy of the English stage was very well-known to Londoners in and after 1717.[86]

Part of his comic value also related to his potential role as a medicine. A debate between Fossile and two fellow doctors (Nautilus and Possum) on the undecided sex of the new mummy gives ways to some parodic moralising on the vanity of this long-dead Egyptian, 'who by his pyramid and pickle thought to secure to himself death immortal'. 'His pyramid', agrees Fossile, 'alas! is now but a wainscot case', and his pickle (adds Possum) 'can scarce raise him to the dignity of a collar of brawn'. The relative familiarity of the mummy is once again refigured here, with the astonishing achievements of Egyptian embalmers reduced to a homely 'pickling', and the equally homely 'collar of brawn' perhaps echoing the tendency for corpse medicine to sink down from the level of physic to that of food. Nautilus, however, does assert that, 'by your favour, Dr. Possum … he is better to be taken inwardly than a collar of brawn' and Fossile backs him up, giving the audience scope for nudging and chortling when he agrees, 'an excellent medicine! He is hot in the first degree, and exceeding powerful in some diseases of women'.

An ensuing debate between Nautilus and Possum about whether the mummy is preserved with 'asphaltion' or 'pice asphaltus' is mediated by Fossile, who asks them to 'turn your speculations on my alligator'. This effort in turn prompts further comic tension when Nautilus offers to prove (*pace* Possum) that its hide *can* be penetrated by a sword ('draws his sword'), and Possum remarks, 'in the mean time I will try the mummy with this knife, on the point of which you shall smell the pitch, and be convinc'd that it is the pice-asphaltus' ('takes up a rusty knife'). The tension is prolonged when Fossile objects ('hold, sir: You will not only deface my mummy, but spoil my Roman sacrificing knife'), after which Townley enters, whispering aside, 'I must lure them from this experiment, or we are discovered'.[87] The expectant audience is rewarded with more farce as she distracts the doctors; the mummy and the alligator run for the door, find it locked, and swiftly run back. Presently they are at last discovered, and some tortuous explanations ensue. It is fairly clear that the audience is expected to feel distant from the arcane speculations of Possum and Nautilus about Pliny, Dioscorides, and the true form of pitch. Part of the joke seems to hinge on the doubtful authority of physicians per se, whilst there is also some implied criticism of their irreverent willingness to so briskly dissect a mummy in pursuit of their learned quibbles.[88]

That kind of satire of élite medicine is employed at great length in James Miller's cannibalised version of Moliere's *Le Malade Imaginaire*, published in 1734 as *The*

Mother-in-Law, or the Doctor the Disease.[89] Shortly after the central character, Sir Credulous Hippish, has been lamenting the vast bills of his apothecaries, we hear his daughter's maid, Primrose, opining that 'this Dr. Mummy and Mr. Galleypot divert themselves finely, at the expense of your carcass. They have a rare milch-cow of you; and I'd gladly know what distemper you have, that your maw must be thus perpetually stuffed with physic'. Whilst Sir Credulous briskly responds, 'peace, ignorance. 'Tisn't for you to contradict the prescriptions of art', it is clear that the audience is imagined to feel otherwise.[90] Naturally enough, much of this play, like its original source, works on the logic that physicians are dislikable merely by being physicians.

Breaking down this axiomatic notion, we find that their greed and unjust wealth (already implied by Primrose) is one cause of such antipathy. When Primrose objects that Belina, Sir Credulous's daughter, should not marry Mummy's son, Mr Looby, the father tells her that 'this Mr. Looby is Dr. Mummy's only heir ... and Dr. Mummy has a good five thousand a year'. 'Mercy on us!' (responds Primrose) 'what a world of people must he have killed to get such an estate!'.[91] Next – echoing the opening sally between Primrose and Credulous – we have a repeated hostility to supposedly learned theory, tyrannising over both obvious realities and the sound common sense of the ordinary citizen. One unhappy patient of Dr Mummy complains (with a notably mock-rustic diction) 'zir, my father can hold it no longer, his head rages at the most grievous rate!', to which Mummy: 'the patient's a fool; the distemper, according to Galen, does not lie in his head, but in his spleen'. Having fobbed off this unhappy customer ('well, I'll visit him in two or three days' time, but if he should die before, be sure you send me word of it, for 'tis not proper that a physician should visit the dead'), Mummy is accosted by a woman whose husband 'grows worse and worse'. Learning that he has been bled (on Mummy's own instructions) 'fifteen times ... within this fortnight', the doctor avers learnedly, 'that's a sign his distemper is not in his blood; we'll purge him as many times, to see if 'tis not in his humours; and at last, if nothing will do – why, we'll send him to the Bath'.[92]

This kind of arrogant contempt for the empirical realities of suffering (occurring as they do so far below the lofty peaks of medical theory) reaches its comic nadir when Dr Mummy and his fellow doctor mistakenly begin trying to diagnose Mummy's nephew Looby (who his uncle does not recognise after an absence of fifteen years). The nephew is not ill, merely hungry, but out of country deference answers the various diagnostic queries until Mummy concludes:

> as it so is, that no malady can be cured, unless we are acquainted with it; and as we cannot be acquainted with it without establishing an idea of it, by symptoms diagnostic and prognostic; permit me, my ancient friend and brother, to observe, that our patient here present is unfortunately affected, possessed, and oppressed with that sort of madness which we justly term hypochondriac melancholy; so called not only by the Latins, but also by the Greeks, which is very necessary to be taken notice of in this case.

The triumph of ancient theory over immediate reality is nicely highlighted when Looby finally states plainly that he is not sick, only to be told by Mummy, 'a bad symptom – a patient not to be sensible of his illness. Look ye, sir, we know how ye are, better than you do your self ... '.[93]

This and a good deal more of the play's satire plainly hinged on an inferred general hostility to physicians. One did not write or adapt a popular play without a good sense of popular attitudes. We will see in a few moments that the implied image problem of élite medicine was quite closely linked to the attempts of some physicians to distance themselves from corpse medicine, and other now seemingly dubious or arcane ingredients of the Pharmacopeias. What needs emphasising most of all about Miller's play, however, is just that one basic detail of the chief physician's stage identity. For what seems to have been the first time ever, a physician is parodically labelled 'Dr Mummy'.[94] At one level, this again assumes the ready complicity of London audiences. It is obvious what this will mean to them: if you want to create a stock physician, and shade a little more darkly the penumbra of disrepute which he naturally attracts, then associate him precisely with one of the more disreputable medicines of his trade. Indeed, if Miller was assuming a rough equation between the easy identity of the apothecary (Galleypots) and that of the physician, then the axiomatic ease of the link between mummy and dubious physic becomes all the stronger.[95]

At the level of longer historical perspective, the name could hardly be more apt (even if an astute cultural critic had invented it himself). For decades physicians had by various means kept themselves at a certain distance from corpse medicines. Just occasionally, as in some of Fuller's sharper outbursts, that distance seemed at risk of collapse. In the later seventeenth century, popular perceptions threatened to roughly shove physicians and mummy into uncomfortably intimate proximity. The repeated 'beating to mummy' of literature and drama must ultimately have reflected a public attitude which saw physicians in nearer physical contact with such substances, simply pounding human matter, where once they had stood back behind a veil of learned theories. No less aptly, it was at this time that mummy began, effectively, to merge with the bodies of those who were at least potential clients of it. The aged in particular now *become* mummy, or mummies. Finally, having managed with remarkable adroitness to keep out of these grubby jokes for so long, the physician himself merges, in 1734, with that substance he had kept at such a convenient distance. Again, the slow process of osmosis is itself neatly symbolic. Just as mummy did not immediately 'become merchandise', so physicians prescribed and profited from corpse medicines many decades before the association stuck too tightly and too negatively to their personae. And we will now see that Miller's label evidently had an importance as much practical as symbolic.

Horrid medicines: reason, disgust and enlightenment

We met the physician Robert James earlier, as a supporter of the use of human fat. In his *Pharmacopœia Universalis: or, a New Universal English Dispensatory* of 1747, James drily notes what he considers to be a popular superstition: namely, the belief that human skull renders the body 'so impenetrable as not to be pierced with a musket bullet'. He then alludes to the opinion of a German physician named Rieger on the moss of the skull, and emphatically agrees with him that there is 'no necessity why a physician should disgrace his profession by prescribing it'. James does not deny that usnea actually works. But, he insists, other substances work equally well. And these, he adds, 'no patient will refuse on account of the horror and nausea they produce'.[96]

In 1751 this stance is broadly echoed by the physician and botanist John Hill. Hill's *Materia Medica* openly laments that 'we cannot be content with medicines without running to our own bodies for them'; and he, unlike James, does deny the efficacy of skull–moss, asserting that the moss of the human skull 'possesses no more virtues than that which grows on a stick or a stone'. Delusions about its powers are themselves, however, 'less shocking, than the swallowing the flesh and bones of our fellow creatures'. 'The mummy and the skull alone of all these horrid medicines retain their places in the shops', Hill adds, 'and it were much to be wished they were rejected too'.[97] Hill reiterates this attitude in his *Useful Family Herbal* of 1754. 'There is not', he asserts, 'any particular kind of moss growing upon the human skull, nor does any moss by growing upon it acquire any particular virtues, whatever fanciful people may have imagined'.[98] Three years later, publishing under the name of Christian Uvedale, Hill's tone is yet stronger: 'their folly is hardly less than their beastliness, who expect good from the dung of animals, from rotten human skulls, from the moss that has grown upon them, or from the ill-preserved remains of human carcasses, which they call mummy. Reason banishes these detestable medicines, which decent delicacy should never have admitted. They were always shocking to the imagination; and they are now known to be void of efficacy'.[99]

1755 brings us not a medical landmark, but a literary one: the publication of Samuel Johnson's *Dictionary*. Johnson's entry for 'mummy' quotes at some length from Hill's opinions of 1751. In doing so, it gives a quite thorough description of two different types of the drug and their respective qualities and textures. Although the entry edits out some of Hill's more indignant comments, it condemns trade in mummy as generally disreputable, given that 'what our druggists are supplied with is the flesh of executed criminals, or any other bodies the Jews can get' – these being treated with common bitumen and baked in ovens so as to resemble embalmed corpses. Johnson's entry then goes on to insist that 'at present, we are wise enough to know, that the virtues ascribed to the parts of the human body, are all either imaginary, or such as may be found in other animal substances'. And it concludes with yet more emphatic condemnation, quoting Hill's statement, 'the mummy and the skull alone of all these horrid medicines retain their places in the shops'.[100] By 1782 the physician William Black seems, if possible, still more emphatic than Johnson or Hill, as he celebrates the professional discrediting of 'loathsome or insignificant' remedies such as 'Egyptian mummies' and 'dead men's skulls powdered'. These 'and a farrago of such feculence, are all banished from the pharmacopeias'.[101]

This brief overview of the eighteenth-century opposition to corpse medicines encapsulates all the key themes of the new hostility. Such substances, James asserts, disgrace the medical profession. Secondly, they are disgusting: 'shocking', 'loathsome', 'beastly'; an offence against 'decent delicacy' – or, in Black's especially memorable phrase, 'a farrago of … feculence'. Thirdly, they do not work. Any supposed efficacy is a result of the 'fanciful' imaginations of patients or practitioners. A fourth key point is hinted at by Hill and Johnson: 'at present, we are wise enough to know, that the virtues ascribed to the parts of the human body, are all either imaginary, or such as may be found in other animal substances'. The 'present' wisdom of the Enlightenment features frequently in attacks on corpse medicines, and is very much in evidence when Hill triumphantly asserts: 'reason banishes these detestable medicines … ', writing a kind of unofficial motto for later-eighteenth-century attitudes. Often, as we will see, the antipathy of Reason to such alleged Superstitions is so great that it prompts the ultimately irrational rewriting of medical history.

The medical profession

I have selected these four authors partly because of their weight of influence across the mid- and later eighteenth century. But there is also another reason. Johnson produced what is now recognised as the first substantial dictionary of the English language. Despite its not containing an entry for that much loved English comestible, the sausage, this work naturally became a standard point of reference for many educated people of the day. We have to ask ourselves, then, how far Johnson artificially accelerated the early opposition to corpse medicines. If you were, say, merely ambivalent about such substances, might you not become fixedly hostile on reading what seemed to be the authoritative stance of the great doctor? The reason for raising that point here is that Johnson was also a friend of that other key early opponent, William James. Although Johnson does not openly cite James, this may in part be just because Hill is slightly fiercer in his condemnation. If James did influence Johnson, then in that early phase of antipathy, we find a very tight-knit cluster of powerful authorities, whose views were at once potent, and (arguably) less than wholly representative.

It is important to emphasise that James, whatever his influence, has a different tone to that of Hill. He begins with droll irony toward superstitions about the human skull, rather than the apparent moral indignation of Hill, for whom such therapies are 'shocking'. And his chief concern is that a physician should not 'disgrace his profession'. With this crucial notion of 'disgrace', James signals a very different idea of what medicine is – or, at least, what it should become. Where Hill is emotionally disturbed, James is cannily pragmatic. At one level, he is concerned for the image of the medical 'profession' just because – as historians have shown – this now widely accepted entity was, at that time, still struggling to establish itself.[102] As Gay and Miller both made amply clear, physicians were an easy, indeed natural, target for abuse, resentment, and satire.

And James himself was in many ways a perfect example of the kind of selfish drive for personal gain which we saw Culpeper attacking decades earlier, and Miller echoing in 1734. As T.A.B. Corley emphasises, the most famous (or notorious) thing about James was his invention and personal monopoly of 'James's fever powder'.

Although numerous practitioners had attempted to fence off the profits of their supposed panaceas, the scale of James's success makes him an interesting forerunner of
those global medical corporations who now patent and monopolise cures which
might otherwise be available to the sick poor of the developing world. 'Having taken
out a patent, in 1747 James furnished the court of chancery with a description of the
contents and the method of manufacture; yet experts soon found these could not
make the kind of powder being sold, and indeed the doses varied in quality over
time'. Corley here shows that James was at once eager to monopolise all profits via an
official patent, whilst unofficially refusing to make clear to anyone what was in his
miraculous powder. Although Corley adds that results of the powders were mixed,
and that 'James's reputation as a doctor was diminished by his ... strenuous claims for
the powders', overall the patent clearly brought James great wealth: 'a veritable pantheon of authors lauded them and their efficacy, Thomas Gray and William Cowper
demurely, Horace Walpole ecstatically, and Richard Cumberland in many stanzas of
inflated verse'. They were used by George III, and 'as late as the 1860s they were to
be found in Queen Victoria's medicine chest'.

It perhaps hardly needs stressing that James's concern for the image of the medical
profession was largely selfish, rather than altruistic or public-spirited. Like modern
corporations, James probably assumed that 'public image' might be conveniently
detached from actual practice. What you do matters less than what you seem to do,
or what you say. Indeed, Corley further notes that, although (according to Johnson),
James 'never drew a sober breath during the final twenty years of his life', 'this scarcely impaired his medical practice as he was extremely adept at concealing' his actual
condition. Ultimately, the kind of personal eccentricity or arrogance which are
sniped at in *The Doctor the Disease* were stronger in James than was his superficial
concern about corporate public image. This is confirmed generally by his opportunism in plundering wholesale from numerous authors, in order to concoct the various
books that went under his name.[103] And, in particular, James in fact cited Johann
Schroeder at great length in 1747, giving no personal comment or hint of opposition
when listing over a page of substances drawn from the human body.[104]

James's seeming inconsistency only confirms that his brief, arguably atypical
hostility to skulls and skull-moss was coolly pragmatic. Yet, if James was not sufficiently angry or unnerved about corpse medicines to avoid such inconsistencies,
others clearly were. Of fifteen hostile references to these remedies in the eighteenth
century, only three occur before 1734. Is this merely coincidence? Influential
physicians or scientists often lived in London, and were often (like James) jovial men
about town. It seems unlikely that those working in the capital could have been
unaware of Miller's comedy of 1734. Opening at the New Theatre in the Haymarket
on 12 February, the play was still running (now at the Theatre Royal in Drury Lane)
come June 1736.[105] There must, accordingly, be a strong chance that here (not for
the first or last time) life imitated art. It was one thing for people to be occasionally,
covertly ambivalent about physicians and their use of human skull or blood or flesh.
It was quite another for a physician to be publically labelled as 'Doctor Mummy',
with this long-used remedy now clinging to him like an unwanted garment as he was

mocked upon the common stage. Once literature had caught up with you in this embarrassingly public way, it was time to move on, extricating your would-be 'profession' from the muck of the past, and remaking it in the cool light of reason and progress.

This brings us back to John Hill. Not only was Hill notable for vigorously attacking corpse medicine three times before 1760; he was also, in every sense, a man of many parts. As Barry O'Connor explains, 'Hill's fascination with the theatre' vied 'with his interest in botany as chief among his lifelong preoccupations'. Although the report that Hill 'was a strolling player from 1730 to 1735' remains unsubstantiated, Hill definitely was acting various roles from the late 1730s onwards. Initially engaged by 'the second duke of Richmond, Lennox, and Aubigny ... to collect specimens for him from England and Wales' in 1739, Hill went on to take up residence at Richmond's Sussex seat, Goodwood House, where he 'met a number of the theatrical community including Owen MacSwinney, David Garrick (then at the beginning of his career), and Peg Woffington', and acted on Goodwood's private stage. O'Connor adds that, whilst Hill's 1750 treatise *The Actor* drew heavily on a French original, the work was nonetheless 'the first English acting treatise to discuss the personal and emotional attributes of the actor rather than the rhetorical conventions of performance that had characterized earlier acting manuals'.[106] Add to all this the fact that Hill 'was apprenticed to the London apothecary Edward Angier in 1730–31', and we realise that he was in every way suited to be the reactive agent between Miller's play and the world of élite London medicine.[107] Whether or not Hill was acting himself by this time, he could scarcely have failed to be aware of the ludicrous physicians paraded at the Haymarket's New Theatre from 12 February 1734.

William Black would have missed out on this, as he was born only in 1749. But for Black, the recent existence of corpse medicines (surviving, he admits, into 'part of the present' century) was plainly a source of outrage, rather than merely a matter of pragmatic concern.[108] His remarks are telling not just for their obviously emotive language, but also because 'loathsome and insignificant' is an arguably contradictory phrase. The latter term may be another way of saying that these things did not work, but the two words so close together do look odd: these cures were not so 'insignificant' that they failed to generate violent feelings in Black's mind. As so often, eighteenth-century opponents of corpse medicine feel very strongly about it, but do not entirely know what their feelings are. Although Black does not openly talk, like James, about such ingredients disgracing the 'medical profession', the very nature of his book makes it clear that he is keenly interested in this emergent entity. The work's full title is 'An Historical Sketch of Medicine and Surgery, from Their Origin to the Present Time; and of the Principal Authors, Discoveries, Improvements'. Black is writing an early form of medical history. As will become all too clear in a few moments, for many of those working in this field in the twentieth century, corpse medicine was so appalling that it was all but written out of the history books. Black is less dishonest about medicinal cannibalism than many of those later authors, or than certain of his peers. But it is telling that, when seeking to explain how now discredited ingredients had survived so long, he cites an earlier doctor, Robert Pitt. Pitt picks chiefly on the apothecaries rather than the physicians, claiming that the former were simply trying to increase their profits by selling unnecessary substances, shrouded in what Black terms 'mystery and pomposity'.[109]

Just a few years after Black, in 1789, the eminent Royal Physician William Cullen cites 'cranium humanum' as one of various ingredients which, 'if they were to appear in prescription, would, in Britain at least, effectually disgrace a practitioner'.[110] Cullen had links with the medical or scientific societies of Paris, Madrid, Copenhagen, Dublin and Philadelphia.[111] In the passage in question he discusses some now generally discredited cures which are still accepted only in Paris, and it may be that it is France to which he implicitly opposes the changed attitude of the British public. Given its enduring reputation as an importer of human skulls, Germany is another possibility. Whoever this backward nation (or nations) may be, Cullen's basic stance is clear. He does not personally register disgust, and in fact does not directly question the efficacy of human skull. His concern seems to be solely the public image of the 'medical profession' in Britain.[112]

Disgust

We saw that disgust was not a known English word at the start of the seventeenth century. Even in following decades, it was evidently not an influential one in the field of medicine. But in the later eighteenth century, many of the words flung so violently at corpse medicine are sharply spiced with this special human emotion. Black's authority Pitt gets in surprisingly early, when in 1703 he laments the fact that 'mummy had the honour to be worn in the bosom next the heart' (presumably, as an amulet) 'by the kings and princes and all others who could then bear the price, in the last age, in all the courts of Europe'. Pitt's biographer M.P. Earles states that this physician and anatomy lecturer was noted for a general 'desire to reform the practice of medicine'. This drive led Pitt to attack various ingredients beside human ones (and especially those which were exotic or expensive). He does not especially single out human substances, and interestingly, on the page on which he derides mummy, it is actually the hearts, skins, guts and lungs of various animals which, he believes, 'ought to be rejected as loathsome and offensive'. Similarly, his attack on 'the famed skulls of a dead man' is embedded amidst derision of elk's, rhinoceros', and unicorn's horns, and swallows' nests and snake skins. Yet Pitt does preface his discussion of mummy with an assault on those who 'thrust into the stomach of their patients, not only the most loathsome, but the parts of animals' which, being dead, are merely 'a dry and unactive earth', and it is telling that, in this early manifesto for reform, the word 'loathsome' appears a number of times.[113]

Similarly, in 1733 the physician Thomas Apperley adumbrates Black with remarkable precision when describing 'mummy, and the dried hearts, livers and spleens of animals burned to a powder' as 'loathsome, and useless medicines', neatly cementing the parallel when he adds that 'the powder of vipers … and preparations of human skull, are insignificant'.[114] Some time before 1743, the poet and playwright Richard Savage was satirical (and perhaps uneasy) about both dissection of women, and the sourcing of human skulls, which he assumed to be derived from grave theft:

Grudge heroes not your heads in stills inclosed!
Grudge not, ye fair, your parts ripped up exposed!
As strikes the choice anatomy our eyes;
As here dead skulls in quick'ning cordials rise …

And this prompted him to reflect, too, on other areas of corpse supply, in lines which might have consciously been echoing Thomas Browne:

From Egypt thus a rival traffic springs:
Her vended mummies thus were once her kings;
The line of Ninus now in drugs is rolled,
And Ptolemy's himself for balsam sold.[115]

After James, Hill and Johnson the tone gets more heated, expansive and assertive. In 1770 the physician and botanist Charles Alston states unequivocally, 'mummies are, in my opinion, detestable stuff, and unworthy of a place in any dispensatory', earning himself, also, a place in a small élite when he adds, 'human flesh is no better than … a hog's, nor cannibals [diet?] so wholesome as that of other people'.[116] Even when emphatically not cannibalistic, corpse materials could rouse yet fiercer language in some. Thus Moses Browne, editor of a 1750 version of Izaak Walton's *Complete Angler*, citing various unguents previously reputed good baits, felt them to be things 'the bare naming of which, in persons of humane and delicate tempers, must excite horror, and sound more like witches' spells, as a mixture of human fat, man's skull, or bones powdered, mummy' and 'the earth taken off a fresh grave, sprinkled on the worms'.[117]

Was this new phase of opposition a matter of medical ethics? One way of answering this question is to emphasise that the very concept, or even phrase, was still in its infancy in the late eighteenth century.[118] The first book bearing this title was published by the dissenter and physician Thomas Percival only in 1803. Percival's religious background must be significant in this respect, and it is notable that he is sometimes credited with having coined the phrase 'medical ethics'.[119] Another answer is that, even for those who talked, self-consciously or otherwise, of something broadly resembling medical ethics, this was very unlikely to mean anything approaching 'human rights'. For many opponents of corpse medicine, hostility arose from the new sensibilities (recall Hill's 'delicate decency') of patient or doctor, or from a related anxiety about medicine's corporate image. After all, if physicians were really so concerned about the rights of human beings per se, why did the use of human fat persist so widely in this era?

In 1799 the Scottish physician James Makittrick Adair did object to this substance, along with various others, citing illegitimate medicines, which were 'found to consist of the most insignificant ingredients, as pith of bread, brick-dust, sheep's dung etc, or, the most disgusting, as the human skull, fat, placenta etc, the venders depending for success on the strength of the patient's imagination, and the liveliness of their faith'.[120] But if we should imagine that this indignant practitioner was appalled on behalf of unwilling human donors, we might like to bear in mind that he in fact practised his trade in Antigua, and vigorously 'defended the island's slave owners in his *Unanswerable Arguments against the Abolition of the Slave Trade*' of 1790.[121]

'The days of superstition'

A third habit of opponents in this period was to artificially distance corpse medicine by various means. In some cases the technique was to straightforwardly pitch the general use of such substances back in time. In 1756, for example, one Robert Colborne wrote, rather oddly, that 'about a century ago, mummy was often given inwardly for hurts, falls and bruises; at the same time it was used plaster wise to comfort and strengthen'. On one hand, Colborne himself admits that there is plenty of mummy (albeit fake) in the shops at this stage.[122] On the other, he is clearly uneasy about its use. He cites a potion for bruises containing powdered rhubarb, madder, mummy, and pomegranate juice, and then adds that 'it is likely the powder of rhubarb alone would do as well'. Another such powder comprises Irish slate, mummy, and the salt of amber, and in this case Colborne thinks that this is 'but an indifferent compositiion, the two first ingredients being of little use'. Again, describing a powder containing valerian, human skull and placenta, Colborne notes that it was 'greatly depended on in former days', before asserting that 'the simple powder of valerian root is' now 'thought to be as effectual'.[123] It may well have been true that, by 1756, mummy was less widely used than previously. But any historian reading Colborne's book alone would probably be surprised to learn that (as Hill and Johnson pointed out) skulls were indeed still on sale at this time (to say nothing of being listed in the period's books of import duty).

Other ways of distancing one's age from Europe's cannibals could be more oblique. Listen again, for example, to John Hill: 'reason banishes these detestable medicines, which decent delicacy should never have admitted. They were always shocking to the imagination; and they are now known to be void of efficacy'.[124] Those opening words, a fitting Enlightenment motto for new attitudes to the human body, are effectively echoed by a new mindset so powerful that it not only rejects the past, but recreates with one bold sweep the mentality of hundreds or thousands of Renaissance patients and practitioners: 'they were *always* shocking to the imagination ... '. Needless to say, they were not. Hill has no evidence, and the evidence we have seen shows that almost no one expressed such shock in around 200 years. If Hill cannot actually deny the previous existence of corpse medicine, he can at least assert that it was as mentally abhorrent to past minds as it is to his own.

Writing some time before 1737, the German chemist Caspar Neumann (1683–1737) shows no signs of disgust when he describes his own chemical analysis of human skull (and is also happy to taste the resulting extract). But his attitude changes sharply when he reflects on previous medical use of the skull. Having listed other, similarly backward medical ingredients (such as fox's lungs) with derision, he opines: 'to such lengths of extravagance have the sons of physic been carried by the blind superstition of former ages!'[125] Although this pre-Enlightenment folly was to prove a popular target amongst opponents of corpse medicine, derision of such misguided beliefs was arguably in good faith by comparison with another of this era's scapegoats.

Whilst Johnson's *Dictionary* entry for 'mummy' arguably had undue influence on eighteenth-century perceptions, we should not overlook the 1741 edition of the long-running Chambers' *Cyclopaedia*. Under 'mummy, mumia', there is first a description of Egyptian mummies. The entry then states: 'mummy is said to have been first brought into use in medicine by the malice of a Jewish physician, who wrote that flesh thus embalmed was good for the cure of diverse diseases, and particularly bruises'. One can only marvel at the powers of this (tellingly unnamed) Jewish physician – a man who single-handedly managed to catalyse a vast systematic trade amongst the suggestible Christians of the early modern era. The potent flavour of Christian paranoia is here strengthened especially by the belief that this Jewish culprit not only triggered over two centuries of corpse medicine at the stroke of a pen, but also did so out of deliberate 'malice' – clearly not believing in any of these claims himself.[126] It is no small irony that many decades earlier Edward Browne, watching the blood-drinking in Vienna, had the insight to observe that 'of all men the Jews, who suffer no blood to come into their lips, must most dislike it'.[127] We have also seen that it was in fact only Jewish users of mummy who took the trouble to secure a formal religious ruling on the legitimacy of this substance.

In 1780 the physician John Aikin discusses Mayerne's book, *Praxeos Mayerniae* (posthumously published in 1690 by Mayerne's godson Sir Theodore de Vaux). In this work, notes Aikin, 'vestiges of ancient superstition frequently appear. The secundines of a woman at her first labour, who has been delivered of a male child, the bowels of a mole cut open alive, mummy made of the lungs of a man who has suffered a violent death, the liver of frogs, and the blood of weasels, are articles of his *materia medica*'.[128] Secundine or placenta was most likely to be used by Paracelsians, who would (like the Protestant Mayerne) usually consider themselves at the furthest remove from the 'superstitious' habits of Roman Catholics. And, if Mayerne was unusual in preferring 'mummy' derived from human lungs, we know that corpses perished of violent deaths were the absolutely standard requirement of innumerable physicians in his day. It hardly needs re-emphasising that Mayerne was one of the most eminent physicians of his era, attending to more monarchs than any of his peers. What is especially telling is the way that Aikin artificially constructs such ingredients as '*vestiges* of ancient superstition'. They effectively become the mere marginal remnants of some mythically backward age, rather than part of a mainstream tradition which was often vigorously theorised by educated exponents such as van Helmont.

When Aikin further lists Mayerne's use of 'balsam of bats' for 'hypochondriacal persons', and 'adders ... sucking whelps, earth-worms, hog's grease, the marrow of a stag, and the thigh-bone of an ox' as 'ingredients fitter for the witches' cauldron in Macbeth than a learned physician's prescription' we are reminded of Moses Browne, to whom the older fish baits of human fat and skull sounded 'more like witches' spells'.[129] In each case, there is a subtle but effective displacement of corpse ingredients. For Aikin especially, in 1780, witchcraft is now so absolutely incredible as to be both incomprehensible, and (again) part of a mythically primitive era. Hence the fact that even the witches he derides are themselves fictional ones, and rooted in a fiction which itself vapours away into the mists of Scottish history. As with William Black, it is no accident that this stance occurs in an early version of medical history, Aikin's book being titled *Biographical Memoirs of Medicine in Great Britain from the Revival of Literature to the Time of Harvey*.

Seven years later, in 1787, the antiquary Francis Grose is no less confident of the cultural superiority of his age. 'It will be scarcely be conceived', he writes, 'how great a number of superstitious notions are still remaining and prevalent', even in London itself. From among these he cites the credulous belief that 'moss growing on a human skull, if dried, powdered, and taken as snuff, will cure the headache'.[130] Grose clearly assumes that his educated readers share certain of his basic attitudes. It is not necessary to *persuade* them that such beliefs are 'superstitious'. This is interesting, because Grose is doing something which in that era was still quite unusual. As Peter Burke explains: 'it was in the late eighteenth and early nineteenth centuries, when traditional popular culture was just beginning to disappear, that the "people" or the "folk" became a subject of interest to European intellectuals'.[131] And, sure enough, Grose's book is entitled *A Provincial Glossary, with a Collection of Local Proverbs, and Popular Superstitions*. This implies at least two things. One: there is now (as Burke and other historians have noted) a growing split between popular and élite culture – an important departure from the days when Francis Bacon or Robert Boyle would use usnea just as readily as a peasant who chanced on an unburied skull near some lonely battlefield. Secondly, these beliefs are being singled out as an object of study in their own right. One consequence of that is a further distance between Grose and his readers, on one hand, and those who still stubbornly adhere to such fallacies on the other: almost as if the latter are a strange species of animal, or a remote tribe studied by late nineteenth-century anthropologists.

Still more intriguing details surface when we analyse a reference to usnea which appeared in 1794, in an English translation of *Herman of Unna*, a German historical romance by Benedict Naubert. At one point the hero, wounded and suffering severe blood loss, is cured by an old shepherd, oracle of the village, with the moss of a human skull. What is most interesting is the translator's footnote which purports to 'explain' this episode: 'the moss which grows on the skull of a man unburied, was celebrated, in the days of superstition, for its medicinal virtues'.[132] What does this tell us? First, the treatment is assumed to *need* explaining. It seems unlikely that this was really so: in 1755, Johnson admits, human skull remained on sale in apothecaries' shops. John Cruso was still recommending it in 1771, and Benjamin Moseley in 1792, and it was still subject to import duty in 1778.[133] As when Charas saw these skulls some decades before, some must have come complete with a growth of moss.

Should we remain in any doubt about the translator's stance, we need only turn to the preface which they have added to the work. Here, a brief discussion of tyranny attributes this vice in part to the ignorance of past ages, after which the writer triumphantly exhorts readers: 'let us … congratulate ourselves that we are born in an age of illumination, when the artifices of superstition and tyranny are fated to vanish before the torch of truth'.[134] Clearly, then, the footnote betrays a deliberate attempt to actively and artificially distance the enlightened world of 1794 from that of the superstitious past. (The translator may, indeed, even be seeking to actively flatter readers, assuming that such ancient oddities are far beneath the refined circles in which they live.) Still more artfully, the reference to usnea occurs in a tale which advertises itself as 'a series of adventures of the fifteenth century', implying that such remedies were in fact not used after these 'days of superstition'. Corpse medicine is thrust back into an almost absolutely distant medieval age, some three centuries, rather than just three decades, ago.

In reality, certain educated patients must have still been using corpse medicine at this time. If they were not, Moseley could hardly have enjoyed such a thriving career at the close of the eighteenth century. Even in the sixth edition of Johnson's *Dictionary*, in 1785, mummy was still listed as a medicine. Whilst the entry insists that any mummy available in England is fake, this still implies sufficient demand to prompt counterfeiting.[135] Corpse medicine was not usually cheap. But, as our examination of sources has shown, human bones and the moss of the skull may in some areas have been readily available for free. This is an important consideration, especially given that the rising prosperity of eighteenth-century England was limited to a small fraction of the population as a whole.[136] Moreover, given that Germany in particular was noted as a chief importer of human skulls, the original German reference to this practice may well have reflected a far more persistent tradition of medical usnea than that surviving in other countries.

The great whitewash: corpse medicine in medical history

We can close this survey of increasing hostility by looking at a kind of antagonism which should be quite different, but which is in many ways very similar to that seen above. Why has the subject of European medical cannibalism been so strikingly absent from the very field which should have dealt with it most comprehensively? The stance of the later Enlightenment was one of buoyant optimism about human scientific progress, coupled with a no less vigorous denunciation of a superstitious, backward, perhaps even 'barbaric' past. It hardly needs adding that such an attitude easily slides into blind self-congratulation. For a long time, this position was an all too common intellectual tone among medical historians. Take, for example, the preface to a 1945 *History of Medicine* by Douglas Guthrie. Reflecting on the nature of medical history in general, Guthrie imagines the gradual construction of a 'mosaic of medical history, each detail as it falls into place revealing a steady and natural sequence. It is a noble theme ... '.[137] What exactly is this 'mosaic'? History is vast, messy, pluralistic, and in many ways finally unknowable. It is not, as Guthrie seems to imply, one self-contained and ornate work of art. Ironically, though, this 'mosaic' image *is* an accurate description of medical history as conceived and constructed by historians such as Guthrie. It is indeed possible to fit fragments into a neat pattern if you, the historian, have already chosen and designed a particular form of medical history. You then simply select examples which suit that design and ... *voila*! they do indeed form a pleasing work of art.[138]

And so, in Guthrie's 'noble' history, mummy appears only as something to be denounced and discarded on the triumphal march toward a modern and enlightened medical outlook. Ambroise Paré, for example, is celebrated because he had dared to write of 'the folly of the physicians in employing such remedies as powdered mummy and unicorn's horn'.[139] Guthrie himself was a consultant ear nose and throat surgeon to the Royal Edinburgh Hospital for Sick Children, and thus typifies the long-standing tendency for medical professionals to write their own history. This cosy dilettante habit has all too often produced highly distorted, selective, self-congratulatory narratives – ones which have more in common with autobiography than with serious history. Indeed, it is perhaps not too whimsical to imagine that consultants in particular, as élite practitioners who enjoy almost wholly unchallenged authority in the present, simply forbid the past to contradict them, any more than their secretary, or some humble unsatisfied patient.

The unstated but undeniable assumption of these older studies was that mummy and similar treatments were simply not 'real' medicine, and that the duty of medical history was to chart the 'steady and natural sequence' by which real medicine and real science arose from the nasty swamps of folklore and magic. This is an utterly impoverished version of history. It obliterates the beliefs and experiences of 'real' people, denying the interest or validity of what such people felt, and how they perceived their bodies and the world around them. Not only that, but in their desire to construct heroic champions of rational medicine, such historians occasionally tell outright lies. Erwin H. Ackerknecht, for some years the director of the Institute of Medical History at Zurich University, might be expected to display more academic rigour than Guthrie. In fact, he merely echoes the attitude to Paré, and pushes it into the realms of fantasy: 'in his treatise on the unicorn and the mummy, two very fashionable remedies of the period, Paré destroyed the reputation of these two fake drugs for ever'.[140] This statement is subtly misleading, in that 'fake drugs' (compare 'mistaken') implies deliberate fraud on the part of physicians. More glaringly, it pushes back the European abandonment of corpse medicine by almost 200 years, producing not a sliver of evidence in support of this wild claim. As Howard Wilcox Haggard indeed points out, Paré's statements on mummy 'excited the violent opposition of the whole Paris Faculty of Medicine'.[141]

It is hard not to suspect that Ackerknecht, rather like the Naubert translator, with his supposedly 'medieval' moss of the skull, simply wants to shove the embarrassing topic of medicinal cannibalism as far back into the past as he possibly can. In each case ideology triumphs over facts. Ironically, given the broadly Enlightenment mentality of both writers, the zeal for Scientific Progress produces moments of irrationality rivalling that of the traditional Christianity which eighteenth-century science broadly opposed. William S. Keezer (also writing, like Ackerknecht, in the 1960s) is reasonably accurate on dating, but more or less Enlightenment in his indignant tone: 'the apothecary shop of the seventeenth century still contained many nostrums such as the mumia, the unicorn, and the bezoar stone. Mumia was probably the most monstrous remedy that ever entered the pharmacopeias. It is hard to believe that until two centuries ago the remains of Egyptian mummies had been widely used as a remedy … '.[142] Another irony lurks here – Keezer would surely have been far *more* horrified to hear of (say) John French, mashing up human brains and spinal marrow into his monstrous cannibal pâté. But, thanks to the great whitewash of medical history, he has been spared this and various other colourful details. When the American medical doctor Harry Bloch writes, three years after a 1988 reprint of Ackerknecht's book, that, in 1582 Paré 'exposed the therapeutic frauds of mummy, bezoar stone and unicorn horn', the statement looks rather like a direct echo of Ackerknecht's earlier one.[143] Moreover, the small but telling cluster of 'therapeutic frauds' puts mummy into the company of exotic quackery, rather than within the widespread tradition of corpse medicine. Yet again, the latter is subtly but definitely distorted and marginalised.

Medical history as a whole has, of course, become far more diverse and sophisticated in recent years. Heroic or misleading histories such as Guthrie's or Ackerknecht's are now relatively marginal to the discipline. In a sense, though, the changing intellectual stance of most writers only makes the continuing neglect of corpse medicine all the more striking. Indeed, given how widespread such neglect is, one begins to suspect that even those scholars less committed to writing Great White Enlightenment narratives find themselves unconsciously shying away from this particularly powerful taboo. As we saw in chapter one (p. 9–10), Vivian Nutton's 1995 reference to classical uses of fresh blood subtly distorts Celsus's attitude to the practice. Moreover, Nutton's phrasing ('a remedy for epilepsy *involving* the blood of a dead gladiator') does not make it clear that the blood was drunk, and that it had to be drunk fresh and warm. In reality, the gladiator was not even quite dead when the blood was consumed. In the same book, Roy Porter notes how 'the fifth *London Pharmacopeia* (1746) ... eliminated human fat, spider-webs, moss from human skulls, unicorn's horn ... bones from the stag's heart, and the like'.[144] As we just have seen, corpse medicine certainly did decline in credibility from around that time. But human fat, ironically, remained one of the most enduring corpse agents of the Georgian era. Moreover, Porter seems also to echo older historians, in that he refers to mummy *only* as it is being abandoned. Imagine, by comparison, a history book which referred to significant men and women only to note their deaths.

One of the most telling responses to corpse medicine is that of F.M. Valadez and C.D. O'Malley. Discussing the use of human skull to treat Lord Leominster in 1711, these authors describe such therapies as 'irrelevant and nasty'.[145] It is no small irony that the phrase as a whole echoes the tone of William Black, who in 1782 condemned mummy and skull as 'loathsome and insignificant'. The word 'nasty' looks particularly out of place in an academic article, and betrays a powerful and unanalysed sense of personal repugnance. But the word 'irrelevant' is still more revealing. It simply cannot mean anything unless one assumes that such medicine is 'irrelevant' to modern notions of pharmacology. While this is presumably the unstated prejudice of the authors, a general reader might easily assume that powdered skull was 'irrelevant' to the medical theory of the early-eighteenth century. Clearly, it was not. Once more, in an otherwise serious and valuable article, we find that the history of the past is anachronistically distorted by the values of the present.

Although Valadez and O'Malley were themselves writing back in 1971, it would be rash to assume that their attitude has wholly vanished from the realm of medical history. Another way of dealing with the embarrassing problem of European cannibalism is simply to ignore it altogether. Time after time, medical histories, or even books specifically devoted to early modern medicine, have nothing to say about corpse medicine. Some authors do a little better. In a 1,000-page history of early modern medicine in France, first published in 1997, we are treated to one single mention of human skull. Lawrence Brockliss and Colin Jones inform the reader that, 'every drug had to have at least one ingredient from the animal realm' and that 'even human remains were thought to be efficacious ... Epileptics were to be given a drug which contained the shavings of a human skull'. Whilst these authors do admit that 'use of a human skull in epilepsy was advocated in many theses', even this brief reference is consigned – tellingly – to a footnote.[146] As for so many older historians, here medicinal cannibalism is at best a footnote in the progressive narrative of human enlightenment, and at worst a dirty secret.

The very few words found in this monumental book are themselves misleading: '*even* human remains ... '. This would have puzzled many of the medical practitioners or proto-scientists who supposedly form the subject of that book. Such a statement turns the original logic of corpse medicine inside out. The whole point about the human body was that it was the pinnacle of creation – a first resort, and not a desperate last one. As we saw in chapter six, it was a French author who, around 1664, insisted that mummy had 'received, not only while it was animated, but afterwards, all the influences whereof the human body is susceptible' – thus becoming 'the abstract of all the celestial powers'. Such, he added, was the special potency of 'man ... the abridgement of the world'.[147] Moise Charas put the point yet more plainly. Asserting that 'the body of man ... affords parts which are in truth medicaments, as the brains, the blood, the fat, the hair, etc' he explains: 'thus great is the benignity of the good Creator, who hath not suffered man to be destitute of excellent remedies contained in his own body'. Such medicines, Charas adds, are 'far superior to those that are comprehended in the bodies of any other creature'.[148]

'*Even* human remains' ... Not only is this misleading; on closer scrutiny, it is uncannily similar to that seminal eighteenth-century attack on corpse medicine by Dr Johnson's source, John Hill. In 1751 Hill had regretted that 'we cannot be content with medicines without running to our own bodies for them'. For most of the long history of medicinal cannibalism, no one seems to have imagined patients or doctors 'running to [their] own bodies'. This figure implies distance; that one is thus going to strange or exotic extremes; that such therapies are, so to speak, 'far-fetched'. If this was true of Egyptian mummy, it was not so of ordinary human flesh, blood, bone, or fat. Charas makes it absolutely clear that God's wisdom and goodness had put such substances *close* to hand. In the case of one's own body, they could hardly be closer: however forgetful we may be, we always take it with us. Recall, too, that this portable medicine chest could well have saved the lives of those injured men who had fresh urine (rather than dirty water) splashed upon their wounds. As with Hill, the 'even' used by Brockliss and Jones puts the human body at a distance. Once it was a relatively natural choice, at once divine and yet familiar. After that status changes, attitudes to it can remain oddly consistent, across some 250 years.

In 1694 Pomet, noting that the Parisian apothecaries 'sell human fat or grease, which is brought us from several parts', had added: 'as everybody knows in Paris, the public executioner sells it to those that want it, so that the druggists and apothecaries sell very little'.[149] In the late seventeenth century, everybody knew it; by the late twentieth century, almost everybody has forgotten it – even professional academics ... One is at times tempted, indeed, to say 'especially professional academics'. As I stated in the introduction, I myself was in some danger of overlooking the wider significance of this topic when I first began researching it. And it was just around that time, in 2003, that a reasonably thorough discussion of the subject was published. It appeared as a chapter of a creative and ingenious book on peculiar uses of human corpses, titled *Stiff*, and written by the American author Mary Roach.[150] Almost twenty years after Dannenfeldt's academic article appeared, the most thorough treatment of corpse medicine to be published was found in a popular book, penned by a journalist. I emphasise this not to deride journalists, but to point up how academics had really missed their chance here. They had, indeed, largely missed the chance to even inform what Roach included. Although she appears to have overlooked Dannenfeldt's essay, she otherwise made do with what she could find. Her chief sources for the chapter were works all but mummified in their own right: one was first published in 1910, the other in 1929.[151] And it was perhaps no accident that one of these was a book titled *The Art and Mystery of the Apothecary* – yet again, the wily physician has slipped out of sight here. Blame is effectively shifted onto his humble assistant – a figure who in most cases could never have prepared or sold anything which the élite physicians had not first sanctioned, published, and prescribed.

'Why don't I know about this?' That bewildered question (put to me by a man with a PhD in history) has been an invaluable prompt during the writing of this book. As so often with the question 'why ... ?' the answer can be twofold. The above discussion is one answer. You don't know because, for various reasons, medical historians have very rarely talked about it (and, when they did, the discussion was often far from helpful or accurate). There again: *why* did they not talk about it? What we can say is that the data has been there in secondary form since 1910, and again since 1985.[152] The neglect, then, seems to have been due to discomfort or embarrassment, rather than to practical reasons.

We can also say, more confidently, that both the unease and its effects have notably persisted into the twenty-first century. One effect of academic neglect of this subject has been to produce a general misconception oddly like that seen in eighteenth-century discussions. Corpse medicine belongs to 'the days of superstition'. The days of superstition are often held, also, to be ones of cruelty and general barbarity – and, as any fan of Quentin Tarantino could tell you, such days are, basically, 'medieval'. Hence, in 2001, a popular book on Egyptian mummies tells us that 'stolen pieces of mummy were used to make medicine and paint in the Middle Ages (from about AD 1000 to AD 1450)'.[153] Rather neatly, this author's end point for the mummy trade is more or less that at which it begins in earnest. Indeed, as I have argued above, in terms of corpse materials more generally, there was very possibly more on sale in Britain in 1750 than there was in 1450 or 1550. The point would apply all the more strongly to Germany.

In a nominally academic article of 2004, moreover, this basic misunderstanding makes its way into the very title of the piece in question. An anonymous essay in the journal *Science News* is headed, 'Medieval Cure-All May Actually Have Spread Disease'. The ensuing paragraphs curiously mingle fact and fiction:

> One of medieval Europe's most popular concoctions for treating disease might instead have been an agent of germ transmission, new research suggests ... In the Middle Ages, merchants in [sic] apothecaries often dispensed mumia, or bitumen, a black asphaltlike substance thought at the time to alleviate ailments as diverse as epilepsy, gout, and plague. When natural supplies of [this] ran short, merchants turned instead to Egyptian mummies as a source of the material, says Barb'ra Anne Carter [of California State University]. That's because the practitioners mistakenly believed that bitumen had been used to create the dark-skinned mummies ... When import restrictions interrupted the supply of Egyptian mummies, European merchants ... turned to readily available local imitations.

The piece goes on to argue that certain micro-organisms instrumental in transmission of plague can survive for some time in recently dead corpses (i.e. the 'local imitations').[154] This itself is interesting, and adds one more nice irony to the history of corpse medicine. People were eating disease in order to cure disease. But they were certainly not doing so in the medieval period. Although the phrasing of this article is somewhat compressed and therefore unclear (and there is no actual date given anywhere) the broad sequence presented above seems to correspond to the introduction of both 'counterfeit mummy' (conscious frauds baked up by merchants and their accomplices in Alexandria and elsewhere) and Paracelsian mummy. In the second case especially, we are very far from the medieval period. In Britain the zenith of Paracelsian mummy fell around the mid- to later seventeenth century. (And we should recall that it still had an ardent follower *c.*1739, in the form of the Reverend John Keogh of County Cork.) We must indeed suspect, then, that Naubert's Enlightenment aims have been effectively fulfilled by writers such as Ackerknecht. By the late eighteenth century, corpse medicine was already 'getting medieval'; and in some people's view, it had not shifted beyond this (perhaps mythically antique) status come 2004.

In one other case of distortion, however, corpse medicine is shifted back so far that the medieval period looks more or less like last week by comparison. The following words occur in a general survey of cannibalism written by the journalist and author Reay Tannahill: 'to make tincture of mummy, says an ancient Egyptian medical prescription, "select the cadaver of a red, uninjured, fresh, unspotted malefactor, twenty-four years old, and killed by hanging, broken on the wheel, or impaled ... cut it in pieces, sprinkle with myrrh and aloes; then marinate it for a few days, and pour on spirits"'. A case, it may be thought, of the cure being worse than the disease – whatever the disease may have been. 'The papyrus does not say'.[155] This recipe probably looks familiar. Its historical location, of course, does not. To us, this perhaps seems at first like a faintly comical misunderstanding. General information on medicinal mummy was so thin when Tannahill wrote her book that she automatically assumed that it was the Egyptians themselves who used their own mummified dead for therapeutic ends. In itself this conclusion is already striking, and also profoundly ironic: the Egyptians had suffered quite enough plunder and indignity in the era of the mummy trade, surely, without then having the whole phenomenon recast as their own invention (and – take note – solely their invention, in Tannahill's account). It is difficult to know just how or why this author managed to overlook the odd details of her 'Egyptian' formula: who, after all, had ever heard of the Egyptians hanging malefactors, or breaking them on the wheel (or, indeed, being noted for their red hair)?[156] One plausible inference as to her seeming carelessness is this: the phenomenon of medicinal cannibalism was so odd to her, already so unreal, that it seemed naturally to be something best-suited to the realms of a mythically distant antiquity, contradictions notwithstanding.

It would be easy enough to dismiss the three references I have cited if, around this time, there had actually been other available views to counter them. But in an area so thoroughly characterised by neglect or distortion, a little misinformation can go a surprisingly long way. Whilst Tannahill's book was originally published in 1975, the above quotation comes from the revised, 1996 edition of the work; and the book seems, moreover, to have sold in considerable quantities. Comical as the error may look to us, it would by contrast have left many of its original readers genuinely convinced that the only known tradition of medicinal cannibalism occurred in Egypt, several thousand years ago.

Thus much of neglect. Unease also lingers on. In 2004 I submitted an article on medicinal cannibalism to the journal *Social History of Medicine*. Two anonymous readers made various suggestions as to how the piece might be amended or expanded. Among their generally useful comments was one all too familiar attitude. I should, it was recommended, 'drop the word cannibalism'. Why, you might ask, should an author remove what is surely one of the most central and interesting elements of such a study? Presumably, we must infer, because it made the reader uncomfortable. When I recounted this tale to various people, most were bewildered. And it should be added that, when David Musgrove asked me 'why don't I know about this?', that conversation was made possible only because I included the word 'cannibalism' in the title of the article, and the list of associated keywords.

If we were to pursue discussion of the nature of medical history extensively, the present book could very easily turn into two books. Let us therefore conclude by just briefly returning to one of corpse medicine's most famous users. We saw that Charles II fell ill in February 1685. In theory, no one had more eminent physicians than the king. And, by all accounts, no one imbibed a greater or more costly kaleidoscope of drugs than Charles in that final week of his life. For decades now, it has been a minor historical tradition to assert, with faintly bemused condescension, that Charles II was murdered by his doctors, rather than by the more general forces of age and nature.[157]

In the words of Haggard: 'as the first step in treatment the king was bled to the extent of a pint from a vein in his right arm. Next his shoulder was cut and the incised area "cupped" to suck out an additional eight ounces of blood. After this homicidal onslaught the drugging began'. This involved 'an enema containing antimony, sacred bitters, rock salt, mallow leaves' and several other ingredients. Meanwhile,

> for external treatment a plaster of Burgundy pitch and pigeon dung was applied to the king's feet. The bleeding and purging continued, and to the medicaments were added melon seeds ... slippery elm, black cherry water ... and dissolved pearls ... The king's condition did not improve, indeed it grew worse, and in the emergency forty drops of extract of human skull were administered to allay convulsions. A rallying dose of Raleigh's antidote was forced down the king's throat; this antidote contained an enormous number of herbs and animal extracts ... As a sort of grand summary to this pharmaceutical debauch a mixture of Raleigh's antidote, pearl julep, and ammonia was forced down the throat of the dying king. King Charles was helpless before the drugging of his physicians ... [158]

I have chosen Haggard's version of this oft-repeated 'homicidal onslaught' just because his work is in other ways relatively balanced and neutral. For all that, his critical acumen dissolves at the bedside of monarchy, rather like the poise of some humble subject, temporarily stunned by the heady influence of royal blood. In general terms, the account is hopelessly wayward. Why would any physicians possibly want to kill their most eminent customer? He not only commanded fabulous amounts of wealth, but acted as the ultimate medical showpiece: save the king, and every affluent patient in the land would hear of it. Looking at this strange hostility from another angle, we might begin to wonder if Haggard is unconsciously seeking to tame a wider sense of bewilderment, by conveniently blaming the medical theories of an entire epoch on just a few desperate physicians. The general madness of past beliefs is thus somehow limited in the figures of a few specially culpable individuals. And this leads us to another very basic general criticism. Clearly, Charles's doctors all *believed* in what they were doing. Their attempts were quite as genuine and serious as those of the doctors who attended (for example) the Queen Mother just before her death in April 2002.[159] Yet, in Haggard's loosely farcical sketch, the whole drama is reduced to a two-dimensional comedy, a 'debauch' or a kind of whimsical licensed murder.

The details of Haggard's language are also interesting. Although less pronounced, his attitude to 'Raleigh's antidote' faintly echoes that of Valadez and O'Malley. This remedy, he states, 'contained *an enormous number* of herbs and animal extracts' (italics mine). The phrasing is subtly but unmistakably indignant. This is curious in one way, as modern advertisements for medical and other products will still positively boast that they comprise a large number of ingredients. And it is curious, again, given that Raleigh's antidote was still being used by the physician James Keill many years later. But most revealing of all is the way that Haggard constructs Charles as 'helpless'.

Twice we are told that the physicians 'forced' drugs down his throat. Haggard's general tone and attitude imply that this word is not used neutrally. It could of course mean that the king was too weak to swallow actively. But in such a biased context it seems to once again reflect Haggard's sense of the king being personally and maliciously attacked. Beyond that, it sets up another kind of opposition between monarch and doctors. For Haggard, Charles is not just a physical victim. Rather, he is also effectively set apart from the pre-scientific follies of his medical attendants. The drugs are 'forced' on him because, in his full strength and with a clear head, he would not have consented to take them. Once more, anachronism distorts the historical picture. For in reality, Charles, like most educated men and women, accepted these treatments. He had long since consented to all these procedures by choosing these physicians himself, and accepting their prescriptions earlier in his life.

And what is of course most striking about Haggard's account is the way it indiscriminately lists extract of human skull without any further comment. Not only did Charles generally subscribe to the validity of this: he was said to have paid £6,000 for the recipe, and he seems to have personally distilled it himself.[160] He dosed himself with the treatment at the very start of his final illness, even before his physicians had been summoned. The remedy was so closely associated with him that it was indeed known as 'the King's drops'. At a casual glance, a general reader of Haggard's outline would scarcely have inferred any of this. A narrative which presented Edward Jenner as pinned down on a bed, being forcibly vaccinated by sadistic doctors, could hardly have been more misleading.

For a long time charges of cannibalism were used as a highly effective slur against tribal peoples in the Americas and Australasia. It was perhaps partly this which prompted the anthropologist William Arens to write his 1979 book, *The Man-Eating Myth*, claiming that anthropophagy was an entirely fictitious affair. Most scholars in relevant fields now accept that ritual cannibalism has occurred for centuries. We have seen that it was probably still occurring in Brazil in the 1960s. When studying early modern medicine, we need as far as possible to know what happened, and why. What did it mean to those engaged in it? How have taboos and allegedly 'universal instincts' changed radically over time? How entirely rational and homogeneous (by contrast) is the medicine of an age where doctors tell you to take your cold to bed, and pharmaceutical companies tell you to take it to work? For a long time historians have behaved rather like Arens. They have sought to protect medicine as a whole, and perhaps the past itself, from the potent slur of cannibalism. Like good anthropologists, those studying medical history need to see the past as interestingly different, rather than dangerously wrong.

CONCLUSION

Afterlives

Why did corpse medicine end? Even when tackling just its demise amongst the privileged in the late eighteenth century, it is not possible to give a single reason, nor even possible to choose one dominant factor out of those which appear to be involved in its decline. The chief causes seem to have been: the rise of Enlightenment attitudes to science, superstition, and the general backwardness of the past; a desire to create a newly respectable 'medical profession'; a changing attitude toward hygiene, the body and disgust; and the radically changed nature of the human body itself.

The first of these two areas has been discussed at some length in the previous chapter. The second was noted some time ago by Lawrence Stone, when he observed that, from around 1700 'the quality' increasingly marked itself off from other classes by 'the substitution of forks for fingers in eating ... of handkerchiefs for fingers or clothes for nose-blowing ... control of spitting' and 'the introduction of washbasins, portable bath-tubs and soap', among other things.[1] This broad sketch is supported and nuanced by G.J. Barker-Benfield, who cites various pieces of contemporary evidence. The writer Mary Ann Radcliffe (c.1746–c.1810), for example, now believes that the '"refinement and delicacy" of the "well-bred female" distinguishes her from the "poor and abject"', whilst James Fordyce, in 1766, exclaims: '"a dirty woman – I turn from the shocking idea"'.[2]

Both those instances suggest that such changes affected women more strongly than men, and it may be that changing attitudes to corpse medicine and other 'disgusting' therapies were initially objected to by female patients more widely than by male ones. To this evident gender division, we can add a chronological one which fits the narrative of medicinal cannibalism. As we saw, the first wave of opposition to this comes only around the middle of the eighteenth century. This seems to hold, also, for changing attitudes to hygiene. Lawrence Wright, for example, believes that, 'in the first half [of the eighteenth century] the rougher ways of the seventeenth century persist'.[3]

As chapter eight has suggested, the way in which such factors operated could well have been complex, with change often involving a subtle interplay between patients and practitioners, or between practitioners and the public per se (recall, most notably, the case of 'Dr Mummy'). Some of those turning against corpse medicine may have been motivated by new feelings about disgust and nature in general; some by more abstract ideals concerning Enlightenment and the backward past. Others, again, must have been influenced by the increasingly mechanised model of the human body: an entity now drained (at least for the educated) of its animistic, essentially cosmic vitality. Although people continue to talk of the 'spirits' in physiological terms, the link between spirits and soul, undermined to some extent in the later seventeenth century, has essentially been broken come the eighteenth. In this area, then, the point is not that the body as medicine is disgusting, but that this new body no longer resonates the animistic forces of an earlier Christian era. Thus John Hill, in 1751, deriding the moss of the skull, which now 'possesses no more virtues than that which grows on a stick or a stone'.[4]

My main interest in this concluding chapter, however, is in the various afterlives which corpse medicine enjoyed beyond the eighteenth century. In these closing pages I will look, first, at persistent medical use of the human body in popular culture. Whilst this itself cannot easily be detached from magic, it is my second section which deals most thoroughly with a startling occult tradition: the making of candles from human fat. Thirdly, we find that those swallowing human materials (especially blood) after the Enlightenment are increasingly likely to sexualise such activity. A fourth and final section broadens out these discussions by examining a recurring and widespread fantasy: the belief that the powerful will kill you in order to use your body for medical ends.

Medicinal cannibalism after the eighteenth century

The persistence of corpse medicine in this era can be split into two broad categories: a semi-official use, in which human materials were sold, and that of popular culture, in which they usually had to be obtained more or less illicitly, and often with some difficulty.

The first class offers some surprisingly late instances. C.J.S. Thompson, writing around 1929, could state that 'mummy is still sold in the drug-bazaars as a remedial agent in the Near East'.[5] In Europe, we find that, according to Raphael Patai, 'in Upper Bavaria, "mumie" or "wild human flesh" was sold in pharmacies as late as the nineteenth century, as a remedy against consumption'.[6] Camporesi states that in Italy the medical virtues of human fat were still being praised in print at the start of the nineteenth century.[7] In 1899 the *London Standard* could note with some warmth how, 'so late as 1852 a bottle was found on the shelves of a chemist at Leamington, labelled "Moss from a dead man's skull"'.[8] In 1862 one doctor near Liverpool was allegedly 'very fond of giving' his patients 'earthworms and toads, vipers and their excreta, precipitate of human blood, undiluted human excretions ... and the oil of human fat', as well as '*facullas stercoris humani*' – something which this critic considers is 'best left, probably, in its nice classic dress'. Isolated as this case may have been, it was not quite unique: 'only the other day', adds the indignant author, 'a London physician of considerable repute was actually prevented by the college, under pains and penalties, from using, as he had then been doing, *several of the above compounds!*'.[9]

A more ambiguous phenomenon at the cusp of the Victorian era was the lingering advocacy of 'the king's drops'. In the 1823 edition of his immensely popular cookery book the epicure and writer William Kitchiner (1778–1827) included various medical recipes. For convulsions in children he recommended 'five or six drops of king's-drops, or spirit of harts-horn, in two spoonfuls of black cherry water, sweetened with syrup of male peony'.[10] The association with convulsions, and the alternative 'spirit of harts-horn' (so often found in company with spirit of skull in earlier decades) are both notable. So too is the presence in the book of broadly similar medical ingredients, such as peacock's dung and horse dung (both to be swallowed).[11] Moreover, the opportunistic Kitchiner had in fact plundered these and other recipes directly from a work attributed to Mary Kettilby, first published at the start of the eighteenth century, when corpse medicines still persisted in mainstream educated culture.[12]

By Kitchiner's time, however, many people were evidently under the impression that the 'king's drops' were in fact 'made by distilling the finest raw silk that could be procured'. So said the *Scots Magazine*, for example, in 1798 – also compounding the ironic 'patent' bought by Charles II when it explained that Charles, 'who was an excellent chemist, invented a medicine which went under the name of the King's Drops'.[13] The belief in silk as chief ingredient went back at least as far as 1748, when it was stated by the physician Robert Poole.[14] For all that – and whatever his own beliefs – Kitchiner's work could certainly have given authority or encouragement to anyone possessing the cannibalistic recipe for the drops in the early nineteenth century.

Turning to popular culture, we find that the bodies of hanged criminals retained for some time the powers credited by Fludd in England, and by so many anonymous men and women in German countries. A good way into the nineteenth century Thomas Hardy's story 'The Withered Arm' has a young woman taking some trouble to touch the corpse of a recently hanged man to cure the arm in question, and at this point the rope is still 'sold by the inch' after the hanging.[15] Evidently set slightly before the author's own birth in 1840, Hardy's tale reminds us of what might have been occurring away from London – either in provincial towns, or indeed – as in this story – at the secluded cottage of the hangman himself.[16] As Jacqueline Simpson points out, someone had indeed enacted a very public version of this cure at a hanging in Brighton in 1835.[17] Whether or not this influenced Hardy, his dating was clearly accurate. In New England, W.J. Hoffman found the Germanic settlers of Pennsylvania still convinced, circa 1889, that 'if the hand of a corpse be rubbed over the goitre, the afflicted may be certain of recovery'.[18] This was also a persistent treatment for scrofula in the nineteenth century in the Scottish Highlands and Islands; and the belief itself (if not the practice) was still known in Indiana circa 1950.[19]

As late as 1892 *The Yorkshire Herald* could report that headaches were being treated by the use of skull-moss (as snuff) or by tying the hangman's rope around the patient's head.[20] (This last cure may well have worked, simply because of the application of sufficient pressure.) We saw that gibbets were themselves abolished in Britain only in 1834.[21] Those prepared to resort to such bodies for cures could have done so in relative secrecy; and the same would hold for those patients who – after the removal of public gibbets – turned to the hangman himself. Such practices, then, could have continued for a long time in certain areas without easily attracting educated notice or condemnation.

Throughout the nineteenth century (and possibly beyond) a number of people were still making cannibalistic (or at least very intimate) uses of the human skull for medicine. Writing some time before his death in 1829, the physician John Armstrong stated: 'producing a powerful impression on the mind will cure epilepsy, and in this way the powder of human skulls will cure it, horror at the dose having the effect of stopping the epilepsy. I have seen the powdered skull of a monkey, used under the name of powdered human skull, succeed in curing epilepsy'.[22] As Armstrong was born only in 1784, this incident almost certainly fell within the nineteenth century. Although the idea of a psychosomatic cure is interesting (especially given the cases of spontaneous remission noted by Moog and Karenburg), this thesis is clearly too sweeping: by Armstrong's time those given human skull were often not told what they were swallowing.

In or shortly before 1847 a Bradford man consulted 'one of those half quacks, half "wise men"' about his daughter's epilepsy, and was told to 'get the skull of a young woman, not decayed, and ... pound it small, mix it with treacle, and give it in small doses to the young woman'. 'After some trouble', adds the report, 'the father obtained the nauseous compound' and administered it – allegedly without effect. When the reporter (for the *Leeds Mercury*) insists: 'our correspondent vouches for the accuracy of this statement, so extraordinary and disgraceful to the age', we are left in little doubt as to educated opinion on such treatments. This kind of attitude is further reflected in the article's heading, 'Appalling instance of Credulity', and in the rapidity with which reprints of the tale circulated through the press during that month. On 19 February the *Liverpool Mercury* told of how 'a young woman ... has actually swallowed ... a human skull powdered', and by 24 February the piece had also made *The Lancet*, where it featured under the heading 'Credulity'.[23]

Much of the detail of this case remains tantalisingly uncertain. It is quite possible, for example, that the man who prescribed the treatment was highly respected by those who could not afford (or were otherwise alienated from) professional medicine, and that in some cases he provided valuable services. It is also just possible that the skull, obtained only 'after some trouble', was actually derived from the murkier recesses of some backstreet Bradford apothecary. If not, we have to suspect connivance with a local sexton or gravedigger. What is beyond doubt is that this instance was a thoroughly urban phenomenon. In this sense the report is especially valuable, given how we might otherwise assume nineteenth-century corpse medicine to be lingering on only in rural fringes.[24]

Other data – limited though it is – indeed supports such an assumption. Writing in 1887, Gordon Cumming refers to belief in the medical (or magical) powers of a suicide's skull, stating that 'the Reverend T.F. Thiselton-Dyer quotes an instance of it in England in 1858'.[25] Over the western border, meanwhile, at Ruabon in Wales in 1865, a collier's wife 'applied to a sexton for "ever so small a portion of human skull for the purpose of grating it similar to ginger"', and mixed it into a powder for her daughter, who suffered from fits.[26] Cumming adds that 'it is only a few years since the skull of a suicide was used in Caithness as a drinking cup for the cure of epilepsy', and that a 'Dr Arthur Mitchell knows of a case in which the body of such a one was disinterred in order to obtain her skull for this purpose'.[27] In the Highland parish of Nigg in the nineteenth century an epileptic boy was given powder from the skull of a suicide – to obtain which, 'a journey of well over sixty miles had to be made'.[28] Also reporting this case, Cumming – who puts the distance at 'nearly a hundred miles' – shows us that this instance occurred before 1887, and notes that the boy was ignorant as to what he was drinking. He also adds that, in the adjoining county of Sutherland, one cure for consumption was to make the patient drink warm blood from their own arm. A James Simpson, and the doctor, Mitchell, had both known this, and the latter had heard of it several times.[29]

Mary Beith reinforces the impression that such habits lingered in remoter parts of Scotland. The cure reported by Mitchell and Simpson occurred again as late as 1909, when an epileptic man resorted to a healer in Lewis after two years of professional treatment in Edinburgh. (You did not, it seems, necessarily have to live in rural Scotland to try such remedies.) In this case, 'blood was taken from the patient's left foot and given him (the patient) to drink'. Along with numerous magical rituals, 'the sufferer was also directed to drink out of a *copann-cinn* (skull-pan) taken from an old cemetery on a small island, which he did for some weeks, reporting … that "the peculiar taste was fresh in the mouth the next morning as it was on the previous night"'.[30] Writing in 1995, Beith adds that the 'well of Annat near the head of Loch Torridon in Wester Ross' was famed for its healing powers, and 'within living memory … a man suffering from epilepsy undertook the ancient regime of drinking the well water from a suicide's skull every sunrise and sunset for two weeks'.[31] In Kirkwall, Orkney, meanwhile, 'part of a human skull was taken from the churchyard, grated and administered to the epileptic'; whilst on the west coast a variant remedy for epileptics involved drinking water 'in which a corpse had been washed'.[32]

One final instance from popular culture brings us back to the cannibal priest of Mitchelstown, John Keogh. A specially ironic measure of how the Keoghs' healing reputation covered not just distance but considerable time is found when, around 1883, William George Black writes: 'a peculiar sanctity is attached in Ireland to the blood of the Keoghs. In Dublin, the blood of a Keogh is frequently put into the teeth of a sufferer from toothache. A friend of my own in Belfast writes that his foreman, on whose word he can depend, says he knew a man named Keogh whose flesh had actually been punctured scores of times to procure his blood'. Black goes on to complain that, despite a query in *Notes and Queries*, this and other 'such inquiries [have] brought me no information … [about] any incident in the history of the Keogh family which might have given distinction to the family blood'.[33]

Does *Notes and Queries* accept answers over 120 years late? What we can say more certainly is this: by 1883 the educated world had forgotten John Keogh's impressively cannibalistic medicine chest. But the less privileged retained an oblique memory of it, along with notably sanguine confidence in the powers of a Keogh's body. It seems almost certain that this enduring reputation must have ultimately derived from the medical status of the Keoghs in the eighteenth century (especially given the popularity of the belief in Dublin). Of course, if one characterises the Keoghs not as charitable healers but as cannibals (as Victorians might well have done) this may indeed seem to be a striking case of the sins of the fathers being visited upon the children. Whether or not the cannibal habits of one generation should justly prompt later ones to be habitually vampirised, however, only God can say.

By their very nature, cases such as these were unlikely to come to the attention of the educated public. The main factors influencing more general awareness would seem to be locality (just how remote or otherwise was the region involved?) and the difficulty of obtaining the ingredients in question. This latter point suggests two related matters. First: in popular culture, users of corpse medicine were now having to make do chiefly with what they could source more or less covertly and unofficially. This meant that they were necessarily limited to bone, skull-moss, and blood (as we can see, not necessarily just that of the patient). Second: if for various reasons it was not so difficult to obtain human skull or blood, then such remedies could well have persisted invisibly in certain areas for quite some time. It must be added that a family which catalysed a journey of over sixty miles, in Scotland in the nineteenth century, was one which had an impressively powerful belief in such a cure.

If we were limited to these points alone we would feel the need to be open-minded about the extent and historic persistence of popular corpse medicine. Beyond that, scholarly caution would restrain us from drawing any more emphatic conclusions. But there is in fact a wealth of additional evidence which suggests that corpse medicine considerably exceeded the few surviving examples listed above. When seen in context, nineteenth-century corpse medicine is just one small thread in a dense and durable web of popular medicine per se. Most of these cures would now be understood as folk medicine. And, for almost all of history, for the vast bulk of the human population, folk medicine *was* medicine. Its modern scientific descendant may now have won out in terms of efficacy and accuracy. But in purely statistical terms scientific medicine is the minority version. In many parts of Europe and North America, the immediate medical option of country dwellers some way into the twentieth century was a cure or recipe which to the scientific eye would look like magic or superstition.[34]

Here we can only skim the thinnest surface layer of this rich ocean of popular custom and belief. We can first add that the Ross-shire boy for whom the suicide's skull was fetched had initially been treated by the use of mole's blood dripped onto his head (this cure itself dating back at least to Hildegard of Bingen, in the twelfth century).[35] And we can next turn back to the notorious incident of the Bradford skull-dosing. In 1854 one Caroline A. White recalled this in an article on medical 'Simples, and their Superstitions'. Interestingly, White's use of this story is a quite enlightened one, verging on cultural relativism. She repeats it after citing Kenelm Digby's wound salve recipe, with its blend of mummy, human fat, blood and skull.

Whilst clearly staggered at this (and expecting a similar reaction from her readers) White then continues: 'let not modern wisdom, however, laugh at the folly of its forefathers, when we find in a newspaper of 1847 an account of a woman swallowing a human skull ... '. She then adds that, 'even this, disgusting as it seems' is mild by comparison with 'tearing the heart of a black hen while living, to roast and powder it for a similar purpose; or dividing, alive, a snow-white pigeon, to bind the separated halves to the feet' of an epileptic patient. 'Both these last atrocious experiments have been perpetrated', she claims, 'to our own knowledge within the last few years' – one in an Essex village just twenty miles from London, the other in 'an interior hamlet in Kent'.[36] White may have been yet more traumatised to find that, in New England around 1889, an epileptic 'must drink the warm blood of a freshly-killed dove', it being better 'if the head be cut off and the blood taken directly from the neck'.[37]

The sharp-eyed reader will notice, too, that these latter cures are remarkably close echoes of remedies prescribed by the educated in the early modern period. Come the Victorian era they may be among the more startling remedies of popular medicine; but they were almost certainly repeated, in less drastic form, by innumerable Americans and Europeans in following decades. And, if we glance briefly at one more comment from White, we can remind ourselves of the wider cultural context in which such habits persisted. After citing the wound salve formula, and before comparing it to the Bradford story, White first remarks: 'there is a scent of witchcraft about it worthy of Hecate and the three weird sisters, whose "charmèd pot" scarcely contained items more hideous ... '.[38]

In thus broadly linking witchcraft and corpse medicine, White was more accurate than she perhaps realised. Although those using or prescribing corpse medicines in Digby's time would usually be pious Christians fiercely hostile to witchcraft, the two phenomena were culturally related. And this relationship continued into and beyond White's own era. Along with the widespread persistence of folk medicine, it is beliefs in witchcraft and the supernatural which further clarify the status of corpse medicine after the eighteenth century. To put the point simply: in many rural areas of Europe and North America, the everyday beliefs and habits of ordinary people were ones which would have utterly astonished their educated peers.[39] As is probably already clear, popular Victorian uses of corpse materials or blood cannot easily be separated from the realm of magic, and the same holds for much of popular medicine in general. And magical beliefs dominated the lives of numerous country dwellers for a surprisingly long time.

For perhaps 200 years after the British Witchcraft Act of 1736 formally outlawed further witch trials, in many parts of Britain witchcraft was habitually used to explain the most routine accidents or misfortunes of everyday life. Witches still caused sickness of humans and animals.[40] Come the age of mechanisation, they damaged machinery.[41] Perhaps most of all: time and again, witches stole or dried up the milk of livestock.[42] Whilst these beliefs themselves are striking enough, it is the persistent physical attacks on witches which attest most strongly to the force of popular belief. In Scotland supposed witches were cut severely by their 'victims' in 1820 and 1826.[43]

In 1935, meanwhile, M.R. Taylor could quote a Poole doctor as saying: 'in a Dorset village an old woman lives whose back and chest are covered with scars. She was accused of bewitching someone, and the victim made her take off the spell by "blood". She had twenty two wounds which required stitching up'.[44]

In some of these cases the attackers and their beliefs may have been in the minority. But much evidence suggests otherwise. Taylor – writing again in 1935 – tells of a witch murder in the west of the country about fifty years since, which brought 'long terms of imprisonment' for the killers. Yet, in this case, 'all the county sympathised with them'.[45] In almost all cases of violence, the attacks themselves were not merely vengeful, but magical, designed to 'disinfect' a witch or take away her powers. Less tragic but not less supernatural was the peculiarly witch-haunted village of Canewdon in Essex – a place routinely avoided by outsiders until the early twentieth century. Here many locals lived in awe or outright terror of one George Pickingale, a well-known male witch who died in 1909, aged 93.[46]

None of the uncanny happenings of Canewdon attracted legal attention, and even serious attacks (such as that of 1820) were evidently often unprosecuted. Over in Germany Johann Kruse, a schoolteacher who cited significant witch attacks from the 1950s and 60s, could assert – after forty years studying this subject – that most such crimes went unreported by their female victims.[47] Such evidence strongly suggests that data from legal records was just a small part of widespread popular belief in magic. At times, fairy beliefs could prompt violence equalling or surpassing that of witch attacks. For centuries, those whose children were in some way abnormal seriously believed that their own infant had been 'taken by the fairies', with this damaged substitute being left in its place. In seeking to make the fairies reverse the switch, relatives or neighbours of the suspect child committed startling acts of violence. Carole G. Silver recalls cases of beating, starving, near-drowning, and immersion in poisonous foxglove essence from 1843, 1878, and the 1890s – with the latter instance ultimately proving fatal.[48]

Once again, many of the more remote or less harmful incidents of 'changeling abuse' must have gone unrecorded. A case which instead enjoyed sensational publicity was the 1895 trial of Michael Cleary, from Clonmel in Ireland. In the previous year Cleary had murdered not an infant, but his twenty-six-year-old wife, Bridget, in the belief that she was a fairy changeling. This affair in particular revealed the gaping intellectual chasm between the various classes of one nominally unified country. There was no question about Cleary's own opinions. For, as Silver emphasises, an initial 'charge of wilful murder was dropped in favour of manslaughter, it being clear, as *The Cork Examiner* commented, that Bridget Cleary was not deliberately murdered, but "killed in the belief that an evil fairy had taken possession of her"'.[49] At the same time, the educated public were convulsed with morbid fascination – incredulous at an extreme manifestation of a popular belief which most had never even suspected.

Many of those confronted with the Bradford or Ruabon skull-dosings could scarcely have been more startled than late Victorian city dwellers as they trembled over their newspapers in 1895. Let us now revisit the framing question of this final chapter.

When did corpse medicine end? In some parts of Europe and North America, corpse medicine probably survived as long as did the powerful traditions of popular medicine and popular magic. For all the educated theology and all the educated science of élite culture, the majority of people lived their lives in defiant independence of such ideas. For most people, to believe anything was to believe in magic. Almost 2,000 years after the Garadene swine, such people routinely sought to transfer their diseases or skin blemishes to plants, animals or other people. In doing so, they might use standard medical formulae themselves, or consult one of those local 'wise men' or women. The Canewdon male witch, George Pickingale, supposedly cured a local woman of rheumatism 'by "transferring the disease to her father"'.[50]

There were probably various reasons why ordinary people continued to believe in magic, witchcraft and fairies so long after 1736, and so near to the space age. But a very basic one is this: all those things were useful. For those who were uneducated, and who lacked mental, social or technological aids against accidents, sickness, or severe weather, all those beliefs offered forms of mental and physical control.[51] If the educated really wished to outlaw these beliefs, then they had also to outlaw the social conditions which sustained them. In this sense, then, corpse medicine, folk medicine, and magical beliefs in general were all very robustly connected.

To understand the afterlives of corpse medicine, we need to do something remarkably difficult. We need to accept that what we take for granted as scientific reality is, historically, the minority view. I emphasise this, in part, just because it is fascinating to see that, for decades after the Enlightenment, most people existed, believed and acted wholly outside of educated intellectual culture. But I emphasise it too for another, more precise reason. In writing this conclusion I am immensely indebted to the extraordinary fragments of belief recovered by folklorists. Regrettably, however, the very category of folklore has an unfortunate smell of the marginal and arcane. It did not feel that way to those who attacked witches in 1820, those who attacked changelings in 1894, or those who tore the live heart from a chicken circa 1834. For many of those who lived deep within the resilient web of magic, there was probably little distinction between orthodox piety and illicit sorcery. Nature was relatively supernatural, and the supernatural relatively natural. There might indeed have been wonder, horror or awe. But again, most basically of all, there was a desire to get greater control over your life and your surroundings. Magic and practical utility must at times have interwoven with seamless ease in a world at once vibrantly uncanny and brutally pragmatic. If one had godlike power over culture and language, then perhaps the best label to cover all the folklore research of past decades would be, simply, 'Life'.

Given the peculiarly dark realms of magic into which we are now about to descend, it should be added that popular belief needs to be treated with sensitivity and nuance. There must have been some very poor, nominally uneducated people who were unusually modern or sceptical in their outlooks. There must have been some who passionately adhered to certain magical beliefs, and fervently shunned others. We can no more bluntly describe all this as 'magic' than we can crudely generalise all of early modern Europe as 'very religious'.

Human candles

As we saw in chapters three and eight, one of the most enduring (and probably efficacious) substances in the corpse medicine chest was human fat. Even as the eighteenth century turned against mummy, skull, and other 'horrid medicines', human fat lingered with a stubbornness perhaps all too familiar to the weary dieters of modern times. Come 1866, its place in Charles Kingsley's novel *Hereward the Wake* is ostensibly very different. When the Anglo-Saxon hero briefly visits a witch's hovel, he sees in one corner 'a dried human hand, which he knew must have been stolen off the gallows, gripping in its fleshless fingers a candle, which he knew was made of human fat. That candle, he knew, duly lighted and carried, would enable the witch to walk unseen into any house on earth'.[52] Taken alone, all this could hardly be more fantastical or Gothic. As with the supposedly 'medieval' use of skull-moss, Kingsley deploys this macabre candle as a marker of eleventh-century witchcraft. He would, we can well imagine, have been more than a little surprised to find that that one Liverpool doctor was still prescribing 'oil of human fat' just three years earlier.

But this, as we will see, was just the mildest and most mundane instance to be found in the nineteenth century. There is arguably a small book to be written on the largely forgotten history of human fat. We have already seen the surprising roles it played in early modern warfare, and in South America from around 1500 to the present day. Here I will limit myself chiefly to the subject of candles. Given that this topic is a relatively marginal one come the Victorian age, we should briefly remind ourselves how widespread belief in the occult powers of fat had once been.

In Thomas Middleton's play *The Witch* we find Hecate 'giving the dead body of a child' to her assistant Stadlin, with the instructions

> Boil it well; preserve the fat:
> You know 'tis precious to transfer
> Our 'nointed flesh into the air,
> In moonlight nights, o'er steeple tops.[53]

In the Jacobean period such a speech was not purely fantastical. Recall Jonson, in his 1609 *Masque of Queens*, ventriloquising a witch who had 'kill'd an infant, to have his fat'. This – along with the lines from *Macbeth* and from *The Witch* – was something which, at very least, made sense to early modern viewers. In a marginal note to the witch's speech, moreover, Jonson quite soberly reasserts this and other witch atrocities, underpinning them with various scholarly authorities.[54]

Yet more striking still are certain witchcraft accusations of 1613, made against Ellen and Jennet Bierley by one Grace Sowerbutts in Lancashire. Jonson, and especially Middleton – whose play is conjecturally dated 1615 – may well have been paying close attention to this case.[55] Having supposedly killed an infant by occult means, the two sisters were alleged to have then removed it from Salmesbury churchyard, and at Jennet's house 'did boil some thereof in a pot, and some did boil on the coals'. Having eaten some of the roasted and boiled flesh themselves, they then allegedly offered these delicacies to their accuser (Grace) and her daughter, who refused. Afterwards, the sisters 'did seethe the bones of the said child in a pot, and with the fat that came out of the said bones, they said they would annoint themselves, that thereby they might sometimes change themselves into other shapes'. Whilst this part of the accusation is quite explicit, the description of the child's killing is also notable. We are told that the Bierleys stole the infant from the bedroom of Thomas Walshman and his wife. Downstairs by the fire Jennet then 'thrust a nail into the navel of the said child: and afterwards did take a pen and put it in at the said place, and did suck there a good space, and afterwards laid the child in bed again'. According to Sowerbutts, after this 'the said child did thenceforth languish, and not long after died'.[56] What was Jennet sucking out of the child's body? It may possibly have been breath, or spirits, or the soul itself. But it could equally have been fat. The way that this was achieved without visible signs or immediate injury, and yet afterwards proved fatal, quite closely mirrors the actions of the Bolivian kharisiri, whose assault was unknown, at first, even to his victims.[57]

Come the time of George III, with educated Britons perhaps still in denial about the witch craze of the last century, the occult powers of human fat were held to have migrated to the colonies. A famous Negro robber, 'Three Fingered Jack', was killed in Jamaica in January 1781 after terrorising the island in the previous year. Jack was repeatedly associated with the practice of African magic, part of which involved an 'Obi' – in this case the end of a goat's horn filled with 'grave dirt, ashes, the blood of a black cat, and human fat, all mixed into a kind of paste'.[58] Ironically, this eyewitness description of the Obi came from none other than the physician Benjamin Moseley, who around this time was one of the latest official supporters of corpse medicine.[59]

The history of human fat and candles takes us back to the sixteenth century, and leads us on a strange and winding path through the criminal and magical worlds of several European countries. In 1577 the Nuremberg executioner Franz Schmidt broke on the wheel at Bamberg 'a man who had committed three murders for the sake of the fat of his victims'.[60] Later, on 21 April 1601, Schmidt dispatched one Bastian Grübl of Gumpnhoffen. Grübl had been convicted of twenty murders, including five pregnant women. He had – Schmidt wrote in his diary – 'cut them open and cut off the hands of the infants and made candles of their hands to be used in burglaries'.[61] Extraordinary as this last charge may seem, we will see in a few moments that if such an act could have been committed anywhere, it would almost certainly have been in Germany.

In 1652, an account of the alleged atrocities committed against Protestants in Ireland circa 1641 claimed that one Scotchman had had 'his belly ripped up' and 'his small guts tied to a tree', and fully unravelled, 'that they might try (said they) whether a dog's or a Scotchman's guts were longest'. Meanwhile, 'another young fat Scotchman who was murdered' had 'candles made of his grease'.[62] In few cases is it so hard to distentangle fact from fiction as in English accounts of The Irish Massacre. We should, however, remind ourselves that a broadly similar mutilation clearly was carried out by Protestants in Ostend in 1601; and that far worse things were reported of Catholic troops in Piedmont, in April 1655.

In 1691 an anonymous British author writes of the belief (not, at this time, strictly popular) that 'candles compounded of human fat', if 'set up lighted in any part of the house' will 'keep them sleeping that are asleep'.[63] The writer goes on to tell of a criminal gang which had carried out many robberies and murders by (and for?) this means, and whose leader was finally 'drawn in a cart through the chiefest city of Norway', where 'at the corner of every street [he] had his flesh tore with red hot pincers, until he was dead, to deter others from this magical practice'.[64]

Come the nineteenth century, a number of cases of murder for the sake of human fat are found in Germany. An especially startling and well-detailed account is reported by Frederick Elworthy, who derived it from an 1877 edition of *The Gentleman's Magazine*. 'In 1834, in the forest of Plantekow, in Pomerania, an old herdsman, named Meier, was murdered', and 'a triangular piece of flesh was found to have been cut from his body, below the heart'. The killing remained a mystery for over a year, until a woman named Berger accused her husband. Presently both were arrested, and the wife told of how 'her father had more than once told her husband that the possessor of a "thief's candle" could enter a house and rob it, without those in the house being able to wake' – and that this candle 'was fashioned out of human fat'. On the day of the murder, she continued, her husband 'produced the fat he had cut off from under the dead man's ribs, and … they melted it, twisted a wick of cotton, and poured the fat into a mould'. They found, however, that the fat would not set, and had to be thrown away.

After some time in prison the husband – who was a known thief – 'confessed that he had murdered the man at the instigation of his wife and her father', who often told him that such a candle would allow them to '"rob and steal in any house at night without anyone waking and seeing us."' At the trial it also 'came out … that they had borrowed a candle mould from a neighbour'; and it was further established by prosecutors that human fat will not set like ordinary tallow in a mould. Berger was executed in 1838, by this time protesting his innocence of the murder. In 1844 a sailor about to be executed for another crime confessed that he had murdered Meier, and it was then revealed (by the wife?) that Berger had merely chanced on the dead body, and cut out the fat to make the candle.[65]

Anyone who has read early modern witchcraft accusations knows that one cannot necessarily believe a story just because of its detail. In the above case, however, the detail is often sober, rather than fantastical or bizarre, and the points about the candle mould in particular are mundanely convincing (reminding us, also, that ordinary people were used to making their own tallow candles, whether of animal or human grease). Our next case, occurring even as Berger languished in prison, also comes from Germany.

In April 1836 *The Times* told of how:

> a man has just been arrested at Insterburg in Prussia, on a charge of having murdered a shepherd about twelve months ago. He has been examined as to his motives for committing the murder, and has confessed that his object was to get a sufficient quantity of human fat, with which to make a torch to render

himself invisible. His superstitious belief was that the possession of such a talisman would have this effect.[66]

In 1888, a similar crime occurred in the Kursk district of Russia. Sentenced to between eight and twenty years' penal servitude for the October murder of a young girl, Lukeria Cherkuahina, four peasants confessed that they had wished to 'procure some "magic candles" before entering on a series of predatory expeditions'. A local man had narrowly escaped being their victim (as he was armed with a wood axe), as had an 'abnormally stout' priest who fortunately chanced to be out administering sacraments when they called upon him. Finally, the thieves followed Lukeria into some woods, and after murdering her, 'removed certain parts of the body, which they afterwards boiled'. They escaped detection for some time, until a handkerchief containing human fat was found in their rooms, and identified as being that of the murdered girl.

Reporting this case in November 1888, the *Pall Mall Gazette* insisted that the murderers' belief was shared by 'the lower classes throughout the length and breadth of Russia', while in Austria, Dr Josef Bloch claimed that the notion existed among the criminal classes of Germany, and that specific punishments for such crimes had in fact been written into the country's legal codes in the seventeenth and eighteenth centuries.[67] Did the belief also have some currency in London's East End, between April 1888 and February 1891? Across this period, the unsolved Whitechapel Murders of 'Jack the Ripper' involved some especially horrible mutilations of the female victims, and prompted at least one commentator to conclude that the murderer was motivated by a desire to gain human fat for magical ends. Bloch himself supported this inference, noting that, in eighteenth- and nineteenth-century Germany, it was female corpses in particular which were mutilated for such purposes.[68] Citing Bloch in an article of October 1888, *The Star* told of how thieves' candles, made from the uterus and other organs, had 'played an important part in the trials of robber bands at Odenfald and Westphalia', in 1812 and 1841. It told, also, of how at the trial of a German robber Theodor Unger (executed at Magdeburg in 1810) authorities 'discovered that a regular manufactory had been established by gangs of thieves for the production of such candles'.[69]

Whilst Britain's part in this impressively long-running tradition remains uncertain, it is notable that, time and again, the trail leads back to Germany. During the Russian case, however, it was also asserted that the belief in question was common throughout that country. Indeed, come 1927 an American minister, John R. Crosby, could write of a Marie Kountzik, supposedly the 'only surviving professional witch in the state of Pennsylvania'. Kountzik was a member of a Russian sect called the Throndakians, whose emigration had originally been prompted by persecution of their magical habits in 1898. Although Crosby is somewhat unclear as to whether or not Throndakian witch gatherings were still occurring in 1927, he does state very precisely that these meetings were 'popularly supposed to be illuminated with a candle made out of human fat, which renders the celebration invisible to all except initiates'.[70]

The 1810 trial suggests that such candles were actually made. Elworthy also cites an instance from Ningpo in China in 1870, which shows that little skill was needed to produce a crude version of this occult lighting apparatus. One of the Tai Ping rebels was here supposed to have butchered and boiled a human body, and when sufficient fat floated to the surface, to have simply used 'a roll of cloth … soaked in this human oil, and tightly rolled up into a torch'.[71]

Before snuffing out the fitful illuminations of the human candle we can briefly turn its uncanny light more fully upon the dead hand described in Kingsley's novel. Elworthy shows that this, for all its air of Gothic fantasy, was in fact part of a genuine tradition, now usually labelled 'the hand of glory'. Versions of this vary, but its logic is essentially that of the thief's candle. It will render the bearer invisible, or produce (or maintain) sleep in the house to be burgled. According to John Aubrey, writing in the seventeenth century, it was generally believed, '"when I was a schoolboy, that thieves, when they broke open a house, would put a candle into a dead man's hand' to keep the residents asleep. Here, although the nature of the candle itself is uncertain, we find the belief evidently well known in early modern Britain. Elworthy also cites a report that thieves in Ireland had, in 1831, entered a house using such a hand, with the human candle in its grasp. Are dead hands able to grasp very effectively? It may have been for this reason that another form of the occult hand was rather simpler: you simply lit its fingers – which, in many stories, could prove remarkably hard to extinguish. 'Elworthy emphasises that there are at least two pictures of such hands – one engraved in 1568, and another engraved after a painting by David Teniers the younger (d.1690).[72]

In a case partly recalling the Norwegian execution, we hear of a Lithuanian who, in 1619, was 'tortured with red hot pincers and afterwards burnt alive', having confessed to several murders 'for the purpose of obtaining sinews … to form wicks for "thieves' candles"'. He also used 'the fingers of infants for the same purpose'. A cook named Schreiber was involved in this case, and was said to have actually manufactured the candles. Whilst the detail of the infants' fingers echoes the 1601 execution of Grübl, a case from 1638 reminds us of the numerous instances of corpse mutilation cited by Evans. A man 'imprisoned for a month at Ober-Haynewald for cutting off the thumb of a dead felon' admitted that he had intended (with admirable economy) to 'use it as a "thief's candle"'.[73] Here we find a general link with the numerous other magical uses of criminal relics, and a probably quite particular one with the removal of felons' hands or fingers.

It is hard to say exactly what inspired the strange beliefs in the magical power of human fat. Perhaps most obviously, the notion was of course more likely to arise amongst those who were habitually using animal fat as their only source of light (hence the use of the candle mould in 1834). It also seems likely that these supposed powers were at least partly inspired by the more routine efficacy of human (or animal) fat as treatments for ulcers, wounds, and rheumatic complaints. These cures could be seen as natural; but for many nature itself was already a partly magical realm: its forces were not understood scientifically. In this sense, it might be said that even those who committed horrific crimes and mutilations had ultimately a greater reverence for the supernatural or religious forces animating the humblest levels of nature. For these people, the early modern holism of matter and spirit (recall Fludd and the vital spirits tugging at his flesh) had by no means died out.

What we can say with particular certainty is that, if we now asked people from North America or much of Europe about the magical substances of the human body in past eras, most would probably select blood as the obvious candidate. Folklorists and historians aside, few or none would choose fat. Accustomed as we are to this relatively new taboo, it is worth reflecting briefly on how complete this revolution in attitude has been. Fat can be disliked, shunned, joked about – levels of antipathy vary from person to person. But overall, fat is demonised. For some, it is disgusting – and not infrequently this disgust has a tacit but powerful charge of moral hostility. For those suffering from bulimia or anorexia, fat can be more disgusting than those waste substances and fluids which are habitually tabooed by society. In the former case, after all, vomit is a welcome form of elimination and weight control, and even in the latter ordinary excretion must have something of the same value.

It is perhaps obvious enough that these tragic medical conditions belong to a world in which it is no longer difficult to get fat. For many, in most of history, extra body fat must have been a formidable luxury – perhaps a kind of life insurance, at times, against a hard winter or bad harvest. It was only a few decades ago, indeed, that those at Bathsheba Everdene's shearing supper could scrupulously judge the exact size of the knobs of fat which went into a pudding.[74] At times, the potential irrationality of human behaviour depends on the angle from which you view it. From certain angles, it is indeed irrational to believe in 'thieves' candles'. There again: is this definitely more irrational than those who die of starvation amidst abundant wealth and food sources?[75] Or even those who weigh six stone in similar circumstances?

Love magic

The use of blood or other bodily fluids or substances as a love potion evidently goes back a very long way. It was believed, for example, to have been known among the Roman élite, who 'used man's blood against this intoxication' – most notably in the case of 'Faustina, daughter to the Emperor Antoninus Pius, and wife to Antoninus the philosopher, who fell madly in love with a sword-player'. Asking advice of various 'wizards', Antoninus was recommended to 'put to death this sword-player', and then make 'Faustina … drink up a good draught of his warm blood' before going 'to bed to her husband'. This advice was followed, and from this unnaturally heated conjunction there later sprang the notorious Emperor Commodus. So, at any rate, thought the Caroline physician James Hart, who held all of this to have been inspired by Satan, and who notably referred to love in general as 'this intoxication'.[76]

For all that, as given by Hart the Roman tale is relatively chaste, the cure being designed to restore proper matrimonial harmony and to quell irregular lusts. Matters are rather different come the eighteenth and nineteenth centuries. One Monday in autumn 1720, for example, 'a gentleman and a lady came in a Hackney coach to a surgeon's in Leadenhall Street, where both being bleeded, they drank each other's blood out of the porringers, paid a guinea, and went away about their business'.[77] Just under twenty years later, a less consensual version of this amorous vampirism occurred in Bristol. A journal of 1738 tells of

> a love affair that happened without Lawford's Gate; in which a young damsel having smitten a young fellow, he strongly importuned her with his addresses; but she giving him the deaf ear, he took an opportunity on Sunday last to give her a proof of his passion in the following manner; she having occasion to be blooded for a slight disorder, the operator had no sooner closed her vein but he eagerly seized the dish which held her blood, and drank it off. Tis thought if this young damsel will not take this for sufficient proof of the young man's integrity, she will never meet with such a humble servant.[78]

We cannot very definitely interpret either of these striking incidents on the brief accounts given here. But associated data suggests the following. The later case does not obviously imply high status among the two involved (the woman is not 'a lady', nor the youth 'a gentleman'). And, assuming that they were relatively humble, then the educated author's reading of the event may well be some way off the mark. Rather than being a startling 'proof' of his love, the youth's illicit draught may instead have been an attempt to magically further its mutual success. In magical terms the more common formula is to get the beloved to drink your blood (or sweat, among other things). But magic has all sorts of variations, and quite often defies ordinary logic (and we should also bear in mind that getting the woman to swallow *his* blood would have required a good deal of planning and perhaps bribery on the youth's part).

It was probably in popular magic that such potions were used most frequently. In the early twentieth century Géza Roheim found them amongst gypsies, and noted that in Silesia one could mix sweat or blood or hair into the food or drink of the desired person. At Amboina, meanwhile, lovers did indeed 'drink each others blood'. At Nagylebgyel in Hungary 'a man will drop a few drops of blood from his finger into a glass of wine the girl is about to drink'; whilst both German and Serbian women were known to 'mix their menstrual blood into the coffee or wine' of husbands or those they sought to win.[79] In the late nineteenth century W.J. Hoffman heard of a Pennsylvanian woman who, besotted with a boatman who failed to reciprocate, used the following method '*to compel him to love her even against his will*. With the blade of a penknife she scraped her knee until she had secured a slight quantity of the cuticle, baked it in a specially prepared cake and sent it to him'. Whilst the result, admits Hoffman, remained unknown, the woman herself was 'said to have had the utmost faith in the charm'.[80] More generally, Gillian Bennett reports that those Christians who credited blood libel tales sometimes believed that the stolen blood 'could be used as a love potion'.[81]

What of the earlier case in Leadenhall Street? There is no doubt that the couple were privileged. They are explicitly identified as 'a gentleman and a lady'; they travel in a hackney coach; and they pay a guinea. Accordingly – although we should not rule out magical aims – it seems likely that this mutual blood pact had some degree of proto-Romantic psychology behind it. In order to understand the associated motivations, we can turn to a literary version of their act which was penned just before the close of the eighteenth century.

In 1796 there appeared a work entitled *Horrid Mysteries*. This itself was an English translation of a lurid Gothic novel, *Memoirs of the Marquis of Grosse*, by the self-styled German 'marquis', Karl Grosse. The book featured an occult and powerful secret society, allegedly modelled on a real organisation of the fifteenth century, the Illuminati, which began as an intended counterweight to political tyranny, but ultimately degenerated into a corrupt and satanic sect.[82] The society does indeed undertake the drinking of blood as one of its rituals. By way of initiation, the character called Carlos is stabbed and has his blood drunk by its brethren.[83] But our interest lies with a vampiric love pact made between Carlos and his beloved, Rosalia. The two have very recently met and fallen into an extravagance of mutual passion. Remarkably potent for their time, the descriptions of the couple's ardour must have ranked high among those passages which allegedly 'tarnished the name' of Minerva Press, the work's earliest English publishers:

> I felt myself closely encircled … a quivering, balsamic lip burned on my languishing mouth; my breast heaved against a panting bosom; all my senses were entranced; my blood fermented … a virgin fulness enchanted my senses … We roved through the garden arm in arm, melted, as it were, into one being, and frequently dropped half fainting on the swelling grass to exchange our souls in burning kisses.

Just moments later it is Rosalia who pulls out a dagger in order to effect their marriage by blood: 'she bared my arm, and opened a vein, sucking the blood which flowed from the orifice in large drops; and then wounded her arm in return, bidding me to imbibe the roseate stream, and exclaimed, "thus our souls shall be mixed together!"[84]

Come 1818, this incident was sufficiently well known for Thomas Love Peacock to parody it – with tellingly coded brevity – in his satirical novel *Nightmare Abbey*. The chief protagonist, Scythrop, dwells in a gloomy mansion in the wilds of Lincolnshire, and has often been seen as a parodic recreation of Percy Shelley. Scythrop's passion for his attractive cousin, Marionetta, prompts him to urge: "'do as Rosalia does with Carlos, divine Marionetta. Let us each open a vein in the other's arm, mix our blood in a bowl, and drink it as a sacrament of love. Then we shall see visions of transcendental illumination, and soar on the wings of ideas into the space of pure intelligence'". Although Peacock's version of the pact verges on outright slapstick (Marionetta, who 'had not so strong a stomach as Rosalia' promptly 'turned sick at the proposition' and fled away along the corridors of the house) it is nevertheless a useful comparison in some ways.

When the original Rosalia exclaimed, "'thus our souls shall be mixed together!'" she certainly did not mean what an early modern lover might have done by such a phrase. For one thing, some early modern writers evidently did believe that kisses alone could literally do this. And if they could do so for Rosalia and Carlos, then why bother opening veins? Hence, when Scythrop hopes to 'soar on the wings of ideas', he captures at least something of the essentially Romantic psychology of the earlier love pact. The 'ideas' that impel such an act are now intellectual and philosophical, rather than narrowly Christian. Here, to drink blood is to drink a new kind of self, rather than an old kind of God.

But Peacock's rewriting is also useful for its notably tamer phrasing. Even when merely described, rather than actually performed, the blood pact is – as it were – relatively anaemic. In proper English fashion it will be taken from bowls – a sanitised vampirism which only serves to remind us how potently transgressive Rosalia and Carlos were. In a society where sexual activity was fiercely monitored and tabooed, we find a man and a woman sucking fluid directly from one another's bodies. It is important not to underestimate the genuine sensuous charge this must have had, circa 1796. All the torrid quiverings and fermentings of the encounter may look faintly comic to us. But – as the 'tarnished' reputation of Minerva Press alone implies – they had a far great density and power some 200 years ago. They had, indeed, the unsteady force of something newly discovered: an openly sexualised and intimate individuality. Here is a kind of magic for the privileged classes of Europe – a celebration of the transformative powers of sex which aptly marks the shift from general charms to personal charm.

Was there anything of this kind of psychology in the barber-shop incident of 1720? There must, at least, have been a quite powerful atmosphere of sensuality: in that case, after all, the couple literally drank blood, rather than merely writing about it. And it seems likely that, whilst such behaviour was hardly common, this was probably not the only time that it occurred amongst the gentry. Frustratingly uncertain as that early piece of love vampirism may be, we can certainly see a much clearer social shift under way in the bloodlusts of the early nineteenth century. Just a year after Peacock's novel, Polidori published his sexually charged tale, *The Vampyre*. From this tellingly Byronic yarn through *Carmilla* (1871–72) and *Dracula* (1897) the broad pattern is clear. For a society at once obsessed by and profoundly ambivalent about sex, tales of blood-drinking are no longer religious or medical or scientific. Rather, they are a convenient way of experimenting with what is otherwise unspeakable, allowing the terror of supernatural demons to craftily merge with a Victorian terror of the sexual body.

Just four years before Stoker's novel, for example, the sexologist Richard von Krafft-Ebbing, in his *Psychopathia Sexualis* of 1893 told of how he had once been visited by a married man with many scars on his arms. Krafft-Ebbing explained that: 'when he wished to approach his wife, who was young and somewhat "nervous", he first had to make a cut in his arm. Then she would suck the wound, and during the act became violently excited sexually'.[85]

By the Edwardian period, even medicinal cannibalism itself has been absorbed within this newly sexualised paradigm of what we might call 'intimate transgression'. In November 1910, Rupert Brooke penned a poem entitled 'Mummia', whose opening verses run thus:

As those of old drank mummia
To fire their limbs of lead,
Making dead kings from Africa
Stand pander to their bed;
Drunk on the dead, and medicined
With spiced imperial dust,
In a short night they reeled to find
Ten centuries of lust.
So I, from paint, stone, tale, and rhyme,
Stuffed love's infinity,
And sucked all lovers of all time
To rarefy ecstasy.[86]

That third quatrain, in which the speaker claims to have 'sucked all lovers of all time' into some strangely heady distillation, leaves us in little doubt that the associated 'mummia' is at once potent and sensual – as indeed does the single night which somehow compacts 'ten centuries of lust'. But this new form of mummy is not something which early modern patients or physicians would have recognised. Aptly sea-changed by the tides of post-Romantic sexuality, corpse medicine is now transformed into an aphrodisiac. The transformation is the more intriguing given that Brooke might have been expected to know a little more about medicinal mummy than his peers.[87] His interest in the substance may have been partly sparked by London or Cambridge Egyptology. (Intriguingly, Brooke admitted to envying his friend Hugh Popham's post at the British Museum, as he (Brooke) 'had often dreamed of sneaking into the museum at dead of night to embrace a female mummy'.[88]) But it was almost certainly derived more directly from his thesis on John Webster, which he was researching in 1911. In *The White Devil*, the lines on Lodovico explicitly identify mummy as 'physic', and in *The Duchess of Malfi* the association with the 'salvatory' gives at least a hint at mummy's medical nature.[89]

This kind of telling cultural revision is found in yet more startling forms in later decades. We saw that, in Germany in 1824, one man was prepared to kill in order to make medical use of his victim's blood. By 1957, the motivation for such a crime was very different. In Vineland New Jersey that summer, a forty-seven-year-old Puerto Rican farm labourer, Juan Rivera Aponte, was charged with the murder of a thirteen-year-old-boy, Roger Carlotto. Aponte's aim, he told authorities, was to powder the skull (found drying out by his kerosene stove) and then make 'a love potion to cast spells on women'.[90]

By this stage, the potion is explicitly identified as 'black magic' by Aponte and those reporting the crime. And the case was clearly an exceptional one. For all that, we can see at one level how it relates to older, more benign forms of cannibalistic love magic. And we can also remind ourselves, at another level, that perhaps the most startling case of sexual cannibalism of all time occurred consensually, between two educated Germans, less than ten years ago. In 2001 Armin Meiwes posted an Internet advertisement requesting 'a well-built 18 to 30-year-old to be slaughtered and then consumed'. He in fact received several responses from people who later backed out of the proposed transaction. Finally, on 9 March, Bernd Jürgen Brandes went to Meiwes' home, having conscientiously made his will and booked a day off work. Meiwes severed Brandes' penis, which would have been eaten had it not been badly overcooked (with garlic, pepper, wine and salt) by Meiwes. Later, Meiwes butchered Brandes' corpse quite systematically and ate parts of it for some time after the killing.

There is no ambiguity about the basic facts of this case: the events are on videotape. Whilst Meiwes and Brandes obviously fall into a very small minority in one sense, it is surely no accident that this event occurred in the early twenty-first century, rather than (say) the early seventeenth. Whatever the exact nature of its psychology, the pact was broadly a product of an era in which sexuality is a very basic form of cultural and personal definition. Perhaps strangest of all is the evidently consensual nature of the killing and cannibalism. Whilst Brandes' mental state has been queried, the case made legal history just because it was so difficult to accuse Meiwes of straightforward murder, and he was ultimately convicted only of manslaughter, thus being sentenced to just eight years' imprisonment. The apparent agreement of the two men makes the incident very different from the many cases of cannibalistic sexual murder documented throughout the twentieth century. It is almost as if, so deep inside the post-Romantic era, Meiwes and Brandes took this step in order to enter into new realms of cannibal intimacy, after so many tamer variants of such psychology had been enacted. We must also bear in mind that, even if Meiwes and Brandes themselves were just a minority of two, several people did initially respond to the request.

People who are prepared to kill or die for sex or for love potions clearly have to be taken seriously. At the same time, whilst their startled peers are able to at least partly comprehend their behaviour (in a way that Milton or Marlowe probably could not have done), such people are engaging in actions which are socially meaningful, rather than cosmically meaningful. They are not, like so many patients of the early modern era, using human skull or skull-moss in the belief that it contains emanations from the stars, or a distillation of the human soul.

It might well seem apt to end a book full of strange and disgusting facts with the strange and disgusting tale of the two German love cannibals. But there remains one late element of the afterlives of medicinal cannibalism which is arguably just as strange, and which now has a topical counterpart that is no less shocking than the pact of 2001.

Social and medicinal cannibalism

In our own times there have been a few relatively benign (arguably even commendable) uses of the human body which can be broadly linked to the traditions of medicinal cannibalism. For a long while mummy was used in paint. 'Artists declared' (notes Cumming) 'that mummy-powder beaten up with oil, gave richer tones of brown than any other substance'.[91] How discerning one has to be to spot such tones in the National Gallery is difficult to say; but in the present day small amounts of this cannibalised pigment do survive: the Brighton artist Stig Evans, for example, still possesses a quantity of it.[92]

A much more recent development has been the use of human fat as fuel. In 2005 the Australian sportsman Peter Bethune had about 100 millilitres of fat removed from his own body, in order to contribute to the fuel for his boat, *Earthrace*, when it attempted a round-the-world speed record. As Mr Bethune weighed in at just 70 kilos, surgeon Martin Rees had considerable trouble finding anything at all, and the resulting fuel was sufficient to power the boat for just 2 kilometres. Bethune himself added that recovery was 'rather like waking up the day after a hard rugby game'.[93] There again, *Earthrace* was no ordinary vehicle. According to Jenna Higgins, of the National Biodiesel Board, a gallon of grease gives a gallon of fuel, with the same mileage obtained from conventional diesel. This potential was recently harvested by a Beverley Hills liposuction surgeon, Craig Allen Bittner, who for some time ran the SUVs of himself and his girlfriend on fat which (he claimed) had been willingly granted by his patients. Despite that, Bittner was in violation of human tissue laws, and in November 2008 he closed his once thriving practice and disappeared to South America.

Some environmental campaigners may feel that human tissue laws should be amended to exploit the green potential of unwanted human fat. Consider, for example, the aims of the Estonian company, Lipotechnica, with its vigorous promotion of 'Humanfuel' as a way to 'help commercial customers improve their environmental stewardship practice'. Although Lipotechnica's website (www.lipotechnica.com) is in fact an elaborate spoof, it is a spoof which has a certain resonance and significance in the era of rising fuel costs, melting ice caps, and Bittner's 'lipodiesel'. Perhaps one day scientists and green governments will unite to produce SUVs in which the driver can plug themself into a literally 'auto-motive' liposuction fuelling system, wolfing hamburgers as they drive, instead of pulling into petrol stations.

As we saw in chapter three, however, this kind of notion would have genuinely dark overtones for those native Bolivians and Peruvians still haunted by the kharisiri and the pishtaco. These strange roaming demons offer us probably the most memorable and potent encapsulation of a surprisingly widespread and enduring fear: powerful and invasive outsiders will quite literally carve up and process your body in the interests of science, industry, or medicine. Although in many cases this kind of attack is not actually cannibalistic, it falls under that label in at least two senses. First: it draws on the feeling that cannibalism is a fundamental form of invasion. Second: it quite overtly matches popular uses of the verb, 'to cannibalise', in which this term is taken to imply some degree of illegitimate (rather than just creative) re-use of 'parts from one unit for incorporation in, and completion of, another' (*OED*).

To put it another way: for those political minorities who genuinely believe that the powerful will do this to them, such fears project the taboo of cannibalism into a form of social myth. There is nothing that these powers will not do to us if we let them: they will even cannibalise us. In this area, the line between truth and fantasy can be a peculiarly hard one to draw. And, even when such tales are clearly false, as in the case of the 'fat for skin-creams' scandal of November 2009, these stories can have a certain socio-historical logic of their own.

In the Indian region of Simlah a few years prior to 1858, 'a report got abroad among the hillmen' at the sanatorium that 'the Governor-General had sent orders to have a certain quantity of human fat prepared and sent down to Calcutta; and that for this purpose the authorities were engaged in entrapping hill men, who were then killed, and boiled down for their fat'. Martin Richard Gubbins, the British civil servant who cited this rumour, lamented the 'working of ignorant and barbarous minds' and the 'suspicious credulity' which those 'residing in the enlightened countries of Europe' could scarcely have imagined.[94] Clearly, Gubbins had been talking to the wrong kind of Europeans: it was in Germany, among other places, that people *were* actually murdered for their fat, and for reasons arguably more credulous than these.

Moreover, whilst the fears of the Simlah Indians probably were unfounded, the British élite of this era evidently was capable of using human bodies in a more or less systematic, utilitarian way in the fields of industry and medicine. In his 2004 play *The History Boys*, Alan Bennett has the schoolteacher Hector contextualise Hardy's poem, 'Drummer Hodge', by telling his students how remarkable it is for this character to even bear a name. By contrast, the fate of most soldiers until this time had been not only anonymous but horrifically utilitarian: 'there was a firm in the nineteenth century (in Yorkshire, *of course*) which swept up their bones from the battlefields of Europe in order to grind them into fertiliser'. We could scarcely be further, here, from some of the early modern attitudes which underpinned medicinal cannibalism. Outwardly, the irreverence of practitioners was at times just as great as that of Victorian industry. Yet beneath all the graverobbing, dissection, pulping, grinding and processing there remained a stubborn thread of cosmic holism. Once, it had been religion which made the human body good enough to eat. In Bennett's tale, it is science which makes it too useful to waste.

Ruth Richardson, discussing an inquiry into Lambeth bodysnatchers in 1795, implies that in a sense the bone fertiliser of the nineteenth century was merely a larger-scale version of certain earlier, more ad hoc practices. For the Lambeth investigation was told that, 'human flesh has been converted into a substance like spermacetti, and candles made of it, and ... soap has also been made of the same material'.[95] As we know, whilst most of the anatomy specimens of this and later years came from grave theft, the furthest extreme of the medical corpse trade descended into outright murder.

And the crimes of Burke and Hare lead us not merely to Edinburgh, but up into the Highlands and Islands of Scotland. Beith explains that: 'the alarm spread by the activities of the notorious body-snatchers Burke and Hare ... had its repercussions well beyond urban Scotland'. Beith seems to believe that some Scottish country dwellers were actually murdered by those aiming to sell corpses to anatomists. But, she adds, 'there is also no doubt that the popular imagination could magnify and distort the extent of gruesome practice. Legends abounded'. Dr James Logan of the Caledonian Medical Society had often heard of

the 'wild' or 'black' doctors, a fearful brotherhood, whose great object was to obtain human bodies, and who 'scrupled not to take away life for their own evil ends'. Their feared weapon was the *black patch* – a highly adhesive plaster which, when suddenly applied over the mouth and nose, stopped all cries, and produced speedy suffocation. The feeing market at Inverness was said to be a special hunting-ground for luring country girls to a dreadful fate, doubtless before as well as after death. Thus far the stories might be credible, but the public imagination added a truly inventive rider. The object of the 'black doctors', it was claimed, was not anatomical, but pharmaceutical: the bodies being boiled down yielding a broth of such marvellous healing quality that people who were wasted with disease and racked with pain were speedily restored to perfect health and comfort by its use. Dr Logan added: 'I also heard it hinted that this terrible process was the source of castor oil!'[96]

Whatever the final truth of these fears, the details themselves stand as a potent distillation of alienation: both from medical science, and from those with political power over ordinary lives. Here the entire body is boiled into broth, producing a tonic of almost miraculous efficacy, a kind of densely fantastical human stock which seems to fuse the qualities of older blood medicines with the human pâté mashed up by French in the 1650s.

And, as Beith shrewdly notes, the broader context in which such terrors flourished was one which the Indian hillmen of the British Empire would have understood all too well. Adding that 'people who lived through that Highland era of dispossession and uncertainty might be excused for believing that such horrors were likely', she goes on to state that, when Sutherland men were required for the Crimean War in 1854, not one of the younger men enlisted: '"we have no country to fight for. You robbed us of our country and gave it to the sheep"'.[97] The date at which this minor social rebellion occurred amongst younger Scots might indeed have been exactly that of the Simlah fat panics, said by Gubbins to have fallen just a few years before 1858.

The belief in these Scottish 'black doctors' shows how such terrors could arise within what was nominally one unified country. Something similar was evident – on a smaller scale – amongst those Parisians who in 1750 'rioted over the disappearance of children from the city's streets, claiming that the king [Louis XV] had had them carried off for the sake of their blood – children's blood being the purest of all – to cure his rumoured leprosy'.[98] Around forty years later, indeed, some of those seen as responsible for the social oppression of that era were themselves partially eaten during the French Revolution. Back in Latin America, meanwhile, we cross the line from fantasy to stark reality, in a case which also occurred within one country. In the early 1990s in Colombia, death squads were more or less systematically murdering the urban poor. In such a context, we can well imagine terrified street people huddled together, exchanging yet more horrific tales of murdered friends or relatives, sold to the anatomy schools for dissection. Here there was a crucial difference. Such tales were true. Corpses were indeed being bought by Baranquilla medical school: we know this because one Oscar Rafael Hernandez actually survived the attempted killing and subsequent transaction in Colombia in 1992.[99]

We find ourselves, then, in a strange borderland, where the boundary between fact and fiction is thinly policed. Here the shadows of social demons flare up and retreat with the uncanny swiftness of London resurrection men, slipping through the lamplight into a Victorian alleyway. Take, for example, Stephen Frears' 2002 film, *Dirty Pretty Things*. After a hotel porter finds a human heart in a toilet bowl, he slides into an underworld of illicit organ surgery and a black market in human transplantation: a startling realisation of the 'urban myth' which sees a person waking from anaesthetic, in a bath filled with ice, and a telephone at their side to call the hospital. Perhaps this was just fantasy. Perhaps it was also a (well-motivated) mixture of terror and hatred which led Palestinians to believe that Israeli soldiers shot them with surgical precision, so that their organs could later be removed and sold on the black transplant market.

But amongst those who held them, these were very real beliefs. 'On April 4 1994', writes David Samper, 'in the Guatamalan village of San Cristobal Verapaz, American tourist June D. Weinstock was assaulted by a mob and suffered eight stab wounds, several broken limbs, and a fractured skull'. Weinstock was in fact lucky to escape with her life. She had been seen saying hello to a group of children, and with an eight-year-old boy temporarily missing, there was sparked a rumour that she had kidnapped him in order to have him killed, and his organs harvested for transplant back in North America. As Samper explains, neither tear gas nor the efforts of several dozen police could save Weinstock from the crowd of over a thousand local people when they smashed down the doors of the police station, dragged out the supposed culprit, and beat her with metal pipes. She ultimately escaped only because the police constable, José Israel Morales, persuaded her attackers that she was already dead. In Verapaz, then, this seemingly fantastical belief was not only fervent but very general. And Samper emphasises, moreover, that it 'surfaced and resurfaced in Latin America' from the mid-1980s to the late 1990s.[100] Once again, we do not have to believe it to see how it seemed possible to those involved.

As I write on 17 December 2010, the history of medical cannibalisation continues to unfold into ever darker regions. In November 2008 at Pristina airport in Kosovo, 'a 23-year-old Turkish man, Yilman Altun, fainted in front of customs officials … while he waited for his flight to Istanbul'. Officials 'lifted his shirt and discovered a fresh scar on his abdomen'. The next day, Kosovo police drove down a dirt road to a farmhouse some six miles away. Here they raided an establishment known as 'Medicus', where they discovered 'a 74-year-old Israeli, Bezalel Shafran, who … revealed he had paid €90,000 for a stolen kidney. Both "donor" and recipient identified' the Turkish surgeon Yusuf Ercin Sonmez as having been involved in the surgical procedure'.

This story derives from *Guardian* articles by Paul Lewis.[101] Futher details, and the wider context of this trade, are yet more startling. At the very top of the pyramid is said to be the Kosovan prime minister, Hashim Thaçi. Lewis wrote from Pristina, where a court assembled on the 14th heard of how 'desperate Russians, Moldovans, Kazakhs and Turks were lured into the capital "with the false promise of payments" for their kidneys. European Union prosecutor Jonathan Ratel told the court the organs had been illegally removed from victims and transplanted into wealthy recipients in the [Medicus] clinic ... Those who paid up to €90,000 (£76,400) for the black-market kidneys included patients from Canada, Germany, Poland and Israel, Ratel said ... He estimated there were 20–30 victims in the first eight months of 2008 alone, all tricked into believing they would be paid for their organs by middle men in Istanbul'.

'The story would be shocking enough', Lewis continues, 'if it ended there. But what the court did not hear is that the Medicus clinic has been linked in a Council of Europe report to a wider network of Albanian organised criminals. They are said to have had close links to senior officials in Kosovo's government, including ... Thaçi. Their supposed links to the underground organ market allegedly go back more than a decade when, in its most gruesome incarnation, the operation is said to have involved removing kidneys from murder victims'. Human rights activist Dick Marty claimed that, 'after medical checks and blood tests', a handful of Serbian captives 'were moved to a farmhouse in Fushë-Krujë, a town north of the Albanian capital, Tirana. According to the report, some of these prisoners became aware of the fate that awaited them, and are said to have pleaded not to be "chopped into pieces". The report adds: "the testimonies on which we based our findings spoke credibly and consistently of a methodology by which all of the captives were killed, usually by a gunshot to the head, before being operated on to remove one or more of their organs"'.

Lewis adds that 'organs are believed to have been shipped to Istanbul, in a criminal racket operated by Yusuf Sonmez, the same Turkish doctor wanted by Interpol for his alleged involvement in the Medicus clinic'. Nor was Sonmez the only medical professional involved. 'Huddled in the centre of the [court]room, in overcoats, were seven defendants alleged to have played some role in the racket. Among them were some of Kosovo's most respected physicians, including a former permanent secretary of health who is accused of abusing office to grant Medicus a false licence, and Dr Lutfi Dervishi, a urologist at the university hospital alleged to have set up the operation'.

Rightly or not, many of us probably find the involvement of professional doctors one of the most shocking parts of this tale. Amidst the almost limitless abyss of Nazi atrocities, those committed by doctors still remain especially chilling. Such feelings are not easy to analyse. They must come, in part, from the discomforting friction between ordinary medical ethics and ideals, and selfish criminal complicity in medical exploitation (or murder). Our sense of repulsion must also often be produced by the impression of a peculiarly cold-blooded scientific detachment (something all the more prominent in those Nazi experiments which were not motivated by desire for financial gain). Here the 'necessary inhumanity' once recommended to eighteenth-century medical students by the surgeon William Hunter has shifted radically beyond the necessities of orthodox medicine.[102]

Could all of the doctors involved in this practise have been oblivious of the murders of Serbian captives in 1999? We should remind ourselves that, in the case of Burke and Hare, the Edinburgh surgeon Dr Robert Knox has often been plausibly attacked merely for his failure to ask more searching questions as to where the anatomy murderers' oddly ready corpses were coming from. Beyond this, we have the figure of

Sonmez. Lewis reports that, after the alleged murders, the victims' kidneys 'were flown to Istanbul in ischemia bags ... A Washington-based intelligence source said the kidneys were sold to Sonmez'. As I write, this fifty-three-year-old surgeon remains the subject of an international manhunt.

It would be rash to make glib decisions as to whether or not Sonmez should take more blame for these crimes than Thaçi. The latter, after all, can reasonably be seen as more power hungry than a mere surgeon – he did not get to be Kosovan prime minister by accident. But there is very good reason for thinking that many public observers have stronger feelings about Sonmez than about Thaçi. The surgeon's two most popular nicknames at present are 'Doctor Vulture' and 'Doctor Vampire'. Once again, the historic echoes of medicinal cannibalism lead us back to that coffined lair of the Western world's most successful other-worldly spectre. In one realm, this demon might seem relatively benign – even useful (certain publishers and film-makers, indeed, could well be accused of drinking its blood with insatiable thirst). Tracking its blood-clotted footprints from the discreet blood-drinking of early Georgian barber shops, on through to Polidori, Stoker, and the oddly Victorian repressions of *Twilight*, we find the vampire acquiring much of its enduring popularity through its post-Enlightenment sexualisation. Somehow, drinking blood is much more darkly elegant than chewing even the most well-cooked flesh.

With Sonmez, we are on very different ground. His alleged crimes present a shadowy alliance between the vampire, the doctor, and that cannibal who 'cannibalises' 'parts from one unit for incorporation in, and completion of, another' (*OED*). For many, his supposed activities must seem to form the darkest possible inversion of ordinary medical practice and ethics. Is it worse to shoot someone in the head, or to painstakingly incise them, and utilise formidable surgical skills in removing their kidneys, knowing that they have been murdered for this purpose? Readers must decide this for themselves. But the collective decision of those who christened and rechristened 'Doctor Vampire' seems to have already been made. The broad logic of the label is clear enough – its bearer stands accused of plundering the most basic stuff of human life for illegitimate ends. Yet the term is clearly a little inexact for all that: the vampire, motivated by the grim necessity of survival, is surely less culpable than someone impelled by a cold drive for profit.[103]

How does this ongoing story compare to the broader sweep of the present book? Over 500 years ago Marsilio Ficino (a man who, in his time, was far more eminent than either Sonmez or Thaçi) proposed that the aged might rejuvenate themselves if they would 'suck the blood of an adolescent' who was 'clean, happy, temperate, and whose blood is excellent but perhaps a little excessive', drinking it 'the way leeches do, an ounce or two from a vein on the left arm barely opened'. We do not know for certain that this ever happened. But the notion would recur for some decades, and versions of it were indeed practised, through the proto-scientific mediations of men such as Robert Boyle. If it did happen? Well, those with vivid imaginations may be struck by the picture of a well-dressed old man, comfortably seated as he gulps down the hot red fluid from the punctured arm of his impoverished young donor. Yet, if you had a strong stomach, this was far from being the worst way to earn money which the Renaissance would offer. If all went well, you survived unharmed – perhaps also believing that some superfluous blood had been usefully removed from your veins.

By comparison, we have the Turkish donor Altun (described by Lewis as 'a desperate young Turk'). The beneficiary of his suffering, Bezalel Shafran, was 'a 74-year-old Israeli who had paid £76,400 for the black-market kidney he hoped would prolong his life'. Just what Shafran knew about the exact mechanics of that transaction we cannot yet say. But we can well imagine that some observers would see yet one more vampire at the centre of this tale. Altun was lied to, and treated so shoddily by the doctors involved that he would later faint in an airport queue. Perhaps just as seriously: Altun sold some of his old life in the utopian hope of a new life, a radically different future which he might gain by having his insides carved out. Perhaps the dashing of these hopes was as cruel as anything else in the whole extraordinary episode.

The case of Innocent VIII's blood transfusion is the closest parallel to that of Altun and other black-market organ donors. But the status of that tale finally remains uncertain. We have no definite evidence that physicians or their agents ever killed anyone solely for the purposes of corpse medicine. After death, they were certainly mutilated, dissected, plundered, torn and pulped – recast into a myriad startling new forms, their skulls rarefied into liquid distillations, flesh marinaded into scarlet tinctures, their skin belted around the waists of pregnant women, or even tugged onto the hands of those wearing Keogh's medicinal gloves. But the main crime was very clearly the dishonour of those already dead. As the long strange career of the medicinal cannibals finally began to disappear down the mossy byroads of popular culture and magic, a parodic physician on the London stage briefly acquired the disreputable label of 'Doctor Mummy'. But even this figure and his real-life counterparts never dreamed of the crimes supposedly performed by a twenty-first-century 'Doctor Vampire'.

It is in fact in the nineteenth century that we find one of the closest parallels to the alleged transplant murders of 1999. In Russia and Germany, people were very occasionally murdered solely for their fat. Yet the parallel quickly breaks down into the strangest irony. Those earlier killings must have appeared to educated peers to represent the nadir of primitive superstition and backwardness. But it was in part the post-Enlightenment striving for rational improvement which created the conditions that permitted the killings of 1999. Without numerous forms of medical and scientific technology, and without the professional training of the surgeons involved, the organs could not have been successfully removed, transported, and re-implanted. Here, some might say, is one result of scientific progress in a world which yet preserves radical social inequalities.

If the Kosovan organ murders were indeed a reality, then it is surely no accident that they should occur where and when they did. This region and this conflict saw some of the worst recent instances of tribal hatred and tribal atrocities. At first glance it might be tempting to compare some of these (and the organ murders themselves) with the tribal cannibalism of the Huron or Tupinamba. In each case we find violence inspired by a radical sense of otherness: enemies who confirm your identity by the hatred you bear them and the harm you do them. In each case such harm can be strikingly prolonged, calculating, painstaking. But finally there is something vital missing from such a parallel. That element is honour. Amongst the cannibal tribes, we find this embedded at the heart of the most unimaginable violence – deciding, for example, the post-mortem fate of the Antis' victim, who had (or had not) shown any sign of pain as he was carved and eaten alive.

We do not, by contrast, seem to find any honour in the case of the French Protestant who, in Auxerre in the 1570s, was ritually executed before having his heart 'plucked out, chopped in pieces, auctioned off, cooked on a grill and finally eaten with much enjoyment'.[104] Nor was it evident when Protestants in Piedmont had their organs spontaneously fried and eaten in 1655 – one of them allegedly being roasted alive on a pike.[105] The Brazilian cannibals who performed more honourable versions of such treatment had told Thevet that their victims 'have been always [our] mortal enemies'. In Europe, Christians managed to reproduce the same level of hatred amongst themselves in just a few generations.

It hardly needs emphasising that there was no shred of honour in the web of lies and calculation which ensnared Altun and others, and which in an earlier version may have impelled outright murder. But it is worth adding that to some this latter case might seem a grimly ironic conclusion to a century of technologically enabled atrocities, from the strafing of trench machine guns, through the gas chambers and the atom bomb. By comparison with the cruelties inflicted by the Huron upon their cannibal victim, the suffering undergone by Altun may seem slight. But after the hours of inconceivable tortures performed by this Canadian tribe, the subject died honourably, before the god held to be watching in the form of the rising sun. Between Altun and Shafran, by contrast, we find only the briefest, perhaps most accidental whisper of human contact: 'the Turkish donor and the Israeli recipient', writes Lewis, 'were laid down on beds beside each other before the kidney was exchanged. Both men would later confirm that their eyes met for a brief few seconds before the anaesthetic took effect'.[106]

NOTES

Introduction notes

1 At times Charles's chemists may have done this work; but, as we will see, it is almost certain that his personal interests prompted him to undertake it personally on more than one occasion (a view held by C.J.S. Thompson (see: *The Mystery and Art of the Apothecary* (1929; repr. Detroit: Singing Tree Press, 1971), 205)).

2 *The Apology and Treatise of Ambroise Paré* (1585), ed. Geoffrey Keynes (London: Falcon, 1952), 143.

3 *King Charles II* (London: Weidenfeld & Nicholson, 1979), 50.

4 See Malcolm Oster, 'Jonathan Goddard', new DNB. Thompson gives the sum as £1,500 (*Mystery and Art*, 205).

5 Fraser, *King Charles II*, 445.

6 Fraser, *King Charles II*, 441.

7 Ronald Hutton, *Charles the Second: King of England, Scotland, and Ireland* (Oxford: Clarendon Press, 1989), 421. Cf., also, Charles's request for the torture, in 1684, of certain suspects of the Rye House Plot (see Tim Harris, *Restoration: Charles II and his Kingdoms, 1660–1685* (London: Penguin, 2006), 365–66).

8 Keith Richards, with James Fox, *Life* (London: Weidenfeld & Nicholson, 2010), 546.

9 Daniel Korn, Mark Radice and Charlie Hawes, *Cannibal: A History of the People-Eaters* (London: Channel 4/Macmillan, 2001), 9–10.

Corpse medicine from the Middle Ages to Caroline England notes

1 Perhaps partly because it affected consciousness, epilepsy was at this time known as 'the sacred disease'.

2 Leo Kanner, 'The Folklore and Cultural History of Epilepsy', *Medical Life* 37.4 (1930): 167–214, 198; citing Pliny the Elder.

3 Vivian Nutton, in Lawrence I. Conrad, Michael Neve, Vivian Nutton, Roy Porter, and Andrew Wear, *The Western Medical Tradition: 800 BC to AD 1800* (Cambridge: Cambridge University Press, 1995), 55.

4 'Some have freed themselves from such a disease by drinking the hot blood from the cut throat of a gladiator: a miserable aid made tolerable by a malady still more miserable' (Celsus, *On Medicine*, trans. W.G. Spencer (London: Heinemann, 1948), I, 339).

5 Ferdinand P. Moog and Axel Karenburg, 'Between Horror and Hope: Gladiator's Blood as a Cure for Epileptics in Ancient Medicine', *Journal of the History of the Neurosciences* 12.2 (2003): 137–43, 139. Cf. also ibid. on Tertullian, who showed familiarity with the practice in around 197 AD.

6 'Between Horror and Hope', 138.

7 Owsei Temkin, *The Falling Sickness: A History of Epilepsy from the Greeks to the Beginnings of Modern Neurology* (Baltimore: Johns Hopkins University Press, 1994), 23. Cf. also 'Between Horror and Hope', 139.

8 *The Healing Hand: Man and Wound in the Ancient World* (Cambridge, Mass.: Harvard University Press, 1991), 401–3.

9 Moffett (d.1604), *Health's Improvement* (1655), 139–40. Democritus lived from *c.*460–370 BC; 'Miletus' is presumably the Greek philosopher, Thales of Miletus (*c.*624–546 BC); the physician Artemon is thought to have lived some time in or before the first century AD; Apollonius is evidently either the father or son of this name, both of whom were physicians in the second or first century BC. On Democritus see also Thorndike, *History*, IV, 61, who notes that a magician, Osthanes, living at the time of the Persian Wars, proposed blood-drinking as a medical remedy. Cf. also James Hart (*Klinike, or the Diet of the Diseased* (1633), 347), attacking those of the ancients who 'set down' the drinking of fresh blood 'as a remedy ... against ... the epilepsy'.

10 *Theatrum Mundi*, trans. John Alday (1566), T3r–v.

11 On Ancient Egyptian uses of the brain in medicine, see C.J.S. Thompson, *The Mystery and Art of the Apothecary* (1929; repr. Detroit: Singing Tree Press, 1971), 209. Other instances beyond Europe include Teflis (or Tbilisi) in Georgia, where in the late seventeenth century Sir John Chardin (1643–1713) heard from a wise woman that 'for inward pains of what sort soever', one should 'take potions of mummy', as well as drinking it 'for all sorts of falls, bruises and hurts' (*The Travels of Sir John Chardin into Persia ...* (1686), 234); and (allegedly) Turkey (see: *British Weekly Mercury* (London), Saturday, 29 January 1715).

12 Louise Noble, '"And Make Two Pasties of Your Shameful Heads": Medicinal Cannibalism and Healing the Body Politic in *Titus Andronicus*,' *ELH* 70.3 (2003): 677–708, 681–82.

13 *Falling Sickness*, 23.

14 Richard J. Evans, *Rituals of Retribution: Capital Punishment in Germany, 1600–1987* (Oxford: Oxford University Press, 1996), 94–95.

15 Cited in Temkin, *Falling Sickness*, 23.

16 *Falling Sickness*, 23; 'Between Horror and Hope', 139. Debate persists as to just when Aretaeus lived and wrote, with some claiming that he was dead by 90 AD, and others that his era was in fact that of the third century (Timothy S. Miller, Review of Giorgio Weber, *Areteo di Cappadocia* (1996), in *Bulletin of the History of Medicine* 73.1 (1999): 141–42).

17 'Between Horror and Hope', 139–40.

18 Simon Cordo of Genoa (d.1303) was a papal physician and the author (among other things) of *Synonyma Medicinae* (1292). On Cordo's travels in search of plants, see R.A. Donkin, *Between East and West: The Moluccas and the Traffic in Spices up to the Arrival of Europeans* (Philadelphia: American Philosophical Society, 2003), 123. On the *Synonyma* ('one of the most cited medical treatises of the 13th century'), see Lynn Thorndike, 'Some Thirteenth Century Classics', *Speculum* 2.4 (1927): 374–84, 379.

19 Karl H. Dannenfeldt, 'Egyptian Mumia: The Sixteenth Century Experience and Debate', *Sixteenth Century Journal* 16.2 (1985): 163–80, 163–65.

20 See Dannenfeldt, 'Egyptian Mumia', 165–67, on the enduringly mistaken belief that all mummies had been embalmed with bitumen; as well as on the role of the thirteenth-century Baghdad physician Abd Allatif. On the continuing value of mineral pitch in the late seventeenth century, see John Fryer (d.1733), *A New Account of East-India and Persia ... being nine years travels begun 1672 and finished 1681* (1698), 318.

21 Cf., however, the medieval physician Peter Aponensis (b.1250 AD), who apparently commended mummy, frankincense and dragon's blood against diseases of the heart

(*Treasure of Euonymus*, 272–73). Aponensis was also known as Petrus de Abano or Peter of Apona (for further details, see Lynn Thorndike, 'Peter of Abano and the Inquisition', *Speculum* 11.1 (1936): 132–33).

22 'Egyptian Mumia', 166–67.

23 'Egyptian Mumia', 167.

24 *A Most Excellent and Learned Work of Chirurgery*, trans. John Hall (1565), 65. Although some of this work is by Hall himself, the preface (by Hall's surgeon friend Thomas Gale) states that Hall's own explanatory table (which includes 'mumia' (72–73)) aimed to gloss terms *used by* Lanfranc (sig. Air). On Collenucius, see Thorndike, *History*, IV, 598. Brian A. Curran briefly notes the medical use of mummy from the twelfth century, but gives no further details (see *The Egyptian Renaissance: the Afterlife of Ancient Egypt in Early Modern Italy* (Chicago: University of Chicago Press, 2007), 283–84).

25 *The Treasure of Euonymus*, trans. Peter Morving (1559), 118.

26 *The Cure of Old Age*, trans. Richard Browne (1683), 108. 'Mine' here is evidently used in the sense of 'an abundant or constant source of supply; a store from which (something specified) may be obtained in plenty or whose supply is by no means exhausted' (*OED*, 1c fig.).

27 Quoted in Conrad Gesner, *The New Jewel of Health*, trans. George Baker (1576), 170r–v. Gustav Ungerer's DNB article on Baker points out that this work was 'a revamped translation of Gesner's *Thesaurus Euonymi Philiatri de Remediis Secretis* (1552)'.

28 Thorndike notes that there were at least three different versions of this letter. One was cited, around 1426, by a Sante Ardoini of Pesaro as 'The Book of the Distillation of Human Blood' (*History*, III, 78–80).

29 Thorndike points out that in one version of Arnold's letter the 'miracle' allowed the dying man (in that case a Count) to receive last rites (*History*, III, 78–80).

30 *New Jewel*, 169v–170r. Thorndike notes that the *Icocedron* of the fourteenth-century monk Walter of Odington (fl. 1330–47) contained a chapter on the separation of different elements from human blood, and that the fourteenth-century alchemist and prophet, John of Rupecissa, also gave instructions on its chemical analysis (*History*, III, 128–30, 358). For more on Walter's treatment of a distilled 'air', see: Robert James Forbes, *A Short History of the Art of Distillation* (Chicago: Chicago University Press, 1970), 64.

31 Cf., also, the tendency to associate the 'barbarity' of cannibalism with aggressive or martial drinking of enemies' blood: John Speed, *England, Wales, Scotland and Ireland Described and Abridged* (1627), Y5r.

32 While the *Oxford English Dictionary* still informs readers that 'vampire' was first used in English in 1734, the scholar Katherina Wilson has shown that it was in fact employed as a metaphor back in 1688 ('The History of the Word Vampire', *Journal of the History of Ideas* 46 (1985): 580–81).

33 On poison, see Heinrich Nolle (fl. 1612–19), *Hermetical Physic*, trans. Henry Vaughan (1655), 24–25.

34 On tubercles, see Paul Barbette (d.1666?), who mixes mummy with human fat and various other ingredients (*Thesaurus Chirurgiae* (1687), 214; cf. also ibid., 197, on a dram of human skull against ulcer of the bladder).

35 A relatively early reference (1575) to the efficacy of skull against epilepsy and fever comes from Giovanni Francesco Olmo, a Brescian physician who (notably) opposed 'superstitious remedies' (Thorndike, *History*, V, 230, 233). On the precise area of skull, see Thomas Bartholin, *Bartholin's Anatomy* (1668), 336.

36 See Barbette, *Thesaurus*, 162.

37 *Loimotomia, or, The Pest Anatomized* (1666), 150.

38 *The Encyclopedia of Folk Medicine: Old World and New World Traditions*, ed. Gabrielle Hatfield (Oxford: ABC Clio, 2004), 326.

39 *The Herbal or General History of Plants* (1633), 1263. This was first published in 1597.

40 Cf. British Library Sloane MS 104, which has 'Arabian' mummy from poorer corpses; 'Egyptian' from those of the nobility; mineral pitch; and 'Libyan' (i.e., sand mummies);

along with Paracelsus' new formula as a fifth kind (fols 74–75). I am very grateful to Arnold Hunt for bringing this manuscript to my attention. Piero Camporesi similarly subdivides mummy into that from dearer and cheaper forms of embalming. He omits mineral pitch and includes counterfeit mummies '"those made with *pissaphaltum*"' (*Bread of Dreams: Food and Fantasy in Early Modern Europe*, trans. David Gentilcore (Oxford: Polity Press, 1996), 49).

41 On these last two terms see, respectively, Fryer, *New Account*, 318, 333; and Adrian von Mynsicht, *Thesaurus and Armamentarium Medico-chymicum, or, A Treasury of Physic*, trans. John Partridge (1682), 68. The term 'common mummy' is used ambiguously by Girolamo Ruscelli (*A Very Excellent and Profitable Book [of] Medicines*, trans. Richard Androse (1659), 13). The Paracelsian Joseph Duchesne uses it to indicate mummy from embalmed corpses, rather than fresh ones (*A Brief Answer of Josephus Quercetanus*, trans. John Hester (1591), 33v–34r).

42 On Egyptian mummy, see Samuel Purchas, *Purchas his Pilgrimage* (1613), 466–67; for Paracelsian usage, see John Headrich, *Arcana Philosophia* (1697), 73. On 'mumia sincere' see Cornelius Schilander, *Cornelius Shilander his Chirurgery*, trans. S. Hobbes (1596), C3v. Cf. also Vincent Leblanc, *The World Surveyed*, trans. F.B. (1660), 168–69, for yet another category of 'right mummy'. This term is used ambiguously in Lemnius Levinus (d.1568), *An Herbal for the Bible*, trans. Thomas Newton (1587), 37.

43 For the former term, see Mynsicht, *Thesaurus*, 100; for the latter, see the surgeon John Hall in *A Most Excellent and Learned Work of Chirurgery* (1565), 72.

44 See, for example, Joannes Jonstonus, *An History of the Wonderful Things of Nature*, trans. anon. (1657), 97. Cf. John Hall: 'differing from this [mineral pitch] is that which the most of the Arabians do mention: who affirm it to result of the embalming or spicery of dead bodies at their burials' (*A Most Excellent ... Work*, 72). A 1653 English translation of a German work of 1629 uses 'Arabian mummy' to signify 'a certain composition of aloes, myrrh, crocos, and balsamum with which they do ... embalm dead bodies'. Although 'they' here might seem to imply the Arabians, the author's description of 'Egyptian mummy' as a distinct category suggests otherwise. This type comes from 'the common people', who 'were usually embalmed with asphaltos'. This implies that the 'Arabian mummy' is derived from the bodies of Egyptian nobles, and that Egyptian mummy was subdivided according to the class of the dead. It could also imply that high demand for Egyptian mummy had prompted use of all available corpses (see Andreas Tentzel, *Medicina Diastatica*, trans. Ferdinando Parkhurst (1653), 2; the same classification is found in Johann Schroeder, *Zoologia*, trans. anon. (1659), 52–53). Tentzel also shows that sand mummies could be described as 'Lybian mummy' (ibid., 3).

45 *A Most Excellent ... Work* (1565), 72.

46 Wilhelm Adolf Scribonius, *Natural Philosophy, or, A Description of the World* (1621), 30.

47 Interestingly, such writers occasionally present mineral pitch as the dominant element in Egyptian mummy. In the 1661 *Glossographia* of Thomas Blount, for example, the entry for '*Mumie* or *Mummie*' actually seems to prefer the variety which is 'digged out of the graves ... of those bodies that were embalmed' over 'the second kind', which 'is *only* an equal mixture of the Jews' Lime and bitumen, in Greek *pissasphaltum*' (first italic mine). Yet anyone who read just the very opening words of the entry would gather merely that 'mumia' was 'a thing like pitch sold by apothecaries', being 'hot in the second degree, and good against all bruisings, spitting of blood, and divers other diseases' (*Glossographia* (1661), Ddr; cf. also Edward Philips, *A New World of English Words* (1658)). Similarly, a work of 1580 is well aware that mummy is derived from Egyptian corpses, but opines that it is 'not much different from bitumen indaicum' (Thomas Newton, *Approved Medicines and Cordial Receipts* (1580), 32). Gordon Braden in new DNB notes that this book was compiled rather than written by Newton, who was a Church of England clergyman. Cf., also, the physician John Pechey, noting in 1694 that 'some think the virtue of mummy proceeds wholly from the aloes, wherewith bodies were wont to be embalmed' (*The Complete Herbal of Physical Plants* (1694), 201).

48 Pious readers may however be interested to know that some believed bitumen to have been employed by those 'who builded the tower of Babel', who 'used this in stead of mortar, as appeareth in Gen. chapter the 11' (Swan, *Speculum*, 302).

49 *Bread of Dreams*, 47. Camporesi here cites Carpi from a work of 1518, in which the author refers specifically to 'the old people of our family'.

50 On Montagna, see V.L. Bullough, 'Duke Humphrey and his Medical Collections', *Renaissance News* 14.2 (1961): 87–91, 91.

51 *The Noble Experience of the Virtuous Handy Work of Surgery*, trans. anon. (1525), MIv, R3v–R4r, O1r, O4v, N2r, N1v, O1v. For more on Brunswick, see Patsy A. Gerstner, 'Surgical Instruments, from Brunschwig's Cirurgia', *Technology and Culture* 7.1 (1966): 70–71.

52 *Noble Experience*, N1v, R3v.

53 *Noble Experience*, R4r.

54 If the blood was indeed drunk, it would of course have been metabolised like ordinary food, rather than transferred into the bloodstream.

55 For much more on this incident, see: Lauro Martines, *April Blood: Florence and the Plot Against the Medici* (London: Pimlico, 2003), esp. 111–37.

56 People of course grew up rather more quickly in the Renaissance. Both Francis Bacon and John Donne entered university at age twelve, and their peers would have been only two or three years older.

57 On Alexander's suitably ironic death, see J.N.D. Kelly, *Oxford Dictionary of Popes* (Oxford: Oxford University Press, 1997), 254.

58 Innocent's Bull of 1484 – 'Summis Desiderantes' – specifically accused men and women of using devilish aid to kill cattle and spoil vines, fruits and harvests (see *Witchcraft in Europe, 400–1700: a Documentary History*, ed. Alan Charles Kors and Edward Peters (Philadelphia: University of Pennsylvania Press, 2001), 178). H.P. Broedel emphasises that Kramer and Sprenger used the Bull as a preface to *Malleus* and that 'the text proclaimed itself to be as authoritative as the authors' ingenuity could make it' (*The Malleus Maleficarum and the Construction of Witchcraft* (Manchester: Manchester University Press, 2003), 19). Brian Levack argues that Innocent's Bull was quite similar to other such papal documents, and that its notoriety derives from its use in *Malleus* (*The Witchcraft Sourcebook* (London: Routledge, 2004), 119).

59 Innocent was paid off by Bayazid II to keep his captive brother and rival Djem from returning to Turkey (see: Kelly, *Oxford Dictionary of Popes*, 252; Bernhard Schimmelpfennig, *The Papacy*, trans. James Sievert (Oxford: Blackwell, 1992), 250).

60 Schimmelpfennig, *Papacy*, 242; Kelly, *Oxford Dictionary of Popes*, 252. For further details of Innocent's military engagements, see also David Chambers, *Popes, Cardinals and War: the Military Church in Renaissance and Early Modern Europe* (London: I.B. Tauris, 2006), 89–93.

61 For overviews of the blood libel and its variants, see: *The Blood Libel Legend: A Casebook in Anti-Semitic Folklore*, ed. Alan Dundes (Madison: University of Wisconsin Press, 1991); Bill Ellis, 'De Legendis Urbis: Modern Legends in Ancient Rome', *Journal of American Folklore* 96.380 (1983): 200–208; James Shapiro, *Shakespeare and the Jews* (Columbia University Press, 1996). On the impressive persistence of the myth, see especially: Frank Felsenstein, *Anti-Semitic Stereotypes: A Paradigm of Otherness in English Popular Culture, 1660–1830* (Johns Hopkins University Press, 1995), xiii; Shapiro, *Shakespeare and the Jews*, 89. In 2007 the historian Ariel Toaff (himself the son of a rabbi) published *Pasque di Sangue: Ebrei d'Europa e Omicidi Rituali* ('Passovers of Blood: The Jews of Europe and Ritual Murders'), in which he argued that that some Christian children may have been killed by '"a minority of fundamentalist Jews of Ashkenazi origin"'. After considerable controversy, Toaff finally withdrew the first edition of the book from circulation. The revised, 2008 edition of the work accepted that blood libel tales were Christian fabrications. For more details, see Sabina Loriga, 'The Controversies over the Publication of Ariel Toaff's "Bloody Passovers"', *Journal of The*

Historical Society 8.4 (2008): 469–502. I am very grateful to Mauro Spicci for drawing Toaff's work to my attention.

62 Hunter was talking specifically about anatomy, and there is some reason for thinking that his notion was influenced by Enlightenment views of medicine and science. Yet – while such a tactic could have been a problematic one for an era which preferred to see the physician as 'the helper of God' – versions of this mentality can be seen in figures such as the medieval surgeon Henri de Mondeville (1260–1320) and the French royal surgeon Ambroise Paré (Hunter cited by Ruth Richardson, *Death, Dissection and the Destitute* (London: Phoenix, 2001), 31; on Mondeville, see Marie-Christine Pouchelle, *The Body and Surgery in the Middle Ages*, trans. Rosemary Morris (Cambridge: Polity, 1990), 76–77; for Paré see Lawrence, Conrad, and Neve, *Western Medical Tradition*, 298).

63 *Countess Dracula: the Life and Times of the Blood Countess, Elisabeth Báthory* (London: Bloomsbury, 1997), 229.

64 Louis XI (1423–83) was thought to have drunk the blood of children to cure his leprosy (for the belief, see: *The Memoirs of Philip de Comines* (1723), 76; Reay Tannahill, *Flesh and Blood: a History of the Cannibal Complex* (London: Abacus, 1996), 87, citing Soane, *NQ* 28 February 1857, 162 ('he vehemently hoped to recover by the human blood which he took and swallowed from certain children'); Tannahill's source does not look wholly reliable). In the seventeenth century Andreas Tentzel, stating that 'a bath made of the blood of infants, for curing the leprosy … hath rendered certain kings hateful to the common people' (*Medicina Diastatica*, 76), implies that versions of this story tended to cluster about unpopular rulers. P.M. Kendal claims that, during his last sickness, Louis sent a sea captain in search of great sea tortoises, hoping to drink their blood for his supposed leprosy (in fact only a skin inflammation). Kendal believes that this may account for the story 'put about by the princes after his death, that he drank infants' blood' (*Louis XI* (London: Allen & Unwin, 1971), 365).

65 For more on the fifteenth-century attempt to have Albertus canonised, see: David J. Collins, 'Albertus, *Magnus* or *Magus*? Magic, Natural Philosophy, and Religious Reform in the Late Middle Ages', *Renaissance Quarterly* 63.1 (2010): 1–44.

66 *The Book of Life*, trans. Charles Boer (Texas: University of Dallas Press, 1980), 57. I owe the initial reference to Ficino's blood theory to Piero Camporesi, who records it in *Bread of Dreams*.

67 *Book of Life*, 56.

68 Valerie Fildes, who cites this, notes also that human milk was a common treatment for pulmonary tuberculosis from the fourteenth to the nineteenth century (*Wet Nursing: A History from Antiquity to the Present* (Oxford: Blackwell, 1988), 73, 34).

69 See, for example, Ambroise Paré: 'milk is none other thing than blood made white by the power of the kernels that are in the dugs' (*Works*, trans. Thomas Johnson (1634), 946–47).

70 Cf. also the physician Robert Bayfield, who in a work on tumours in 1662 advises that liver spots and accompanying fevers can be treated by 'man's blood distilled with breast-milk' (*Tractatus de Tumoribus Praeter Naturam* (1662), 68).

71 *Bread of Dreams*, 45. There is a certain degree of irony in this, given that it was broadly such a cure which aimed to save one pope's life, and that his next-but-one successor then effectively murdered the more famous Savonarola, who was indeed Giovanni's grandson. Whilst Thorndike (*History*, IV, 183) gives 1464 as the date of Savonarola's death, Y.V. O'Neill thinks that he may have lived until 1468 (see 'Michele Savonarola and the Blighted Twin Phenomenon', *Medical History* 18 (1974): 222–39, 222). Another Italian work of 1566 implies that distilled blood was quite familiar by this time, referring as it does, with relatively coded brevity, to 'the elixir, or medicine to conserve the life of man'. While the author thinks that human blood should not be used (for medical reasons) he implies that others generally do so, and elsewhere recommends 'human blood rectified' as an alchemical ingredient (Giovan Battista Agnello, *A Revelation of the Secret Spirit*, trans. R[obert] N[apier] (1623)), 63–64, 55.

Agnello's work first appeared in Italian in 1566, and was itself a translation of an anonymous Latin book of just eight pages (Thorndike, *History*, V, 624). For more on Agnello (who was living in London in Elizabethan times), see: Katherine Shrieves, 'Mapping the Hieroglyphic Self: Spiritual Geometry in the Letters of John Winthrop, Jr, and Edward Howes (1627–40)', *Renaissance Studies*, published online, 14 January 2010; Deborah E. Harkness, *The Jewel House: Elizabethan London and the Scientific Revolution* (London: Yale University Press, 2008), 9, 142–43, 149, 158, 170, 174–78, 213, 282. Harkness not only identifies Napier as the 'R.N.' of the translation, but shows that certain of Agnello's interests were sufficiently worldly to attract a visit from William Cecil in 1577. The fifteenth-century murderer Gilles de Rais was supposedly persuaded by a monastic alchemist that the blood of the children he murdered for sexual purposes could be used in alchemy (see Tannahill, *Flesh and Blood*, 92–93).

72 *The Virtuous Book of Distillation* (1528), M2r–v. This work first appeared in German in 1512.

73 *Juice of Life: The Symbolic and Magic Significance of Blood* (New York: Continuum, 1988), 31. In a 1580 translation of some of Fioravanti's writings there are several references to dangerously wounded men cured by 'our quintessence' (33v, 35r–v, 37v–38r). Although Fioravanti does not give the full recipe for this, his 'syrup of quintessence' is indeed said to have revived 'those that are half dead' and to have 'done miracles'. This contains twelve ounces of a 'pure rectified *aqua vitae*' which sounds very much like the 'rectified' fifth essence of human blood (*A Short Discourse … Upon Chirurgery*, trans. John Hester (1580), 55v (cf. also the 'elixir vitae' of Arnold of Villanova (*New Jewel*, 170r)). This work was partially translated by Thomas Hill and passed to Hester on Hill's death in 1574 (Harkness, *Jewel House*, 88–89). For more on Hill, see John Considine, new DNB. Cf. also, more broadly, the Italian natural philosopher Giambattista della Porta, on a mummy elixir which, 'being anointed on the lips or nostrils, reviveth the soul … ' (*Natural Magic*, trans. anon. (1658), 275; this work first appeared in 1558).

74 *Juice of Life*, 29–30.

75 *The Vanity of Arts and Sciences*, trans. anon. (1676), 302–3.

76 'Egyptian Mumia', 176, citing *Paradoxorum Medicinae* (Basle, 1535).

77 Thorndike, *History*, V, 445, 454. Thorndike also notes that the anatomist Alessandro Benedetti and the German physician Euricius Cordus opposed the use of corpse medicines around this time (V, 454).

78 Gesner, *New Jewel of Health*, 145r; Suavius (born Jacques Gohorry) is cited by Thorndike (*History*, V, 637, 639). In the view of Charles Webster, Gesner 'regarded his fellow countryman Paracelsus with a mixture of admiration and fright' (*From Paracelsus to Newton: Magic and the Making of Modern Science* (Cambridge: Cambridge University Press, 1982), 5).

79 Quoted in *Medicina Diastatica*, 8. On Paracelsus' iconoclasm, see Robert Burton: 'Paracelsus did that in physic, which Luther in divinity' (*Anatomy of Melancholy* (1621), 467). Cf. Laurence Brockliss and Colin Jones on the 'Paracelsian heresy' (*The Medical World of Early Modern France* (Oxford: Clarendon Press, 1997), 119).

80 Lynn Thorndike notes that most of Paracelsus' writings existed only in manuscript form when he died, but that they began to be published extensively around twenty years after his death (*History*, V, 618, 620).

81 Jonstonus, *An History* … , 98.

82 *Secreti Nuovi* first appeared under Ruscelli's pseudonym, Alexis of Piedmont. On this and the work's popularity, see: William Eamon and Françoise Paheau, 'The Accademia Segreta of Girolamo Ruscelli: A Sixteenth-Century Italian Scientific Society', *Isis* 75.2 (1984): 327–42, 330.

83 *A Very Excellent … Book*, 20, 12; 19–20 (2nd set of pages). Ruscelli's phrase in the second case is 'the wolf', now glossed by the *OED* as 'a name for certain malignant or erosive diseases in men and animals' (7a).

84 *The Third and Last Part of the Secrets of the Reverend Master Alexis of Piemont* (1562), 3r, 32.

85 *Theatrum Mundi*, trans. John Alday (1566), T3r; *New Jewel*, 44v, 66v, 137v.

86 *New Jewel*, 227v–228r. As we have seen, this book also recommends what looks like human fat ('grease of mumia' (*New Jewel*, 145r)) in a balm to treat wounds of the bones.

87 *The Apology and Treatise of Ambroise Paré* (1585), ed. Geoffrey Keynes (London: Falcon, 1952), 143.

88 On this and related issues, see: Nicholas Jewson, 'Medical Knowledge and the Patronage System in 18th-Century England', *Sociology* 8 (1974): 369–85; Margaret Pelling, *Medical Conflicts in Early Modern London* (Oxford: Oxford University Press, 2003), 226.

89 Cf. John Carvel, 'Patients to Rate and Review their GPs on NHS Website', *Guardian*, 30 December 2008.

90 Howard Wilcox Haggard, *Devils, Drugs and Doctors: the Story of the Science of Healing from Medicine-man to Doctor* (Wakefield: EP Publishing, 1975), 324.

91 See: Mabel Peacock, 'Executed Criminals and Folk Medicine', *Folklore* 7 (1896): 268–83, 270.

92 For France, see also Joseph Duchesne, *A Brief Answer*, 33v–34r.

93 Thorndike points out that Brasavola, for example, was using dissections as a source of human fat (*History*, V, 454).

94 Allen G. Debus notes that, despite their involvement with France, the early Paracelsians Severinus and Guinter 'did not affect the development of chemical medicine' during their years in France (*The French Paracelsians: The Chemical Challenge to Medical and Scientific Tradition in Early Modern France* (Cambridge: Cambridge University Press, 1991), 21). Laurence Brockliss and Colin Jones state that 'most first-generation Paracelsians in France were not graduate physicians'. They add that the Protestant rulers of the independent kingdom of Navarre patronised Paracelsian healers from the mid-sixteenth century, and court patronage continued to be important into the next century, despite changes of monarch. Even though the universities managed to promote a judgement threatening death for those who taught '"any maxim contrary to ancient and approved doctors"', Paracelsians were protected by Richelieu around this time, and were especially prominent from 1624–42 (*Medical World*, 123–25).

95 Cited in Camporesi, *Bread of Dreams*, 47.

96 *A Most Excellent … Work*, 72–73.

97 See, for example, Pierre Pomet, *A Complete History of Drugs*, 3rd edn (1737), 229. Cf. also James Howell, *Lustra Ludovici* (1646), 5.

98 Unless otherwise stated, all biographical details on Bullein are from DNB article by Patrick Wallis. The relative novelty of some of Bullein's therapies may have been partly responsible for an accusation of poisoning made against him in 1560.

99 The Greek word 'theriac', originally relating to venomous animals and later to antidotes, came to mean 'treacle' in the Middle Ages.

100 *Bullein's Bulwark Bulwark of Defence Against all Sickness* (1562), 32r (third set of pages), 62v. Cf. also 62v for a mixture of 'dragon's blood, plantain water, madder', 'mumia, tempered together and drunk' for 'great bruises, bloody fluxes', and (applied topically) to staunch wounds. 'Cassiafistula' is another name for senna leaves.

101 *Bulwark*, 12r–v, 38v (3rd page set). In the second case, the *OED* defines Bullein's term 'epithem[a]' as 'any kind of moist, or soft, external application'.

102 *Bulwark*, 62v. I have been unable to find out precisely what 'mariarum water' is.

103 *A Needful, New, and Necessary Treatise of Chyrurgery* (1575), 56r, 21r.

104 *Antidotary Chyrurgical* (1589), 3, 4, 5, 6, 9, 13, 14, 15, 22, 64, 69, 72, 89, 98, 101, 195, 208, 215; for ulcers and inflammations, see 14, 22, 89–90; for a Paracelsian plaster, see 265.

105 *A Proved Practise for all Young Chirurgians* (1588), 27–28, 49–50. On the friendship of Banister and Clowes, see I.G. Murray, 'William Clowes', new DNB.

106 Cf. Harkness, *Jewel House*, 83, who emphasises that Banister was 'one of the few men in England' licensed 'to practice both physic and surgery'.

107 Although the Lumleian started in 1584, Gweneth Whitteridge argues that the first actual dissection was in 1588 (see *William Harvey and the Circulation of the Blood* (London: Macdonald, 1971), 86). When Holinshed states that the lectures were 'to

begin to be read in London, in Anno 1584, the sixth day of May' (*Chronicles*, 3 vols (London, 1586), II, 1349, 1369) he could well be referring to purely oral lectures, without dissection (and this would also fit 6 May, a rather late, possibly warm, date for handling corpses). For more on the probable influence of the surgeons, see Elizabeth Lane Furdell, *Publishing and Medicine in Early Modern England* (Woodbridge: University of Rochester Press, 2002), 20–21.

108 Search made 15 March 2010.

109 Richard Hakluyt, *Principal Navigations* (1599), 201. For Turberville, see below.

110 Wecker, *A Compendious Chirurgery*, trans. John Banister (1585), 296–97, 311–12, 316, 347; Levinus Lemnius, *An Herbal for the Bible*, trans. Thomas Newton (1587), 37; *A Brief Answer of Josephus Quercetanus*, 2r, 6v, 33v–34r; *The Sclopotary of Josephus Querceta-nus*, trans. John Hester (1590), 52, 69, 77; *A Hundred and Fourteen Experiments of ... Paracelsus*, trans. John Hester (1596), 62, 67, 68; *Cornelius Shilander his Chirurgery*, C3r–v.

111 Cf., also, its titular self-description as 'gathered from the most worthy learned, both old and new'. One of the few people in England to rival Hall's early interest in Paracelsus was John Dee (see Webster, *From Paracelsus to Newton,* 5).

112 *A Most Excellent ... Work*, 20, 21, 43, 61, 66. Petrus Andreas Matthiolus (1500–1577), was an Italian physician and author of a 1544 commentary on Dioscorides. For more on Matthiolus, see John M. Riddle, *Contraception and Abortion from the Ancient World to the Renaissance* (London: Harvard University Press, 1992), 149–51; Harkness, *Jewel House*, 78. For Banister, see *Antidotary*, 143, 265, 292. On the relative rarity of the word 'mummy' in the sixteenth century, see also: Philip Schwyzer, 'Mummy is Become Merchandise: Literature and the Anglo-Egyptian Mummy Trade in the Seventeenth Century', in *Re-orienting the Renaissance*, ed. Gerald Maclean (London: Palgrave, 2005), 66–87.

113 Harkness explains that Baker in fact received 'an incomplete draft translation of *The New Jewel* from Thomas Hill, a collector of books and manuscripts and an avid student of nature who died before completing his project' (*Jewel House*, 88).

114 *The Method of Physic* (1583), 32. As well as pointing out that this book went through seven editions to 1652, K.A. James in the new DNB also notes that 'Barrow's is an empirical medicine, one in which practice – and practical knowledge – serve to extend the boundaries of the art of medicine. "Arte", argues Barrow, "is weake without practise"'. Part of Barrow's treatment for epilepsy, which uses two red-hot frying pans held over the patient's head (ibid.), is nothing if not ingeniously empirical.

115 *The Whole Course of Chirurgery* (1597), Ii3r–v. As well as having founded the Glasgow Faculty of Physicans and Surgeons, Lowe was surgeon to Henri IV while in France, and Helen M. Dingwall thinks that he may also have 'become a master surgeon (academic, or "gown-surgeon") of the College of St Côme' (DNB).

116 *Jewel House*, 57–96.

117 *Jewel House*, 61.

118 Indeed, it is also possible that such remedies were personally employed by Clowes and Baker, who at one point fell to blows (Harkness, *Jewel House*, 84). On the far more common tendency to settle arguments by violence in this period, see Lawrence Stone, *The Family, Sex and Marriage in England 1500–1800* (Harmondsworth: Penguin, 1979), 77–78. For individual cases see also, Leonardo Fioravanti, *A Short Discourse* (1580), 30r; Lucinda Beier, 'Seventeenth-century English Surgery: the Casebook of Joseph Binns', in *Medical Theory, Surgical Practice: Studies in the History of Surgery*, ed. Christopher Lawrence (London: Routledge, 1992), 48–84, 50–51, 58, 59; Arthur Ponsonby, *More English Diaries* (London: Methuen, 1927), 66; *Universal Spectator and Weekly Journal*, 23 October 1736.

119 Thorndike, *History*, V, 224. All information on Russwurin from Harkness, *Jewel House*, 78–79; see also ibid., 56–96, and 81, for the opinion of the Paraclesian John Hester, who thought Russwurin '"a wise alchemist"'.

120 Charles Goodall, *The Royal College of Physicians of London ... [with] an historical account of the College's proceedings against empirics and unlicensed practisers* (1684), 351–52. F.V. White

in new DNB states that Anthony was brought before the College six times; that he narrowly escaped prison in the last instance; and that he ultimately became rich, perhaps partly because of the patronage of James I. For more on Plat (or Platt), see article in new DNB (Sidney Lee, rev. Anita McConnell).

121 *Medicine and Magic in Elizabethan London: Simon Forman, Astrologer, Alchemist, and Physician* (Oxford: Clarendon Press, 2005), 214. On the rather different status of itinerant, unofficial practitioners in Italy, see: David Gentilcore, *Medical Charlatanism in Early Modern Italy* (Oxford: Oxford University Press, 2006).

122 *Christ's Tears over Jerusalem*, 2nd edn (1594), *Works of Thomas Nashe*, II, 184.

123 It is also worth noting that, in *The Unfortunate Traveller*, in 1594, Nashe's description of the Jewish physician Zachary tells how, 'out of bones, after the meat was eaten off, he would alchemize an oil that he sold for a shilling a dram'. This may or may not signal Nashe's awareness of medicines distilled from human bones; but the fact that Zachary uses animal bones does not rule out the possibility (*Unfortunate Traveller* (1594), M2v).

124 *The Merry Wives of Windsor*, 5.3, 16–18.

125 *Book of Falconry*, 78.

126 The early modern term for this would probably have been 'imagination' or 'fancy' (cf. for example Robert Boyle, *Of the Reconcileableness of Specific Medicines to the Corpuscular Philosophy* (1685), 126–27).

127 *Book of Falconry*, Biir.

128 *Book of Falconry*, 215–16. 'Castings' in this context refers to the *OED*'s sense 3c: in *Falconry*, 'anything given to a hawk to cleanse and purge her gorge, whether it be flannel, thrummes, feathers, or such like' (Latham, *Falconry* (1615)).

129 *Book of Falconry*, 218, 255.

130 On diet, see ibid., 280–81.

131 We should note, however, that the prefatory poem was Turberville's own work.

132 *Book of Falconry*, 280–81, 343.

133 *Book of Falconry*, 280.

134 Given that it seems to be Turberville himself speaking when he says that 'this is a very good receipt [of Cornarus], but not so good as this' of Manoli, it is possible that he himself had some practical experience when he wrote.

135 *Ornithology* (1678), 400, 431.

136 *The Gentleman's Recreation in Four Parts, viz. hunting, hawking, fowling, fishing* (1686), 81, 84. Although Turberville is not credited at these points, phrasing is almost identical to that of 1575. For citations of Turberville, see 7, 111, 123. Cf., also, 50.

137 The author adds sharply that 'such manner of feeding of them is stark naught, and maketh their flesh unsavoury in eating, and very prejudicial unto health' but does not seem to doubt that the practice occurs (*Maison Rustique*, trans. Richard Surphlet (1616), 646). Estienne's work first appeared in Latin as *Praedium Rusticum* in 1554. A French version, translated by Estienne's son-in-law Jean Liébault, was published as *Maison Rustique* in 1564.

138 See: César de Rochefort, *The History of the Caribby-Islands* (1666), 305; Gervase Markham, *The Husbandman's Jewel* (1695), 35; Pomet, *Complete History of Drugs* (1694), 229. De Rochefort's book was first published anonymously in Rotterdam in 1658.

139 S. Mendyk's new DNB article on Blome states: 'Blome has been accused of lack of originality and of employing hack writers for a pittance ... He acted more as compiler or editor than as author of his best-known work outside of the cartographic field, The Gentleman's Recreation (1686) ... More credit for this work has been given to Nicholas Coxe and to prominent engravers employed in its production'.

140 *The Gentleman's Recreation in Two Parts* (1686), 191. For another recipe, see Gervase Markham, *The Husbandman's Jewel* (1695), 35.

141 *Sermons*, IV, 326–27, Whitehall, Lent, 1622/3.

142 *Sermons*, IV, 333.

143 *Gentleman's Recreation*, 182.

144 Cf. 'white great maggots … to be fed with sheeps tallow, and beasts' livers cut small' (ibid., 182). The Belgian chemist Jean Baptiste van Helmont also claimed to have cured the wounds of horses using mummy (albeit in his own distinctive way; see *A Ternary of Paradoxes*, trans. Walter Charleton (1650), 55).

145 *Mystical Bedlam* (1615), 51.

146 John Keogh, *Zoologia Medicinalis Hibernica* (Dublin, 1739), 102. For a satirical glance at this problem, see also: John Webster, *The Tragedy of the Duchess of Malfi* (1623), D1v.

147 For Donne's belief in witches, see: *Sermons*, IX, 96. Rather differently, even the commendably sceptical Reginald Scot believed that 'to bring apparitions and spirits they make a strange fume of a man's gall, and the eyes of a black cat' – taking this as one of 'many *natural* compositions, which have very stupendous effects of themselves' (*Discovery of Witchcraft* (1665), 69, 68, italic mine; this book first appeared in 1584).

148 *The Works of Benjamin Jonson* (1616), 951. The performance of 1609, including the queen, occurred at Whitehall on 2 February. Cf., also, a note keyed to the same work at 946. On use of infants' fat by witches, see also: *Macbeth*, 4.1, 23; William Foster, *Hoplocrisma-spongus: or, A Sponge to Wipe Away the Weapon-salve* (1631), 7–8; Heywood, *The Hierarchy of the Blessed Angels* (1635), 606 (on use of this and adult fat, as well as bone, to render them impervious to pain); John Banks, *Cyrus the Great* (1696), 5. For a male magician's imagined use of the fat of strangled infants to feed his familiar spirit, see: John Crown, *The History of Charles the Eighth of France* (1672), 61.

149 Cf., however, the famous reference to 'witches' mummy' in *Macbeth* (4.1, 24).

150 On the legendary associations between the earliest Christians and cannibalism, (as cited by Tertullian (*c*.150–220 AD)), see: Ellis, 'De Legendis Urbis', 201–3.

151 Featley, *The Grand Sacrilege of the Church of Rome* (1630), 293–94.

152 *Grand Sacrilege*, 268–69.

153 *Transubstantiation Exploded* (1638), 83–85.

154 *Maison Rustique* (1616), 457.

155 As well as English, the work was translated into German, Dutch, Italian and Scandinavian languages.

156 *Maison Rustique*, 206, 42.

157 Joan Lane, *John Hall and his Patients: The Medical Practice of Shakespeare's Son-in-Law* (Stratford: Alan Sutton, 1996), 53–55. I am grateful to Margaret Pelling for alerting me to this reference.

158 *Sylva Sylvarum* (1627), 261.

159 *Sylva Sylvarum*, 265.

160 *Poems*, 65, 384. For this latter view, cf. also: Donne, *Sermons*, VII, 257; and the variant of John Oldham: 'Vilest of that viler sex, who damn'd us all! … / … Mummy by some dev'l inhabited' ('A Satire upon a Woman … ', *Works* (1684), 142). For another possible echo, see Cyrano de Bergerac, on woman as 'that precious mummy' (*Satyrical Characters* … , trans. 'a person of honour' (1658), 60).

161 'Donne and Paracelsus: An Essay in Interpretation', *Review of English Studies* 25.98 (1949): 115–23, 115–16, 117–18. Donne's reference to a 'cold quicksilver sweat' may also be relevant here ('The Apparition', *Poems*, 43).

162 *Letters,* I, 178, to Sir H[enry] G[oodyer], n.d.

163 *Anatomy*, l.57, *Poems*, 272.

164 *Fifty Sermons* (1649), 214, Whitehall. Cf. Donne's poetical version of this in his verse letter to the Countess of Bedford, 'Reason is our soul's left hand' (*Poems*, 225).

165 *Sermons*, II, 81, n.d. For a close parallel with this, cf. Walter Pagel on '"Balsam"' or '"Mummy"', the terms which Paracelsus used to describe 'the natural healing power of the tissues [in] counteracting putrefaction' (*Paracelsus: An Introduction to Philosophical Medicine in the Era of the Renaissance* (New York and Basle: S. Karger, 1958), 101). In his recent book on Paracelsus, Charles Webster seems to separate 'mumia' and 'balsam' in a way that neither Donne nor Murray do: 'the status of mumia was high, but it was not as elevated as balsam. The former gave resilience to the body, but the latter reached

over to the world of the immortal spirit'. He does, however, also note that 'balsam was intrinsic to physical bodies while at the same time belonging to the spiritual realm', and one can see that such a substance would have strong appeal for Donne (*Paracelsus: An Introduction*, 151). Webster's sense of balsam is arguably evident when Paracelsus states that 'the life, then, is … a certain astral balsam, a balsamic impression, a celestial and invisible fire, an included air' and that 'the spirit is in very truth the life and balsam of all corporeal things' (*Paracelsus: Essential Readings*, trans. Nicholas Goodrick-Clarke (Crucible, 1990), 179).

166 Cf. John Carey, *John Donne: Life, Mind and Art* (London: Faber & Faber, 1981),149–50.

167 For poetry, see *Anatomy*, 159–60, *Poems*, 274.

168 *Ignatius His Conclave*, ed. T.S. Healy, SJ (Oxford: Clarendon Press, 1969), 19–25. Where, for example, Paracelsus takes a conveniently 'devilish' attitude to the pox in *Ignatius* (23–24), his attitude to syphilis in *Biathanatos* (written in 1608) is notably pious (*Biathanatos* (1644), 215). It is also telling that, even as Ignatius derides Paracelsus, he displays Donne's precise awareness of one of Paracelsus' key followers: 'Neither doth *Paracelsus* truly deserve the name of an innovator, whose doctrine, Severinus and his other followers do refer to the most ancient times' (*Ignatius*, 25).

169 *Letters*, I, 175. As Ramie Targoff notes, while this letter was assigned to Sir Thomas Lucy in the 1651 edition of the *Letters*, 'there is strong reason to believe it was written to Goodyer. According to Roger E. Bennett, it is "one of several of Donne's efforts to encourage Goodyer to be constant in his religion" … M. Thomas Hester, one of the editors of the forthcoming edition of Donne's letters, agrees with this conclusion' (*John Donne: Body and Soul* (Chicago: University of Chicago Press, 2008), 187n25, citing Bennett, 'Donne's Letters from the Continent in 1611–12', *Philological Quarterly* 19 (1940): 66–78, 65 n40.)

170 *Sermons*, II, 76–77, Lincolns Inn, n.d.

171 See Geoffrey Keynes, *A Bibliography of Dr. John Donne*, 4th edn (Oxford: Clarendon Press, 1973), 273, L135. He also refers specifically, in another sermon, not just to balsamum, but to balsamum as applied by a medical 'plaster' (*Fifty Sermons*, 139, Lincoln's Inn). For other, evidently positive, references to Paracelsus, see: *Essayes in Divinity*, ed. Evelyn M. Simpson (Oxford: Clarendon Press, 1952), 11; *Biathanatos* (1644), 172. *Biathantaos* was written in 1608. When Donne refers to dew as '*Coeli sudor*, a sweaty excrement of the heavens, and *siderum saliva*, the spittle, the phlegm of the stars' (*Sermons*, III, 233, April 1621) he is evidently drawing on Pliny (rendered, in Philemon Holland's translation, as 'a certain sweat of the sky, or some unctuous jelly proceeding from the stars' (Holland, I, 315)). But Paracelsus' reference to celestial emanations as the '"smell, smoke, or sweat" of the stars' is surely worth noting (Paracelsus, *Paramirum*, I, viii, *Der Bucher und Schrifften* (Basle, 1589–90), I, 15; quoted by Gardner in *The Songs and Sonnets*, ed. Helen Gardner (Oxford: Clarendon Press, 1978), 186).

172 See: Kate Frost, 'Prescription and Devotion: the Reverend Doctor Donne and the Learned Doctor Mayerne: Two Seventeenth-century Records of Epidemic Typhus Fever', *Medical History* 22.4 (1978): 408–16, 409; Anthony Raspa, in *Devotions upon Emergent Occasions*, ed. Anthony Raspa (Oxford: Oxford University Press, 1987), 144.

173 'Precription and Devotion', 409.

174 Both Moffett and Mayerne were influential figures (on Moffett, see Frances Dawbarn, 'New Light on Dr Thomas Moffet: The Triple Roles of an Early Modern Patronage Broker', *Medical History* 47 (2003): 3–22, 6; Roy Porter, *The Greatest Benefit to Mankind: A Medical History of Humanity from Antiquity to the Present* (London: Fontana Press, 1999), 205–6). But the role of Moffett has been seen as problematic by Dawbarn ('New Light', 15–22).

175 Cf. a royal proclamation of the same year, which commanded 'all apothecaries of this realm, to follow the dispensatory lately compiled by the College of Physicians of London' (*By the King. A Proclamation Commanding all Apothecaries* … (1618), t–p).

176 Mummy is an ingredient in various plasters in the edition of 17 December 1618 (see 166, 172, 176). For Moffet's hostility, see *Health's Improvement* (1655), 139–40. Whatever Moffet's influence on English Paracelsianism, his effect on the *Pharmacopeia* was

necessarily slighter than that of Mayerne, as he died in 1604. For Moffett's links to continental ideas, and involvement with the relatively neglected 'Lime Street naturalists' of Elizabethan London, see Harkness, *Jewel House*, 27, 33, 44–45. Harkness also notes (85–86) that the initial 1585 committee on the possibility of an English *Pharmacopeia* arose out of struggles to secure space in London's medical marketplace. Another possible influence is the apothecary and herbalist John Parkinson. Parkinson, notes Juanita Burnby, 'became so well respected in his profession that he was one of the five apothecaries who were consulted by the College of Physicians during the compilation of the first Pharmacopoeia Londinensis' (new DNB). As Thorndike points out, Parkinson's *Theatrum Botanicum* (1640) lists mumia along with bezoar stone and amber (*History*, VIII, 62–63).

177 See: Hugh Trevor-Roper, *Europe's Physician: The Various Life of Sir Theodore de Mayerne* (New Haven: Yale University Press, 2006), 4; 'Precription and Devotion', 409.

178 *Europe's Physician*, 270.

179 *Europe's Physician*, 269. Brian Nance argues that, as well as possibly encouraging James 'to look out for his health', this letter would, 'should some serious illness befall the king ... show Mayerne to be vigilant and careful, and the king to be reckless and unrestrained' (*Turquet de Mayerne as Baroque Physician: The Art of Medical Portraiture*, Clio Medica 65 (Amsterdam: Rodopi, 2001), 183). On Mayerne's excellent clinical records, see also: Elizabeth Lane Furdell, *The Royal Doctors 1485–1714: Medical Personnel at the Tudor and Stuart Courts* (New York: University of Rochester Press, 2001), 103.

180 For more on James's routine health problems, see Furdell, *Royal Doctors*, 103–4.

181 *Europe's Physician*, 275.

182 Ferdinand, in *Duchess of Malfi* (1623), L3r.

183 *Treatise of the Gout*, trans. Thomas Shirley (1676), 48, 59–60.

184 *Opera Medica* (1703), 95, 139, 64, 99–100; *Medicinal Counsels*, trans. Thomas Shirley (1677), 127.

185 See: John Aikin, *Biographical Memoirs of Medicine* (1780), 262–63.

186 Even Raspa, in a notably meticulous commentary, fails to offer any gloss of the mummy reference in *Devotions upon Emergent Occasions*.

187 'Prescription and Devotion', 408.

188 'Prescription and Devotion', 415, 412. For other memorable therapeutic ingredients, see also Furdell, *Royal Doctors*, 104.

189 'Prescription and Devotion', 409.

190 'Prescription and Devotion', 412. Frost also notes (413) that Mayerne used a theriac (or treacle) containing a large and variable number of ingredients. Although the theriacs in the 1618 *Pharmacopeia* do not include mummy, we should recall that the 'Galenic treacle' cited by Bullein did.

191 Cf., for example, the anti-spasmodic opiate for epilepsy of Lazare Riverius, published in 1640 and containing coral, pearl, bezoar stone and human skull (cited in Brockliss and Jones, *Medical World*, 163).

192 'Prescription and Devotion', 411–12.

193 We get some broad sense that this may have mattered to Donne when, in Meditation 9, he writes: 'where there is room for consultation, things are not desperate. They consult; so there is nothing rashly, inconsiderately done; and then they prescribe, they write, so there is nothing covertly, disguisedly, unavowedly done' (*Devotions* (1624), 207).

194 On Donne and Foxe, see: R.C. Bald, *John Donne: A Life* (Oxford: Clarendon Press, 1970); 452; Raspa, in *Devotions upon Emergent Occasions*, 28.

Corpse medicine from the Civil War to the eighteenth century notes

1 Patrick Curry in new DNB. Last quotation from: L. Fioravanti, *Three Exact Pieces*, 1652, preface.

2 Cf. especially Curry on the way 'Culpeper continued to criticize the self-interest of the college physicians, whom he had already classed with priests and lawyers: "The one

deceives men in matters belonging to their soul, the other in matters belonging to their bodies, and the third in matters belonging to their estates'" (*A Physical Directory*, 1649, 'To the reader').

3 *Pharmacopoeia Londinensis* (1653), 52–53. On Culpeper's political commitment, cf. also Curry (DNB) who notes that in 1643 Culpeper, fighting for the Parliamentarians, 'received a serious chest wound from a musket ball, which probably hastened his death'.

4 *Physical Directory* (1649), 151, 295–96, 304, 309, 321–22.

5 *Culpeper's Directory for Midwives* (1662), 244–45.

6 *English Physician* (1652), A4v, 209.

7 *Physical Directory*, A1v–A2r. For more on Culpeper's work and ethos, see: Elizabeth Lane Furdell, *Publishing and Medicine in Early Modern England* (Woodbridge: University of Rochester Press, 2002), 41–45.

8 *Approved Medicines* (1651), 32.

9 Nicolaas Fonteyn, *The Woman's Doctor* (1652), 37, 66. The convulsions in question appear to be psychosomatic, and fall under the general heading of 'epilepsy in the matrix' (60).

10 On this new market, see Jukka Tyrkkö, '*A Physical Dictionary* (1657): The First English Medical Dictionary', in *Selected Proceedings of the 2008 Symposium on New Approaches in English Historical Lexis (HEL-LEX 2)*, ed. R.W. McConchie, Alpo Honkapohja, and Jukka Tyrkkö, 2009 (Somerville, Mass.: Cascadilla Press), 171–87 (www.lingref.com (document 2175)). Tyrkkö notes that this first medical dictionary (another significant product of the Interregnum) cites mumia (ibid., 7–8).

11 *The Great Instauration: Science, Medicine and Reform 1626–1660* (London: Duckworth, 1975); *Paracelsus: Medicine, Magic and Mission at the End of Time* (New Haven: Yale University Press, 2008).

12 For Philipott's political allegiance, see his poem on the royalist Arthur Lord Capel (*Capellus Virbius* (1662)).

13 See Antonio Clericuzio, new DNB, 'George Thomson'.

14 *A Ternary of Paradoxes*, trans. Walter Charleton (1650), 3–4. This translation first appeared in 1649.

15 *Ternary*, 30. Cf. this belief with Camillo Brunori (1726) as cited in Camporesi, *Bread of Dreams: Food and Fantasy in Early Modern Europe*, trans. David Gentilcore (Oxford: Polity Press, 1996), 45–46.

16 *Ternary*, 27.

17 *Ternary*, 25. Cf. Donne, on dew and honey as derived from '*Coeli sudor*, a sweaty excrement of the heavens, and *siderum saliva*, the spittle, the phlegm of the stars' (*Sermons*, III, 233, April 1621).

18 *Ternary*, 4.

19 *Ternary*, 25–26.

20 Cf., broadly, Camporesi on those 'superstitious soldiers' who believed themselves safe from all dangers in battle after drinking from a human skull (*Bread of Dreams*, 45).

21 For another version, cf. van Helmont on Saint Hubert of Arduenna: 'a small lock of wool, from the stole or upper garment of the Saint ... is artificially inclosed within the skin of the forehead' of one bitten by a mad dog; after which, the person is immune to attacks by any animal (*Ternary*, 26).

22 *Ternary*, 106. For a recent discussion of Kenelm Digby's writings on the wound salve, see: Elizabeth Hendrick, 'Romancing the Salve: Sir Kenelm Digby and the Powder of Sympathy', *British Journal for the History of Science* 41.2 (2008): 161–85.

23 *Ternary*, 17.

24 *Ternary*, D2v.

25 *Ternary*, 12, 29, D3r. This may be the first use of 'mumial' in English (albeit via translation). The term is used by a number of others shortly after 1650. Cf. also Elisha Coles, *An English Dictionary* (1677): '*Mumial*, belonging to *Mumy, Mummy, l. Pissa sphaltum, Picibitumen*, a pithy substance, either from bodies embalmed in Arabia, or made of Jews lime and bitumen'.

26 *Ternary*, E1r–v.

27 A very similar version of the recipe, given by the German pharmacologist Johann Schroeder (b.1600) is cited from a work of 1677 by Camporesi (*Bread of Dreams*, 49). This version, however, only makes general mention of a 'violent death'. On the original reference in the 1609 *Basilica Chymica*, see Thorndike, *History*, VIII, 414.

28 *Bazilica Chymica*, trans. 'a lover of chemistry' (1670), 155.

29 For other instances of chemical or alchemical interest in mummy on the continent around this time, see Thorndike: *History*, VII, 192–93, on the alchemist Johannes Conradus Rhumelius (1597–1661), who credited human mumia as 'the most universal medicine' in a work of 1635; and VIII, 145, on Carolus Ludovicus de Maets, a professor of chemistry at Leyden who left manuscripts of his 'secret chemical college' in which he described the preparation of 'artificial mumia'.

30 *History*, VIII, 414.

31 Andreas Tentzel, *Medicina Diastatica,* trans. Ferdinando Parkhurst (1653), a2r–v.

32 See, for example, *Medicina Diastatica*, 116.

33 *Medicina Diastatica,* 102.

34 *Medicina Diastatica,* 128. Other Paracelsian references around this time include mummy as an ingredient in two different unguents for gunshot wounds (Giles Everard, *Panacea* (1659), 52r–v, 54v–55r); and a powder made from rhubarb, mummy, and cress seeds to dissolve clotted blood (John Tanner, *The Hidden Treasures of the Art of Physic* (1659), 406. Respective title pages describe Everard as a doctor, and Tanner as 'student in physic and astrology'. Noah Biggs is probably referring to Egyptian mummy when he compares the 'balm' of the blood to 'that of Memphis' (*Mataeotechnia Medicinae Praxeos, The Vanity of the Craft of Physic* (1651), 161). In his new DNB article on Biggs, Malcolm Oster notes that Biggs seems more a disciple of van Helmont than Paracelsus (a belief supported by Biggs's reference to 'that acute philosopher and ingenious Helmont' (69)). Biggs at one point criticises those physicians who make opportunistic and careless use of Paracelsian remedies (13–14). He cites Paracelsus approvingly at 34, but criticises him to some extent on 217.

35 *Polypharmakos kai Chymistes, or, The English Unparalell'd Physician and Chyrurgian* (1651), 133. Although this looks like a near verbatim quotation of Fioravanti, Border writes as though he is making the claim himself (for Fioravanti, see Piero Camporesi, *Juice of Life: The Symbolic and Magic Significance of Blood* (New York: Continuum, 1988), 31). On Border's career, see J. Max Patrick, 'The Arrest of Hugh Peters', *Huntington Library Quarterly* 19.4 (1956): 343–51, 345–46.

36 *Polypharmakos*, 134.

37 *Polypharmakos*, 124.

38 *Polypharmakos*, 33.

39 *Polypharmakos*, 133. Cf. 82–83, which offers a recipe for a balsam for 'wounds, aches and pains', and cramp, containing (amongst many other things) 'hog's grease … oil of wax and man's grease'.

40 *Polypharmakos*, 134. Cf. also the more familiar opinion, that, 'from the forepart of a man's skull there is drawn by distillation, a water, an oil, and a salt, which is most profitably used against the falling sickness' (ibid.).

41 Webster notes that this work was 'derived from sixteenth century works, with sections from' the German chemist, Johann Rudolph Glauber (*Great Instauration*, 279).

42 Unless otherwise stated, this and all other biographical information on French is from Peter Elmer's article in new *DNB*.

43 *Great Instauration*, 297–98.

44 *The Art of Distillation* (1653), 89–90. On 'magistery', see *OED*, sense 5a alchemy. 'A master principle of nature, free of impurities; a potent transmuting or curative quality or agency; (*concr.* [concretely]) a substance, such as the philosopher's stone, capable of transmuting or changing the nature of other substances'.

45 *Art*, 90.

46 Malcolm Oster in new DNB notes of Goddard that he was on the management committee of the Savoy Hospital from 1653.

47 *Art*, 91. For an oblique echo of this status a few years later, see Samuel Pordage's devotional and mystical poem, *Mundorum Explicatio* (1661), 248.

48 *Art*, 91.

49 *Occasional Reflections upon Several Subjects* (1665), 197.

50 *Art*, 92–93.

51 *Art*, 92.

52 *Art*, 90.

53 Cf. Webster: 'records indicate that dissections were carried out as a matter of routine in the [London] hospitals' (*Great Instauration*, 299).

54 Irvine offers an interesting case of someone who appears broadly Paracelsian (see for example ibid., 45, 51, 59, and 102 (referring to that 'noble chemist Crollius')) but who at one point emphatically opposes medical 'sects' and any who 'should swear himself a slave to Galen' or 'to Paracelsus', for 'these were great men, but when these gave themselves to contentious disputes to defend their own opinions, they much erred many times from the truth' (56).

55 Unless otherwise stated, all biographical information on Irvine is from Helen M. Dingwall's article in new DNB.

56 *Medicina Magnetica: or, The Rare and Wonderful Art of Curing by Sympathy* (1656), 99.

57 See: Robert Burton, *Anatomy of Melancholy*, 2 vols (1800), I, 429. Whilst this reference is distinctly contemptuous, it is not found in the 1651 edition of the *Anatomy*, and is the work of a later editor. Walter Charleton is no less incredulous (see: *The Darkness of Atheism Dispelled by the Light of Nature* (1652), 201. For Robert Boyle's more ambivalent views, see below (p. 61).

58 Cf. Roy Porter, who notes that the four primary humours 'may have been suggested by observation of clotted blood: the darkest part corresponded to black bile, the serum above the clot was yellow bile, the light matter at the top was phlegm' (*The Greatest Benefit to Mankind: A Medical History of Humanity from Antiquity to the Present* (London: Fontana Press, 1999), 57).

59 A possible influence on Irvine's notion of 'insensible transpiration' may have been the Italian Sanctorius Sanctorius (1561–1636). Describing Sanctorius as 'a much cited medical author', Thorndike notes that his *Medicina Statica* of 1614 was translated into English and Dutch (*History*, VIII, 406). Virginia Smith explains that Sanctorius claimed to have proved the existence of '"insensible perspiration"' by obsessively monitoring his diet, and frequently weighing himself in a special 'balance chair', thereby 'measuring the shortfall between his intake and outgo' (see *Clean: A History of Personal Hygiene and Purity* (Oxford: Oxford University Press, 2007), 202–3).

60 *Medicina Magnetica*, 86. In Irvine's time and for decades afterwards, people habitually shared beds with those of the same sex, either for reasons of economy or warmth.

61 *Medicina Magnetica*, 86. Cf. the herbs with the idea that one could improve one's health or absorb nourishment by means of a lump of turf placed on the chest or belly (see, for example: Eirenaeus Philalethes [i.e., George Starkey], *Collectanea Chymica* (1684), 163).

62 *Medicina Magnetica*, 86. Irvine notes also that 'Paracelsus (though obscurely) makes often mention' of such phenomena.

63 *Medicina Magnetica*, 97–98. Thorndike notes that this cure was cited by Johann Ernst Burggrav (or Burgravius) in his *Biolychnium* of 1611 (*History*, VIII, 414). The same point is made by van Helmont (*Ternary*, 12) who adds that Burggrav took the cure from Paracelsus. To understand certain passages in Irvine it is necessary to be aware that he at times uses the word 'wight' to mean not 'a man' but 'a living being in general; a creature' (*OED*, 1a obsolete); that is, an animal.

64 See Lauren Kassell, *Medicine and Magic in Elizabethan London: Simon Forman, Astrologer, Alchemist, and Physician* (Oxford: Clarendon Press, 2005), 188.

65 *Medicina Magnetica*, 73.

66 Thorndike, *History*, VIII, 199. Kate Frost, commenting on Donne's case in 1978, noted that this 'remedy is still in use in some parts of southern North America for snakebite. The animal used is usually a small mammal or a bird, probably due to their high body temperatures' (Kate Frost, 'Prescription and Devotion: The Reverend Doctor Donne and the Learned Doctor Mayerne: Two Seventeenth-Century Records of Epidemic Typhus Fever', *Medical History* 22.4 (1978): 408–16, 414). For a close Paracelsian comparison with Irvine's theories of transfer or transplantation, see *Medicina Diastatica*, 67ff.

67 Mark 5.1–18, Luke 8.27–37.

68 For more on the New Testament context, see John M. Hull, *Hellenistic Magic and the Synoptic Tradition* (London: SCM Press, 1974), 104.

69 Matthew 9; Luke 8; Mark 5. Cf. Greece, *c*.1962: 'When he was healing, Jesus took the sins of others upon himself; eventually he died from this. That's like with the healers here; when Maria, for example, cures others of pain, that pain is transferred to her, but she has no place to put the bad after that' (Richard and Eva Blum, *The Dangerous Hour: The Lore of Crisis and Mystery in Rural Greece* (London: Chatto & Windus, 1970), 81).

70 Cited in Naomi Janowitz, *Magic in the Roman World: Pagans, Jews and Christians* (London: Routledge, 2001), 14.

71 Cf., specifically, Irvine's insistence that a good physician should 'follow Nature everywhere, plain and simple' (*Medicina Diastatica*, 56).

72 For more on the relationship between spirits in a living body, and in its distant 'excrements', see *Medicina Magnetica*, 28–32.

73 *Medicina Magnetica*, 66–67.

74 Cf. Tentzel, who claims that 'if we could feed on living creatures, it would be much more conducible to the nourishing and preservation of our bodies and spirits' as a body which is 'sound, and vivacious, is more nutrimental than any which a disease hath killed, and thereby deprived it of its spirit or mummy' (*Medicina Diastatica*, 5–6).

75 *Medicina Magnetica*, 79.

76 It is worth noting, however, that early modern anatomists were known to influence the mode of death used on the condemned, preferring drowning, because of the relatively slight damage inflicted on the body as specimen (see Roger French, *Dissection and Vivisection in the European Renaissance* (Aldershot: Ashgate, 1999), 3, 238).

77 For more on this, see *Medicina Magnetica*, 30–31 (the story is broadly true, though Irvine's interpretation is mistaken); and Roy Calne, *Renal Transplantation*, 2nd edn (London: Edward Arnold, 1967), 4–5. I am very grateful to Richard Newell for clarifying this story, and bringing Calne's book to my attention.

78 John Henry, 'Samuel Boulton', new DNB.

79 *Medicina Magnetica*, A3r–v.

80 Of relevance here is Boulton's claim that he had his work ready for publication as early as 1646. He adds (in 1656) that 'I have locked it up fast for this ten years space in the most secret corners of my closet' (Preface to the reader). If by this he means his own copy, and not the original MS, then it is possible that the MS passed to others (including Irvine) in the years after 1646.

81 See, again, *Anatomy* (1800), I, 429. As we have seen, van Helmont also attributes the transference cures to Burgravius.

82 Referring at one point to Paracelsus as 'that monarch of medicine', Bolnest lists as other respected authorities Duchesne, Daniel Sennert, John Hartmann and Croll (*Medicina Instaurata* (1665), 63, 60). Although relatively little is known about Bolnest, he may have had formal medical training. He is described by Anthony Wood as an 'M.D.' (*Athenae Oxonienses* (1692) 470), and referred to as 'Dr Bolnest' by two contemporary authors, one of whom (the astrologer John Gadbury) also calls Bolnest 'my worthy friend' (Hortolanus Junior, *The Golden Age* (1698), 79–80; Gadbury, *London's Deliverance Predicted* (1665), 38–39). Bolnest's *Medicina Instaurata* was still being offered for sale in a catalogue of 1800 (John Cuthell, *A Catalogue of Books for the Year 1800* (1800), 387).

83 *Aurora Chymica* (1672), 6–8.

84 *Aurora Chymica*, 9–12. On medical use of bones around this time, see also Thomas Bartholin, *Bartholin's Anatomy* (1668), 336.

85 *Aurora Chymica*, 2.

86 *Great Instauration*, 246–50. Cf. also Bolnest's belief that his quintessence of salt 'retardeth old age' and keeps back 'grey hairs', and his hope to effect 'the restoration, or recovery, of the decayed, or lost health of man' (*Medicina Instaurata*, 57, 149).

87 See the article on Bolnest in new DNB by Lawrence M. Principe.

88 *Medicina Instaurata*, 151.

89 Anon., *An Advertisement from the Society of Chymical Physicians* (1665).

90 *Aurora Chymica*, 8, 10.

91 *Medicina Instaurata*, 148–49.

92 Unless otherwise stated, all biographical details are from Antonio Clericuzio's article in new DNB. Earlier, Thomson had been unable to attend either Oxford or Cambridge due to the death of his father. In the long run, his education probably benefited. Clericuzio notes that in 1665 Thomson was 'among the Helmontians who projected a college of chemical physicians to challenge the college's monopoly'.

93 For more on this experiment, see: Charles Webster, 'The Helmontian George Thomson and William Harvey: the Revival and Application of Splenectomy to Physiological Research', *Medical History* 15 (1971): 154–67.

94 See DNB; and *Galeno-pale, or, A Chemical Trial of the Galenists* (1665), 109–15.

95 See: Anon., *An Advertisement …* (1665).

96 *Ortho-methodoz itro-chymike: or the Direct Method of Curing Chemically* (1675), 123. Webster notes that, 'after the restoration' Thomson 'took over [George] Starkey's role as the most active Helmontian pamphleteer' (*Great Instauration*, 282).

97 *Ortho-methodoz itro-chymike*, 77, 122. Cf. also 'blood flowing from the nose', which 'stops excessive haemorrhages' (122).

98 *Loimotomia, or, The Pest Anatomized* (1666), 150.

99 *Ortho-methodoz itro-chymike*, 122.

100 *Ortho-methodoz itro-chymike*, 123.

101 *Ortho-methodoz itro-chymike*, 84.

102 Cf., also, Simon Forman, who thought that it could be used to anoint lepers (Kassell, *Medicine and Magic*, 188).

103 *Ortho-methodoz itro-chymike*, 122, 124.

104 Cf. Clericuzio, new DNB, 'George Thomson': 'it is apparent that already in the 1650s Thomson had regular recourse to chemically prepared medicines'; if these worked, it was not always by the power of suggestion, as one patient was the dog on whom Thomson performed the live splenectomy.

105 Cf. Webster on George Thomson, who 'approved of Harvey's discoveries and himself conducted vivisection experiments' (*Great Instauration*, 286). Given the influence of van Helmont on certain of these figures, we should also bear in mind that 'Helmont's son, the exotic cabbalist Franciscus Mercurius … was feted when he arrived in England in 1670', attracting the attention of Lady Anne Conway and Lady Damaris Masham (see Charles Webster, *From Paracelsus to Newton: Magic and the Making of Modern Science* (Cambridge: Cambridge University Press, 1982), 9).

106 *Choice Manual*, 149–52, 183.

107 *Choice Manual*, 3. 'Endive' is another name for chicory leaves.

108 See Jonathan Sawday, *The Body Emblazoned: Dissection and the Human Body in Renaissance Culture* (London: Routledge, 1995), 60–61.

109 'The deaths in infancy of her brothers, and her father's quarrel with his brother, who was heir to his titles, made Elizabeth and her two sisters great heiresses'. Considine adds that, though her father died in 1616, Elizabeth's inheritance was delayed for twenty years by family wrangling.

110 On Freke, see Elaine Leong, 'Making Medicines in the Early Modern Household', *Bulletin of the History of Medicine* 82.1 (2008): 145–68. Among Freke's reading notes

were selections from John Gerard, Culpeper's 1649 *Pharmacopeia*, and the French physician Moise Charas, who listed a powder containing human skull against fever, poisoning and smallpox ('Making Medicines', 151; Charas, *The Royal Pharmacopeia* (1678), 122). At the risk of distorting early modern respect for class hierarchy, one could argue that awareness of figures such as Freke might be tied to other research which has helped correct the heavily male-dominated world of printed medicine. Back in the Elizabethan period, we have Harkness's valuable study of popular London healers such as '"the old woman at Newington ... unto whom the people do resort, as unto an oracle", "the woman on the Bankside ... " and "the cunning woman in Sea Coal Lane"' (*Jewel House*, 71). Cf. also Deborah E. Harkness, 'A View from the Streets: Women and Medical Work in Elizabethan London', *Bulletin of the History of Medicine* 82.1 (2008): 53–85. For more on the role of women publishers in late Elizabethan and early Stuart London, see Furdell, *Publishing and Medicine*, 91–112.

111 'Making Medicines', 147.

112 'Grace Mildmay', new DNB.

113 Northampton County Record Office, Westmorland, 66. Dating is from personal communication, 9 June 2010: 'Most of the recipe books span a long time period. Most of the ones cited in the database were created during the "long 17th century." Grace Mildmay's is the earliest – most likely she started it late 16th century and many of the other mss dip into the early 18 century'.

114 See: Freke (BL additional ms 45718), 228r, 226v; Chesterfield (wellcome western 751), b2r, b3v, b4r, b32v; Monmouth House (Bod MS don.3.11), 14r; fol-chest (Folger v.b. 286), 14, 89–90; hoghton (Folger v.a. 365), 15v, 21r; Hughes (wellcome western ms 363), 191v, 220v; Fairfax (arcana fairfaxiana), 54; greenway (NLM ms b 261), 21; danby (HM 60413), 18r; evelyn (BL Additional MS 78337), 60v; read (alphabetical book of physical secrets), 41, 68, 131, 218–20; queen (queen's closet opened), 95–96; Bertie (Elizabeth Bertie – Bod Ms Eng Misc D), 21–24, 113. A Fairfax cure for wounds made from skull-moss, human blood and earthworms is later cited in *The Leeds Mercury*, Saturday, 19 November 1892.

115 Chesterfield, e2r, fol-chest, 45.

116 Chesterfield, e1r; Monmouth House, 31r; fol-chest, 7; queen, 130; Monmouth House, 40v; read, 31; kent, 68; ladies, 180; ladies, 163–64; Fairfax, 41; greenway, 75; fol-chest, 106; greenway, 113; tc, 32.

117 Fairfax, 8.

118 Chesterfield, d12r, b32bv.

119 For discussion of those more privileged women who shifted back to maternal breast-feeding as the seventeenth century progressed (and the contrasting continental situation), see: David Harley, 'From Providence to Nature: the Moral Theology and Godly Practice of Maternal Breastfeeding in Stuart England', *Bulletin for the History of Medicine* 69 (1995): 198–223.

120 Fildes notes that, unlike many parents, 'higher aristocracy' tended to have wet nurses in their own homes, which would obviously have made adult use of milk easier. She also shows that 'sucking glasses' were used to express milk in the seventeenth century (usually to improve milk flow in dry breasts). See Valerie Fildes, *Wet Nursing: A History from Antiquity to the Present* (Oxford: Blackwell, 1988), 79, 88.

121 On quantities, see 'Making Medicines', 145–46. A broad comparison with the independent medical arts and supplies portrayed by Leong is offered in Stephen Bradwell's *Helps for Sudden Accidents Endangering Life* (1633). This features internal and external mummy recipes for falls and bruising (79–84), and explicitly advertises itself to 'those that live far from physicians or chirurgions' but who may yet 'happily preserve the life of a poor friend or neighbour, till such a man may be had to perfect the cure' (t–p). For more on Bradwell (or Bredwell) and this book's status as the first English 'first aid guide', see: Norman Gevitz, '"Helps for Suddain Accidents": Stephen Bredwell and the Origin of the First Aid Guide', *Bulletin of the History of Medicine* 67.1 (1993): 51–73.

122 *Great Instauration*, 255. Leong's inference, that Freke used eight pints of her 'aqua mirabolus' between 1710 and 1712, further suggests that such remedies were being fairly widely distributed ('Making Medicines', 164).

123 John Considine's new DNB article on Grey states: 'This work has often been ascribed to Elizabeth herself. However, W.I. Gent, who also produced a book of remedies for the plague in 1665 (his name may have been William Jervis), makes it clear in his prefatory matter that the collection was made by him for Elizabeth's use: "this small Manuall ... was once esteemed as a rich Cabinet of knowledge, by a person truely Honorable"'. Whilst it seems fairly certain that the recipes had diverse sources or authors, W.I.'s phrasing in his preface to Letitia Popham is by no means as clear as Considine claims (see *A Choice Manual* (1653), A2r–A3r).

124 'Women, Health and Healing in Early Modern Europe', *Bulletin of the History of Medicine* 82.1 (2008): 1–17, 9. Cf. Furdell, who describes Kent's book as 'sought after', and notes that at least seven of its earlier editions were published by Gertrude Dawson (*Publishing and Medicine*, 109). On Hannah Woolley, author of the 1680 work *The Queen-like Closet*, see: L.F. Newman, 'Some Notes on Folk Medicine in the Eastern Counties', *Folklore* 56.4 (1945): 349–60, 351–53; *Women's Worlds in Seventeenth-Century England*, ed. Patricia Crawford and Laura Gowing (London: Routledge, 2000), 101–3.

125 *Hermetical Physic* (1655) 24–25. On Vaughan's medical practice, see Alan Rudrum in new DNB. Cf., also, the influential educational reformer and admirer of Francis Bacon, Samuel Hartlib, who in this same year commended mummy against ulcers (*Chymical, Medicinal, and Chyrurgical Addresses* (1655), 96).

126 *Reliquiae Baxterianae* (1696), 106.

127 *The Anatomy of Human Bodies*, trans. William Salmon (1694), 118. For more on various errhines and their mode of operation, see Charas, *Royal Pharmacopeia*, 60–61.

128 Johann Schroeder, *Zoologia*, trans. anon. (1659), 39.

129 *Zoologia*, 42.

130 *Zoologia*, 48.

131 *Zoologia*, 48–51.

132 *Zoologia*, 58, 61.

133 *Zoologia*, 52–53.

134 *Zoologia*, 56–57. In 1660 Daniel Beckher's *Medicus Microcosmus* was published in England. As well as a surprising number of ingredients from living bodies, Beckher's work features human skin and brain, as well as the more predictable fat, cranium and mummy (Thorndike, *History*, VIII, 415). This work was first published in Rostock in 1622. Beckher died in 1655.

135 For usnea, see *Choice and Experimented Receipts* (1675), 27.

136 *A Choice Collection of Rare Secrets and Experiments in Philosophy* (1682), 197. For details on Digby's life I am indebted to the article by Michael Foster in the new DNB. This book was published after Digby's death (in 1665) by Hartman.

137 See Lawrence Stone, *The Family, Sex and Marriage in England 1500–1800* (Harmondsworth: Penguin, 1979), 115.

138 *Adenochoiradelogia, or, An Anatomic-chirurgical Treatise of Glandules and Strumaes or, Kings-evil-Swellings* (1684), 115–16. Browne was also surgeon at St Thomas's Hospital from 1683–91 (see Ian Lyle in new DNB). Elizabeth Furdell notes that Browne, originally from Norfolk, was mentored by Sir Thomas Browne (Elizabeth Lane Furdell, *The Royal Doctors 1485–1714: Medical Personnel at the Tudor and Stuart Courts* (New York: University of Rochester Press, 2001), 182). For remedies involving skull and mummy at this time, see also Sir Robert Sibbald, *Scotland Illustrated* (1684), 87, 5 (second reference from second page set); and Robert Johnson, *Enchiridion Medicum, or, A Manual of Physic* (1684), 6.

139 *Two Discourses Concerning the Soul of Brutes*, trans. Samuel Pordage (1683), 160. This first appeared in Latin in 1672.

140 See, for example, the Spanish physician Antonio Colmenero de Ledesma (*A Curious Treatise of the Nature and Quality of Chocolate*, trans. Don Diego de Vades-forte (1640));

Anon., *The Virtues of Chocolate East-India Drink* (1660). Cf. also Henry Stubbe, *The Indian Nectar, or, A Discourse Concerning Chocolata* (1662). Dedicated to 'my learned friend, Dr Thomas Willis', this provides Willis with 'the discourse I promised you, of chocolata'; describes the medicinal qualities of chocolate; and includes a chemical analysis by Charles II's chemist, Nicaise Lefebvre. One Richard Mortimer, in Sun Alley in East Smithfield mixed up prescriptions from the recipes which Stubbe had given him (ibid., A6r–A7r). On 24 November 1664 Samuel Pepys records going 'to a coffeehouse, to drink jocolatte, very good'. See also Philippe Sylvester DuFour, *The Manner of Making of Coffee, Tea, and Chocolate*, trans. anon. (1685), 57–99, on the medical qualities of cocoa and those ingredients then typically mixed with it.

141 Unless otherwise stated, all biographical information on Willis is from Martensen's article in new DNB. Martensen further notes that, whilst Willis 'left the bulk of his estate to his son Thomas ... the three surviving younger children each received £3000'.

142 For Willis's piety see especially Martensen, on the illicit prayer meetings of the Interregnum. On Willis's avant-garde and scientific treatment of the brain, see Richard Sugg, *The Smoke of the Soul: The Animated Body in Early Modern Europe* (Michigan: University of Michigan Press, forthcoming), ch. 9.

143 *Dr Willis's Practice of Physic* (1684), 137, 138.

144 *Practice of Physic*, 69, 207, 79.

145 *Practice of Physic*, 149–50, 204, 159, 213.

146 *An Essay of the Pathology of the Brain*, trans. Samuel Pordage (1681), 71. This work first appeared in Latin in 1667. For epilepsy it also recommends 'human skull prepared' (23), and a head plaster using powdered skull (24).

147 *Practice of Physic*, 160. The reference came originally from Willis's 1672 book *Two Discourses Concerning the Soul of Brutes*, where Willis locates the incident 'six years ago'.

148 *Practice of Physic*, 160. Willis dedicated both his *Essay on the Pathology of the Brain* and *Two Discourses* ... to Sheldon.

149 *Practice of Physic*, 159, 137.

150 *Medicinal Experiments* (1694), 51–52; *Medicinal Experiments* (1693), 37. Some of these recipes date from an earlier book, *Some Receipts of Medicines ... Sent to a Friend in America* (1688). Cf. Michael Hunter in new DNB: 'He also brought out a collection of medical recipes in 1688; initially this was privately printed but a properly published edition appeared posthumously in 1692, with sequels appearing thereafter.'

151 *Occasional Reflections upon Several Subjects* (1665), 197–98.

152 On Boyle's piety, see: Michael Hunter, new DNB: 'The central fact of Boyle's life from his adolescence onwards was his deep piety, and it is impossible to understand him without doing justice to this. His friends remarked after his death how "the very Name of God was never mentioned by him without a Pause and a visible stop in his Discourse"'. On Boyle's evident hostility to incipient deism, see Michael Hunter, *Boyle: Between God and Science* (London: Yale University Press, 2009), 203–4. On Boyle's anonymous theological works, see Joseph Agassi, 'Robert Boyle's Anonymous Writings', *Isis* 68 (1977): 284–87. On his piety and his strong belief in 'an active supernatural realm', see Michael Hunter, 'Alchemy, Magic and Moralism in the Thought of Robert Boyle', *British Journal for the History of Science* 23.4 (1990): 387–410, 388, 396, *et passim*.

153 *Some Considerations Touching the Usefulness of Experimental Natural Philosophy* (1663), 253.

154 *Of the Reconcileableness of Specific Medicines to the Corpuscular Philosophy* (1685), 126–27.

155 *Of the Reconcileableness ...* (1685), 124–26.

156 When discussing Paracelsian ideas of transferring disease, Boyle is indeed relatively open-minded (see especially *Memoirs for the History of Humane Blood* (1683), 249–50).

157 Two of Boyle's sisters, Mary Rich, Countess of Warwick, and Katherine Jones, Viscountess Ranelagh, were especially likely to know 'great people'. However, Katherine was particularly close to Boyle. Moreover, she was, from 1643, closely associated with

the Hartlib circle, and despite being forced to leave Ireland after the 1641 uprising, remained closely involved with the country in various ways (Sarah Hutton, new DNB). It therefore seems more likely that she would be interested in medicine, and that she would have more Irish contacts than her sister. Boyle's family per se was of course immensely powerful in Ireland; Boyle's father, Richard, was the richest man in the country, with an income of £18,000 by 1641 (see Ciaran Brady and Jane Ohlmeyer, 'Making Good: New Perspectives on the English in Early Modern Ireland', in *British Interventions in Early Modern Ireland*, ed. Ciaran Brady and Jane Ohlmeyer (Cambridge: Cambridge University Press, 2005), 1–27, 11). For more on Ranelagh, see: Ruth Connolly, 'A Proselytising Protestant Commonwealth: The Religious and Political Ideals of Katherine Jones, Viscountess Ranelagh (1614–91)', *The Seventeenth Century* 23.2 (2008): 244–64.

158 'Locke's Contribution to Boyle's Researches on the Air and on Human Blood', *Notes and Records of the Royal Society of London* 17.2 (1962): 198–206, 198, 201.

159 'Locke's Contribution', 201. Cf. also Locke's studies of blood under the microscope (*An Essay Concerning Humane Understanding* (1690), 140).

160 'Locke's Contribution', 201, 203.

161 *Memoirs*, 255–56; 40, 53–54, 57. Cf. also *Certain Physiological Essays* (1669), 240.

162 *Memoirs*, 328. The initial scepticism of this passage is echoed when Boyle refers to Burgravius and his lamp explicitly at *Memoirs*, 248–49.

163 *Some Considerations*, 327; *Memoirs*, 208–9.

164 For the value he set by these, cf. *Memoirs*, A3v.

165 *Some Considerations*, 326, 388.

166 *Some Considerations*, 329.

167 Michael Hunter, 'Robert Boyle', new DNB. Peter Elmer, on French, states that 'according to Anthony Wood, French died in October or November 1657, at or near Boulogne in France' (new DNB). Not only was this late in the year, but, given the distance, the news of his death may have taken some time to reach Boyle.

168 Boyle was also evidently discussing blood chemistry with natural philosophers on the continent; see, for example, *Electronic Enlightenment* (online resource, http://www.e-enlightenment.com/): translation from Latin into English of Israel Conradt to Robert Boyle, The Hague, 8 May 1672.

169 Boyle credits this formula to 'some loose papers' sent to a friend (perhaps Locke?) 'many years ago'. If this too was written *c.*1657, then Boyle's recipe presumably dates back to at least 1650, if not earlier (*Some Considerations*, 326–27).

170 *Some Considerations*, 333–34.

171 *Some Considerations*, 276.

172 *Memoirs*, 210–12. If this is the same case as mentioned in *Some Considerations*, it probably predates the late 1650s; and this broadly matches the sense of distance implied in the *Memoirs*, where Boyle opens the story with 'as I remember'.

173 *Memoirs*, 334.

174 *Some Considerations*, 332.

175 *Memoirs*, 212–14.

176 Agassi, 'Robert Boyle's Anonymous Writings', 284.

177 See *Family Magazine* [1747], 85, 151, on blood and moss of the skull.

178 A letter (apparently written after April 1666) detailing the skull-moss and bloodletting case appears in *Works*, vol. 1 [1772], lxxxii. Cf. also: *Works* (1725), vol. 1, 92, 445, vol. 3, 574; *Works* (1772), vol. 5, 106.

179 One exception was Jonathan Swift, who sometime before 1745 referred to 'Goddards' Drops' in a burlesque death speech (*Works* (1765), XVI, 392).

180 *The European Magazine* (1789), XV, 272–73.

181 Quoted in: *Women's Worlds*, 37–38.

182 *The Diary of William Cartwright*, ed. Joseph Hunter (BiblioBazaar, 2009), 26.

183 George Willis, *Willis's Current Notes* (London, 1853), 25.

184 *Mystery and Art*, 205.

185 For more on Chiffinch, see Ewan Fernie in new DNB.

186 *Notes of Me*, ed. Peter Millard (Toronto: University of Toronto Press, 2000), 224–25. I am very grateful to David Thorley for his prompt assistance with this reference.

187 Quoted by: David Allen, 'The Political Function of Charles II's Chiffinch', *Huntington Library Quarterly* 39.3 (1976): 277–90, 277.

188 *The Court at Windsor: A Domestic History* (London: Longmans, 1964), 69.

189 The work was popular in both France and England, with a first edition of the English translation appearing in 1712, and a third in 1737.

190 See, for example, César de Rochefort, *The History of the Caribby-Islands* (1666), 305; Gervase Markham, *The Husbandman's Jewel* (1695), 35.

191 Moise Charas (1618–98), a highly respected Jewish physician who had converted to Christianity, published his *Royal Pharmacopeia* in Paris in 1676. Charas himself further noted the use of a powder containing 'shavings of a man's skull that died a violent death' against fevers and poisoning, adding that the remedy 'prevails wonderfully against the small-pox' (*The Royal Pharmacopeia* (1678), 122).

The bloody harvest notes

1 As readers are probably aware, the Egyptians took the afterlife very seriously indeed. It is perhaps less widely known that in this culture the deceased were actually judged by a special panel of other citizens: 'if it was proved that the life of the deceased had been impious and scandalous, his memory was branded with infamy, and his body deprived of the rites of sepulture' ('Antiquities of Egypt', in Q. Curtius Rufus, *The History of …Alexander the Great*, trans. from French (1755), xxiv).

2 We know that Berengario da Carpi saw 'nearly intact' Egyptian mummies in Venice sometime before 1518 (see: Piero Camporesi, *Bread of Dreams: Food and Fantasy in Early Modern Europe*, trans. David Gentilcore (Oxford: Polity Press, 1996), 47).

3 For more on bribery, see Philip Schwyzer, 'Mummy is Become Merchandise: Literature and the Anglo-Egyptian Mummy Trade in the Seventeenth Century', in *Re-orienting the Renaissance*, ed. Gerald Maclean (London: Palgrave, 2005), 66–87, 74.

4 Details for this re-creation are derived from: John Ray, *A Collection of Curious Travels and Voyages* (1693), 139–47; John Greaves, *Pyramidographia* (1646), 85–86; Richard Hakluyt, *Principal Navigations* (1599), 200. Sir Thomas Browne (d.1673) acknowledged Greaves as 'the learned describer of the pyramids' (*Certain Miscellany Tracts* (1683), 39).

5 For various details on the apothecaries of the period I am indebted to Penelope Hunting, *A History of the Society of Apothecaries* (London: Society of Apothecaries, 1998).

6 'Dragon's blood' was in fact only tree gum. For centuries red earth had been dug from the Greek isle of Lemnos; it was thought to be a particularly effective antidote to poisons.

7 See Alan Ford on Ussher, in new DNB.

8 The very earliest were in fact older, with modern estimates now dating these around 3200 BC. For early modern estimates, see George Abbot (d.1633), *A Brief Description of the Whole World* (1664), 157–58: bodies 'unputrefied for divers hundred years; and all learned men think thousands of years'; and Jean Dumont, *A New Voyage to the Levant* (1696), 214–15 ('preserved entire, perhaps above 4000 years'). Abbot's reference first appeared in an edition of 1605.

9 Indeed, according to certain pre-Christian calculations, the pyramids were in fact older than the earth (see, for example, Greaves, *Pyramidographia*, 16–17).

10 *Pyramidographia*, 70.

11 *A New Voyage to the Levant* (1696), 211. For more on the relationship between Renaissance Rome and Egypt, see: Brian A. Curran, *The Egyptian Renaissance: The Afterlife of Ancient Egypt in Early Modern Italy* (Chicago: University of Chicago Press, 2007), 4–9.

12 For a discussion of native bog mummies (animal and human), see Charles Leigh, *The Natural History of Lancashire, Cheshire, and the Peak in Derbyshire* (1700), 58–65.

13 On Italian saintly mummies, see Camporesi, *The Incorruptible Flesh: Bodily Mutation and Mortification in Religion and Folklore*, trans. Tania Croft-Murray (Cambridge: Cambridge University Press, 1988), 7. On the body of a young woman, found preserved in oil in Italy in the time of Pope Paul III, see *Diary of John Evelyn*, ed. William Bray (London: F. Warne, n.d.), 121.

14 *Diary*, VII, 367–68, 12 November 1666.

15 Anon., *A Full and True Account of ... an unknown person that was found ... within the top of a chimney ...* (1701), title page; *Morning Chronicle and London Advertiser*, 29 April 1774. Cf., also, a piece of preserved 'petrified flesh' found in an old burial ground 'and presented to Mr Roger North, of Rougham in Norfolk' (*Lloyd's Evening Post and British Chronicle*, 23 April 1762). Oddly enough, two such bodies seem to have been found in chimneys in 1701 (the coincidence being possibly due to high winds which damaged buildings in London). For the second case, see *Post Boy*, 11 October 1701.

16 As modern pathologists are now aware, some corpses naturally develop a condition called adipocere, which slows or prevents their decomposition. In 1702 an Englishman saw in a Wiltshire family vault a young woman who, though buried some ten years, 'looked as though she had been but just dead' (*Post Angel or Universal Entertainment*, March 1702, Issue 3). Cf., also, the 'human skull covered all over with the skin' on display in Gresham College, and thought to have 'been buried ... in some limey, or other like soil, by which it was tann'd or turn'd into a kind of leather' (Nehemiah Grew, *Musaeum Regalis Societatis* (1685), 7). For a discussion of the impressively artful preservation techniques of Fredrik Ruysch (1638–1732) and Lodewijk de Bils (1624–49), see: Dániel Margócsy, 'Advertising Cadavers in the Republic of Letters: Anatomical Publications in the Early Modern Netherlands', *British Journal for the History of Science* 42.2 (2009): 187–210.

17 Johann Michael Vansleb, quoted in: Ray, *Collection*, 147.

18 Pomet (d.1699), *A Complete History of Drugs*, 3rd edn (1737), 230 (a hint of uncertainty appears in Pomet's cautious 'if we dare believe tradition'). For a whimsical but seemingly genuine admiration of the lost 'secret of the ancient Aegyptians', see also: Monsieur de Voiture (d.1648), *Familiar and Courtly Letters* (1700), 140–41.

19 Bacon, *Sylva Sylvarum* (1627), 200.

20 At this time such status must have been cemented by the rarity of intact mummies (as artefacts) within Europe. For a rare exception, see Stephen Mullaney on the antiquarian Walter Cope, who (by the 1590s) possessed the mummy of a child ('Strange Things, Gross Terms, Curious Customs: The Rehearsal of Cultures in the Late Renaissance', *Representations* 3 (1983): 40–67, 40).

21 Across this period Vansleb was travelling in both Egypt and Syria. In the account given here he refers to his second visit to Egypt.

22 Ray, *Collection*, 142.

23 Ray, *Collection*, 139–47.

24 Ray, *Collection*, 146.

25 See, for example, Johann Schroeder, *Zoologia*, trans. anon. (1659), 58; John Keogh, *Zoologia Medicinalis Hibernica* (Dublin, 1739), 103.

26 Karl H. Dannenfeldt, 'Egyptian Mumia: The Sixteenth Century Experience and Debate', *Sixteenth Century Journal* 16.2 (1985): 163–80, 174.

27 Cited in *Bread of Dreams*, 47; italics mine.

28 Schwyzer, 'Mummy is Become Merchandise', 75.

29 *Arcana Microcosmi* (1652), 263.

30 *New Voyage* (1696), 214–15. On the alleged scarcity of Egyptian mummy *c.*1675, see also George Thomson, *Ortho-methodoz itro-chymike* (1675), 123.

31 *The Bridle of Pegasus: Studies in Magic, Mythology and Folklore* (London: Methuen, 1930), 171. The Guanche (or Guancho) were one of the aboriginal peoples of the Canaries, until displaced by the Spanish.

32 *A True Historical Discourse of Muley Hamet's Rising ...* (1609), K3r–v. For early sixteenth-century references to sand mummies, see Dannenfeldt, 167–68.

33 *The Life of our Blessed Lord and Saviour* (1693), 109.
34 Ray, *Collection*, 147. Cf. also Vincent Leblanc on the difficulty of navigation and the alleged size of some of these travelling convoys. If 'ten or twelve thousand persons' really were involved, the resultant supply would indeed have been plentiful. Leblanc also notes very precisely that these travellers would 'ride upon camels in wainscot cabins for the great dust and heat, with small holes for air and light, where they both eat and sleep' (*The World Surveyed*, trans. Francis Brooke (1660), 279; Leblanc himself died in 1640).
35 Ray, *Collection*, 147.
36 *Arcana Microcosmi*, 263.
37 *A Most Excellent ... Work* (1565), 73.
38 Cited in: Thomas Blundeville, *M. Blundeville his Exercises* (1594), 260.
39 *World Surveyed*, 169.
40 In: Robert Boyle (d.1691), *General Heads for the Natural History of a Country* (1692), 58, 61. This occurs in a part of the work added by an anonymous editor (see 'Preface to the Reader'). Boyle's original article was first published in 1666 in the *Philosophical Transactions* of the Royal Society (see Michael Hunter, *Boyle: Between God and Science* (London: Yale University Press, 2009), 152–54).
41 On the Polish grottos of Kiow, see Patrick Gordon, *Geography Anatomized* (1699), 128–29.
42 *The Royal Commentaries of Peru*, trans. Paul Rycaut (1688), 262. This book was first published as *Comentarios Reales de los Incas*, in Lisbon in 1609. Roy L. Moodie notes that art could also be employed in this region, where bodies were sometimes eviscerated, 'heavier muscle mass was removed, and the remains cured by "smoking"' (*Roentologic Studies of Egyptian and Peruvian Mummies* (Chicago: Field Museum of Natural History, 1931), 20).
43 Ross, *Arcana Microcosmi*, 96. Bacon noted that the Turks' peculiar diet of water, rice, and 'other food of small nourishment, maketh their bodies so solid, and hard' that it permitted them to indulge in the otherwise damaging habit of frequent washing (*Sylva Sylvarum*, 191–92).
44 I am very grateful to Daniel Hartley for suggesting this parallel. The word was clearly rare by the sixteenth century. It does not appear in the *OED*, and I have found just two instances besides Cottington's (Chaucer, *Plowman's Prologue*; Patrick Hume, *Annotations on Milton's* Paradise Lost (1695)). The accent of the period may have encouraged a link between 'manna' and 'munna'.
45 Pomet, *Complete History*, 228.
46 Pomet, *Complete History*, 229.
47 Dannenfeldt, 'Egyptian Mumia', 168.
48 See: Schwyzer, 'Mummy is Become Merchandise', 73–75; Dannenfeldt, 'Egyptian Mumia', 174, 169.
49 *Du Bartas his Divine Weeks*, trans. Joshua Sylvester (1611), 353. Du Bartas' *La Sepmaine: ou, Creation du Monde* had first appeared in French in 1578. The current stanza comes from the unfinished *Seconde Sepmaine* of 1584. Given that Protestant authors were more likely to refer to mummy as 'balsamum', it is worth recalling that Henri of Navarre (under whom du Bartas served) was an influential patron of Paracelsian healers (Laurence Brockliss and Colin Jones, *The Medical World of Early Modern France* (Oxford: Clarendon Press, 1997), 123–25). This stanza was often quoted in geographical works of the seventeenth century (see, for example, Peter Heylyn, *Cosmography* (1652), 5).
50 *Complete Works of Ben Jonson*, IV, 2.1, 56–59, 68–69. Ian Donaldson in new DNB states that *Poetaster* was 'performed at Blackfriars by the Children of Her Majesty's Chapel probably in the spring of 1601'.
51 *A Brief Description of the Whole World* (1605), K3r. As Fincham notes, this work did not appear under Abbot's name until after his death in 1633. Abbot became archbishop in 1611.
52 *Brief Description*, K3r. There is also a good chance that what he saw was sand mummy, given the reference to 'flesh clung to the bones'. Cf., in 1612, the Scottish traveller

William Lithgow, who saw 'whole bodies, hands, or other parts' taken from the Egyptian mummy pits to 'make the mummia which apothecaries use' (quoted by Schwyzer, 'Mummy is Become Merchandise', 75).

53 The Act which asserted this in March of that year noted that such duty had existed before the Civil War, so it is also likely that mummy was being taxed as an import earlier in the century (*An Act for the Redemption of Captives* (1650), 1, 32, 6). On duties, cf. also Schwyzer, 'Mummy is Become Merchandise', 75.

54 See Lucinda McCray Beier, *Sufferers and Healers: the Experience of Illness in Seventeenth-century England* (London: Routledge & Kegan Paul, 1987), 161.

55 *Three Reports of the Select Committee … on … the East Indies, China, Japan and Persia* (1793), 111. Others included tortoiseshells, serge, broadcloth, quicksilver and saffron.

56 *An Universal European Dictionary of Merchandise* (1799). This work first appeared in Hamburg in 1797.

57 Pomet, *Complete History*, 228.

58 *The Works of Beaumont and Fletcher*, intro. George Darley, 2 vols (London: Routledge, 1866), II, 5.3, 332. Gordon McMullan's new DNB article on John Fletcher notes that this play was unfinished at Fletcher's death (in 1625) and was licensed in 1626.

59 *Speculum Mundi* (1635), 302–3.

60 'Anthropophagy in Post-Renaissance Europe: the Tradition of Medicinal Cannibalism', *American Anthropologist* 90.2 (1988): 405–9, 407.

61 Pomet, *Complete History*, 228–29.

62 See: Mary Roach, *Stiff: The Curious Lives of Human Cadavers* (London: Penguin, 2003), 49–50.

63 *A Brief Account of Some Travels in Divers Parts of Europe* (1685), 155.

64 Cf. Leo Kanner, who dates the drinking, running, and also whipping of the patient back to the Middle Ages ('The Folklore and Cultural History of Epilepsy', *Medical Life* 37.4 (1930): 167–214, 199).

65 Kanner, 'Folklore and Cultural History of Epilepsy', 199.

66 *Rituals of Retribution: Capital Punishment in Germany, 1600–1987* (Oxford: Oxford University Press, 1996), 90–91.

67 Schroeder, *Zoologia*, 48; Keogh, *Zoologia*, 101.

68 Dr Richard Newell (until recently anatomy lecturer at Cardiff University) kindly informs me that: 'patients who have received blood transfusions for various therapeutic reasons do show in many cases a rapidly occurring sense of wellbeing, sometimes disproportionate to the amount of blood transfused'. Medical student Naishal Patel adds that the absorption of iron happens relatively quickly, occurring 'in the upper section of the small intestine – the sections directly after the stomach called the duodenum and upper jejunum'.

69 For this and other details on Browne, see Kees Van Strien, in new DNB.

70 On the status of epileptics in the pre-scientific world, see *Rituals*, 95–96. In 1930, Kanner could write that 'the Swabians still believe that the saliva of epileptics is poisonous' ('Folklore and Cultural History of Epilepsy', 176).

71 Kathy Stuart, *Defiled Trades: Honour and Ritual Pollution in Early Modern Germany* (Cambridge: Cambridge University Press, 1999), 158–59. Although Evans's accounts (like that of Browne) tend to be late seventeenth century at the earliest, the editors of *A Hangman's Diary*, which spans the years 1573–1617, also note 'that sick people sometimes bribed the executioner to allow them to drink the blood streaming from the trunk of the newly beheaded'. Sadly, we have no exact date (or dates) in this case, as the edition of the *Diary* comprises selections from an original manuscript, and the blood scenes were not transcribed (see: *A Hangman's Diary: Being the Journal of Master Franz Schmidt, Public Executioner of Nuremberg, 1573–1617*, ed. A. Keller, trans. C. Calvert and A.W. Gruner (London: Philip Allan, 1928), 63).

72 *Rituals*, 90.

73 *Rituals*, 92–93.

74 Kanner, 'Folklore and Cultural History of Epilepsy', 199. Woytasch himself was shocked at this sight, and had to have its rationale explained to him by another witness.

75 Cited in Ferdinand P. Moog and Axel Karenburg, 'Between Horror and Hope: Gladiator's Blood as a Cure for Epileptics in Ancient Medicine', *Journal of the History of the Neurosciences* 12.2 (2003): 137–43, 142.

76 Mabel Peacock, 'Executed Criminals and Folk Medicine,' *Folklore* 7 (1896): 268–83, 270–71. Cf. also *The Encylopedia of Folk Medicine*, which notes that 'human blood has been widely used to treat epilepsy' (39).

77 Ruth Richardson, *Death, Dissection and the Destitute* (London: Phoenix, 2001), 52.

78 *Itinerary* (1617), 205.

79 It is also possible that the executioner was actually drunk (cf. Moryson, *Itinerary*, 205, on a drinking bout ending in murder by another executioner).

80 *Philosophical Letters* (1664), 228.

81 *Curiosities in Chymistry* (1691), 86. Cf. also: Daniel Sennert, *The Sixth Book of Practical Physic*, trans. Nicholas Culpeper and Abdiah Cole (1662), 81; Andreas Tentzel, *Medicina Diastatica*, trans. Ferdinando Parkhurst (1653), 76. It is Sennert who refers the tale back to Matthiolus' 1544 *Diascordium*.

82 On epilepsy and shock, see Kanner, 'Folklore and Cultural History of Epilepsy', 173.

83 See, for example, Edward Topsell, *The History of Four-footed Beasts* (1607), 686–87.

84 For an especially notorious example of this in Germany in 1800, see Evans, *Rituals*, 194.

85 *Rituals*, 92.

86 *Three Books of Occult Philosophy*, trans. J.F. (1651), 85.

87 *Rituals*, 91–92, 93, 92.

88 'Executed Criminals', 271. Such methods echo the prescription cited by Alexander of Tralles in the sixth century: '"take a bloody rag of a slain swordsman or executed man, burn it, mix the ashes into wine, and with seven doses you will free the patient of epilepsy"' (cited in 'Between Horror and Hope', 142).

89 *Defiled Trades*, 149–85, 157.

90 *Defiled Trades*, 163–64. Cf. also a reference to the hangman's repute in treating open wounds (ibid., 173) which would almost certainly have involved use of human fat.

91 Pomet, *Complete History*, 229.

92 Pomet, *Complete History*, 229–30.

93 Giovanni Ferrari, 'Public Anatomy Lessons and the Carnival: The Anatomy Theatre of Bologna', *Past and Present* 117 (1987): 50–106, 100–101. Ferrari's Italian sources derive, like Pomet's comments, from the late seventeenth century.

94 *Rituals*, 89.

95 Moryson, *Itinerary*, 143. At certain times there were evidently unusually high numbers of executions (and sometimes even hangings in the cases of private feuds). See, for example: William Drummond, *History of Scotland* (1655), 14, on the 300 people hung on one occasion in Scotland in 1426; Alexander Shields, *A Short Memorial of the Sufferings ... of the Presbyterians in Scotland* [Edinburgh?, 1690], 34 on a spontaneous hanging without trial; and E.C., *A Faithful Account, of the Present State of Affairs ... Since the Discovery of the Horrid Popish Plot, anno 1678 to this present year, 1689* (1690), 60–72.

96 Anon., *A Short Account of a Late Journey to Tuscany, Rome, and other parts of Italy* [1741], 65–66. This account suggests that the belief of Evans, that 'only in very exceptional cases ... is the use of the blood of the beheaded for medico-magical purposes recorded in Catholic societies' needs reconsidering (*Rituals*, 98). It may, for example, have gone unrecorded in Italy just because the educated were complicit in it, and thought it too unremarkable to record. On this question, cf. also Stuart, *Defiled Trades*, 180–81.

97 That behaviour overlaps to some extent with the Germans who painted blood on their doors against fire (see below); but clearly differs insofar as the Italians were prepared to actually drink it.

98 *Rituals*, 98.

99 For the vivid account of the execution given by Patricia Fumerton, see *Cultural Aesthetics: Renaissance Literature and the Practice of Social Ornament* (Chicago: University of Chicago Press, 1991), 3–10.

100 Charles I, William Fulman, Richard Perrinchief, and John Gauden, *Basiliká: the Works of King Charles the Martyr* (1687), 58. For the relics, we know that long afterwards devout Royalists wore lockets in which curls of Charles's hair were kept.

101 The comparison of course also extends to Paul, who in Acts 19.11–12 was performing numerous cures by proxy, merely by sending to the sick handkerchiefs or other items which he had touched. Cf., also, the legend of Saint Veronica, supposed to have wiped away Christ's sweat and blood en route to Calvary, with a handkerchief which thereafter became 'an apotropaic talisman' (quotation from: Andrew Sofer, 'Absorbing Interests: Kyd's Bloody Handkerchief as Palimpsest', *Comparative Drama* 34.2 (2000): 127–53, 146). As Andrew Lacey points out, the handkerchiefs dipped in Charles's blood were held to have effected various cures some time after his death. Mary Bayly was cured of the king's evil in 1649; and (echoing the irony noted above) we find that a three-year-old boy was also cured via a handkerchief belonging to a Parliamentarian, Major Gouge (*The Cult of King Charles the Martyr* (Woodbridge: Boydell Press, 2003), 62–63).

102 Cf. also the woman who touches the hem of Christ's garment (Luke 8.42–48), allegedly in order to secure an impersonal power (*dunamin*) of healing: 'the faith is in the power. What the woman wants is the power, not the Christ; the water, not the fireman' (Friedrich Preisigke, cited by M. Hull, *Hellenistic Magic and the Synoptic Tradition* (London: SCM Press, 1974), 109).

103 Howard Wilcox Haggard, *Devils, Drugs and Doctors: The Story of the Science of Healing from Medicine-man to Doctor* (Wakefield: EP Publishing, 1975), 328.

104 *Rituals*, 194, 91–92.

105 See, again, Ferrari, 'Public Anatomy Lessons', 100–101.

106 Andrew Hadfield (citing Arthur Marotti), 'A Handkerchief Dipped in Blood in *The Spanish Tragedy*: An Anti-Catholic Reference?', *Notes and Queries* 46.2 (1999): 197. (Many thanks to Willey Maley for passing this piece on.)

107 Willy Maley's new DNB article on Riche notes that data on his life is thin; the article shows that Rich was not known to be in England in 1611, but we cannot be certain that he was definitely present at the execution.

108 Barnabe Rich, *A Catholic Conference* ... (1612), 5v–6r; cited in: Patricia Palmer, '"A headlesse Ladie" and "a horses loade of heades": Writing the Beheading', *RQ* 60.1 (2007), 25–57, 42–44.

109 *Boswell on the Grand Tour: Italy, Corsica, and France, 1765–1766*, ed. F. Brady and F.A. Pottle (London: Heinemann, 1955), 194.

110 *Itinerary*, 205. Moryson's interest in Germanic infamy shows that this phenomenon was far more pronounced there than in England. Jonathan Sawday (*The Body Emblazoned: Dissection and the Human Body in Renaissance Culture* (London: Routledge, 1995), 78–84) does seem to have exaggerated the 'infamy' surrounding the English executioner (see Mark S.R. Jenner, 'Body, Text and Society', *Social History of Medicine* 12 (1999): 143–54, 145–46).

111 *Rituals*, 56–58. For the associated range of other demeaning or death-related tasks which German executioners tended to perform, see ibid., 60–63. Given that the touch of the executioner was an especially potent source of infamy or pollution, it seems likely that the curious 'death machine' observed by Edward Browne arose from a desire to avoid it: 'at Pressburg they have a strange way of execution, still used at Metz, and some other places, by a maid, or engine like a maid finely dressed up with her hands before her. The malefactor salutes her first, and then retires. But at his second salute she opens her hands and cuts his heart in sunder' (*Brief Account*, 155).

112 *Rituals*, 62.

113 *Defiled Trades*, 149–85.

114 *The Spectacle of Suffering: Executions and the Evolution of Repression: from a Preindustrial Metropolis to the European Experience* (Cambridge: Cambridge University Press, 1984), 32.

115 Peacock, 'Executed Criminals', 270. Peacock cites the entry under 'Bourreau' from Collin de Plancy's 1825 *Dictionnaire Infernal (Dictionary of Demonology)*. Plancy himself does not date the custom. See also his 'Hand of the Hanged Man', in *Dictionary of Demonology*, ed. and trans. Wade Baskin (London: Peter Owen, 1965), 100.

116 For further discussion of this seeming paradox, see: Stuart, *Defiled Trades*, 149–50.

117 Cf. Evans, *Rituals*, 95, on offenders as 'both polluting and healing', as well as for an interesting parallel with the dualistic status of epileptics.

118 *Rituals*, 93–94, 377.

119 All references and quotations from: Henry Goodcole, *Heaven's Speedy Hue and Cry Sent After Lust and Murder* (1635), reissue, STC 12010.5, C4r–v.

120 *The Works of Benjamin Jonson* (1616), 951.

121 Anon., *The Manner of the Death and Execution of Arnold Cosby* (1591), A2v.

122 *An Account of the Life and Dying Confession of William Anderson Horner* [Edinburgh, 1708].

123 See Tim Marshall, *Murdering to Dissect: Grave-robbing, Frankenstein, and the Anatomy Literature* (Manchester: Manchester University Press, 1995), 93. On the tactical economy of gibbet locations (usually out of towns), see Pieter Spierenburg, *The Spectacle of Suffering: Executions and the Evolution of Repression: From a Preindustrial Metropolis to the European Experience* (Cambridge: Cambridge University Press, 1984), 57–58.

124 *Rituals*, 87–88.

125 See *Itinerary*, 207, 210. Evans notes that the criminal code of the Holy Roman Emperor Charles V, published in 1532, prescribed the death penalty for 'treason, blasphemy, conjuring, witchcraft, rape, abortion, unnatural sex, forgery, highway robbery, robbery with violence (actual or threatened) and theft at the third conviction' (*Rituals*, 29).

126 *Itinerary*, 207.

127 *Rituals*, 93–94.

128 Ironically, it seems as if certain anatomy specimens may have endured longer than some gibbeted bodies. In Vienna in winter or early spring 1668–69, Edward Browne saw 'a public anatomy of a woman' which 'lasted so long, that the body was nineteen days unburied' (*Account*, 140).

129 *Rituals*, 27–28. Evans here cites the eyewitness report of a wheel-breaking which John Taylor the water-poet saw in Hamburg in August 1616. While Moryson (above) uses the common phrase 'broken upon a wheel', in Germany felons were actually broken with a wheel, after being tied fast to the ground – something confirmed generally by Evans, and by Taylor's own detailed description. For breaking *on* the wheel (usually with an iron bar) in France, see: John Reynolds, *The Triumphs of Gods Revenge* (1635), 14, 42, 111, 211, 336–37. On an unexplained theft from a gibbet in Amsterdam in 1689, see Spierenburg, *Spectacle*, 90.

130 See S.J. Connolly, *Religion, Law, and Power: The Making of Protestant Ireland 1660–1760* (Oxford: Clarendon Press, 2002), 224.

131 C.D. O'Malley, *Andreas Vesalius of Brussels: 1514–1564* (Berkeley: University of California Press, 1964), 64.

132 William Harvey, *Lectures on the Whole of Anatomy*, trans. C.D. O'Malley, F.N.L. Poynter, and K.F. Russell (Berkeley and Los Angeles: University of California Press, 1961), 5.

133 An entry for 24 February 1608 in the *Annals of the Royal College of Physicians of London* records the decree that 'the bodies dissected by the anatomy lecturers should afterwards be buried in wooden coffins at the expense of the College' (*RCP*, III, i, 6). What exactly was in these coffins is another matter. It would seem likely that fat in particular might have been regarded as a necessary casualty of the dissection process.

134 From around 1624 or 1625 the Physicians also held an annual winter dissection (usually in December). The 'Goulstonian lecture' appears to have been inaugurated by 1625 (*RCP*, III, i, 188), to have occurred around 10 December in 1628 (*RCP*, III, ii, 260) and in 1629 definitely took place on 11, 12, and 14 December (*RCP*, III, ii, 269).

135 *The Annals of the Barber-Surgeons of London*, ed. Sidney Young, 2 vols (London: Blades, East & Blades, 1890), II, 320.

136 *Defiled Trades*, 158, 173.

137 See: Helen Dingwall, *A Famous and Flourishing Society: The History of the Royal College of Surgeons of Edinburgh, 1505–2005* (Edinburgh: Edinburgh University Press, 2005), 101. In this case Bell may have wanted the body parts for private study, rather than personal gain.

138 2.2, 153–54.

139 Although Fludd was considered unorthodox by some doctors, he was a close friend of William Harvey, and became a full member of the College of Physicians in June 1608. (On this and the College's initial resistance to Fludd as a (possibly) anti-Galenic physician, see the DNB article by Ian Maclean.) On the private anatomy, see: *Mosaical Philosophy* (1659), 250. (This work was first published in Latin in 1638.). Fludd evidently began dissecting for public lectures in or after 1624 (see *RCP*, III, i, 188, 30 October 1624). Maclean's article on Fludd states that he lectured on 27 June 1620; but this was probably a purely oral lecture, given that actual anatomies were confined to the cooler months of the year, in the absence of efficient refrigeration or preservative agents.

140 *Mosaical Philosophy*, 250.

141 See *Defiled Trades*, 163.

142 Anon., *The Strange and Wonderful Discovery* ... (1684), 1–2.

143 On the still more cavalier treatment of a dissection specimen in London 1740, see: *Daily Post* (London), 9 June 1740.

144 'We know from a scribbled note by Aubrey in *Monumenta Britannica* that Toope excavated at the Sanctuary in the first instance (which he refers to in the letter to Aubrey) in 1678. The letter is 1685, and as Aubrey states he was lately there again, 1685 could be a reasonable date for his second foray' (Jonathan Trigg, personal communication, 19 June 2010).

145 Jonathan Trigg kindly informs me of 'the unusual fact that the burial chambers were backfilled in prehistory with a mixture of earth and artefacts, and possible midden material. Piggott argues that, where he excavated, Toope had only dug down three feet, leaving five feet unexcavated before the bones would have been encountered. This backfilling of burial chambers is unique in British megalithic tombs as far as I know' (personal communication, 19 June 2010).

146 Stuart Piggott, 'The Excavation of the West Kennet Long Barrow 1955–56', *Antiquity* 32 (1958): 236–37. Trigg notes that 'Took' was apparently a drily apt nickname reflecting Toope's irreverent plunder: 'it seems to be a slightly derogatory sobriquet given him by varying Wiltshire locals, in relation to his activities. It is recorded by Stukeley in his papers and I presume he was told it by the locals' (personal communication, 20 June 2010).

147 Letter quoted in: *Wiltshire Archaeological and Natural History Magazine* (www.archive. org/stream/wiltshirearchaeo04wilt/wiltshirearchaeo04wilt_djvu.txt). Trigg kindly informs me that, besides Bristol (where Toope wrote that letter), Toope's 'various other possible abodes include Bath, Marlborough and Oxford' (personal communication, 20 June 2010). We know that Toope wrote a letter to the chemist Robert Boyle from Bath on 5 April 1683, and in this stated that he had been resident in Marlborough in February 1678. Toope also asks Boyle for 'a taste of that blessed oil, which you promised the way of confecting' – a request which may refer to Boyle's oil of human blood (Boyle, *Works*, vol. 5 [1744], 645–46). Although we do not know just when Toope moved, he clearly came to be well associated with the Spa in later years. In 1725 the physician Thomas Guidott refers to Toope (perhaps then deceased) as 'sometime since a laudable practitioner at the Bath' (*A Collection of Treatises Relating to the City and Waters of Bath*, 280). It is just possible that Toope did the digging himself (he writes, 'I came next day and dug for them'). In his era, however, it would be unusual for the genteel to engage unaided in manual work.

148 See Stuart Piggott, *The West Kennet Long Barrow Excavations 1955–56* (London: Stationer's Office, 1962), 4.

149 Pomet, *Complete History*, 229. Presumably 'heads' here is just another word for 'skulls'.
150 *The Family Physician* (1678), 127. By contrast, mummy was only five shillings and 4 pence a pound, and other common medical ingredients far cheaper again. Fox lungs, for example, cost just two shillings a pound, with rasped ivory coming in at a mere four pence.
151 *Bread of Dreams*, 45–46, citing Cammilo Brunori.
152 We should recall, too, that it was a crime to take property (such as jewellery) from a grave, but not to take the corpse itself.
153 Cf. Richardson, however, on the more amateur and piecemeal bodysnatching of the early eighteenth century (*Death, Dissection and the Destitute*, 54; on the general phenomenon, see ibid., 52–72). For a very recent Italian case, see: Tom Kington, 'Vatican Cardinal Faces Corruption Inquiry over Rome Property Deals', *Guardian*, Sunday, 20 June 2010.
154 *Bell's Weekly Messenger* [?1798–?1799], 80.
155 Samuel Jackson Pratt, *Liberal Opinions, upon Animals, Man, and Providence* (1775–77), VI, 129–30.
156 'The Progress of a Divine: A Satire', in *Works* (1777), 119.
157 *Times*, 7 August 1798. One of the most notorious of them was evidently not. Ruth Richardson notes that although Sir Astley Cooper underwent a post-mortem after his death, 'from the size of his stone sarcophagus it would seem that he made quite sure that he would not personally undergo dissection' (*Death, Dissection and the Destitute*, 117).
158 *The Bury and Norwich Post*, Wednesday, 22 October 1817.
159 See Colin Dickey, *Cranioklepty: Grave Robbing and the Search for Genius* (Columbia: Unbridled Books, 2009).
160 *Works* (London: William Pickering, 1835), III, 478.
161 This is because, he adds, death can 'in a moment can so disfigure us that our nearest friends, wife, and children stand afraid and stare at us' (*Religio Medici* (1642), 76). Although Browne's skull was not (as far as we know) used for a drinking bowl, it was stolen and sold in 1840 by an unscrupulous sexton – later spending a good deal of time on public display in a Norwich museum.
162 'Cultures of Death and Politics of Corpse Supply: Anatomy in Vienna, 1848–1914', *Bulletin of the History of Medicine* 82.3 (2008): 570–607, 580. For a case of grave violation prompted by medical/magical aims in the Swiss town of Saanen in 1795, see Evans, *Rituals*, 93. On the late Victorian collection of skulls and their use in phrenology, see: Helen Macdonald, *Human Remains: Dissection and its Histories* (London: Yale University Press, 2006), 96–135. Macdonald notes that the Victorian doctor, Joseph Barnard Davis, had amassed 1,474 skulls in his Staffordshire home by 1867.
163 See Elizabeth T. Hurren, 'Whose Body is it Anyway? Trading the Dead Poor, Coroner's Disputes, and the Business of Anatomy at Oxford University, 1885–1929', *Bulletin of the History of Medicine* 82.4 (2008): 775–819, 811–12.
164 Quoted in: Tentzel, *Medicina Diastatica*, 8.
165 *Daily Gazetteer*, 4 October 1736. Vanessa Harding notes that even the graves of the better off may have been relatively shallow by modern standards. In the parish of St Stephen Coleman in 1542 a burial order specified minimums of just three foot for children and four for adults, with the six foot standard being prompted in 1582 by reason of plague (Vanessa Harding, *The Dead and the Living* in Paris and London, 1500–1670 (Cambridge: Cambridge University Press, 2002), 64).
166 Peter Elmer's new DNB article on French states that he began working at the Savoy at the end of the first civil war (in 1646).
167 *Miscellaneous Remarks ... in a Late Seven Years Tour through France, Italy, Germany and Holland* [?1758], 56–57. Cf. Vanessa Harding: 'those who were buried from the [Parisian] hospitals ... were treated pragmatically and sometimes it seems callously, with inadequate protection either for themselves or for the public' (*Dead and the Living*, 231).

168 Roach, *Stiff*, 42. On pauper burials in nineteenth century England, see Elizabeth Hurren and Steve King, '"Begging for a Burial": Form, Function, and Conflict in Nineteenth-Century Pauper Burial', *Social History* 30.3 (2005): 321–41.

169 *Poems*, 75.

170 In the sixteenth and seventeenth centuries especially the death rate frequently exceeded the birth rate by some distance (see E.A. Wrigley and R.S. Schofield, with R. Lee and J. Oeppen, *The Population History of England: 1541–1871: A Reconstruction* (Edward Arnold, 1981), 161–62, 164, 167, and Pullout 1).

171 For more on such forms of decoration, see Philippe Ariès, *The Hour of our Death*, trans. Helen Weaver (London: Penguin, 1987), 59–61. On the rather more mundane forms of overcrowding in London, *c.*1839, see David Brandon and Alan Brooke, *London: City of the Dead* (Stroud: The History Press, 2008), 88: in St Anne's churchyard in Soho '"you may see human heads, covered with hair"' and '"human bodies with flesh still adhering to them"'.

172 Harding, *Dead and the Living*, 64, 65.

173 Harding, *Dead and the Living*, 112.

174 John Gerard (d.1612), *The Herbal or General History of Plants*, ed. Thomas Johnson (1633), 1563. Vanessa Harding suspects that most London charnel houses were cleared away at the Reformation; the parish of St Alphege, for example, took its down in 1547 (*Dead and the Living*, 64). Nevertheless, in 1687 the preacher John Scott could ask his listeners at a funeral sermon to 'go down into the charnel-house, and there survey a while the numerous trophies of victorious Death'; while in 1695 the rector of Drumglass, Edward Arwaker, could still write that, 'every charnel-house will present us with as many skulls, that still retain their hair and teeth, as that had lost those ornaments, before they saw corruption' (*A Sermon Preached at the Funeral of Sir John Buckworth* (1687), 10; *Thoughts Well Employed* (1695), 126). On the medieval charnel house in London's Spitalfields, see Nic Fleming, 'Secrets of the Charnel House … ', *Daily Telegraph*, 11 July 2005.

175 *Hour of our Death*, 59, 60.

176 See Brandon and Brooke, *London: City of the Dead*, 86. On St Bride's see also Harding, *Dead and the Living*, 65.

177 Christian Uvedale, *The Construction of the Nerves* (1758), 51. Although Uvedale seems to try and push this and other corpse medicines back into the past ('it was believed that [usnea] had thence great virtue') it seems odd that the pieces of skull should remain in the garden if there was a universal hostility to such substances in 1758.

178 *Aurora Chymica* (1672), 11.

179 For the sometimes remarkably precise knowledge a gravedigger might have of his cemetery and its variously decomposing bodies, see Ariès, *Hour of our Death*, 59.

180 'Contesting Sacred Space: Burial Disputes in Sixteenth-Century France', in *The Place of the Dead: Death and Remembrance in late Medieval and Early Modern Europe*, ed. Bruce Gordon and Peter Marshall (Cambridge: Cambridge University Press, 2000), 131–48, 131–32.

181 For a concise scholarly account of the massacre, see: Barbara B. Diefendorf, *Beneath the Cross: Catholics and Huguenots in Sixteenth-century Paris* (New York: Oxford University Press, 1991), 93–106, *et passim*.

182 *A True History of the Memorable Siege of Ostend*, trans. Edward Grimeston (1604), 54–55. The original version seems to have been in Dutch, and was after translated into German and then French. Grimeston's translation draws only on some of the full account, which did not appear in entirety until 1605. In his translation a preface by 'the author' is signed 'A.V.' (A3r).

183 On fat and wounds, see *Dr Fludd's Answer unto M. Foster* (1631), 13.

184 *The Spoil of Antwerp* (1576), B7v–C1r.

185 For examples in the case of Antwerp, see Gascoigne, *Spoil*, B7r, C1v–C3r.

186 Geoffrey Parker, *The Thirty Years' War* (London: Routledge, 1984), 215.

187 Ronald G. Asch, *The Thirty Years' War: the Holy Roman Empire and Europe, 1618–1648* (Basingstoke: Macmillan, 1997), 185.

188 Samuel Gardiner, *The Thirty Years' War, 1618–1648* (New York: Greenwood, 1969), 213–14.

189 Philip Vincent, *The Lamentations of Germany* (1638), 62.

190 For a possible case of grave theft for food in fourteenth-century Ireland, see: William C. Jordan, *The Great Famine: Northern Europe in the Early Fourteenth Century* (Princeton: Princeton University Press, 1996), 114–15. This occurred on a greater scale during the Munster famine in the early 1580s, 'when the starving … dug corpses out of the ground' (many thanks to Willey Maley for this information (personal communication, 29 October 2010)).

191 *A True Relation of … the Travels of … Thomas Lord Howard* (1637), 10–11.

192 On the dissection, see, again, *Basiliká* (1687), 58.

193 *Richard Baxter's Penitent Confession* (1691), 42.

194 James Heath, *A Chronicle of the Late Intestine War* (1676), 61. Rather frustratingly, there is no trace of any habitation called Kendal on modern maps of this area, a few miles west of the City of York. The bell to which the author, James Heath, refers would seem to indicate a church, but there are several of these encircling the Moor within a radius of five miles or less. In terms of close proximity the nearest are probably those of Tockwith, around two miles to the south-west, and Hessay, a similar distance to the north-east. The only nearby location which sounds remotely like Kendal is the ancient village of Cattal, a few miles to the north-west of the battle site.

195 See Markku Peltonen, 'Francis Bacon' in new DNB. Peltonen notes that the treatise, 'Certain considerations touching the plantation in Ireland', was not published, but was given to James I as a new year's gift.

196 Cited in: Nicholas P. Canny, *The Elizabethan Conquest of Ireland: A Pattern Established, 1565–1576* (Sussex: Harvester, 1976), 119. Given Davies' legal training, his argument was probably inspired by the Roman legal theory of 'res nullius'. For its use as justification of invasion and settlement, see: Donne, *Sermons*, III, 274; Walter S.H. Lim, *The Arts of Empire: The Poetics of Colonialism from Raleigh to Milton* (London: Associated University Press, 1998), 79–80.

197 Patricia Palmer, *Language and Conquest in Early Modern Ireland: English Renaissance Literature and Elizabethan Imperial Experience* (Cambridge: Cambridge University Press, 2001), 75. See also ibid., 40–73, on the English attitude towards Gaelic in this period.

198 Cf., again, John Speed, citing the mid-fourth-century chronicler, Gaius Julius Solinus, and the classical geographer and historian, Strabo (c.64 BC–19 AD), on the alleged incest, cannibalism and blood-drinking of the Irish (*England, Wales, Scotland and Ireland Described and Abridged* (1627), Y5r). This book was reprinted as late as 1676.

199 *Man and the Natural World: Changing Attitudes in England 1500–1800* (London: Allen Lane, 1983), 42–43.

200 Quoted in: Andrew Murphy, *But the Irish Sea Betwixt Us: Ireland, Colonialism, and Renaissance Literature* (Lexington: University Press of Kentucky, 1999), 11–12.

201 Raymond Gillespie, 'Temple's Fate: Reading *The Irish Rebellion* in Late Seventeenth-Century England', in *British Interventions in Early Modern Ireland*, ed. Ciaran Brady and Jane Ohlmeyer (Cambridge: Cambridge University Press, 2005), 315–33, 316.

202 Elaine Murphy notes, for example, that during the 1640s, the parliamentary navy frequently denied ordinary military law to Irish prisoners of war, who were summarily executed in situations in which Royalists, by contrast, were spared (see: 'Atrocities at Sea and the Treatment of Prisoners of War by the Parliamentary Navy in Ireland, 1641–49', *The Historical Journal* 53.1 (2010): 21–37, 30).

203 See S.J. Connolly, *Contested Island: Ireland 1460–1630* (Oxford: Oxford University Press, 2007), 4–5.

204 New DNB, article on Sir Humphrey Gilbert. Unless otherwise stated, all information on Gilbert is from this article.

205 Connolly, *Contested Island*, 145. On the reward, and its ultimate collection by William Piers, see Hiram Morgan, '"Treason against Traitors": Thomas Walker, Hugh O'Neill's would-be Assassin', *History Ireland* 18.2 (2010): 18–21, 18.

206 'Although Churchyard himself dates his service under Sir Humphrey Gilbert and Sir Thomas Morgan to 1569, it is most likely to have been in the unsuccessful expedition of 1572, the year of the siege of Tergoes where he probably served' (Raphael Lyne, 'Thomas Churchyard', new DNB).

207 *A General Rehearsal of Wars* (1579), Q3v–Q4r. For more on the especially high number of extra-judicial beheadings under English rule, see, again, Palmer, '"A headlesse Ladie"'.

208 *General Rehearsal*, Q2r.

209 Connolly, *Contested Island*, 146.

210 Owing to variant forms of dating in the period this battle is also sometimes dated 3 January 1602 (Edmund Curtis, *A History of Ireland* (London: Methuen, 1961), 217–18).

211 *The Complete Herbal of Physical Plants* (1694), 132.

212 Pomet, *Complete History*, 229. This statement may have been added by another author. The original French text of 1694 has instead: '"these skulls mostly come from Ireland, where they frequently let the bodies of criminals hang on the gibbet til they fall to pieces"' (quoted in: A.C. Wootton, *Chronicles of Pharmacy*, 2 vols (London: Macmillan, 1910), II, 6). The 1712 English translation refers both to gibbets and to the Irish Massacre (*Complete History* (1712), 229).

213 Samuel Clarke (d.1682), *A New Description of the World* (1689), 61. Cf. *A New Description* (1657), 148. The passage also implies that this region of Germany was well-situated to trade with Paracelsian Denmark, just to the north. On trade in this area between the Italians and Bruges, see also Fynes Moryson, *Itinerary*, 96.

214 Curtis, *History*, 244.

215 Some decades earlier, the Irish had also won the Battle of the Yellow Ford, on 15 August 1598, when around 1,500 English soldiers were killed (Curtis, *History*, 212–13).

216 Micheál Ó Siochrú, *Confederate Ireland, 1642–1649: a Constitutional and Political Analysis* (Dublin: Four Courts Press, 1999), 11, 29.

217 In terms of transport between Ireland and England, we know that ships were regularly sailing from Bristol to Ireland with supplies for settlers, in the Restoration era and beyond (see Gillespie, 'Temple's Fate', 315). Although such skulls were most obviously chosen because of their growths of moss, most German practitioners must have been using the skull itself – not least because of the cost involved.

218 Andrew Canessa, 'Fear and Loathing on the Kharisiri Trail: Alterity and Identity in the Andes', *The Journal of the Royal Anthropological Institute* 6.4 (2000): 705–20, 705. I am very grateful to Rachel Bailin, who confirms via a Bolivian friend, Carmen Velasco, that this fear remains a living one in 2010.

219 Anthony Oliver-Smith, 'The Pishtaco: Institutionalized Fear in Highland Peru', *The Journal of American Folklore* 82.326 (1969): 363–68, 363–64. See also Canessa, 'Fear and Loathing', 706. Steve J. Stern also attributes the figure of the kharisiri to the habitual Spanish use of human fat in the early colonial period (*Resistance, Rebellion and Consciousness in the Andean Peasant World* (Madison: University of Wisconsin Press, 1987), 170–71, cited by Canessa, 'Fear and Loathing', 706).

220 Thomas Gage, *The English-American, his Travail by Sea and Land* (1648), 40. Gage cites reports that Cortez used those already slain in fighting, stating also that the Indians, 'who were cruel and bloody butchers, using sacrifice of man's flesh, would in this sort open the dead body and take out the grease'. See also Samuel Purchas, *Purchas his Pilgrims* (1625), 1,121–22, where Cortez' act is partly due to desire for vengeance. In 1642, the preacher Thomas Fuller seems to confirm the value of animal fat to New World settlers when he claims that 'in the West-Indies thousands of kine are killed for their tallow alone, and their flesh cast away' (*The Holy State* (1642), 426).

221 Cited by Oliver-Smith, 'The Pishtaco', 364.

222 *Beware the Cat* (1584), C5r.
223 *Dr Fludd's Answer*, 13.
224 Both animal and human fats, however, were also chemically treated from a quite early stage in the history of corpse medicine (see, for example, *A Brief Answer of Joseph Quercetanus*, trans. John Hester (1591), 36v).
225 Cf., also: L.F. Newman, 'Some Notes on Folk Medicine in the Eastern Counties', *Folklore* 56.4 (1945): 349–60, 358, on hogs' grease for sore feet.
226 See: *The Encyclopedia of Folk Medicine: Old World and New World Traditions*, ed. Gabrielle Hatfield (Oxford: ABC Clio, 2004), 153.
227 W.J. Hoffman, 'Folk-Medicine of the Pennsylvania Germans', *Proceedings of the American Philosophical Society* 26.129 (1889): 329–52, 335.
228 Canessa also suggests an ironic possible source of the kharisiri which gives further evidence for Spanish use of human fat. Bethlehemite friars working in the Andes 'travelled alone throughout the countryside, collecting alms at often-remote crossroads. These friars were primarily physicians ... and it is supposed they used the human body fat in administering to the sick'. Moreover, the founder of their order, Pedro de San Joseph de Betancur, was 'supposed to have adopted the practice of cleaning sores and rotting wounds with his mouth as an exercise in humility'. As Canessa points out, any Indians who saw or heard of this might well have 'thought he was sucking the life out of his victims' ('Fear and Loathing', 706).
229 For further details, see: Lewis Hanke, *Aristotle among the American Indians* (London: Hollis and Carter, 1959); Richard Sugg, *John Donne* (London: Palgrave, 2007), 154–85
230 Las Casas' *Brief Relation of the Destruction of the West Indies* was first published in Seville in 1552.
231 Canessa, 'Fear and Loathing', 705–6.
232 On Greek vampires and sudden unexplained deaths (notably, of those who were alone), see Leone Allacci (1645), cited by Montague Summers, *The Vampire: His Kith and Kin* (1928), abr. Nigel Suckling, chapter one, 7 (www.unicorngarden.com/vampires. htm). I am very grateful to Nigel Suckling for making this version available. On fairies, see Mary Ellen Lamb, 'Taken by the Fairies: Fairy Practices and the Production of Popular Culture in *A Midsummer Night's Dream*', *Shakespeare Quarterly* 51.3 (2000): 277–312.
233 On the whiteness of the kharisiri, and for an overview of analyses of the kharisiri as an emblem of colonial oppression, see Canessa, 'Fear and Loathing', 706. On the pishtaco, see Oliver-Smith, 'The Pishtaco', 363: 'In the vast majority of tales the *pishtaco* is a white or mestizo ["a person of mixed American Spanish and American Indian descent" (*OED*)] male ... *Pishtacos* are often associated with the richest and most educated positions in highland society'.
234 [J.P. Gilmour], 'Literary Notes' *British Medical Journal* 2.2493 (1908): 1122.
235 *Freeman's Journal and Daily Commercial Advertiser* (Dublin), Thursday, 28 August, 1856: 'The Revue de geneve lately published an extraordinary account of the [sic] peasant of the mountains having, with the concurrence of his wife, killed his little girl seven years of age, in order to boil the body and procure human fat, which he had been told would cure him of a severe rheumatism. The Savoy Gazette gives a positive contradiction to this revolting story'.
236 *The Gentleman's Magazine*, VI (1736), Kkkkr. The story is headed 'Thursday, 7 [October]', although it is not clear if this is the date of the suicide or of the sale.
237 *Daily Gazetteer*, 19 October, 1736. For this version, cf. also: *Universal Spectator and Weekly Journal*, 23 October, 1736. Overall, there is clearly some uncertainty about dating, as the Gazetteer puts the actual suicide 'last week' (i.e. sometime after the seventh).
238 *Treatise*, trans. Henry Crantz (1775), 107.
239 *London Daily Post and General Advertiser*, 9 June, 1740.
240 *Some Considerations Touching the Usefulness of Experimental Natural Philosophy* (1663), 327; *Memoirs for the History of Humane Blood* (1683), 208–9.

241 *Dr Fludd's Answer*, 12–13.

242 *Book of Life*, 57.

243 Charas, *The Royal Pharmacopeia* (1678), 98.

244 Mortimer is described as 'a writer on trade and finance' in new DNB (Christabel Osborne, rev. Anne Pimlott Baker).

245 *The Student's Pocket Dictionary* [1777].

246 Thomas Churchyard, *Churchyard's Challenge* (1593), 92. Cf. also the royal surgeon John Browne, who noted that good blood should taste 'sweet' (*A Complete Treatise of Pre-ternatural Tumours* (1678), 38). We know of the advertising practice because the Barber-Surgeons' Company attempted in 1566 to forbid barbers from using it (see Young, ed., *Annals*, I, 181). They may or may not have been successful in this attempt.

247 *Zoologia*, 49, 50.

248 *Polypharmakos*, 33.

249 *Memoirs*, 333–34.

250 *Memoirs*, 27, 29, 35.

251 Dewhurst, 'Locke's Contribution', 201.

252 Cf. the Tupinamba Indians of Brazil, who used sharpened animal teeth to break the vein for routine blood-letting, and who may have been less influenced by medical theory than European Galenists (see: *Hans Staden's True History: an Account of Cannibal Captivity in Brazil*, ed. and trans. Neil L. Whitehead and Michael Harbsmeier (Durham: Duke University Press, 2008), 79–80).

253 There, admittedly, the situation was broadly reversed; but by comparison with this revolutionary experiment, blood-letting was at least mundanely familiar.

254 *The Art of Curing Sympathetically* (1700), 72.

The other cannibals notes

1 See: William Arens, *The Man-eating Myth: Anthropology and Anthropophagy* (New York: Oxford University Press, 1979); Frank Lestringant, *Cannibals: The Discovery and Representation of the Cannibal from Columbus to Jules Verne*, trans. Rosemary Morris (Cambridge: Polity Press, 1997), 6–7.

2 *Consuming Grief: Compassionate Cannibalism in an Amazonian Society* (Austin: University of Texas Press, 2001), 65–86.

3 There does also seem to have been some habitual cannibalism which was a matter of routine nourishment. On the evidence for this 'homicidal cannibalism' in Cheddar Gorge, some 14,700 years ago, see Robin McKie, *Observer*, 20 June 2010. For a kind of magical cannibalism used against vampirism, see: Agnes Murgoci, 'The Vampire in Roumania', *Folklore* 37.4 (1927): 320–49, 324.

4 Keith Richards, with James Fox, *Life* (London: Weidenfeld & Nicholson, 2010), 546.

5 For this and many other intriguing details on the history of pop and rock, see Simon Napier-Bell, *Black Vinyl, White Powder* (London: Ebury Press, 2001). Many thanks to Jason Draper for sending me a copy of this work.

6 As Conklin explains, 'Wari'' is pronounced 'Wah-REE', while the apostrophe 'denotes a glottal stop, a quick cut-off of the preceding sound in the back of the throat' (*Consuming Grief*, 252).

7 *Consuming Grief*, 76–84.

8 *Consuming Grief*, xv–xvii.

9 See Roger Boyes, *Times* (London), 13 December 2002.

10 *Consuming Grief*, xxii.

11 See Hermann Helmuth, 'Cannibalism in Paleoanthropology and Ethnology', in *Man and Aggression*, ed. Ashley Montagu (New York: Oxford University Press, 1973), 229–54, 235; *Consuming Grief*, xv.

12 Daniel Korn, Mark Radice and Charlie Hawes, *Cannibal: A History of the People-Eaters* (London: Channel 4/Macmillan, 2001), 14 (citing Timothy Taylor); 15.

13 *Cannibal*, 92.

14 In this case the 'donor' was a young Taiwanese woman, later diagnosed as mentally unstable (*Cannibal*, 90).

15 *Cannibal*, 91. The authors also cite a pathologist who admits that, although probably very few survived such a procedure, the liver is noted for its impressive regenerative powers. In rats, for example, it will regrow even after 70 per cent of its volume has been removed. Cf.: Leonardo Fioravanti, *A Short Discourse ... upon Surgery*, trans. John Hester (1580), 35v. For examples of these practices (sometimes also called 'gegan' and 'gegu') in Chinese literature, see: Tina Lu, *Accidental Incest, Filial Cannibalism, and Other Peculiar Encounters in Late Imperial Chinese Literature* (London: Harvard University Press, 2008), 147–48, 152–56.

16 Herodotus, IV, 26, cited by R.S. Charnock, 'Cannibalism in Europe', *Journal of the Anthropological Society* 4 (1866): xxv.

17 Charnock, 'Cannibalism', xxv.

18 Information on the Calatians (sometimes also Calandians) is scarce. One early modern source notes that they were besieged by the Greek conqueror Lysimachus (*c*.355–281 BC) some centuries later.

19 *Ductor Dubitantium, or, the Rule of Conscience* (1660), 227. Some versions of this tale attribute the query not to Darius but to Alexander the Great.

20 *Consuming Grief*, xviii. A further reference to the Calatians, occurring in the 1753 supplement to Chambers' *Cyclopaedia*, remarks that they 'eat their parents, that they might in some measure be revived in themselves'. Although slightly opaque, this could well imply that desire to conserve a vital principle (essentially, to eat the soul) which features in many cannibalistic funerals.

21 *Another Collection of Philosophical Conferences* (1665), 493.

22 *Varieties* (1635), 163.

23 *Cannibals*, 66.

24 See, for example, *The New Found World* (1568).

25 *Discovery of ... Guiana* (1596), 43.

26 His account of endo-cannibalism reappears in Chambers' *Cyclopaedia* in 1753.

27 Cited as 'Letter to London', 10 November 1675, in: Thomas Hutchinson, *A History of the Massachusetts Bay Colony*, 2 vols (1764), I, 296. Although Hutchinson emphatically states that this tale confirms the 'savage' nature of the native Indians, he is in fact relatively balanced in his attitude to them in many parts of the history, noting here that the justice of the execution was itself doubtful (and see, also, I, 79–80).

28 Quoted in Robert Viking O'Brien, 'Cannibalism in Edmund Spenser's *Faerie Queene*, Ireland, and the Americas,' in *Eating their Words: Cannibalism and the Boundaries of Cultural Identity*, ed. Kristen Guest (New York: State University of New York Press, 2001), 35–57, 37. For more on the literary and cultural context of this statement, and Spenser's role in Ireland, see: Andrew Hadfield, 'Edmund Spenser', new DNB; Andrew Hadfield, 'Spenser's Description of the Execution of Murrough O'Brien: An Anti-Catholic Polemic?', *Notes and Queries* 46.2 (1999): 195–96. (Thanks, again, to Willy Maley for this last piece.)

29 *Cannibals*, 60–64.

30 *Cannibals*, 60–64.

31 *Cannibals*, 65.

32 *Hans Staden's True History: an Account of Cannibal Captivity in Brazil*, ed. and intro Neil L. Whitehead; trans Michael Harbsmeier (Durham, N.C.: Duke University Press, 2008), 54, illustration 51. Cf. also the verbal taunts of triumph and vengeance (ibid., 127).

33 *Hans Staden's True History*, 129–37.

34 *Divine Hunger: Cannibalism as a Cultural System* (Cambridge: Cambridge University Press, 1986), 125.

35 Sanday, *Divine Hunger*, 141.

36 Again, as Daniel Korn, Mark Radice, and Charlie Hawes point out, among the Fijians (as encountered by European travellers in the first half of the nineteenth century)

'cannibalism was part of an absolutely fundamental religious and social understanding of the world ... founded on the worship of ancestor spirits' (*Cannibal*, 66). For early Peruvian cases of ritual cannibalism (*c.*500 AD) possibly designed to consume the strength or vitality of captured prisoners, see: John Verano, 'Paleonthological Analysis of Sacrificial Victims at the Pyramid of the Moon, Moche River Valley, Northern Peru', *Chungará* 32.1 (2000): 61–70, 61. I am very grateful for Jonathan Trigg for bringing this article to my attention. For a much later incident, see Stephen Brumwell, who notes that the Indians who ate the heart of Captain James Dalyell before watching British captives in 1763 'were paying Dalyell a back-handed compliment: by devouring his heart they hoped to imbibe his bravery' (*Redcoats: The British Soldier and War in the Americas, 1755–1763* (Cambridge: Cambridge University Press, 2002), 181n65).

37 *Cannibal*, 67. Cf., also, the aggressive cannibalism of the Asabano, occurring in Papua New Guinea until the 1970s: Roger Ivar Lohmann, 'The Afterlife of Asabano Corpses: Relationships with the Deceased in Papua New Guinea', *Ethnology* 44.2 (2005): 189–206, 189.

38 Sanday, *Divine Hunger*, 6. For some interesting beliefs on spirits and aggressive cannibalism among the Wari', see *Consuming Grief*, 33.

39 Cf., again, the Moche sacrifices, which clearly had powerful cultural importance, and in which it was evidently only élite priests or priestesses who consumed the blood.

40 First published in France in 1567, the account is given here in a 1568 English translation of Thevet's book, *The New Found World*. Cf. Staden: 'they do all this because of their great hatred' for one another (*Hans Staden's True History*, 127).

41 Cf. these figures with Gang Yue, who (also citing Zheng Yi) notes that eighteen bodies were stripped of all flesh; that the official number of cannibal participants was 400, whilst Zheng Yi estimated 10,000 to 20,000 (*The Mouth That Begs: Hunger, Cannibalism, and the Politics of Eating in Modern China* (London: Duke University Press, 1999), 230).

42 All details and quotations from *Cannibal*, 97–98. For a fuller discussion of these incidents and their implications, see Yue, *Mouth That Begs*, 228–52. For examples of revenge cannibalism under the Tang dynasty in the eighth and ninth centuries, and other forms of cannibalism in twentieth-century China see ibid., 54, 128.

43 This interpretation also matches the youth of the participants (cf. Paolo Viola on the similar age of those involved in exo-cannibalism in the French Revolution ('The Rites of Cannibalism and the French Revolution', 165–68 (http://www.library.vanderbilt.edu/quaderno/Quaderno3/Q3.C10.Viola.pdf)).

44 This kind of area is a special challenge to the scholar. While the most educated men were capable of believing what now appear to be wholly incredible slanders, some seemingly 'barbaric' activities look more plausible. The relatively sympathetic Thomas Hutchinson tells in 1764 of an Indian party on the march who, 'their hunting failing ... were kindling a fire to roast a child of one Hannah Parsons, when a strange dog, falling in their way, supplied the child's place' (*History*, II, 164). Again, the report is at least broadly comparable with tales of children eaten by Christians during severe European famines.

45 See Professor J.H. Trumbull, cited in *OED*.

46 On Columbus' first encounter with the Caribs, and on the distinction between 'cannibalism' and 'anthropophagy' in the period, see Philip P. Boucher, *Cannibal Encounters: Europeans and Island Caribs, 1492–1763* (Cambridge, Mass.: Harvard University Press, 1992), 15–16.

47 See *OED*, 'Cannibal' (etymology). It is also notable that relatively enlightened travellers admired both the dignity and strength of New World tribes in general. See, for example, Sir Walter Raleigh's meeting with the chief of the South American Orenoqueponi in 1595 (*Discovery of ... Guiana*, 64). For discussion of the few surviving Caribs (and their still formidable hunting skills) in the twentieth century, see: Patrick Leigh Fermor, *The Traveller's Tree: A Journey Through the Caribbean Islands* (London: John Murray, 1951), 115–16.

48 *The Doctrine of the Synod of Dort and Arles* (1631), 161. See also, Twisse, *A Discovery of D. Jackson's Vanity* (1631), 550.

49 *A Just Invective* (1661), 1, 34.

50 *Full and Easy Satisfaction* (1674), 86.

51 Cf. also: William Leigh, *The First Step, Towards Heaven* (1609), 197.

52 *A Sermon Preached before the Right Honourable the Lord Mayor* (1673), 4–5.

53 *Nosce Teipsum* (1599), 97.

54 Roger Williams, *A Key into the Language of America* (1643), 49.

55 de la Vega, *Royal Commentaries of Peru* (1688), 278–79. Ironically, de la Vega claims that the only thing the Spanish did achieve was the elimination of funerary cannibalism (279).

56 *Sylva Sylvarum* (1627), 7.

57 See Edward Daunce, *A Brief Discourse of the Spanish State* (1590), 28–29. For further discussion of the syphilis–cannibalism link, see: William Eamon, 'Cannibalism and Contagion: Framing Syphilis in Counter-Reformation Italy', *Early Science and Medicine* 3.1 (1998): 1–31.

58 John Norden, *A Pathway to Penitence* (1626), 229–30. On cannibal usurers, see also: *Complete Works of Ben Jonson*, IX, 477. For biblical attacks on usury, see: Leviticus 25.36, 37, Ezekiel 18.10, 12, 13, Exodus 22.25, Psalms 15.1, Luke 6.35. (The attentive reader will note that most of these are from the Old Testament, and therefore in fact Jewish.)

59 *Countess Dracula: The Life and Times of the Blood Countess, Elisabeth Báthory* (London: Bloomsbury, 1997), 21, citing an account by Pàlöczy Horrrath (1944).

60 See Harold Jenkins, *The Life and Work of Henry Chettle* (London: Sidgwick & Jackson, 1934), 86–87. Again: the mingling of exo- and endo-cannibalism practised by the vengeful Hungarian élite is echoed by numerous reports of people forced to eat parts of their own relatives, during recent wars in Liberia and the Congo.

61 *The Incorruptible Flesh: Bodily Mutation and Mortification in Religion and Folklore*, trans. Tania Croft-Murray (Cambridge: Cambridge University Press, 1988), 21.

62 For some fascinating examples, see: Susan Griffin, *The Book of the Courtesans: A Catalogue of their Virtues* (London: Pan Macmillan, 2002), 172–74. For other examples of seemingly arbitrary (even 'savage') social codes and customs, see: Wilfrid Hooper, 'The Tudor Sumptuary Laws', *English Historical Review* 30.119 (1915): 433–49; Liza Picard, *Elizabeth's London: Everyday Life in Elizabethan London* (London: St Martin's Press, 2005), 152–53; John Andrew Boyle, 'A Eurasian Hunting Ritual', *Folklore* 80.1 (1969): 12–16, 13, 12; D.H. Madden, *The Diary of Master William Silence: a Study of Shakespeare and of Elizabethan Sport* (London: Longmans, Green, 1897), 62–65.

63 *Oracle Bell's New World*, 11 September 1789.

64 *Memoirs*, trans. A.S. Kline (2005), Bk IX, ch. 3, §1 (http://tkline.pgcc.net/PITBR/Chateaubriand/ChateaubriandMemoirsBookIX.htm).

65 *Evening Mail*, 21 September 1792.

66 See 'Rites of Cannibalism', 165–68.

67 *Evening Mail*, 17 October 1792. This alleged cannibalism occurred during an event which was certainly marked by extremes of violence, now known as 'the September Massacres'. Hundreds of Royalists were slaughtered, and several bodies mutilated. For a Homeric instance of the desire for exo-cannibalistic violence, see: James M. Redfield, on Achilles' slaying of Hector (*Nature and Culture in the* Iliad: *The Tragedy of Hector* (Chicago: University of Chicago Press, 1975), 199. On the essentially tribal violence of Homeric culture, see also: R.B. Onians, *The Origins of European Thought* (Salem: Ayer, 1987), 3–4). For the more habitual violence of everyday European life, see: Henry Goodcole, *The Adultress's Funeral Day* (1635), A4v; Picard, *Elizabeth's London*, 200; Lawrence Stone, *The Family, Sex and Marriage in England 1500–1800* (Harmondsworth: Penguin, 1979), 77–78, 80; Anon., *An Exact Relation of the Bloody and Barbarous Murder, Committed by Miles Lewis, and his Wife, a Pinmaker upon their Prentice* (1646); *The Diary of John Evelyn*, ed. J. Bowle (London: Oxford University Press, 1983), 133–35 (7 May 1650); *More English Diaries* ed. Arthur Ponsonby (London: Methuen, 1927), 65–66.

68 For some particularly vivid examples, see the 1686 persecution of the Waldenses in Piedmont (Gilbert Burnet, *The History of the Persecution of the Valleys of Piedmont* (1688), 30–34).

69 *Essays*, trans. John Florio (1613), 104.

70 *Cannibals*, 80.

71 *A General Martyrology* (1660), 420, 421–22, 423–24, 425.

72 *Cannibals*, 1–2.

73 *The Raw and the Cooked: Introduction to a Science of Mythology* (London: Cape, 1970).

74 *A Year with Swollen Appendices* (London: Faber, 1996).

75 *Cannibal*, 66.

76 Cornelius Walford, 'The Famines of the World: Past and Present', *Journal of the Statistical Society of London* 41.3 (1878): 433–535, 435–37, 441. Unless otherwise stated all famine references are to Walford's article.

77 *Mercy in the Midst of Judgment* (1670), 8.

78 See: Harding, *The Dead and the Living*, 112. Cf., also an alleged famine among the Arabians, in which 'the people was driven to pluck out the dead bodies out of their graves, and … suck the marrow of their bones' (Thomas Lupton, *A Thousand Notable Things* (1579), 180).

79 *A Field of Blood* (1641), 46.

80 Vincent, *Lamentations of Germany*, A7r–A8v. There is no obvious reason for Vincent to have fabricated these tales, and they are supported by German legal authorities, as well as the ministers who wrote to Vincent narrating these events.

81 *Bread of Dreams*, 40. Cf. George Starkey, who had 'heard many travellers deliver of their own knowledge and experience, that a man may live ten or twelve days by sucking of his own blood' (Eirenaeus Philalethes [i.e., George Starkey], *Collectanea Chymica* (1684), 164). Cf. also the siege of Colchester in 1648, when the famished Royalists surrendered after having eaten cats, dogs, rats and mice (*The Journal of William Schellinks' Travels in England 1661–1663*, trans. Maurice Exwood and H.L. Lehmann (London: Camden Society, 1993), 33).

82 Brunwell, *Redcoats*, 178.

83 *Cannibals*, 74–78. On Léry's suspicion that the old woman was – like Ficino's aged bloodsuckers – possibly trying to renew her vitality, see ibid., 77.

84 *Cannibals*, 69.

85 César de Rochefort, *History of the Caribby Islands*, trans. J. Davies (1666), 329.

86 For all its extremity, Rochefort's description is not implausible. There is a reliable account of a Jesuit prisoner being killed and eaten in roughly this way (although his flesh was first roasted) by the Canadian Iroquois in the seventeenth century (see Sanday, *Divine Hunger*, 126–27). For a similar case in the Old World (minus the eating), see the Russian execution of John Michaelovits Wiskowaty, in 1570 (J. Crull, *The Ancient and Present State of Muscovy* (1698), 336–38).

87 For a fictional version of such blood-drinking in New England, see Frances Brooke, *Emily Montague* (1769), 23.

88 On raw cannibalism in Peru, see also John Locke, *Two Treatises of Government* (1690), 72–73, citing de la Vega. For more details on the Antis, see: Anon., *Virtue Rewarded* (1693), 66–67.

89 *Miscellany Poems* (1691), 54.

90 *A Geographical Description* (1657), 69–70. This and the Samuel Clarke of *A General Martyrology* are different people. For an interesting British parallel with this attitude to meat, see also Richard Franck on those in 'the country of Southerland … a rude sort of inhabitants … almost as barbarous as cannibals' (*Northern Memoirs* (1694), 177).

91 *A World of Words* (1598); *Queen Anna's New World of Words* (1611). It is probably no accident that the newest, most shocking term 'cannibal', rather than 'antropophago', is used here.

92 *Wit's Commonwealth* (1634), 734.

93 *Geographical Description*, 70.
94 *Cannibals*, 69.

Dirty History, filthy medicine notes

1 Nicholas Culpeper, *Pharmacopoeia Londinensis, or, The London Dispensatory* (1653), 52–53. Culpeper's work was first published in 1649.
2 On its supposed origin, see: Thomas Lupton, *A Thousand Notable Things* (1579), 259–60. For Bacon's belief in it, see *The History of Life and Death* (1638), 133. 'East bezoar' came from Persian goats, the Western variety from deer.
3 Although synthetic musk is now used extensively, civet cats are still kept for this purpose in some parts of the world.
4 *King Lear*, 4.6, 130–31, ed. G.K. Hunter (London: Penguin, 1980).
5 See the MS of Boyle's *Medicinal Experiments* (1694), 20; and MS read, alphabetical book of physical secrets, 72. Boyle commends this against cataracts; and the read MS against 'fistula or cold sores'. (Again, I am indebted to Elaine Leong for these references.)
6 *The Mysteries of Opium* (1700), 192. For more on Jones, see Stuart Handley in new DNB.
7 Brockliss and Jones, *Medical World*, 136.
8 Thorndike, *History*, V, 560.
9 *History of Four-footed Beasts* (1607), 581.
10 Boyle, *Medicinal Experiments* (1694), 47. The *OED*'s exact definition of erysipelas is: 'a local febrile disease accompanied by diffused inflammation of the skin, producing a deep red colour; often called St. Anthony's fire, or "the rose"'.
11 *Antidotary* (1589), 34r, 85r.
12 *The Autobiography of Benvenuto Cellini,* trans. George Bull (London: Penguin, 1998), 343.
13 Thorndike, *History*, II, 147.
14 Thorndike, *History*, II, 497.
15 Thorndike, *History*, VII, 176.
16 Thorndike, *History*, II, 496.
17 For further discussion of seventeenth-century amulets, see: Martha R. Baldwin, 'Toads and Plague: Amulet Therapy in Seventeenth-Century Medicine', *Bulletin of the History of Medicine* 67.2 (1993): 227–47.
18 *Religion and the Decline of Magic* (London: Weidenfeld & Nicholson, 1971), 189.
19 Thorndike, *History*, VII, 176. On elk's hoof, cf. Leo Kanner, who reports the seventeenth-century experience of a French huntsman, de la Martinière: 'in an elk hunt in Norway, one of the animals fell down suddenly in an epileptic fit, and his host immediately made him the present of the elk's left [sic] hind claw'. De la Martinière, 'somewhat skeptical, remarked: If the remedy is really efficient, it is rather strange that the animal was not able to cure itself. He was informed that this is often actually the case; the elk does cure himself by putting the claw in his ear' ('The Folklore and Cultural History of Epilepsy', *Medical Life* 37.4 (1930): 167–214, 191).
20 Thorndike, *History*, VII, 176. Some could take a relatively scientific view of amulets. The Dutch physician Henning Michael Herwig thought that, 'growing hot by touching the body', they 'send forth atoms, and little particles and effluviums, when we perceive them not', with these being absorbed through the patient's skin (*The Art of Curing Sympathetically* (1700), 65–66).
21 Kanner, 'Folklore and Cultural History of Epilepsy', 177, 188, 193, 190, 188, 193, 200, 198.
22 John Keogh, *Zoologia Medicinalis Hibernica* (Dublin, 1739), 99–100.
23 *Shakespeare: A Life* (Oxford: Oxford University Press, 1998), 15, 17–18.
24 These figures derive from contemporary 'Bills of Mortality', lists introduced in the sixteenth century with the specific aim of recording plague deaths. At its outset, the bubonic plague of 1348 had decimated the English population by something like 40 per cent. It was not until the mid-seventeenth century that the population returned to

its pre-plague level. Over on the European continent and in the Near East, as much as one third of the populace was wiped out by this first plague epidemic in the years 1347–51.

25 On some parts of the continent outbreaks could be still worse. Cf. Vincent, *Lamentations of Germany* (1638), 62: 'the very plague consumed in Saxony the other day in the space of two months, no less than sixteen thousand'.

26 F.P. Wilson, *The Plague in Shakespeare's London* (Oxford: Oxford University Press, 1963), 106–7.

27 Wilson, *Plague*, 98.

28 *Medicina Magnetica: or, The Rare and Wonderful Art of Curing by Sympathy* (1656), 73.

29 Wilson, *Plague*, 8–13. The same principles underlay the use of sheep to test the safety of a house in plague time; you took two or three sheep, shortly before the full moon, and shut them in for a month. Removing the animals (which had presumably had some kind of food) you then washed them in warm water, and gave the water itself to pigs. If the pigs lived, the house was clean.

30 *Tragedy of the Duchess of Malfi* (1623), D1v.

31 On this range of cures, see again Wilson, *Plague*, 8–13.

32 Barbette, 354–55; 366–67. On mummy against the plague, see also *A Brief Answer of Josephus Quercetanus … ,* trans. John Hester (1591), 33v–34r.

33 See, again, *Aurora Chymica* (1672), 8, 10; and George Thomson, *Loimotomia* (1666), 150.

34 *A Book, or Counsel Against the Disease Commonly Called … the Sweating Sickness* (1552), 9r.

35 *The Haven of Health* (1636), 316.

36 As Porter adds, the precise nature of this affliction 'remains a riddle' (*The Greatest Benefit to Mankind: A Medical History of Humanity from Antiquity to the Present* (London: Fontana Press, 1999), 168). On possible causes and possible cures, see: Caius, 14v; Bacon, *History of the Reign of King Henry the Seventh* (1629), 9; Caius, 21v–22r; Cogan, 316–17.

37 See David E. Shuttleton, *Smallpox and the Literary Imagination 1660–1820* (Cambridge: Cambridge University Press, 2007), 1.

38 Shuttleton, *Smallpox*, 1. For more on leprosy, see Steven Mullaney, *The Place of the Stage: License, Play, and Power in Renaissance England* (Ann Arbor: University of Michigan Press, 2007), 32–40.

39 Arthur Grenke, *God, Greed and Genocide: The Holocaust Through the Centuries* (Washington: New Academia, 2005), 137–38. For more on the history of smallpox and biological warfare, see: David A. Koplow, *Smallpox: The Fight to Eradicate a Global Scourge* (Berkeley: University of California Press, 2003), 58–103. Koplow adds that some estimates put the death toll as high as 500 million for the twentieth century alone.

40 We do know that the population expanded dramatically in the sixteenth and seventeenth centuries. It was around 50,000 in 1500, and around 200,000 in 1700.

41 E.A. Wrigley and R.S. Schofield, with R. Lee and J. Oeppen, *The Population History of England: 1541–1871: A Reconstruction* (Edward Arnold, 1981), 333. The remaining five fell in the eighteenth century.

42 *Devotions* (1624), 1–2.

43 In relative terms, Ann Donne's plight was not especially severe. In this era many women suffered perhaps ten or twelve childbirths (and occasionally as many as twenty) and sometimes prolonged labour, without the benefit of modern anaesthetic. In cases of caesarean section it was taken for granted that only the child could survive: the mother would inevitably bleed to death. For a recent discussion of early modern childbirth, see: Louis Schwartz, *Milton and Maternal Mortality* (Cambridge: Cambridge University Press, 2009).

44 *Sermons*, II, 83. Cf. a passage on the worm-eaten corpse, delivered not at a funeral, but at a wedding (*Sermons*, VIII, 106).

45 Cited by Liza Picard, *Elizabeth's London: Everyday Life in Elizabethan London* (London: St Martin's Press, 2005), 24–25.

46 *Diary*, 48, 50–51, 14–15 August 1661. As my phrasing suggests, Peters was not strictly executed as a regicide (see article in new DNB by Carla Gardina Pestana).

47 See Alasdair Raffe, 'Nature's Scourges: The Natural World and Special Prayers, Fasts and Thanksgivings, 1541–1866', in *God's Bounty?: the Churches and the Natural World* (Woodbridge: Boydell & Brewer, 2010), 237–47, esp. 240.

48 *The Art of Patience* (1694), 75.

49 *Letters from James, Earl of Perth*, ed. W. Jerdan (London: Camden Society, 1845), 7.

50 See especially: Phillipe Ariès, *Hour of our Death*, trans. Helen Weaver (New York: Oxford University Press, 1991), 559–601.

51 *The Letters of Pietro Aretino*, ed. Thomas Caldecot Chubb (Archon Books, 1967), 10 December 1526, 24.

52 In warfare as a whole, even the basic treatment of non-fatal wounds could be more cruel than the violence of enemy soldiers. Until Ambroise Paré one day ran out of his usual supplies and accidentally discovered the effectiveness of rose oil, egg whites and turpentine in such cases, a routine procedure was to stop bleeding with a coat of boiling pitch.

53 *The Diary of John Evelyn*, ed. John Bowle (Oxford: Oxford University Press, 1985), 245.

54 Clowes, *A Proved Practise* (1580), 26–28; *Antidotary*, 215.

55 Barbette, *Thesaurus* (1687), 31–32, 75, 171–72. Cf. also Culpeper, *Directory for Midwives* (1662), 214, on a mixture of 'herb robert, verbascum or moulin, scabious, caprifolium, or honeysuckles, dill', and man's grease for post-surgical treatment of certain cancers.

56 Evelyn himself had indeed personally witnessed a severe episode of judicial torture in France in March 1651, and it is perhaps telling that his response then ('the spectacle was so uncomfortable, that I was not able to stay the sight of another') was very similar, although if anything slightly less emphatic (*Diary*, 139–40). For discussion of the cultural context in which ether arose in Britain in 1846, see: Alison Winter, 'Ethereal Epidemic: Mesmerism and the Introduction of Inhalation Anaesthesia to Early Victorian London', *Social Hisory of Medicine* 4.1 (1991): 1–27.

57 Lucinda Beier, 'Seventeenth-century English Surgery: the Casebook of Joseph Binns', in *Medical Theory, Surgical Practice: Studies in the History of Surgery*, ed. Christopher Lawrence (London: Routledge, 1992), 48–84, 58, 59, 50–51. For genteel violence and honour, see, again: Evelyn, *Diary*, 133–35 (7 May 1650); *More English Diaries*, ed. Arthur Ponsonby (London: Methuen, 1927), 65–66.

58 *Gentleman's Magazine* (1731), 1.3, 130.

59 John Hester (d.1593), *The Pearl of Practise ... for Physic and Chirurgery* (1594), 7.

60 Quoted in Lawrence Stone, *The Family, Sex and Marriage in England 1500–1800* (Harmondsworth: Penguin Books, 1979), 82.

61 *The Private Diary of Dr John Dee*, ed. J.O. Halliwell (London: Camden Society, 1842), 16, 25, 38. Cf. also ibid., 5 August 1588, 28.

62 *Experimenta et Observationes Physicae* (1691), 67–71. For examples of the dangers of hunting in the eighteenth century, see also: *Gentleman's Magazine* (1731), 1.8, 352–53.

63 William Gouge, in: Nicholas Byfield, *A Commentary: or, Sermons upon ... Saint Peter* (1623), A6v–A7r.

64 *The Diary of John Manningham of the Middle Temple 1602–1603*, ed. Robert Parker Sorlien (Hanover, N.H.: University Press of New England, 1976), 54.

65 Evelyn, *Diary*, 224–25. An early modern, or 'real tennis' ball would have been slightly smaller than its successors.

66 *Diary*, 132–33 (3 May).

67 *Thesaurus*, 31.

68 *Adenochoiradelogia* (1684), 115–16; *Antidotary*, 90v–91r.

69 Kathy Stuart, *Defiled Trades: Honour and Ritual Pollution in Early Modern Germany* (Cambridge: Cambridge University Press, 1999), 163–64.

70 For further details, see Manningham, *Diary*, 46; John Woodall (d. 1643), *The Surgeon's Mate* (1655), 66; Angelo Sala, *Opiologia: or, A Treatise Concerning ... Opium* (1618).

Woodall's book was first published in 1617. Dictionaries of 1661 and 1677 make no reference to laudanum's role as a painkiller (Thomas Blount, *Glossographia* (1661); Elisha Coles, *An English Dictionary* (1677)).

71 Cited by Ruth Padel, *In and Out of the Mind: Greek Images of the Tragic Self* (Princeton: Princeton University Press, 1992), 49.

72 Mayerne, *Treatise,* 1676, 59–60; *Thesaurus*, 155.

73 N.H. Keeble, DNB.

74 Quoted by Keeble, ibid. For further discussion of Baxter's persistent ill heath, see: Tim Cooper, 'Richard Baxter and his Physicians', *Social History of Medicine* 20.1 (2007): 1–19.

75 See Baxter's work, *The Certainty of the World of Spirits* (1691), 16.

76 *More English Diaries*, 57 (3 January 1621, 15 August 1653, 2 November 1635, 1 December 1651).

77 *The Diary of Walter Powell ... 1603–1654* (www.archive.org/stream/diarywalterpowe00 powerich)

78 Virginia Smith points out that sugar and sugared foods would later wreak havoc with the teeth of the more affluent, come the eighteenth century. Ironically (Smith adds) this was just when 'a new vogue for ... the smile began to affect French manners', with 'the first romantic open smile' of 'European art history' appearing in a painting of 1787 (*Clean: A History of Personal Hygiene and Purity* (Oxford: Oxford University Press, 2007), 230).

79 Park Honan, *Shakespeare: A Life* (Oxford: Oxford University Press, 1999), xi.

80 Cited by Picard, *Elizabeth's London*, 162.

81 For a late nineteenth-century instance, see: *Kilvert's Diary*, ed. William Plomer, 3 vols (London: Jonathan Cape, 1969), III, 191–92.

82 Cf., again, Moffett, on Apollonius curing 'bad gums with dead men's teeth' (*Health's Improvement* (1655), 139–40).

83 Thorndike, *History*, II, 496.

84 Thorndike, *History*, II, 767.

85 *Incorruptible Flesh*, 114–15.

86 Edward Reyner, *The Twelve Wonders of England* (1655), 3–4.

87 *Helminthologia* (1668), title page. For a broadly similar opinion, see: M. Bromfield, *A Brief Discovery of ... the Scurvy* (1694), 3–4. On worms in the liver, see Diemerbroeck, *Anatomy* (1694), 85.

88 *Helminthologia*, 32–45.

89 *Helminthologia*, 4.

90 The picture can be found between pages 16 and 17 (image 17, on *Early English Books Online* (http://eebo.chadwyck.com/home)). It does, admittedly, seem doubtful that the serpentine worm at top left could actually attain a span of 'above three hundred foot long'.

91 All quotations and case studies are from: Jan Bondeson, *A Cabinet of Medical Curiosities* (London: I.B. Tauris, 1997), 58–71.

92 Stone, *Family*, 65.

93 *An Essay of the Pathology of the Brain*, trans. from Latin by S.P. (1681), 69, 71, 70. This work first appeared in Latin in 1667.

94 Howard Wilcox Haggard, *Devils, Drugs and Doctors: the Story of the Science of Healing from Medicine-man to Doctor* (Wakefield: EP Publishing, 1975), 328.

95 For more on Mather and inoculation, see: Haggard, *Devils, Drugs and Doctors*, 223–24; Thomas Hutchinson, *A History of the Massachusetts Bay Colony*, 2 vols (1764), II, 275; M.G. Hall, 'Cotton Mather', DNB. For more on the history of smallpox vaccination per se, see: *Bulletin for the History of Medicine* 83.1 (2009): Special Issue, 'Reassessing Smallpox Vaccination'.

96 *Clean*, 12.

97 *The Anatomy of Disgust* (London: Harvard University Press, 1997), 25–27.

98 See, for example, the Dutch traveller William Schellinks, who in July 1661 exchanged his inn bed at Gravesend for a 'night's rest on a hard bench' rather than fall prey to a 'hungry and bloodthirsty mob' of English fleas (*The Journal of William Schellinks' Travels*

in England 1661–1663, trans. Maurice Exwood and H.L. Lehmann (London: Camden Society, 1993), 35). As for lice, even in the early nineteenth century (notes Lawrence Wright) William Cobbett advised those choosing a wife to look carefully behind her ears (*Clean and Decent: the Fascinating History of the Bathroom and the Water Closet* (1960; repr. London: Penguin, 2000), 138–39).

99 *Anatomy of Disgust*, 20, 163. It may also be for similar reasons that dedicated 'bug destroyers' (even then used only by the rich) appeared in England only at the very end of the seventeenth century (see Wright, *Clean and Decent*, 139–40).

100 There is some faint trace of later attitudes in George Thomson's discussion of the medical use of 'various superfluous excrescences of living bodies' (see: *Ortho-methodoz itro-chymike: or the Direct Method of Curing Chemically* (1675), 98–99). By contrast, however, an Irish clergyman can write in 1739 of the medical use of 'the wax, or filth of the ears' with no obvious sense of repugnance (Keogh, *Zoologia*, 99). There is considerable evidence that children of our own time learn disgust as they grow up. Miller cites an experiment on children under two: '62% ate imitation dog feces realistically crafted from peanut butter and smelly cheese; 58% ate a whole, small, dried fish; 31% ate a whole sterilised grasshopper; but only 8% would tolerate a lock of human hair' (*Anatomy of Disgust*, 55–56). R.W. Moncrieff tells, similarly, of an experiment made by P. Ottenburg, M. Stein, and N. Roulet on 300 children aged 3–12. They inhaled (twice) with their eyes closed from bottles containing '"synthetic faeces" (a chemical mixture built up to have a faecal odour), synthetic sweat, and amyl acetate'. They were asked to state either like or dislike. 'Most of the three and four-year olds rated all three odours as pleasant; at the age of five there was a significant change and they then disliked faeces and sweat' (*Odour Preferences* (London: Leonard Hill, 1966), 246). Cf. also ibid., 194, on the differing 'bodily requirements' of children and adults. For various experiments on smell and adult sexual psychology, see: D. Michael Stoddart, *The Scented Ape: The Biology and Culture of Human Odour* (Cambridge: Cambridge University Press, 1990), 135–41. On the limited 'cultural variability' of attitudes to urine, excrement, sweat and so on, see Jesse J. Prinz, *Gut Reactions: A Perceptual Theory of Emotion* (Oxford: Oxford University Press, 2004), 154. For more on the interaction between nature and nurture in the acquisition of adult disgust (and the specific area of the brain involved), see Smith, *Clean*, 12–13.

101 Even Miller himself (who is American) seems to betray something of the distinctively North American stance occasionally (see *Anatomy of Disgust*, 79, 92).

102 The most fatal form of cholera (the 'asiatic' variety) was in fact a late historical arrival in Europe. The Renaissance had known the less ferocious 'cholera morbus', a serious but not usually fatal attack of fever.

103 On London, see Trygg Engen, *The Perception of Odors* (London: Academic Press, 1982), 12; on Paris, see Alain Corbin, *The Foul and the Fragrant: Odor and the French Social Imagination* (Leamington Spa: Berg, 1986), 222–23. For further discussion of both cases, see also David S. Barnes, 'Confronting Sensory Crisis in the Great Stinks of London and Paris', in *Filth: Dirt, Disgust and Modern Life*, ed. William A. Cohen and Ryan Johnson (London: University of Minnesota Press, 2005), 103–29.

104 *Foul and Fragrant*, 225, 227.

105 See, for example, Miller, *Anatomy of Disgust*, 76–77. For a sustained discussion of various aspects of the relationship between smell and recollection, see: *Memory for Odors*, ed. Frank R. Schab and Robert G. Crowder (Hove: Laurence Erlbaum, 1995).

106 Quoted by Dominique Laporte, *History of Shit*, trans. Nadia Benabid and Rodolphe el-Khoury (Cambridge, Mass.: MIT Press, 2000), 10.

107 Cf. Wright, who notes that 'the language of the toilet is indeed an etymologist's nightmare' – its confusions and displacements being at least partly a response of the need for euphemism and evasion (*Clean and Decent*, 118).

108 Patrick Suskind, *Perfume: The Story of a Murderer*, trans. John E. Woods (London: Penguin, 1986), 3–4.

109 Even Louis, however, preferred being 'dry-cleaned' ('rubbed ... down with scented linen cloths') to using the lavish bathing chambers which he had had built at Versailles (see Smith, *Clean*, 194).

110 A. Weldon, *Court of King James* (1650), 178 (I am grateful to Barbara Ravelhofer for alerting me to this reference).

111 *The Royal Doctors 1485–1714: Medical Personnel at the Tudor and Stuart Courts* (Rochester, N.Y.: University of Rochester Press, 2001), 104.

112 *Diary*, 319 (6 February 1685). (It is perhaps telling that Evelyn cannot refrain from stressing this point, even though the king had been dead just a bare few hours as he wrote.)

113 Keith Thomas, *Man and the Natural World* (Oxford: Oxford University Press, 1996), 104.

114 Marcellus Laroon, *Criers and Hawkers of London* (Aldershot: Scolar, 1990), 86.

115 It should be stressed that this and similar contrasts are with the modern developed world (for the dangers of sanitation in modern Dhaka, see Larry Elliott, 'Where Death by Water Is Part of Daily Life', *Guardian*, 26 November 2007).

116 Leona Skelton points out, however, that early use of flushing lavatories was in fact quite problematic, as the addition of water to human waste vastly increased the basic volume of material disposed of.

117 On the very fine, sometimes lockable ones owned by various monarchs, see Wright, *Clean and Decent*, 69–71. Cf., also ibid., 71–75, on the very early prototype of the flushing lavatory designed by Elizabeth's godson, Sir John Harington. Wright adds that this was installed at Richmond Palace, but not generally copied until some 200 years later.

118 See Picard, *Elizabeth's London*, 46. There were clearly also less official 'public lavatories' in various cities; recall the French Protestant whose corpse was buried by Catholics in '"in a place where everyone was accustomed to urinate and defecate"' (Penny Roberts, 'Contesting Sacred Space: Burial Disputes in Sixteenth-Century France', in *The Place of the Dead: Death and Remembrance in late Medieval and Early Modern Europe*, ed. Bruce Gordon and Peter Marshall (Cambridge: Cambridge University Press, 2000), 131–48, 131–32).

119 Norbert Elias, *The Civilizing Process: The History of Manners*, trans. Edmund Jephcott (Oxford: Blackwell, 1978), 136.

120 See Wright, *Clean and Decent*, 115.

121 Laporte, *History*, 150–51n11; citing letter of 9 October 1694, to Electress of Hanover.

122 All quotations from Elias, *Civilizing Process*, 129–32.

123 Corbin, *Foul and Fragrant*, 174.

124 *Civilizing Process*, 131.

125 Cf. Robert Boyle, *General History of the Air* (1692), 212–13.

126 Compare an advice book of 1547, cited by Picard: 'wash your hands and wrists, your face and eyes, and your teeth with cold water' (*Elizabeth's London*, 162).

127 Bacon, 191–92. Cf. Walter Bruel, advising baths for convulsives, but warning that 'the patient must not stay long in the bath, because it doth resolve the strength too much' (Walter Bruel, *Praxis Medicinae* (1632), 71); and Keith Thomas, 'Cleanliness and Godliness in Early Modern England', in *Religion, Culture and Society in Early Modern Britain: Essays in Honour of Patrick Collinson*, ed. Anthony Fletcher and Peter Roberts (Cambridge: Cambridge University Press, 1994), 56–83, 58.

128 *A Relation of a Journey of ... My Lord Henry Howard from London to Vienna, and thence to Constantinople* (1671), 181.

129 *Clean and Decent*, 75.

130 'Cleanliness and Godliness', 58.

131 *Clean*, 206.

132 *Foul and Fragrant*, 37. For a broad comparison with this belief among the eighteenth-century poor, see Thomas, 'Cleanliness and Godliness', 77.

133 On musk and 'eau de mille fleurs' see Corbin, *Foul and Fragrant*, 63, 230, 67. The suggestion concerning the privy is that of Robert Boyle, as cited by Corbin (67).

134 *Scented Ape*, 7. For more on musk, and the use of Calvin Klein's 'Obsession' as an animal aphrodisiac, see *Clean*, 14.

135 On early modern wall construction, see Picard, *Elizabeth's London,* 51; Wilson, *Plague*, 2.

136 *Perfume*, 4.

137 David Brandon and Alan Brooke, *London: City of the Dead* (Stroud: The History Press, 2008), 87–88. Tellingly, the chapel was a private speculative venture, set up in 1823.

138 *A Chronicle of the Late Intestine War* (1676), 61.

139 Samuel Clarke, *A General Martyrology* (1640), 92.

140 One aim of such strategies was of course to spread disease. As Barbara Ravelhofer kindly points out, during the siege of Vienna by the Turks in 1683, civic authorities enforced draconian regulations on the burial of those dying within the city walls for just this reason.

141 Vincent, *Lamentations of Germany*, 62.

142 *Foul and Fragrant*, 223.

143 Miller, *Anatomy of Disgust*, 158–59.

144 *The Anatomy of Human Bodies* (1694), 10. Whilst Smith notes that Thomas Sydenham (1624–89) shifted older attitudes in this area, it seems likely that his views may have been minority ones for some time (*Clean*, 217–18).

145 *Journal of the Very Rev. Rowland Davies*, ed. Richard Caulfield (London: Camden Society, 1857), 50–52.

146 *Diary*, 245 (24 March 1672).

147 *History of the Persecution* (1688), 40.

148 Quotation from *Foul and Fragrant*, 49.

149 *Foul and Fragrant*, 146.

150 *Foul and Fragrant*, 54.

151 Cf. Thomas, 'Cleanliness and Godliness', 77, on the belief that lice and millipedes 'were thought to have therapeutic value'.

152 For relatively recent survivals of this more animal relationship to scent, see Stoddart, *Scented Ape*, 10, on the habit of 'greetings by smell' amongst both Esquimaux and Indian hill people.

153 Cf. also Lupton, *Thousand Notable Things*, 89, for the use of smell to forecast the imminent death of a consumptive.

154 *Foul and Fragrant*, 41. Cf., by contrast, the allegedly delightful smell emitted by the body of the Bishop Polycarp, burned *c.*155 AD: Susan Ashbrook Harvey, *Scenting Salvation: Ancient Christianity and the Olfactory Imagination* (Berkeley: University of California Press, 2006), 11–12.

155 All from Corbin, *Foul and Fragrant*, 41, 39.

156 *Nosce Teipsum* (1599), 46.

157 *Diary*, 87.

158 See *Criers and Hawkers*, 110

159 For more on 'moral disgust', see Prinz, *Gut Reactions*, 154–55.

160 *Man and the Natural World*, 104.

161 *Man and the Natural World*, 102. For a particularly extreme version of such habits, see Richard Franck, *Northern Memoirs* (1694), 177.

162 For further details, see Emily Cockayne, *Hubbub: Filth, Noise and Stench in England 1600–1770* (New Haven: Yale University Press, 2007), 187.

163 *History,* 32.

164 Leona Skelton, 'Beadles, Dunghills and Noisome Excrements: Regulating the Environment in Seventeenth-Century Carlisle', MA dissertation, Department of Modern Languages and Cultures (University of Durham, 2008), 25. Cf., also, one Cuthbert Carr of Hexham, whose will of 1649 specifically bequeathed the small parcel of land which he used to site his dunghill (Northumberland Archives, Woodhorn, NRO/PHU/C2). Again, I am very grateful to Leona Skelton for supplying this record.

165 Highland Archive Centre, Bught Road, Inverness, Inverness-shire, IV3 5SS, BI/1/1/1: Burgh Court Book, 1556–67. Many thanks once again to Leona Skelton for this gem.

166 Laporte, *History*, 33, 35. On human excrement in Britain, see Liam Brunt, 'Where There's Muck, There's Brass: The Market for Manure in the Industrial Revolution', *Economic History Review* 60.2 (2007): 333–72. I am indebted to Skelton for drawing Brunt's essay to my attention.

167 See Monica Burguera, 'Gendered Scenes of the Countryside: Public Sphere and Peasant Family Resistance in the Nineteenth-Century Spanish Town', *Social History* 29.3 (2004): 320–41, 326–28.

168 On this pronunciation, see *Criers and Hawkers*, 136. For further details on this area, see Beverly Lemire: 'Consumerism in Pre-industrial and Early Industrial England: the Trade in Second-hand Clothes', *Journal of British Studies* 27.1 (1988): 1–24; 'The Theft of Clothes and Popular Consumerism in Early Modern England', *Journal of Social History* 24.2 (1990): 255–76.

169 Cockayne, *Hubbub*, 187.

170 See, again: Burguera, 'Gendered Scenes', 326–28.

171 *Healing Threads: Traditional Medicines of the Highlands and Islands* (Edinburgh: Polygon, 1995), 173. Beith herself notes that this was 'based on theories once held in orthodox medicine'.

172 Cited by Laporte, *History*, 99.

173 Cited by Conrad Gesner, *The New Jewel of Health*, trans. George Baker (1576), 170v.

174 *Maison Rustique*, trans. Richard Surphlet (1616), 456.

175 *Medicina Magnetica*, 78–79, 82–83.

176 *Choice Manual* (1687), 46. It is not clear if one should bind both coal and turd to the wound; but clearly the procedure was messy at best, and painful at worst.

177 Charas, *The Royal Pharmacopeia* (1678), 96; Boyle, *Medicina Hydrostatica* (1690), 191–92. Moreover, Boyle here suggests that spirit of urine is an acceptable substitute for the notably more expensive aqua fortis – a preparation which contained gold. For non-medical experiments, see *Certain Physiological Essays* (1669), *passim*; *Experimenta*, 46–47, 101. Boyle also notes that the then Duke of Holstein (who was held to be a 'great chemist') prepared spirit of urine for unspecified uses (*Physiological Essays*, 270).

178 *Experimenta*, 193.

179 *Medicinal Experiments* (1693), 38. Cf. also ibid., 71, 112, 121.

180 Thorndike, *History*, VIII, 141, 144.

181 C.J.S. Thompson, *The Mystery and Art of the Apothecary* (Philadelphia: J.B. Lipincott, 1929), 210.

182 *Anatomy* (1694), 201.

183 Keogh, *Zoologia*, 99–100.

184 Cf., rather differently, the eighteenth-century physician, John Hill, lamenting on how 'the dung of peacocks has been poured down many throats' (Christian Uvedale [i.e., Hill], *Construction of the Nerves* (1758), 51).

185 *Works* (1684), 61, 67–69, 93, 151–53, 222. Cf. also John Pechey on 'distilled water of horse-dung' against pain in the joints (*The Store-house of Physical Practice* (1695), 280). Leo Kanner noted in 1930 that peacock's dung was still being used against epilepsy in western Bohemia and Ruthenia ('Folklore and Cultural History of Epilepsy', 195).

186 Laporte, *History*, 101, citing Gaston Bachelard.

187 Cited by Camporesi, *Bread of Dreams: Food and Fantasy in Early Modern Europe*, trans. David Gentilcore (Oxford: Polity Press, 1996), 48.

188 *A Short Discourse … upon Surgery*, trans. John Hester (1580), 32v–33r.

189 *Healing Threads*, 188. In World War One, troops sometimes used cloth soaked in urine as protection against gas attacks (the alkaline of the urine counteracting the chlorine in the gas).

190 *Short Discourse*, 35v. For more on Fioravanti, see: David Gentilcore, *Medical Charlatanism in Early Modern Italy* (Oxford: Oxford University Press, 2006), esp. 267–68. 'Charlatanism' in this context is not a straightforwardly negative term (see ibid., 1–3).

191 *The Surgeon's Directory* (1651), 129.

192 *A Journal of a Voyage Made into the South Sea* (1698), 192.
193 *Works*, trans. Thomas Johnson (1634), 644.
194 *Panacea* (1659), 35. This work first appeared in Latin in 1587.
195 *Helps for Sudden Accidents* (1633), 38–39. Cf. the use of child's urine on hornet, bee or wasp stings (46). Cf. Paré, *Works*, 784.
196 Kenelm Digby, *Choice and Experimented Receipts in Physic and Chirurgery* (1675), 25.
197 *Thesaurus*, 87.
198 *The Accomplish'd Lady's Delight* (1675), 174, 176.
199 *Bullein's Bulwark of Defence Against all Sickness* (1579), fol. 3v.
200 *Healing Threads*, 188.
201 *Journal of William Schellinks*, 43. This was a general custom among the privileged, at times extending to the face also.
202 Laporte, *History*, 98, 102, 106, 107.
203 This point naturally applies a little differently to the illiterate. Cf., however, Suzy Knight on that 'oral and unlettered culture' in which 'the natural world offered … an abundance of raw materials which could be used to protect and to heal' ('Devotion, Popular Belief and Sympathetic Magic Among Renaissance Italian Women: The Rose of Jericho as Birthing Aid', in *God's Bounty?*, 134–43, 134).
204 Stuart, *Defiled Trades*, 183.
205 *Hamlet*, 2.2, 283–84, 3.4, 92–94.
206 For exceptions or ambivalence, see Richard Sugg, *Murder after Death* (Ithaca: Cornell University Press, 2007), 162.
207 As Pepys's editors point out, it was in fact not unique. Cf. Sunday 22 June 1662 (*Diary*, IV, 48n3). If Wells had been taken by surprise, she was not alone. Cf. John Manningham, *Diary*, 132, February 1603.
208 The full entry reads: 'Mr Pickering tells me the story is very true of a child being dropped at the ball at Court; and that the King had it in his closet a week after; and did dissect it; and making great sport of it, said that, in his opinion, it must have been a month and three hours old; and that, whatever others think, he hath the greatest loss (it being a boy, as he says) that hath lost a subject by the business' (17 February 1663). The phrase 'the King had it in his closet a week after' is ambiguous. It may mean that he took possession of it a week later, rather than keeping it for a week. Even in that case, the corpse had still been tolerated by somebody for seven days, and would have been in Charles's presence some time while he accomplished a dissection.
209 See: William Harvey, *Lectures on the Whole of Anatomy*, trans. C.D. O'Malley, F.N.L. Poynter, and K.F. Russell (Berkeley and Los Angeles: University of California Press, 1961), 13.

Eating the soul notes

1 *Devotions upon Emergent Occasions*, ed. Anthony Raspa (Oxford: Oxford University Press, 1987), 66.
2 Or, if he was, we must say that fancies of this kind had far greater weight in 1624 – something we can infer in part just from the immense popularity of *Devotions* in that and following years.
3 *French Virtuosi* (1664), 183–84.
4 *Ternary* (1650), 8–9. For a recent discussion of piety and nature in early modern Ireland, see: Raymond Gillespie, 'Devotional Landscapes: God, Saints and the Natural World in Early Modern Ireland', in *God's Bounty?*, 217–36 (and 235 on the animate qualities of nature).
5 Eirenaeus Philalethes [George Starkey], *Collectanea Chymica* (1684), 6–8.
6 It should be remembered, however, that in this period minerals were indeed considered to be organic substances, with gold, for example, thought to be slowly ripening in the womb of the earth (cf. Pomet's 'breed in the entrails').

7 *Summa contra Gentiles*, trans. the Fathers of the English Dominican Republic, 5 vols (London: Burns Oates and Washbourne, 1923), II, 180.

8 For further discussion of this scene, see: Richard Sugg, *The Smoke of the Soul: The Animated Body in Early Modern Europe* (Michigan: University of Michigan Press, forthcoming), ch. 4.

9 See: Helkiah Crooke, *Somatographia Anthropine* (1616), Table 19 [EEBO image 52].

10 *The Happiness of the Church* (1619), 428. This page number occurs twice, firstly in place of (inferred) pages 426–27. The quotation is from second (actual) 428. Crooke (412) cites a French physician, Ulmus of Poitiers, who believes the vital spirit to be prepared in the spleen.

11 Helkiah Crooke, *Microcosmographia* (1615), 516. On the distinctive structure of the wonderful net, see, again, Crooke: 'this net compasseth the glandule … and is not like a simple net, but as if you should lay many fishers' nets one above another' and is 'admirable' because 'the replications of one are tied to the replications of another so that you cannot separate the nets asunder' (*Microcosmographia*, 470). On the variety of attitudes to the wonderful net, and its increasingly problematic status (hinted at obliquely by Crooke's labelling of 1616 ('the rete mirabile … as it is found in the heads of calves or oxen')), see *The Smoke of the Soul*, ch. 9.

12 *Sylva Sylvarum* (1627), 90.

13 Reginald Scott, *The Discovery of Witchcraft* (1584), 485–86.

14 *Sylva Sylvarum*, 251. Cf., also, Virgilio Malvezzi, *David Persecuted*, trans. Robert Ashley (1647), 85–86.

15 *Arcana Microcosmi* (1652), 97.

16 *Sylva Sylvarum*,184.

17 *Sylva Sylvarum*, 31. Cf. M. Flamant: 'all our actions are performed by the assistance of the vital and animal spirits; and 'tis their commerce which maintains that perfect union, between the heart and the brain, which are the principal organs of the body' (*The Art of Preserving and Restoring Health* (1697), 9).

18 *The French Academy*, Pt II, trans. Thomas Bowes (1594), 578, 563. On the close physiological relationship of soul, spirits and blood, see also Flamant, *Art*, 11; John Woodall, *The Surgeon's Mate* (1655), 204; Thomas Powell, *Human Industry* (1661), 131.

19 *Letters*, II, 260.

20 Charas, *The Royal Pharmacopeia* (1678), 122. The powder also contained – among other things – roots of male peony gathered in the decrease of the moon, shavings of unicorn's horn, ivory, hoof of an elk, oriental musk, and leaves of finest gold.

21 'The Life of the Corpse: Division and dissection in late Medieval Europe', *Journal of the History of Medicine and Allied Sciences* 50 (1995): 111–32, 115.

22 Katharine Park, 'The Life of the Corpse: Division and dissection in late Medieval Europe', *Journal of the History of Medicine and Allied Sciences* 50 (1995), 111–32, 116.

23 Park, 'Life', 115.

24 *Ternary* (1650), 65–66.

25 *Two Sermons* (1654), 35.

26 *The Wonders of the Little World* (1673), 92. The phenomenon could also operate in reverse, with the murderer bleeding in presence of the victim's body (see: Henry Goodcole, *Heaven's Speedy Hue and Cry Sent After Lust and Murder* (1635), reissue, STC 12010.5, C3r). By the end of the seventeenth century, we find one Charles Gildon treating the idea with contempt (*The History of the Athenian Society* (1691), 16).

27 Park, 'Life', 116.

28 Park, 'Life', 125.

29 In pre-Christian cultures this persistent (and sensible) deterioration could also take place, whilst being more emphatically located in the afterlife itself. Michael Clarke argues that not only were the Homeric 'shades' of Hades wasted and enfeebled, but that in fact they *continued* to waste away in Hades (see: *Flesh and Spirit in the Songs of Homer: a Study of Words and Myths* (Oxford: Clarendon Press, 1999), 161).

30 Park, 'Life', 130.
31 Cf. Park, 'Life', 129–30, on the different attitudes to the display of severed body parts as judicial deterrent.
32 'Tractate on Melancholy', in *Votivae Angliae* (1643), 90–91.
33 Catholics of course believed that almost all humans would be detained in purgatory before reaching their allotted afterlife destination.
34 See: *Letters*, I, 174–76, Mitcham, 9 October [1607].
35 *Ternary*, 4. Notably, Paracelsus himself seems to have believed that 'the quintessence … (a certain matter corporally extracted out of all the things, which Nature hath produced; and also out of every thing that hath a life in its self' could only be extracted from plants or minerals. For 'the spirit of the life of a thing is permanent, but of man mortal; from whence may be understood, that a quintessence cannot be extracted from the flesh or blood of a man; and that for this reason, because the spirit of life, which also is the spirit of virtues, dies, and the life exists in the soul, which then afterwards is not in the substance' (*Paracelsus, his Archidoxis*, trans. John Hester (1660), 35–36)). Just how this can be squared with Paracelsus' remarks about the value of a three-day-old corpse is difficult to say. Ultimately, however, we are not concerned with the unitary consistency of Paracelsus' (imputed) writings, but with the ideas of later Paracelsian and Helmontian chemists.
36 See Miroslav Verner, *The Pyramids: Their Archaeology and History*, trans. Steven Rendall (London: Atlantic Books, 2002), 37.
37 *Pyramidographia* (1646), 45 (see also 47). Greaves was Professor of Astronomy at Oxford. Francis Maddison notes in the DNB that Greaves' trip to the Levant was indeed 'one of the first scientific expeditions' to the region. He visited the pyramids in the years 1638–39.
38 *The World Surveyed*, trans. Francis Brooke (1660), 269. Greaves might at first seem to be merely citing a non-Christian belief with careful descriptive accuracy. (He has indeed borrowed the above description from a Roman author, Maurus Servius). Yet his attitude in fact appears rather more ambiguous. He further notes that for Plato 'the long duration' of Egyptian mummies had seemed 'to prove the immortality of the soul'. And he presently goes on to talk of how the Egyptians had 'by art found out ways to make the body durable, whereby the soul might continue with it, *as we showed before*' (58, italics mine). What does that last phrase mean? Is it just a rather clumsy paraphrase of what the Egyptians themselves thought? Or does Greaves indeed consider the idea to be a valid one? As he observes in the same section of his book, the influential Church Father St Augustine 'truly affirms, that the Egyptians alone believe the resurrection, because they carefully preserve their dead corpses' (47). For a whimsical Restoration variant of this idea, see Thomas Duffett, *The Amorous Old-Woman* (1674), 13.
39 *A Discourse upon Prodigious Abstinence* … (1669), 9–10. For Reynolds's links with the Royal Society, see the book's preface.
40 Hair and nails can continue to grow, as Pierre Pomet noted (*A Complete History of Drugs*, 3rd edn (1737), 229). More subtly, corpses can show an illusion of growth. Skin and gums shrink back from the nails and the teeth, which are thus more visible, though at the same time no larger than those of any ordinary body. Paul Barber notes, however, that the teeth of folk vampires were far less often emphasised than those of fiction (*Vampires, Burial, and Death: Folklore and Reality* (New Haven: Yale University Press, 1988), 44).
41 *An Essay of Transmigration, in Defence of Pythagoras* (1692), 119–21.
42 *Aurora Chymica* (1672), 11.
43 Cited by John Manningham, *Diary*, 7. The phrase seems to have been proverbial, at least in later years (cf. Robert Bolton, *Some General Directions* … (1626), 198; cf. also Thomas Willis, who noted that the souls of some animals 'serve chiefly to preserve them only for a little time, and as it were pickle them to keep them from putrefaction' (*Two Discourses Concerning the Soul of Brutes*, trans. Samuel Pordage (1683), 4)).

44 For a startling example of the seemingly residual life of a severed head, in September 1602, see: *A Hangman's Diary: Being the Journal of Master Franz Schmidt, Public Executioner of Nuremberg, 1573–1617*, 181. On epilepsy and the soul, see also: Leo Kanner, 'The Folklore and Cultural History of Epilepsy', *Medical Life* 37.4 (1930): 167–214, 168: 'the Topantumatu, a tribe of Central Celebes, actually believe that the spell is precipitated by a sudden temporary expulsion from the body of the patient's soul'. On the New Testament, and similar Muslim beliefs, see Matt 17.14–18; Kanner, ibid., 168. More routinely, in popular Christian belief, the soul could literally be sneezed out of the body. Until it returned, one was at risk of demonic interference – hence the 'bless you' traditionally addressed to one who had sneezed.

45 It is possible that the Brazilian Wari' had a similar notion, given that they fed the flesh of enemies to tribal elders in particular.

46 Porta, *Natural Magic*, trans. anon. (1658), 275; italics mine.

47 *Electronic Enlightenment* (online resource, http://www.e-enlightenment.com/): Rev. John Beale to Robert Boyle, Yeovil, 10 April 1666.

48 Ironically (given that Beale was alluding to Deuteronomy or Leviticus) such a belief was consistent with what the Ancient Hebrews understood 'soul' to be. In the Old Testament humans (and animals) had a quantity of vitality, not 'a soul', and this was simply recycled, like a kind of impersonal gas, into Yahweh upon a person's death (see: H. Wheeler Robinson, 'Hebrew Psychology', in *The People and the Book: Essays on the Old Testament*, ed. A.S. Peake (Oxford: Clarendon Press, 1925), 353–82; W.E. Staples, 'The "Soul" in the Old Testament', *The American Journal of Semitic Languages and Literatures* 44.3 (1928): 145–76). 'Transanimation' usually referred to Pythagorean metempsychosis.

49 Piero Camporesi, *Bread of Dreams: Food and Fantasy in Early Modern Europe*, trans. David Gentilcore (Oxford: Polity Press, 1996), 49, citing Johann Schroeder, *Pharmocopeaia Medico-Chymica* (Frankfurt, 1677), 327. The case of the mummified body found in a London chimney in October 1701 very clearly shows that in a certain environment even an untreated body could 'cure' itself; no one detected this corpse via its stench (see: Anon., *A Full and True Account of … an unknown person that was found … within the top of a chimney …* (1701), title page).

50 Cf., again, Camporesi, *Juice of Life: The Symbolic and Magic Significance of Blood* (New York: Continuum, 1988), 29.

51 Jole Shackelford, 'Paracelsianism and the Orthodox Lutheran Rejection of Vital Philosophy in Early Seventeenth-Century Denmark,' *Early Science and Medicine* 8.3 (2003): 210–52, 245.

52 *The Differences of the Ages of Man's Life* (1607), 4. Cf., also, the medical doctor Sir Thomas Browne, on varying lengths of life and personal vitality: 'though the radical humour contain in it sufficient oil for 70, yet I perceive in some it gives no light past thirty: men assign not all the causes of long life, that write whole books thereof. They that found themselves on the radical balsam, or vital sulphur of the parts, determine not why Abel lived not so long as Adam … ' (*Religio Medici*, in *Works*, ed. Geoffrey Keynes, 6 vols (London: Faber, 1928), I, 53.)

53 Although Cuff adds, sceptically, 'his own hasty leaving of his life, was confutation sufficient' of this 'false ostentation, or extreme madness', Donne also plays with the idea in his poem 'The Good Morrow', when alluding to the mixture of different humours or elements which made up an individual's 'temperature' (Cuff, *Differences of the Ages of Man's Life*, 71; cf. Donne, 'The Good Morrow', *Poems*, 60).

54 *Sylva Sylvarum*, 263.

55 Thorndike, *History*, VIII, 414–15. Thorndike adds that 'Tentzel's book continued to find readers after 1666 when it was reprinted at Erfurt … Thomas Bartholinus cited cases from it for 15 pages as a postscript to his letter on the transplantation of diseases'.

56 See R.B. Onians, *The Origins of European Thought* (Salem: Ayer, 1987), 171–73.

57 Tylor, extract from *Primitive Culture* (1871; repr. in: *From Primitives to Zen: A Thematic Sourcebook of the History of Religions*, ed. Mircea Eliade (London: Collins, 1967), 178). Citing Frazer, Onians (*Origins*, 172) also finds something similar among the Society Islanders. Cf. Ovid (born 43 BC) who, when Cephalus accidentally and fatally wounds Procris, has the former state: 'My lips her soul receive, with her last breath:/Who, now resolved, sweetly smiles in death' (*Ovid's Metamorphosis*, trans. George Sandys (1628), 200).

58 *Medicina Diastatica,* trans. Ferdinando Parkhurst (1653), 75.

59 Quoted in *Medicina Diastatica*, 8. On Paracelsus' iconoclasm, cf. Robert Burton: 'Paracelsus did that in physic, which Luther in divinity' (*Anatomy of Melancholy* (1621), 467). Cf. Laurence Brockliss and Colin Jones on the 'Paracelsian heresy' (*The Medical World of Early Modern France* (Oxford: Clarendon Press, 1997), 119).

60 See John's gospel, ch. 11.

61 Cf., also, the raising of Jairus's daughter, and the meaning of 'death' among the African Dowayos (Luke 8.51–55; Nigel Barley, *Dancing on the Grave: Encounters with Death* (London: Abacus, 1997), 46). For the strikingly reversible nature of 'death', in the Apocrypha, see: *Acts of Peter,* 'The Gardener's Daughter'; *Acts of John*, v.62–86 (*The Apocryphal New Testament: A Collection of Apocryphal Christian Literature in an English Translation*, ed. J.K. Elliott (Oxford: Oxford University Press, 1993), 398–99, 328–35.

62 Frederick S. Paxton, *Christianizing Death: The Creation of a Ritual Process in Early Medieval Europe* (Ithaca: Cornell University Press, 1990), 21.

63 Daniel Korn, Mark Radice and Charlie Hawes, *Cannibal: A History of the People-Eaters* (London: Channel 4/Macmillan, 2001), 67.

64 'Russian Peasant Beliefs and Practices Concerning Death and the Supernatural Collected in Novosokol'niki Region, Pskov Province, Russia, 1995. Part I: The Restless Dead, Wizards and Spirit Beings', *Folklore* 111.1 (2000): 67–90, 72.

65 A. Murgoci, 'Customs Connected with Death and Burial Among the Roumanians', *Folklore* 30.2 (1919): 89–102, 95–96.

66 Warner, 'Russian Peasant Beliefs and Practices Concerning Death and the Supernatural Collected in Novosokol'niki Region, Pskov Province, Russia, 1995. Part II: Death in Natural Circumstances', *Folklore* 111.2 (2000): 255–81, 265.

67 See Barber, *Vampires,* 20.

68 *Dr Fludd's Answer unto M. Foster* (1631), 68, 128. Fludd writes 'forasmuch as the text saith' without giving that text. Job 12.10 seems to be the nearest possible match: 'In whose hand [is] the soul of every living thing, and the breath of all mankind'. Cf., also, Diemerbroeck, who specifically identifies spirits and blood with Leviticus 17.11 (*Anatomy* (1694), 5).

69 Lauren Kassell, *Medicine and Magic in Elizabethan London: Simon Forman, Astrologer, Alchemist, and Physician* (Oxford: Clarendon Press, 2005), 116, citing from a work of 1607.

70 He does not say how old the corpse was, or if the flesh was treated according to the popular Paracelsian recipes.

71 *Mosaical Philosophy* (1659), 248. Sadly, Fludd does not say how this extraction was performed.

72 Joseph Mede, *Works* (1664), 235–36. Mede died in 1638. His *Works* first appeared in 1648.

73 *Sylva Sylvarum*, 184. Cf. also Juan Luis Vives, *The Passions of the Soul: the Third Book of De Anima et Vita*, trans. Carlos G. Norena (Lewiston, N.Y.: Mellen, 1990), 103. All further references to Vives are to this work and edition.

74 Cited in: Mary Roach, *Stiff: The Curious Lives of Human Cadavers* (London: Penguin, 2003), 222.

75 Lefebvre does not, however, seem to have been straightforwardly Paracelsian, but to have drawn on a range of traditions, including Neoplatonic, Paracelsian, Helmontian, and Aristotelian ideas.

76 *Medicina Diastatica*, 33–34.

77 On medical use of the heart, see Johann Schroeder, *Zoologia*, trans. anon. (1659), 58; John Keogh, *Zoologia Medicinalis Hibernica* (Dublin, 1739), 103. On Mayerne and the lungs, see John Aikin, *Biographical Memoirs of Medicine* (1780), 262–63.

78 Camillo Brunori (1726), cited by Camporesi, *Bread of Dreams*, 45–46.

79 Thorndike, *History*, VIII, 417.

80 'Erotic Hangings in "Cyclops"', *James Joyce Quarterly* 34.3 (1997): 345–48. It is estimated that the practice causes between 250–1,000 deaths per year in the United States (J.L. Uva, 'Autoerotic Asphyxiation in the United States', *Journal of Forensic Sciences* 40 (1995): 574–81).

81 On the growth of the mandrake from the semen or urine of a hanged man, see Raymond J. Clark, 'A Note on Medea's Plant and the Mandrake', *Folklore* 79.3 (1968): 227–31. For a seemingly open-minded discussion of hanging and mandrakes, see: Bureau d'adresse et de rencontre, *Another Collection of Philosophical Conferences of the French Virtuosi* (1665), 338–40.

82 *Sylva Sylvarum*, 264.

83 *Medicina Diastatica*, 74.

84 On this latter custom see Patricia Fumerton, in *Renaissance Culture and the Everyday*, ed. Patricia Fumerton and Simon Hunt (Pennsylvania: University of Pennsylvania Press, 1999), 1–2.

85 *Countess Dracula: The Life and Times of the Blood Countess, Elisabeth Báthory* (London: Bloomsbury, 1997), 228.

86 In 1616, for example, Harvey's first Lumleian anatomy occurred from 16–18 April (see Geoffrey Keynes, *The Life of William Harvey* (Oxford: Clarendon Press, 1966), 86).

87 See: Roger French, *Dissection and Vivisection in the European Renaissance* (Aldershot: Ashgate, 1999), 3, 238.

88 *A Hangman's Diary* (1573–1617), 116. Richard Evans explains, more generally, that 'drowning was mainly though not exclusively reserved for female offenders, and … applied above all to crimes against morality and religion, such as adultery and heresy' (*Rituals of Retribution: Capital Punishment in Germany, 1600–1987* (Oxford: Oxford University Press, 1996), 30).

89 'Indulco and Mumia', *The Journal of American Folklore* 77.303 (1964): 3–11, 8–9.

90 Cited in *Bread of Dreams*, 47; italics mine.

91 *Transubstantiation Exploded* (1638), 83–85.

92 *Good Thoughts in Worse Times* (1647), 100–101.

93 *The Great Instauration: Science, Medicine and Reform 1626–1660* (London: Duckworth, 1975), 386–87, 394–402.

94 For more on the early stages of microscopy, see Catherine Wilson, *The Invisible World: Early Modern Philosophy and the Invention of the Microscope* (Princeton: Princeton University Press, 1995), 79–81, 220–23.

95 *Juice of Life*, 31.

96 Charas, *Pharmacopeia*, 98.

97 *Medicina Diastatica*, 76.

98 *Two Treatises of Government* (1690), 72–73. Vega's claim may be true, although he and Locke have misunderstood its significance. The eating of a child born to a tribal woman and her surrogate outsider husband was something which we witnessed in chapter four, in the case of the Tupinamba.

99 Notice, too, how the relatively scientific and empirical Irvine here definitely rejects the older, essentially Scholastic idea that the soul is merely 'everywhere and nowhere' in the body.

100 *Medicina Magnetica*, 90–91.

101 *Electronic Enlightenment* (online resource, http://www.e-enlightenment.com/): translation from French into English, letter from Georges Pierre Des Clozets to Robert Boyle, Caen, 24 March 1678. For more on Des Clozets and the homunculus, see: Lawrence Principe, *The Aspiring Adept: Robert Boyle and His Alchemical Quest* (Princeton: Princeton University Press, 2000), 115, 119, 132–2.

102 Philip Schwyzer, 'Mummy is Become Merchandise: Literature and the Anglo-Egyptian Mummy Trade in the Seventeenth Century', in *Re-orienting the Renaissance*, ed. Gerald

Maclean (London: Palgrave, 2005), 66–87, 71 (citing Fray Luis de Urreta's *History of Ethiopia* (1610–11)).

103 *Mosaical Philosophy*, 236–37. Cf. George Chapman, *Bussy D'Ambois* (c.1603), on a flatterer as 'worse than the poison of a red-haired man' (*Bussy D'Ambois*, ed. Nicholas Brooke (Manchester: Manchester University Press, 1964), 3.1, 15–18). On dating, see Mark Thornton Burnett, new DNB.

104 The Jewish stereotype is further reinforced by the fact that, as Fludd claims, the mythical Jew also sold the potion 'at an excessive rate'. In yet one more version of the story, Fludd has a wicked Catholic cardinal similarly distilling poison from the living breasts of his red-haired mistress.

105 Andrew Wear, *Knowledge and Practice in English Medicine, 1550–1680* (Cambridge: Cambridge University Press, 2000), 86–87. Hence, for example, the more orthodox medical use made of vipers (see Michael Foster's DNB article on Sir Kenelm Digby's various experiments).

106 *The History of the Holy War* (1639), 90. Cf. also Conrad Gesner, *The New Jewel of Health*, trans. George Baker (1576), 145r, effectively using poison against poison, with his recipe for an antidote which includes live scorpions, boiled for some four hours.

107 *Mosaical Philosophy*, 236–37.

108 On this physiology, see Donne: 'For if the sinewy thread my brain lets fall/Through every part,/Can tie those parts, and make me one of all'; 'As doth the pith, which, lest our bodies slack,/Strings fast the little bones of neck, and back' ('The Funeral'; 'Of the Progress of the Soul', *Poems*, 59, 203).

109 *Bread of Dreams*, 44–46.

110 Cf. the Jewish anatomist of Nashe's *The Unfortunate Traveller*, as discussed in Richard Sugg, *Murder after Death* (Ithaca: Cornell University Press, 2007), 177–88.

111 See Webster, *Great Instauration*, 282–84.

112 *Course of Chemistry*, trans. anon. (1720), 507–8. This work was first published in 1675. Once again, the head must be that of a healthy young man, killed by a violent death.

113 *Pharmacopeia*, 2

114 *The Labyrinth of Man's Life* (1614), B1r.

115 *Lustra Ludovici* (1646), 5.

116 *Jacob Behmen's Theosophic Philosophy* (1691), 377.

117 *Theosophic Philosophy*, 80.

118 Despite asking an anatomy lecturer, I have not been able to learn what these might be.

119 On mummy and the Eucharist, cf. also Karen Gordon-Grube, 'Anthropophagy in Post-Renaissance Europe: The Tradition of Medicinal Cannibalism', *American Anthropologist* 90.2 (1988): 405–9, 408.

120 To be more precise, we must say that for Catholics this failure to decay was important; for the Greeks it was usually an extremely negative phenomenon, linked to sin, excommunication and vampirism (see, for example, Paul Ricaut, *The Present State of the Greek and Armenian Churches* (1679), 280–82).

121 John Hooper, 'Monumental Church Dedicated to Controversial Saint Padre Pio', *Guardian*, 2 July 2004.

122 *The Incorruptible Flesh: Bodily Mutation and Mortification in Religion and Folklore*, trans. Tania Croft-Murray (Cambridge: Cambridge University Press, 1988), 36–43, 46–48.

123 Vivian Nutton, in Lawrence I. Conrad, Michael Neve, Vivian Nutton, Roy Porter, and Andrew Wear, *The Western Medical Tradition: 800 BC to AD 1800* (Cambridge: Cambridge University Press, 1995), 175.

124 See, for example: John Bridges, *A Sermon, Preached at Paul's Cross* [1571], 126; George Goodwin, *Babel's Balm* (1624), 65.

125 Caroline Walker Bynum, *Holy Feast and Holy Fast: The Religious Significance of Food to Medieval Women* (Berkeley: University of California Press, 1988), 171–72.

126 For more on the psychology of the act and the sick woman's response, see *The Anatomy of Disgust* (London: Harvard University Press, 1997), 158–63.

127 For a rather different view of the relationship between religious piety and disgust, see: Alexandra Cuffel, *Gendering Disgust in Medieval Religious Polemic* (Notre Dame, Ind.: University of Notre Dame Press, 2007).

128 Compare particularly Catherine's subsequent vision, in which Christ told her '"you forced yourself to swallow without a qualm a drink from which nature recoiled in disgust ... As you then went far beyond what mere human nature could ever have achieved, so I today shall give you a drink that transcends in perfection any that human nature can provide ... "' Christ then put Catherine's mouth to his wounded side and let her drink his blood (Bynum, *Holy Feast*, 172). This passage offers not only a strong instance of spirit over matter, but an especially striking instance of Christian endo-cannibalism. Assuming that the 'vision' was self-produced, it also confirms Catherine's egotism.

129 Bynum, *Holy Feast*, 144–45. Titus 1.15.

130 *Conflicts and Comforts of Conscience* (1628), 100.

131 See, for example: Carola Scott-Luckens, 'Propaganda or Marks of Grace? the Impact of the Reported Ordeals of Sarah Wight in Revolutionary London, 1647–52', *Women's Writing* 9.2 (2002): 215–32; Rebecca Bullard, 'Textual Disruption in *Anna Trapnel's Report and Plea* (1654)', *The Seventeenth Century* 23.1 (2008): 34–53.

132 *Britain's Remembrancer* (1628), 44r.

Opposition and ambivalence notes

1 Karl H. Dannenfeldt, 'Egyptian Mumia: The Sixteenth Century Experience and Debate', *Sixteenth Century Journal* 16.2 (1985): 163–80, 176, citing *Paradoxorum Medicinae* (Basle, 1535).

2 See *The Glory of Women*, trans. from Latin (1652). This was first written around 1509.

3 *The Vanity of Arts and Sciences* (1676), 302–3.

4 Thorndike, *History*, V, 446, VIII, 414.

5 While Gesner's original text reads 'nether', in context this evidently means 'neither' rather than 'never'.

6 *A Treasure of Easy Medicines* (1771), 120.

7 *Essays*, trans. John Florio (1613), 104.

8 *The Apology and Treatise of Ambroise Paré* (1585), ed. Geoffrey Keynes (London: Falcon, 1952), 145.

9 *The Case Reports and Autopsy Records of Ambroise* Paré, ed. and trans. W.B. Hamby, from J.P. Malgaignes, *Oeuvres Completes d'Ambroise Paré, Paris 1840* (Springfield, IL: Charles C. Thomas, 1960); cited by A.N. Williams, '"Labor improbus omnia vincit"; Ambroise Paré and Sixteenth-Century Child Care', *Archives of Disease in Childhood* 88 (2003): 985–89. The use of an animal-skin for severe bruising was still known in Greece in the twentieth century: when one old man of 83 fell from a balcony, 'his people put him in the skin of a freshly-killed lamb ... to heal him' – after which he lived to be 95 (Richard and Eva Blum, *The Dangerous Hour: The Lore of Crisis and Mystery in Rural Greece* (London: Chatto & Windus, 1970), 65).

10 'Treatise on Mummy', cited in Karen Gordon-Grube, 'Anthropophagy in Post-Renaissance Europe: The Tradition of Medicinal Cannibalism', *American Anthropologist* 90.2 (1988): 405–9, 407.

11 *Apologie and Treatise*, 145.

12 *Works*, trans. Thomas Johnson (1634), 1029.

13 *Health's Improvement* (1655), 139–40. Victor Houliston notes, in the new DNB, that this was probably compiled about 1595.

14 It was also in James's time, in 1611, that 'the Paris student Guillaume Desclames attacked a long list of popular occult cures for epilepsy, which included semen collected under a waning moon' and 'powders concocted from a human skull, human bones, and cuckoo's ashes' (Laurence Brockliss and Colin Jones, *The Medical World of Early*

Modern France (Oxford: Clarendon Press, 1997), 136). Again, this attack is not obviously or solely directed at corpse medicine.

15 *The Visions of Dom Francisco de Quevedo Villegas*, trans. R.L. (1667), 32. Though composed between 1606 and 1622, Quevedo's original Spanish work was considered controversial by official censors, and did not appear in Spain until 1627. A translation of some parts of the work was published by the poet Richard Crashaw in 1640.

16 *The World Surveyed*, trans. F.B. (1660), 280.

17 *Hoplocrisma-spongus: or, A Sponge to Wipe Away the Weapon-salve* (1631) (1631), 7–8. Interestingly, Foster also fuses claims of devilish aid with more precisely material attacks, noting that, as there are so many different recipes for the salve, the only effective common factor must be Satanic agency (see Ibid., 54–55).

18 *Klinike, or the Diet of the Diseased* (1633), 365–66, 347. Hart does also glance at the New World ('hence have we so many sacrifices of mankind' which 'even unto these our times … still continue; as our Spanish narrations make mention of the Western parts of the world') but this could refer just to the Aztecs, rather than to more routine types of exo-cannibalism.

19 *Christ's Tears, Works of Thomas Nashe*, II, 184.

20 Richard Hakluyt, *Principal Navigations* (1599), 201.

21 Not all medical clients would allow a doctor to impose on them at this time. It has been argued by medical historians that the whole concept of the modern 'patient' was an alien one until relatively recently. Those sufficiently educated and affluent to use physicians, it has been said, were often far from passive or deferential (see, for example: N. Jewson, 'Medical Knowledge and the Patronage System in 18th-Century England', *Sociology* 8 (1974): 369–85; Margaret Pelling, *Medical Conflicts in Early Modern London* (Oxford University Press, 2003), 226; Dorothy Porter and Roy Porter, *Patient's Progress: Doctors and Doctoring in Eighteenth-Century England* (Palo Alto, Calif.: Stanford University Press, 1989), 53–69).

22 *A Help to Memory and Discourse* (1630), 31–32. Notably, this passage does not occur in earlier editions of Basse's popular work.

23 *Seven Deadly Sins of London* (1606), 39.

24 Jonson, *Works*, 4.4, 14. On dryness, see also a broadside ballad of 1635, *The Old Bride, or The Gilded Beauty*.

25 *Honest Man's Fortune* (1647), 5.1, 223–25. This play was first performed around 1613 and published in 1647 (see E.K. Chambers, *The Elizabethan Stage*, 4 vols (Oxford: Clarendon, 1923), III, 227). Cf. also S.S., *The Honest Lawyer* (1616), Act 3, 25–30.

26 *A Christian Turned Turk* (1612), 1.5, 126–27.

27 Ira Clark notes that this play was both produced and published in 1633 ('James Shirley', new DNB).

28 Shirley, *Bird in a Cage* (1633), C1r.

29 It must be emphasised that religious prejudice was at this time far more likely than racial antagonism.

30 *The White Devil* (1612), D3r. David Gunby states that 'The White Devil was first performed by Queen Anne's Men at the Red Bull in Clerkenwell, probably early in 1612' ('John Webster', new DNB).

31 *White Devil*, B1r. A broad comparison with this image of exploitative, calculating consumption, is offered by Sir Toby Belch, in *Twelfth Night*, 3.2, 60–62 (see Richard Sugg, *Murder after Death* (Ithaca: Cornell University Press, 2007), 62–66).

32 It seems also to have been Webster who inserted the insult 'rotten mummy' into Marston's play *The Malcontent*, in the revised version of 1604 (see *The Malcontent* (1604), Greg, I, 203(c), B4v; and cf. the earlier printing, *The Malcontent* [1604], Greg, I, 203(a); on revision see James Knowles, 'John Marston', new DNB). A more plainly negative reference comes, in 1621, from the clergyman William Loe, who asks: 'shall the church-man, because he cannot preach to every palate, be censured in his ministration? Who knows not that manna is worse then mummy to some?' (*Vox Clamantis* (1621), 12). Here

the force of the rhetoric plainly depends on the assumption that these two substances are poles apart. It may also have been assisted by a pronunciation which could make 'manna' sound relatively like 'munna' (cf., again, Robert Cottington, *True Historical Discourse* … , K3r–v; and Hume, *Annotations on Milton's Paradise Lost*, 57).

33 John Webster, *The Tragedy of the Duchess of Malfi* (1623), K1r.

34 Cf. *OED*: 1612 Woodal, *Surg. Mate* Wks. (1653) 16 'The Salvatorie if it contain six severall unguents, it is sufficient for any present use'. See, also, John Banister ('mixed with a little unguent out of his salvatory') in Clowes, *A Proved Practice* (1580), B4r–v.

35 'Can houses, lands, can gold or silver give/To minds distract, heart's-mummy to relieve?' (*Labyrinth* (1611), K1r).

36 *A Pathway to Penitence* (1626), 229–30.

37 *Good Thoughts in Worse Times* (1647), 100–101.

38 'Thomas Fuller', new DNB.

39 *Holy State* (1642), 156.

40 For a broad comparison, cf. Donne on blasphemy: *Sermons*, I 308, 19 April 1618. Cf. also *Sermons*, III, 218.

41 Fuller's remark on illegitimate jests was repeated by David Lloyd, writing on Fuller in 1668 (see *Memoires of the Lives … of those … that Suffered … for the Protestant Religion* (1668), 524).

42 *The Holy State*, 426.

A broad comparison with this figuring of tyranny is found in a poem by Hester Pulter:

> You know the royal eagle finds it good
> In his old age he lives by sucking blood
> [fol. 116v] Nay if you're loath, great kings have done the same
> For which they live still in the book of Fame
> For fatting of their nobles up in cages
> Eating their mummy with the blood of pages
> To an old tyrant melancholy grown
> No music pleaseth but the dying groan
> Of innocents …
>
> (Leeds Brotherton MS Lt q 32, 116r–v)

Here 'mummy' is used in part as a general synonym for 'flesh' (cf., again, Falstaff's 'mountain of mummy'). I am very grateful to Alice Eardley for this poem, derived from her forthcoming edition of Pulter's writings (*Lady Hester Pulter: Complete Works* (Toronto: Centre for Reformation and Renaissance Studies, forthcoming, 2012)). Eardley dates the poem *c.*1650–60. She is clearly right to suspect that 'Pulter may have had Thomas Fuller's account of tyrants in mind when she wrote this' (see: *Holy State* (1642), 426).

43 The basic aptness of Fuller's repeated equations between plunder and mummy is neatly underlined by a parallel usage from the French Revolution: 'their fanatical confidence in the omnipotence of church plunder, has induced these philosophers to overlook all care of the public estate … With these philosophic financiers, this universal medicine made of church mummy is to cure all the evils of the state' (Edmund Burke, *Reflections on the Revolution in France* (1790), 338).

44 *A Pisgah Sight of Palestine* (1650), 79. It was believed that in the three-year Old Testament siege of Samaria by the Assyrians mothers were forced to eat their own children (see, for example, George Abbot, *An Exposition upon the Prophet Jonah* (1600), 221).

45 Almost as if conscious of the need to regain control, Fuller then shifts gear again, adding more soberly: 'however, whilst some squeamish stomachs make faces to feed on the dead, perhaps their hard hearts at the same time, eat up the living as if they are dead, either by fraudulent contracts or forcible oppressions' (citing Psalms 14.4). Even this suggests to us that Fuller has a more general sense of public unease about mummy.

46 *Threnoikos the House of Mourning … delivered in LIII sermons preached at the funerals of divers faithfull servants of Christ* (1660), 546. This collection is credited to 'Daniel Featly, Martin Day, John Preston, Ri. Houldsworth, Richard Sibbs, Thomas Taylor … Thomas Fuller and other reverend divines'. Fuller's parenthetical 'seeming' evidently refers to the ghostly, 'apparitional' status of the Old Testament (summoned by Saul and the so-called 'witch of Endor'); it is not *actually* Samuel, hence the qualification. Although sermons themselves are not individually credited, there seems no doubt as to Fuller's authorship of this one. We are not told whose funeral this was for. For a possible hint as to dating, see ibid., 546–47. It seems certain that the sermon fell somewhere after 1640, as an earlier edition of this collection appeared (twice) in that year, without Fuller's name amongst those credited.

47 It must be added that, even in this last attack, there is some sense of the Egyptians being blamed for the phenomenon of medicinal cannibalism, rather than European consumers.

48 *Memoirs for the History of Humane Blood* (1683), 333–34.

49 *Memoirs*, 334.

50 *A Treatise of the Asthma* (1698), 85.

51 Similarly, the Royal Society fellow Nehemiah Grew believes that mummy does not work ('let them see to it, that dare trust to old gums, which have long since lost their virtue') but has nothing to say about its ethical status (*Musaeum Regalis Societatis* (1685), 3). Over on the continent, Paul Ammann, director of the medical garden at the University of Leipzig in 1675, opposes mumia but not usnea (Thorndike, *History*, VIII, 98).

52 *Du Bartas his Divine Weeks*, trans. Joshua Sylvester (1611), 353.

53 *Kingdom's Intelligencer* (1661), 23 December 1661. On the continent, one could see 'the mummy of an Egyptian Prince above 1800 years old' in the University of Leiden's famous anatomy theatre (Gerard Blancken, *A Catalogue of all the Chiefest Rarities in the Public Theatre and Anatomy-Hall, of the University of Leiden* (1697), 7). For a discussion of those pre-eighteenth-century collections which would only later become 'museum pieces', see: Amy Boesky, '"Outlandish-Fruits": Commissioning Nature for the Museum of Man', *ELH* 58.2 (1991): 305–30.

54 For uses which are negative but not comic, see: Dryden, *Amboyna, a Tragedy* (1673), 62; Charles Goodall, *Poems and Translations* (1689), 162.

55 Cf. Richard Head *The English Rogue* (1668), 267: 'I basted him soundly, till that I had made jelly of his bones, and that his flesh lookt like Egyptian mummy'.

56 *Sir Martin Mar-All* (1668), 4.1, 508–9.

57 *Innocent Mistress* (1697), 29. For other instances of beating, see: 1662 R. Brathwait *Chimneys Scuffle* 3 (*OED*); Richard Head, *The English Rogue Pt 1* (1665), 241; Roger Boyle, *Mr. Anthony* (1690), 28; George Powell, *A Very Good Wife* (1693), 30; William Winstanley, *The Essex Champion* (1699), 103; Jonathan Swift, *Travels into Several Remote Nations of the World. By Captain Lemuel Gulliver* (1726), II, 191. For making or selling, see: Anon., *The Bloody Duke* (1690), 8.

58 *The Fond Husband* (1677), 27.

59 See for example George Villiers (d.1687), *Miscellany Poems* (1692), 52; Thomas Duffett, *The Amorous Old-Woman* (1674), 13.

60 An early version of this echoes *Volpone*, combining Voltore's proverbial dryness with the hint that the aged have little value except for the material utilities offered by their bare physical matter: 'If 'twere thy plot I do confess/For to make mummy of her grease,/Or swap her to the paper mill,/This were extracting good from ill' ('To my honoured Friend Mr. *T. C.* that asked me how I liked his mistress being an old widow', John Cleveland (d.1658), *Works* (1687), 263).

61 Lewis Maidwell, *The Loving Enemies* (1680), 23.

62 Robert Gould, *The Rival Sisters* (1696), 10.

63 *The World in the Moon* (1697), 11.

64 Thomas Duffett, *The Amorous Old Woman* (1674), 13, 41.

65 *Familiar Letters* (1697), 189–90, T. Brown to W. Knight at Ruscombe.

66 *Bury-Fair* (1689) 17. Cf., also, Oldwit when drunk: 'Old spouse, mummy; thou that wrap'st thy self every night in sear-cloths!' (39).
67 *The Plain Dealer* (1677), 33.
68 *Lustra Ludovici* (1646), 5.
69 For other instances of age and dryness, see: William Chamberlayne, *Love's Victory* (1658), 3; Sir Robert Howard, *The Surprisal*, in *Five New Plays* (1692), 1; Charles Hopkins, *Neglected Virtue* (1696), 2; Howard, *Poems* (1696), 93; David Craufurd, *Courtship a-la-Mode* (1700), 20. An early usage of this sense from William Davenant appears to derive from a 1635 ballad. Where that version had 'lips', Davenant has 'hips' (*Love and Honour* (1649), 22). One such instance echoes Falstaff as a 'mountain of mummy', and refers to 'Don Bertran', who is evidently fat, but also precisely defined in dramatis personae as 'an humorous *old* man' (italic mine; John Corye, *The Generous Enemies* (1672), 57). For a usage attacking female cosmetics (and thus implying that those decried are all surface and no substance), see Anon., *England's Vanity* (1683), 103.
70 *Psyche Debauched* (1678), 18.
71 All references from *The Sacrifice* (1687), 9–13.
72 Fane's dedication to the Earl of Dorset, quoted by J.P. Vander Motten, new DNB.
73 *Canidia, or, The Witches* (1683), 29. Noting that this poem was originally ascribed just to one 'R.D.', Jason McElligott, in his new DNB article on Dixon, argues that it probably was written by Dixon the clergyman.
74 For a broad parallel with this instance, see Richard Burridge, *The Shoemaker Beyond his Last* (1700), 12.
75 *Canidia*, 76.
76 *Canidia*, 24. Cf. also those illusory 'gods' who are really 'but sepulchral jars:/Crocks and dust, mummy at best' (84).
77 Fuller arguably does this when he remarks, 'they it seems being cannibals, who feed on man's flesh for food, though not for physic' (*Threnoikos*, 546). But it is important to note that this statement is relatively brief by comparison with the attacks made by Montaigne and Boyle.
78 Richard Lower performed the first roughly modern blood transfusions in 1666, switching the fluid directly between the veins and arteries of dogs (rather than introducing the blood orally). In 1667 a human volunteer survived after receiving the blood of a sheep. Such procedures were halted when a French subject died in that same year. Even before that, these first transfusions were of course novel and (for some) dangerously impious.
79 Daniel Korn, Mark Radice and Charlie Hawes, *Cannibal: A History of the People-Eaters* (London: Channel 4/Macmillan, 2001), 9–10.
80 *Occasional Reflections upon Several Subjects* (1665), 194–200. Michael Hunter's new DNB article on Boyle notes that parts of this work date back to the 1640s.
81 Gunpowder is usually composed of 75 per cent saltpetre, 15 per cent carbon, and 10 per cent sulphur (or, in early modern terms, saltpetre, charcoal, and brimstone (cf. Thomas Fuller, *History of the Worthies of England* (1662), 318–19)). Whilst saltpetre seems in this period to have often been extracted from ordinary earth, a popular source was also clearly animal or bird excrement. Morland (whose scientific interests imply some specialist knowledge of its production) may be referring here to dungheaps in which human and animal excrement were indiscriminately mingled. On saltpetre and non-human excrement, see: Fuller, *History*, 278; Henry Stubbe, *Legends no Histories* (1670), 51–52, 85; John Fryer, *A New Account of East-India and Persia* (1698), 257. Stubbe at one point possibly implies the value of human organic matter, reporting the belief that 'no place yields petre so plentifully as the earth in churches' (*Legends*, 51–52). Cf. van Helmont the younger, on the production of saltpetre from 'privies or stables' (Franciscus Mercurius van Helmont, *The Paradoxal Discourses of F.M. Van Helmont* (1685), 62). The professional role of 'salt-petre men' was sufficiently well-known to allow the preacher John Boys, in 1613, a sly pun during a commemorative gunpowder

sermon: 'again these S. Peter men (and as I have warrant to term them on this day salt Peter men) err from the true meaning of our text ... ' (*An Exposition of the Last Psalm ... fifth of Nouember, 1613* (1613), 5).

82 *The Urim of Conscience* (1695), 92–93. Alan Marshall in new DNB notes that Morland had to turn down work from 1690 onwards because of blindness. In the preface to *The Urim of Conscience* Morland writes, 'it having pleased almighty God, to deprive me of the sight of both my eyes, for above three years already past; and being thereby disabled to do my king or country any further service, I thought it might not be amiss, to employ some part of my time ... in recollecting some observations and reflections, which I have heretofore made' (*Urim*, 3–4). This would seem to place the composition of the work around 1693 or 1694, at a time when Morland was likely to be expecting death. He finally died on 29 December 1695. For discussion of Morland's scientific and mathematical interests and inventions, see: J.R. Ratcliff, 'Samuel Morland and his Calculating Machines *c*.1666: the Early Career of a Courtier-Inventor in Restoration London', *British Journal for the History of Science* 40.2 (2007): 159–79.

The eighteenth century notes

1 Leo Kanner, 'The Folklore and Cultural History of Epilepsy', *Medical Life* 37.4 (1930): 167–214, 190.

2 F.M. Valadez and C.D. O'Malley, 'James Keill of Northampton, Physician, Anatomist and Physiologist', *Medical History* 15.4 (1971): 317–35, 328.

3 Henry Curzon, *The Universal Library: or, Complete Summary of Science*, 2 vols (1712), I, 531; J. Quincy (ed.), *The Dispensatory of the Royal College of Physicians* (1721), 86, 221. Cf., also, Thomas Fuller, *Pharmacopoeia Domestica* (1723), 17, where *cranium humanum* is listed without comment amongst various ingredients. It is important to note that Curzon's work is a compilation.

4 Jean Jacob Berlu, *The Treasury of Drugs Unlocked* (1738), 39; Poole, *A Physical Vade Mecum ... Wherein is Contained, the Dispensatory of St. Thomas's Hospital* (1741), 295. Berlu's book first appeared in 1690. Cf., also: John Allen, *Synopsis Medicinae* [1740], 184–85. This cites *cranium humanum* for epilepsy on the authority of Ettmuller, and expresses no objection.

5 *Daily Courant*, 21 June 1709; *Daily Advertiser*, 7 January 1743. See also: George Bate, *Pharmacopoia Bateana: or, Bate's Dispensatory* (1720), A4v; Sir Richard Blackmore, *Discourses on the Gout* (1726), 123; George Cheyne, *The English Malady* (1735), 221, 232. Although Thomas Sydenham himself died in 1689, his works were still vigorously recommending Goddard's drops as late as 1769 (*The Entire Works of Dr Thomas Sydenham* (1769), xxvi). As we see in the conclusion, certain writers now held the active ingredient of Goddard's drops to be silk, not skull.

6 *A Treasure of Easy Medicines* (1771), 102; *A Treatise on Tropical Diseases* (1792), 339.

7 For Boyle's generally high reputation in the fields of eighteenth-century medicine and science, see: Benjamin Allen, *The Natural History of the Mineral-waters of Great-Britain* (1711), 7; Anon., *An Account of a Medical Controversy in the City of Cork* (1749), 33; Charles Alston, *Lectures on the Materia Medica* [1770], 300.

8 *Works* (1772), V, 106.

9 We owe this information to a physician and Fellow of the Royal Society, John Allen. Allen himself preferred to use 'acid mixture with florence wine' for this purpose (*A Summary View of the Whole Practice of Physic* (1733); this work first appeared in Latin in 1733.)

10 Christian Uvedale (i.e., John Hill), *The Construction of the Nerves* [1758], 51, italics mine.

11 *Useful Family Herbal* (1754), 252–53.

12 *Treasure*, 102.

13 'Anthropophagy in Post-Renaissance Europe: The Tradition of Medicinal Cannibalism', *American Anthropologist* 90.2 (1988): 405–9, 408.

14 See, respectively: John George Hansel, *Joannis Georgii Hanselii Medicina Brevis* (1714), 111–12; and James Alleyne, *A New English Dispensatory* (1733), 253, 351. In his Preface (ix) Hansel describes himself as a chemist and pharmacist, and states 'I honour Galen, Hippocrates, and Paracelsus'.

15 *Syphilis: A Practical Dissertation on the Venereal Disease* (1737), 76–77.

16 See: *De Morbis Cutaneis. A Treatise of Diseases Incident to the Skin* (1736), 366–67; *The Art of Surgery* (1741–42), 469.

17 *A Collection of Receipts in Physic* (1754),13–14. For more on Broxholme (1686–1748), see new DNB (article by Gordon Goodwin, rev. Kaye Bagshaw).

18 *The British Dispensatory* [1747], 130. On blood and epilepsy, see Gordon-Grube, 'Anthropophagy', 407.

19 *Aristotle's Complete and Experienced Midwife* [1760?], 141.

20 *A New Practice of Physic*, 2 vols (1728), II, 492–93.

21 *A Course of Lectures, upon the Materia Medica* (1730), 85–86.

22 For more on Bradley, see Frank N. Egerton in new DNB.

23 *Schola Medicinæ Universalis Nova* ... (1794), 100. Rowley (d.1806) 'was the physician at the Marylebone Infirmary and his practice in London was considerable' (new DNB, Norman Moore, rev. Elizabeth Baigent).

24 All references from: *A New Medical Dictionary* [1791], 526. It must be significant that the evidently Paracelsian Motherby 'practised in Königsberg, where he won great renown for his work in vaccination against smallpox, which practice he is said to have brought to the city about 1770'. He was said to be 'a physician of eminence at the court of Prussia' (see Elisabeth Baigent in new DNB).

25 *A Treatise of the Diseases of the Bones* (1726), 489; *Dictionaire Oeconomique: or, the Family Dictionary*, 2 vols (1758), I, Uuu2r. Cf. also mummy in an ointment for fistula (Fffff2v).

26 *Chirurgia Curiosa* (1706), 114, 213–14; Lorenz Heister, *A General System of Surgery*, trans. anon., 8th edn [1768], 108. Philip K. Wilson describes Heister as an 'influential German physico-chirurgus' (*Surgery, Skin and Syphilis: Daniel Turner's London (1667–1741)* Clio Medica 54 (Amsterdam: Rodopi, 1999), 23).

27 *Poverty and Nobleness of Mind*, trans. Maria Geisweiler (1799), 102–3.

28 *The Art of Angling* (Birmingham [1790?]), 98. Cf. also ibid. on another version made with mummy, barley and honey.

29 For more on Birch (historian, compiler, and sometime secretary to the Royal Society), see David Philip Miller in new DNB.

30 *St. James's Chronicle*, 20 June 1761.

31 *Morning Chronicle and London Advertiser*, 16 June 1788.

32 On rickets and gout, see, respectively: *The Family Guide to Health* (1767), 273; and Thomas Garlick, *An Essay on the Gout* (1729), 32. Against the pains of syphilis, see John Astruc, *A Treatise of the Venereal Disease* (1737), 173. Michael Ettmuller used it against ulcers, wounds, and cramps (*Etmullerus Abridged* (1703), 213, 259, 495). It still formed part of the wound salve around 1743 (Herman Boerhaave, *An Essay on the Virtue and Efficient Cause of Magnetical Cures*, trans. anon. (1743), 55). For other uses, see: Thomas Fuller, *Pharmacopœia Extemporanea*, 5th edn (1740), 444; *The Family Magazine* (1743), 296; Lorenz Heister, *A Compendium of the Practice of Physic* ... , trans. Edmund Barker, MD (1757), 370.

33 *The Ladies' Friend and Family Physical Library* (1788), 350. Cf. a reprint of Culpeper's *Directory for Midwives*, which still recommended human fat as one ingredient able to dissolve cancer of the breast (*A Directory for Midwives* [1755], 283–84).

34 For more on Wiseman (sometime surgeon to Charles I), see John Kirkup in new DNB.

35 *An Essay on Scirrhous Tumours, and Cancers* (1759), 20–21.

36 *A Treatise on the Effects and Various Preparations of Lead ... for Different Chirurgical Disorders* [1780?], 38–39.

37 *Pharmacopœia Universalis* (1747), 470–71.

38 *A Medicinal Dictionary* (1743), L1v.

39 *A New Method of Preventing and Curing the Madness Caused by the Bite of a Mad Dog* (1743), 22–24. It should be emphasised that James uses Desault in part to underline the supposed efficacy of mercury against rabies.

40 *A New Method*, 27–29. See, also: James, *A Treatise on Canine Madness* (1760), 31–32.

41 *A Treatise on the Venereal Distemper*, trans. John Andree (1738), 234–35.

42 *Treatise on Canine Madness*, 136. For another approving citation of Desault's methods, see also: Daniel Peter Layard, *An Essay on the Bite of a Mad Dog* (1768), 77–79.

43 On Crell, see: Jean Antoine Claude Chaptal, *Elements of Chemistry*, trans. anon. (1791), 364.

44 Antoine-François de Fourcroy, *Elements of Chemistry and Natural History*, trans. William Nicholson, 3 vols (Edinburgh, 1800), III, 287–88.

45 *Pharmacopœia Universalis: or, a New Universal English Dispensatory* (1747), 126.

46 *A Treatise on the Nervous Sciatica* (1775), 107. This appeared in Italian in 1764.

47 Although data on the prices of corpses for anatomy is limited, Ruth Richardson cites a charge of two guineas and a crown for an adult body in the 1790s (*Death, Dissection and the Destitute* (London: Phoenix, 2001), 57).

48 [J.P. Gilmour], 'Literary Notes', *British Medical Journal* 2.2493 (1908): 1122.

49 One source of difficulty must have been the need to get a body in which the fat was still relatively liquid.

50 That is, a patient would probably imagine a human skull as dry, even though the remedy was sometimes given in liquid form. Human fat would presumably be absorbed when used, for example, on ulcers, as in 'a salve of fox-oil, dill-oil, turpentine, man-grease, and the like' (Paul Barbette, *Thesaurus Chirurgiae* (1687), 91).

51 Cf. Webster, *Great Instauration*, 254–55.

52 New DNB.

53 John Keogh, *Zoologia Medicinalis Hibernica* (Dublin, 1739), 98–103. Keogh also thought that human excrement could be processed or distilled into 'occidentale civet' ('the essence of man's dung, brought to a sweetness for digestion'), though he does not say what for.

54 Cf. Johann Schroeder, *Zoologia*, trans. anon. (1659), 57: gloves made from human skin combat 'the withering and contraction of the joints'.

55 Anon, *A Full and True Account of … an unknown person that was found … within the top of a chimney …* (1701), title page.

56 *Stiff: The Curious Lives of Human Cadavers* (London: Penguin, 2003), 51.

57 See Schroeder's own *Zoologia* of 1659, 39–57. Given this continental influence, it is possible that the 'John Keogh of County Dublin, who received his Reims degree in 1752', and who 'claimed to have gained his MA at Ingolstadt in 1743, then to have spent four years studying medicine at Prague' was a son of John Keogh the younger (see: Laurence Brockliss, 'Medicine, Religion and Social Mobility in Eighteenth- and Early Nineteenth-Century Ireland', in *Ireland and Medicine in the Seventeenth and Eighteenth Centuries*, ed. Fiona Clark and James Kelly (Farnham: Ashgate, 2010), 73–108, 84).

58 *An Universal European Dictionary of Merchandise* (1799). This work first appeared in Hamburg in 1797.

59 *Dictionary of the English Language*, II.

60 See: *An Additional Book of Rates of Goods and Merchandizes Usually Imported* (1725), 157; *An Abridgment of the Public Statutes in Force and Use Relative to Scotland …* 2 vols, (1755), I, Y1r; Timothy Cunningham, *The Merchant's Lawyer* (1768), 434.

61 Edward Burrow, *A New and Complete Book of Rates* (1778), 222.

62 Burrow, *New and Complete Book of Rates*, 222.

63 *Treasury* (1733), 139. On moss, see 153: 'we have seen it in some skulls brought from Ireland'.

64 Trade with Germany may also have been growing, given the enduring use of other corpse medicines in that country. In 1727, Paul Hermann, professor of botany at the University of Leiden, implies possible demand in Holland, when stating that the skull of one perished from a violent death 'is given sometimes in epileptic cases in powder', and, further, is the subject of chemical analysis ('in distillation it affords a volatile spirit

and a foetid oil'). Hermann himself is opposed to it, though not denying its anti-epileptic virtues 'there are so many other good remedies, we need not this' (*Materia Medica*, trans. Edward Strother MD (1727), 135–36).

65 *Treasury*, A2r; title page.

66 *History of the Materia Medica* (1751), 876.

67 For examples, see, respectively: Thomas Brown (1663–1704), *The Cornuted Beaux*, in *Remains* (1720), 99; William Forbes, *Xantippe* (1724), 5; and (again) Swift, *Travels into Several Remote Nations of the World*, 2 vols (1726), II, 191. See, also, a miser who seems to have mummified himself by his own austerities (Thomas Park, *Sonnets* (1797), 28).

68 *Dictionary of the English Language*, II. It may be pure accident that Johnson's chosen quotation takes the form 'beat to *a* mummy' (rather than the more familiar 'beat to mummy', which more obviously implies corpse medicine). Whatever the reasons, this relatively unusual phrasing is at once subtly misleading, and emblematic of the slowly shifting status of Egyptian mummies in this period.

69 *The Dispensary* (1714), 17–18.

70 'The Earth: a Philosophical Poem', from *Poetical Essays on Several Occasions* (1733–35), 92.

71 'The Demagogue', in *The Poetical Works* [1796], 103.

72 *Lustra Ludovici*, 5.

73 And also, at times, to the humbler classes; see, for example, the elephant and mummy brought from Turkey 'as presents to eminent merchants of this city' in 1756 (*London Evening Post,* 26 February 1756). In this changing context, we are not always sure whether a reference to 'the mummy trade' implies medicine, personal collection, or both. For example, see a burlesque poem of 1765: 'Quin's Soliloquy on seeing Duke Humphry at St Albans' (*Public Advertiser* (London), 11 September 1765).

74 *Daily Advertiser* (London), 7 October 1742. For the later sale of 'a very curious Egyptian mummy' of a tall slender female of about six foot, see: *London Evening Post*, 16 May 1767.

75 *London Evening Post* , 24 October 1767, citing letter from Paris, 12 October.

76 *Connoisseur* (London), 30 May 1754.

77 George Keate, *An Epistle to Angelica Kauffman* (1781), 9. This poem also twice implies that mummy was now being used in paint (see 11, 26).

78 *The Belle's Stratagem* (1781), 32. On mummy genealogy, cf. also William Kenrick, *The Duellist* (1773), 24.

79 J.S. Chamberlain notes that the plays of Bacon (who was a clergyman as well as a writer) may never have been performed (see 'Phanuel Bacon', new DNB).

80 *The Trial of the Time Killers* (1757), 24–25.

81 Mummies and human skulls, along with various kinds of poison, are heaped on an immense pyre constructed to aid necromancy (see: *Vathek*, ed. Roger Lonsdale (London: Oxford University Press, 1970), 29–44). This novel was originally written in French in 1782.

82 Unless otherwise stated, all information on Woodward is taken from J.M. Levine's article in new DNB.

83 'John Gay', new DNB.

84 *Prefaces, Biographical and Critical, to the Works of the English Poets* (1779–81), 8–9. It is possible that Johnson is implying 'disgust' at the indecency of the scene. (Cf. Nokes, DNB, on the 'eight pamphlets appeared attacking the play's alleged obscenity').

85 On the assistance of Pope and Arbuthnot, see also: *Revels History of Drama in English, 1660–1750*, ed. J. Loftis, Richard Southern, Marion Jones, and A.H. Scouten, 8 vols (London: Routledge, 1996), V, 236.

86 Cf., also, Dr Johnson on Cibber, who in productions of *The Rehearsal*, 'said, that he once thought to have introduced his lovers disguised in a mummy and a crocodile' (*Prefaces, Biographical and Critical, to the Works of the English Poets* (1779–81), 201–2). In addition to its immediate publication in 1717, the comedy was also published again in 1758 (see Nokes, new DNB).

87 Robert D. Hume thinks that this scene was inspired by Edward Ravenscroft's *The Anatomist* (1697); see: *The Rakish Stage: Studies in English Drama, 1660–1800* (Carbondale: Southern Illinois University Press, 1983), 257; and, in the play, 17–19.

88 In this case the jibe probably also depends on public attitudes toward anatomists; Fossile himself states during this scene, 'I think it no degradation to a dead person of quality, to bear the rank of an anatomy in the learned world'.

89 On the play's origins, see: Paula O'Brien, 'James Miller', new DNB; and *Mother-in-Law*, Dedication ('Moliere, Madam, is, properly, the author of this play: for most of the scenes in it are translated from one or other of his Comedies'). Along with *Le Malade Imaginaire*, Miller's comedy also made use of Moliere's *Monsieur de Pourceaugnac*. *Le Malade Imaginaire* was first published (illegally) in 1674.

90 *The Mother-in-Law, or the Doctor the Disease* (1734), 4–6.

91 *Mother-in-Law*, 8–9.

92 *Mother-in-Law*, 26.

93 *Mother-in-Law*, 29–31.

94 Moliere's central physician was originally called Monsieur Purgon. It may well be significant that two other eighteenth-century uses of the name 'Dr Mummy' in stage plays are both employed to label men associated with the collecting of antiquities (see: Samuel Foote, *Taste* (1752), 17, 24–25; Arthur Murphy, *The Spouter, or the Triple Revenge* (1756), 39).

95 The association implied in the name of the secondary physician, Doctor Diascorditum, is similar, but was probably not quite so obvious ('diascord' or 'diascordium' was 'a medicine made of the dried leaves of *Teucrium Scordium*, and many other herbs' (*OED*)).

96 *Pharmacopœia Universalis* (1747), 470–71.

97 *History of the Materia Medica*, 876.

98 *Useful Family Herbal* (1754), 252.

99 *Construction of the Nerves*, 51.

100 *Dictionary of the English Language*, II. On mummy fraud and the Jews, see also: John Barrow, *Dictionarium Medicum Universale* (1749), Cc2r.

101 *An Historical Sketch of Medicine and Surgery* (1782), 218–19.

102 For an early example of this struggle (and some discussion of popular attitudes to physicians) see Jeremiah Whittaker, *An Essay on the Principles and Manners of the Medical Profession* (1783). Tellingly, a search for 'medical profession' on *Eighteenth Century Collections Online*, gives just seven references between 1700 and 1770, and 276 between 1770 and 1800. *Early English Books Online* yields just seven references, in only two authors, for the entire period prior to 1700 (see: Noah Biggs, *Mataeotechnia Medicinae Praxeos* (1651), b2r; John Webster: *Metallographia* (1671), 38; *The Displaying of Supposed Witchcraft* (1677), preface). Both searches made 18 June 2010. On changes in medical culture more generally from the late eighteenth century on, see *British Medicine in an Age of Reform*, ed. Roger French and Andrew Wear (London: Routledge, 1991), 1. For a broad overview of changing medical education in the late eighteenth and early nineteenth centuries, see T.N. Bonner, *Becoming a Physician: Medical Education in Britain, France, Germany, and the United States, 1750–1945* (Oxford: Oxford University Press, 1996), 61–157. On the relationship between medical reform and quackery, see Roy Porter, *Quacks: Fakers and Charlatans in English Medicine* (Stroud: Tempus, 2000), 222–35.

103 See, again, Corley, new DNB.

104 *Pharmacopeia Universalis*, 511–12; cf. Schroeder, *Zoologia* (1659), 39ff. This rather undermined James's seeming preference for 'mumia' derived from mineral pitch (ibid., 285).

105 See, respectively: *Daily Journal* (London), 19 February 1734; and *London Daily Post and General Advertiser*, 2 June 1736.

106 The original was *Le Comédien* by Pierre Rémond de Sainte-Albine. O'Connor further emphasises that 'the second edition of The Actor in 1755 expanded on the first, making more extensive reference to the English stage; this version was translated back into French'.

107 It is also worth noting that in Miller's popular 1730 comedy, *The Humours of Oxford*, a female scientist, finally convinced of the folly of her ambitions, vows, 'I will destroy all my globes, quadrants, spheres, prisms, microscopes … send all my serpent's teeth, mummy's-bones, and monstrous births, to the Oxford Museum; for the entertainment of other as ridiculous fools as my self' (79).

108 *Historical Sketch*, 218.

109 *Historical Sketch*, 219–20.

110 *A Treatise of the Materia Medica*, 2 vols [1789], I, 33.

111 See *Treatise of the Materia Medica*, title page. On Cullen more generally, see W.F. Bynum, new DNB.

112 For more on the medical profession, and the early formation of the history of medicine, see: John C. Burnham, 'How the Concept of Profession Evolved in the Work of Historians of Medicine', *Bulletin of the History of Medicine* 70 (1996): 1–24.

113 All references to *The Craft and Frauds of Physic*, 2nd edn (1703), 42–44. For 'loathsome', see ibid., 16, 48, 163. In 1727, Paul Hermann describes mummy as 'a resinous substance made in Egypt and Persia, sometimes of human flesh and sometimes of blood [sic]'. Although, 'this medicine is out in use' in Holland, Hermann seems to have no personal objection to it, adding that 'if any would make it, it were easily done with any muscle, seasoned with myrrh, saffron and aloes. It is said that Francis I … always wore a piece of mummy about him, and rhubarb, as anodynes … ' (*Materia Medica*, 147).

114 *Observations in Physic* (1733), 171.

115 Savage (d.1743), 'The Progress of a Divine: A Satire', in *Works* (1777), 119. It is not clear why Savage effectively inverts the real sequence of the corpse trade, in which local supply was used when the Egyptian variety became less available. In 1753 the Edinburgh physician George Young is sceptical about the 'cephalic' powers of human skull, but expresses no unease or disgust (*A Treatise on Opium* [1753], 9). On human skull, see also the physician Richard Brookes, who states that the ingredient 'is now justly banished' from treatments for epilepsy, with valerian root being substituted instead (*The General Practice of Physic*, 2 vols (1754), II, 308). For the little that is known of Brookes, see article in new DNB (G.T. Bettany, rev. Claire L. Nutt).

116 Charles Alston, *Lectures on the Materia Medica* [1770], 544. It is perhaps significant that Alston here uses 'mummies', not 'mummy'. Cf. also 525, where Alston laments the fact that 'cranium humanum … too long passed for a specific antiepileptic'.

117 *The Complete Angler* (1750), 104–5.

118 A search of *Eighteenth Century Collections Online* (made 18 June 2010) for variant spellings of this phrase yields just seven references, most from the later eighteenth century.

119 Although the term was used prior to Percival's book, it may be fair to say the prominence he gave it justifies crediting him with its origins. Dorothy and Roy Porter, noting that this work was 'written at the close of the eighteenth century', add that its aims were by no means wholly selfless (see: *Patient's Progress: Doctors and Doctoring in Eighteenth-Century England* (Palo Alto, Calif.: Stanford University Press, 1989), 19).

120 *An Essay on Regimen, for the Preservation of Health* (1799), 201.

121 For this and other information on Makittrick Adair, see DNB, W.P. Courtney, rev. Michael Bevan.

122 *A Complete English Dispensatory* (1756), 112.

123 *Dispensatory*, 325, 326, 328–29.

124 *Construction of the Nerves*, 51.

125 *Chemical Works*, 2 vols (1773), II, 360.

126 *Cyclopaedia*, 2 vols (1741), II. For an impressively late instance of this association, see W.G. Clark, in his 1878 edition of *Macbeth* (*Macbeth*, ed. W.G. Clark and W.A. Wright (Oxford: Clarendon Press, 1878), 143). It is worth adding that Chambers is oddly equivocal about mummy and cannibalism. The former is referred to several times in different editions of the *Cyclopaedia*. But it seems to be just once that it is linked to cannibalism. In 1753, under the entry 'Anthropophagi', we find this reflection: 'it may

be asked, whether the use which is made of certain parts of the human body in physic come under the denomination of *Anthropophagy*? How many tombs have been violated on this occasion? To say nothing of mummies and the like?' (Phrasing here suggests that Chambers refers to the use of fresh corpses as well as Egyptian mummies. Given this, it is especially notable how tentative the link with cannibalism is. It does not occur under entries for mummy, and even in the above instance is framed only as a question (*A Supplement to Mr Chambers' Cyclopaedia*, 2 vols (1753), I)). In the 1741 edition, the penultimate sense of 'mummy' gives a faintly baffled summary of the ideas of Irvine and van Helmont on spiritual transfer.

127 *A Brief Account* (1685), 155.

128 *Biographical Memoirs of Medicine in Great Britain* (1780), 262–63.

129 *Biographical Memoirs*, 262.

130 *A Provincial Glossary* (1787), 56 (there are two sets of page numbers; reference is to second set).

131 *Popular Culture in Early Modern Europe* (London: Wildwood House, 1988), 3.

132 *Herman of Unna*, 2 vols (1794), II, 172. This note is followed by 'T', which evidently means 'Translator'. The original was published at Leipzig in 1788.

133 See, again, Burrow, *New and Complete Book of Rates*, 222.

134 *Herman of Unna*, vii.

135 *Dictionary*, 2 vols (1785), II. Ironically, this entry is arguably less negative than that of 1755–56, as the reference to 'horrid medicines' is now absent.

136 Given the contemporary fondness for the glorious England of Jane Austen, it is interesting to note that, shortly before Austen's birth in 1775, certain English families were so poor that they starved to death. In or shortly before 1760 Margaret Graham and her two children starved to death in Walbeck, Cumberland. In January 1769, James Eaves and his wife and two children all starved to death in their cottage in the village of Datchworth in Hertfordshire. They were almost entirely naked when discovered (see, respectively: Anon., *The Cumberland Tragedy* [1760?], broadsheet ballad; and Philip Thicknesse, *An Account of the Four Persons found Starved to Death, at Datchworth in Hertfordshire* (1769), 2–3).

137 *A History of Medicine* (London: Nelson, 1945), vi.

138 The following is just one example of the kind of detail best omitted from such a mosaic. The Chamberlens, having invented the revolutionary Chamberlen forceps to aid delivery of children, then kept these as a profitable family secret for a full 200 years (J. Willocks, 'Scottish Man-Midwives in 18th Century London', in *The Influence of Scottish Medicine*, ed. D.A. Dow (Park Ridge, N.J.: Parthenon, 1988), 45–61, 45.)

139 Douglas Guthrie, *A History of Medicine* (London: Nelson, 1945), 144.

140 *A Short History of Medicine* (New York: Ronald Press, 1968), 111.

141 Howard Wilcox Haggard, *Devils, Drugs and Doctors: the Story of the Science of Healing from Medicine-man to Doctor* (Wakefield: EP Publishing, 1975), 324.

142 'Animal Sources of Early Remedies', *Bios* 35.2 (1964): 86–91, 89. It should be added that even Keezer shows up Ackerknecht's stance, noting that 'even Ambroise Paré ... considered mumia an efficient remedy for internal use, in cases of pains, bruises and sprains' (89).

143 'Ambroise Paré (1510–90): Father of Surgery as Art and Science', *Southern Medical Journal* 84.6 (1991): 763–65, 764.

144 Lawrence I. Conrad, Michael Neve, Vivian Nutton, Roy Porter and Andrew Wear, *The Western Medical Tradition: 800 BC to AD 1800* (Cambridge: Cambridge University Press, 1995), 423–24.

145 'James Keill of Northampton, Physician, Anatomist and Physiologist', *Medical History* 15.4 (1971): 317–35, 328.

146 Laurence Brockliss and Colin Jones, *The Medical World of Early Modern France* (Oxford: Clarendon Press, 1997), 161.

147 *French Virtuosi* (1664), 183–84.

148 *The Royal Pharmacopeia* (1678), 2.

149 Pierre Pomet, *A Complete History of Drugs*, 3rd edn (1737), 229.

150 *Stiff*, 221–47. Perhaps not surprisingly, this brief account is not flawlessly accurate. Roach states, for example, that Paré 'hastened to add that he never prescribed' mummy (223; cf. Paré's own admission, that he had tried mummy 'an hundred times' without success). Meanwhile, when she writes of how 'Pierre Pomet ... wrote in the 1737 edition of *A Compleat History of Druggs* that his colleague Guy de la Fontaine had travelled to Alexandria' and seen fake mummies, she seems under the impression that the two men were contemporaries, and that Pomet was still alive in 1737 (223; Fontaine was in Egypt in 1564, whilst Pomet was born in 1658, and died in 1699).

151 A.C. Wootton, *Chronicles of Pharmacy*, 2 vols (London: Macmillan, 1910); C.J.S. Thompson, *The Mystery and Art of the Apothecary* (Philadelphia: J.B. Lipincott, 1929).

152 Cf., also, the discussion of corpse medicine by W.R. Dawson: *The Bridle of Pegasus: Studies in Magic, Mythology and Folklore* (London: Methuen, 1930), 162–73.

153 Paul Mason, *Mummies* (London: Belitha Press, 2001), 26.

154 *Science News* 165.14 (2004): 222.

155 *Flesh and Blood: A History of the Cannibal Complex* (London: Abacus, 1996), 49.

156 It is rather hard to defend Tannahill here, given that her source for the reference (E.A. Wallis Budge, *The Divine Origin of the Craft of the Herbalist* (London: Society of Herbalists, 1928), 5) quotes the recipe in the context of a discussion of Culpeper; makes no mention of a 'papyrus' (or of Ancient Egypt); and gives a reference (J.H. Baas, *Outlines of the History of Medicine* (New York: Vail & Co., 1889)., 436) directly beneath the quotation.

157 An exception to this habit is found in Antonia Fraser's biography of Charles II, where the author admits that the disease would itself have probably killed Charles (*King Charles II* (London: Weidenfeld & Nicholson, 1979), 450). For an early instance of the more common tradition, see T.B. Macaulay's *History of England*: 'a loathsome volatile salt, extracted from human skulls, was forced into his mouth' (*OED*, 'loathsome', citing T.B. Macaulay, *The History of England* (1849), iv, I, 432). Ronald Hutton adds that Charles's was 'one of the best-chronicled death agonies in history, several observers having left accounts of these last days' (*Charles the Second: King of England, Scotland, and Ireland* (Oxford: Clarendon Press, 1989), 443).

158 Haggard, *Devils, Drugs, and Doctors*, 334–35.

159 Cf. Fraser, *King Charles II*, 445, who notes that the physician who bled Charles was later paid £1,000.

160 See Thompson, *Mystery and Art*, 205.

Conclusion notes

1 Lawrence Stone, *The Family, Sex and Marriage in England 1500–1800* (Harmondsworth: Penguin Books, 1979), 412–13.

2 *The Culture of Sensibility: Sex and Society in Eighteenth-Century Britain* (Chicago: University of Chicago Press, 1992), 290–91. Cf., also ibid., on *The Gentleman's Magazine* 1791, which suggested that 'only the lowest class now used the word "sweat"'.

3 *Clean and Decent: the Fascinating History of the Bathroom and the Water Closet* (1960; repr. London: Penguin, 2000), 112. Cf., however, Joseph Addison, who, in *The Spectator* in 1714 can already state, of cleanliness: '"no-one, unadorned with this virtue, can go into company without giving manifest offence"' (Virginia Smith *Clean: A History of Personal Hygiene and Purity* (Oxford: Oxford University Press, 2007), 226).

4 *History of the Materia Medica*, 876. For the changing status of spirits (amongst a minority) in the seventeenth century, see Harvey, cited in Richard Sugg, *Murder after Death* (Ithaca: Cornell University Press, 2007), 210–11; Willis, in Richard Sugg, *The Smoke of the Soul: The Animated Body in Early Modern Europe* (Michigan: University of Michigan Press, forthcoming), ch. 9.

5 C.J.S. Thompson, *The Mystery and Art of the Apothecary* (1929; repr. Detroit: Singing Tree Press, 1971), 213.

6 'Indulco and Mumia', *The Journal of American Folklore* 77.303 (1964), 8.

7 *Bread of Dreams: Food and Fantasy in Early Modern Europe*, trans. David Gentilcore (Oxford: Polity Press, 1996), 48–49.

8 *The Standard*, 28 August 1899.

9 *Liverpool Mercury*, 17 February 1862, signed: 'One of the Committee', Liverpool, 15 February 1862. Admittedly, this commentator probably had a basic agenda of his own, given that he was a homeopath, and explicitly described the Liverpool offender as 'an allopath of note'.

10 *The Cook's Oracle* (Boston: Constable, 1823), 255.

11 *Cook's Oracle*, 117–18, 159–60.

12 *A Collection of Above Three Hundred Receipts in Cookery, Physic, and Surgery*, 2nd edn (1719), 69. This work is described as 'by several hands' and as 'printed for Mary Kettilby'. Kitchiner's plagiarism seems consistent with the fact that he also lied about attending Eton, and about holding a Glasgow medical degree (see Anita McConnell, new DNB).

13 *Scots Magazine* (November 1798), 729.

14 *The Chymical Vade Mecum* (1748), 283. Cf also *The Tatler* (1797), I, 187–88.

15 *Wessex Tales*, ed. F.B. Pinion (London: Macmillan, 1977), 76.

16 The hanging occurs either 'near twenty years' or 'near twelve years' after 1813, with this latter date being used for the edition of 1912 (see *Wessex Tales*, 374). Rural gibbets also seem to have been reasonably common (see, for example, M. Gillett, 'The Gibbet on Inkpen Beacon', *Folklore* 34.2 (1923): 160–61).

17 *The Folklore of Sussex* (London: Batsford, 1973), 82.

18 'Folk-Medicine of the Pennsylvania Germans', *Proceedings of the American Philosophical Society* 26.129 (1889): 329–52, 338. Cf. also William S. Keezer, 'Animal Sources of Early Remedies', *Bios* 35.2 (1964), 90, on a corpse cure cited in an 1837 list of North American family recipes.

19 Mary Beith, *Healing Threads: Traditional Medicines of the Highlands and Islands* (Edinburgh: Polygon, 1995), 170; Violetta Halpert, 'Folk Cures From Indiana', *Hoosier Folklore* 9.1 (1950): 1–12, 9.

20 *The Yorkshire Herald, and The York Herald*, 17 December 1892.

21 Even after the abolition, the gibbets themselves sometimes remained. A Sussex minister's wife, Mrs Latham 'describes how her childhood walks on Beeding Hill in the 1840s were spoilt by her terror of an ancient gibbet which stood there' and by her nurses tales of it, including one of a woman cured of a wen on her neck by touching a dead felon's hand at the gallows (*Folklore of Sussex*, 82).

22 *Lectures on … Acute and Chronic Diseases*, ed. Joseph Rix (London, 1834), 755.

23 *Liverpool Mercury*, 19 February 1847; *Lancet*, 24 February 1847, 216. I am immensely grateful to Christine Alvin for bringing this tale to my attention.

24 The powdered skull of a stillborn infant is noted as a supposed cure for rabies in 1889 in a Blackburn paper, but here there is no actual case or date cited, nor link to the town itself (*The Blackburn Standard and Weekly Express*, 15 June 1889).

25 'Strange Medicines', *Popular Science Monthly* 31.6 (1887): 750–67, 756–57.

26 Felix Grendon, 'The Anglo-Saxon Charms', *Journal of American Folklore* 22.84 (1909): 105–237, 123.

27 'Strange Medicines', 756–57.

28 See: Anne Ross, *The Folklore of the Scottish Highlands* (London: Batsford, 1976), 80. Ross also notes that a holy well used for cures (still, occasionally, as she wrote) gained this power because of association with the skull of a suicide (81–82).

29 'Strange Medicines', 756–57. Tannahill cites a less benign use of blood in China in the 1870s, where a number of lepers at Whampoa were said to have attacked and killed '"healthy men, that they might drink the blood and eat the intestines of those killed"'

as cure for their disease. The account is a contemporary one, and given China's history of cannibalism and medicinal cannibalism we have to be open-minded about this claim (Reay Tannahill, *Flesh and Blood: a History of the Cannibal Complex* (London: Abacus, 1996), 87).

30 *Healing Threads*, 101.

31 *Healing Threads*, 131. The cure was supposed to have been highly successful, though Beith thinks that this was due to an injunction to drink very little alcohol.

32 *Healing Threads*, 183. The Orkney usage is not dated.

33 William George Black, *Folk-Medicine: A Chapter in the History of Culture* (London: Folklore Society, 1883), 140. There were evidently various reasons why one 'clan' attracted such a reputation. Black adds, for example, that 'the blood of the Walches, Keoghs, and Cahills, is considered in the west of Ireland an infallible remedy for ery-sipelas', and we hear elsewhere that the islanders of Lewis placed special value on the blood of a Munro (*The Encyclopedia of Folk Medicine: Old World and New World Traditions*, ed. Gabrielle Hatfield (Oxford: ABC Clio, 2004), 39). But in this instance it seems unlikely that the habits of John Keogh the younger could be mere coincidence.

34 See, for example: Kate Lawless Pyne, 'Folk-Medicine in County Cork', *Folklore* 8.2 (1897): 179–80; Dorothy Brewer, 'Current Belgian Folk Medicine', *Folklore* 40.1 (1929): 84–85; L.F. Newman, 'Some Notes on Folk Medicine in the Eastern Counties', *Folklore* 56.4 (1945): 349–60.

35 'Strange Medicines', 756–57.

36 'Simples, and their Superstitions', *The Ladies' Cabinet* (London), 1 November, 1854, 247.

37 'Folk-Medicine of the Pennsylvania Germans', 338.

38 'Simples, and their Superstitions', 247.

39 For a particularly memorable example, see: *Kilvert's Diary: Selections from the Diary of the Rev. Francis Kilvert*, ed. William Plomer, 3 vols (London: Cape, 1960), I, 300–1, 1 February 1871.

40 See: Elizabeth Cloud Seip, 'Witch-Finding in Western Maryland', *Journal of American Folklore* 14.52 (1901): 39–44; W. B. Carnochan, 'Witch-Hunting and Belief in 1751: The Case of Thomas Colley and Ruth Osborne', *Journal of Social History* 4.4 (1971): 389–403.

41 Eric Maple, 'The Witches of Dengie', *Folklore* 73.3 (1962): 178–84, 180.

42 See: Ross, *Folklore of the Scottish Highlands*, 67–73; Lizanne Henderson, 'The Survival of Witchcraft Prosecutions and Witch Belief in South-West Scotland', *The Scottish Historical Review* 85.219 (2006): 52–74, 73.

43 M.M. Banks, 'Scoring a Witch Above the Breath', *Folklore* 23 (1912): 490; 'Survival of Witchcraft Prosecutions', 72–73. For a threat of murder against a witch in 1890, see: 'Witches in Cornwall', *Folklore* 2.2 (1891): 248.

44 M.R. Taylor, 'Witches and Witchcraft', *Folklore* 46.2 (1935): 171–72. Cf. also: M.R. Taylor, 'Witches and Witchcraft', *Folklore* 46.2 (1935): 147–48.

45 'Witches and Witchcraft', 147–48.

46 Eric Maple, 'The Witches of Canewdon', *Folklore* 71.4 (1960): 241–50

47 George Hendricks, 'German Witch Mania', *Western Folklore* 23.2 (1964): 120–21.

48 *Strange and Secret Peoples: Fairies and Victorian Consciousness* (Oxford: Oxford University Press, 1999), 62–63.

49 *Strange and Secret Peoples*, 64–65.

50 'Witches of Canewdon', 247. For other examples, see: Hoffman, 'Folk-Medicine of the Pennsylvania Germans', 332, 342; Brewer, 'Current Belgian Folk Medicine', 84–85; George Bundy Wilson, 'Notes on Folk Medicine', *Journal of American Folklore* 21.80 (1908): 68–73, 70, 72; Richard and Eva Blum, *The Dangerous Hour: The Lore of Crisis and Mystery in Rural Greece* (London: Chatto & Windus, 1970), 81.

51 On weather and violence against witches, see especially: Edward Miguel, 'Poverty and Witch Killing', *Review of Economic Studies* 72.4 (2005): 1153–72, 1153.

52 *Hereward the Wake, 'Last of the English'*, 2 vols (London: Macmillan, 1881), II, 140.
53 *Thomas Middleton: the Collected Works and Companion*, ed. Gary Taylor and John Lavagnino (Oxford: Oxford University Press, 2007), 1.2, 16–19. Many thanks to Danielle Yardy for reminding me of this scene.
54 *Works* (1616), 951.
55 On dating see Gary Taylor, 'Thomas Middleton', new DNB.
56 Thomas Potts, *The Wonderful Discovery of Witches in the County of Lancaster* (1613), L1v–L2r. I am very grateful to Danielle Yardy for bringing this tale to my attention.
57 For a broadly similar (though not fatal) type of witch-magic in Montenegro, see: Leo Kanner, 'The Folklore and Cultural History of Epilepsy', *Medical Life* 37.4 (1930): 167–214, 173.
58 This word (pronouced 'obeah') has various meanings, the chief of which is given by the *OED* as, 'in the Onitsha and western Igbo area of Nigeria: a king, a chief'.
59 *Medical Tracts* (1800), 197.
60 *Horns of Honour: and Other Studies in the By-Ways of Archaeology* (London: John Murray, 1900), 187.
61 *A Hangman's Diary: Being the Journal of Master Franz Schmidt, Public Executioner of Nuremberg, 1573–1617*, 176–77.
62 *An Abstract of ... Those Barbarous, Cruel Massacres and Murthers of the Protestants and English in ... Ireland* (1652), 12. Cf. Benjamin Keach, *Distressed Sion Relieved* (1689), 110, 137. For a vivid illustrated account of what was believed to have been done to some victims, see James Cranford, *The Tears of Ireland* (1642).
63 The author himself seems to believe this is possible, but that the effect is achieved by the Devil, not by the candle itself.
64 *Athenian Gazette or Casuistical Mercury* (London), 19 December 1691.
65 *Horns of Honour*, 187–89.
66 *The Times*, 18 April 1836, 7.
67 *The Pall Mall Gazette*, 24 November 1888; *The Star* (Saint Peter Port), 11 October 1888.
68 Similarly, the Kursk murder was itself frequently dubbed 'a Whitechapel murder' by the newspapers of the day.
69 *The Star*, 11 October 1888.
70 'Modern Witches of Pennsylvania', *Journal of American Folklore* 40.157 (1927): 304–9, 304–5.
71 *Horns of Honour*, 190–91.
72 *Horns of Honour*, 180–84. Although Elworthy credits the pre-1568 painting to Jan Breugel, he must mean Pieter Breugel the elder (d.1569), as Jan Breugel the elder was born only in 1568.
73 *Horns of Honour*, 186–87.
74 *Far from the Madding Crowd* (London: Macmillan, 1912), 174.
75 In 2008 Rosemary Pope, then a pro-vice-chancellor of Bournemouth University, died at aged 49 after a long history of anorexia. By the time she fatally collapsed, her heart had shrunk to the size of a child's.
76 *Klinike, or the Diet of the Diseased* (1633), 347.
77 *Applebee's Original Weekly Journal* (London), 24 September 1720.
78 *Common Sense or The Englishman's Journal* (London), 23 December 1738. Although the place name given beside the incident's date (6 December) is illegible, this would seem to be Lawford's Gate in Bristol.
79 *Animism, Magic, and the Divine King* (London: Kegan Paul, 1930), 98–101, citing sources from 1886, 1907, and 1908.
80 'Folk-Medicine of the Pennsylvania Germans', 349–50.
81 *Bodies: Sex, Violence, Disease, and Death in Contemporary Legend* (Jackson: University Press of Mississippi, 2009), 269.
82 For this and further details, see Devendra P. Varma, in *Horrid Mysteries* (London: Folio Society), xii.

83 *Horrid Mysteries*, 61.
84 *Horrid Mysteries*, 64–68.
85 Cited in *Dracula*, ed. J.P. Riquelme (Boston: St Martin's, 2002), 396–97.
86 *The Poetical Works of Rupert Brooke*, ed. Geoffrey Keynes (London: Faber & Faber, 1952), 81. Brooke sent the first two stanzas to Jacques Raverat in a letter of 8 November 1910; the full poem was published in *The New Age* on 16 November 1911 (see: Nigel Jones, *Rupert Brooke: Life, Death and Myth* (London: Richard Cohen, 1999), 144).
87 Without wishing to labour the point, it is worth adding that recent oblivion as to the past existence of corpse medicine is further illustrated by the words of Brooke's biographer, Jones, when he mistakenly declares that 'the poem's central image ... is grotesquely original' (*Rupert Brooke*, 145). This is of course true insofar as Brooke shifts from medicine to aphrodisiac, but Jones seems to have no idea of the medical history of 'mummia'.
88 Jones, *Rupert Brooke*, 145.
89 It is possible, of course, that Brooke was aware of the medical nature of mummy. But if so he does seem to risk exposing himself to some ridicule by verses which give no hint of such awareness.
90 Eileen S. Barr and Roger K. Brown, 'Human Skull for Love Potion', *Western Folklore* 17.1 (1958): 61–62.
91 'Strange Medicines', 758.
92 Many thanks to Martyn Bennett for this detail.
93 See: www.solarnavigator.net/earthrace.htm.
94 *The Examiner* (London), 21 August 1858.
95 *Death, Dissection and the Destitute* (London: Phoenix, 2001), 97.
96 *Healing Threads*, 116–17.
97 *Healing Threads*, 117.
98 See Tannahill, *Flesh and Blood*, 87
99 Mary Roach, *Stiff: The Curious Lives of Human Cadavers* (London: Penguin, 2003), 49–50.
100 David Samper, 'Cannibalizing Kids', *Journal of Folklore Research* 39.1 (2002): 1–32, 1–2.
101 Paul Lewis, 'Kosovo PM is Head of Human Organ and Arms Ring, Council of Europe Reports', *Guardian*, 14 December 2010; 'The Doctor at the Heart of Kosovo's Organ Scandal', *Guardian*, 17 December 2010. All further quotations are from second article.
102 See *Murder after Death*, 166.
103 For the harsh realities of the vampire diet, see especially the 2008 film *Let the Right One In* (dir. Thomas Alfredson).
104 Frank Lestringant, *Cannibals: The Discovery and Representation of the Cannibal from Columbus to Jules Verne*, trans. Rosemary Morris (Cambridge: Polity Press, 1997), 80.
105 *A General Martyrology* (1660), 420, 421–22, 423–24, 425.
106 Whilst Samper has convincingly shown that the often strikingly detailed stories of Latin American children killed for organ theft have never been proved ('Cannibalizing Kids', 6–12), we should note that Sonmez has also been linked to illicit transplant operations in Ecuador (Lewis, 'Doctor at the Heart of Kosovo's Organ Scandal').

INDEX